RALPH NADER PRESENTS

CIVICS FOR DEMOCRACY

A JOURNEY FOR TEACHERS AND STUDENTS

BY KATHERINE ISAAC

A PROJECT OF
THE CENTER FOR STUDY OF RESPONSIVE LAW AND ESSENTIAL INFORMATION

Readers are encouraged to send their comments on *Civics for Democracy* to:

Civics for Democracy
CSRL
P.O. Box 19367
Washington, DC 20036

Published by Essential Books
P.O. Box 19405, Washington, DC 20036

Cover photograph © 1989 Beverly Orr
Housing Now march and rally, October 7, 1989, Washington, DC

Cover design by Kathy Cashel

Printed by McArdle Printing Company, Upper Marlboro, MD

Library of Congress Catalog Card Number: 92-97031

ISBN 0-936758-32-5

 Printed on 50% Recycled Stock With 10% Post-Consumer Waste

Contents

Contents

FOREWORD

At a certain level of abstraction, there is widespread agreement in our country that "good citizenship" builds a better democracy which, in turn, contributes to a stable society of opportunity and justice. However, as one moves closer to the fields of life's practice, the grand consensus increasingly crumbles, revealing two camps — the many, who believe that people should have adequate rights and remedies even though they do not possess wealth or power; and the few who are not troubled by today's inequities. The assumption underlying *Civics for Democracy: A Journey for Teachers and Students* draws on the old adage that when a society is in trouble, the solution is not less democracy but more democracy.

Is our society in trouble? Most people would reply in the affirmative and proceed to give very similar examples of what they mean by "trouble." According to the recent Kettering Report, *Citizens and Politics: A View from Main Street America*, "Public participation in voting is low, and seems to be reaching lower levels at each election. People's frustration about politics is high. A sense of political efficacy among citizens is missing."

One logical response to this characterization of the popular mood is to look at our schools, where the next generation of citizens is spending a considerable portion of its waking days. Corporate involvement in the public schools has raised concerns among educators about excessive commercialism, symbolized by the controversy over Whittle Communications' Channel One. At the same time, the programs of teacher conventions, especially social studies teachers, are filled with seminars and workshops about the need for greater "civic competence," "civic literacy" and "citizenship skills." It seems that teachers are competing these days, not successfully, with the time youngsters spend watching television, videos and other big time corporate entertainment shaped for their various age groups.

Learning "good citizenship" needs to become a high priority in our schools because it combines a requirement of proficiency in basic education with experience. It connects knowledge to its application fueled by the student motivation that proceeds from being taken seriously and given responsibility in association with adults from the community. Unfortunately, "good citizenship" is not accorded a serious status within the curriculum of most schools. As Ernest L. Boyer, president of the Carnegie Foundation for the Advancement of Teaching observed, "Moral and civic education have almost disappeared. We've become increasingly preoccupied with the economic impact of education."

Practicing civics, becoming a skilled citizen, using one's skills to overcome apathy, ignorance, greed or abuses of power in society at all levels invites knowledge of civic history, understanding of civic rights and strategies and sharing in a growing civic culture of regular participation. Bridging the gap between classroom learning and community experience is a way of connecting students to purposeful learning that transcends the listlessness and restlessness on the one hand, and the excessive vocational or trade school instrumentalism, on the other hand.

Throughout this book, written by Katherine Isaac, in consultation with a deep reserve of classroom teachers, general educators and experienced citizens, is a steady though little recognized theme of American history. That is, beyond its battles, its elections, its enterprise and its calamities, there runs a steady, steadfast and sturdy civic energy ranging from minorities of one to mass movements of Americans that have rescued their country from shame, error, cruelty and decline. But the latter forces keep re-emerging and place ever more complex and time-absorbing demands on citizens to build and rebuild movements of reconstruction and redress. The demands on our practice of citizenship grow with the expansion of a complex, interdependent society. Our supply of citizenship must keep up, equipped with modern democratic tools suited more to the 21st century than to the 18th century. This need logically brings us back to our schools, where civic education has lacked educational fortitude. Civics as a course of instruction seems to invite more than its share of collective yawns inside and outside the classroom. This is so because instructional materials have been shorn of the grist of civic history which is controversy, struggles over injustice between parties and interests having proper names, brand names and heroic names. The neuterizing of the civics curriculum, through a soporific excess of self-censorship, joins with the paucity of civic experience afforded students. Where different conditions have prevailed, where teachers and principals and School Boards have shed their inhibitions to confront realities past and present, students are given problems to analyze and solutions to ponder and advance in their own neighborhood, community, state, nation or right inside their own school. The fresh initiatives of free, critical, intellectual and normative school and community experiences tap into the multiple intelligences of students and provoke them to levels of confidence, attentiveness and participation neither they nor their teachers thought possible. The emphasis of this book is meant to stimulate these very characteristics.

Without this modest level of fortitude regarding the substance of civics for democracy, education at all levels will continue to stripmine this part of the curriculum of its metabolism, its motivating force to take the students from instruction to learning to knowledge to application until the acme of pedagogical ambition is reached — the sustained onset of educational self-renewal of, by and for the student.

Fortitude, history, skills and experience are the threads that are woven throughout *Civics for Democracy*, so that many journeys are undertaken by teachers with their students. Journeys that students desire to continue long after graduation. For civic participation is a formula for human happiness — both private and public. It is more than a slogan to be intoned or even a duty to be self-imposed; it is a delight to be savored as an essential quality of life that makes democracy an authentic reality. Indeed, there can be no daily democracy without daily citizenship. But rights are not enough. There must be added skills and experience so that these rights are exercised by an educated mind. For it is superior to foresee and forestall than to react and repair.

Everyone at some time comes to some definition of democracy. Permit me to offer one: a democracy is a society where less and less courage and risk are needed of more and more people to spread justice and the blessings of liberty throughout the land.

Such a society starts with dedicated attentions to the nurturing of civic cultures. Civics can be a grand and regular nurturer. The Center for Study of Responsive Law nurtured this volume and this orientation as its response to nearly a generation of requests by teachers and others that we make a contribution, arising from our experience of working with students on many projects, to the forward march of civic educational quality and retention. May the following pages find their uses in the minds and hearts of young citizens eager to build a more just, sustainable and happy world.

Ralph Nader
Washington, DC
August 1992

PREFACE

Numerous reports have documented a "citizenship crisis" — a lack of knowledge of the basic concepts of citizenship and a disconnectedness and alienation of young people in the United States from engaging our system of government. For example, a 1989 survey commissioned by People for the American Way concluded, "Young Americans today have absorbed only half of democracy's story, perceiving the virtue of our system of government only in the rights and freedoms it provides, not in the accompanying responsibilities it bestows."[1]

When asked to describe a "good citizen," students responded that "the task of being a good citizen carries no additional meaning or special responsibilities beyond simply being a 'good person.'"[2] The basic civic duty to vote was mentioned by only 12 percent of the respondents as a component of citizenship.[3]

However, the People for the American Way survey concluded that "[m]embers of today's younger generation are not, by and large, selfish or apathetic; they seem instead to be well-meaning people with weak civic skills."[4] Although most students were not involved in any kind of community service or political action, they indicated a willingness to become involved. Of the students surveyed, 51 percent favored making community service a requirement for high school graduation and 89 percent agreed that volunteer service work should be rewarded with school credit.[5]

If apathy or selfishness are not major factors; then what prevents people from participating in the affairs of their communities? Community organizer Si Kahn writes that one of the biggest barriers to participation is fear.[6] People often fear that they are not competent enough to give a speech in public or fear that they will appear ignorant when asking a question or voicing an opinion. People also fear what will happen — losing their job or being harassed or intimidated, for example — if they do speak out about problems in the workplace or community.

While some of these fears may be justified, "sometimes this fear is exaggerated," writes Kahn, because we are not taught that citizen participation is "basic to how the American system of democracy and representative government is supposed to work."[7] We do not learn that almost all significant social change in this country was brought about by citizen action — from Rosa Parks refusing to tolerate segregation on the Montgomery, Alabama buses to, more recently, Lois Gibbs demanding that she and her neighbors at Love Canal in New York be protected from toxic waste contamination.

Because our schools teach so little about how citizens have participated throughout U.S. history, it is difficult for many citizens to imagine themselves becoming involved. As historian Lawrence Goodwyn writes, "One cannot construct what one cannot imagine."[8] Citizens must be aware not only that problems exist (as students living with problems including poverty and violent crime already do) but that possibilities to diminish these problems exist as well. Citizens must be able to imagine what can happen when people try to make change.

Even if citizens overcome their fears and envision a better world, they still need concrete civic skills to be effective in their efforts. Because many people do not know how to "proceed from where we are to where we wish to be,"[9] they focus on private, individual gain to the exclusion of a public, civic life.

By encouraging students to participate in their schools and communities, this book is intended to help students learn firsthand that citizenship involves more than freedoms and liberties. By learning that citizen action has a long tradition in the United States, students overcome their fears and imagine a world made better by their involvement in it. By practicing citizen tools and skills in the laboratory of the community, students gain the confidence and experience to continue their involvement throughout their lives.

The first section, PROFILES OF STUDENTS IN ACTION, dispels the idea that young people are not involved by telling seven stories of students who have worked to make positive change. From the high school students in Coral Springs, Florida who successfully campaigned to save the largest stand of cypress trees in their county to the elementary school students in Washington, DC whose energy patrol saved their school thousands of dollars in energy bills, these examples are meant to inspire students all over the United States that their actions can, and do, make a difference.

The second section, HISTORY OF CITIZEN MOVEMENTS, offers a history of five citizen movements — civil rights, labor, women's rights, consumer and environmental — to show students how people have effected change over the course of U.S. history. Although each of these topics may be mentioned in high school history texts, the following chapters are an attempt to bring teachers and students more detailed material that illuminates the role of the citizen, rather than government or other institutions, in effecting change. The lives of a number of individual activists are profiled to reveal how and why people overcome their fears to become involved in the issues and problems of their communities.

The third section, TECHNIQUES FOR PARTICIPATION, describes some of the many strategies that citizens throughout U.S. history have used and continue to use to effect change. These citizen tools include direct actions such as boycotts and demonstrations, the steps involved in citizen lobbying to change or create laws, how citizens can use the courts, how to propose a ballot initiative and how to get a message to the media.

Section four, STUDENT ACTIVITIES, offers 10 projects that students can undertake within the school or in the community. Some active civics courses call for students to visit city hall or invite government officials to speak at school. But the activities in this book offer students a more indelible opportunity to practice solving problems themselves — in the laboratory of their own community or school.

Students profile their elected officials by looking at voting records, campaign finances and press coverage and release their results to voters in their communities. Students learn about energy efficiency, conduct a wastehunt in their school to identify wasteful energy practices and recommend and implement changes. And students survey area stores for toys that do not meet federal or state safety standards, issue their findings to parents and teach younger children about toy safety. And with the Time Dollar, a system of trading time for services developed by Dr. Edgar Cahn, teachers and students have an excellent opportunity to build a base for community service within the school.

In addition, 75 STUDENT ACTIVITY IDEAS are offered to inspire students to look at their own schools and communities to decide what issues they want to resolve. An extensive list of RESOURCES — citizen groups, publications, teaching materials and videos — will help students and teachers in their search for information about issues in which they choose to become involved.

SUGGESTIONS FOR USING *Civics for Democracy*

As a one year or one semester course on participatory civics:

■ Combine all sections of the book to shape a vibrant civics course in which students learn about citizen participation in U.S. history, the skills of citizen action and the practical application of these tools to improve their schools and communities.

As a supplement to U.S. history courses:

■ Use each of the chapters from HISTORY OF CITIZEN MOVEMENTS to enhance traditional history textbook discussions.

■ Supplement current events discussions with issues that face the movements for civil rights, women's rights, labor, environmental and consumer protection today.

■ Add a discussion of citizen movements which many U.S. history textbooks do not cover.

As a supplement to U.S. government courses:

■ Use the background material from the following STUDENT ACTIVITIES — Profiling Members of Congress, Community Profile of Voter Participation, Using the Freedom of Information Act, Representativeness in the Jury Selection Process and Evaluating Local Television News — to discuss barriers that often diminish citizen participation, including the campaign finance system, voter registration, the lack of access to government information, restrictions on jury service and lack of citizen access to the media. Discuss proposals for reform.

As a guidebook for an after-school club:

■ Combine material from the HISTORY OF CITIZEN MOVEMENTS with a STUDENT ACTIVITY. For example, provide students in an after-school environmental club with examples of how other citizens — including high school students — have won environmental victories. Follow the activity guides to conduct an energy wastehunt or make your school a green consumer. Use the TECHNIQUES FOR PARTICIPATION to choose citizen tools for solving environmental problems in your community.

ACKNOWLEDGMENTS

Contributing Writers:

Amy Allina, Joanne Manning Anderson, Jennifer Kassen, Holley Knaus, Ben Lilliston, Leslie Woodside

Reviewers:

Dr. Edgar Cahn, professor, D.C. School of Law; Dr. Helen Caldicott, author; Todd Clark, executive director, Constitutional Rights Foundation; Greg Clevenger, teacher, Rochester Adams High School, MI and NCSS teacher of the year; John Dempsey, president Sandhills Community College, NC; Charles DeVeney, teacher, Coral Springs High School, FL; Frank Dirks, Youth Service America; James Donahue, Essential Information; Joanne Doroshow, Empowerment Project; Peter Dykstra, Greenpeace; Marilyn Golden, Disability Rights Education and Defense Fund; Patti Goldman, Freedom of Information Clearinghouse; Lawrence Goodwyn, professor, Duke University; Mary Haas, professor of curriculum and instruction, West Virginia University; Dr. John Haefner, Professor Emeritus, Social Studies Education, University of Iowa; Mildred Hinkle, teacher, and her AP American Government class, Marion, IN; Barbara Lewis, teacher and author of *The Kid's Guide to Social Action*; Brian Lipsett, Citizens Clearinghouse for Hazardous Waste; Michael Merrill, professor, Rutgers Labor Studies program; Sanford Newman, Project Vote; Robert Paehlke, professor, Trent University, Ontario; Isidore Starr, Professor Emeritus of Education, Queens College - CUNY; Karl Stehle, teacher, West Milford High School, NJ; Jon Stubenvoll, OSPIRG; Margery Tabankin, Hollywood Women's Political Committee; Robert Weissman, *Multinational Monitor* and Marilyn Zola.

Thanks to John Richard and Bill Day for their editorial assistance and to the staff of the Center for Study of Responsive Law and Essential Information for production assistance. Special thanks to Claire Riley and Jim Donahue for their feedback and support. And finally, a special thanks to Ralph Nader whose inspiration and commitment to citizen participation fueled this project.

About the Author

Katherine Isaac, as project director at the Center for Study of Responsive Law, edited two consumer guides, *Being Beautiful* and *Eating Clean* and was editor of *Buyer's Market*, a monthly consumer newsletter. She is a contributing writer to the *Multinational Monitor* magazine. She is a contributor to *CIVITAS: A Framework for Civic Education*. Isaac is a graduate of the College of William and Mary with a B.A. in American Government.

Section One

Profiles of Students in Action

Saving What's Left of Florida
Channel One Boycott
Energy Patrols in Washington, D.C.
Public Interest Research Groups
Polystyrene Foam Ban in New Jersey
Study Group Report on Nursing Homes
Utah Pupils Fight Toxic Waste

PROFILES OF STUDENTS IN ACTION

Kids Against Pollution, a nationwide group started by Closter, New Jersey students, is calling for an amendment to the U.S. Constitution to guarantee the right to clean air, water and land.[1] Student journalists from Hazelwood, Missouri challenged school censorship of their student newspaper in the U.S. Supreme Court.[2] And students in Roxana, Missouri raised almost $6,000 to buy 10 acres of endangered rainforest in Costa Rica.[3] Students all over the United States are working to improve their schools, community, country and world. The following profiles of students in action serve as inspiring examples that show students can and do make a difference.

SAVING WHAT'S LEFT OF FLORIDA

It all started in 1987, when Charles DeVeney, a teacher at Coral Springs High School in Florida, was biking to work and saw that land near the school was slated to be cleared for development. He spoke to his outdoor education class about the rapid rate of deforestation in southern Florida and of his desire to preserve some of the area's nature for future generations. The students wanted to know what they could do.[4]

So DeVeney and his students formed a club, called Save What's Left, to try to save the 68 acres of dense wetlands, including a large stand of cypress trees, that were to be cut down to build soccer fields. The students began by writing letters to anyone they could think of who might be able to stop the destruction of the trees.[5]

At first, no one in the community listened. So Save What's Left students began to gather signatures on petitions to protest the development. Standing on the sidewalk in front of their school, they held signs asking drivers passing by in their cars to stop to sign the students' petition. The response was so overwhelming that on the second day of petitioning, the highway patrol had to direct traffic. Save What's Left eventually gathered 3,500 signatures from community residents concerned about the rapid rate of development.[6]

Upon further investigation, the students discovered that the developers had skirted regulations concerning development of wetlands. Because more than 10 acres of wetlands were at stake, the developers needed federal permission to build. But instead of going through the federal Environmental Protection Agency (EPA), which would have required public scrutiny of the project, the developers obtained two special permits - each for less than 10 acres - from the Army Corps of Engineers. The Corps, which is authorized to issue permits when less than 10 acres are involved, issued two permits in different names to allow the developers to bypass the EPA. Because the permits had already been issued and because the conflict involved federal agencies, local officials' hands were tied.[7]

But Save What's Left never gave up. The students spoke at city and county council meetings and gathered petitions to convince the City and County Commissions to ask residents to vote to buy the land. After two years, the issue was put on the ballot for the voters to decide. In March of 1989, Broward County voters approved a $75 million bond issue to buy the 68 acres of Coral Springs trees as well as 13 other sites in the county. The 68 acres turned out to be the largest cypress tree stand left in Broward County.[8] County Commissioner John Hart said, "It was because of people like these kids in Save What's Left that this got done."[9]

The city of Coral Springs and Save What's Left have since begun a project to completely restore the land over the next few years. Eventually it will be used as an outdoor classroom in which to teach environmental appreciation and to inspire other environmentalists to use their power to "save what's left." The outdoor education class that Save What's Left advisor Charles DeVeney teaches is so popular that some students wait two years to enroll.[10]

Save What's Left has grown to 300 members at Coral Springs High School and has expanded to schools in five other states as well as Yugoslavia and Colombia. Soon it will expand to Bolivia and Puerto Rico. And, in its four years of existence, the club has compiled an impressive list of achievements. Students collected over 25 tons of phone books for recycling. They participate in annual beach cleanups. They protested a proposed garbage incinerator, initiated a school recycling program and launched dozens of other school and community projects.[11]

Save What's Left students also picketed to protest the building of a strip shopping center. They argue there is no need for another shopping center, especially in an environmentally sensitive area. DeVeney and 10 club members were invited by Governor Lawton Chiles to attend 1991 Earth Day celebrations at the state capital.[12] And the students have been featured in several local and national newspapers and magazines. DeVeney was named Coral Springs High School Teacher of the year for 1987-88 and Citizen of the Year by the *Coral Springs News*.

In October 1990, Save What's Left members posted signs throughout Coral Springs near land being cleared for development. The students attached signs to trees reading "Please Save These Trees" and "Don't Let Them Kill Me." "It was a silent protest," said advisor DeVeney, "because the trees can't speak for themselves."[13]

The "silent protest" caused quite a stir in the community. The students, their advisor and the school board received threatening letters from Coral Ridge Properties, the developer involved, charging that the students had trespassed and insinuating that DeVeney should be fired.[14] Several newspapers supported the students' right to protest and attorneys in the community offered their services, if needed. Parents enthusiastically supported DeVeney and convinced the school board to endorse his activities.[15]

Asked why the club members are waging their campaigns, student Jennifer Swanberg answered, "I just got scared. I thought that one day I'd have kids with three heads because of all the pollution. We have to do something about it."[16]

The club once again took on developers to protest proposed changes in the city's tree ordinance. The students protested the city's Planning and Zoning Board proposal to allow developers and homeowners to replace each tree they remove — no matter how old or large — with a smaller, younger tree. Save What's Left students drafted their own ordinance for evaluation by the Planning and Zoning Board.[17]

"There will always be another game or another party," said Save What's Left member Alex Pomareda. "But there might not be another chance to save the environment."[18]

Save What's Left is setting up a computer network that will allow access to information and suggestions for starting a branch of this environmental group. Contact Charles DeVeney at Save What's Left, c/o Coral Springs High School, 7201 West Sample Road, Coral Springs, FL 33065.

CHANNEL ONE BOYCOTT

Students at North High School in Fargo, North Dakota returned to school in September, 1990 to find a newly-created 20-minute home room class.[19] School administrators created the class, by cutting the students' lunch period, to require students to watch Channel One, a television news program with commercials that is beamed into classrooms across the United States via satellite.[20] North High School agreed with Whittle Communications, the producer of Channel One, to require students to view the program every day in exchange for a TV satellite dish, two video cassette recorders and 37 television sets.[21]

Students at North High quickly objected to Channel One. Said student Leslie Doran, "I was looking forward to the program until I actually saw it. But the news lacked any kind of depth."[22] Student Jared Eide said of Channel One's news program, "You get more out of reading the newspaper headlines."[23] Other students objected to the cut in lunch time and to the mandatory viewing.

The concerns of students at North High School were not the first. Critics around the country objected to the viewing of commercials (advertisers pay Whittle Communications $150,000 for each 30-second commercial aired on Channel One) during classroom time. Only two minutes of the program is national news, another two minutes is advertisements, and the other 10 minutes is devoted to stories on topics from new hairstyles to new cars.[24] These stories often feature a product — one segment, for example, showed how Nike running shoes are manufactured.[25]

New York and Rhode Island banned their public schools from entering into contracts with Channel One. And California's superintendent of education has told California schools that "signing up violates the state's constitution."[26] California will withhold state funds, equal to the two minutes students spend watching commercials each day, from any school that signs up with Channel One.[27]

According to John Murray, professor at Kansas State University, "[A]n analysis of Channel One showed that it provided more in-depth coverage in the advertising than the news: A typical episode would devote only 125 seconds to seven news stories - 18 seconds per story - as opposed to 120 seconds for four television commercials."[28] Furthermore, the dialogue in both news and advertising runs at a pace of 140 words per minute, twice as fast as normal speech.[29]

In-depth, commercial-free news programs are available. Cable News Network (CNN) Newsroom is offered to schools without charge and has "longer, more clearly focused news stories — one news story was nearly four minutes long, as opposed to a maximum of 40 seconds on Channel One. And the dialogue on CNN Newsroom was more normal in pace — about 90 words per minute."[30] A number of public television stations around the country also produce news programs for students.[31]

Encouraged by a history teacher, the North High students planned a boycott of Channel One. On the first day, 250 students skipped home room. The next day, 600 of North High's 850 students stayed away from class. North High's principal made a deal with the students; if they returned to class, they could present their views to the school board.[32]

One week later, at a school board meeting, the student protestors made their case against Channel One. Student body president Erika Hovland told the board members, "Channel One has no educational value.

The school gets $50,000 in free equipment, but the students gain nothing."[33] Jared Eide advocated alternatives to Channel One, which do not contain commercials and emphasize more serious news. Eide also said students were willing to raise money to pay for the equipment obtained in the Channel One agreement.[34]

The students' walkout prompted the Board of Education to set up a committee made up of students, teachers and parents to study student complaints about the program. The committee examined five episodes in depth and issued a 25-page report of their findings. The committee concluded that Channel One should cover fewer stories in more depth on each program and that minority issues needed to be covered with more sensitivity.[35]

Channel One responded to the walkout and report by sending a company representative to meet with the students in March 1991. Gary Belis, a spokesperson for Whittle Communications, told the Associated Press in October 1990 that "Out of 4,000 schools on line, this is the only one raising a protest."[36]

The school board decided to eliminate the home room period, but students must view Channel One at the end of the day. The board formed another committee (without student representatives) to study the situation further. Says Erika Hovland, "It's a positive change, but our main goal is still to get rid of Channel One."[37] The students, who attracted media attention nationwide, vowed to continue their protest if the board decides to keep Channel One. Says student Leslie Doran of the boycott, "When you believe in something, you take a stand."[38]

ENERGY PATROLS IN WASHINGTON, DC

Students in the District of Columbia roam the halls of their elementary schools in search of open windows, leaky faucets and other forms of energy waste. Since 1984, energy patrols, teams of students wearing bright orange jackets and armed with clipboards, have contributed to an effort that has lowered the energy consumption and utility bills of District schools.[39]

Students patrol their schools in the morning and afternoon, and during recess, making note of broken windows, open doors and lights left on in empty classrooms. The patrols report their findings to a sponsoring teacher who in turn reports them to the principal or school custodian. Sometimes, the patrols leave notes or citations, advising teachers or students of energy violations.[40]

The purpose of the program is to lower utility bills and to teach students about energy conservation. The savings reported by some of the participating schools indicate that the students have been successful in meeting the program's goals: Principal Erma Fields credits the energy patrol with reducing the 1990 utility bill of J.O. Wilson Elementary School by $43,000.[41]

According to Lily Lewis of the D.C. Energy Office, almost 90 percent of D.C. public elementary schools participate in the program and more students are eager to join the patrols. Since the Energy Office can afford to give out only 10 jackets to each school, sponsoring teachers have implemented a policy of alternating the students on the patrol, so everyone has a chance to participate.[42]

One of the most enthusiastic participants in the program is the patrol at Park View Elementary School which is organized by science teacher Barry Sprague. As of March 1991, about 40 students were on a waiting list to join the 12 member patrol, which helped the school to save over $1,500 in utility bills in 1990. Sprague became concerned that students were only interested in the program because they liked to wear the orange jackets. So, he took the jackets away for a few weeks and was pleased to find the students still excited about energy conservation. The students "like the idea of being in charge,"[43] says Sprague, who describes the program as giving students the power "to accomplish something constructive"[44] through means as simple as switching off a light.

Park View School paid to have patches and baseball hats made for the patrollers to wear with their jackets. The students had a chance to show off their outfits when they appeared on a Cable News Network segment about the patrols.[45]

PUBLIC INTEREST RESEARCH GROUPS

State University of New York at Buffalo student Jill Siegel, at age 19, successfully lobbied the New York state legislature to pass a bill designed to protect consumers from fraud in sales of hearing aids, despite intense opposition from the hearing aid industry. Siegel's campaign was part of her legislative internship with the student group New York Public Interest Research Group (NYPIRG).[46] "From being a nervous and up-tight sophomore, I became more aggressive and poised as I went along," says Siegel.[47]

NYPIRG students at Queens College had released a study revealing that hearing aid dealers regularly convinced elderly customers to buy the devices whether or not they needed them and that dealers failed to alert customers who needed further medical attention. Siegel and the NYPIRG staff proposed that a law be passed to require all hearing aid customers to obtain a doctor's prescription before purchase to ensure that only those who need the device buy it. "Once when our bill got stalled, we held a press conference with the sponsors," says Siegel. "We put together a good campaign — lots of letters and telegrams — from hundreds of people. On such a relatively obscure issue, that much support is unexpected. It makes people pay a lot of attention."[48]

NYPIRG formed a coalition with senior citizen groups, doctors and audiologists which effectively pressured the legislature to pass the bill.[49] Siegel says, "Being there first hand was what really taught me about the legislature ... I always have felt that through college most of my true learning was gleaned from working with NYPIRG."[50]

College students around the country, as part of campus-based Public Interest Research Groups (PIRGs), actively participate in shaping issues facing their communities. PIRGs, which are student-run and student-funded organizations, exist on 175 campuses in 25 states and Canada. Each PIRG hires a small professional staff of lawyers, scientists and researchers to assist students in their various campaigns and to provide continuity to efforts sometimes interrupted by summer or semester breaks in the school year. Writes Kelley Griffin in *More Action for a Change,*

"Through PIRGs, students have uncovered everything from auto repair rip-offs to deadly toxic chemicals in drinking water sources, from dangerous and banned children's toys being sold in department stores to the lack of planning for emergency evacuation of people living around nuclear power plants."[51]

PIRG students launch campaigns on issues concerning the environment, university governance, government ethics, standardized testing, voter registration and many others. They encourage student activism by providing students with the skills and materials that they need to become involved in the issues that interest them. PIRGs teach students how to run a campaign, plan a rally, recruit students to join a group, attract media attention for an event and use many other organizing skills.

One of the most common tactics that PIRG activists use is research. As Kelley Griffin writes, research "may mean compiling and comparing tenant laws, or it may mean interviewing people in the community or workplace to compile statistics on anything from consumer purchasing habits to job safety. PIRG researchers may go over voting records of legislators or monitor campaign contributions."[52] But research is just the first step.

PIRGs also lobby the legislature, use the courts, act as a watchdog over government and corporations and educate the public. For example, New Jersey PIRG (NJPIRG) conducts regular "streamwalks" to monitor industry compliance with federal and state laws regulating what and how much of a pollutant may be discharged into waterways. Writes Griffin, "Equipped with hipboots, maps of streams, data sheets, and a list of industries and their discharge permits, students would hike or canoe along stream beds and make systematic assessments of sources of pollution."[53] NJPIRG students then release the results to encourage government agencies to enforce the laws. In one New Jersey county, streamwalkers stopped more than 20 plants from discharging wastes without a permit. The Environmental Protection Agency (EPA) gave NJPIRG a grant to produce a how-to manual for streamwalkers, and awarded former NJPIRG director Ed Lloyd its Special Award of Merit for citizen environmental activism.[54]

In 1983, several state PIRGs created the U.S. Public Interest Research Group, with headquarters in Washington, DC, to work at the national level on state PIRG issues, including support for voting reform, federal environmental legislation, including the Superfund to clean up hazardous waste and the Clean Air Act, utility rate reform and opposition to nuclear power.[55] U.S.PIRG also acts as a resource center and clearinghouse for state PIRG activities.

PIRG founder Ralph Nader writes in *More Action for a Change*, "The one underlying principle behind all PIRGs is that students are citizens, and that therefore their education should include experience in recognizing and solving society's shortfalls."[56]

POLYSTYRENE FOAM BAN IN NEW JERSEY

Students at West Milford High School in New Jersey, were required to write a current events paper for a social studies class in which they were studying Thomas Paine and the American Revolution. Sophomore Tanja Vogt wrote an essay about the danger to the environment of polystyrene foam (known by the trade name styrofoam) trays used by the school cafeteria. The trays contain chlorofluorocarbons which contribute to depletion of the ozone layer. The trays take up landfill space and are made with styrene, a central nervous system depressant.[57] Vogt noted that the Board of Education preferred to use polystyrene foam trays because they cost a nickel less than trays made of paper; Vogt, however, believed that students would be willing to pay the extra five cents to protect the environment. Social studies teacher Karl Stehle challenged his class to respond to the problem the way that Paine might have: to initiate a boycott campaign to ban the cafeteria's polystyrene foam trays.[58]

Class members surveyed other students, asking whether they would be willing to pay extra for paper trays. Their results — 86 percent of students at the high school and 92 percent of students at Macopin Middle School said yes — impressed Edward Vogel, the business administrator for the Board of Education. Vogel had the class set up a test week in which students could buy lunch on foam trays for $1.20 and on paper for $1.25.[59]

7

A group of about 200 students spent the week convincing others of the importance of banning polystyrene foam. Some even loaned nickels to students without the extra change. By the end of the week, it was clear that paper trays were preferred by most students: 72 percent of high school students, and 86 percent of middle school students had paid the extra nickel.[60]

The test week convinced the school board to institute an all-paper policy for township schools in February 1989.[61] A few months later, the school board, citing economic and environmental reasons, switched again from paper to reusable hard plastic, and from throwaway plastic utensils to silverware in six of the township's eight schools.[62]

The West Milford students expanded their campaign to a state-wide level, writing letters to over 700 New Jersey schools to request that they follow West Milford's lead and ban polystyrene foam. Their efforts attracted the attention of the State Commissioner of the Environment, Christopher J. Daggett, who visited West Milford High School in March, 1989 and promised students that the state would stop using immediately polystyrene foam products stockpiled in the department's cafeteria in Trenton.[63]

State Assembly member William J. Pascrell, Jr., inspired by a meeting with Tanja Vogt and the other students, proposed legislation that would require New Jersey to recycle half of its trash by 1992. Pascrell commented, "Young people led us to see the light on civil rights and the Vietnam war, and they're going to do it again. Young people are going to lead us to a cleaner and safer America."[64]

The students formed an environmental club which was an active participant in the successful nationwide boycott of McDonald's restaurants protesting the fast-food chain's use of polystyrene foam food containers. (For more on the boycott, see page 256). The students staged protests at their local McDonald's; student Kurtiz Schneid dressed in a clown outfit as "Ronald McToxic," alerting others to the dangers posed by polystyrene foam products.[65] The West Milford High environmental club began work in 1991 to convince the New Jersey legislature to pass a bottle deposit bill to encourage recycling of bottles and cans.[66]

In April, 1989 Tanja Vogt was asked to speak at the United Nations at a day-long forum sponsored by the U.N. Environment Project. Her message to the hundreds of students gathered at the conference: "Don't ever let anyone tell you that one person cannot make a difference."[67]

STUDY GROUP REPORT ON NURSING HOMES

In 1969, the U.S. Senate released a report, *Developments in Aging*, which outlined the dismaying plight of the elderly in the United States: older people were likely to be living lives of what consumer advocate Ralph Nader termed "poverty, sickness, loneliness and powerlessness."[68] Nader, believing that these conditions were focused most intensely in the nation's nursing homes, organized a task force to study nursing home conditions and the responsibility of the federal government to elderly residents. What made this task force distinctive was its membership. Nader suggested that a group of six high school seniors run the project, contributing their energy and enthusiasm to an effort of young citizens reaching out to older citizens.[69]

The task force determined that a broad-based study was necessary to trace the reasons for nursing home conditions and make suggestions for improvement. Over the summer of 1970, the student task force worked in three nursing homes, and visited over 20 others, to gain firsthand knowledge of the situation. The team then divided their task into specific areas of responsibility, each member studying individually a different aspect of the problem.[70]

Claire Townsend and Patricia Pittis investigated government involvement in nursing homes. Catherine Morgan was responsible for analyzing legislation affecting the elderly. Three of the students examined issues directly related to the day-to-day operation of nursing homes: Lallie Lloyd looked at the financial aspects, Janet Keyes studied personnel, health care and overall environment, and Margaret Quinn made a detailed study of drugs used in nursing homes. Social and economic conditions of the elderly outside of the nursing home were studied by Elizabeth Baldwin.[71]

While the task force was advised by an instructor, a research assistant and Ralph Nader, it was the six students who conducted the project. They spent months examining government reports and documents on aging. They interviewed more than 85 officials of the federal government, state agencies, the nursing home industry and the medical profession. They also conducted interviews with staff and residents of the nursing homes that they visited.[72]

The students were horrified at the neglect and poor treatment of the elderly they witnessed in nursing homes: patients tied down in beds or wheelchairs, sedatives freely prescribed and emergency call button signals ignored.[73] These findings were incorporated into a 346-page report, later published as a book, which recommended specific measures that the federal government, the nursing home industry and the medical profession should take to improve the lives of nursing home residents.[74]

In December 1970, the task force testified along with Nader before a Senate Subcommittee on Aging. Claire Townsend told the subcommittee that 80 percent of homes receiving public tax dollars did not meet federal standards of care. Nader urged the subcommittee to pressure President Richard Nixon's administration to force nursing homes to comply with minimum standards and called for a national retired peoples' "liberation movement."[75]

In her preface to the book, Claire Townsend argues that the youth of the task force was an asset in producing a fair, critical report: "We have no vested interests to serve, no reason to keep silent about what we see, no cause to dole out praise or blame, no excuses to make on behalf of anyone or anything."[76] As she said before the Senate subcommittee, "Age really has nothing to do with it. It's your dedication and devotion that counts."[77]

UTAH PUPILS FIGHT TOXIC WASTE

Teacher Barbara Lewis' goal was to create environmental awareness among her pupils at Jackson Elementary School in Salt Lake City, Utah. "I had no idea I was unleashing a tiger," says Lewis.[78] But when her fourth, fifth and sixth grade pupils discovered a toxic waste site three blocks from their school, they went into action.

The site contained a stockpile of over 50,000 barrels, including many that held dangerous chemicals. Some of the barrels were rusted and corroded and were leaking residue onto the ground. The students set out to determine if the leakage had contaminated the community's groundwater supply.[79]

Local health department officials told Lewis, "There's nothing children can do. They'll be in high school before they see any results."[80] When the students themselves called the officials, Lewis says, "[T]hey were shooed away like pesky flies."[81]

The students refused to buy into the pessimism of the health department. They conducted a door-to-door survey of their neighborhood, informing residents about the dangers of hazardous wastes and searching for wells from which health officials could take water samples. They devoured newspaper and magazine articles about hazardous waste and telephoned and wrote letters to health department officials, the national and regional offices of the Environmental Protection Agency and the local power company which owned the land where the hazardous waste was located.[82]

Their efforts attracted the attention of the media, and eventually of Mayor Palmer DePaulis, a former schoolteacher, who promised to work toward completing a clean-up effort within 18 months. A few weeks later, workers started removing barrels from the site.[83]

In June 1987, the day of the students' sixth-grade graduation party, EPA researchers came to Utah to test the site. The students left the party to watch officials dig wells to test the water. Nine months later, student Heather Hilliard received the test results which indicated that harmful chemicals, solvents, coal tars, pesticides and heavy metals had polluted the soil and groundwater at the site. In the Salt Lake Valley, drinking water is collected and mixed — the dump, therefore, threatened the health of over 477,000 people. It was soon recommended for placement on EPA's National Priorities List.[84]

The students' concern spread to other dumps around the state. They raised $2,700 which they wanted to donate to the state to help clean up any hazardous waste site. However, no legal mechanism existed through which Utah could accept the funds. Undaunted by the messy politics surrounding the issue, the students wrote a resolution proposing a Utah State Superfund and then lobbied for the bill in the state legislature.[85]

They called the offices of the legislators; they spoke before the senate; they passed out flyers decorated with crayon. One senator said, "No one has more effectively lobbied us than these young kids. And they didn't even have to buy us dinner."[86] The bill passed unanimously.

After these students went on to junior high school, Lewis' new pupils took up the cause of social change, applying the lessons learned by the older children to their own projects. When they discovered that a single tree, in its average 50-year lifetime, will contribute $62,000 worth of air pollution control, they worked to receive two city grants, totalling $3,600, to plant 187 trees in their neighborhood. Later, they too took on the Utah State Legislature, successfully arguing for a law that created $10,000 in grants for children in Utah to plant trees. And through a petition and letter writing campaign, the students helped persuade the U.S. Congress to make money for tree-planting available to students through the America the Beautiful Act of 1990.[87]

Lewis insists that her pupils are not any smarter or any more privileged than other students. In fact,

Jackson Elementary has the lowest per capita income in the city's school district. What is special about these students is their belief in their ability to solve some of the problems they see around them. Lewis says, "[O]ne thing they do have is courage. They don't give up easily. They believe that the future depends on them. They're not afraid to attack things that other people say can't be done."[88]

Barbara Lewis has written a practical guide for students called *The Kids Guide to Social Action: How to Solve the Social Problems You Choose — And Turn Creative Thinking into Positive Action*; see bibliography below.

BIBLIOGRAPHY

Bell, Thomas. "Schools Put Power in Students' Hands: Energy Patrols Boost Morale, Lower Utility Bills," *The Washington Post*. February 7, 1991.

Bendavid, Naftali. "It's Not Easy Being Green, But Push by Broward Students Takes Root," *The Miami Herald*. April, 21, 1991.

Clark, Chuck. "The Fourth 'R:' Recycling Finds Niche in School Curriculums as Teen Activists Rally Behind the Environment," Fort Lauderdale *Sun-Sentinel*. January 20, 1991.

Curreri, Gary. "Students do Speaking for Trees," *Coral Springs News*. October 24, 1990.

DeVeney, Charles. *Save What's Left: Centuries to Create, Seconds to Destroy*. Coral Springs, FL: Save What's Left, 1991.

Griffin, Kelley. *More Action for a Change*. New York: Dembner Books, 1987.

Healy, Michelle. "Despite Static, Channel One Has Strong First Year," *USA Today*. March 5, 1991.

Henderson, Lynne. "Commissioners Delay Approval of Tree Ordinance Modifications," *Coral Springs News*. November 14, 1990.

Hutt, Katherine. "Drastic Plastic: West Milford Kids 'Recruit' Dr. Ruth," The North Jersey *Herald and News*. June 8, 1989.

James, George. "Pupil Starts A Revolution of Her Own: Ban Plastics," *The New York Times*. April 28, 1989.

Kahn, Larry. "Dispute Continues Over Protest," *Coral Springs Forum*. November 15, 1990.

Kelly, Robert. "Pupils Putting Funds Where Forests Are," *St. Louis Post-Dispatch*.

Lardner, George, Jr. "Nursing Home Conditions Hit By Nader Unit," *The Washington Post*. December 18, 1970.

Lewis, Barbara A. *The Kid's Guide to Social Action: How to Solve the Social Problems You Choose — And Turn Creative Thinking into Positive Action*. Minneapolis: Free Spirit Publishing, 1991. (800) 735-7323.

Murray, John. "TV in the Classroom: News or Nikes?," *Extra!* September/October 1991.

Ridgeway, James and Dan Bischoff. "Fighting Ronald McToxic: Children Lead a Crusade Against the Clown and His Clamshells," *Village Voice*. Vol. XXXV. No. 24. June 12, 1990.

Taylor, Stuart, Jr., "Court, 5-3, Widens Power of Schools to Act as Censors," *The New York Times*. January 14, 1988.

Townsend, Claire. *Old Age: The Last Segregation*. New York: Bantam Books, 1971.

"TV Trouble at North High," *Zillions*. April/May 1991.

"Young Take Environmental Concern to United Nations," *The Sussex Herald*. May 2, 1989.

Section Two

A History of Citizen Movements

Civil Rights Movement
Labor Movement
Women's Rights Movement
Consumer Movement
Environmental Movement

A HISTORY OF CITIZEN MOVEMENTS

INTRODUCTION

Historian Howard Zinn compares the task of the historian to that of the mapmaker, who, "in order to produce a usable drawing for practical purposes, must first flatten and distort the shape of the earth, then choose out of the bewildering mass of geographic information those things needed for the purpose of this or that particular map."[1] A map for bicyclists, then, would emphasize information quite different from the information on a map made for airplane pilots.

But the choices historians make about what to emphasize are not merely for technical purposes. Rather, any emphasis necessarily supports "some kind of interest, whether economic or political or racial or national or sexual."[2] The interest supported by many history textbooks used in schools in the United States today is simply an effort to "please everyone and offend no one,"[3] concluded a review of textbooks commissioned by People for the American Way. The review found a pattern in which "textbook publishers have removed or downplayed subjects that are controversial."[4] As a result, "the dynamic sense of government and politics — the fierce debates, colorful characters, triumphs and tragedies — is lost."[5]

The histories in this book — of the civil rights, labor, women's rights, consumer and environmental movements — emphasize and illuminate the role citizens (rather than government and other institutions) have played and continue to play in winning and securing rights and achieving access to and participation in the process of government. This emphasis was chosen to serve the interest of inspiring and informing students about the tradition of citizen action in the United States.

By highlighting the successes and failures and the wide variety of tactics and strategies in these citizen movements, students will learn that controversy and conflict are a normal part of change. Citizen activists, in addition to challenging the policies of government and other institutions, often disagreed among themselves about the best way to achieve the same goal. Women working for the right to vote disagreed over the best strategy and thus launched both a campaign

for a federal amendment to the U.S. Constitution and a campaign to win the right to vote on a state-by-state basis.

Furthermore, these activists were not always fair and tolerant even when challenging the government to be fair and tolerant. For example, male abolitionists originally excluded women from their activities. Many of these women began the campaign for woman suffrage and later white suffragists excluded African American women working for the same goal.

Studying these strategies and conflicts can help students learn to think critically about their government and about the role of citizens in a democracy.

The five movements discussed here do not begin to cover the wide range of citizen activism in U.S. history. Rich histories of activism and resistance are also evident in the movements of populist farmers and of students, for an end to war and the arms race and for the rights of Native Americans, Latinos, disabled people (see pages 241-242) the elderly and gay and lesbian Americans. For example, Native Americans, from fish-ins at Puget Sound to the occupation of the Bureau of Indian Affairs in Washington, DC, have worked to protect their tribal cultures and religions as well as land and water rights.

Advocates for the elderly have protested mandatory retirement and have worked to alleviate the problems of poverty and health care costs among the aged. At the age of 66, Maggie Kuhn founded the Gray Panthers to work for better housing, medical care and employment opportunities for the aged and to connect the younger and older generations. These movements had varying successes and many setbacks, but each one placed on the national agenda concerns not previously addressed, and each group continues to secure and protect basic rights.

Many of the activists in the movements described in the following pages did not succeed in every campaign. But many persevered and in so doing changed their own lives and the lives of others. They were part of a struggle to make the world a better place and in so doing demonstrated that the pursuit of justice is a central precondition to the pursuit of happiness.

A History of the Civil Rights Movement

Introduction

Civil rights are basic rights, privileges and protections which belong in principle to every citizen of the United States. Though civil rights are constantly evolving, most agree that civil rights minimally constitute the freedom of speech and of religion, rights of those accused of crimes (to representation and trial by jury), rights to participate in the political process and the right to equal treatment under the law. Although the U.S. Constitution guarantees these basic rights, many groups have had to fight for the opportunity to enjoy them.

The U.S. Constitution, at the time it was written and for nearly a century afterward, considered African Americans to be property, not citizens. Interpretations of the Constitution in the late 18th and early 19th centuries continued to legitimize slavery. As late as 1857, the Supreme Court, in the *Dred Scott* decision, affirmed that even free black people "had no rights which the white man was bound to respect; and that the negro might justly and lawfully be reduced to slavery for his benefit."[1]

Only after a devastating civil war was the Constitution amended to abolish slavery, with the Thirteenth Amendment in 1865. The Fourteenth Amendment, ratified in 1868, was designed to guarantee the rights of free black people by providing that no state could "deprive any person of life, liberty or property, without due process of law; nor deny to any person within its jurisdiction the equal protection of the laws." The Fifteenth Amendment, ratified in 1870, was an attempt to protect the right of African American men to vote. But the legal end to slavery by no means guaranteed most basic civil rights to African Americans.

The Civil Rights movement usually refers to a series of protests, which employed a variety of tactics, by African Americans and others in the 1950s and 1960s against injustices dating back to slavery. Though the modern movement is the most well-known period of African American activism, it was by no means the beginning. During 250 years of slavery, black women and men overtly and covertly resisted their brutal treatment. After the Civil War, African Americans organized community groups and national movements to protest and change their continued unequal treatment. Such organizing and activism existed in varying degrees throughout the 19th and 20th centuries. Although African Americans are not the only Americans who have experienced repression and unequal treatment, the black Civil Rights movement dramatically changed the country and inspired subsequent citizen action to obtain and protect basic rights.

Slavery

By 1619, one million Africans had already been brought to Spanish and Portuguese colonies in South America and the Caribbean to work as slaves.[2] The first Africans arrived in the English colony of Jamestown, Virginia in 1619. Some historians write that these Africans were used as indentured servants, freed after a certain period of servitude. But in any case, the colonists quickly made the Africans slaves for life.[3] Slavery in the British colonies grew as the plantation system grew. By 1700, there were 6,000 African slaves in Virginia. By 1763, that number was 170,000 — about half of the population.[4]

Slavery tore families apart; slavery did not recognize marriages and did not allow children to attend school. Slaves performed backbreaking labor from dawn to dusk while subsisting on a minimum of nourishment. White people could legally beat or kill slaves for no reason. Slaves were prohibited from making contracts, owning property and learning to read and write.[5]

By 1830, slavery had been abolished in most areas of the North and was confined largely to the southern states, where slave labor was key to the plantation economy.[6] Many slaves produced cotton, the backbone crop of southern agriculture. Providing free labor to a developing country; slaves, while reaping no benefits, created the affluence needed for a strong and stable economy.[7]

The myth that slaves enjoyed and benefited from their enslavement was perpetuated by white Americans to justify slavery.[8] Yet slaves resisted by running away and engaging in "sabotage, slowdowns, and subtle forms of resistance which asserted, if only to themselves and their brothers and sisters, their dignity as human beings."[9]

In the early 1800s, free black people and white people in the North campaigned for an end to slavery by launching the abolitionist movement.[10] In 1829, David Walker, son of a slave, distributed a pamphlet, *Walker's Appeal*, calling on black people to fight for their freedom.[11] Another former slave, Frederick Douglass, escaped to the North in 1838, "where he became the most famous black man of his time, as lecturer, newspaper editor, writer."[12] Douglass spoke out and wrote about ending slavery. He often disagreed with the moderate tactics of white abolitionists.[13] As historian Howard Zinn writes, African Americans were often "more willing to engage in armed insurrection, but also more ready to use existing political devices — the ballot box, the Constitution — anything to further their cause. ... Moral pressure would not do it alone, the blacks knew; it would take all sorts of tactics, from elections to rebellions."[14]

During the 1850s, thousands of slaves escaped to the North, Canada and Mexico, many aided by the Underground Railroad. Harriet Tubman, who escaped slavery as a young woman, escorted more than 300 slaves to freedom.[15]

When civil war divided the nation, President Abraham Lincoln issued the Emancipation Proclamation on January 1, 1863 to free the slaves of all regions of the country engaged in rebellion against the Union. But the Proclamation did not address slavery in states belonging to the Union. Abolitionists flooded Congress with petitions asking for legislation to end all slavery. Congress adopted the Thirteenth Amendment, making slavery illegal, in 1865.[16]

Stokely Carmichael, a leader in the modern movement for civil rights, writes in *Black Power*, "The fact of slavery had to have profound impact on the subsequent attitudes of the larger society toward the black man."[17] The emancipation of slaves did not abolish racial prejudices ingrained for hundreds of years. Carmichael writes, "When some people compare the black American to 'other immigrant' groups in this country, they overlook the fact that slavery was peculiar to the blacks. No other minority group in this country was ever treated as legal property."[18]

White Americans were surprised when suddenly, nearly 100 years after slavery had been abolished, African Americans protested. But as Howard Zinn writes, "The memory of oppressed people is one thing that cannot be taken away, and for such people, with such memories, revolt is always an inch below the surface. For blacks in the United States, there was the memory of slavery, and after that of segregation, lynching, humiliation. And it was not just a memory but a living presence — part of the daily lives of blacks in generation after generation."[19] Many laws had been passed and decisions made which were meant to guarantee the rights of black citizens; yet, these initiatives were largely meaningless, having no real effect on their lives.

FROM RECONSTRUCTION TO JIM CROW

For a time after emancipation, under the Reconstruction Acts of 1867 and 1868, the Republican-dominated Congress forced radical Reconstruction on the South, consequently protecting the rights of African Americans to vote and hold office. Voters elected hundreds of local, state and federal black officials, including two U.S. Senators and 20 U.S. Representatives.[20] However, white Southerners, outraged by sudden black political potency, were determined to reverse Reconstruction gains and the federal government pulled out the troops charged with enforcing Reconstruction laws.[21]

Southern governments instituted a series of laws, beginning in the late 1880s, which disenfranchised southern black people via poll taxes, literacy requirements and other barriers to voter registration.[22] Because 95 percent of freed slaves were illiterate and because they possessed no capital in the form of cash or land, the new laws shut African Americans out of the political process.[23] (For more on disenfranchisement laws, see page 228). In addition to legal barriers, white men practiced violence to keep African Americans from voting.[24]

Under the Jim Crow system of segregation, African Americans were completely segregated from white southern society. Black Southerners were prohibited from using the same water fountains, rest rooms, railroad cars, lunch counters, department store dressing rooms and much more.[25] Although the Fourteenth Amendment to the U.S. Constitution was ratified in 1868 to guarantee "equal protection" under the law to freed slaves, many southern state and local governments enacted laws mandating segregation.[26]

In 1887, Florida passed the first state law mandating segregation on railroad cars, and was quickly followed by Mississippi, Texas and Louisiana. Louisiana's 1890 "Act to promote the comfort of passengers," required railroad companies to provide "equal but separate accommodations" for black and white passengers.[27]

Black citizens of Louisiana organized to test the law. On June 7, 1892, Homer Adolph Plessy boarded a railroad car reserved for white passengers and was arrested, as expected. Plessy argued before New Orleans District Court Judge John H. Ferguson that racial segregation was illegal under the Fourteenth Amendment to the U.S. Constitution. Ferguson ruled against Plessy and the case was appealed to the Louisiana Supreme Court and then to the U.S. Supreme Court.[28]

In 1896, the Supreme Court ruled in *Plessy* v. *Ferguson* that the segregation of races was constitutional as long as facilities were "separate but equal."[29] Life in the South was already rigidly segregated, but *Plessy* sanctioned that separation. White Southerners ignored the "equal" provision: public facilities and services for black citizens continued to be inferior or did not exist at all.[30]

In addition to political exclusion and social segregation from white America, African Americans contin-

ued to suffer economically. During Reconstruction, Congress debated whether to compensate newly freed slaves for centuries of servitude by confiscating land from plantation owners and giving it to former slaves.[31] Congress rejected this proposal. Even if former slaves could have afforded to buy land, white Southerners would not sell it to them because they knew that land provided an economic power base which would threaten white domination.[32]

Sharecropping, living on and farming land owned by someone else and paying crops to the owner as rent, became the most common employment for freed slaves, often on the same plantations on which they had worked as slaves. The system kept black sharecroppers dependent on the plantation. In 1917, the Supreme Court ruled that such a system was unconstitutional, but federal authorities did little to enforce the ruling.[33]

In the late 1800s and early 1900s, more African Americans began to escape sharecropping by moving to southern cities or to the industrial North. Southern government officials and landlords attempted to prevent them from leaving by requiring labor recruiters to obtain expensive licenses and by intimidating emigrants.[34] Yet, this did not stop the ever-increasing migration. Though they had no money, many black Southerners packed up their few belongings and moved to the city.

The small number of African Americans who lived in the North in the late 1800s and early 1900s did not experience the same violence and strict racial codes as their counterparts in the South. However, economic opportunities were limited severely. Factories discriminated against black workers and most labor unions (with the notable exception of the Knights of Labor) refused to admit black members. Black workers often faced intimidation and violence from white workers who were afraid of losing their jobs. Those with factory jobs received less pay for the same work as white immigrants and were rarely hired for or promoted to skilled jobs, so they could not obtain qualifications which would allow them to advance.[35]

Black citizen organizations pressured government officials, employers and union leaders to remove the barriers to equal opportunity. They pointed out to unions that unorganized black workers were a threat to white unions because black workers could often only find employment as strikebreakers. But still the American Federation of Labor (AFL) stalled and made no real attempt to integrate its affiliates.[36]

Despite the concerted, almost overwhelming effort to prevent African Americans from achieving equality, black activists, little by little, forced the government to address their concerns. They organized their own unions, associations, clubs and societies to advance the cause of economic, political and social justice and equality.

Black workers formed their own unions, such as the Workingmen's Association of Pensacola of 1868 and the Labor League of Jacksonville of the early 1870s, to protest discrimination both by industry and white unions. In 1869, a group of black laborers formed the National Labor Union.[37] In 1881, a group of black women formed the Washerwomen's Association of Atlanta. They struck for better pay, but the strike failed due to the economic intimidation of the city council and landlords.[38] Later, in 1925, A. Philip Randolph organized the black porters and maids who worked for the Pullman railway company into the Brotherhood of Sleeping Car Porters.[39] (See page 68 for more on the Brotherhood).

In 1891, Thomas Fortune founded the Afro-American League to fight for "the full privileges of citizenship"[40] for African Americans. During the period from 1890 to 1920, northern middle-class black women initiated a women's club movement to aid poor black people migrating from the South. The clubs "stressed community betterment, education and self-improvement ... [and] continual emphasis on race pride and on advancement for all black people."[41]

Stemming from the club movement was a campaign against the mass lynchings of black men in the South. Black journalist Ida B. Wells-Barnett travelled around the country to document lynchings, distribute her pamphlet *Southern Horrors* and organize anti-lynching societies. In 1895, Wells-Barnett wrote:

> *Not all or nearly all the murders done by white men, during the past thirty years in the South, have come to light, but the statistics*

as gathered and preserved by white men, and which have not been questioned, show that during these years more than ten thousand Negroes have been killed in cold blood, without the formality of judicial trial and legal execution ... no white man has been lynched for the murder of colored people.[42]

Lynchings often took place with the tacit consent of the local and state government. According to historian Richard Kluger, "It was the exceedingly rare white man who was tried for participating in a lynching, and a conviction was unheard of."[43]

Another organization dedicated to improving the lives of African Americans, the National Association for the Advancement of Colored People (NAACP), was

NAACP flyer urging action against lynching of African Americans, 1919

founded in 1909 by a group of middle-class black and white men and women, including Mary White Ovington, W.E.B. DuBois, Ida B. Wells-Barnett and William English Walling. They called for a national conference on the "Negro question." Of the six officers of the organization, only one was black: W.E.B. DuBois, an educated, middle-class scholar. DuBois was involved in an all-black scholarly movement called the Niagara movement. Its members were encouraged to join the NAACP since the two groups had nearly identical platforms, including "freedom of speech and criticism, an unfettered and unsubsidized press, manhood suffrage, the abolition of all caste distinctions based simply on race and color, the recognition of the principle of human brotherhood as a practical present creed ... a belief in the dignity of labor and united effort to realize these ideals under wise and courageous leadership."[44]

But Wells-Barnett and other black activists criticized the NAACP for its moderation and patronization of black members. When writing the new organization's statement of purpose, Wells-Barnett advocated an anti-lynching resolution which the NAACP leadership did not adopt.[45]

As more black people migrated North, some white people began to sympathize with the black people who lived in poor conditions in urban ghettoes. In 1910, an interracial group of New Yorkers concerned about the plight of black people advocated cooperation among existing organizations so that efforts would not be duplicated. Representatives from a number of groups met to form what later was called the National Urban League. Again, the founders were primarily middle-class men and women. Their goals were the study of conditions for black people in cities, establishment of "betterment" agencies when necessary and the training of young men and women for social work.[46]

While the NAACP and the National Urban League advocated working with the white establishment to improve conditions for African Americans, Marcus Garvey offered a radically different proposal. Garvey, a native of Jamaica, founded the Universal Negro Improvement Association (UNIA), and established the first U.S. branch of the organization in New York in 1917. He organized thousands of urban black people to promote racial pride, self-help and independence.[47] The UNIA events were characterized by elaborate marches, military uniforms and flags of red, black and green to symbolize a united African nation.[48]

A gifted speaker, Garvey verbalized what many African Americans had been thinking. Garvey criticized the NAACP and the National Urban League as white-dominated and elitist and instead called for the establishment of a united Africa where "all the Negro peoples of the world [would unite] into one great body to establish a country and government absolutely their own."[49] To this end, Garvey formed an all-black steamship company to return African Americans to their native Africa. The Black Star Line would be entirely run by African Americans, offering even the poorest a chance to buy a share in the company.[50]

Garvey was convicted of fraudulent use of the mails to sell Black Star stock, "though there was no evidence that he was guilty of anything more than poor management, inexperience, and bad judgment in choosing some of his associates."[51] In 1927, he was deported as an undesirable alien.[52] He went to Jamaica, where he was given a hero's welcome. He organized new UNIA chapters in Jamaica and cabled weekly inspirational messages to a black newspaper in New York.[53] His ships never sailed to Africa but his movement gave many African Americans a sense of racial pride and hope for the future.

These and other movements and organizations created by and for black men and women had mixed success, but they attest to the spirit of protest always alive among African Americans.

World War I created an industrial boom in the North, attracting black workers in search of better pay and better treatment to cities including Chicago and New York. As more and more black Southerners migrated North, some white people resorted to mob violence. In the "Red Summer" of 1919, riots broke out in 25 cities, injuring and killing many black people.[54] In the 1920s, extreme racism in both the North and the South was evidenced by a resurgence in Ku Klux Klan (KKK) membership, which climbed to between three and five million.[55]

Despite such harsh conditions, black communities in the North flourished culturally. In the 1920s, urban black artists, most notably in Harlem, made outstanding contributions to art, literature and music, in a period known as the Black or Harlem Renaissance.[56] Much of their work expressed anger at the injustices committed against them. Langston Hughes' poem, *Lenox Avenue Mural*, foreshadowed the movements which would take place in the 1950s and 1960s:

> *What happens to a dream deferred?*
> > *Does it dry up*
> > *like a raisin in the sun?*
> > *Or fester like a sore -*
> > *And then run?*
> *Does it stink like rotten meat?*
> *Or crust and sugar over -*
> *like a syrupy sweet?*
>
> *Maybe it just sags like a heavy load.*
>
> *Or does it explode?*[57]

The Great Depression was a difficult time for African Americans in both the North and the South. Farm prices plummeted and insects and floods destroyed crops. The New Deal Agricultural Adjustment Act hurt black sharecroppers because the government paid growers to destroy some of their crops and to reduce production so as to raise the prices of farm products by creating a shortage. Land owners then threw many of their black tenants off the land without giving them any of the government subsidy.[58] Because land owners dominated the local offices which administrated New Deal programs, black sharecroppers generally received smaller relief payments and their complaints were the last to be addressed.[59] Sharecroppers made several attempts to form unions and collectives, but economic gains were minimal and the attempts often resulted in violent retaliation from white landowners and police officials.[60]

The depressed economy led white workers, desperate for work, to look for jobs previously filled only by black workers. Many white workers demanded that black workers be fired and white workers hired in their place.[61] Black workers were thus displaced from nearly every type of employment. And New Deal provisions for a minimum wage and social security did not cover the few types of employment in which black workers dominated, such as sharecropping and domestic service.[62]

Black workers protested discrimination in hiring. Black people boycotted the businesses which refused to employ them in "Don't Buy Where You Can't Work" campaigns.[63] But it was U.S. production of materiel for the war in Europe that created jobs which brought many more black workers to northern cities from the South. The shift to a war economy meant some improvement in job prospects for all Americans, including African Americans. Skilled jobs were now available to more black workers and their median income rose in proportion to that of white workers.[64]

However, discrimination in hiring practices was far from eliminated. Black workers, the last to be hired, remained disproportionately poor and concentrated in unskilled and menial jobs.[65] In 1941, African Americans, led by A. Philip Randolph of the Brotherhood of Sleeping Car Porters, threatened President Franklin Roosevelt with the embarrassing prospect of 100,000 black protestors marching on the nation's capital during a war, unless he outlawed discrimination in hiring by the war industries.[66] The threat from the March on Washington movement forced Roosevelt to issue Executive Order 8802 on June 25, 1941, the first presidential directive for African Americans since Reconstruction, which not only banned hiring discrimination in defense and government work, but also established a Fair Employment Practices Commission (FEPC) to ensure compliance with the executive order.[67]

Though the unaddressed injustice of segregation in the World War II army and the weakness of the FEPC continued to anger many African Americans,[68] the March on Washington victory was impressive. African Americans began to speak of a "Double V" campaign: victory in the war and victory against racism at home.[69]

Yet the war itself did not lead to victory for African Americans. When the soldiers returned home to their old jobs, black workers, who had been the last hired, were the first to be fired.[70]

ROOTS OF THE CIVIL RIGHTS MOVEMENT

Many historians cite World War II as an important turning point for African Americans.[71] This period was the first since Reconstruction in which the federal government, for a variety of reasons, took seriously African Americans' demands for justice. First, black workers had made significant gains through campaigns including the March on Washington movement in eliminating employment discrimination and making their voices heard in policy making decisions. Second, as Constance Baker Motley, who was an NAACP attorney in the 1940s, recalled, "Here we were as a nation involved in a war to make the world safe for democracy, and one of the embarrassing features was that blacks were segregated in our armed forces, and they resented it. And here we were trying to represent ourselves as a democratic nation."[72]

After World War II ended, the United States began an ideological battle with the Soviet Union to establish influence in the Third World. Many of the African independence movements of this time allied with the Soviet Union. America's treatment of African Americans gave the Soviets a powerful weapon in the war for allies, for it was easy to imagine how badly a country which did not treat its own citizens equally would treat citizens of Asia and Latin America.[73]

President Harry Truman appointed, in 1946, a Committee on Civil Rights. Truman was blunt about the motivation for his sudden interest in rights for African Americans, an issue the federal government had ignored since Reconstruction: "We cannot escape the fact that our civil rights record has been an issue in world politics .... Those with competing philosophies have stressed — and are shamelessly distorting — our shortcomings .... The United States is not so strong, the final triumph of the democratic ideal is not so inevitable that we can ignore what the world thinks of us or our record."[74]

THE CAMPAIGN FOR SCHOOL DESEGREGATION

Many people who worked for civil rights thought that one of the keys to achieving social and economic equality was an integrated school system.[75] Black schools, from elementary, high school and college to graduate and professional schools, were for the most part substandard or nonexistent. For example, in 1930, South Carolina spent 10 times more on each white student than it did on each black student, and Alabama, Florida, Georgia and Mississippi spent five times more.[76] According to the *Journal of Negro Education*, black teachers were paid less than half what white teachers were paid; 17 of the 19 states with statutes authorizing school segregation had no graduate or professional schools for black students; and in some of the northern states where no laws mandated segregation, some communities practiced it.[77]

The NAACP decided to challenge school segregation in the courts. The NAACP reasoned that the refusal of states to provide adequate schools for black students violated the equal protection clause of the Fourteenth Amendment, and that with persistence, the courts would uphold the Constitution and require states to integrate the education system.[78]

In 1935, the NAACP hired as its chief legal counsel Charles Houston, the dean of the law school at Howard University, the largest black college in the United States. Houston's strategy was to begin to test segregation at the graduate and professional school level, where the lack of equal facilities was most pronounced. In addition, Houston decided that integrating graduate schools was less threatening to white Americans than integrating elementary schools.[79]

One of Houston's former students, Thurgood Marshall, suggested that the NAACP take the case of Donald Gaines Murray, who was denied admission to the University of Maryland law school due to his race.[80] In 1935, Marshall and Houston argued in court that since Maryland had no black law schools, Murray must be allowed to attend the white university. The municipal court ruled in Murray's favor, and the state court upheld this ruling on appeal in *Murray* v. *Pearson*.[81] According to Juanita Jackson Mitchell of the Baltimore NAACP, "The colored people in Baltimore were on fire when Thurgood did that. They were euphoric with victory.... We didn't know about the Constitution. He brought us the Constitution as a document like Moses brought his people the Ten Commandments."[82]

In 1938, Houston and Marshall argued a similar case, *Missouri ex rel. Gaines* v. *Canada*, before the Supreme Court and won, entitling Lloyd Lionel Gaines to attend the University of Missouri School of Law. Thurgood Marshall took Houston's place when he left the NAACP in 1940 and continued to win cases regarding segregation in graduate and professional schools.[83]

Although lawyers at the NAACP differed somewhat in their proposed strategy to challenge unequal schooling at the elementary and secondary level, on the goal of ending segregation, all agreed, believing that even if black and white schools were made materially equal, segregation was an inherently unequal arrangement.[84] They thought that segregating black children from white children instilled in them feelings of inferiority. In June 1950, a NAACP conference resolved that all future legal battles would "be aimed at obtaining education on a non-segregated basis and that no relief other than that will be acceptable."[85] Then NAACP lawyers began to search for cases across the nation to test the *Plessy* v. *Ferguson* separate but equal doctrine.[86]

One case involved a high school in Prince Edward County, Virginia. The NAACP did not find the case; the case found the NAACP. Prince Edward County built Robert R. Moton High School in 1939, the first high school in the county that black children were allowed to attend. Though the school had few facilities compared to white Farmville High School and its teachers were paid less than the those at the white high school, the black community in the county greeted its opening with enthusiasm.[87] The building soon held twice as many students as it was intended to accommodate.[88] Barbara Rose Johns, a student at Moton, recalled, "What really bothered us was the time some of the boys in the vocational program visited the shop at the white school and came back telling us how nice their whole school was — and how well equipped. The comparison made me very angry, and I remember thinking how unfair it was."[89]

Barbara Johns, committed to rectifying this inequality, recruited a group of students to attend PTA and school board meetings where they lobbied, unsuccessfully, for a new black high school. Johns then decided to take direct action. On the morning of April 23,

1951, she asked another student to call the school principal and tell him that two students were in trouble at the bus station and needed to be picked up. When the principal left the school, Johns forged his signature to notes announcing an assembly that morning. When the students and teachers arrived at the assembly, Johns asked the teachers to leave, saying that the students were planning a surprise event. With the teachers gone, Johns spoke to her fellow students about her dream of having a decent school and her plan for a student attendance strike to achieve that goal. She pointed out that if they acted in solidarity, the town jail could not hold them all. When the principal returned, he asked them not to strike, but did not stop their meeting. The students decided to begin the strike the following day. Johns recalled, "We knew we had to do it ourselves and that if we had asked for adult help before taking the first step, we would have been turned down."[90]

Johns and the high school president, Carrie Stokes, wrote a letter to the NAACP legal staff asking for their help. Two NAACP lawyers, Oliver Hill and Spottswood Robinson, were arguing a case in Roanoke, Virginia, and decided to visit the Moton students. The lawyers planned to tell the students to go back to school and wait while the NAACP fought segregation in the courts in the more cosmopolitan cities.[91] But, Hill recalls, "These kids turned out to be so well organized and their morale was so high, we just didn't have the heart to tell 'em to break it up."[92]

The NAACP agreed to proceed with the students' case under the conditions that the suit would be to end segregation itself and that their parents agreed. At a mass meeting on May 3, 1951, support among black residents of Prince Edwards county for a lawsuit to fight segregation was overwhelming. On May 23, Robinson filed suit on behalf of 117 students. The NAACP lost the case, *Davis* v. *County School Board of Prince Edward County*, at the Federal District level and appealed to the U.S. Supreme Court.[93]

Davis was one of five school segregation cases which the Supreme Court agreed to hear. The five cases (from South Carolina, Virginia, Delaware, the District of Columbia and Kansas) were consolidated under the name of one of the cases, *Brown* v. *Board of Education of Topeka, Kansas*. The *Brown* case involved an eight-year-old girl, Linda Brown, who traveled one mile to reach her all-black school, though an all-white school was only three blocks from her home.[94] Supreme Court Justice Tom Clark explained the use of *Brown* as the case under which the others were consolidated: "We felt it was much better to have representative cases from different parts of the country, so we consolidated them and made *Brown* the first so that the whole question would not smack of being a purely Southern one."[95]

When the NAACP lawyers learned that the Supreme Court would hear cases challenging school segregation, they immediately began the difficult work of writing briefs and preparing oral arguments.[96] Thurgood Marshall recalls, "We'd rarely get any sleep. We'd fuss 'n' fight all night."[97] The NAACP lawyers practiced at Howard University law school, where mock judges drilled them on every aspect of the cases.[98]

The Supreme Court heard the cases in December 1952. The courtroom was filled to capacity, and half of the seats were filled with black attendees. Marshall argued that, "The only thing [segregation] can be is an inherent determination that the people who were formerly in slavery, regardless of anything else, shall be kept as near that stage as is possible. And now is the time, we submit, that this Court should make it clear that is not what our Constitution stands for."[99]

After months of discussion and an inability to reach unanimity, the Court asked for a reargument. Before the reargument took place, Chief Justice Vinson died suddenly in the summer of 1953 and was replaced by California Governor Earl Warren. Marshall later said that President Dwight Eisenhower had pressured Earl Warren not to overturn school segregation.[100]

The reargument took place in December 1953. Finally, the Court delivered its unanimous opinion on May 17, 1954. Chief Justice Warren said of black students, "To separate them from others of similar age and qualifications solely because of their race generates a feeling of inferiority as to their status in the community that may affect their hearts and minds in a way very unlikely ever to be undone. We conclude, unanimously, that in the field of public education the doctrine of 'separate but equal' has no place. Separate

educational facilities are inherently unequal."[101] Thurgood Marshall later said that the *Brown* decision "probably did more than anything else to awaken the Negro from his apathy to demanding his right to equality."[102]

Implementing the decision was far more complex and difficult than any of the NAACP lawyers had imagined. Some communities, such as Washington, DC, Baltimore, Louisville and St. Louis, complied and began to desegregate their schools voluntarily.[103] However, several states chose to fight the decision; some communities closed their schools rather than integrate.[104] During this period, Thurgood Marshall took on cases to enforce *Brown*, including the case of nine students who attempted to integrate Central High School in Little Rock, Arkansas.[105]

Officials in Little Rock, Arkansas planned to allow integration to proceed slowly, even though most white people in Arkansas opposed complying in any way with the *Brown* decision.[106] The Little Rock School Board developed a plan for gradual desegregation in which several hundred black children were to enroll at Central High School, the largest all-white school in Little Rock, beginning in the fall of 1957.[107]

But as the first day of school approached, as NAACP lawyer Wiley Branton recalls, "Little Rock decided that 'Oh, my God, this thing is on us,' [and] they started putting up all kinds of barriers," such as requiring students to register, screening students and attempting to dissuade parents from sending their children to Central. In the end, only nine black students were scheduled to start Central High School that fall.[108]

On the first day of school, September 3, officials asked the black students to wait "until this dilemma is legally resolved." A federal judge had ruled, on August 30, on an NAACP lawsuit, that integration should proceed. In response to the hesitation of the school board, the judge reaffirmed the order.[109]

The following morning, eight of the nine children met Daisy Bates, president of the Arkansas NAACP and editor-in-chief of the *Arkansas State Press*, to face together the violent crowd which would meet them at the school. The ninth child, Elizabeth Eckford, only

15 years old, unaware of this meeting, went alone.[110] She later recalled that, as she walked toward the entrance of the school:

> I walked up to the guard who had let the white students in .... When I tried to squeeze past him, he raised his bayonet and then the other guards closed in and raised their bayonets .... They glared at me with a mean look and I was very frightened and didn't know what to do. I turned around and the crowd came toward me.... Somebody started yelling, "Lynch her! Lynch her!" I tried to see a friendly face somewhere in the mob someone who maybe would help. I looked into the face of an old woman and it seemed a kind face, but when I looked at her again she spat on me .... Someone hollered, "Drag her over to this tree! Let's take care of the nigger."[111]

Finally, a white woman helped her board a bus away from the mob.

Mobs continued to attack any black person who arrived at the school, making international news. President Eisenhower could not remain silent, though he had spoken against the *Brown* decision, since Arkansas Governor Orval Faubus was violating a federal law. The Little Rock situation had become a battle between federal and state power. If Eisenhower, who, as President, was charged with upholding federal law, had not taken action, the incident would have set a precedent weakening the power of the federal government.[112] Eisenhower federalized the National Guard, sent soldiers to Little Rock and commanded them to assure the students' safety at Central High. At last, on September 25, 1957, the Little Rock Nine went to school.[113]

Though the battle had ended in the eyes of the media and the nation, the daily battle for the children continued. The troops remained at the school to protect them, but Melba Patillo Beals, another of the Little Rock Nine, recalled "[T]hey couldn't be with us everywhere. We'd be showering in gym and someone would turn your shower into scalding. You'd be walking out to the volleyball court and someone would break a bottle and trip you on the bottle. I have scars on my right knee from that."[114] The students experienced constant ostracism and psychological and physical intimidation.

In June of 1958, one of the Little Rock Nine, Ernest Green, became the first black student to graduate from Central High School. In September of that year, Governor Faubus closed all of the public high schools in Little Rock. One year later, the Supreme Court ruled his action unconstitutional.[115]

26

On June 13, 1967, Thurgood Marshall became the first African American to sit on the U.S. Supreme Court. In addition to his many years as a civil rights lawyer, Marshall served on the U.S. Court of Appeals and as Solicitor General, the attorney who represents the government before the Supreme Court.[116] Although some senators on the Judiciary Committee, including the pro-segregation Strom Thurmond of South Carolina, made Marshall's Senate confirmation process for Supreme Court justice difficult, Marshall was confirmed by a vote of 69 to 11.[117]

© NATIONAL GEOGRAPHIC SOCIETY/U.S. SUPREME COURT HISTORICAL SOCIETY

social engineers rather than lawyers."[122] Marshall graduated first in his class in 1933.[123] For three years he worked in private practice in Baltimore, often helping low-income black defendants. In 1936, Houston invited Marshall to join the NAACP legal team.[124]

During his long career fighting segregation, Marshall had to endure the very injustices he was working to combat. For example, in the early 1940s, while he was waiting for a train in a small Mississippi town, he recalls, "[T]his white man came up beside me in plain clothes with a great big pistol on his hip. And he said, 'Nigger boy, what are you doing here?' And I said, 'Well, I'm waiting for the train to Shreveport.' And he said, 'There's only one more train comes through here, and that's the 4 o'clock, and you'd better be on it because the sun is never going down on a live nigger in this town.'"[125]

Marshall was born in Baltimore, Maryland in 1908. Marshall recalls, "The only thing different between the South and Baltimore was trolley cars. They weren't segregated. Everything else was segregated."[118] Marshall's family taught him to adjust to segregation rather than fight it.[119]

In 1925, Marshall started college at Lincoln University in Pennsylvania, where he took courses in preparation for dental school. At first, he cared little for civil rights struggles, yet one of his classmates, poet Langston Hughes, began to discuss with him the lack of black professors at Lincoln. A school-wide vote on the issue of integrating the faculty resulted in two-thirds support for keeping the faculty all white (Marshall voted with the majority). Hughes called the vote evidence of the Lincoln students' "belief in their own inferiority."[120] Through conversations with Hughes and a favorite professor, Marshall began to change his mind and resolved that he must fight segregation.[121]

Instead of going dental school, Marshall decided to attend law school. In 1930, he enrolled at Howard University law school, where Charles Houston, who later became the NAACP's chief legal counsel, was dean. Marshall recalls that Houston said that "lawyers were to bear the brunt of getting rid of segregation, and he made public statements that we would become

In addition to his legal victories in the campaign for school desegregation, Marshall's successes in the fight for civil rights included ending the use of policies which prevented African Americans from buying homes, ending the all-white primary election in Texas and equalizing black and white teachers' salaries.[126] By the time he was appointed to the Supreme Court, Marshall had argued more cases before the Supreme Court than any of his colleagues on the Court. Of those 32 cases, he won 29.[127]

Marshall argues that the civil rights legislation of the 1960s did not address or solve all the problems facing African Americans. Speaking at Howard law school in 1979, he said "I am ... amazed by people who say, 'You ought to go around the country and show yourself to Negroes and give them inspiration.' For what? These Negro kids are not fools. They know when you tell them there is a possibility that someday they'll have a chance to be the O-N-L-Y Negro on the Supreme Court, that those odds aren't too good....

Well, all I am trying to tell you is there's a lot more to be done."[128]

In September 1989, Marshall criticized the increasingly conservative Supreme Court, stating that its decisions "put at risk not only the civil rights of minorities but the civil rights of all citizens."[129] Marshall also criticized President Ronald Reagan for his hostility to civil rights issues.[130]

During the celebration of the bicentennial of the U.S. Constitution, Marshall gave a speech criticizing the document's failure to include women and non-whites. He refused to attend a reenactment of the writing of the Constitution, stating, "If you are going to do what you did 200 years ago, somebody is going to give me short pants and a tray so I can serve coffee."[131]

According to historian John Hope Franklin, "If you study the history of Marshall's career, the history of his rulings on the Supreme Court, even his dissents, you will understand that when he speaks, he is not speaking just for black Americans but for Americans of all times. He reminds us constantly of the great promise this country has made of equality, and he reminds us that it has not been fulfilled. Through his life he has been a great watchdog, insisting that this nation live up to the Constitution."[132]

BEGINNINGS OF THE MODERN CIVIL RIGHTS MOVEMENT: THE MONTGOMERY BUS BOYCOTT

Though the Montgomery bus boycott is the most well-known example, it was not the first time African Americans had organized an effective boycott of a bus company. Black protesters launched a month-long bus boycott in Harlem in 1941 to protest the exclusion of black workers from employment by private bus lines in New York City. The black community, led by the Reverend Adam Clayton Powell, Jr. (later a Member of Congress), employed nonviolent direct action protests including picketing bus stops and holding rallies to generate support. They also organized car pools and worked with the Transportation Workers Union, which represented white workers at the bus companies, to successfully pressure the bus companies to change their hiring practices.[133]

In Montgomery, Alabama, in the mid 1950s, most of the riders on the buses were black people. Yet, segregation laws subjected them to indignities such as paying at the front and then entering the bus at the back and being forced to vacate an entire row of seats if a single white person was standing.[134]

Rosa Parks was an active member of the black community in Montgomery. She had been secretary of the Montgomery branch of the NAACP and was the NAACP Youth Council advisor. She also had a history of resistance to the bus segregation laws. One driver had evicted her from his bus in 1943 for refusing to enter through the back door.[135] On December 1, 1955, she boarded a bus after work and sat at the front of the "colored" section in the rear. As the bus made its stops, all the seats filled up. When a white man boarded the bus, the driver asked all the black passengers in Parks' row to give up their seats. The other three did, but she decided not to tolerate such an unjust practice and so did not stand up. In explaining her decision she said, "[T]his is what I wanted to know: when and how would we ever determine our rights as human beings?"[136] She had found a way to begin.

The driver had her arrested and the police charged her with violating a segregation law. From jail she called her mother, and news of her arrest soon reached E.D. Nixon, president of the state NAACP and regional officer of the Brotherhood of Sleeping Car Porters.[137] Nixon went to bail her out and said, "Mrs. Parks, this is the case we've been looking for. We can break this situation [segregation] on the bus with your case."[138]

Nixon immediately called all of the black leaders he knew in Montgomery, including a recently arrived Baptist minister, Dr. Martin Luther King, Jr. The leaders decided to hold a mass meeting to rally community support for a city-wide bus boycott. Jo Ann Robinson, an English professor at Alabama State College and president of the Women's Political Council, a group of black professional women founded in 1946, organized a massive leaflet campaign to tell black residents about the boycott and the mass meeting.[139] E.D. Nixon leaked the story to a newspaper reporter, who made Robinson's leaflets front page news and thus assisted the boycott.[140]

On the first day of the boycott, December 5, 1955, Dr. King had hoped for 60 percent participation. He woke up early to observe the outcome. Nearly 100 percent of black Montgomery residents had chosen to boycott the bus system.[141] King later wrote, "[A] miracle had taken place. The once dormant and quiescent Negro community was now fully awake."[142] Thousands gathered at the mass meeting that night and voted unanimously to continue the boycott. The leaders formed the Montgomery Improvement Association and elected King spokesperson.[143]

Meanwhile, attorney Fred D. Gray defended Parks in court, but the judge convicted her of disobeying the segregation law. King wrote, "I am sure that supporters [of segregation] would have acted otherwise if they had had the prescience to look beyond the moment,"[144] for Parks' arrest gave Gray the opportunity to bring the case to the U.S. District Court to challenge the constitutionality of bus segregation.

For over a year black residents of Montgomery refused to ride the buses. They organized car pools or simply walked to work. The city of Montgomery "retaliated by indicting one hundred leaders of the boycott, and sent many to jail. White segregationists turned to violence."[145] Both King's and Nixon's homes were bombed in an attempt to intimidate the boycotters, but it only served to deepen their conviction.[146] Coretta Scott King recalled that "[T]he more we got into it, the more we had the feeling that something could be done about the situation, that we could change it."[147]

Two months after the boycott began, the bus system had lost 65 percent of its income. About three months later, the bus company announced that it would no longer practice segregation, but the city went to court for an order to prohibit bus desegregation.[148] In June 1956, the District Court ruled for the Montgomery Improvement Association. The city of Montgomery appealed the decision, and on November 13, the Supreme Court affirmed the lower court's decision outlawing segregation. Finally, on December 20, the written Court mandate arrived in Montgomery and the next day the boycott, which had lasted more than one year, ended.[149]

Buses were no longer segregated, but riders were harassed and even attacked.[150] And every other aspect of Montgomery life remained completely segregated. Yet the victory served as an inspiration to many black Southerners who saw how large an effect their actions could have. Boycotts spread to Birmingham and Mobile, Alabama, and Tallahassee, Florida.[151] Black citizens were taking literally what King had said in a speech on the first night of the boycott: "[O]ne of the great glories of democracy is the right to protest for right."[152]

As boycott leader Jo Ann Robinson said years later:

> *We felt that we were somebody. That somebody had listened to us, that we had forced the white man to give what we knew [was] our own citizenship ... And if you have never had the feeling that ... you are [no longer] an alien, but that this is your country too, then you don't know what I'm talking about. It is a hilarious feeling that just goes all over you, that makes you feel that America is a great country and we're going to do more to make it greater.[153]*

The momentum created by the boycott did not fade after the victory. Southern black religious leaders formed an organization called the Southern Christian Leadership Conference (SCLC) and elected King president. The SCLC began to work against segrega-tion and disenfranchisement in the South. King began to give speeches throughout the country and "his message and eloquence were met with rapt attention and enthusiastic support."[154]

In May 1957, civil rights groups held the Prayer Pilgrimage in Washington, DC, with 25,000 people attending on the third anniversary of the *Brown* Supreme Court decision.[155] Three months later Congress passed The Civil Rights Act of 1957, which established a Commission on Civil Rights to investi-gate allegations of voting discrimination and autho-rized the Justice Department to bring federal suits against voting discrimination.[156] Although weak, the act was the first major legislative victory for African Americans since Reconstruction. But by 1960, only 6 percent of the schools in the South had started to desegregate. And fewer than one in four black citizens of voting age in the South could register and vote.[157]

THE STUDENT MOVEMENT FOR CIVIL RIGHTS

The student movement for civil rights began spontane-ously, with very little organization, with sit-ins at segregated restaurants and lunch counters. Black activists in northern and southern cities had used sit-ins as early as 1943, yet the media had not paid much attention. By 1960, however, the *Brown* Supreme Court decision and the Montgomery boycott forced Americans to acknowledge the student sit-ins as part of a larger phenomenon.

On February 1, 1960, four seventeen-year-old students from North Carolina A & T, a black college in Greensboro, sat down at a Woolworth lunch counter to protest that the lunch counter only served white customers. Denied service, they stayed until closing time. The manager did nothing, saying, "They can just sit there, it's nothing to me."[158] Yet, when they returned daily and were joined by other students, both white and black, the lunch counter could no longer do business since all of its seats were full of people who the manager refused to serve. By the fall of 1960, Greensboro's lunch counters agreed to serve black customers.[159]

The sit-in movement received national publicity. Within two weeks following the first sit-in, the idea had spread to 15 cities in five southern states.[160] In the next 12 months more than 50,000 people had participated in 100 cities and 3,600 people had been jailed.[161] In addition to sit-ins, students staged 'kneel-ins' in churches, 'sleep-ins' in motel lobbies, 'swim-ins' in pools, 'wade-ins' on restricted beaches, 'read-ins' at public libraries, 'play-ins' in parks, even 'watch-ins' in movie theaters,"[162] and other demonstrations wherever black people were denied access.

Most of the protests were nonviolent and as historian Clayborne Carson writes, "Nonviolent tactics, particularly when accompanied by a rationale based on Christian principles, offered black students an appealing combination of rewards: a sense of moral superiority, an emotional release through militancy and a possibility of achieving desegregation."[163]

Students in Nashville, led by Vanderbilt University theology student James Lawson, had staged test sit-ins in the fall of 1959.[164] Lawson had chosen to go to prison rather than serve in the military in the Korean War and had spent three years as a missionary in India, studying Gandhi's theories on nonviolence.[165] Lawson conducted workshops on nonviolence for students, which Diane Nash and Marion Barry, later to become mayor of Washington, DC, attended. Their rules for nonviolence included: "Don't strike back or curse if abused ... Show yourself courteous and friendly at all times ... Report all serious incidents to your leader in a polite manner. Remember love and nonviolence."[166]

Diane Nash, a student at Fisk University, led students in organizing the Nashville Student movement.[167] Police arrested 82 Nashville students for sitting in. They refused to pay bail and served their one-month terms in jail. Nash issued the following statement, "[W]e feel that if we pay these fines we would be contributing to and supporting the injustice and immoral practices that have been performed in the arrest and conviction of the defendants."[168] Thus the students filled up the jails as well as the lunch counters. In May of 1960, Nashville's lunch counters began to serve black customers.[169]

In Atlanta, students launched sit-ins at private lunch counters as well as at bus station and city hall cafeterias to test segregation of government facilities.[170] One focus of the students' efforts was Rich's Department Store, where many Atlanta black shoppers had charge accounts. First the students appealed to customers to close their accounts, saying "[C]lose out your charge account with segregation, open up your account with freedom."[171] Students then appealed to Martin Luther King, Jr., who had already received national attention as a spokesperson for civil rights, to sit down with them at Rich's lunch counter. King joined them and was jailed in a maximum security prison because he was on probation after being convicted of failing to exchange his Alabama driver's license for a Georgia license after he moved to Atlanta.[172] King's participation attracted national attention to the students' cause. In fall of 1961, Atlanta's lunch counters were desegregated.[173]

The students' activities did not go unnoticed by civil rights leaders. Ella Baker, the executive director of the SCLC, saw the momentum and energy of the students and feared that unless they organized, this spontaneous movement would disappear. Baker recalled that communication among those who participated in sit-ins was limited or nonexistent. "They were motivated by what the North Carolina four had started, but they were not in contact with each other, which meant that you couldn't build a sustaining force just based on spontaneity," said Baker.[174]

To help the students create an organization, Baker called a conference for students at Shaw University in Raleigh, North Carolina, in the spring of 1960. The purpose of the conference was to achieve "a more unified sense of direction for training and action in Nonviolent Resistance,"[175] Baker's opening address, "More than a Hamburger," urged the students to think beyond integrating lunch counters to changing the whole social structure. Over 300 students from the North and South attended.[176]

Representatives from the NAACP, SCLC and two other civil rights groups, Congress of Racial Equality (CORE) and Fellowship of Reconciliation (FOR), attended the conference. CORE and FOR had a long history of using nonviolent direct action to achieve social reform. These groups wanted the student activists to become the youth arm of their organizations. But as student James Forman recalled, Ella Baker "felt the students had a right to determine their own structure — if they wanted one at all at that point; that it was their right to explore all possibilities and make their own decisions, since thus far it was they who had propelled the sit-in movement to national and international importance."[177] The students, many of whom were critical of the existing civil rights groups, rejected the invitations and instead formed an independent organization called the Student Non-violent Coordinating Committee (SNCC).

The students at the Shaw conference agreed with Baker that it was "important to keep the movement democratic and to avoid struggles for personal leadership."[178] SNCC was authorized to speak for the movement only "in a cautious manner in which it is made quite clear that SNCC does not control local groups."[179] All SNCC actions required the support of two-thirds of the members present. Emphasizing group rather than individual concerns, SNCC took part in most of the civil rights protests in the 1960s and was a vital part of the Civil Rights movement.[180]

The sit-in movement stirred up the older generation as well. As historian Harvard Sitkoff writes, "An intangible yet profound shift in the psychology of the black community became manifest. The sit-ins dramatically illustrated the power of individuals to shape their own history, and a renewed will to struggle for civil rights appeared."[181]

SNCC leader James Forman writes, "Ella Baker is one of those many strong black women who have devoted their lives to the liberation of their people. She has an endless faith in people and their power to change their status in life. She believes strongly in the organized will of the people as opposed to the power of a single leader. She has served black people without fanfare, publicity or concern for personal credit."[182]

Ella Baker was born in 1903 in Norfolk, Virginia and was raised in North Carolina. After graduating as valedictorian of her class from Shaw University in Raleigh, North Carolina, Baker moved to New York City where, because of her race, the only work she could find was waiting tables and factory work.[183] While working, she attended graduate school at the New School for Social Research.[184]

During the Great Depression in New York, Baker became involved in a movement for consumers' rights. She helped found the Young Negroes' Cooperative League in 1932 where she began organizing consumer cooperatives.[185] Baker was hired by President Franklin Roosevelt's Works Progress Administration (WPA) to continue her speaking, writing and teaching about consumer affairs.[186]

Baker also joined and worked for the NAACP, becoming national director of its local branches in 1942 and later president of the New York chapter.[187]

During her work with the NAACP, Baker traveled extensively throughout the South, organizing membership campaigns. According to Baker:

> *The major job was getting people to understand that they had something within their power that they could use, and it could only be used if they understood ... how group action could counter violence even when it was perpetrated by the police or, in some instances, the state. My basic sense of it has always been to get people to understand that in the long run they themselves are the only protection they have against violence or injustice. ... People have to be made to understand that they cannot look for salvation anywhere but in themselves.[188]*

Through the NAACP Baker helped to initiate community action against *de facto* segregation in the New York public schools. In 1958, she traveled to Atlanta to help set up the Southern Christian Leadership Conference and stayed on for two years as it executive director.[189]

Ella Baker left her position with the SCLC to advise the SNCC students. Baker's leadership philosophy was profoundly different from that of her male counterparts in the SCLC.[190] Critical of the "leader-centered group" which grew up around Martin Luther

King, Jr., Baker favored "group-centered leadership," in which the only purpose for individual leadership development was to benefit the group. Baker stated:

I have always felt it was a handicap for oppressed peoples to depend so largely upon a leader, because unfortunately in our culture, the charismatic leader usually becomes a leader because he has found a spot in the public limelight ... which means that the media made him, and the media may undo him. There is also the danger in our culture that, because a person is called upon to give public statements and is acclaimed by the establishment, such a person gets to the point of believing that he is the movement. Such people get so involved with playing the game of being important that they exhaust themselves and their time, and they don't do the work of actually organizing people.[191]

Baker advised the SNCC students while carefully keeping a distance and letting them make their own decisions as to goals and tactics. Personally Baker would not have chosen nonviolent action as a tactic.

She recalled, "I frankly could not have sat and let someone put a burning cigarette on the back of my neck as some young people did. Whether this is right or wrong or good or bad, I have already been conditioned, and I have not seen anything in the nonviolent technique that can dissuade me from challenging somebody who wants to step on my neck. If necessary, if they hit me, I might hit them back."[192]

Baker continued her work in the Civil Rights movement, advising SNCC and helping to found the Mississippi Freedom Democratic Party (MFDP). She gave the keynote address at MFDP's founding convention. Later, Baker was on the staff of the Southern Conference Educational Fund, an organization formed to encourage white and black people to work together in the South. And she was active in groups supporting freedom struggles in Zimbabwe and South Africa.[193]

Said Baker, "I have never thought in terms of my 'making a contribution.' I just thought of myself as functioning where there was a need. And if I have made a contribution I think it may be that I had some influence on a large number of people."[194]

THE FREEDOM RIDES

In 1946, the Supreme Court, in *Morgan* v. *Virginia*, declared unconstitutional state laws forcing segregation in vehicles engaged in interstate transportation.[195] The following year, an interracial group of members of CORE and FOR tested this ruling with a "journey of reconciliation" on an interstate bus through the South.[196] Twelve of the riders were arrested and one was beaten but the media paid little attention. Despite the 1946 ruling, segregation on interstate buses persisted into the 1960s because the federal government did not enforce the law.[197] Again, African Americans had to make up for the lack of enforcement of laws meant to protect their rights.

In 1960, the Supreme Court, in *Boynton* v. *Virginia*, extended the 1946 ruling to include accommodations, such as waiting rooms and restaurants, in interstate bus and train terminals.[198] Another group of CORE members decided in 1961 to test for compliance, this time calling the protest a Freedom Ride. James Farmer, CORE's director, explained the rationale for the Freedom Rides:

> *Federal law said that there should be no segregation in interstate travel. The Supreme Court had decided that. But still state laws in the southern states and local ordinances ordered segregation of the races on those buses. Why didn't the federal government enforce its law? We decided it was because of politics. If we were right ... then what we had to do was to make it more dangerous politically for the federal government not to enforce federal law. ... This was not civil disobedience, really, because we would be doing merely what the Supreme Court said we had a right to do. The whites in the group would sit in the back of the bus, the blacks would sit in the front of the bus, and would refuse to move when ordered. ... We felt that we could then count upon the racists of the South to create a crisis, so that the federal government would be compelled to enforce federal law. That was the rationale for the Freedom Ride.[199]*

CORE recruited a group of riders and trained them extensively in nonviolence. The CORE Freedom Ride began on May 4, 1961, and as the buses travelled deeper into the South, violations of rights and brutality became increasingly frequent.[200] In Charlotte, North Carolina, a Freedom Rider was arrested for attempting to get a shoe shine at a white barber shop; in Rock Hill, South Carolina, a group of white people beat two riders for attempting to enter a white waiting room.[201]

In Alabama the attacks were far worse. At Anniston, six members of the Ku Klux Klan (KKK) boarded the first bus, threw black riders to the back and instructed the driver to go on to the next stop, Birmingham. At Birmingham, a mob beat the riders with pipes. No police were present to stop the violence. James Peck, who had been a rider in the Journey of Reconciliation, required 53 stitches.[202]

The second bus fared even worse. At Anniston, the riders faced a mob with guns, chains, clubs and knives and the riders, to stay alive, decided not to get off the bus. But the mob slashed the bus' tires and followed it to the outskirts of town until the tires blew out. The mob then surrounded the bus and prevented the riders from exiting. A member of the mob broke a window and threw a firebomb into the bus. The riders barely escaped before the bus blew up.[203]

National and international newspapers published photographs of the events in Alabama, greatly embarrassing President John Kennedy, who had voiced support of a strong federal role in protecting civil rights. Attorney General Robert Kennedy sent his administrative assistant John Seigenthaler to fly the Freedom Riders safely out of Birmingham, where the riders faced another angry mob.[204]

SNCC members decided to continue the rides despite the violence and voted to take over where CORE had left off. They elected Diane Nash to coordinate the rides. Nash recalled, "Some of the students gave me sealed letters to be mailed in case they were killed. That's how prepared they were for death."[205] When the SNCC members arrived in Birmingham, the police commissioner, Eugene "Bull" Connor, put the riders in jail, in 'protective custody.'[206] The riders launched a hunger strike to protest. The next day Connor's police officers drove the riders 120 miles across the state line to Tennessee and left them there. Undeterred, the riders returned to Birmingham.[207]

John Seigenthaler met with the governor of Alabama, John Patterson, who reluctantly agreed to protect the riders in Alabama. The Freedom Rides continued from Birmingham to Montgomery. Just outside Montgomery, the patrol cars and airplanes that had been protecting the riders disappeared. Upon arrival in Montgomery, a mob of men, women and children attacked the riders with bats, chains, bricks and pipes. No police were present to protect the nonviolent Freedom Riders from the attack.[208] The Montgomery Police Commissioner said "[W]e have no intention of standing guard for a bunch of troublemakers coming into our city."[209] Finally, Governor Patterson's assistant ordered state troopers to stop the attack, but not before several protesters were badly injured and John Seigenthaler was knocked unconscious. President Kennedy ordered 600 federal marshals to an Air Force base outside Montgomery to stand ready in case of further trouble.[210]

The next day, over 1,000 people attended a rally at Reverend Ralph Abernathy's First Baptist church in Montgomery, Alabama, where Martin Luther King, Jr. was scheduled to speak.[211] Angry white people gathered around the church hurtling firebombs through the windows. Finally, the U.S. marshals arrived and attempted to disperse the mob with tear gas, but were unable to control the situation. Gas began to seep inside the church. Governor Patterson declared martial law and sent in the Alabama National Guard.[212]

Still undaunted, 27 Freedom Riders boarded buses to Jackson, Mississippi on May 24, 1961. Despite threats of ambush and destruction of the bus, they encountered no violence in Mississippi. Robert Kennedy had made a deal with Mississippi Senator James Eastland that Kennedy would not protest the riders' arrests in exchange for a promise from Mississippi authorities that the riders would not encounter more violence. When the riders arrived in Jackson, police immediately arrested and sentenced them to 60 days in a maximum security penitentiary. Despite the harsh conditions in the prison, Freedom Riders continued to travel to Mississippi and face imprisonment. By the

end of the summer, over 1,000 activists had participated in the Freedom Rides and over 300 had been arrested, with most of those serving time in the state penitentiary.[213]

Conditions for the Freedom Riders in the Mississippi prisons included "endless rounds of questioning and beatings, the pain of battery-operated cattle prods, the terror of wristbreakers and the sounds of friends groaning and crying; the back-breaking work in the fields from sunup to sundown, the execrable food, and the filthy cots in bug-infested cells ... Jail broke some. It strengthened others ... They went to work for SNCC, SCLC and CORE changed men and women,"[214] writes historian Harvard Sitkoff.

Finally, Robert Kennedy petitioned the Interstate Commerce Commission (ICC) for regulations which increased federal power for enforcing the laws against segregation. On September 22, 1961, the ICC required signs on buses and trains and in terminals declaring that seating is "without regard to race, color, creed or national origin."[215]

REGISTERING VOTERS IN THE DEEP SOUTH

By the end of 1961, SNCC was divided into two factions: those who favored continued nonviolent direct action campaigns and those who wanted to put energy into registering black citizens to vote.[216] The former group feared that SNCC would lose its spirit and momentum by solely registering voters, a plan encouraged by the Kennedy Administration. SNCC finally decided to try both tactics.[217] As voter registration efforts encountered resistance, Ella Baker later recalled, "[SNCC] began to see that they wouldn't have to abandon their nonviolence. In fact, they would be hard put to keep it up."[218]

Amzie Moore, head of the NAACP in Cleveland, Mississippi, had been fighting for voting rights for black Mississippians using the favored NAACP tactic: the legal battle.[219] Yet, despite laws to the contrary, black citizens still could not vote. For example, Hartman Turnbow of Tchula, Mississippi, testified in 1964 before a U.S. Commission on Civil Rights hearing that his home was firebombed after he attempted to register. When he ran outside, a white man shot at him. Turnbow also testified that "[T]he minute the news spread abroad that I had [attempted to register] ... all of my credit was cut off.... And ... many other colored people right there at Tchula right now — well, they won't attempt to register."[220]

The lack of results led Moore to advocate direct action. The NAACP did not support such tactics, so Moore asked Bob Moses, a teacher from Harlem and a member of the more militant SNCC, to bring SNCC workers into Mississippi to help black people register to vote.[221] Moses began the first voter education and registration project in McComb, Mississippi, where in 1960 fewer than 200 black citizens registered to vote out of an adult black population of more than 8,000.[222]

SNCC workers canvassed from door-to-door, held workshops to teach black citizens to pass the tests required for registration and then recruited volunteers to go to the courthouse to try to register. Bob Moses was soon arrested. White violence against both the SNCC workers and those citizens who attempted to register increased.[223]

SNCC's Marion Barry also arrived in McComb and began organizing high school students who sat in at the Woolworth lunch counter. Two students were arrested and sentenced to 30 days in jail. After another sit-in, high school students were given eight month sentences and one, Brenda Travis, was sentenced to one year in a state institution for delinquents.[224]

Despite SNCC's efforts, resistance from white McComb residents prevented most black residents from registering. Federal Bureau of Investigation (FBI) agents did nothing to uphold federal law.[225] SNCC decided to retrench and give up, at least temporarily, on McComb.

Meanwhile in Albany, Georgia, SNCC workers Charles Sherrod and Cordell Reagon arrived to conduct a voter registration project. Within weeks, black residents formed the Albany movement to win not only the vote but total desegregation. Of the 23,000 black residents in Albany, over a thousand went to jail for protesting segregation and discrimination.[226]

In 1962, SNCC, CORE, SCLC and the NAACP formed a coalition called the Council of Federated Organizations (COFO) to prevent competition and promote cooperation among the organizations. COFO received money from the Voter Education Project which was set up by the Kennedy Administration in an attempt to steer the movement away from direct action.[227]

COFO organizers went to Greenwood, Mississippi, where every demonstration they conducted led to massive arrests.[228] The LeFlore County Board of Supervisors, to discourage the protests, cut off the county's participation in a federal program which provided food for the poor. Poor families in Greenwood, mostly black, faced severe food shortages. In response, SNCC organized a food drive in which SNCC workers picked up donations in the North and then delivered food and medical supplies to low-income families in Greenwood. Some participants were arrested for bringing "narcotics" (the medical supplies) into the state.[229]

The presence of the SNCC workers politicized the community and black people began to line up at the courthouse to register, despite white violence. Greenwood resident Jimmy Travis was shot in the head and shoulder while driving down a highway.[230] And in Jackson, Mississippi, NAACP field secretary Medgar Evers, who was leading a boycott of Jackson businesses, was shot outside his home and died on June 12, 1963. The fingerprints on the gun belonged to a member of the white Citizens' Council in Greenwood. Murder charges were dropped after two trials in which juries failed to reach a verdict.[231]

Even when African Americans were registered to vote, the Democratic Party barred them from its meetings, so they had no power to influence the selection of candidates. In the fall of 1963, COFO held a mock election called the Freedom Vote to show that apathy was not the reason that African Americans in the South did not vote.[232] COFO recruited northern white students to help attract media attention. Approximately 80,000 black Mississippians cast ballots in the Freedom Vote to protest being denied the vote.[233]

EXCERPTS FROM THE CONSTITUTION

Part 1. In case of the removal of the president from office, or of his death, resignation, or inability to discharge the powers and duties of the said office, the same shall devolve on the vice-president, and the congress may by law provide for the case of removal, death, resignation or inability, both of the president and vice-president, declaring what officer shall then act as president, and such officer shall act accordingly, until the disability be removed, or a president shall be elected.

Part 2. In all cases affecting ambassadors, other public ministers and consuls, and those in which a state shall be a party, the supreme court shall have original jurisdiction.

Part 3. In all the other cases before mentioned, the supreme court shall have appellate jurisdiction, both as to law and fact, with such exceptions, and under such regulations as the congress shall make.

Part 4. Neither slavery nor involuntary servitude, except as a punishment for crime whereof the party shall have been duly convicted, shall exist within the United States, or any place subject to their jurisdiction.

INSTRUCTION "C"

(After applicant has read, not aloud, the foregoing excerpts from the Constitution, he will answer the following questions in writing and without assistance:)

1. In case the president is unable to perform the duties of his office, who assumes them? _____

2. "Involuntary servitude" is permitted in the United States upon conviction of a crime. (True or False)_____

3. If a state is a party to a case, the constitution provides that original jurisdiction shall be in_____

4. Congress passes laws regulating cases which are included in those over which the United States Supreme Court has_____ jurisdiction.

I hereby certify that I have received no assistance in the completion of this citizenship and literacy test, that I was allowed the time I desired to complete it, and that I waive any right existing to demand a copy of same. (If for any reason the applicant does not wish to sign this, he must discuss the matter with the board of registrars.)

Signed: _____ (Applicant)

Literacy test developed for use in Alabama in the 1950s and early 1960s.

Despite the efforts of COFO, few black voters succeeded in registering to vote from 1961 to 1963. It was clear that without federal intervention and national attention, voter registration on a large scale could not take place.

FAIR EMPLOYMENT AND DESEGREGATION: BIRMINGHAM

In 1963, George C. Wallace became governor of Alabama with the words "segregation now ... segregation tomorrow ... segregation forever."[234] During the Montgomery bus boycott, Alabama had banned the NAACP from the state. Members of the KKK in Birmingham, Alabama were particularly violent. Black churches and homes were bombed so frequently that the black section of town was known as Dynamite Hill.[235]

Fred Shuttlesworth, a black Birmingham minister who helped to found the SCLC, was convinced that Birmingham should be the next focus of the Civil Rights movement. Wyatt Tee Walker, another SCLC member, planned Project C: "C" stood for confrontation in Birmingham.[236] Walker later recalled, "[M]y theory was that if we mounted a strong nonviolent movement, the opposition would surely do something

to attract the media, and in turn induce national sympathy and attention to the everyday segregated circumstance of a black person living in the Deep South."[237]

Project C protesters directed their demands less toward the local or state government and more toward white Birmingham businesspeople. They demanded desegregation of downtown stores and the hiring of black sales clerks. Some thought the best way to obtain these demands was to wait for the newly elected mayor to make changes promised during his campaign. However, according to Shuttlesworth, many "didn't think that any system of government at that time would do what we needed to do. To the outside it looked like it meant change, but to us it had been superficial."[238]

Project C protests began on April 3, 1963, with demonstrations in downtown Birmingham. The first protests were not well-attended and received little media attention. Then, in a controversial move, the SCLC began to organize elementary and high school students, teaching them the methods of nonviolent civil disobedience. On May 2, hundreds of students marched downtown and Eugene "Bull" Connor, the Birmingham police commissioner, ordered 600 children, aged six to eighteen, arrested.[239] The next day another 1,000 protesters gathered and Connor ordered the police to use vicious attack dogs and fire hoses which delivered 100 pounds of pressure per square inch to break up the protest.[240] Patricia Harris, one of the young protesters, later recalled that she "was really afraid, but I wasn't afraid enough to just say 'well, I don't want to go on any longer.'"[241]

At the heavy cost of such brutality, the protesters finally attracted media attention. Dramatic images of children being rolled across the street with fire hoses and of attack dogs biting them were televised across the United States. Many American viewers were impressed by the protesters' nonviolence, which leaders went to great lengths to preserve.

Finally, Birmingham businesses agreed to some desegregation and jobs for black residents, and advocated the release of the 3,000 protesters from jail if the Project C demonstrations stopped. The SCLC agreed. That night, however, the KKK denounced the white businesspeople for negotiating and bombed several homes and businesses owned by black residents.[242]

Yet much had been accomplished. President Kennedy could not ignore the violence which stunned white Northerners as they watched the evening news. He proposed a civil rights bill which President Lyndon Johnson pushed Congress to pass in 1964 after Kennedy's death. The Civil Rights Act of 1964 prohibited discrimination in voting, education, jobs and public accommodations. Congress had passed civil rights acts in 1957 and 1960, but lack of enforcement rendered them ineffective.[243]

MARCH ON WASHINGTON

In the summer of 1963, 73-year-old labor organizer A. Philip Randolph organized the March on Washington to support the proposed civil rights legislation. It was at this gathering of more than 200,000 people that King delivered his eloquent "I have a dream" speech which encouraged black and white people to work together peacefully for change.[244]

But some criticized the established civil rights leaders for allowing the Kennedy administration to control the event.[245] SNCC leaders were resentful when the March leaders asked SNCC chairperson John Lewis to make his remarks more moderate.[246] And Malcolm X in a speech declared:

> *The Negroes were out there in the streets. They were talking about how they were going to march on Washington ... and tie it up, bring it to a halt, not let the government proceed. ... It was the grass roots out there in the street. It scared the white man to death, scared the white power structure in Washington, D.C. to death ... This is what they did with the march on Washington. They joined it ... became part of it, took it over. And as they took it over, it lost its militancy. It ceased to be angry, it ceased to be hot, it*

> *ceased to be uncompromising. Why, it even ceased to be a march. It became a picnic, a circus. ... No, it was a sellout. It was a takeover ... They controlled it so tight, they told those Negroes what time to hit town, where to stop, what signs to carry, what song to sing, what speech they could make, and what speech they couldn't make, and then they told them to get out of town by sundown.[247]*

Meanwhile, violence continued to rage against African Americans in the South. In September of 1963, 15 sticks of dynamite exploded in the Sixteenth Street Baptist Church in Birmingham, Alabama, killing four young girls: Denise McNair, Carole Robertson, Addie Mae Collins and Cynthia Wesley.[248]

MISSISSIPPI FREEDOM SUMMER

Following the relative success of the Freedom Vote of 1963, in which white workers had been recruited, a debate ensued within SNCC as to whether to recruit more white volunteers for a registration drive in the summer of 1964. Not surprising to black activists, violence against white activists attracted far more attention from the media and the government than did violence against black citizens.[249]

Though many leaders of the movement feared that including white participants would threaten their autonomy and intimidate rural Mississippi residents, they finally decided that the violence and resistance was so great that such a measure was necessary. SNCC recruited approximately 700 white volunteers from northern universities to register voters, establish freedom schools, community centers and medical and legal clinics. All volunteers were trained extensively in the tactics and philosophy of nonviolence.[250]

Nonetheless, violence erupted. Bombs exploded outside the Mississippi headquarters of COFO, CORE and SNCC and fires destroyed at least six black churches.[251] On June 20, 1964, CORE workers James Chaney and Michael Schwerner and newly recruited student Andrew Goodman disappeared while investigating a church burning near Philadelphia, Mississippi. President Johnson ordered the FBI to search for the missing workers.[252]

On August 4, their bodies were found. All three had been shot and Chaney, who was black, had been so badly beaten that many of his bones were crushed.[253] In December of 1964, FBI agents — who had infiltrated the Mississippi KKK several months earlier — arrested 19 white men including the county sheriff and deputy sheriff. The criminal case for murder was dropped by the state court, but seven of the men were sentenced to prison for three to ten years in 1967 for violating federal civil rights laws.[254]

Despite the loss of the three civil rights workers and other murders and brutal beatings, SNCC members and the northern volunteers continued to register voters during Freedom Summer. SNCC was successful in inspiring many low-income rural black people, who had never heard of the Civil Rights movement, to begin to demand their rights. Many did not know they had the right to vote. Fannie Lou Hamer, a sharecropper on a cotton plantation, was inspired by the SNCC students. When Hamer returned home after being arrested for attempting to register, the owner of the plantation where she worked kicked her out of her house. Despite many threats on her life — and the loss of her job — she became increasingly active in the movement for political rights.[255]

By the end of August, 1964, 80,000 black voters had registered with the Mississippi Freedom Democratic Party (MFDP), which had been organized in the spring of 1964 to challenge the all-white Democratic delegation from Mississippi at the Democratic National Convention.[256] At the convention in Atlantic City, the Democratic Party refused to seat them, but offered a compromise: two of the black delegates would be seated, though they would not officially represent Mississippi, and Mississippi would be prohibited from sending an all-white delegation in the future.[257] Fannie Lou Hamer addressed the entire convention, asking: "Is this America, the land of the free and the home of the brave, where we are threatened daily because we want to live as decent human beings?"[258]

The MFDP delegates rejected the compromise, but most of them supported the Democratic presidential candidate, Lyndon B. Johnson, in the general election and continued to seek entry to the Democratic Party. Others were too disillusioned by the failure of the delegation to be seated to put faith in further coali-

tions with the Democrats.[259] But many local MFDP leaders were elected to office in Mississippi, and MFDP efforts resulted in the 1967 election of Robert Clark, the first black state legislator since Reconstruction.[260]

THE MARCH FROM SELMA TO MONTGOMERY

In 1963, SNCC workers encountered significant resistance to their Alabama voting rights campaign. When prospective black voters lined up to register in Selma, Dallas County Sheriff Jim Clark and his deputies attacked and arrested them.[261] The local courts put restrictions on meetings of civil rights leaders, including a ban on meetings of more than three people at a time without the sheriff's permission.[262] In the fall of 1964, local leaders asked the SCLC and Martin Luther King, Jr. for help.[263]

The SCLC planned an Emancipation Day service on January 2, 1965, in violation of the injunctions against meetings. When that meeting was successful, they continued to hold mass meetings in Brown's Chapel. The SCLC also held daily marches to the Dallas County courthouse to attempt to register to vote. By the end of the month, over 2,000 black marchers had been arrested.[264]

At a march in nearby Marion, members of a white mob sprayed TV cameras with paint and then attacked the protesters. They beat Reverend James Dobynes who was on his knees in prayer. State troopers descended on and brutally killed protester Jimmy Lee Jackson.[265]

In the aftermath of Jackson's death, the SCLC called for a march from Selma to the state capital, Montgomery, to confront Governor George Wallace with its grievances. Wallace prohibited the march, saying it would be impossible to protect the marchers and Martin Luther King, Jr. canceled the march and left for Atlanta. Nonetheless, on March 7, 1965, approximately 600 people set out for Montgomery. To reach the highway which led to Montgomery, they had to cross the Edmund Pettus Bridge. When they got to the top of the bridge, about 200 Alabama state troopers and local police were waiting for them. After ordering the protestors to retreat, the law enforcement officers attacked — as TV cameras filmed them — with chains, cattle prods and tear gas. When the attack was over, 57 marchers needed medical treatment. The incident was soon known as Bloody Sunday.[266]

All over the country, people showed their outrage and support for the marchers by holding sympathy marches. Fourteen students held a seven-hour sit-in at the White House.[267] Martin Luther King, Jr. called for a second march and many supporters traveled to Selma to continue the march to Montgomery. Two days later, 2,000 marchers crossed the bridge. Again, state troopers blocked their path, but this time without violence. The marchers knelt and prayed.[268]

Suddenly King turned the march around, explaining that he did not want to violate a court order from a federal judge who he believed would soon rule in favor of their right to march. Before the march began King had agreed with federal authorities to turn the march around in exchange for assurances that the Alabama police would not use violence. Many SNCC members who had participated in the march disagreed with King's bow to federal authority and left Selma.[269]

Days later, a group of white people attacked three white ministers who were in Selma for the march. Their blow to James Reeb proved fatal; he died of skull fractures two days later. President Johnson called Reeb's family and called a joint session of Congress to request a voting rights bill. Thousands in northern cities protested the death. But once again it took the death of a white person to arouse attention. As Stokely Carmichael later commented, "[I]t means that our life is not worth, even in death, the life of anybody else — that their life is still more precious."[270]

As expected, the federal judge overturned Governor Wallace's prohibition of the march and President Johnson federalized the Alabama National Guard to protect the marchers. On March 21, 3,200 marchers left Selma for Montgomery. By the end of the march five days later, more than 25,000 participants had joined. Martin Luther King spoke at a rally on the steps of the state capitol.[271]

After the march, four members of the KKK shot and killed Viola Liuzzo, a white woman, as she drove to pick up participants in the Selma to Montgomery march.[272] Once again President Johnson spoke out. In August, Congress passed the Voting Rights Act of 1965, which, with Supreme Court decisions and the Twenty-fourth Amendment outlawing the poll tax in federal elections, paved the way for significant black voter participation.[273]

President Johnson signed Executive Order 11246 to require all entities, public or private, with 50 employees or more, receiving at least $50,000 in federal contracts, to file affirmative action plans specifying goals and timetables to correct under-utilization of minorities and women in their workforces. Johnson declared, "You do not take a person who, for years, has been hobbled by chains and liberate him, bring him up to the starting line of a race and then say, 'You are free to compete with all the others,' and still justly believe that you have been completely fair."[274]

Malcolm Little was born in 1925 in Omaha, Nebraska. His parents were active organizers for Marcus Garvey's Universal Negro Improvement Association. Their work created trouble for the family. Two white men burned down their home in 1929, and when Malcolm's father died after being run over by a trolley car in 1931, many thought he had been lynched. The pressure was too much for his mother, who eventually was institutionalized, and the family broke up.[275]

Malcolm had been at the top of his junior high class and the class president in a nearly all-white school, but he dropped out after a teacher discouraged his ambition (because he was black) to be a lawyer. He moved to New York City and eventually turned to a life of crime. He was arrested and sentenced in 1946 to 10 years in prison. There he converted to the Lost-Found Nation of Islam, or the Black Muslims. Leaving prison in 1952, he changed his name to Malcolm X and became a minister of Islam.[276]

The Nation of Islam was founded in 1931 to preach a version of Islam mixed with black nationalism. One in five Africans forced to the Americas as slaves was Muslim, but most were converted to Christianity. The Nation of Islam, led by Elijah Muhammad, advocated total racial separation believing that integration with the "blue-eyed devil" was unthinkable.[277]

Historian Harvard Sitkoff writes, "The Nation of Islam was depicted as an army of black fanatics planning for the inevitable race war. Little or nothing most whites read and heard informed them of Muslim success in rehabilitating blacks that others considered beyond reclamation, or of the Muslim gospel that blacks had to conquer their own shame and poverty by adhering to such traditional American virtues as hard work, honesty, self-discipline, mutual help and self-respect."[278]

© SCHOMBURG CENTER FOR RESEARCH IN BLACK CULTURE/

THE NEW YORK PUBLIC LIBRARY/ASTOR LENOX AND TILDEN FOUNDATION

By the early 1960s, Malcolm X had become a well-known spokesperson for the Nation of Islam. Many civil rights leaders disagreed with Malcolm X, including Martin Luther King, Jr. who advocated integration not separation.[279] But Malcolm X's message appealed to many African Americans as Sonia Sanchez, a CORE member in the early 1960s, recalls:

[H]e knew how to, in a very real sense, open your eyes as to the kind of oppression that you were experiencing .... You see, what he said out loud is what African American people had been saying out loud forever behind closed doors .... He expelled fear for African Americans .... [What he said was] I am not afraid to say what you've been thinking all these years, that's why we loved him .... He took on America for us .... And he made us feel we were worth something finally on this planet Earth.[280]

Malcolm X broke with the Nation of Islam in 1963. The next year he made a pilgrimage to Mecca, the Islamic holy city, and he toured Africa and "began to link the struggles of African Americans with those of Africa and other Third World countries."[281] Malcolm X rejected the Nation of Islam's view that all white people are intrinsically evil and began to work with other leaders of the Civil Rights movement.[282] In June 1964 he founded the Organization of Afro-American Unity (OAAU).[283] Parallel organizations formed in Africa, which allowed Malcolm X to put civil rights violations in the United States on the international agenda and force the U.S. government to acknowledge that it failed to enforce the rights of *all* its citizens.[284]

On February 21, 1965, Malcolm X was assassinated. Three Black Muslims were convicted of the shooting, but the question of who gave the orders for the assassination remains open.[285]

Though the OAAU quickly died out after Malcolm X's death, Stokely Carmichael recalled that Malcolm X's views "had a profound effect upon ... SNCC, and of course, consequently on the country because of the role that SNCC played in the country."[286] Thousands read *The Autobiography of Malcolm X.*[287] "In death, Malcolm X achieved an eminence and a devoted following that he never had in his lifetime," writes Harvard Sitkoff.[288]

The Nation of Islam, led by Louis Farrakhan, had about 10,000 members as of 1990. Based in Chicago, it continues to promote black pride and works in urban communities around the country to address the problems of crime and poverty.[289]

THE LOWNDES COUNTY FREEDOM ORGANIZATION: ELECTORAL REFORM THROUGH A NEW PARTY

At the beginning of 1965, in Alabama, where the State Democratic Party's official motto was "White Supremacy," not a single black resident of Lowndes County, Alabama, was a registered voter.[290] SNCC decided, after the failure of the MFDP to gain access to the Democratic convention, to create a political organization separate from the two established parties and attempt to elect black officials to county posts. SNCC joined forces with local leader John Hulett, who had worked with Martin Luther King, Jr. and had organized the Lowndes County Christian Movement for Human Rights.[291]

Despite the voter registration efforts, only 250 black citizens registered from March to August 1965, due to intimidation from white residents.[292] Hulett recalled:

[W]hile I was waiting for people to go in and take their tests, many of the white mens would ride by in pickup trucks with shotguns. In the summertime when it was hot, they cut the water off so we couldn't get water to drink. And they made peoples come over and over and over again, and they would turn them down. Peoples who lived on plantations and the farms, sharecroppers, they didn't own their own land. If they registered they could not live on the plantation any longer.[293]

Passage of the 1965 Voting Rights Act and the presence of federal registrars theoretically made it possible for many more black voters to register in Lowndes County, but angry white residents stepped up their reign of terror.[294]

On August 14, a group of SNCC workers protested voter registration barriers. An angry mob threatened the students and police arrested and jailed the SNCC workers. After one week in jail, the police suddenly released them without explanation. While they waited outside the jail for other SNCC workers, Thomas Coleman, a part-time deputy sheriff, shot and killed white divinity student Jonathan Daniels and badly wounded Father Richard Morrisroe, a white priest.[295] An all-white jury later acquitted Coleman, whose

defense was that Daniels had attacked him with a knife, and he had fired in self-defense.[296]

Despite this tragedy, SNCC workers continued to organize a new political party. Alabama law allowed the formation of county- level political parties and mandated that parties have symbols. Thus, John Hulett and the SNCC workers formed the Lowndes County Freedom Organization (LCFO) and adopted the symbol of the black panther because it is an animal which fights back when attacked. Some worried that this meant a violent uprising, but as Hulett later explained, "[W]e wasn't violent people. But we were just some people who was going to protect ourselves in case we were attacked by individuals."[297]

The LCFO planned its convention for May 3, 1966, to coincide with the county's Democratic Party primary for seven county offices. The sheriff deputized 550 white men to prevent the convention from taking place. But when word spread that the LCFO would use guns to defend its right to convene, the convention took place without disruption. The SCLC urged black voters to remain loyal to the Democratic Party, but 900 out of 2,000 registered black voters risked violence and economic repercussions to vote at the LCFO convention.[298]

Even though the LCFO candidates did not win in the general election, Hulett said:

[T]his was the first time that the black peoples in this county came together to make the choice of their own candidates for public office. That's why it was important. It was important also because of the numbers of peoples that turned out to that election that day and voted for their candidates and thought that they had done something for themselves to start making changes ....[299]

By 1968, southern black voters were registered in numbers proportionate to white voters.[300] The LCFO later merged with the reorganized state Democratic Party, and in 1970, the voters of Lowndes County elected Hulett sheriff. Meanwhile, the image of the black panther spread across the United States as a symbol of black people fighting back when attacked, a symbol which challenged King's creed of nonviolence. SNCC leader Stokely Carmichael increasingly advocated what the panther represented.[301]

DIFFERENT DIRECTIONS FOR THE MOVEMENT

Conflict among activists with different philosophies, tactics and backgrounds eventually led to division. New leaders began to offer alternatives to Martin Luther King, Jr.'s support for nonviolence and integration, as African Americans saw that, despite 10 years of a civil rights movement which embraced King's creed, many injustices persisted.

Stokely Carmichael was elected chair of SNCC in May 1966 and steered the organization in a more militant direction, creating increasing division between SNCC and SCLC.[302] John Lewis recalled, "[T]here was a sense, this feeling, that somehow and some way this movement must be more black-dominated and black-led ... I think there was a feeling in SNCC ... that they needed someone who would maybe be not so nonviolent, someone who would be blacker, in a sense, that would not preach interracial effort, preach integration."[303]

In the summer of 1966, many black leaders marched in Mississippi to protest the shooting of James Meredith, the first black student to attend the University of Mississippi. Stokely Carmichael and other SNCC members used the march as an opportunity to introduce this new militancy, using the slogan "Black Power."[304] David Dawley, a white student who participated in the march described the shift in focus:

> *Willie Ricks from SNCC asked people what they wanted, and they answered, "Freedom Now." Willie Ricks exhorted the crowd to demand not "Freedom Now" but "Black Power." He kept talking at the crowd, ... until eventually "Black Power" began to dominate until finally everyone together was thundering, "Black Power, Black Power." And that was chilling. That was frightening .... It seemed like a division between black and white .... After listening to Willie Ricks, the atmosphere was clearly different. There was a surface of more anger and more hostility. There was a release of more hostility toward whites.[305]*

SNCC was not the first organization to use the term Black Power but as the concept spread, making headlines across the country, it became associated with violence.

Andrew Young, an SCLC member, recalls that King, who disagreed with the tactics of Black Power, said that "in a pluralistic society, to have real power you have to deny it. And if you go around claiming power, the whole society turns on you and crushes you. It was not black power that [King] was against, it was the slogan Black Power, because he said, 'If you really have power you don't need a slogan.'"[306]

Many students broke with the older leaders, and white activists began to drift away from the movement, many becoming involved in anti-Vietnam War protests. Vice President Hubert Humphrey, generally a supporter of the Civil Rights movement, called Black Power reverse racism. Some white people feared that Black Power meant a war between the races.[307]

Martin Luther King, Jr.'s approach began to change as well. In 1966, King said, "I am appalled that some people feel that the civil rights struggle is over because we have a 1964 civil rights bill with 10 titles and a voting rights bill. Over and over again people ask, What else do you want? They feel that everything is all right. Well, let them look around at our big cities."[308]

King was expressing a shift in the concerns of many African Americans which began to surface in the mid 1960s, 10 years after the beginning of the Civil Rights movement. The movement made significant gains in ending segregation, particularly of schools, and in securing voting rights. Despite these gains, African Americans continued to face high rates of poverty and unemployment.

THE BLACK PANTHERS

In Oakland, California, two black men who worked at a neighborhood antipoverty center, Huey Newton and Bobby Seale, founded the Black Panther Party for Self-Defense in October 1966, to help black people to defend themselves against widespread police brutality and to put their definition of Black Power into practice. Creating the Black Panther Party was not the first action that Newton and Seale took to abolish police brutality. Seale recalled:

> *We got [5,000] signatures ... to get the city council to try to set up a police review board to deal with complaints of police brutality. Well, the city council ignored us. So the phenomenon was that the city council was just a racist structure which could care less about the [48] percent black and Chicano people who lived in the city of Oakland. So there we are, trying to figure out what to do. We finally concluded through those months that we had to start a new organization.[309]*

Newton was a part-time law school student and made use of his knowledge of the law in monitoring the activities of the police. California law allowed people to carry guns if they were not concealed. The Black Panthers soon became identified with the guns they always carried, along with their black clothing and berets. Though members carried guns, they abided by Party rule number five which said, "no party member will use, point, or fire a weapon of any kind unnecessarily or accidentally at anyone."[310]

The 10-point Black Panther Party program called for "an immediate end to POLICE BRUTALITY and MURDER of black people," power over the destiny of black communities, full employment, financial restitution for slavery and oppression, decent housing, education in black history, exemption from military service, the release of all black people held in prison, black juries for black defendants, and "a United Nations-supervised plebiscite to be held throughout the black colony in which only black colonial subjects will be allowed to participate, for the purpose of determining the will of black people as to their national destiny."[311]

Newton and Seale spread word of their program by using the lists of people on welfare at their anti-poverty center. Newton recalled, "We used those lists to go around and canvass the community in order to find out the desires of the community. So we would go from house to house and explain to people our program."[312]

The Party took on many projects to improve life in the ghetto. Its first action was to go to an elementary school where the lack of a traffic light had resulted in several children being hit by cars. The Black Panthers directed traffic at the intersection and collected signatures until the city council installed a traffic light. They counseled black people in the community on their legal rights, protested evictions, taught black culture and history classes and observed the police to prevent unnecessary use of violence and the violation of the rights of the accused.[313] Elaine Brown, who became a Panther in 1967, recalled:

> *The party reached out mostly to men, to young, black urban men who were on the streets, who knew that there were no options somewhere in their lives, who were gang members because that was all you could be in order to find some sense of dignity about yourself. We reached out to these people because we had something for them to do with the rest of their lives. In most cases, they were used to violence, they were used to struggle, they were used to fighting just to keep alive. We offered them the opportunity to make their lives meaningful.[314]*

The Black Panther Party, however, was simply too threatening to the state and federal government to allow its continued existence. In July 1967, the California legislature passed the Mulford Act which made it illegal to carry loaded firearms. The FBI labeled the Panthers the gravest threat to national security and began to arrange for its destruction.[315] J. Edgar Hoover, the FBI director, formulated a counter-intelligence program (COINTELPRO) "to expose, disrupt, misdirect, discredit, or otherwise neutralize the activities of black nationalist, hate-type organizations and groupings, their leadership, spokesmen, membership and supporters."[316] According to Judith Albert and Stewart Albert in their book, *The Sixties Papers*:

> *FBI special agents sought to divide the Panther organization by spreading false rumors and misinformation. They composed letters to Party members implicating Panther leaders in stealing from the Party treasury, taking money from the police, maintaining secret*

Swiss bank accounts and having sexual liaisons with white women. Local police forces were encouraged to launch raids against Panther headquarters.[317]

Under COINTELPRO, FBI agents monitored phone calls and meetings, raided Panther offices in several states and arranged assassinations of Party members. As historian Howard Zinn writes:

On December 4, 1969, a little before five in the morning, a squad of Chicago police, armed with a submachine gun and shotguns, raided an apartment where Black Panthers lived. They fired at least [82] and perhaps [200] rounds into the apartment, killing 21-year-old Black Panther leader Fred Hampton as he lay in his bed, and another Black Panther, Mark Clark. Years later, it was discovered in a court proceeding that the FBI had an informer among the Panthers, and that they had given the police a floor plan of the apartment, including a sketch of where Fred Hampton slept.[318]

The COINTELPRO campaign succeeded in dismantling the Black Panther movement.

URBAN RIOTS

Urban riots became increasingly common after 1965, attesting to the failure of the civil rights protests and the laws they brought about to effect any real change in the lives of African Americans living in the inner cities.

On August 11, 1965, just five days after President Johnson signed the Voting Rights Act, an incident of police brutality provoked a riot in Watts, an inner city section of Los Angeles, California, with predominately black residents. Police and the National Guard were called in and 34 people were killed, hundreds wounded and 4,000 arrested.[319]

From 1965 to 1968, hundreds of race riots took place across the country.[320] According to studies of the riots, there was logic to the seeming blind fury. The rioters mostly attacked businesses owned by white people, especially those with the reputation for taking advan-tage of black customers. They avoided damaging churches, schools and libraries.[321]

Scholars have disagreed over whether the riots could be labeled protests,[322] but regardless of the intentions of the rioters, they forced white Americans to acknowledge that the problem of race had yet to be solved.[323] African Americans continued to face disproportionate poverty, unemployment two or three times the average, substandard housing, inadequate municipal services, deficient education, high prices, high mortality and sickness rates and police brutality.[324] *The New York Times* reported that, during the 1960s, the suburbs gained 3,000,000 jobs, an increase of 44 percent, while inner cities lost 836,000 jobs.[325]

The particularly violent summer of 1967 prompted President Johnson to appoint a commission on civil disorders, which blamed the riots on the "explosive mixture" of unemployment, poverty and slum conditions in the inner cities. The National Advisory Commission on Civil Disorders warned that "our nation is moving toward two societies, one black, one white — separate and unequal." [326] The commission recommended federal funds to create jobs, housing and welfare programs. Congress responded with the Civil Rights Act of 1968 which strengthened the laws prohibiting violence against African Americans. But Congress exempted law enforcement officers and members of the National Guard or the Armed Forces "who are engaged in suppressing a riot or civil disturbance."[327]

Ironically, the first person prosecuted under the Act was SNCC leader H. Rap Brown on charges of instigating a riot. The Act was also used to prosecute anti-Vietnam War demonstrators at the Democratic Convention in Chicago in 1968.[328]

ASSASSINATION OF MARTIN LUTHER KING, JR.

Increasingly, King made demands that threatened the economic institutions of the United States: "[W]e need massive programs that will change the structure of American society so there will be a better distribution of the wealth."[329] King also linked the poverty issue to the escalating war in Vietnam. Because of this anti-establishment focus, King became, as historian Howard Zinn writes, "a chief target of the FBI, which tapped his private phone conversations, sent him fake letters, threatened him, blackmailed him, and even suggested once in an anonymous letter that he commit suicide. FBI internal memos discussed finding a black leader to replace King."[330]

King planned a "Poor People's Encampment" on Washington in the summer of 1968 to bring national attention to poverty issues. But in early April he travelled to Memphis to support a sanitation workers' strike. There, on April 4, 1968, Martin Luther King, Jr. was assassinated. Urban riots erupted in 125 U.S. cities, in which 46 people were killed, 41 of them black.[331]

THE MOVEMENT LOSES GROUND

Although the Civil Rights movement had achieved significant gains for African Americans, when the goals moved toward economic justice, the movement suffered serious setbacks. Growing violence in the inner cities prompted candidates for office in almost every city to promise law and order. For example, in 1966, Ronald Reagan, who was critical of the Watts' rioters, was elected governor of California.[332]

Also in 1966, for the first time in a decade, Congress rejected a proposed civil rights bill. The election in 1968 of Richard Nixon, who spoke against open housing and school busing, underscored the changing mood. George Wallace, the governor of Alabama who had promised segregation forever, received almost 14 percent of the vote when he ran for President on a third party ticket.[333]

In 1968, the Supreme Court mandated in *Green* v. *County School Board* that each school district end *de facto* segregation, stating, "[T]he burden on a school board today is to come forward with a plan that promises realistically to work, and promises realistically to work now." And, in 1971, the Court gave power to the federal district courts to ensure desegregation, by busing children out of highly segregated schools if necessary.[334]

By 1973, 46.3 percent of the black children in the South were attending schools in which the majority of the students were white, yet in the North and West only 28.3 percent of black children attended white

majority schools.[335] This phenomenon, caused by housing segregation and white flight to the suburbs, is called *de facto* segregation, since it is not mandated by law, but exists in fact. On a NAACP Legal Defense Fund challenge, the Supreme Court ruled in 1973 that if a school district had policies which led to *de facto* segregation, it must remedy the situation. Thus northern school districts were subjected to measures which had previously been reserved for the South.[336]

Yet in 1974, the Court weakened its commitment to school integration by ruling in *Milliken* v. *Bradley* that desegregation plans did not have to include the suburbs.[337] By 1980, the Court had completely rejected busing as a method for improving black schooling but offered no alternative. The number of single-race schools increased rapidly.[338]

Civil rights activists continued to lose ground throughout the 1970s and 1980s. President Gerald Ford maintained Nixon's welfare funding freeze, fought against school busing and open housing and vetoed legislation aimed at helping low-income black people.[339]

In 1976, Jimmy Carter's campaign promises included helping the poor and disadvantaged of the nation, and he earned 94 percent of the black vote. Carter appointed many prominent African Americans to federal positions, but financial aid, school lunch programs and health care suffered under his administration.[340]

Affirmative action came increasingly under fire. For example, in 1978, the Supreme Court ruled in *Regents of the University of California* v. *Bakke* that a quota for the admission of racial minorities to the University of California at Davis medical school was unconstitutional.[341]

Upon taking office in 1981, President Ronald Reagan reduced social spending, scaled down welfare and food stamp programs, attempted to reverse affirmative action, opposed laws against discrimination in awarding federal contracts, tried to reverse the provision that private schools which discriminated would lose tax-exempt status, weakened the Civil Rights Commission, fought a strengthened Voting Rights Act, sought to abolish the Department of Education and cut back student loan programs.[342]

According to Ralph G. Neas, executive director of the Leadership Conference on Civil Rights, "[T]he Reagan administration compiled the worst civil rights record of any [administration] in more than a half-century."[343] President Reagan became the first President to veto civil rights legislation in 122 years.[344]

President Reagan applied his philosophy on civil rights to his judicial appointments: during his eight years in office he named over half of the judges on the Federal bench and his appointees dominate the circuit courts of appeal. Reagan also appointed three Supreme Court justices, including the Chief Justice.[345] A series of Supreme Court decisions in 1989 "did more damage to civil rights laws in four weeks in June than had occurred in the previous four decades," according to Ralph Neas.[346] In one of the cases, *Wards Cove* v. *Antonio*, the Court overturned a 1971 Court decision, placing on employees the burden of proof in discrimination cases.[347]

Despite the many setbacks of the 1970s and 1980s, gains in the number of African Americans participating in the political process increased dramatically. From 1940 to 1984, the voter registration rate for African Americans in the South increased from 3.1 percent to 66.9 percent. And turnout of black registered voters increased in the South from 13 percent in 1952 to 85 percent in 1984.[348]

In the mid-1960s, before the passage of the Voting Rights Act of 1965, only approximately 280 African Americans served as elected officials in the United States — at all levels of government. As of 1988, the number was 6,200 — still only about 2.1 percent of all elected officials, although African Americans make up over 12 percent of the population.[349]

Despite the gains in civil and political rights, African Americans' economic status overall improved little from World War II to the 1990s. Modest socioeconomic gains achieved in the 1970s were completely reversed in the 1980s. The National Urban League's *State of Black America, 1989* describes the Reagan administration as a time of "stagnation and retrogression in the economic status of black Americans ... no progress was made in reducing the longstanding economic disparities faced by blacks ... In fact, racial inequality in American economic life actually increased by many of the standard indicators."[350]

Comparison of levels of income, poverty, wealth ownership and employment reveal that African Americans fall economically far behind white Americans. Although family income grew at a slower rate in the 1980s than in the 1970s for all American families, black family income grew significantly slower than white family income.[351] Black unemployment averaged 11.8 percent in 1988 compared to only 4.7 percent white unemployment. And unemployment among black teenagers in 1988 was 33.4 percent compared to 13.3 for white teenagers.[352]

In 1987, one-third of African Americans lived in households with incomes below the poverty level. The proportions were even higher for black children, who experienced a poverty rate of 45.1 percent. Moreover, over half of all families headed by women had poverty level incomes in 1987.[353]

The consequences of poverty are devastating. In 1986 a black infant born in the United States was more than twice as likely to die as a white infant born that year.[354] The black infant mortality rate among the youngest black infants (under 28 days of life) rose nationally in 1985 for the first time in over 20 years. Even black children's immunization status is sliding backwards. In 1985, one in every ten nonwhite children, one to four years of age, received no doses of polio vaccine — nearly double the percentage in 1980.[355]

Medicaid served fewer poor children in 1986 than in 1979, when there were nearly one-third fewer poor children. In the 15 years following Medicaid's enactment, black infant mortality fell 49 percent, nine times the rate in the 15 years before it was enacted. But between 1976 and 1986, the percentage of poor families covered by Medicaid fell from 65 percent to 46 percent, until in 1987 Medicaid served less than 50 percent of the eligible poor.[356]

CURRENT ISSUES AND ACTIVISM

Despite the setbacks, civil rights groups continue to work to protect civil rights legislation and court decisions as well as to improve the economic status of African Americans.

Congress proposed civil rights legislation in 1990 to overturn a number of 1989 Supreme Court rulings against civil rights and to strengthen Title VII of the Civil Rights Act of 1964.[357] President George Bush opposed the bill, stating his concern that it would encourage businesses to establish "hiring quotas," under which they would attempt to maintain a statistically balanced workforce to avoid lawsuits. Congress responded by revising the bill to state that it does not require or encourage quotas and passed the Civil Rights Act of 1990 with approximately 64 percent majorities in each house.[358] President Bush vetoed the bill on October 22, 1990. The Senate failed to override the veto by one vote.[359]

Civil rights organizations continued their campaigns for civil rights legislation. The Leadership Conference on Civil Rights (LCCR) began meeting with the Business Roundtable, a group of 200 chief executive officers of major U.S. corporations. Both groups wished to reach compromises on the latest version of the legislation offered by Congress.[360] They developed

a "definition of business necessity that employers could meet without being forced to hire by the numbers."[361] And all over the country, coalitions of civil rights, women's, gay and lesbian, disability rights and religious organizations worked together in a concerted fight for the civil rights act.[362]

The Civil Rights and Women's Equity in Employment Act of 1991, passed the House on June 5, 1991, 273 to 158.[363] But the bill stalled in the Senate, as proponents tried to render it both effective in its goal of strengthening civil rights laws and veto-proof. Suddenly, in October 1991, negotiations between White House and Senate leaders began to produce substantial agreement on a bill that would overturn the Supreme Court decisions of 1989 which restricted civil rights. On October 25, Bush endorsed a compromise bill, which Congress passed. On November 21, Bush signed the Civil Rights Act of 1991 into law.

Yet the debate was not over. Two White House lawyers wrote a proposed executive order which "would have ended government affirmative action and hiring guidelines that benefit women and minorities."[364] The statement was leaked to the media and created such a furor among civil rights leaders as well as government officials that President Bush disavowed it the next day. Ralph Neas of the LCCR, said, "There is no question that the Bush administration will continue to do everything possible to undermine the Civil Rights Act of 1991...."[365] Officials predicted that the order would be reissued when "the furor dies down."[366]

Some of the concerns and tactics of African American activism have changed since the height of the civil rights movement in the 1950s and 1960s. Civil rights groups still work for legislative and judicial remedies for discrimination and its effects but also now work for self-help and economic remedies. At a recent conference, the first Summit of Black Organizations, Benjamin Hooks, executive director of the NAACP, stated "Much of what needs to be done within the African American community must be done by ourselves and for ourselves."[367] The participants in the Summit formed the National Association of Black Organizations, which will focus on developing self-help programs.[368]

Ralph Neas of the LCCR believes that civil rights activists so far largely have ignored issues of economic justice and equality.[369] Yet many groups are beginning to address economic development in minority communities. And a number of groups have banded together as consumers to encourage the business community to respond to problems and goals of African Americans.

Operation PUSH, headed until recently by Jesse Jackson, negotiates "economic covenants" with companies doing a large proportion of their business with black consumers. Operation PUSH asks the company to hire black employees in a proportion similar to the proportion of business done with the black community. In several instances, Operation PUSH organized nationwide boycotts of companies which did not agree to such covenants.[370]

In July 1990, PUSH officials met with executives of Nike, a company which does $200 million of business annually with African Americans. PUSH documented that Nike hires few black workers, does not purchase products or services from black businesses and has no black directors on its board. Nike officials seemed to be sympathetic, yet in August they published a letter attacking PUSH. There would be no economic covenant. On August 11, PUSH launched a nationwide boycott of Nike products. According to journalist Salim Muwakkil, "[M]ost African Americans overwhelmingly support PUSH's goals."[371]

According to Muwakkil, "[M]ost analysts conclude that PUSH's covenants have aided the cause of racial parity."[372] Both the NAACP and the SCLC also practice this strategy, called "tradism." Jackson explains that while African American consumers do "more business each year with corporate America than Russia, China and France combined,"[373] corporations hire few black workers and purchase few goods or services from black businesses. Jackson states that economic leverage may be a more effective tool for change than political pressure.[374]

Many African American citizen groups address issues in which race, gender and economics overlap. The National Black Women's Health Project addresses issues such as availability and affordability of health care.[375] Other activism includes working against housing discrimination, drugs and the AIDS epidemic.

CONCLUSION

According to the National Urban League's report, *The State of Black America 1989*:

The initial struggles are over; Jim Crow laws are gone; and there are no longer segregated drinking fountains and "separate but equal" schools. But the war is far from won; the battles have simply taken on a new personality. The struggles today are in some ways more important, for they will decide whether blacks and whites will live in a harmonious and productive America or one convulsed by the divisive cancer of racism, suspicion and ignorance. The fight at the back of the bus 30 years ago is now centered over much more

powerful issues — education, jobs, values and money.[376]

This statement sums up both the progress of and the continuing problems facing African Americans.

BIBLIOGRAPHY

Adams, Frank with Myles Horton. *Unearthing Seeds of Fire: The Idea of Highlander.* Winston-Salem, NC: John F. Blair, 1975.

Albert, Judith Clavir and Stewart Edward Albert, eds. *The Sixties Papers: Documents of a Rebellious Decade.* New York: Praeger, 1984.

Aldred, Lisa. *Thurgood Marshall: Supreme Court Justice.* New York: Chelsea House Publishers, 1990.

Aptheker, Herbert. *Afro American History: The Modern Era.* Secaucus, NJ: The Citadel Press, 1971.

Baldwin, James. *The Fire Next Time.* New York: Dial Press, 1963.

"Black Muslims: From Fringe to Bedrock," *U.S. News and World Report.* Vol. 109. No. 14. October 8, 1990.

Cantarow, Ellen with Susan Gushee O'Malley and Sharon Hartman Strom. *Moving the Mountain: Women Working for Social Change.* Old Westbury, NY: The Feminist Press, 1980.

Capeci, Dominic J., Jr. "From Harlem to Montgomery: The Bus Boycotts and Leadership of Adam Clayton Powell, Jr. and Martin Luther King, Jr.," *The Historian: A Journal of History.* Vol. 41. No. 4. August, 1979.

Carmichael, Stokely and Charles V. Hamilton. *Black Power.* New York: Vintage Books, 1967.

Carson, Clayborne. *In Struggle: SNCC and the Black Awakening of the 1960s.* Cambridge: Harvard University Press, 1981.

Civil Rights Monitor. Washington, DC: Leadership Conference Education Fund. Fall 1990.

Civil Rights Monitor. Washington, DC: Leadership Conference Education Fund. Summer 1991.

Clark, Septima Poinsette. "Literacy and Liberation," *Freedomways: A Quarterly Review of the Negro Freedom Movement*. First Quarter, 1964. Vol. IV. No. 1.

Clark, Septima Poinsette. Edited with an introduction by Cynthia Stokes Brown. *Ready from Within: Septima Clark and the Civil Rights Movement*. Navarro, CA: Wild Trees Press, 1986.

Cronon, E. David. *Black Moses: The Story of Marcus Garvey and the Universal Negro Improvement Association*. Madison: The University of Wisconsin Press, 1981 [1955].

Cruse, Harold. *Plural But Equal: A Critical Study of Blacks and Minorities and America's Plural Society*. New York: William Morrow, 1987.

Davis, Marianna W., ed. *Contributions of Black Women to America*. Columbia, SC: Kenday Press, Inc., 1981.

Devroy, Ann. "President Signs Civil Rights Bill," *Washington Post*. November 22, 1991.

Dewart, Janet, ed. *The State of Black America 1989*. New York: The National Urban League, 1989.

Edds, Margaret. *Free at Last: What Really Happened When Civil Rights Came to Southern Politics*. Bethesda, MD: Adler and Adler, 1987.

Eight Men and a Lady: Profiles of the Justices of the Supreme Court. Bethesda, MD: National Press, 1990.

"End of the Quota Non-Issue?" *New York Times*. April 24, 1991.

Evans, Sara M. and Harry C. Boyte. *Free Spaces: The Sources of Democratic Change in America*. New York: Harper and Row, 1986.

Fager, Charles E. *Selma, 1965*. New York: Charles Scribner's Sons, 1974.

Finch, Minnie. *The NAACP: Its Fight for Justice*. Metuchen, NJ: The Scarecrow Press, Inc., 1981.

Forman, James. *The Making of Black Revolutionaries*. Washington, DC: Open Hand Publishing, Inc., 1985.

Friedman, Leon, ed. *The Civil Rights Reader*. New York: Walker and Company, 1968.

Giddings, Paula. *When and Where I Enter: The Impact of Black Women on Race and Sex in America*. New York: William Morrow and Company, Inc., 1984.

Goldman, Peter Louis. *The Death and Life of Malcolm X*. New York: Harper and Row, 1973.

Grant, Joanne, producer, director, writer. *Fundi: The Story of Ella Baker* Film. Vols. I & II. 1982.

Haley, Alex. *The Autobiography of Malcolm X*. New York: Grove Press, 1965.

Hampton, Henry and Steve Fayer. *Voices of Freedom: An Oral History of the Civil Rights Movement from the 1950s through the 1980s*. New York: Bantam Books, 1990.

Harding, Vincent. *There Is A River: The Black Struggle for Freedom in America*. New York: Harcourt Brace Jovanovich, 1981.

Harris, William H. *The Harder We Run: Black Workers Since the Civil War*. New York: Oxford University Press, 1982.

Hughes, Langston. *Langston Hughes Reader*. New York: George Braziller, Inc., 1958.

Jordan, Winthrop D. and Leon F. Litwack. *The United States*. Seventh Combined Edition. Englewood Cliffs, NJ: Prentice Hall, 1991.

Justice for Wards Cove Workers Act. Fact sheet. Washington, DC: Leadership Conference on Civil Rights.

King, Martin Luther, Jr. *Stride Toward Freedom: The Montgomery Story*. New York: Harper and Row, 1958.

King, Martin Luther, Jr. *Why We Can't Wait*. New York: Harper and Row, 1963.

King, Martin Luther, Jr. *Where Do We Go From Here: Chaos or Community?* Boston: Beacon Press, 1967.

King, Mary. *Freedom Song: A Personal Story of the 1960s Civil Rights Movement*. New York: William Morrow and Company, Inc., 1987.

Kluger, Richard. *Simple Justice*. New York: Vintage Books, 1975.

Koonz, Claudia."The Auxiliary of Hate," *New York Times Book Review*. January 5, 1992.

Lerner, Gerda, ed. *Black Women in White America: A Documentary History*. New York: Pantheon Books, 1972.

Levine, Lawrence W."Marcus Garvey's Moment," *The New Republic*. October 29, 1984.

Litwack, Leon F. *Been in the Storm So Long: The Aftermath of Slavery*. New York: Alfred A. Knopf, 1979.

Litwack, Leon F. *North of Slavery: The Negro in the Free States 1790-1860*. Chicago: University of Chicago Press, 1961.

Morris, Aldon D. *The Origins of the Civil Rights Movement: Black Communities Organizing for Change*. New York: The Free Press, 1984.

Muwakkil, Salim."An Organized PUSH for Black Participation," *In These Times*. September 12-18, 1990.

Muwakkil, Salim."Black Leaders Favor 'Self-Help' Over Integration," *In These Times*. October 10-16, 1990.

Neas, Ralph G."The Civil Rights Legacy of the Reagan Years," *USA Today: The Magazine of the American Scene*. Society for the Advancement of Education. Vol. 118. No. 2538. March, 1990.

O'Reilly, Kenneth. *Racial Matters: The FBI's Secret File on Black America, 1960-72*. New York: The Free Press, 1989.

Ovington, Mary White. *How the National Association for the Advancement of Colored People Began*. Pamphlet. Washington, DC: NAACP, originally published in 1914.

Powledge, Fred. *Free at Last?: The Civil Rights Movement and the People Who Made It*. Boston: Little, Brown, 1991.

Raines, Howell. *My Soul is Rested: The Story of the Civil Rights Movement in the Deep South*. New York: Penguin, 1977.

Redmond, Pat."Women of Color Set Agenda," *New Directions for Women*. September 1990.

Robinson, Jo Ann. *The Montgomery Bus Boycott and the Women Who Started It*. Knoxville: University of Tennessee Press, 1987.

Rose, Thomas and John Greenya. *Black Leaders: Then and Now*. Garrett Park, MD: Garrett Park Press, 1984.

Schuman, Howard, Charlotte Steeh and Lawrence Bobo. *Racial Attitudes in America: Trends and Interpretations*. Cambridge: Harvard University Press, 1985.

75th Annual Conference Program. New York: National Urban League, 1985.

Shaw, Nate. With Theodore Rosengarten. *All God's Dangers*. New York: Vintage Books, 1984.

Sitkoff, Harvard. *The Struggle for Black Equality: 1954-1980*. New York: Hill and Wang, 1981.

Sterling, Dorothy. *Black Foremothers: Three Lives*. New York: The Feminist Press, 1988.

Summary of the Civil Rights Act of 1991. Fact sheet. Washington, DC: Leadership Conference on Civil Rights.

Wells-Barnett, Ida B. *Crusade for Justice*. Chicago: University of Chicago Press, 1970.

Wilkinson, J. Harvie, III. *From* Brown *to* Bakke: *The Supreme Court and School Integration: 1954-1978*. Oxford: Oxford University Press, 1979.

Williams, Juan. *Eyes on the Prize: America's Civil Rights Years, 1954-1965*. New York: Viking, 1987.

Zinn, Howard. *SNCC: The New Abolitionists*. Boston: Beacon Press, 1965.

Zinn, Howard. *A People's History of the United States*. New York: Harper and Row, 1980.

A HISTORY OF THE
LABOR MOVEMENT

INTRODUCTION

As workers first entered factories, with the onset of the Industrial Revolution, they lost the ability to independently earn a living and became employees rather than self-employed producers. Factory conditions often were oppressive and wages low. Yet the factory also brought workers together where they began to form organizations to lessen the hardships of industrial work.

Workers who practiced the same trade or possessed the same skill or training formed trade unions to protect their jobs from unskilled workers. Other workers organized by industry, to win improvements in wages and working conditions as well as to increase their control of workplace decisions. Workers at times created their own political parties such as the workingmen's parties, the Socialist Party and the Farmer-Labor Party. The labor movement also has a rich history of workers banding together to pursue a better world outside the workplace.

WORK AT THE TIME OF
THE AMERICAN REVOLUTION

At the time of the American Revolution, the workforce was made up of skilled artisans, such as blacksmiths, silversmiths, tailors and shoemakers — who owned their own shops and hired journeymen and apprentices to work for them — as well as farmers, common laborers, indentured servants, household servants and African slaves.[1] White women worked mostly in the home "weav[ing], spin[ning], mak[ing] lace, soap, shoes, and candles, as well as car[ing] for their households and families."[2]

The skilled artisans were proud of their trade. As the tanners, curriers and cord-wainers (shoemakers) of Philadelphia wrote, "Our professions rendered us useful and necessary members of the community, proud of that rank, we aspired no higher."[3] Great autonomy existed in the workplaces of skilled artisans, who lived mostly in the cities. As historian

Alfred Young writes, "[T]here was a thick web of custom by which skilled workers set the pace on the job and defined what went on in the workshop."[4] In the shoemakers' shop, the owner "took in work and ... neighbors, came in there and sat down and made shoes right in their laps, and there was no machinery. Everybody was at liberty to talk ... there was absolute freedom and exchange of ideas."[5]

INDUSTRIALIZATION: A REVOLUTION
IN THE NATURE OF WORK

As industrialization increased, the nature of work changed dramatically. Factories with modern machinery produced commodities more quickly and inexpensively than the artisans' shops. Old-style shops were forced out of business by the availability of cheaper, mass-produced goods. Skilled artisans, once in business for themselves, now sought work in factories.[6] The work in the factories often required no skill or training. Instead of making a shoe, from start to finish, for example, an individual factory worker made one part of a shoe, performing the same task over and over, with other workers making other, separate parts. Much of the pride that the artisans took in completing a project was lost.

Factory conditions were often dismal. Long hours and unsafe conditions were common. Historian Franklin Rosemont writes:

A half-century after the Revolution, it was not unusual for workers to labor seven days a week and twelve hours a day. For many families to make ends meet, even small children had to work the same long hours, but at even lower pay. Most workplaces and dwellings lacked adequate ventilation, sanitation, and rubbish removal. Medical care remained beyond the means of working-class families; mortality rates were high. Recurring epidemics decimated cities and towns. Even in good times workers' lives were hard; but there were also hard times, long periods of unem-

ployment, inflation, and economic collapse brought on by financial panics.[7]

EARLY ATTEMPTS AT WORKER ORGANIZATION TO RESIST INDUSTRIALIZATION

Workers reacted to the growing inequalities in society, linking them to not just individual factories but also the power of monopolies and of wealthy interests in government. They believed the promises of the Declaration of Independence were not being fulfilled for the vast majority of Americans. Workers began to organize not only for improvements in working conditions but to preserve the way of life threatened by industrialization.[8]

Resistance to industrialization often took an individual form. "In massive numbers, workers refused to bend to the new disciplines of the industrial setting. They came late or not at all to work. They refused to let the factories control their children. Most of all, they quit and moved elsewhere," write historians Sara Evans and Harry Boyte.[9]

The earliest organizations to give expression to workers' sympathies were the workingmen's parties that, starting in Philadelphia in 1828, spread to every state.[10] Although they were led mostly by native-born, white, male, skilled workers, the workingmen's parties attempted to include women, immigrants, Native Americans, slaves and unskilled workers.[11]

In one of their declarations, they proclaimed, "There appears to exist two distinct classes, the rich and the poor; the oppressor and the oppressed; those that live by their own labour, and they that live by the labour of others ..."[12] They criticized political favoritism such as government-granted, exclusive monopolies to business which contributed to the growing inequality between rich and poor.[13] They proposed a wide variety of reforms to allow working people greater access in many areas of public life, including extending the right to vote to all adults, free public education, direct elections, civil service reform, simplification of the legal system and more equitable taxation. They also advocated better working conditions, a shorter workday and an end to child labor.[14]

"The new movement's most characteristic rallying cry, however, was for free land," writes Franklin Rosemont.[15] The workingmen's parties urged the federal government to let eastern workers settle the governments' vast holdings of land in the West. Free land advocates argued that large numbers of workers from the eastern cities, where more workers than jobs existed, moving west would solve the unemployment problems, and eventually raise wages and shorten the workday of workers in the East.[16]

The workingmen's parties, opposed to both major political parties, ran their own candidates in numerous elections.[17] In New York in 1829, the workingmen's party elected Ebenezer Ford, a carpenter, to the State Assembly.[18] The workingmen's parties published newspapers, books, pamphlets and verses.[19] During the 1830s, the major parties adopted some of the workingmen's proposals, and although the workingmen's parties could not compete, their movement "instilled immeasurable confidence in working people" and "gave powerful momentum to the trade union movement."[20] Tens of thousands of workers joined trade unions (organizations of workers who practice the same craft or trade or possess the same skill or training) in the 1830s.[21]

As unions recognized their common concerns, they combined forces to form a national federation of unions. The National Trades Union (NTU), formed in 1834 by delegates from Boston, Philadelphia, Brooklyn, Poughkeepsie and Newark, represented 25,000 workers. This union was part of a national labor upsurge that called more than 100 strikes over the next few years.[22] The NTU dissolved under the pressure of the financial panic of 1837.[23]

Courts ruled, as early as 1806, that organized activities of workers, including strikes, pickets and boycotts, were "criminal conspiracies" because the activities interrupted the free flow of trade. Throughout the 1800s, judges continued to rule on the legality of union activities on a case-by-case basis.[24] Since workers could not predict whether the courts would hold their organizing strategies to be criminal acts, they could not use these tactics to win concessions from their employers without fear of legal reprisals.

WOMEN AND CHILDREN ENTER THE WORKFORCE

White women, as well as children, began to work in factories by 1814.[25] Women in the first half of the 19th century worked in over 100 industrial occupations. Historian Eleanor Flexner writes that "At first, some of these occupations, the making of cloth, garments and hats, and the sewing of shoes, were carried on in the home where [women] had first engaged in them as housewives. But with the invention of the spinning jenny and the power loom, home work shrank; there was a steady demand for women workers in the textile mills."[26] Women typically earned much less than men for the same work; one newspaper in 1833 suggested that most women were paid less than one-fourth the earnings of men.[27]

Young women working in the textile factories in Lowell, Massachusetts, left their rural homes and lived together in factory-owned dormitories. The women engaged in activities from publishing a literary magazine and sponsoring social and cultural events to forming labor organizations, which became more active as speed-ups and wage cuts became more frequent.[28]

In 1845, after witnessing a series of unsuccessful turnouts (strikes) in protest of long hours and low wages, five young women workers in Lowell met to plan a campaign to win the 10-hour-day. These women recruited 600 members into the Lowell Female Labor Reform Association. Women formed several chapters of the Association in other New England towns. Sarah Bagley, president of the Association, wrote articles for the *Voice of Industry*, defending women workers' right to organize.[29]

The women won numerous victories through the Association. For example, "When one of the larger mills in Lowell tried to increase the work load from three to four looms, at the same time reducing wages a cent per piece, a meeting of the Association pledged that no such increased load would be accepted unless accompanied by an increase in pay. Almost every woman weaver working for the mill signed a pledge to this effect, and stuck to it; the attempted speed-up was canceled," writes Eleanor Flexner.[30]

The Female Labor Reform Association also collected signatures petitioning the Massachusetts state legislature for a 10-hour-day law. Eventually the state did appoint a committee to investigate working conditions in the mills, but the committee, after hearing eight witnesses from the mills (six of whom were women) and visiting Lowell themselves (for which the mills were cleaned up), decided to make no recommendation for a 10-hour-day law.[31] The committee was "satisfied that the order, decorum, and general appearance of things in and around the mills could not be improved by any suggestion of theirs or by any act of the legislature."[32] Women in the mills continued to protest the long hours and low pay.

The state of child labor was equally grim during the 1800s. Young children spent long hours in dark, dirty factories doing boring and often dangerous work for little pay.[33] The government did not regulate child labor. In Paterson, New Jersey, one series of mill strikes was started by children workers who marched off the job when the company unexpectedly tried to postpone their lunch hour from noon to 1:00 p.m. Other workers joined the children's strike, demanding 10-hour-day policies. The children returned to work when the company threatened to bring in armed guards. The company fired the strike leaders, but their efforts were not entirely in vain; before long the company changed the lunch hour back to noon.[34]

THE EVE OF CIVIL WAR

The two decades before the Civil War were characterized by massive immigration of industrial workers from northern Europe and a series of economic crises. Employers often encouraged resentment among the groups of immigrants from different countries and between immigrants and native-born workers to discourage them from organizing together against the employer. Many new immigrants, who without specific skills could easily be replaced by other workers and who faced constant crises in the national economy that jeopardized their jobs, were initially reluctant to organize.[35] The crisis of 1857 threw so many out of work that thousands of recent immigrants went back to Europe.[36]

But eventually, immigrant workers organized within their own national groups, and in a wave of strikes and union-building in the 1850s, they organized across ethnic and national lines to improve wages and working conditions (including a campaign for the 10-hour workday).[37] Groups of workers, including "hat-finishers, cigarmakers, typesetters, plumbers, painters, stonecutters, shoemakers and iron-molders" formed national unions in the decade before the Civil War that laid the groundwork for larger and more successful efforts after the war.[38]

In 1860, shoemakers in Lynn, Massachusetts launched a massive strike (the largest the nation had yet seen), which eventually involved 20,000 workers, to oppose the layoffs and wage cuts brought by the introduction of the sewing machine.[39] With the issue of slavery prominent on the national agenda, the Lynn workers expressed their desire for freedom from what many called "wage slavery."[40] The shoemakers, who worked for wages instead of for themselves, compared their situation to that of slaves. Eight hundred female strikers marched through the streets of Lynn carrying a banner proclaiming: "American ladies will not be slaves: Give us a fair compensation and we labor cheerfully."[41]

Yet one worker said, "[W]e are not a quarter as bad off as the slaves of the South, though we are, by our ... foolishness, 10 times as bad off as we ought to be. They can't vote, nor complain, and we can. And then just think of it; the slaves can't hold mass meetings, nor 'strike,' and we haven't lost that privilege yet."[42]

Although many northern workers feared that freed slaves would compete for their jobs, and although many workers were racist, few believed in slavery. Some northern labor leaders encouraged workers to support the abolition of slavery because, ultimately, slavery was a labor issue. Both northern workers and slaves were trying to gain control over their labor and their lives.[43]

However, as historian Howard Zinn writes of the Civil War and workers:

White workers of the North were not enthusiastic about a war which seemed to be fought

for the black slave, or for the capitalist, for anyone but them. They worked in semislave conditions themselves. They thought the war was profiting the new class of millionaires. They saw defective guns sold to the army by contractors, sand sold as sugar, rye sold as coffee, shop sweepings made into clothing and blankets, paper-soled shoes produced for soldiers at the front, navy ships made of rotting timbers, soldiers' uniforms that fell apart in the rain.[44]

Southern white workers were not always enthusiastic about the war either. Two-thirds of white Southerners did not own slaves, and many, like their northern counterparts, were reluctant to fight to protect the interests of the rich. The draft law discriminated against workers by allowing the rich, in both the North and the South, to buy their way out of the draft, while workers who were drafted had no alternative but to fight. Draft riots, expressing anger toward the rich and toward African Americans, broke out in several northern cities.[45] Once the war began, most workers were diverted from labor organizing campaigns. The federal government often jailed critics of President Abraham Lincoln's policies and intervened to break strikes interfering with the war effort.[46]

POST-CIVIL WAR ECONOMIC CONDITIONS

After the Civil War, industrialization intensified and wealth became increasingly concentrated among fewer and fewer individuals who gained control over various industries, including oil, steel and railroads.[47] Some employers campaigned to weaken or eliminate workers' organizations using methods including: forcing workers to sign "yellow-dog" contracts (a promise not to join any workers' organization), maintaining blacklists (lists of workers who had attempted to form unions) and refusing to hire blacklisted workers; and seeking court injunctions to stop worker activities such as strikes and pickets.[48] Economic crises continued to erupt. During the depression of 1873, which lasted more than five years, three million workers lost their jobs. In New York City, 90,000 families were evicted from their homes. Previous gains in unionization were wiped out.[49] The crises strengthened the most established monopolists and threw smaller companies out of business.[50]

Workers became increasingly angry about the influence of the wealthy in national affairs. For example, in 1876, the Workingmen's Party of Illinois declared, "The present system has enabled capitalists to make laws in their own interests to the injury and oppression of the workers. It has made the name Democracy, for which our forefathers fought and died, a mockery and a shadow, by giving to property an unproportionate amount of representation and control over Legislation."[51]

Workers also responded to the growing concentration of wealth with a series of strikes. The largest of these was the Great Uprising of 1877, when railroad workers, who belonged to no national union, went on strike spontaneously. Railroad workers' wages had been reduced several times since the beginning of the depression in 1873. In March of 1877, executives from four of the largest railroads met to adopt a plan to cut wages further. When the strikes broke out, federal and state troops intervened, resulting in violence in many areas. The government intervention angered workers and the strike quickly spread to 14 states.[52] Tens of thousands of workers went on strike, and over 100 people were killed and millions of dollars worth of property was destroyed. Although the strikers did not succeed in raising wages or controlling corporate power, the Great Uprising "marked the beginning of a revival of the labor movement."[53]

Although the two to three decades after the Civil War often are characterized simply as a long series of violent strikes, like the Great Uprising, most workers in the United States were not involved in this violence.[54] Instead, the changes associated with industrialization came slowly to small towns and rural areas where people knew one another well and workers successfully resisted many of the changes.[55]

Employers in the large cities could easily replace workers rather than bargain with them. The upper-class, far removed in their daily lives from most workers, had little sympathy for workers' concerns. When the massive depression of 1873 led employers to cut wages, newspapers in the large cities expressed satisfaction that the depression would end workers' attempts to organize.[56]

In small towns, however, industrialists could not replace their workers as easily as in the cities. The middle-class and working class lived and worked together and had a sense of community. Workers in small towns had more political clout than their counterparts in large cities, since they voted in large numbers and participated in local politics. Workers held political office as well as other positions within the community. Small-town newspapers were often independent of industrial interests. Furthermore, middle-class citizens of small towns often resisted the changes industrialization brought to their communities and many took seriously the grievances of workers.[57]

Industrialists generally had more difficulty passing on the costs of the depression of 1873 to workers in small towns because of the workers' strength in their communities. Employers often had to look outside the community for help; they used the state militia or hired guards to end strikes, aggravate racial and ethnic tensions, and evict striking workers from company-owned houses.[58]

A case in point is the strike in the coal mining town of Braidwood, Illinois, which had a population of 6,000 in 1873. By March 1874, at least 25 percent of the miners were unemployed due to a drop in demand in coal as a result of the nationwide depression. The largest of the coal mine employers cut wages significantly.[59]

When the miners refused to sign a contract under the new conditions, the company shut down the mines, recruited unskilled workers from nearby Chicago and brought special armed security police to the town. The Braidwood miners convinced most of the new workers to return to Chicago and even paid for their railway tickets. The middle-class (small business owners, storekeepers and public officials) defended, and the local police actively protected, the miners. Eventually, the mine operators gave in and signed an agreement acceptable to the miners.[60] Historian Herbert Gutman writes that "[R]ural, or at least small-town America ... remained in this period a stronghold of freedom for the worker seeking his economic and social rights."[61]

WORKER ORGANIZATIONS OF THE LATE 19TH CENTURY

Although their membership rolls were relatively small, worker organizations in the late 19th century confronted problems including unemployment, concentration of wealth, low wages, political corruption and lack of control of the workplace with a variety of tactics and visions for the future.

THE KNIGHTS OF LABOR

The Knights of Labor (KOL), which held its first convention in 1878, was labor's first strong national organization.[62] The Knights' goal was to organize all workers, regardless of race or sex, into one big union to address the interests of both skilled and unskilled workers.[63] Membership reached 750,000 at its height.[64] Their slogan was "An injury to one is the concern of all!"[65]

The KOL launched educational campaigns through reading rooms, traveling lecturers and "journals such as the *Labor Enquirer* and the *Knights of Labor*; organized community boycotts against employers; and lobbied public officials on behalf of ... short hours."[66] The Knights stirred debate throughout the country about the nature of rights in the workplace. They emphasized the nobility of the working class, on whom industrial society depends, and criticized the owners of capital for abusing their power.[67] By the late 1880s, the KOL leadership abandoned unskilled workers in favor of organizing skilled workers and soon competed with and lost members to the American Federation of Labor.[68]

THE AMERICAN FEDERATION OF LABOR

While the Knights of Labor attempted to include workers across all industries, the American Federation of Labor (AFL), established in 1886, continued the trade union tradition of organizing workers separately by craft, or particular skilled job.[69] Samuel Gompers, leader of the Cigar Makers Union, was elected president. Gompers witnessed a violent police attack on striking workers at Tompkins Square in New York City in 1874. While this incident led many labor leaders to lose faith in the potential of the existing system of government to address their concerns, Gompers decided that instead of working to change the whole system, skilled workers "should build craft unions to defend their immediate economic interests."[70] Craft, or trade, unions left out the majority of American workers, who were unskilled. The AFL saw itself as a business, with the labor of the workers as the product it offered to employers.[71]

To protect the jobs of skilled workers, who were generally white, native-born men, the AFL, under Gompers, refused to admit black, women or immigrant workers. The membership of the AFL rose from 150,000 in 1886 to over one million after 1900. Gompers' "pure and simple," or "business," unionism focused on skilled workers' immediate economic interests instead of on broader social issues.[72] Gompers and the AFL worked for better working conditions, shorter hours and better pay for skilled workers; Gompers believed these changes would eventually improve the lot of all workers.[73]

An exception to the AFL policy of organizing by craft was the AFL-affiliated United Mine Workers (UMW), formed in 1890, which organized workers throughout the mine industry.[74] The UMW included black miners in their organizing efforts.[75]

EUGENE DEBS AND THE SOCIALIST PARTY

Eugene Debs, a railway worker, organized craft unions in the 1870s.[76] Yet Debs eventually came to believe that protecting only the narrow interests of skilled workers divided the working class. In 1893, Debs, as well as members of the Knights of Labor, helped found the American Railroad Union (ARU), with the intention of uniting all railway workers. They sought to organize by industry instead of by trade.[77] Debs wanted to include black railway workers in the ARU, but at its convention in 1894, a majority of ARU members voted to exclude black workers from the union.[78] A strike the next year in Pullman, Illinois further changed Debs' views of the best ways to advance the goals of workers.

Nine miles south of Chicago, George Pullman had created a city for his company, which made railroad cars. In this city, which he named Pullman, he owned everything — the factories, the houses, the churches, the stores and the library. As the depression of 1893 (the worst of the 19th century) deepened, Pullman lowered wages without lowering the rent for the 12,000 people who lived there.[79] In May of 1894, a committee of workers tried to discuss their concerns with Pullman; he refused to consider their proposals, and then fired three of the committee members. On June 27, the ARU called on its 150,000 members to refuse to work on Pullman railway cars. Since nearly every passenger train included Pullman cars, this call amounted to a nationwide strike of railway workers.[80]

An association of railroad owners hired 2,000 armed guards to break the strike. The federal government had a court issue an injunction against strikers who were blocking trains. Workers continued the strike, stopping railroad service out of Chicago, and President Grover Cleveland responded by sending federal troops to stop the strike. On July 7, 1894, the state of Illinois sent in its militia, which, along with the police, killed, wounded and arrested many strikers. The 14,000 police, militia and troops crushed the strike. Black workers, excluded from the ARU, were not inclined to help the strikers, which contributed to the strike's failure.[81]

On July 10, 1894, Debs, president of the ARU, was arrested for violating an injunction which prohibited doing or saying anything to further the strike. Debs spent six months in prison, where he read and discussed political and economic theory, including ideas about socialism, a political theory which envisions society with "common ownership of the economy and popular control of the government."[82] This was the turning point in Debs' career; for the next three decades he was a leader in the U.S. Socialist movement.[83]

During the 1880s and 1890s, "despite the strenuous efforts of government, business, the church, the schools, to control their thinking, millions of Americans were ready to consider harsh criticism of the existing system, to contemplate other possible ways of living," writes historian Howard Zinn. For example, Edward Bellamy's popular utopian novel *Looking Backward*,[84] a vision of the ideal Socialist society of the future, sold over one million copies and more than

100 groups formed around the country to work toward Bellamy's vision.[85] Workers' as well as farmers' movements, writes Zinn, "went beyond the scattered strikes ... of the period 1830-1877. There were nation-wide movements, more threatening than before to the ruling elite, more dangerously suggestive. It was a time when revolutionary organizations existed in major American cities, and revolutionary talk was in the air."[86]

After forming the Socialist Party of America in 1901, Debs ran for President of the United States four consecutive times. Although Debs was never elected, the Socialist candidates did succeed in electing mayors in at least 80 cities and towns and 1,200 local officials and state representatives. The Socialist Party elected Victor Berger, its first member of Congress, in 1910.[87] Socialists published eight daily newspapers and more than 300 periodicals, of which the largest three had over one million readers.[88] Their platform called not only for worker ownership of the economy but for the abolition of monopolies, voting rights for women, initiative, referendum and recall, direct election of the President, abolition of all laws discriminating against women and the abolition of war.[89]

INDUSTRIAL WORKERS OF THE WORLD

Two hundred Socialists, anarchists and radical trade unionists around the country held a convention in Chicago in 1905, where they created the Industrial Workers of the World (IWW), or the Wobblies, to organize by industry as an alternative to the AFL.[90] Among the speakers at this convention — the "Continental Congress of the Working Class" — were Eugene Debs, leader of the Socialist Party, Mother Jones, organizer for the United Mine Workers of America and Big Bill Haywood of the Western Federation of Miners.[91]

The IWW envisioned a Socialist society where the land and machines were owned collectively by all people. They worked to achieve this goal by creating one big union open to all workers. Under their plan, when the union was strong enough, workers would hold a nationwide general strike to shut down all businesses. The capitalist system would come to an end, and socialism could begin to take over.[92] The

IWW worked to create a new society, not in the voting booth, but by using nonviolent direct action: organization, strikes and sabotage. To the Wobblies, sabotage meant "striking on the job" — "demonstrating inside the factories, subverting production, withholding labor," but not necessarily destroying any property.[93]

In the textile strike of 1912 in Lawrence, Massachusetts, 10,000 workers — Slavs, Italians, Irish, Greeks, Portuguese, French-Canadian, English, Russian, Lithuanian, German, Polish, Belgian — a total of two dozen language groups in all, joined together to fight mill owners who reduced wages when the 56-hour work week took effect.[94] Led by organizer Elizabeth Gurley Flynn, the IWW organized soup kitchens and clothing distribution, and with the Socialist Party, arranged for the strikers' children to stay with families in other cities during the strike.[95]

The American Woolen Company gave in and offered the workers a 5 to 10 percent raise and time-and-a-quarter pay for overtime work. On March 14, 1912, the strikers voted to end the strike.[96] The strikers won an "immeasurable moral triumph" which inspired workers all over the eastern United States to join together.[97]

Wobbly organizers traveled across the country; "they organized, wrote, spoke, sang, spread the message and their spirit."[98] IWW organizer Joe Hill was the best known of the Wobbly songwriters. His songs, poems and cartoons filled the pages of the Wobbly magazines and newspapers distributed in 10 or more languages.[99] "The Wobbly creed spread like wildfire in the eastern immigrant ghettoes and across the Mississippi among the workers of the West, in the mines, timber forests, port towns, and among the migrant workers and hoboes who rode the boxcars," writes historian Harvey Wasserman.[100]

At first, the Socialist movement and the IWW were united in supporting political action. After 1907, under the leadership of Big Bill Haywood, the IWW began to see political struggles as fruitless and unnecessary, and subsequently turned more attention to building the "One Big Union" and conducting nonviolent and orderly strikes.[101]

The Progressive Reform era was largely a response to the surge in popular support for Socialists and Wobblies. Federal and state governments passed numerous laws and reforms, including government regulation of the railroads, telephone and telegraph systems, monopolies, money and the banking system as well as regulation of workers' hours and wages and compensation for injured workers. However, historian Howard Zinn writes that the reforms were "aimed at quieting the popular risings, not making fundamental changes."[102]

WOMEN ORGANIZE THEIR OWN UNIONS

The AFL made little effort to organize women workers since most women were employed in low-paid, unskilled positions.[103] However, groups made up largely of middle-class women made a number of attempts to improve the working conditions of women. The National Consumers League was founded in 1899 to pressure businesses to improve working conditions and the Women's Trade Union League, founded in 1903, helped women workers organize into trade unions.[104] These groups advocated protective labor legislation for both women and children. By 1907, 20 states had passed "hour laws," limiting the number of hours employers could require women to work.[105]

Women working in the garment industry in cities including New York, Philadelphia and Chicago organized unions to protest working conditions and low wages. Eleanor Flexner writes of the factories:

> *For the most part the shops were small, housed in filthy old buildings which were never cleaned and where sanitary conditions and fire hazards were unbelievably bad. Windows were nailed shut and little light came in the grimy panes. The hissing of power belts and grinding of machinery were deafening. The workers were largely foreign-born, newly arrived in this country. Their limited knowledge of English, their youth, inexperience, and desperate need for work put them at the mercy of boss and foreman. There were endless fines: for talking, laughing, or singing, for stains from machine oil*

on the goods, for stitches either too crooked or too large which had to be ripped out at the risk of tearing the fabric, resulting in more fines. Hours not infrequently ran until 10 at night, with no overtime pay and only a sandwich for supper.[106]

Women shirtwaist makers, most of them between the ages of 16 and 25 years, at two of the larger shops in New York City went on strike in 1909 to protest intolerable working conditions. It was the first large strike of women, including both black and white women; between 10,000 and 30,000 workers participated. The Women's Trade Union League took the issue to the public and solicited money from wealthy women in New York City to provide bail for hundreds of women arrested for picketing. The strike lasted for 13 weeks with settlements being made on a shop-by-shop basis. Although the gains were few, the strike had a large impact on the labor movement, proving that women could successfully organize.[107]

That conditions in the shops did not improve is evidenced by a tragic fire in 1912 at the Triangle Shirt-Waist Company in which 146 workers died. Eleanor Flexner writes, "Some of the horrified onlookers carried with them all their lives the sight of bodies leaping out of the windows with clothing ablaze because there was no other way out; others perished jammed against the doors to the stairways which were barred."[108]

Few working women participated in the woman suffrage movement at that time. As Eleanor Flexner writes, for women working under dangerous conditions for little pay, equal rights "was a question of more than education or getting the vote. For them equality also meant better pay for their labor, security from fire and machine hazards or the unwanted attentions of a foreman, and a chance to get home to their domestic tasks before complete exhaustion had overtaken them."[109]

"[W]herever desperate workers went on strike, wherever exploited child laborers cried for help, this querulous, gray-haired, black-bonneted woman with a high-pitched voice and piercing stare appeared to lead them on," writes Joseph Gustaitis about Mary Harris Jones.[110]

Born in Ireland on May 1, 1830, Mary Harris immigrated with her family to the United States in 1838. She attended school in Toronto, Canada and, as a young woman, worked as a dressmaker and as a schoolteacher. In 1861, she married George Jones, an iron molder and strong union supporter. Six years later, her husband and four children died in a yellow fever epidemic.[111]

© HARRISON EWING, FROM THE TERRENCE VINCENT POWDERLY COLLECTION/CATHOLIC UNIVERSITY

Mother Jones often organized the women in mining towns to become an active and vital part of the struggle for workers' rights. One tactic she used was the "dishpan brigade." When coal miners were on strike in Arnot, Pennsylvania, in 1900, Mother Jones organized the women to prevent replacement, or scab, workers from taking the striking workers' jobs. The women gathered at the mine, banging together their pots, pans, brooms and mops, while screaming and shouting at the scab workers. "From that day on the women kept continual watch of the mines to see that the company did not bring in scabs. Every day women with brooms or mops in one hand and babies in the other arm, wrapped in little blankets, went to the mines and watched that no one went in. And all night long they kept watch," wrote Mother Jones.[117]

Mary Jones moved to Chicago where she opened a dressmaking business, but soon after, her home was destroyed in the great Chicago fire of 1871. Taking refuge in a church basement, she wandered into nearby meetings of the Knights of Labor. She became involved in the labor movement, a cause to which she remained committed the rest of her life.[112]

Determined to encourage and support workers' organizing efforts, she travelled all over the country to inspire them with fiery speeches and words of encouragement. Over her long career as a union organizer, Mary Harris Jones, better known as Mother Jones, organized coal miners, child textile workers, street carmen, steel workers and metal miners.[113]

Although she often clashed with its leadership, Mother Jones worked as an organizer for the United Mine Workers of America for much of her life.[114] She dedicated 40 years to helping coal miners in West Virginia and Pennsylvania win union representation.[115] "In the miners' cause she waded creeks, faced machine guns, and taunted many a mine guard to shoot an old woman if he dared," writes historian Priscilla Long.[116]

Mother Jones was particularly outraged by the conditions in which children worked in textile mills and coal mines. To learn firsthand about the conditions of child workers, she worked in textile mills in the South.[118] While in Kensington, Pennsylvania in 1903 to help organize support for a textile workers strike, Mother Jones described the plight of children working in the mills: "Every day little children came into Union Headquarters, some with their hands off, some with the thumb missing, some with their fingers off at the knuckle. They were stooped little things, round shouldered and skinny. Many of them were not over 10 years of age, although the state law prohibited their working before they were twelve."[119]

Jones led a march of child workers from Philadelphia to ask President Theodore Roosevelt, vacationing at his summer home in Oyster Bay, New York, for a federal law "prohibiting the exploitation of children."[120] President Roosevelt refused to see them but the march did draw attention to their cause, and the Pennsylvania legislature soon passed a child labor law.[121]

Mother Jones, who lived to be 100 years old, shared the struggles and successes of workers around the country. Her motto was "Pray for the dead, and fight like hell for the living."[122]

WORLD WAR I

By the time the United States entered World War I in 1917, animosity between the AFL (which supported U.S. entry into the war) and the IWW and Socialist Party (which led the opposition) was intense. The Socialists made huge gains at the polls, since most workers opposed the war. President Woodrow Wilson rewarded the AFL's leader, Samuel Gompers, with a war-time governmental post which Gompers used to strengthen the AFL while weakening his rivals — the Wobblies, Socialists and other union organizers.[123]

In 1917, Congress passed the Espionage Act, which in effect made it illegal to speak out against the war.[124] About 900 people, including Socialist Party leader Eugene Debs, were imprisoned under the Act.[125] In September 1917, Department of Justice agents made raids on IWW meeting halls across the country, seizing literature and correspondence to use as evidence in court, and then arrested 165 IWW leaders for conspiring to hinder the draft and encourage desertion. Of those arrested, 101 went on trial; all were found guilty.[126] With its leaders jailed, the IWW was crushed and lost most of its members to the AFL.[127]

The organizing efforts of the IWW, however, had a lasting effect on workers around the country. The IWW showed that including all workers — regardless of race, sex or nationality — could benefit all workers.[128] The aims of the IWW helped convince union members to work toward goals more ambitious than higher wages or shorter hours. "Higher wages, better conditions, a good union contract alone — no self-respecting Wobbly would consider these adequate accomplishments. The vision of self-rule, of a free people charting their own destiny, remained alive so long as a single American worker refused to accept the status of slave to an alarm clock and a bankbook," writes historian Paul Buhle.[129]

EMPLOYERS TAKE THE OFFENSIVE: SCIENTIFIC MANAGEMENT

A financial panic, collapse and crisis occurred in 1907, leading industrialists to look for ways to cut their costs of production. One approach, developed in

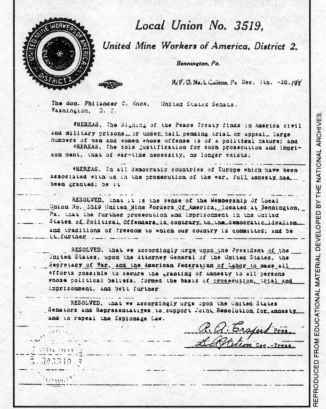

United Mine Workers letter urging release of Americans imprisoned under the Espionage Act.

1911, was "scientific management," or "Taylorism," under which every job in a factory was closely analyzed and a detailed system worked out to divide the work into segments and increase the work done by machines. This system allowed management to control every detail of a worker's energy and time, taking control of many of the decisions in the factory away from workers.[130] The changes de-skilled and demoralized the work force, while boosting the strength and productivity of industrial employers.

Workers launched a movement in the 1920s for control of the workplace in response to business's scientific management techniques.[131] Industrial workers began to resist the changes and demanded that the factory be put under the collective direction of workers.[132] According to historian David Montgomery, "[M]iners, metal workers, railroad employees and others simultaneously forced their employers to rescind various aspects of the new managerial practice and demanded the immediate adoption of their own plans for the reorganization of work relations from below."[133]

THE FARMER-LABOR PARTY

Between the two world wars, workers and farmers in North Dakota formed successful political coalitions which had a profound effect on the decision making process in those states. In Minnesota, the coalition of farmers and workers formed a labor party to compete with the Democratic and Republican Parties. The Farmer-Labor Party became the strongest political force in the state.[134]

Shortly after the end of World War I, Socialists in North Dakota created the Nonpartisan League (NPL). "The success of the movement was almost miraculous. ... it created a state bank, grain elevators, hail insurance, workmen's compensation, income and inheritance taxes, home buyer's assistance, restriction on injunctions in strikes, and the country's best mine safety law. No more dramatic demonstration of democracy has occurred in American history," proclaims historian David Montgomery.[135]

The NPL spread to Minnesota, where it formed a third party, the Farmer-Labor Party (FLP) and, in the 1922 election, won more votes than the Democratic Party. The FLP differed from traditional political parties. It had a dues-paying membership and its own press and educational bodies. Women held prominent roles in the FLP, at least in the beginning. During the 1920s, when nationwide voter participation fell below 50 percent, between 90 and 95 percent of the eligible voters came to the polls in every Minnesota election. The FLP had control of the governorship between 1930 and 1938.[136]

The success of the NPL and the FLP prompted efforts to organize a national third party to represent workers and farmers. These efforts collapsed in 1936 due to desertion from the coalition of a few key groups, including the Congress for Industrial Organizations and the Socialists.[137]

In 1938, accusations that the FLP was dominated by Communists triggered an investigation by the newly formed Un-American Activities Committee in the House of Representatives. In response, the FLP changed its platform, and by 1940 its membership was only 4,000. In 1944, the FLP merged with the Democratic Party.[138]

As early as 1867, the Pullman Palace Car Company, based in Chicago, decided to hire only black workers as porters and maids on its railroad sleeping cars.[139] Freed slaves, encouraged by the prospect of Pullman (as well as other) jobs, moved north after the Civil War. By World War I, the Pullman company was the largest employer of black workers in the United States. Black porters and maids had no opportunity to advance to higher, better paid positions in the company.[140]

Despite many indignities of the job, such as the requirement that porters use their own money to purchase polish to shine the shoes of sleeping car passengers, a porter's annual income, including tips, exceeded the income of a black school teacher and thus attracted many well-educated African Americans who were shut out of other professions.[141]

During World War I, the federal government operated the railroads and allowed unions to represent railroad workers. After the war, the Pullman company refused to recognize the war-time unions and instead established a company union, called the Pullman Porters' Employee Representation Plan (ERP). As was typical of company unions, Pullman paid ERP's leaders, who did not challenge the company's power or try to convince the company to remedy the grievances of the

porters and maids. At the same time, Pullman allowed conductors, who were white, to organize their own union.[142]

Some porters attempted to form a union to demand recognition as the legitimate bargaining agent for the porters and maids. They recruited A. Philip Randolph, the editor of the well-known African American publication, *The Messenger*, to lead the union. Because Randolph did not work for Pullman, he could not be threatened with losing his job for participating in union activities. In August 1925, porters and maids officially formed the Brotherhood of Sleeping Car Porters.[143]

The union worked to gain recognition by the Pullman company as the official representative of the maids and porters, with the right to bargain for improved wages and working conditions, and to gain an international charter from the AFL. The union, with its motto "Service not Servitude," was an inspiring example to African Americans fighting their status as second-class citizens.[144]

Randolph traveled the country, speaking and generating publicity to gather support for the union. The campaign to win recognition for the Brotherhood of Sleeping Car Porters was more than a struggle for union recognition, it was a struggle for racial equality, and Randolph became a leading spokesperson for the rights of African Americans.[145]

Yet the Brotherhood encountered many obstacles. The Pullman company, in 1925, began to hire Filipino porters to demonstrate that the company could easily replace black workers. The company also fired union supporters and paid workers loyal to the company to spy on union activities.[146]

The Great Depression almost destroyed the Brotherhood. Because of the scarcity of jobs, many workers did not want to risk joining a union and jeopardizing their jobs. Yet a few dedicated union leaders kept the organization alive. The union participated in many civil rights protests during the Depression and picketed the AFL to protest its refusal to organize black workers. At its 1935 convention, the AFL refused to expel unions that discriminated against black workers, but it did grant a charter to the Brotherhood of Sleeping Car Porters.[147]

In 1934, Congress passed the Amended Railway Labor Act which guaranteed railway workers the right to organize (the following year, the Wagner Act guaranteed all workers that right). The Brotherhood of Sleeping Car Porters once again demanded recognition from the Pullman company and once again was turned down. But this time the Brotherhood appealed to the National Mediation Board (established under the Amended Railway Labor Act), which ordered an election to determine representation of the Pullman porters and maids. The Brotherhood won an overwhelming majority and, by 1937, the federal government forced Pullman to recognize the union.[148] Pullman and the Brotherhood signed the first agreement between an African American union and a major employer.[149] Randolph continued his activism by leading the campaign for fair employment for African Americans. He organized the March on Washington movement to protest discrimination in war hiring practices and in the armed forces, forcing President Franklin Roosevelt to act.[150] (See page 22 for more on the fair employment campaign).

WORKERS IN THE 1920S
AND THE GREAT DEPRESSION

By 1920, the IWW was destroyed and the Socialist Party was failing. After the war, a Communist Party was organized which "played a leading part in the great textile strike that spread through the Carolinas and Tennessee in the spring of 1929."[151] The AFL lost about two million members during the 1920s. Allied with neither of the two major political parties, the AFL had little power in national politics.[152] Gompers died in 1924, leaving the AFL splintered, disorganized and facing a crisis in leadership.[153]

Unemployment fell through the 1920s and the general level of wages for workers rose. Yet most of the economic prosperity of the 1920s was concentrated among the wealthy.[154] The stock market crashed in 1929, bringing on the Great Depression. Industrial production fell by 50 percent and, by 1933, from one-quarter to one-third of the labor force was out of work.[155] During the Depression, "There were millions of tons of food around, but it was not profitable to transport it, to sell it. Warehouses were full of clothing, but people could not afford it. There were lots of houses, but they stayed empty because people could not pay the rent, had been evicted and now lived in shacks," writes Howard Zinn.[156]

Long before the federal government set up programs to relieve Depression conditions, people organized to help themselves.[157] By the end of 1932, 330 self-help organizations, such as Unemployed Councils, existed in 37 states, with over 300,000 members. But by early 1933, most of these groups had failed; "they were attempting too big a job in an economy that was more and more a shambles."[158] Often, those who had jobs worried that their employer would slow down the rate of production, resulting in some workers losing their jobs. One solution was to arrange for all workers to remain employed, even if everyone subsequently had to work fewer hours. Workers discovered many ways to ensure that everyone had a fair share of the available work, including agreeing not to work more than a certain number of hours. Often agreements of this sort were simply unspoken understandings among workers.[159]

Stella Nowicki, a worker and organizer in a Chicago meatpacking factory in the 1930s, explains how this kind of agreement was enforced in the factory where she worked:

The women themselves had gotten together and they would turn out 144 packages an hour of bacon.... A new girl would come in and the oldtimers would train her. They would help her out so that gradually by the end of a certain period of time she was doing the 144. But they would never let anyone go beyond that 144 packages. They maintained that limit and they did it without a union. One smart-aleck girl came in there once and she was going to show them and go beyond that number because she wanted to earn more money: all the bacon that she got from the girls further up the line was messed up and scrappy and she'd have to straighten it up to put it in the package. She couldn't make a hundred packages an hour.[160]

A NEW DEAL FOR LABOR?

In 1932, Franklin D. Roosevelt was elected President. His New Deal — reform legislation that attempted to bring the country out of the Depression — included the National Recovery Act (NRA), an attempt to stabilize the economy by fixing prices and wages and by limiting competition.[161] The AFL opposed the NRA which although gave mild encouragement to collective bargaining was designed primarily "to head off the alarming growth of spontaneous rebellion in the early years of the Roosevelt administration — organization of tenants and the unemployed, movements of self-help [and] general strikes in several cities."[162]

The Wagner Act, introduced in Congress in early 1934, provided elections for union representation and a labor relations board to settle problems and handle grievances between business and labor.[163] Business opposed the legislation, arguing it conceded too much power to labor. And President Roosevelt did not offer support for the legislation.[164]

But in 1934, nearly one and a half million workers engaged in a variety of protests, from general strikes in Minneapolis, Toledo and San Francisco to a national walkout of nearly 500,000 textile workers from South Carolina to Maine.[165] The strikes "became rallying points for a broader mobilization of working-class forces, including the unemployed."[166] The strikes were in general a rank-and-file (those workers on the job — not paid union leadership) rebellion against their own union leadership as well as against their employers.[167] Many workers called for a labor party as an alternative to the Democratic and Republican Parties.

President Roosevelt took notice and, in part to attract the labor vote, lent his support to the proposed Wagner Act, as well as social security and other measures of the "second New Deal."[168] And in 1935, the Supreme Court declared unconstitutional the unpopular NRA on the grounds that it gave the President too much power.[169] As a result of these policy shifts, President Roosevelt's popularity with labor began to increase.[170]

In 1935, Congress passed the Wagner Act which established the National Labor Relations Board to mediate disputes between labor and business and required businesses to engage in collective bargaining with unions.[171] Due to this government endorsement, union organizing was made easier. Employers, who initially opposed the legislation, began to realize that bargaining with unions was practical — it was much easier than facing wildcat strikes.[172]

To a great extent, these changes in domestic policy represented an attempt on the part of the Roosevelt Administration to control labor uprisings by giving unions legal status and settling some of their grievances and by channelling union activity into officially sanctioned forms of mediation.[173] Thus the work of unions was redirected toward the new system of representation elections, contracts, negotiations and union meetings.[174] Whatever the motivation, the reforms formally acknowledged unions and collective bargaining, although some workers, including farm workers, black tenant farmers and domestic workers, were excluded from these protections.[175]

THE SIT-DOWN WAVE OF 1936-1937

Meanwhile, the AFL also took notice of the rank-and-file rebellions and in response set up the Committee for Industrial Organization (CIO) in 1935 to organize industrial workers who, left out of the AFL trade unions, had begun to organize themselves. In 1936, the CIO broke with the AFL and became an independent group. Changing its name to the Congress of Industrial Organizations in 1938, the CIO operated under the leadership of John Lewis, president of the AFL's strongest industrial union, the United Mine Workers.[176]

The CIO launched recruitment drives to include black industrial workers, who until this time had challenged white-dominated organized labor in a variety of ways, including strikebreaking. The CIO began organizing black workers in the steel and auto industries in 1936 and 1937.[177] Skeptical at first, major black organizations eventually supported the CIO efforts.[178]

But by the time the CIO formed, rank-and-file workers in industry after industry had begun to organize themselves using an effective tactic: the sit-down strike. Historian Barbara Griffith writes:

[T]he sit-down strike was the tool that ... created, in some ways overnight, an enthusiasm that fired workers and organizers with the belief that management's tactics could be overcome. In the end, its effect was as much psychological as organizational because it created a transforming 'moment' that, in many cases for the first time, indicated to workers that they did have a measure of control over their work lives.[179]

In a sit-down strike, workers stop working but remain in the plant to prevent their employer from hiring workers to replace those on strike. Because they remained in the factory, rank-and-file workers had direct control over the bargaining process with the employer and did not have to act through union officials. Employers had to come to the workers directly and bargain with them. Staying in the plant also meant that the strikers were together constantly, increasing their sense of group power. From the rubber factories in Akron, Ohio, the sit-down idea spread quickly because of its high success rate, and brought with it a wave of excitement among industrial workers.[180]

In December of 1936, thousands of workers began the longest sit-down strike of all in the General Motors (GM) Fisher Body plant #1, in Flint, Michigan. The sit-down began when two brothers were fired. Refusing to work or to leave, 2,000 workers stayed in the plant for 40 days.[181] Inside the plant, the workers held meetings to discuss the management of the strike. They strictly enforced rules of conduct, and were careful not to damage company property — "if anybody got careless ... such as sitting on an automobile cushion without putting burlap over it — he was talked to."[182] Members of the community came to the plant to teach classes on government, history, writing and public speaking to the striking workers.[183]

All of the workers who remained in the plant were men, but they depended on the active support of women outside the plant who supplied them with food and confronted the police.[184] Court injunctions prohibited the strike from continuing, but with thousands of armed workers surrounding the plant, police did not attempt to enforce the injunctions.[185] Several violent incidents did occur, however, and a Women's Emergency Brigade was formed to monitor the situation outside the plant and deal with crises.[186] The governor of Michigan summoned the National Guard as the sit-down strike spread to six other GM plants. But before the Guard was called in, workers and GM management settled the strike and signed a six-month contract.[187]

Eventually workers won official recognition by General Motors of the United Auto Workers as their union.[188] This victory was psychologically important for the workers, who emerged from the plant with newly formed friendships and solidarity.[189] Wrote Henry Kraus, who was editor of the GM strike newsletter, "[T]he explosive spontaneity of joy and freedom that seized the city [Flint] late that afternoon and evening was more glorious and significant that anything mere organization could have contrived."[190] The United Auto Workers subsequently became an

important and powerful force within the labor movement.

The sit-down strike, as a tactic to win recognition for unions, quickly spread to nearly every industry, except textiles. In 1936, workers launched 48 sit-down strikes, followed by 477 sit-downs in 1937.[191] By the end of the strike wave, millions of workers had gained recognition for their unions, including the United Rubber Workers, the United Electrical Workers and the United Steelworkers.[192] Union membership, as a result of the sit-down wave of 1936-37, more than doubled from 3.7 million members in 1935 to 8.3 million in 1938.[193]

"The vast social movement that created the CIO and organized basic industry in the United States has been the greatest achievement of the American working class to date. In a matter of a few years, what appeared to be a fragmented mass of individual workers paid at rates and worked at speeds imposed by the employers transformed themselves into an organized force that changed the economic and political fabric of society," writes labor journalist Kim Moody.[194]

THE DEMISE OF THE CIO

The new industrial unions of the CIO differed from the AFL unions which primarily organized by trade and mostly included skilled workers. The CIO made efforts to included African American and women workers. Furthermore, the CIO unions worked for greater worker control of the workplace, for improved working conditions and the lives in general for all Americans and for broader social change while the AFL concentrated on business unionism — winning better wages and working conditions for its own members. But a number of factors contributed to the demise of the goals of the CIO including an improved economy, World War II, growth of union bureaucracy, passage of the Taft-Hartley Act and anti-communism.

The production demands of World War II, which created millions of new jobs at higher wages and brought the U.S. economy out of the Depression, weakened the drive of worker rebellions that characterized the 1930s. Writes Howard Zinn, "It was the war that put almost everyone to work, and the war did something else: patriotism, the push for unity of all classes against enemies overseas, made it harder to mobilize anger against the corporations."[195]

President Roosevelt established the National War Labor Board at the beginning of U.S. involvement in World War II in an effort to regulate labor-business relations for the sake of stability during the war.[196] Both the AFL and the CIO leadership pledged not to call strikes during the war.[197] In return, the War Labor Board agreed to a "maintenance of membership" policy which required workers to join unions and pay dues during the term of a contract. Membership in unions rose from less than nine million to nearly 15 million workers by the end of the war.[198]

During World War II, in part because of the War Labor Board's emphasis on collective bargaining, bureaucratic control of the industrial unions grew.[199] Decisions once made on the shop floor were made increasingly by union officials, further isolating the rank-and-file from decision making.[200] After the war, the rank-and-file membership, which had once been so important, became more alienated from the unions that supposedly existed to serve their interests. As the war-time business-like approach to union negotiating continued, a full-scale union bureaucracy developed.[201]

The rank-and-file fought the bureaucratization of the union and began to protest wage freezes imposed while business profits soared.[202] Many workers challenged the no-strike pledge. Workers launched 14,000 walk-outs and wildcat strikes (not authorized by union leaders) during the war, more than in any comparable period in U.S. history.[203] Although rank-and-file participation and internal union democracy diminished during the war, organized labor emerged from World War II with millions of new members and "a permanent institutional place in American life."[204]

Even before the war ended, strikes took place across the country in anticipation of postwar layoffs. As soon as the war ended, cutbacks in production ended the availability of overtime work and nearly one quarter of all war workers temporarily lost their jobs.[205] To retain economic gains made during the war, workers responded with one of the largest strike waves in the nation's history. The strike wave of 1945-1946 included both general strikes and strikes in particular industries, including steel, electric and auto.[206] Describing the general strikes, historian George Lipsitz writes, "Once the strikes began and ordinary citizens became involved in directing traffic, distributing goods, and managing the affairs of their communities, they got a taste of a new kind of politics — and they liked it. ... The strikes were fun, they were effective in winning their short range goals, and they gave millions of people a glimpse of the politics of direct democracy."[207]

In a strike against General Motors, UAW leader Walter Reuther demanded that wage increases come out of profits and not be passed on to the consumer in the form of higher prices and that GM disclose information about its profits and finances to the public.[208] When GM refused, hundreds of thousands of workers in other industries went on strike. President Harry Truman threatened to use the military to keep vital industries such as the railroads and coal mines in operation.[209]

The strikes were settled with the wage increase but not Reuther's demands, setting an important precedent in labor-management relations.[210] Collective bargaining between labor unions and corporate management began to follow a new pattern, the "wage-price spiral" in which "industry would meet labor's demands by raising prices (higher than necessary to meet the costs of the wage hike), thus passing the cost on to the consumer."[211] For example, immediately following the 1945-1946 strikes, U.S. Steel raised prices by more than double the amount of wage increases. To absorb both the wage increases and the increased price of steel, other corporations, including GM, raised prices. The cost of living increased 18 percent by the end of the year, totally wiping out the gains made by the strikes.[212]

THE TAFT-HARTLEY ACT

The general strikes of 1945-1946 and in particular Reuther's call for wage increases without price increases, generated strong business support for laws restricting unions' rights.[213] In 1947, Congress passed the Taft-Hartley Act which banned labor techniques including secondary boycotts (boycotts which target a company not involved in the major dispute), mass picketing (a tactic used by labor to keep strikebreakers from entering a factory) and sympathy strikes (strikes called by one union in support of another union on strike). Taft-Hartley also curtailed other labor tactics such as the wildcat strike (a strike called by workers without official union support) and allowed state legislatures to pass "right-to-work" laws banning the union shop (a workplace that employs only members of a labor union).[214]

As a result, state legislatures in the South began to pass right-to-work laws and many businesses moved their operations to the southern United States. This coincided with the CIO's unsuccessful campaign — Operation Dixie — to organize textile workers in the South.[215]

ANTI-COMMUNISM IN THE POST-WORLD WAR II ERA

After the war, fear of the spread of Soviet-style communism became widespread in the United States. In 1947, President Truman issued Executive Order 9835 which authorized a program to search out "infiltration of disloyal persons" in the U.S. government. Over the next five years, 6.6 million Americans were investigated. Not one case of espionage was found. Senator Joseph McCarthy (R-WI) began hearings in the Senate to investigate alleged Communists in the government and the House Un-American Activities Committee continued to interrogate Americans about their ties to Communists and Communist organizations.[216]

To win National Labor Relations Board (NLRB) protection for their unions, the Taft-Hartley Act required union officials to file affidavits stating that they were not Communists. In the years that followed, because of pressure from government and society, the leaders of the CIO became increasingly anti-Communist. Both the AFL and the CIO purged their organizations of Communists and Socialists.[217] When 10 CIO-affiliated unions refused to throw out their Communist members, the CIO expelled the unions.[218] The purges resulted in many labor unions losing many of their most active and experienced organizers.[219]

The anti-Communist crusade also "forced the CIO to move closer to the mainstream of the Democratic Party" and restrict their activities to "simple" unionism — improved wages and working conditions — rather than the broader social issues that had characterized CIO campaigns of the 1930s.[220] In addition, the CIO leadership rejected any attempts to form a labor party, and rallied labor's support behind the Democratic Party "to pressure for greater labor influence in party affairs."[221] The Democratic Party soon took the labor vote for granted and labor's electoral power was diminished.[222]

In a matter of a few years, much of the remaining democracy within the unions was abandoned as anti-Communist bureaucrats systematically eliminated opposition and dissent.[223] By the early 1950s, a radical transformation of the CIO's political culture had taken place.[224] With little to distinguish their approaches to unionism, the CIO merged with the AFL in 1955, eliminating one alternative to established, more mainstream unions.[225]

"[L]abor in the postwar period succeeded in winning economic security for a select number of member-workers. But its power as an independent force for social reform and economic justice throughout the whole society was lost in the process," writes historian Marty Jezer.[226]

AFRICAN AMERICAN WORKERS ORGANIZE AFTER WORLD WAR II

Most of the economic advances made by black industrial workers occurred between 1942 and 1945 and were largely lost during the postwar reconversion. The white-dominated labor organizations failed to offer any solution for black workers. In June 1950, black workers held a conference in Chicago which led to the formation of the National Negro Labor Council a year later. In less than a year, 23 Negro Labor Councils (NLCs) were set up across the country. The NLC in Chicago picketed the Woolworth and Scott stores which refused to hire black workers. Business fell by 85 percent and the stores decided to hire black workers. The NLC was particularly active in Detroit, where black workers had been challenging the all-white male leadership of the United Auto Workers to include black workers in UAW leadership positions.[227]

Various leaders within the CIO accused the NLC of being Communist. The action of the CIO leadership paved the way for the House Un-American Activities Committee to harass NLC members which eventually forced the union's demise in 1956.[228] "Racism within the ranks of labor remained an issue, particularly after the merger of the AFL-CIO in 1955. Many black trade unionists saw the merger as a signal of organized labor's declining interest and commitment to the struggle against racism," writes historian Richard Thomas.[229]

Migrant farm workers, who move from farm to farm in search of temporary work harvesting crops, have historically faced many barriers in their attempts to organize unions, including poverty, the short-term nature of jobs, an oversupply of labor and government aid to growers (the employers of farm workers) during strikes. During the 1940s, the Cali-

Cesar Chavez and supporters picket the Dept. of Defense in New York City to protest the Pentagon's purchase of California grapes for shipment to soldiers in Vietnam (1969).

fornia farm labor force included migrants from the "dustbowl" of the United States as well as contract workers (*braceros*) temporarily imported from Mexico by the federal government. By the 1960s, workers of Mexican descent, mostly recent immigrants, made up most of the migrant farm worker labor force.[230]

Migrant workers were paid either a small hourly wage or, more frequently, paid by the piece or the pound, depending on how much of a crop they could harvest or plant. Working conditions for migrant workers were miserable. Employers often forced workers to use short-handled hoes which required hours of stooping over, creating tremendous strain on their backs. In the heat of summer or the cold of winter, migrant workers were in the fields all day without toilet facilities or drinking water. And most migrant workers were exposed to dozens of pesticides, often sprayed while they worked in the fields.[231]

Numerous attempts to organize farm workers failed. But in 1950, Cesar Chavez, who was working on an apricot farm, went to a meeting of the Community Services Organization (CSO) and became involved in efforts to organize Mexican Americans in California. Chavez worked with the CSO for more than 10 years and became its general director.[232] Chavez worked with CSO community organizer Fred Ross from whom Chavez learned organizing techniques such as the house meeting, which he later used to recruit members to a union for farm workers.[233]

But when the CSO board of directors continued to refuse to try to organize farm workers, Chavez resigned and in 1962 began an independent organizing campaign.[234] He distributed cards to residents of the Central Valley of California asking for their names, addresses and how much they thought they should be paid. When the cards were returned by mail, some people had written notes of support. Chavez drove to those people's homes, asking them to join a union.[235] He held the first official meeting of the National Farm Workers Association (later called the United Farm Workers) in September 1962. Though it was difficult to find farm workers who could afford to pay dues, the movement slowly grew. By the summer of 1964, the union had 1,000 members.[236]

The organization first provided economic and social benefits, including a credit union, cooperative buying, life insurance and educational programs.[237] By the summer of 1965, the United Farm Workers (UFW) shifted to union activities.[238] Rose workers, in May 1965, were the first UFW members to call a strike. The workers quickly won a wage increase, but the company would not recognize the union. The union also won wage increases in a grape workers strike.[239]

In the fall of 1965, the UFW joined a large strike against the grape growers of the Central Valley. The union learned a lesson it would learn again and again: strikes alone did not work because of the oversupply of labor and government intervention on behalf of the growers.[240] Dolores Huerta, who was an organizer with the UFW from its beginning and later became its vice president, stated, "We never win with a strike. There are always 10 unemployed workers ready to take the job of the one who strikes."[241]

The UFW changed tactics: it called a boycott of California table grapes in 1965 and millions of Americans, in support of the farm workers, stopped buying grapes.[242] The movement drew increasing support: religious leaders committed acts of civil disobedience, students picketed grocery stores, other unions called sympathy strikes and a few politicians endorsed the UFW.[243] Numerous civil rights and religious organizations offered support and financial backing.[244] In 1968, Chavez went on a 25-day hunger strike. This action united farm workers behind Chavez and brought more outside support to the cause.[245] According to journalist Harry Bernstein, "[T]he UFW retained the aura of a cause even as it took on the structure of a union."[246]

Despite the outpouring of support for the UFW, the police harassed strikers, the U.S. Department of Defense purchased large quantities of boycotted grapes and California Governor Ronald Reagan and President Richard Nixon frequently condemned the union.[247] However, the union finally won. On July 30, 1970, five years after it began, the UFW called off the grape boycott. The loss of millions of dollars in grape sales had forced many growers to sign contracts with the UFW.[248] The contracts included provisions to ban three dangerous pesticides, including DDT, from the fields were farm workers worked.[249] By 1972, the UFW had won over 100 contracts and raised wages for farm workers by almost one-third.[250]

Yet this success was not complete. Some labor laws, including the Wagner Act (requiring employers to recognize union representatives democratically elected by the workers) did not apply to agricultural workers. Many growers resisted the UFW's attempts to win recognition. Even when nearly every worker at a ranch signed a card proclaiming the UFW to be the workers' official representative, the growers could legally ignore them.[251] Recognizing that without laws which enforced the farm workers' right to union representation they could not succeed, the UFW began to lobby for a California law to extend the rights of non-agricultural workers to farm workers. In 1975, the legislature passed the California State Agricultural Labor Relations Act, which Chavez called a "godsend that is without question the best law for workers — any workers — in the entire country."[252]

At first the new law helped the UFW win new contracts. But the growers soon found ways to combat the workers' organizing efforts. They filed numerous lawsuits against the UFW, draining its resources dramatically.[253] The growers also successfully lobbied the state legislature to cut off funding for the California Labor Relations Board, in charge of administering the law. When the UFW proposed a state referendum to insulate the Board from political tampering, the growers raised $2 million for a campaign which helped defeat the measure.[254]

The union has continued to suffer setbacks. In 1982, George Deukmejian was elected governor of California, with the strong support of California growers. Upon election, Deukmejian appointed new members to the California Labor Relations Board who were determined to defeat the UFW by "helping growers fend off workers' complaints of unfair labor practices and defeat the union's organizing attempts."[255] Furthermore, the board offered little or no protection for farm workers fired because of union activities.[256]

Yet the UFW has won many victories for its members such as a medical plan, pensions and other benefits. It forced growers to end the use of the short-handled hoe, which crippled many farm workers. And the UFW continues to fight. In 1985 it launched a new grape boycott, demanding that growers affirm the right to union representation and stop the use of dangerous pesticides.[257] Cesar Chavez again went on a 35-day hunger strike in 1988, to call attention to the grape boycott. Chavez writes of his commitment to the farm worker cause:

There are vivid memories from my childhood — what we had to go through because of low wages and the conditions, basically because there was no union. I suppose if I wanted to be fair I could say that I'm trying to settle a personal score. I could dramatize it by saying that I want to bring social justice to farm workers. But the truth is that I went through a lot of hell, and a lot of people did. If we can even the score a little for the workers then we are doing something. Besides, I don't know any other work I like to do better than this. I really don't, you know.[258]

RANK-AND-FILE REBELLION: ON THE AGENDA AGAIN

By the mid-1960s, profits for U.S. industry began to decline, partly because of competition from overseas and an increase in the price of resources from the Third World.[259] Business, looking for ways to retain profits, asked labor to sign contracts with no-strike clauses, among other concessions. But many rank-and-file workers rejected the contracts and bargaining methods of their unions, and launched a wave of strikes in the 1960s and 1970s. These worker actions expressed widespread worker discontent with management as well as with union leadership.[260]

THE BLACK LUNG CAMPAIGN

The campaign for black lung benefits is one example of a rank-and-file rebellion. In this case, rank-and-file coal miners launched their own campaign because the leadership of the United Mine Workers had failed to work aggressively on behalf of coal miners with black lung disease.

As early as 1869, doctors knew of the connection between coal dust and lung disease.[261] Yet much of the medical profession, the U.S. government, the coal industry and even the United Mine Workers failed to take black lung disease seriously until rank-and-file coal miners organized in the late 1960s to win protection and compensation.[262]

Pneumoconiosis, or black lung, is a respiratory disease which "gradually destroys the lung's ability to function normally."[263] In 1963, the U.S. Public Health Service conducted a study that concluded that at least one in 10 active, and one in five nonactive bituminous coal miners had black lung disease and that the death rate for coal miners was twice that of the general working male population.[264]

Large numbers of miners suffered similar symptoms — breathing difficulties, weakness, early death — but company doctors told the miners that their problems were not related to their work environment. Instead, the doctors said they were caused by the workers' individual habits, such as drinking alcohol and smoking cigarettes. The coal companies were not required

to offer assistance to workers suffering from what was then called miner's asthma.[265] Although the symptoms associated with black lung eventually forced many miners to leave their jobs, in most cases they were not eligible for Medicare benefits.[266] Curtis Seltzer writes, "[M]ost coalfield physicians were still extensions of the coal industry. They had no interest in discovering — and a powerful interest in *not* discovering — that business-as-usual methods were routinely damaging the health of thousands of workers."[267] And although the UMW made safety issues such as preventing accidents and explosions in the mines a major concern, it did little to press the issue of occupational disease.[268]

On November 20, 1968, an explosion in a coal mine in Farmington, West Virginia killed 78 coal miners, bringing nationwide attention to the hazardous working conditions of coal miners.[269] Three doctors, I.E. Buff, Donald Rasmussen and Hawey Wells, Jr., who had been working to expose the role of the medical establishment in downplaying the extent and seriousness of black lung disease, took advantage of the increased attention. The doctors began to travel around West Virginia talking to miners and trying to get press coverage about the disease.[270] They often brought sections of lungs from autopsies of deceased miners and crumbled them into dust to demonstrate what black lung does to its victims.[271]

West Virginia coal miners formed the Black Lung Association in early February 1969 and proposed a state law to compensate miners disabled by black lung disease. A wildcat strike — one not authorized by union leadership — broke out on February 19, 1969.[272] Eventually, 40,000 miners (90 percent of the state's miners) went on strike, shutting down West Virginia coal production.[273] The strike was not authorized by the UMW; the striking miners marched to the state capitol in Charleston, and booed as they passed the UMW headquarters.[274] Writes Robert G. Sherrill, the coal mines "stayed closed for three weeks, opening again only after something of a miracle had been achieved."[275] The West Virginia legislature passed a black lung bill, signed by the governor, and the miners went back to work.[276] That the passage of the legislation was a miracle was due to the power of the coal industry in West Virginia. Writes Curtis Seltzer,

"Coal had dominated West Virginia politics since the 1880s. Many governors and key legislators were coal executives, their lawyers, and their bankers."[277]

Despite intense lobbying by the coal industry, in December 1969, Congress passed the Coal Mine Health and Safety Act which established health and safety standards to prevent mine accidents and occupational diseases such as black lung.[278] The law required coal operators to invest in new equipment, modify existing machines, hire new personnel and comply with federal record keeping.[279]

Enforcement of the new law was slow and at times nonexistent. In the summer of 1970, thousands of miners in West Virginia, Ohio and Pennsylvania went on strike to protest a lack of enforcement of the new law.[280] And in November 1970, the Clay County Poor People's Association in Manchester, Kentucky, organized "hundreds of ex-coal miners, miners' widows, and poor people from eastern Kentucky and West Virginia [who] conducted a mock trial of the administrators of the black lung section of the law."[281] Witnesses at the mock trial reported that the Social Security Administration, responsible for administering black lung benefits, was not properly doing its job: "[O]f the 229,000 claims for black lung benefits filed nationally as of November 6, 43 percent [had] been decided."[282] And in eastern Kentucky, only 22 percent of the claims had been decided, in West Virginia the decision rate was only 24 percent.[283]

Many rank-and-file members of the UMW were unhappy with their union's leadership. Joseph Yablonski decided in May 1969 to challenge the incumbent UMW president in the upcoming election on the platform of returning the union to its members.[284] Yablonski charged the union leadership with corruption and during the campaign unsuccessfully petitioned the federal government to intervene to ensure a fair election.[285] Yablonski lost the election in December 1969. A few weeks later, Yablonski, his wife and daughter were murdered in their home.[286] In early 1970, rank-and-file coal miners formed Miners For Democracy to carry on Yablonski's work. Miners For Democracy won control of the UMW in 1972.[287]

LABOR ON THE DEFENSIVE IN THE 1980s

The defensive tone for labor in the 1980s was set when President Ronald Reagan took office in 1981 and soon thereafter fired Professional Air Traffic Controllers Organization (PATCO) workers who were on strike over grievances that the Federal Aviation Administration had refused to address. President Reagan hired permanent replacement workers to fill the jobs of the striking PATCO workers. Reagan's actions, writes labor journalist Kim Moody, sent the following message: "[T]hat the bargaining atmosphere had changed in both the public and private sectors and that the administration's policies would aid business and undermine labor."[288]

In 1985, the Supreme Court upheld the right — established in a 1938 decision — of employers "to use permanent replacement workers in instances where their workforce strikes for economic reasons."[289] By hiring permanent replacement workers, or threatening to do so, employers "undercut labor's bargaining power by drastically curtailing its ability to make use of its most potent weapon, the strike."[290] The number of strikes called by labor decreased dramatically during the 1980s — from 187 in 1980 to only 54 in 1985 and 44 in 1990.[291]

The power of the strike as a bargaining tool was further diminished as U.S. business increasingly turned to low-wage workers outside of the United States. For example, by 1987, American corporations had built 865 factories in 15 cities along the 1,900-mile border with Mexico to manufacture goods such as televisions, air conditioners and automobile engines. The factories employed nearly 500,000 Mexican workers who made products to be sold in the United States. Wages for the Mexican workers — about 70 percent of whom are women under the age of 21 — are incredibly low, averaging about $22 a week for 48 hours of work.[292] By 1992, the number of U.S. corporations along the border with Mexico had grown to approximately 2,000.[293]

Americans workers lost jobs as U.S. corporations closed factories nationwide and opened new ones overseas. More than ever before, U.S. corporations began to use the threat of relocation or plant closings to force communities to grant tax breaks and unions to grant concessions in wages and benefits in an attempt to save jobs.[294]

NEW STRATEGIES FOR LABOR

Many rank-and-file union members disagreed with their unions' concession policies and developed new strategies for bargaining with business. One such strategy is the corporate campaign, developed by Ray Rogers, which "considers all avenues of pressure and would include the possibility of a strike, a boycott, and other traditional tactics ... timed and coordinated as part of an overall conceptualized strategy."[295] Other tactics used in corporate campaigns include shareholder resolutions and legal challenges under the National Labor Relations Act for violations of workers' rights.[296] Workers have formed coalitions with members of their communities and citizen groups that have an interest in targeting a particular company. This strategy sometimes has been effective in winning contracts for workers, and in forcing employers to recognize and negotiate with newly formed unions.

Rogers' first corporate campaign was an effort to win a union contract for the Amalgamated Clothing and Textile Workers (ACTWU) in the late 1970s with J.P. Stevens and Company. The campaign gathered the support of community, political and religious organizations to pressure banks and other companies with ties to J.P. Stevens to in turn pressure Stevens to change its policy. J.P. Stevens' chief executive officer and another official were forced off the board of directors of Manufacturers Hanover Trust Company, which had begun to worry about the negative publicity and the business it might lose from supporters of the union.[297]

A similar corporate campaign was launched in Austin, Minnesota in 1986, when the United Food and Commercial Workers (UFCW) International Union refused to continue assistance to striking meatpackers working for the Hormel Company. The local union decided to ignore UFCW leadership and undertook a corporate campaign for better wages and benefits from Hormel. The campaign included continuation of the strike, a boycott of Hormel products and pickets and leaflets directed at a bank that finances Hormel operations.[298]

When workers at the BASF Corporation were locked out of their plant in Geismar, Louisiana, in 1984, the Oil, Chemical and Atomic Workers (OCAW) launched a corporate campaign that eventually included a coalition of labor, environmental and community groups. The coalition won a number of victories against BASF in court on safety and environmental issues. In late 1990, BASF agreed to a new contract with locked-out workers which included wage increases and protection from losing jobs to subcontractors.[299]

In addition to the corporate campaign, other economic leverage techniques include working strikes (or slowdowns) and boycotts.[300]

Tony Mazzochi of the Oil, Chemical and Atomic Workers (OCAW) Union is calling for a labor party to give working people in the United States a real voice in government.[301] In a 1989 poll of OCAW members, 53 percent thought it was time for an independent party of working people — 28 percent disagreed with the labor party idea and 19 percent were unsure.[302] Mazzochi formed Labor Party Advocates in 1991 to educate the public about the need for a labor party.

Many rank-and-file union members have organized within their unions to promote greater internal union democracy. Several movements, including New Directions within the United Auto Workers and the Teamsters for a Democratic Union (TDU) work to make union leaders more accountable to the rank-and-file.[303] More than a decade of effort paid off in 1991 when TDU's candidate for president of the Teamsters Union, Ron Carey, won an upset victory.

Working women are organizing to counter discrimination in wage levels, hazardous or intolerable working conditions and job loss. Predominantly Latina women garment workers in El Paso, Texas organized La Mujer Obrera (The Woman Worker) which has taken direct action against sweatshop conditions in the sewing industry on the U.S.-Mexico border. The women have established food cooperatives, health clinics and classes in workers' and women's rights.[304]

The Coalition of Labor Union Women (CLUW) was founded in 1974 to unite labor union women in organizing unorganized women and to increase the participation of women in union leadership and in politics. CLUW's director, Joyce D. Miller, became the first female member of the executive council of the AFL-CIO.[305]

Nine to Five, founded in 1973 to organize women office workers, became affiliated with the Service Employees International Union in 1975. The National Association of Office Workers, among its other activities, holds rallies on National Secretaries Day with the slogan "Raises Not Roses" to call attention to issues facing female office workers.[306]

CONCLUSION

Organized labor in the United States has suffered some serious setbacks in recent years, including the loss of manufacturing jobs to underpaid workers overseas. The proportion of the workforce that belong to unions fell from 32.5 percent in 1953 to 16.1 percent by 1990.[307] Many unions continue to approach problems with a policy of concession. But strategies such as coalitions with citizen groups, the movements for internal union democracy, international links between workers and third party organizing are signs that many workers in the United States want what Jerry Tucker of the New Directions movement calls for: "democratic debate, solidarity, and unionism with a higher purpose."[308]

BIBLIOGRAPHY

American Social History Project, under the direction of Herbert G. Gutman. *Who Built America?: Working People and the Nation's Economy, Politics, Culture and Society.* Volume I. New York: Pantheon, 1989.

Bellamy, Edward. *Looking Backward: 2000-1887.* Boston: Houghton-Mifflin, 1966 [1887].

Bernstein, Harry. "La Causa Lives: 26 Years of Cesar Chavez and the UFW," *Christianity and Crisis.* Vol. 48. No. 2. February 15, 1988.

"Bhopal on the Bayou," *Multinational Monitor.* January/February 1990.

Bollier, David and Joan Claybrook. *Freedom from Harm: the Civilizing Influence of Health, Safety and Environmental Regulation.* Washington, DC: Public Citizen and Democracy Project, 1986.

"The Boys Who Got Excited," *The New Republic.* March 22, 1969.

Buhle, Paul and Alan Dawley, eds. *Working for Democracy: American Workers from the Revolution to the Present.* Urbana: University of Illinois Press, 1985.

Cassidy, Robert. "Appalachian Coal Miners: Life and Death Underground," *The New Republic.* December 12, 1970.

Coles, Robert and Harry Huge. "Black Lung: Mining as a Way of Death," *The New Republic.* January 25, 1969.

"Concessions and Convictions: Striking Meatpackers Face Off Against the UFCW and Hormel," *Multinational Monitor.* March 15, 1986.

"Corporate Campaigns," *Multinational Monitor.* March 15, 1986.

Cupps, Stephen. "Coal Mines: Death By Runaround," *The Nation.* August 31, 1970.

"Death of a Rebel," *Newsweek.* January 19, 1970.

Evans, Sara M. and Harry C. Boyte. *Free Spaces: The Sources of Democratic Change in America.* New York: Harper & Row Publishers, 1986.

Flexner, Eleanor. *Century of Struggle: The Women's Rights Movement in the United States.* Cambridge, MA: The Belknap Press of Harvard University Press, 1975.

"For 35 Days, Water ...," *Food and Justice.* September 1988.

Griffith, Barbara S. *The Crisis of American Labor: Operation Dixie and the Defeat of the CIO.* Philadelphia: Temple University Press, 1988.

Gustaitis, Joseph. "Mary Harris Jones: The Most Dangerous Woman in America," *American History Illustrated.* January 1988.

Gutman, Herbert G. "The Worker's Search for Power: Labor in the Gilded Age," in Wayne Morgan, ed. *The Gilded Age.* Syracuse, NY: Syracuse University Press, 1963.

Harris, William H. *The Harder We Run: Black Workers Since the Civil War*. New York: Oxford University Press, 1982.

Huerta, Dolores. "Reflections on the UFW Experience," *The Center Magazine*. July/August 1985.

Jenkins, J. Craig and Charles Perrow. "Insurgency of the Powerless: Farm Worker Movements (1946-1972)," *American Sociological Review*. April 1977. Vol. 42. No. 2.

Jezer, Marty. *The Dark Ages: Life in the United States 1945-1960*. Boston: South End Press, 1982.

Jones, Mary Harris. *Mother Jones Speaks: Collected Writings and Speeches*. Philip Foner, ed. New York: Monad Press, Distributed by Pathfinder Press, 1983.

Kraus, Henry. *The Many and the Few: A Chronicle of the Dynamic Auto Workers*. Los Angeles: The Plantin Press, 1947.

Leslie, Douglas L. *Labor Law in a Nutshell*. St. Paul, MN: West Publishing Co., 1986.

Levy, Jacques E. *Cesar Chavez: Autobiography of La Causa*. New York: W.W. Norton and Company, Inc., 1975.

Litwack, Leon. *The American Labor Movement*. Englewood Cliffs, NJ: Prentice-Hall, Inc., 1962.

Long, Priscilla. *Mother Jones, Woman Organizer And Her Relations With Miner's Wives, Working Women and the Suffrage Movement*. Boston: South End Press, 1976.

Lynd, Alice and Staughton Lynd, eds. *Rank and File: Personal Histories by Working-Class Organizers*. New York: Monthly Review Press, 1988 [1981].

Lynd, Staughton, ed. *American Labor Radicalism: Testimonies and Interpretations*. New York: John Wiley and Sons, 1973.

Merriam, Eve, ed. *Growing Up Female: Ten Lives*. Garden City, NY: Doubleday, 1971.

Merrill, Michael. "Why There Will Be a U.S. Labor Party by the Year 2000," *Social Policy*. Spring 1990.

Montgomery, David. *Worker's Control in America*. New York: Cambridge University Press, 1979.

Moody, Kim. *An Injury to All: The Decline of American Unionism*. New York: Verso, 1988.

Moore, Michael. "Made in Mexico: Reagan Administration Encourages U.S. Businesses to Move Jobs South of the Border," *Multinational Monitor*. February 1987.

Morgan, Wayne. *The Gilded Age*. Syracuse, NY: Syracuse University Press, 1963.

Nader, Ralph. "Aftermath to Murder: Yablonski's Unfinished Business," *The Nation*. January 26, 1970.

Nader, Ralph. "They're Still Breathing," *The New Republic*. February 3, 1968.

Nathan, Debbie. "Garment Workers: The Long, Last Strike," *Ms*. July/August 1991.

"New Directions for the UAW: An Interview with Jerry Tucker," *Multinational Monitor*. January/February 1990.

Paradis, Adrian A. *Labor in Action: The Story of the American Labor Movement*. New York: Julian Messner, 1975 [1963].

Rogers, Ray. "How to Confront Corporations," *Business and Society Review*. Vol. 38. 1981.

Seltzer, Curtis. *Fire in the Hole: Miners and Managers in the American Coal Industry*. Lexington: The University Press of Kentucky, 1989.

Shaiken, Harley. *Work Transformed: Automation and Labor in the Computer Age*. New York: Holt, Rinehart and Winston, 1984.

Sherrill, Robert G. "West Virginia Miracle: The Black Lung Rebellion," *The Nation*. April 28, 1969.

Shoemaker, Dennis E. "Lasting Imprints in the Fields: The Farmworkers and the Servant Church," *Christianity and Crisis*. February 15, 1988.

A Short History of American Labor. Washington, DC: AFL-CIO, 1981.

Straight Talk on the Fresh Grape Boycott. Flyer. Delano, CA: National Farm Worker Ministry.

Street, Richard Steven. "The Lettuce Strike Story: UFW's March for Justice," *The Nation*. January 19, 1980.

Tyler, Gus. *The Labor Revolution: Trade Unions in a New America*. New York: The Viking Press, 1967 [1966].

Wasserman, Harvey. *Harvey Wasserman's History of the United States*. New York: Four Walls Eight Windows, 1988.

Weissman, Robert. "Replacing the Union: Business's Labor Offensive," *Multinational Monitor*. April 1991.

Whitman, Alden, ed. *American Reformers*. New York: H.W. Wilson Company, 1985.

Zinn, Howard. *A People's History of the United States*. New York: Harper & Row Publishers, 1980.

A HISTORY OF THE
WOMEN'S RIGHTS MOVEMENT

INTRODUCTION

Europeans who immigrated to North America in the 17th and 18th centuries believed women to be of inferior intelligence to men and therefore incapable of participating in many aspects of society on an equal basis with men.[1] This belief was evident in organized religion, in women's lack of access to education and professional careers, in the social conventions that dictated proper behavior for women, in women's exclusion from political life and in women's unequal status relative to men under the legal system.

Although many of the earliest colonists who came to the New World seeking freedom from religious persecution believed in the equality of souls, their religions placed women in a subordinate position.[2] And although women in the colonies had tremendous responsibilities, whether working at home producing food and clothing and caring for children or working as slaves or indentured servants, most women had no access to education.[3] Women's lives also included socially restrictive conventions and double standards for male and female behavior, prohibiting women, for example, from speaking in public or traveling without a male escort.[4]

Furthermore, the framers of the political and legal system of the new nation denied political rights to women, including the right to vote. Much of the republic's legal framework was based on English common law which allowed women few rights.[5] Single women and widows had the legal right to own property, but upon marriage, women "suffered 'civil death,' having no right to property and no legal entity or existence apart from their husbands."[6] And existing laws made it difficult for women to obtain a divorce.[7]

Yet American women continually sought to be included in all aspects of society. In many Native American societies, women had a broad range of economic, social and religious roles as well as some political power and autonomy. As European-Americans forced their way of life (such as male- rather than female-dominated agriculture) on the various tribes, Native American women often resisted the changes that took much of their autonomy away.[8] Anne Hutchinson, in the 1630s, challenged Puritan beliefs about women's participation in religion.[9] And Abigail Adams warned her husband in 1776 as he helped draft laws for the new nation, "If particular care and attention is not paid to the ladies, we are determined to foment a rebellion, and will not hold ourselves bound by any laws in which we have no voice or representation."[10] Despite these early voices, women did not seriously enter the political arena until the early to mid-19th century.[11]

As women entered the political arena in the 1830s through participation in the movement for the abolition of slavery, they recognized both their effectiveness in making change and their unequal status relative to men both within the movement and in society at large. This recognition occurred once again as women participated in the modern civil rights and student movements. Women's activism in these movements was instrumental in bringing about both of the great waves of feminist activity: the campaign for the right to vote (a 72-year struggle) and the women's rights and liberation movement of the 1960s and 1970s.

During the two waves of feminism, thousands of women fought for the right to participate in the decisions that affect their lives and won significant achievements for all American women. But activism for women's rights was not confined to the two waves of feminism. Throughout U.S. history, women have actively protested their unequal treatment, demanding rights not only for themselves, but also the opportunity to make contributions to society.

ACCESS TO EDUCATION

At the time of the American Revolution, writes historian Eleanor Flexner, "It was almost universally believed that a woman's brain was smaller in capacity and therefore inferior in quality to that of a man."[12]

The prevailing attitude was in agreement with the French philosopher Jean-Jacques Rousseau who believed that women's educations (if they received any at all) should be "relative to men. To please them, to be useful to them, to make themselves loved and honored by them, to educate them when young, to care for them when grown, to counsel them, to console them, and to make life sweet and agreeable to them."[13] In addition, many men and women believed that education would cause women to lose their femininity.[14]

Yet because women were responsible for raising their sons to be good citizens of the new republic, they needed some education of their own. In the 1780s, writes historian Sara Evans, "The idea of republican motherhood stimulated a debate on women's education and provoked the founding of female academies, the first institutional settings in which young women could receive serious academic training."[15] These early academies, however, were limited to a small number of white, upper-class women.[16]

However, as demand for teachers in the West increased and as women began to work as teachers and textile mill operators, many women argued their roles in society could extend beyond their duties as the servants and caretakers of men. Some women, including Mercy Otis Warren and Judith Sargent Murray, even began to express the idea that they could, with educations equal to men's, prove women and men to be intellectual equals.[17]

One proponent of this idea was Emma Hart Willard who developed her own teaching methods and trained her students to become teachers themselves. Willard convinced the town council of Troy, New York, to finance the Troy Female Seminary, which opened in 1821 as the first endowed institution for the education of girls. The seminary included sciences such as physiology (the study of the bodily functions of living beings), considered an improper course of study for girls at the time, in its curriculum.[18] Willard continued her innovative teaching methods, and the campaign for the improvement of female education was underway.

Frances Wright, Catharine Beecher and Mary Lyon, although they had quite different perspectives, all made contributions to expanded educational access for women throughout the early 1800s. Their collective efforts widened the curriculum available to women, improved teacher training, expanded education beyond the white upper class and extended the right to education, not just in preparation to be wives and mothers, but for its own sake.[19]

Before the Civil War, education was denied almost completely to African Americans. In the South, it was illegal to teach a slave to read. Eleanor Flexner writes, "To educate [slaves] was to disprove the premise of racial inferiority on which slavery was founded, and also to arm [slaves] for the struggle for freedom."[20] In the North, free black people were denied access to many of the public schools. In Ohio, for example, in the 1840s, the state taxed free black citizens to pay for the schools, but did not allow their children to attend.[21]

Prudence Crandall ran a small girls' school in Canterbury, Connecticut in the 1830s. When she admitted a black student, Sarah Harris, to the school, she faced racist protests which forced her eventually to close the school. Crandall responded by opening a new school and enrolling 17 black girls from towns and cities around the North.[22]

The Connecticut state legislature then passed a law making it illegal for a Connecticut citizen to teach students from another state. Eventually the courts upheld the legality of the school, and the residents of Canterbury resorted to other methods. Eleanor Flexner describes the community's response: "The school's windows were broken; pupils and teachers ... were stoned as they went for walks; manure was dropped in the well; local storekeepers refused to sell food, and doctors denied their services."[23]

In spite of these and other obstacles, the school continued for one and a half years with the help of abolitionists and supporters from nearby communities. But when masked men entered the building at night, destroying the rooms on the bottom floor while the teachers and students waited in terror upstairs, Crandall decided, for the safety of the students, to close the school.[24]

By 1840, the movement to expand education beyond the white, upper-class male population resulted in 38 percent of all white Americans between the ages of five and 20 attending school. And by 1850, most white women could read and write, when in the previous century, about half these women could not sign their names. "As a consequence, more women acquired the tools to analyze and to debate their place and their role in society," writes Sara Evans.[25] The struggle to gain access to education was an important part of the struggle for women to gain opportunities equal to those of men.

WOMEN, SLAVERY AND ABOLITION

Harriet Jacobs, a slave who escaped to the North, wrote in *Incidents in the Life of a Slave Girl*, that "slavery is terrible for men; but it is far more terrible for women."[26] Jacobs documented sexual abuse and rape of black women by white slaveowners and made an appeal for help to women in the North. She hoped that as women, although from a background different from hers, they would understand the suffering of women slaves. Jacobs explained, "I do earnestly desire to arouse the women of the North to a realizing sense of the condition of two millions of women at the South, still in bondage, suffering what I suffered, and most of them far worse."[27]

Many women did join the abolitionist movement in the 1830s. After women formed societies in the 1820s to work for moral and religious reforms such as eliminating prostitution and alcohol abuse, many people in the United States accepted their participation in the struggle to end slavery.[28] Women organized female anti-slavery auxiliaries which supported the work of men's organizations, but some women, including Sarah and Angelina Grimke, expanded that role.[29]

The Grimke sisters were born into a slaveholding family in South Carolina. As adults, they moved to the North and began to participate in the abolitionist movement. They spoke frequently to meetings of female anti-slavery societies, giving eye-witness accounts of the conditions of slavery. They developed a reputation for their zealous anti-slavery sentiments and their speaking skills. A few men became curious and attended some of the meetings where the Grimkes spoke.[30]

The Grimkes' so-called unwomanly behavior, daring to speak in front of an audience of both women and men, soon raised objections from male anti-slavery leaders. In 1837, the Council of Congregationalist Ministers of Massachusetts issued a statement declaring that Angelina and Sarah Grimke were in danger of threatening "the female character with widespread and permanent injury" by speaking in public to men and women.[31] The Grimkes responded by writing articles and pamphlets linking the issues of slavery and women's rights as they realized that gaining rights for women (such as the right to speak in public) was important to the success of their anti-slavery work. Sarah Grimke wrote that "Whatsoever it is morally right for a man to do, it is morally right for a woman to do."[32]

In 1834, the American Anti-Slavery Society conducted a petition campaign to show Congress the extent of public support for the abolition of slavery. Women participated by going door-to-door to collect signatures. As Eleanor Flexner writes, "It took the same kind of courage as that displayed by the Grimke sisters for the average housewife, mother or daughter to overstep the limits of decorum, disregard the frowns, or jeers, or outright commands of her menfolk and go to her first public meeting, or take her first petition and walk down an unfamiliar street, knocking on doors and asking for signatures to an unpopular plea."[33]

In 1840, the World Anti-Slavery Convention met in London, England. In the U.S. delegation to the convention were several women, including future women's rights advocates Lucretia Mott, a Quaker minister and founder of the first Female Anti-Slavery Society, and Elizabeth Cady Stanton, who had attended the Troy Female Seminary.[34] Over the objections of some of the Americans, the organizers of the convention seated only the male delegates, restricting the women to the galleries where they could listen to the men's speeches but not speak or participate.[35] Stanton and Mott, provoked by this event, decided to hold a convention for women's rights in the United States.[36]

After women began working in politics on one issue, male leaders found it more difficult to justify keeping them out of the politics of other issues. One abolitionist writer, Lydia Maria Child, described this change. By urging women to work for moral reform issues through their churches, she wrote, male reform leaders "have changed the household utensil to a living, energetic being, and they have no spell to turn it into a broom again."[37] Once women learned the tools and tactics of political change, they began to envision ways to use them to improve their own lives.

THE FIRST WAVE OF FEMINISM

During the second half of the 19th century, women began working to achieve changes in the conditions which affected their lives. These pioneering women broke down many conventions and opened up many possibilities for the women who followed them. Historians refer to this era of activity as the first wave of feminism.[38]

Although few people believed in women's equality — and even fewer were willing to do anything about it publicly — a small group of advocates began to form. In the summer of 1848, led by Elizabeth Cady Stanton and Lucretia Mott, a group of women placed an advertisement in the Seneca Falls, New York newspaper, inviting women to attend a convention "to discuss the social, civil and religious rights of women."[39] On July 19, 1848, over 300 people came to the Seneca Falls Convention.[40]

The group adopted the Declaration of Sentiments — a paraphrase of the U.S. Declaration of Independence — which included demands for women's equality, including the right to vote. All the provisions of the Declaration were approved unanimously at the meeting, except for the provision calling for the vote for women, which passed by only a small margin.[41] Eleanor Flexner writes, "Beginning in 1848, it was possible for women who rebelled against the circumstances of their lives to know that they were not alone

... a movement had been launched, which they could either join or ignore, that would leave its imprint on the lives of their daughters and of women throughout the world."[42]

Throughout the 1840s and 1850s, women continued their work in anti-slavery societies and simultaneously advocated that the rights of citizenship be extended to women.[43] Women's rights advocates held a national convention in 1850 in Worcester, Massachusetts and again each year over the next decade, with the exception of 1857.[44] Black abolitionists also lent support to the new movement for women's rights. Frederick Douglass attended the Seneca Falls convention where he strongly supported Stanton's resolution for woman suffrage and Sojourner Truth, a freed slave, "electrified conventions with her eloquent insistence that womanhood should include black women."[45]

Early efforts for women's rights concentrated mostly on the right to control property and earnings, the right to obtain divorce, education and employment and the right to sue in the courts.[46] The legal status of women in the United States had changed little by the mid-1800s; "Married women could not sign contracts; they had no title to their own earnings, to property even when it was their own by inheritance or dower, or to their children in case of legal separation."[47]

Ernestine Rose, an immigrant who had successfully contested her arranged marriage in Poland, collected hundreds of signatures for a petition demanding a law guaranteeing property rights to married women in the state of New York. In 1848, the state legislature responded by passing the Married Woman's Property Act.[48]

Susan B. Anthony, who had worked in the temperance and abolition movements, led another petition drive in New York state for guardianship of children in the event of divorce, control of earnings and the right to vote. In 1854, Anthony devised a method for gathering a large number of signatures on the petitions: she chose 60 women, one from each county in New York, to lead petition drives in their areas. Despite the obstacles and ridicule they faced, the women collected 6,000 signatures in 10 weeks. Anthony embarked on an exhausting speaking and petition gathering tour of

New York state. Although legislators initially ridiculed her efforts, they passed a law in 1860 which extended to women the right to collect their own wages and to sue in court.[49] Between 1848 and 1860, many states passed laws giving women the right to collect their own wages, own and sell property, collect rent, bring lawsuits to court and have joint guardianship of their children.[50]

Susan B. Anthony and Elizabeth Cady Stanton joined together to speak, write and organize for women's rights. Writes historian Sara Evans, "The partnership between Stanton and Anthony brought together a brilliant organizer, Anthony, with a charismatic speaker and writer, Stanton."[51] Anthony also lent support to Stanton, whose domestic responsibilities, including caring for her seven children, were often overwhelming.[52]

Stanton's husband Henry voiced objections to her work and her father "temporarily disinherited her when she began public lecturing."[53] In an 1855 letter to Anthony, Stanton wrote:

> *To think that all in me of which my father would have felt a proper pride had I been a man, is deeply mortifying to him because I am a woman. That thought has stung me to a fierce decision — to speak as soon as I can do myself credit. But the pressure on me just now is too great. Henry sides with my friends, who oppose me in all that is dearest to my heart. They are not willing that I should write even on the woman question. But I will both write and speak.*[54]

Many women without Stanton's resolve found the price of speaking out too high.[55]

The movement expanded, attracting a larger number of active members, many of whom embarked on speaking tours around the country. Anthony reported in 1860 to the Tenth National Woman's Rights Convention in New York City that newspapers were paying more serious attention to women's demands and women's educational opportunities were opening up, including admissions to medical school classes.[56] But many state legislatures continued to be unresponsive to demands for property rights for married women, the legal right to separation and to child custody. Without the right to vote, women's rights advocates could not pressure those in the government to change the laws. Woman suffrage advocates could not change the discriminatory laws unless they could vote, but to win the right to vote, they had to change the laws.

THE CAMPAIGN FOR WOMAN SUFFRAGE

During the Civil War, the campaigns for women's rights were put on hold. However, women's rights activists continued to fight for abolition by gathering petitions for passage of the Thirteenth Amendment, making slavery illegal. Stanton and Anthony organized the National Woman's Loyal League in May of 1863. By August of 1864, they had collected 400,000 signatures in favor of the Thirteenth Amendment and presented them to the U.S. Senate.[57]

At the end of the Civil War, many anti-slavery advocates turned their energies to winning the right to vote for black men.[58] Stanton urged that suffrage for women be included in this struggle, but many supporters of black suffrage opposed Stanton's strategy. They believed that, tied to the still unpopular issue of woman suffrage, the right to vote for black men would be more difficult to achieve.[59]

The Fourteenth Amendment to the U.S. Constitution, first introduced in Congress in 1866, provided for equal protection under the law for all U.S. citizens. But the Amendment used the word "male" for the first time in the U.S. Constitution, implying that only men were citizens.[60] Until this point, the question of the right to vote for women was a state, not a federal, issue since the individual state constitutions, not the federal constitution, granted the vote specifically to men. Securing woman suffrage after adoption of the Fourteenth Amendment would thus require another constitutional amendment to name women as citizens and therefore as having the right to vote.[61]

Some women's rights activists, including Stanton and Anthony, opposed ratification of the Fourteenth Amendment because it excluded women and they feared it would make the right to vote for women more difficult to win. But others, including Lucy Stone and Julia Ward Howe, supported it as advancing the cause of equality for black men.[62]

The Fourteenth Amendment was ratified in July of 1868, and six months later, Congress introduced the Fifteenth Amendment which read, "The right of citizens of the United States to vote shall not be denied or abridged by the United States or any State, on account of race, color or previous condition of servitude." Stanton and Anthony argued unsuccessfully that the word "sex" could easily be added to the amendment.[63] Historian Sara Evans writes that, "One consequence, then, of the battles over the political status of black Americans was a more focused women's rights movement which increasingly referred to itself as the 'woman suffrage movement.' ... Suffrage provided a clear agenda around which the women's movement would organize and agitate for more than half a century."[64]

Women's rights activists began to disagree among themselves over the best approach to suffrage and other women's issues. The rival factions, in 1869, each formed their own organizations.[65]

Stanton and Anthony formed the National Woman Suffrage Association (NWSA), open only to women, to work on a variety of injustices faced by women. Their main goal was to ratify a constitutional amendment to give women the right to vote "believing that state-by-state progress would be lengthy, arduous, and difficult to achieve."[66]

The NWSA used a variety of tactics to bring attention to the cause of woman suffrage. Arguing that the Fourteenth and Fifteenth Amendments could be interpreted to apply to women, a number of women in New Jersey; Massachusetts; Washington, DC; New Hampshire; Michigan and New York attempted to cast ballots in several elections. Anthony led a group of women in Rochester, New York to the polls to try to register and to vote in the presidential election of 1872.[67] On November 18, 1872, Anthony was arrested for voting illegally. At her trial, she spoke eloquently about violations of her rights as a citizen, including her right to be tried by a jury of her peers (women

could not serve on juries). The judge fined her $100, which she refused to pay.[68]

Virginia Minor, president of the Missouri Woman Suffrage Association, and her husband Francis Minor sued a registrar who refused to let her vote in St. Louis in 1872 on the grounds that the U.S. Constitution already gave women the right to vote. The logic was that since the Constitution defined citizens as "all persons born or naturalized in the United States" and also guaranteed the right to vote to all citizens, then women should be able to vote.[69] However, the Supreme Court, in October 1874, ruled that the Fourteenth Amendment did not apply to women.[70]

Stanton, Anthony and their colleagues continued to fight for the "Susan B. Anthony Amendment" which read: "The right of citizens of the United States to vote shall not be denied or abridged by the United States or by any state on account of sex."[71] Congress considered the amendment year after year with series of hearings, committees, debates and votes, but always defeated the measure.[72]

Julia Ward Howe, Lucy Stone and her husband Henry Blackwell in 1869 organized the American Woman Suffrage Association (AWSA), which launched state referendum campaigns to win voting rights for women. The AWSA focused exclusively on suffrage to avoid alienating potential supporters. Committed to woman suffrage, the AWSA was not moved by the same visions of equality for women that made Anthony and Stanton willing to face public outrage and condemnation.[73]

The AWSA organized hundreds of state campaigns and saw some victories, though many more defeats. Between 1870 and 1910, 480 campaigns in 33 states were launched to put the issue of woman suffrage to the voters. Only 17 efforts made it to state referenda, held in 11 different states. Only two, Colorado in 1893 and Idaho in 1896, were successful. However, some states did grant partial suffrage to women for elections on issues including schools, taxes and bond issues. By 1890, 19 states had given women the right to vote on school issues.[74]

In 1869, Wyoming became the first territory with full woman suffrage.[75] As women began to vote, their names were added to the list for jury duty, to which many men objected more than woman suffrage.[76] Women in Wyoming also had the right to own property, and female teachers were protected from discrimination.[77] In 1889, when considering Wyoming's application for admittance to the United States, Congress asked that the territory agree to discontinue women's voting rights as a condition of entry. Wyoming refused, and in 1890, it became the first state whose female citizens had full voting rights.[78]

Despite a few victories, women had made little progress in obtaining the vote and "a new generation of [suffrage] leaders saw no utility in the duplication of effort represented by rival organizations."[79] Alice Stone Blackwell, daughter of Lucy Stone, initiated the merger of NWSA and AWSA.[80]

In 1890, the NWSA and the AWSA united to form the National American Woman Suffrage Association (NAWSA) to pool their scarce resources. Elizabeth Cady Stanton served as its president until 1892, but she began to focus her efforts on the role of organized religion in the inferior status of women. She published

The Woman's Bible[81] which analyzed passages of the Bible derogatory to women. Stanton continued writing until her death in 1902.[82]

Susan B. Anthony succeeded Stanton as president of NAWSA and continued to favor the federal amendment approach to winning woman suffrage.[83] Other NAWSA members advocated the state-by-state approach. Sara Evans writes, "Those local campaigns had the virtue of involving and educating thousands of women, as well as a new generation, and building local alliances. As a strategy, however, experience proved state campaigns to be weak indeed."[84]

Two new leaders, Carrie Chapman Catt and Anna Howard Shaw, emerged in the 1890s. Catt led the successful referenda campaigns in Idaho and Colorado where she developed "the flair for planning, for check-up and detail, and for seeking out and training fresh leadership, which were to be the hallmarks of her suffrage work for a quarter of a century."[85] Shaw had a medical degree and worked as a lecturer in the women's temperance movement where she also began to speak about woman suffrage. When Anthony retired from the presidency of NAWSA in 1900, Carrie Chapman Catt took her place for four years, after which she left to devote more time to the grow-

Cartoon of Anti-Suffrage parade, 1912

KAISER WILSON

HAVE YOU FORGOTTEN YOUR SYMPATHY WITH THE POOR GERMANS BECAUSE THEY WERE NOT SELF-GOVERNED?

20,000,000 AMERICAN WOMEN ARE NOT SELF-GOVERNED.

TAKE THE BEAM OUT OF YOUR OWN EYE.

Banner of Woman Suffrage advocates.

ing international movement for woman suffrage. Shaw succeeded Catt in the presidency of NAWSA for the next 11 years.[86]

By the 1890s, black women found that the movement, made up mostly of white, upper-class women, ignored their concerns and refused to fight to enfranchise black women.[87] Northern suffragists often gained support in the South by speaking against black female suffrage.[88] In addition, NAWSA, by allowing its state chapters to determine their own policies regarding membership, permitted the exclusion of black women and the use of white supremacist arguments in the fight for woman suffrage.[89] Although these conditions made participation in the suffrage campaign especially difficult for black women, they formed their own woman suffrage clubs in numerous cities including Tuskegee, St. Louis, Los Angeles, Memphis, Boston, Charleston and New Orleans.[90] And where they could

vote, black women often registered at a higher rate than white women.[91]

Susan B. Anthony remained active in the movement for women's rights until her death in 1906. Writes Eleanor Flexner of Anthony, "Her passing marked the end of an era. She was the last of the giants who had launched the struggle to improve the condition of women to leave the scene. She had lived and worked, without respite and without discouragement, through the years of ridicule, vilification, and apparent hopelessness, which today are all but forgotten. When she died, few thinking people denied either the logic or the inevitability of woman suffrage. The only question that remained was, 'When?'"[92]

VICTORY: THE NINETEENTH AMENDMENT

Eleanor Flexner writes that "the years from 1896 to 1910 came to be known among suffragists as 'the doldrums.'"[93] Six states held suffrage referenda and all were lost. In addition, Congress took no new action on the Anthony Amendment. However, new leaders again began to emerge. Harriet Stanton Blatch, daughter of Elizabeth Cady Stanton, returned to the United States in 1902 after living abroad for 20 years.[94] Blatch, after working in various English social movements, including the campaign for suffrage, returned to find the U.S. suffrage movement "completely in a rut."[95] Blatch founded her own organization, the Women's Political Union (WPU), to try to revive the movement for woman suffrage by making demands more dramatic as well as bringing working women into the movement.[96]

By October 1908, WPU had 19,000 members and was using new tactics including working with labor unions, organizing its membership by political districts, campaigning against legislators opposed to suffrage, serving as poll watchers on election day and organizing parades which became regular events in cities across the country.[97] Despite NAWSA's fears that parades would appear undignified and set back the cause, the *New York Times*, although anti-suffrage, conceded, "The marchers, instead of injuring their cause by conduct that ... was distinctly unfeminine and therefore obnoxious and ridiculous, really accomplished something ... and did not lose but gained respect."[98] In addition, many young women began to call themselves feminists and advocate, in addition to political rights, social and cultural freedoms for women.[99]

In 1910 and 1911, women won the right to vote in the states of Washington and California. Women in California closely monitored activities on election day, from the voting booths where ballots were cast to the tally clerks to the vaults where the counted ballots were held.[100] When the final count was in, the woman suffrage referendum had won by "an average majority of *one vote* in every voting precinct in the state."[101]

In 1912, six states held referenda and women won the right to vote in Arizona, Kansas and Oregon. Early election returns in Michigan showed the woman suffrage referenda ahead, but as the final returns were reported, an increasingly large number of votes were against woman suffrage. The Governor of Michigan accused brewery interests (who opposed woman suffrage out of fear that women voters would support prohibition of alcohol) of tampering in the election, but the final outcome was defeat for women's right to vote.[102]

Congress had not considered the Anthony Amendment since 1896.[103] That changed when Alice Paul, a social worker active in the suffrage movement in England, took up the campaign for a constitutional amendment. Paul used tactics such as civil disobedience and hunger strikes which she learned from the British movement.[104] Lucy Burns, another American who had worked for suffrage in England, joined Paul, originally working with NAWSA.[105] One of their first actions was a parade in Washington, DC the day before President Woodrow Wilson's inauguration. When Wilson arrived in Washington, in March of 1913, his greeters had already left to watch the woman suffrage parade.[106] The parade consisted of 5,000 women and, with little protection from the police, turned into a near-riot, which drew tremendous publicity to the suffrage cause.[107]

Alice Paul split with NAWSA and formed the Congressional Union in 1913 to work solely for passage of a constitutional amendment. The Congressional Union used the British suffrage movement's tactic of

holding the political party in power (at that time the Democratic Party) responsible for inaction on the issue of woman suffrage. Beginning in 1914, the Congressional Union campaigned, especially in the states where women had the right to vote, against Democratic candidates for Congress whether or not they supported woman suffrage.[108] The Congressional Union "claimed at least partial credit for the defeat of 23 out of 43 western Democrats."[109] In 1914, the Senate voted on the woman suffrage amendment, defeating it 35 to 34; and the next year, the amendment was defeated 204 to 174 in the House of Representatives.[110] However, the Congressional Union had succeeded in putting the issue on the agenda again.

Women won the vote in two more states, Montana and Nevada, in 1914. However, in the same year, five more state referenda campaigns were lost.[111] And in 1915, referenda campaigns in New York, Massachusetts, Pennsylvania and New Jersey were all lost.[112]

In June of 1916, the Congressional Union became the National Woman's Party (NWP). In the 12 states where women had the vote, the NWP began to mobilize women for the upcoming presidential election. As a result, both the Republican and the Democratic Party presidential platforms of 1916 supported suffrage. Despite the NWP's campaign against President Woodrow Wilson, he was reelected and the NWP was forced to abandon its electoral strategy.[113]

In January of 1917, the NWP picketed the White House (which had never been done before), silently standing at its gate with banners asking "Mr. President, What Will You Do For Woman Suffrage?"[114] When the United States entered World War I, the banners read "Democracy Should Begin at Home" in response to President Wilson's decree that the war would "make the world safe for democracy."[115]

The banners began to provoke violent reactions from onlookers, and in June of 1917, police began to arrest the picketers on the charge of obstructing sidewalk traffic. According to Eleanor Flexner, "The truth was that the women were violating no law, perpetrating no crime. Their action could legally be classed only as committing a nuisance."[116] But as the violence continued, the Washington, DC courts sentenced the picketers (218 women were arrested, 97 sent to prison) to jail for terms of up to six months. None of the on-lookers, who committed the violence, were ever arrested.[117] On October 20, 1917, Alice Paul was sentenced to seven months in prison for carrying a banner which said, "The Time Has Come to Conquer or Submit."[118]

The women protested their arrests and the poor prison conditions by going on hunger strikes. Prison officials responded with forced feeding.[119] The picketing, the arrests, the jail sentences and the hunger strikes attracted enormous attention. All the picketers were released from jail in November of 1917, and their convictions were overturned the following March.[120]

Meanwhile, Carrie Chapman Catt turned her attention from the international movement back to the United States when she assumed the presidency of NAWSA in 1915. Catt, with her excellent organizational skills, revitalized NAWSA. NAWSA went in an entirely different direction from the NWP by working to convince President Wilson to take a leadership role in advocating woman suffrage. NAWSA, under the leadership of Catt, also developed its "Winning Plan," a detailed six-year strategy for organizing support for both the federal amendment and state referenda. NAWSA lent its support to the war effort but contin-ued to make suffrage its first priority. NAWSA also completely disavowed the picketing tactics of the NWP.[121]

At its conference in December 1917, NAWSA an-nounced that if Congress did not pass the suffrage amendment before the 1918 elections, it would work to replace a sufficient number of senators and repre-sentatives to assure passage in the next Congress.[122] Although the House of Representatives passed the Anthony Amendment in January of 1918, the Senate vote in October fell short by two votes, despite President Wilson's personal plea for support.[123]

NAWSA carried out its threat to work against the reelection of its opponents, contributing to the defeat of two senators and substantially reducing the support of two others.[124] On May 20, 1919, the House of Representatives again passed the amendment, by a vote of 304 to 89.[125] And on June 4, 1919 the Senate

Joint Resolution of Congress for a Woman Suffrage amendment to the U.S. Constitution, 1919.

also passed it, 63 to 30, with 11 of the 13 new senators voting for the amendment.[126]

The fight for state ratification of the Nineteenth Amendment — guaranteeing women the right to vote — proceeded relatively quickly. The NAWSA, which had maintained its organizations even in the states that long ago had passed suffrage referenda, quickly mobilized support for the ratification process.[127] On August 26, 1920 women in every state of the United States won the right to vote.[128]

"I want to stand by my country, but I cannot vote for war. I vote no."[129] Thus spoke Representative Jeannette Rankin (R-MT) in April 1917, on the eve of U.S. entry into World War I, as she cast the first vote of the first woman elected to the U.S. Congress.[130]

Born on June 11, 1880 in Missoula, Montana, Jeannette Rankin earned a degree in biology in 1902 from the University of Montana. After a brief period teaching and working in a settlement house (an institution providing social services to new immigrants and/or the poor — part of the Progressive reform era) in San Francisco, in 1908 Rankin enrolled in the New York School of Philanthropy to train in social work. Frustrated by the lack of laws protecting children, women and the poor, she entered the University of Washington in Seattle in 1910 to study politics. There she worked on the successful campaign for woman suffrage in Washington state and soon returned to Montana to help organize its suffrage campaign.[131]

Rankin became a skilled political organizer as she travelled from county to county, covering more than 9,000 miles, to mobilize support for woman suffrage.[132] Rankin and other suffragists spoke at saloons, town halls, picnics and school houses and on street corners. According to Belle Fligelman Winestine, a Montana suffragist, "No one in Montana, or anywhere else for that matter, had heard of a respectable young woman making a public street corner speech. Yet we knew we would have to adopt all the normal political techniques if we were going to win the vote."[133] The suffragists organized a letter-writing campaign to lobby the state legislature which eventually put a woman suffrage referendum on the ballot. In November of 1914, the male Montana voters approved the measure, making Montana the tenth state in the United States where women had the right to vote.[134]

1917 COURTESY OF THE LIBRARY OF CONGRESS

Rankin decided to run for Congress and remobilized the suffrage organization to work for her campaign.[135] Her platform included support for child welfare laws, the eight-hour day for women factory workers and a federal amendment for woman suffrage.[136] Rankin also supported a number of open government reforms, including public disclosure of the voting records of Members of Congress, a corrupt practices act to limit the influence of the wealthy in elections, direct election of the President (instead of the Electoral College system), proportional representation and the recall, referendum and initiative.[137]

In November 1916, Rankin became the first woman elected to the U.S. Congress, while most women in the United States still could not vote.[138] Articles in the press speculated about Rankin's appearance rather than focusing on her ideas. For example, the *New York Times* editorialized with a poem: "I wonder is she old and stout/Or is she young and pretty/How long the members will stay out/who are on her committee."[139]

Meanwhile, war was escalating in Europe, and in April of 1917, months before Rankin had expected to begin serving as her state's representative, President Woodrow Wilson called Congress into a special session to vote on whether the United States should enter the war. Rankin's views on war were well-known. She had campaigned as a pacifist, yet many suffragists urged her to vote with the majority, in favor of war. They argued that a protest vote would set back the cause for a federal amendment for woman suffrage.[140]

On the morning of April 2, 1917, the day of the special session of Congress, Rankin was honored by both the National American Woman Suffrage Association (NAWSA), which supported the war, and the

National Woman's Party (NWP), which opposed the war. Rankin was "escorted to Congress by 25 flag-draped cars, some decorated with the yellow and white of NAWSA and some with the purple, gold and white of the NWP."[141] Both groups anxiously awaited her vote on the war.

In Congress, Rankin was welcomed with applause and officially seated.[142] President Wilson asked the Congress to approve a war resolution, to "make the world safe for democracy."[143] When the vote was taken, Rankin voted no. Although 55 other Members of Congress also voted against U.S. entry into World War I, "all the anger seemed to be focused on [Rankin]."[144] When Rankin's brother told her she would never be reelected, she said, "I'm not interested in that. All I'm interested in is what they'll say fifty years from now."[145] Once the United States entered the war, Rankin supported her country in hopes of bringing about a faster end to the fighting.[146]

On January 10, 1918, Rankin introduced a constitutional amendment for woman suffrage and became "the only woman ever to vote to give women the vote."[147] Yet her vote against war assured her defeat when she ran for the Senate in 1918.[148]

Rankin stood by her vote against the war and continued to work for peace, particularly by calling attention to the enormous profits that weapons manufacturers made during World War I and arguing that the money spent on defense should instead be spent on social programs.[149] She firmly believed that preparing for war would lead to war since weapons manufacturers profit from war.[150] In 1928, she established the Georgia Peace Society "to raise political awareness and encourage public discussion about creating a peaceful society."[151] She also worked with the Women's International League for Peace and Freedom and the National Council for the Prevention of War.

Whenever someone told her that no one could stop war, she answered, "They said 'You can't stop smallpox' and that 'Women will never vote' - I hate these 'nevers!'"[152] By 1937 polls showed that most U.S. citizens believed that the country should not have entered World War I.[153]

With growing support for pacifism, she ran for Congress in 1940 and was reelected.[154] But calls for pacifism lessened when Japan attacked the U.S. military base at Pearl Harbor in December of 1941. The next day, when President Franklin Roosevelt asked Congress to declare war against Japan, Jeannette Rankin once again voted no. This time she cast the only no vote. During the debate, the speaker of the House refused to recognize her when she demanded speaking time. Her vote angered her friends, family and constituency, and Rankin remarked, "I have nothing left now but my integrity."[155] Rankin became the only member of Congress to vote against U.S. entry into both World War I and II.[156]

Rankin continued her commitment to peace, women's rights and government reform until her death in 1973, at age 92.[157] She traveled to India several times to study Mohandas Gandhi's philosophy of nonviolence.[158] In 1968, she led 5,000 women in a march in Washington, DC to protest U.S. involvement in Vietnam. The women called themselves the Jeannette Rankin Brigade.[159] Rankin called the women's liberation movement of the 1960s and 1970s "encouraging," saying, "The way we know it's growing is that the men make fun of it. They make fun of it because they want it to stop."[160] She advocated a multi-district plan where congressional districts would be combined and voters would elect several representatives from each district. Under such a plan, candidates would not need 51 percent of the vote to win, rather the top candidates would all win a seat, making Congress more representative.[161]

EARLY POLITICAL POWER

In 1920, the National American Woman Suffrage Association (NAWSA) reorganized as the League of Women Voters with the purpose of training women to be good citizens. The League emphasized "an issue-oriented politics based on thorough research and effective public education."[162] The League continued to work on reform issues such as better conditions for working women and restrictions on child labor, but it believed that an organization specifically for women's rights was no longer necessary.[163]

Immediately following the ratification of the Nineteenth Amendment, Congress, fearing that women would vote as a bloc, passed some legislation addressing women's concerns. In 1921, Congress passed the Sheppard-Towner Act for maternal and infant health education programs as a step toward lowering infant mortality rates.[164] However, doctors opposed the bill on the grounds that the government would compete with their practices and funds for the program were cut entirely by the end of the decade.[165] The Classification Act, passed by Congress in 1923, mandated equal pay for federal workers — female and male — yet did not address discrimination in hiring and promotion.[166]

However, it was soon apparent that women, instead of voting as a bloc, voted along party lines, much as men did. As Eleanor Flexner writes, "The politicians relaxed ... when they found that women could not deliver a bloc vote, and that comparatively few of the able and victorious leaders were interested in political careers."[167]

WOMEN MAKE PERSONAL AND ECONOMIC GAINS

The gains many women achieved in the 1920s were not political, but instead were personal and economic. Many of the social conventions that dictated respectable behavior for women broke down. Women went to theaters, movies and dance halls and abandoned restrictive clothing such as corsets and petticoats. And women attended college and worked outside the home in record numbers.[168] Many of these changes began before World War I, but in the 1920s these ideas about what was socially acceptable for women broad-

ened greatly and became the norm.[169] Though many suffragists often were disturbed by the "new woman" (who cared less and less about political rights), their fight for women's rights had opened the door to the "flapper" lifestyle.[170]

The flapper, already a powerful image in 1913, became a symbol of the 1920s "with her bobbed hair, powdered nose, rouged cheeks, and shorter skirts. Lively and energetic, she wanted experience for its own sake. She sought out popular amusements in cabarets, dance halls, and movie theaters that no respectable, middle-class woman would have frequented a generation before. She danced, she smoked, and flaunted her sexuality to the horror of her elders."[171]

During the 1920s, the number of women who attended college rose to 43.7 percent of total college enrollment.[172] Most female college graduates worked, at least during the years before they married and started families.[173] Women made some advances in professional fields, but mostly continued to hold jobs traditionally dominated by women, such as elementary school teaching, library work and social work.[174]

More women entered white-collar jobs as the expansion of business created a demand for female office workers.[175] By 1920, 30 percent of women workers were in clerical and sales work, which remained available mostly to white women.[176] Ten years later, women were in 52 percent of clerical jobs.[177] Although society began to accept women in the workplace, few of these women had any chance for advancement. Women were thought to be in the workplace to look for a husband or to earn money for luxuries, called "pin money."[178]

But single women worked outside the home to support themselves, and many married women worked outside the home to help their families pay rent, food and clothing bills.[179] Black women, who did not benefit from the gains which middle-class white women enjoyed, remained confined mostly to domestic service and laundry work.[180]

PROTECTIVE LEGISLATION V. EQUAL RIGHTS: TWO FACTIONS EMERGE

Although society became more open to diverse roles for women, and women had won the right to vote, they still faced inequalities such as receiving less pay than men for equivalent work and legal restrictions on the rights of married women. Two factions within the women's movement emerged, one dedicated to protecting women in the labor force, the other to securing full equality for women under the law. These different approaches divided the women's movement through the 1960s.

At the turn of the century, because few unions were interested in organizing women, a coalition of middle-class women, including the National Trade Union League and the National Consumers League, formed to mobilize support for legislation to protect working women. The coalition called for "minimum wages, maximum hours, weight restrictions on lifting, and prohibitions on night work."[181] They achieved some successes. By 1907, for example, 20 states had laws limiting the working hours of women.[182]

During World War I, this coalition of women lobbied the federal government to establish an agency called Women in Industry Service to represent women in war work. In 1920, due to pressure from women advocates of protective legislation, Congress made the agency permanent, establishing it within the Department of Labor and renaming it the Women's Bureau.[183] The Bureau, led for 25 years by Mary Anderson, gathered facts and made advisory reports but had no policy making power.[184]

However, another group of women, those affiliated with the National Woman's Party (NWP), opposed protective legislation on the grounds that it "placed women in an inferior position and deprived them of their rights."[185] The NWP began work in 1921 on a state-by-state campaign to pass a constitutional amendment to end all legal discrimination against women.[186] In 1923, the NWP convinced legislators in both houses of Congress to introduce the Equal Rights Amendment (ERA) which read: "Men and women shall have equal rights throughout the United States and every place subject to its jurisdiction."[187]

68TH CONGRESS, 1ST SESSION.

H. J. RES. 75

IN THE HOUSE OF REPRESENTATIVES.

DECEMBER 13, 1923.

Mr. ANTHONY introduced the following joint resolution; which was referred to the Committee on the Judiciary and ordered to be printed.

JOINT RESOLUTION

Proposing an amendment to the Constitution of the United States.

1   *Resolved by the Senate and House of Representatives*
2   *of the United States of America in Congress assembled*
3   *(two-thirds of each House concurring therein),* That the
4   following article is proposed as an amendment to the Con-
5   stitution of the United States which shall be valid, to all
6   intents and purposes, as part of the Constitution when
7   ratified by the legislatures of three-fourths of the several
8   States:

9   ARTICLE XX.

10   "Men and women shall have equal rights throughout
11   the United States and every place subject to its jurisdiction.
12   "Congress shall have power to enforce this article by
13   appropriate legislation."

Joint Resolution of Congress for the Equal Rights Amendment, 1923.

To illustrate the need for an ERA, the NWP pointed to "discrimination against women professionals who were barred from many of the finest schools and relegated to subordinate roles within their professions" as well as the existence of discriminatory legislation in every state, including laws that gave husbands control over their wives' earnings, denied women the right to serve on juries, allowed husbands to determine their wives' legal residence, placed the burden of responsibility for children born to single women on the mother and restricted women's inheritance from their husbands.[188]

The Women's Bureau coalition did not support the ERA because of its potential to provide a basis for repealing protective labor legislation.[189] Many women working with the Bureau accused the NWP of insensitivity toward women working outside the home.[190] They pointed out that the NWP, made up of mostly white, middle- to upper-class, well-educated women, did not need the protective legislation which the Women's Bureau saw as indispensable for low-income women.[191]

Though the two groups worked together on such issues as women's right to serve on juries and worked against laws forbidding the employment of married women during the Depression, two rival coalitions had formed: the Women's Bureau coalition lobbied for equal pay and protective labor laws, while the NWP and a few professional women's organizations worked for an ERA.[192]

WOMEN AND THE GREAT DEPRESSION

Some of President Franklin Roosevelt's New Deal measures, in response to the Great Depression, attempted to equalize wages earned by women and men, but no system of enforcement existed and discrimination against women workers continued. The Federal Economy Act of 1932, for example, mandated that to relieve depression conditions, if a husband and wife both held federal jobs, the wife would lose her job first even if she held a higher position than her spouse.[193] Yet studies by the Women's Bureau showed that many women were the sole support for their families.[194] Single women did not fare much better; in 1934, 75,000 single women in New York City were homeless.[195] The Depression was in general more difficult for black women than white women: by 1931, 42 percent of black women were unemployed, compared to 18 percent of white women.[196] In addition, many government relief programs discriminated against African Americans.[197]

WOMEN AND WORLD WAR II

As U.S. factories produced materiel for the war in Europe in larger and larger quantities, the Women's Bureau of the Department of Labor began to lobby the federal government and private industry by issuing bulletins and reports promoting the employment of women in the war industries.[198] Such ideas were not new; during World War I women worked in oil refineries, steel mills and weapons factories.[199] Despite the efforts of advocates for women workers, openings for women in war industry came only when the departure of millions of male workers for military service created a serious labor shortage.[200] Thus millions of women won access to jobs more challenging and better paying than ever before.[201]

Once the necessity of recruiting women for war work became urgent, the federal government launched a propaganda campaign through the Office of War Information (OWI) both to convince industry to hire women and to convince women to "help out for the duration."[202] The OWI created "Rosie the Riveter," an attractive woman worker who appeared on posters and in news reels and magazines, to reassure the nation that war work would not undermine femininity.[203] The OWI campaign promoted the myth that women had not worked outside the home before the war and would "go home" as soon as the war ended. For example, in a recruitment film, several actors portraying women war workers said they were working because the United States was "in a jam."[204] A pamphlet called *What Job is Mine on the Victory Line?* read, "If you've sewed on buttons, or made buttonholes, on a machine, You can learn to do spot welding on airplane parts. If you've used an electric mixer in your kitchen, You can learn to run a drill press. If you've followed recipes exactly in making cake, you can learn to load shells."[205]

However, women's lives in the 1930s and 1940s were quite different from the OWI's portrayal. Two thirds of women war industry workers had been working outside the home before the war.[206] The vast majority of women worked because they and their families needed the money, not solely to support the war.[207]

The National War Labor Board (NWLB) "promised equal pay with men, declaring wage differentials [lower pay for women than men] based on sex impermissible (partly to lure women to work and partly to keep wage rates up in preparation for the GIs' return)."[208] The NWLB had the power to order equal pay for men and women in the resolution of labor disputes, but only when unions initiated this action in contract negotiations.[209] Unions also supported the principle of equal pay for women because they feared that if women were paid less, industry would continue to employ women to undercut men's wages after the war.[210] One member of the American Federation of Labor explained, "We tried to maintain the rate of the job for women, otherwise, the companies would hire women and men would not have jobs."[211]

Factories with federal government contracts to build war materiel worked on a "cost plus" basis, which meant that the government paid for all the factories' costs and guaranteed a profit above costs. Since the cost of paying equal wages to women was absorbed by the government, industry had an incentive to adopt the practice.[212] From 1942 to 1944, more than 2,200 companies reported voluntary elimination of wage differentials.[213]

The principle of equal pay, however, was narrowly applied. The NWLB often challenged wage differentials within single departments of single plants, letting stand inequalities within a company as a whole.[214] In addition, many companies established different job classifications based solely on the worker's sex. "Female" jobs paid less.[215] Often, the unions sanctioned this practice; for example, the United Auto Workers approved contracts which classified jobs as male and female, with the female jobs paying less.[216] Many unions did not protest the practice, followed by many factories, of keeping separate seniority lists and job classifications for women and black men.[217]

Women in war industry jobs faced many other forms of discrimination. Employers rarely promoted women above entry-level, low-skilled positions or trained them for higher skilled work since their jobs were presumed to be temporary.[218] Women workers also faced a lack of child care facilities. Although the federal government had a great interest in making it easier for women to work, neither the government nor industry offered adequate child care. Some employers provided child care when they could pass the expense on to the federal government under cost plus contracts. And Congress earmarked some money for government-sponsored child care centers, yet it covered only 10 percent of the children who needed it. Congress ended federally funded child care after the war. Most women relied on family and friends or on centers sponsored by religious groups or charities.[219]

The Rosie the Riveter image focused attention on women workers during the war who left their homes to work in factories which produced war materiel. Yet only three million out of the 18 million women who worked during the war worked in defense industries. The majority of women held traditionally female jobs, such as domestic service and clerical work, which always have had lower pay and lower status than traditionally male jobs.[220] Furthermore, about 12 million of the 18 million women workers during the war already worked outside the home for wages.[221]

The political and economic realities of the U.S. involvement in the war had profound effects on non-

War Manpower Commission flyer urging women to work during World War II.

white women. When black workers threatened a protest march in Washington, DC, President Franklin Roosevelt responded by signing Executive Order 8802 in 1941 (see page 22) which outlawed discrimination based on race in defense plants.[222] Despite the Order, black workers (female and male) continued to face discrimination. Most war industry employers refused to hire black women for the high-paying jobs available to white women. In 1942 and 1943, black women held demonstrations for jobs and housing and stormed a Ford automobile factory in Detroit to protest discrimination.[223] Using these tactics, black women achieved gains: between 1940 and 1944 black women's participation in the industrial workforce rose from 6.5 percent to 18 percent and their war-time wages were as much as 1,000 percent higher than their pre-war wages.[224]

The experience of Japanese American women (as well as men and children) during World War II was profoundly different from that of all other American women. On February 19, 1942, President Roosevelt signed an executive order authorizing the evacuation of virtually every Japanese American who lived on the U.S. West Coast.[225] The U.S. government gave families one week to sell all their belongings and then moved them to relocation camps in Utah, Arizona, Colorado, California, Wyoming, Idaho and Arkansas. Life in the camps was extremely difficult. Some women avoided the camps by joining the armed forces or becoming students. One woman, Mitsuye Endo, protested her internment through the U.S. legal system, finally appealing to the Supreme Court, which ruled on December 18, 1944, that the internment of loyal citizens was unconstitutional.[226]

THE POST-WAR ERA AND THE FEMININE MYSTIQUE

When World War II ended, a large majority of women war workers wanted to keep their skilled factory jobs. However, they were laid off at a rate 75 percent higher than that of men.[227] And the U.S. Employment Service no longer offered skilled industrial jobs to women.[228] Women protested this discriminatory treatment with pickets and protests.[229] Black women, who were forced to return to low paying domestic work, attempted to preserve some of the

gains they had made during the war by organizing to keep domestic wages higher and establishing support groups, training programs and job placement agencies.[230]

Along with the layoffs, government and business again launched a campaign, illustrated by the dramatically changing media images of women, to convince women that they belonged in the home and that they must "Give Back Their Jobs" to returning veterans.[231] Munitions worker Margaret Wright remembers that "even the articles in the magazines changed. You know, during the war they was telling you to cook dishes that you cook quick and get on to work. Now, they were telling you how to cook dishes that took a full day. There were more articles in there about raising your child and the psychological development of your children. They never did mention that, you know, before the war...."[232]

The post-war effort to convince women that their roles should be limited to homemakers and mothers created a "mystique of feminine fulfillment [that] became the cherished and self-perpetuating core of contemporary American culture. Millions of women lived their lives in the image of those pretty pictures of the American suburban housewife, kissing their husbands goodbye in front of the picture window, depositing their stationwagonsful of children at school, and smiling as they ran the new electric waxer over the spotless kitchen floor."[233] A bestseller, published in 1947, called *Modern Woman: The Lost Sex*,[234] by Marynia Farnham and Ferdinand Lundberg, was particularly effective in the attempt to convince women to give up their jobs by accusing women working outside the home of depriving their children of needed love.[235]

The post-war message was that "truly feminine women do not want careers, higher education, political rights — the independence and the opportunities that the old-fashioned feminists fought for."[236] As a result, women began marrying at a much younger age and having more children. By the mid-1950s, 60 percent of women dropped out of college to marry. And fewer and fewer women entered professional work.[237]

Although women's participation in the labor force dropped immediately following the post-war layoffs from skilled industrial jobs, many women found new jobs in traditionally female occupations such as teaching, clerical, secretarial, domestic and sales work, and their participation in the labor force continued to grow.[238] "Yet," write Leila Rupp and Verta Taylor, "the public image of women's lives denied the reality of these changes."[239] Despite the number of women workers, a 1945 Gallup poll reported that only 18 percent of the U.S. population approved of a woman working outside the home if she had a husband who could support her.[240]

Furthermore, the idealized white middle-class suburban lifestyle was not a reality for non-white or low-income women, or for any woman working outside the home.[241] The percentage of white married women with children working outside the home rose from 17 percent in 1950 to 30 percent in 1960. The number of female-headed households among the urban poor escalated but the problems of low-income people and of racial minorities were largely ignored.[242]

WOMEN'S ACTIVISM IN THE POST-WAR ERA

The happy homemaker message went much further than convincing women to give up their industrial jobs. Magazines began to ask if women wanted any rights. For example, the *Ladies' Home Journal* published an article which asked "Should Women Vote?"[243] In addition, the general social and political climate of the post-war years, characterized by McCarthyism, was hostile to any kind of social activism.[244] Yet activists continued their work both during and after the war on behalf of women's rights.

During World War II, the two major coalitions within the women's movement (the National Woman's Party and the Women's Bureau coalition) which were established in the 1920s, hoped to capitalize on the public's gratitude for the crucial role women played in the war effort but continued to disagree about what goals to pursue.[245] The National Woman's Party (NWP) created the Women's Joint Legislative Committee (WJLC), an umbrella organization for women's groups which supported the ERA, with a combined membership of five to six million women.[246] The

WJLC convinced Congress to consider the ERA in 1942 and 1943.[247] Alice Paul provided new wording for the amendment: "Equality of rights under the law shall not be denied or abridged by the United States, or by any State, on account of sex."[248] And in 1944, both the Republican and Democratic Parties included the ERA in their platforms.[249]

The Women's Bureau coalition (those groups which supported protective labor laws for women) organized the National Committee to Defeat the UnEqual Rights Amendment (NCDURA) in 1944 to lobby against the ERA.[250] NCDURA recommended repeal of specific state laws harmful to women and in February 1945, proposed a bill mandating equal pay for women. NCDURA had two motivations: the desire to eliminate wage differentials based on gender and the wish to divert attention from the ERA. The National Woman's Party opposed the bill, fearing it would achieve what its proponents hoped. But the equal pay bill did not come to a vote in the Senate in 1945.[251]

On July 19, 1946, the U.S. Senate voted 38 to 35 in favor of the ERA, short of the two-thirds majority needed to approve a constitutional amendment.[252] A *New York Times* editorial commented, "Motherhood cannot be amended, and we are glad the Senate didn't try."[253] The ERA never came to a vote in the House of Representatives.[254]

By 1946, women's contribution to World War II had become a distant memory.[255] The popular image of women as homemakers gave legitimacy to the avoidance of addressing issues such as equal pay. Women's political activities, including the progress of the ERA in Congress, received little media attention.[256] Although out of the spotlight, women's rights advocates did not quit. Through the 1950s, the Women's Bureau continued to promote (although without success) an equal pay law and the NWP continued to work for passage of the ERA.[257]

THE SECOND WAVE OF FEMINISM

By 1960, the dissatisfaction of many women with their limited roles began to surface. Increasingly, women found that their lives were at odds with the images of women presented by the media. Sara Evans writes, "The mass media in 1960, including the *New York Times, Newsweek, Redbook, Time, Harper's Bazaar,* and CBS Television, suddenly discovered the 'trapped housewife.'"[258] After 1957, marriage ages began to rise and birthrates to fall, helped by the introduction in 1960 of the birth control pill.[259]

The larger social and political climate began to change; the civil rights, student and renewed peace movements were in their early stages and John Kennedy, as the newly elected President, encouraged civic participation. Furthermore the United States began to worry that "underemployed women" were a "wasted resource" as the country rushed to compete with the Soviet Union after it sent the first satellite into space in 1957.[260] The stage was set for the second wave of feminism — activism for women's rights and women's liberation during the 1960s and 1970s.

One of the early voices advocating full participation of women in society was Betty Friedan, a homemaker and mother and 1942 graduate of Smith College. Friedan sent questionnaires to her former classmates as a project for their 15th college reunion. Of her classmates who did not work outside the home, most reported that they were not fulfilled by their roles as housewives and they regretted — as did Friedan — not putting their educations to use.[261]

After interviewing hundreds more women, Friedan published *The Feminine Mystique* in 1963, in which she charged that women's magazines, as well as psychologists and educators helped create and perpetuate the myth of the happy homemaker.[262] Friedan wrote of "the problem that has no name — which is simply the fact that American women are kept from growing to their full human capacities — [and which] is taking a far greater toll on the physical and mental health of our country than any known disease."[263] Friedan argued that women did not have to give up their families, but that they could do more; they could have a career, a choice.[264]

Excerpts of her book appeared in magazines, as did articles about Friedan, describing her as an "angry battler for her sex."[265] She began to speak to audiences around the country. Women wrote to thank her, saying that her book had allowed them to see that

their depression and dissatisfaction were normal reactions to the narrow range of experiences life offered them.[266] Friedan wrote that women were "so ashamed to admit [their] dissatisfaction that [they] never knew how many other women shared it."[267]

In the same year that *The Feminine Mystique* was published, 1963, the President's Commission on the Status of Women, created in 1961 by President John Kennedy, published *American Women.*[268] The report "documented in great detail problems of discrimination in employment, unequal pay, lack of social services such as child care, and continuing legal inequality" and strongly supported a federal equal pay act but not the ERA.[269] Eleanor Roosevelt, as chairperson and Esther Peterson, as executive vice-chair, led the federal commission, and most states also set up commissions on the status of women, which created and activated a network of professional women concerned about the issues of equal pay and employment discrimination, among others.[270]

Congress finally passed equal pay legislation in 1963. The Women's Bureau coalition again had initiated a campaign for an equal pay law in 1960, although by that time, women were concentrated in traditionally female jobs, and equal pay legislation would apply to few jobs.[271] The concentration of women into so-called female jobs had "reduced women's wages from 63.9 percent of men's in 1955 to only 60 percent in 1960."[272] The director of the Women's Bureau, Esther Peterson (see page 123), determined to demonstrate the need for an equal pay law, collected statistics and examples of unequal pay from all over the country.[273] When she pressed one manager to explain his practice of paying women lower wages than men for the same work, he said, "Mrs. Peterson, don't do this to me. You know we pay them less because we can get them for less."[274]

Although the bill faced opposition from business (the Chamber of Commerce organized a lobbying campaign to defeat it), as well as objections from the secretary of labor, W. William Wirtz, the bill eventually passed, in large part due to the efforts of Esther Peterson.[275] Congress passed the Equal Pay Act (making wage discrimination illegal), after adding weakening amendments, on June 10, 1963 — 18 years after it was first proposed.[276] The final version excluded many workers and had weak enforcement provisions, yet it symbolized, at last, acknowledgment by the federal government of women's necessary and legitimate participation in the labor force and the need to safeguard women's rights in the workplace.[277]

The next year, Congress passed the Civil Rights Act of 1964 which "strengthened voting rights and access to public education for African Americans and prohibited discrimination based on race in places of public accommodation, in federally assisted programs, and in employment."[278] The NWP campaigned to add the word "sex" to Title VII of the Act, which addressed employment discrimination.[279] The Women's Bureau coalition believed that sex discrimination should be addressed separately and that the proposed amendment might overturn protective labor laws. They also opposed the amendment because it might hurt chances of passing a strong civil rights bill to protect against racial discrimination which many women believed should be addressed before women's rights.[280]

The main force in Congress behind the inclusion of "sex" in Title VII was Martha W. Griffiths of Michigan, who served in the House of Representatives from 1955 to 1975. Griffiths argued that unless gender was added, the Act would fail to address black women. She argued:

In my judgment, the men who had written the ... Act had never even thought about the fact that black women would receive any rights or that white women did not have any. ... The Congress of the United States had never in 188 years considered how any bill would affect women. Women under our laws and our constitution simply were not people. ... Under any circumstances, I made up my mind that if such a bill were going to pass, it was going to carry a prohibition against discrimination on the basis of sex, and that both black and white women were going to take one modest step forward together.[281]

When the bill was discussed on the floor of the House of Representatives, in February 1964, Griffiths remembers the reaction of her colleagues:

During the entire debate [on the Civil Rights Act] there had been little if any laughter. No jokes had been uttered. But when Judge Smith offered the sex amendment and explained it, the House broke in to guffaws of laughter. Various women arose to speak for the amendment, and with each argument advanced, the men in the House laughed harder. [Reps.] Lee [Leonore] Sullivan of Missouri and Edna Kelly of New York were sitting in front of me. Lee turned around and ... said, "Martha, if you can't stop them from laughing, you simply do not have a chance." When I arose, I began by saying, "I presume that if there had been any necessity to point out that women were a second class sex, the laughter would have proved it." There was no further laughter.[282]

Although many supporters of the Civil Rights Act worried that the inclusion of "sex" would hurt the bill's chances of passage, the U.S. House of Representatives voted in favor of the amendment 168 to 133.[283] A woman in the gallery shouted, "We made it! We are human!"[284] Two days later the House passed the entire bill. The Senate also passed the civil rights bill, with the sex discrimination clause included, by a vote of 76 to 18.[285]

Rep. Griffiths recalled the first successful lawsuit under Title VII for women: "The Bell System was sued for back pay for women. They had women who had been ... long distance operators for a period of twenty years who were drawing less than cleaners, all of whom were males, were drawing their first day on the job. Those women sued, and, as I remember, they received $26 million in back pay."[286] By the late 1960s, women began to successfully use Title VII to challenge the practice of companies denying jobs to women because of state protective labor laws.[287]

The Civil Rights Act of 1964 had a particular impact on black women as economic opportunities broadened beyond domestic or other segregated jobs or professional jobs solely within the African American community.[288] "The proportion of black women in clerical and sales jobs increased between 1960 and 1970 from 17 to 33 percent in northern states and from 3 to 11 percent in the South. The proportion of black women in domestic service dropped from 36 percent in 1960 to 15 percent in 1970," writes Sara Evans.[289]

However, at first, the sex amendment was considered a joke by most of the members of the Equal Employment Opportunities Commission (EEOC), the body charged with enforcing it. The administrator of the EEOC commented, "It will give men equal opportunities to be *Playboy* bunnies."[290]

THE NATIONAL ORGANIZATION FOR WOMEN

In April 1966 the EEOC issued guidelines permitting newspapers to segregate help wanted ads by sex without any restriction, despite ruling earlier that, under Title VII of the 1964 Civil Rights Act, want-ads could not be segregated by race.[291] In June, Rep. Griffiths called the EEOC's decision to allow newspapers to continue the practice of segregating jobs as "female" or "male" as "nothing more than arbitrary arrogance, disregard of law, and a manifestation of flat hostility to the human rights of women."[292]

Catherine East, the executive secretary of the President's Commission on the Status of Women, wanted to use the anger in Griffiths' speech to inspire the creation of "an NAACP for women."[293] She made copies of Griffiths' speech to bring to the third National Conference of State Commissions on the Status of Women in June 1966.[294] She spoke to author Betty Friedan about helping to start an organization to represent the interests of women.[295] Friedan and several delegates, including women from the United Auto Workers, discovered that the conference would not allow them to propose any resolutions. Consequently, they decided a women's organization separate from the President's Commission was necessary and met to discuss a name for the organization and make small contributions to its treasury.[296]

On June 29, 1966, the women launched the National Organization for Women (NOW) "to take action to bring women into full participation in the mainstream of American society now, assuming all the privileges and responsibilities thereof in truly equal partnership with men."[297]

The first official act of NOW, in December 1967, was to petition the federal EEOC and picket regional EEOC offices (the first women's rights demonstrations in five decades) to demand a ban on sex segregated help wanted ads based on Title VII of the Civil Rights Act.[298] NOW members "dumped bundles of newspapers onto the floor of the EEOC in protest."[299] After months of pressure, the EEOC ruled in NOW's favor, but the American Newspaper Publishers Association sued the EEOC, claiming that the issue, raised by a "minuscule group of no consequence," would confuse readers and carry high costs.[300] NOW members met with *New York Times* executives, but could not change their opposition to non-segregated ads. NOW members repeatedly picketed the *New York Times* for over a year.[301] Finally, in 1973, the Supreme Court upheld the EEOC ban on segregated help wanted ads.[302]

NOW also petitioned the EEOC to protest the forced retirement of female flight attendants — then called stewardesses — when they married or reached the age of 32.[303] When the chief personnel officer at United Airlines told Martha Griffiths that the reason for this practice was that United Airlines stewardesses had to be young, single and attractive, she wrote to him and asked, "What are you running, an airlines or a whore house?"[304] The EEOC prohibited the policy in 1968.[305]

At NOW's 1968 national conference, NOW members voted to support women's right to reproductive freedom, including abortion. Several lawyers who wanted to concentrate on legal and economic issues left NOW to form the Women's Equity Action League.[306] NOW members also voted to endorse passage of the ERA which caused members of the United Auto Workers to withdraw over the issue of protective labor legislation.[307] But NOW's concentration on the ERA over the next several years resulted in Congress holding hearings on the ERA in 1970.[308]

THE WOMEN'S LIBERATION MOVEMENT

Meanwhile, younger women, many of whom were active in the civil rights and student movements, joined the cause for women's rights. Young women were influenced deeply by the strong leadership roles of women, including Ella Baker and Fannie Lou

Hamer, in the civil rights movement.[309] In addition, the community organizing projects of Students for a Democratic Society (SDS) "offered women opportunities to develop leadership skills and political analysis talents, as well as supplying role models — all of which they later used to begin a new women's movement."[310] Gradually, women involved in the movements of the 1960s became critical of their sexist treatment by male co-workers.

Women's rights leader Robin Morgan recalled of the male student movement leaders, "Thinking we were involved in the struggle to build a new society, it was a slowly dawning and depressing realization that we were doing the same work and playing the same roles *in* the Movement as out of it: typing the speeches that men delivered, making coffee but not policy ..."[311]

In 1965, Mary King and Casey Hayden, active in the civil rights movement with the Student Non-Violent Coordinating Committee, wrote a position paper called "Sex and Caste" which criticized the subordinate role of women in the movement. But the male leaders within the civil rights and student movements did not take the issue of women's rights seriously. When women at a SDS conference the next year demanded a plank addressing their concerns, they were laughed out of the conference.[312]

Many of these women began to meet with each other to form a separate movement. They used their organizing skills to set up small "consciousness-raising" discussion groups, which quickly multiplied across the country. As historian Sara Evans describes these groups, "The early meetings were intense and exhilarating. In a style they had learned in the civil rights movement and the new left, women explored the political meaning of their personal experiences. Again and again, individuals were shocked to discover that their lives were not unique but part of a larger pattern. The warm support and understanding of other women empowered them as they reclaimed the lost legacy of sisterhood."[313]

The younger, more radical women made up what the media called the "women's liberation movement."[314] By the mid-1960s, radical women's groups, including the Redstockings, Cell 16, the Feminists and New

York Radical Feminists, critical of NOW's mainstream values, began to emerge.[315] "Whereas liberal feminism [groups including NOW] sought to include women in the mainstream, radical feminism embodied a rejection of the mainstream itself," writes historian Alice Echols.[316]

The women's liberation groups criticized traditional marriage and family for putting women in an inferior position.[317] They argued that sexism (a term they coined) was not merely an attitude but was "embedded in law, tradition, economics, education, organized religion, science, language, the mass media, sexual morality, child rearing, the domestic division of labor, and everyday social interaction — whose intent and effect was to give men power over women."[318]

The first major campaign of women's liberation groups was to win the right to reproductive freedom, including repeal of laws making abortion illegal.[319] Women held speak-outs, beginning in 1969, where they publicly told of their abortion experiences.[320] The women's liberation movement also helped generate a movement for gay rights and liberation.[321]

The women's liberation movement used various direct action tactics to call public attention to the issues of women's equality. For example, at the 1968 Miss America pageant, protestors picketed to protest the sexist image of women that the pageant promoted.[322] And in March of 1970, 200 women occupied the editorial offices of the popular women's magazine *Ladies' Home Journal* to protest its low ratio of female and minority staff members and lack of equal wages and child care.[323] The publishers responded by allowing the group to edit a one-time supplement to the magazine with articles addressing "sex discrimination in the labor force and education, childbirth, divorce, appearance and beauty, love, sex and how to start a consciousness-raising group."[324]

THE MODERN MOVEMENT MAKES CHANGE: 50 YEARS AFTER SUFFRAGE

The year 1970 marked the 50th anniversary of ratification of the Nineteenth Amendment — guaranteeing women the right to vote. NOW and women's liberation groups organized a national Women's Strike for

Equality on August 26, 1970.[325] Thousands of women marched in demonstrations across the country.[326] The action was designed in part to unite factions of the women's movement and to focus on the unfinished agenda including "equal opportunity for jobs and education, the right to abortion and child-care centers, the right to [women's] share of political power."[327] It was the first nationwide action of women since the campaign for suffrage.[328]

After observing the Women's Strike for Equality march in New York City, columnist Pete Hamill conceded, "The laughing and the snickering are now officially over." What had been "a cocktail party topic, a media fad or a slightly obscene joke" is a movement that is "only beginning."[329]

In May of 1970, Congress held hearings on the ERA for the first time since 1956.[330] The Women's Bureau reversed its long-standing opposition to the amendment, ending nearly 50 years of division on the issue within the women's movement.[331] Rep. Griffiths, who was leading the fight for the ERA, addressed the Judiciary Committee on the merits of the proposed amendment:

> *Women, like their male counterparts, should be judged by the law as individuals, not as a class of inferior beings. This is all the ERA would do. It would not take women out of the home. It would not downgrade the roles of mother and housewife. Indeed, it would give new dignity to these important roles. By confirming women's equality under the law, by upholding women's right to choose her place in society, the ERA can only enhance the status of traditional women's occupations. For these would become positions accepted by women as equals, not roles imposed on them as inferiors.[332]*

Following Griffiths' appeal, the Judiciary Committee moved the amendment to the full House — the first time it had been debated on the floor of the House of Representatives since 1948. By 1972, both the House of Representatives and the Senate had passed the ERA. The amendment retained Alice Paul's wording and a deadline was set for ratification by 1979. By the end of 1972, 22 state legislatures had approved the ERA (amendments must be ratified by the legislatures of or by conventions in three-fourths of the states).[333]

Betty Friedan, Rep. Shirley Chisholm (D-NY) and Rep. Bella Abzug (D-NY), founded the National Women's Political Caucus in 1971 to increase the number of women in politics.[334] Chisholm, the first black woman elected to Congress, ran for the Democratic nomination for President in 1972.[335] And by the 1972 presidential nominating conventions, women's issues had gained enough legitimacy to secure commitments from both the Democratic and Republican Parties on child care and pre-school and after-school programs for children.[336] The number of women participating in the conventions as delegates rose dramatically: women made up 40 percent of delegates to the Democratic Convention (increasing from 13 percent in 1968) and 30 percent at the Republican convention (up from 17 percent in 1968).[337]

In 1971, *New York* magazine published a 40-page special supplement, edited by journalist Gloria Steinem, increasingly a spokeswoman for women's equality. The supplement was named *Ms.*, a term found in a 1930s secretarial handbook as the proper address for a woman when her marital status is unknown. Encouraged by its instant success, its editors raised money to publish *Ms.* on a regular basis. The new magazine, completely controlled by women, quickly became an important voice for the women's movement.[338]

The National Association for Repeal of Abortion Law (later renamed the National Abortion Rights Action League) formed in 1970. That same year, the state of Hawaii repealed its law prohibiting abortion.[339] And in 1973, the Supreme Court ruling *Roe* v. *Wade* invalidated state laws prohibiting abortion in the first three months of pregnancy.[340]

Women's liberation groups held speak-outs on rape, where victims publicly spoke about their experiences.[341] The first "Take Back the Night" march was held in 1977, as "thousands of women across the country marched to show their solidarity and their right to walk the streets at night."[342] Throughout the 1970s, these groups also set up institutions such as rape crisis centers, battered women's shelters and women's health clinics to offer, if not solutions, at least relief from some problems particular to women.[343]

The number of women seeking higher education during the 1970s rose dramatically. In 1970, only 8.4 percent of medical school graduates and 5.4 percent of law school graduates were women. By 1979, those percentages rose to 23 percent for medical school and 28.5 percent for law school.[344] In addition, women fought to include women's history and women's issues in the curricula of universities across the country. Women's studies courses began in 1970 and by 1975, 150 universities offered such programs. By 1980, universities listed 30,000 courses about women.[345]

AFRICAN AMERICAN WOMEN AND THE SECOND WAVE OF FEMINISM

Many African American women rejected the white-dominated women's movement which they saw as ignoring and, in some cases, disrespectful of their needs.[346] The division between black and white women was due in large part to the enormous difference between their experiences. Cynthia Washington, a program director of the civil rights group Student Nonviolent Coordinating Committee, said, "It seemed to many of us ... that white women were demanding a chance to be independent while we needed help and assistance which was not always forthcoming."[347] In addition, many black women concentrated their efforts in the Civil Rights movement, as many believed the fight against racism should take precedence over the fight against sexism.[348]

Furthermore, when white, upper-middle-class women complained about their boring lives in the suburbs, many black women wondered how they could complain about the luxury of not having to work. The issues which were often central concerns for middle-class white women, such as the right to enter the professions on an equal basis with men, were less important to low-income and black women for whom it was often a daily struggle just to feed and house themselves and their families.[349] However, by the late 1970s, a black feminist movement emerged and many women's groups came to the conclusion that racism and sexism could best be addressed together.[350]

WOMEN'S ACTIVISM AND THE BACKLASH AGAINST FEMINISM

The second wave of feminism achieved significant gains for women and forced issues of concern to women onto the public agenda and into the decisions of policy makers. Nevertheless, the women's movement came under siege during the late 1970s and the 1980s as the government, media and new right activists blamed feminism for a range of problems. In her book *Backlash: The Undeclared War Against American Women*, Susan Faludi argues that a "backlash" against the gains of the 1970s women's movement tried to convince women that independence and equality lead to unhappy lives, and has put women, and feminists in particular, on the defensive.[351] However, women's groups continue to work on a wide variety of issues to protect the gains of the second wave of feminism as well as bringing new issues to the public agenda.

In the late 1970s, groups of women, led by Phyllis Schlafly's STOP ERA, began to emerge around the country to oppose ratification of the ERA on the grounds that it would destroy the American family by encouraging more women to work and to leave their children in day care centers.[352] But record numbers of women were entering the workforce in the 1970s without the benefit of the ERA. By 1980, 51.5 percent of all adult women held jobs outside the home including more than 60 percent of women with children between the ages of six and 17.[353]

Although ERA advocates, led by NOW president Eleanor Smeal, successfully lobbied Congress to extend the deadline for ratification of the ERA to 1982, ratification was not achieved.[354] Rep. Griffiths offered an explanation for why the ERA failed, pointing to interests that she believed were operating behind the scenes:

I think what has really happened is that commercial interests opposed ERA ... [including] insurance firms, particularly those that insure health for men and women, because women are ... paying much more than men ... [T]he thing is to me just awful is that the groups who have opposed it, the commer-

*cial groups, have never had the moral cour-
age to say something ... But I am sure that
they are in the background, and that they are
talking to legislators and helping legislators
run campaigns and so forth and so on, and I
think that the second thing that is really
wrong about it is that the press media has to
know this ... [but] [t]hey've never said a
word.*[355]

In addition to the formation of groups opposed to the
ERA, a movement emerged in favor of repealing
abortion laws and further restricting women's reproductive freedom.[356] Aided by the support of both
Presidents Ronald Reagan and George Bush, the anti-
abortion campaign "led to prohibitive rules and
consent and notification regulations in more than 30
states."[357] In 1989, the Supreme Court, in *Webster* v.
Reproductive Health Services, upheld state restrictions
on abortion.[358] However, the majority of Americans
continued to support the Supreme Court's decision in
Roe v. *Wade*, which legalized abortion.[359]

Protection of reproductive rights for women inspired
direct action among women's groups, including the
National Abortion Rights Action League (NARAL),
Planned Parenthood and the National Organization for
Women, in the 1980s and 1990s. Women held marches around the country to support the right of women
to choose whether or not to have an abortion. Many
communities have established networks of people who
can be mobilized on short notice to attend a "clinic
defense," in which pro-choice activists help women to
enter clinics which anti-abortion activists have
blocked. And the National Women's Health Network,
Planned Parenthood and numerous other organizations
encourage development of a wider range of safe and
effective forms of birth control.

Student feminists have been particularly active on the
reproductive rights issue. NARAL, as of 1991, had
more than 500 campus organizers.[360] Students Organizing Students, a network which organizes for
reproductive rights at over 175 schools, launched a
boycott of Domino's Pizza because the company
donated money to anti-abortion organizations. The
boycott helped lead to the resignation of Domino's
CEO Tom Monaghan.[361]

Despite the political and personal gains of the second
wave of feminism, the economic status of a large
number of women worsened. Diana Pearce coined the
phrase "feminization of poverty" in 1978 to describe
how the burden of poverty in the United States was
increasingly being borne by women. Pearce pointed to
several "economic and social consequences of being
female that result in higher rates of poverty."[362] These
consequences include the concentration of women in
low-paying, temporary jobs; the lack of mandated and
enforced child support payments to divorced mothers;
the decline in funding of government programs which
aid low-income, single mothers; and job training
programs which perpetuate female poverty by training
women to work in "traditional, low-paying, predominantly female" occupations.[363]

By 1991, only 9 percent of working women were in
occupations which are not traditionally female-dominated — jobs in which 25 percent or less of the
workforce is female.[364] And working women were
almost twice as likely as men to earn minimum wage
or less.[365] The feminization of poverty affects women
of color in greater proportion than white women.
Women of color, who face the "double discrimination" of race and sex, account for the highest percentage of female-headed households and for the highest
percentage of families that live in poverty.[366]

One consequence of the feminization of poverty is
that, since women tend overwhelmingly to be the
primary caregivers for children, the proportion of
children in poverty increases as poverty for women
increases. And research shows that children raised in
poverty are more likely to grow up to be impover-
ished.[367] The feminization of poverty became more
prevalent during the early 1980s as "budget cuts in
the first four years of the Reagan administration alone
pushed nearly two million female-headed families and
nearly five million women below the poverty line."[368]

A number of women's groups, including the Center
for Women Policy Studies, the Institute for Women's
Policy Research, Wider Opportunities for Women
(WOW) and the Women's Legal Defense Fund,
responded in a variety of ways to bring the economic
problems of women to the public's attention. Wider
Opportunities for Women, founded in 1964, has

advocated economic independence and equal employment opportunity for women and offered skills training and job placement for women.[369] The Women's Legal Defense Fund (WLDF), founded in 1971, works to strengthen the child support awards system to help alleviate the growing poverty among single mothers and their children. WLDF also works to eliminate the double discrimination faced by women of color by working for enforcement of policies and laws that protect employment rights.[370]

One-third of President Ronald Reagan's budget cuts in domestic programs were in programs that predominately serve women.[371] For example, although the number of sex discrimination complaints women filed with the EEOC rose nearly 25 percent between 1982 and 1988, President Reagan cut the EEOC budget in half, forcing the agency to cut back the number of suits it pursued by 300 percent.[372] As a result, according to a report by the House Education and Labor Committee, in the first half of the 1980s, the number of victims receiving compensation for sexual discrimination fell by two-thirds.[373] And while violence against women rose, the federal government stalled funding and defeated bills for battered women's programs and shelters, and shut down its Office of Domestic Violence just two years after it had opened in 1979.[374]

Many groups work to strengthen laws against domestic violence and rape, including the National Clearinghouse on Marital and Date Rape and the National Coalition Against Domestic Violence. Students have raised awareness about date rape as well as sexual harassment on college campuses and forced administrators to adopt stricter disciplinary procedures for dealing with offenders.[375]

Popular culture asserted that women had "made it" — they had achieved full economic, political and social equality. However, full equality was not the reality for the vast majority of women. Journalist Susan Faludi reports that the wage gap between women and men in 1986 was the same as in 1955 — a woman working full-time made only 64 cents to a man's dollar.[376] By the late 1980s and early 1990s, a female college graduate, on average, earned less than a man with no college education; and 80 percent of women still worked in traditional "female jobs" as secretaries, administrative support workers and salesclerks.[377]

Furthermore, women made up less than 8 percent of all federal and state judges, less than 6 percent of all partners in law firms, and less than .5 percent of top corporate managers. Only three states had female governors and only two women held seats in the U.S. Senate.[378]

To promote equality for women, the National Women's Political Caucus has continued to work to elect and appoint more women to government offices with the goal of "gender-balanced government that reflects and supports women in all their diversity."[379] The Fund for the Feminist Majority has campaigned in state legislatures for "gender balance laws" which require "the appointment of equal numbers of women and men to all public boards, commissions, committees and councils."[380] The states of Iowa and North Dakota have gender balance laws in effect which require the appointment of women as much as possible.[381] And at its 1989 annual conference, the National Organization for Women began to explore the possibility of forming a new political party more responsive to women's issues.[382]

The National Woman's Party continues to work for the Equal Rights Amendment. The Party reintroduces the legislation at every session of Congress. Before each session, the Party surveys every member of the House and Senate, asking for support and co-sponsorship. The survey results are entered into a computer data base which records the position of every Member of Congress on the amendment. The Party also works to educate its members and, through coalitions with other women's organizations, spurs ERA supporters across the country to call and write to their congressional representatives to ask them to support the ERA.[383]

CONCLUSION

Media reports in the 1980s made much of "the death of feminism" and the "experiment that failed" and women who refused to call themselves feminists. Women's issues suffered setbacks as the federal government eliminated programs and enforcement efforts.[384] Yet women continued to fight to preserve the gains of the first and second waves of feminism and to bring new issues to the public agenda. And although the issues of women's equality are far from resolved, the accomplishments of women throughout U.S. history have made it easier for women today to make their voices heard and to prepare for a third wave of feminist activity.[385]

BIBLIOGRAPHY

Amott, Teresa and Julie Matthaei. *Race, Gender, and Work: A Multicultural Economic History of Women in the United States*. Boston: South End Press, 1991.

Brown, Dorothy M. *Setting a Course: American Women in the 1920s*. Boston: Twayne Publishers, 1987.

Buechler, Steven M. *Women's Movements in the United States: Woman Suffrage, Equal Rights and Beyond*. New Brunswick, NJ: Rutgers University Press, 1990.

Buhle, Mari Jo and Paul Buhle, eds. *The Concise History of Woman Suffrage: Selections from the Classic Work of Stanton, Anthony, Gage and Harper*. Urbana: University of Illinois Press, 1978.

Campbell, D'Ann. *Women at War with America: Private Lives in a Patriotic Era*. Cambridge, MA: Harvard University Press, 1984.

Cohen, Marcia. *The Sisterhood: The Inside Story of the Women's Movement and the Leaders Who Made it Happen*. New York: Fawcett Columbine, 1988.

Davis, Marianna W., ed. *Contributions of Black Women to America*. Volume II. Columbia, SC: Kenday Press, 1981.

DuBois, Ellen Carol, ed. *Elizabeth Cady Stanton, Susan B. Anthony: Correspondence, Writings, Speeches*. New York: Schocken Books, 1981.

DuBois, Ellen Carol. *Feminism and Suffrage: The Emergence of an Independent Women's Movement in America 1848-1869*. Ithaca, NY: Cornell University Press, 1978.

Echols, Alice. *Daring to Be Bad: Radical Feminism in America, 1967-1975*. Minneapolis: University of Minnesota Press, 1989.

Evans, Sara M. *Born for Liberty: A History of Women in America*. New York: The Free Press, 1989.

Evans, Sara M. *Personal Politics*. New York: Vintage Books, 1980.

Faludi, Susan. *Backlash: The Undeclared War Against American Women*. New York: Crown Publishers, Inc., 1991.

Farnham, Marynia L. Foot and Ferdinand Lundberg. *Modern Woman: The Lost Sex*. New York: Harper and Brothers, 1947.

Field, Connie, producer and director. *The Life and Times of Rosie the Riveter* (film). Emeryville, CA: Clarity Educational Productions, 1980.

Flander, Judy. "Jeannette Rankin Meets Her 'Crush' — Mr. Nader," Washington, DC *Evening Star and Daily News*. September 2, 1972.

Flexner, Eleanor. *Century of Struggle: The Woman's Rights Movement in the United States*. Revised edition. Cambridge, MA: The Belknap Press of Harvard University Press, 1975 [1959].

Frank, Miriam, Marilyn Ziebarth and Connie Field. *The Life and Times of Rosie the Riveter: The Story of 3 Million Working Women During World War II*. Educator's edition. Emeryville, CA: Clarity Educational Productions, 1982.

Friedan, Betty. *The Feminine Mystique*. New York: Laurel Books, 1973 [1963].

Gibbs, Nancy. "The War Against Feminism," *Newsweek*. March 9, 1992.

"Give Back Their Jobs," *Woman's Home Companion*. October 1943.

Griffiths, Martha W. *New York Times* Oral History Program - Former Members of Congress. Number 32: Martha W. Griffiths, Member of Congress from Michigan, 1955-1975.

Gurko, Miriam. *The Ladies of Seneca Falls: The Birth of the Woman's Rights Movement*. New York: MacMillan Publishing Co., 1974.

Harrison, Cynthia. *On Account of Sex: The Politics of Women's Issues 1945-1968*. Berkeley: University of California Press, 1988.

Hartmann, Susan M. *The Home Front and Beyond: American Women in the 1940s*. Boston: Twayne Publishers, 1982.

Houppert, Karen. "Wildflowers Among the Ivy: New Campus Radicals," *Ms.* September/October 1991.

Jacobs, Harriet A. *Incidents in the Life of a Slave Girl, Written by Herself.* Cambridge, MA: Harvard University Press, 1987 [1861].

Kaledin, Eugenia. *Mothers and More: American Women in the 1950s.* Boston: Twayne Publishers, 1984.

Kava, Beth Millstein and Jeanne Bodin. *We, the American Women: A Documentary History.* Revised edition. Chicago: Science Research Associates, Inc., 1983 [1977].

Kerber, Linda K. and Jane Sherron DeHart, eds. *Women's America: Refocusing the Past.* Third edition. New York: Oxford University Press, 1991.

Lapin, Eva. *Mothers in Overalls* (pamphlet). New York: Workers Library Publishers, 1943.

Lerner, Gerda. *The Woman in American History.* Menlo Park, CA: Addison-Wesley Publishing, Co., 1971.

Lerner, Gerda, ed. *Black Women in White America: A Documentary History.* New York: Random House, 1972.

McCulley, Carol and Diana Morley. *Jeannette Rankin: First Woman in Congress.* Windsor, CA: National Women's History Project, 1989.

Milgram, Donna. "Passing the NEW Act," *Women at Work* (Washington, DC: National Commission on Working Women and the Women's Work Force Network of Wider Opportunities for Women). Fall/Winter 1991-92.

Morgan, Robin, ed. *Sisterhood is Powerful: An Anthology of Writings from the Women's Liberation Movement.* New York: Vintage Books, 1970.

Pearce, Diana M. "The Feminization of Poverty: Women, Work and Welfare," *Urban and Social Change Review.* Winter/Spring 1978.

Pressman, Steven. "The Feminization of Poverty: Causes and Remedies," *Challenge.* March/April 1988.

Ross, Susan Deller and Ann Barcher. *The Rights of Women: The Basic ACLU Guide to a Woman's Rights.* Toronto: Bantam Books, 1984.

Rupp, Leila J. and Verta Taylor. *Survival in the Doldrums: The American Women's Rights Movement, 1945 to the 1960s.* New York: Oxford University Press, 1987.

"Sharp Tongue at 91: Across 9 Decades: Jeannette Rankin," *SRS News.* January 1970.

Smeal, Ellie. "Why I Support a New Party," *Ms.* January/February 1991.

Smith, Norma. "The Woman Who Said No to War: A Day in the Life of Jeannette Rankin," *Ms.* March 1986.

Stanton, Elizabeth Cady. *The Woman's Bible.* New York: European Publishing Co., 1892-1898.

United States President's Commission on the Status of Women. *American Women: The Report of the President's Commission on the Status of Women.* Washington, DC: Government Printing Office, 1963.

Walker, Rebecca. "Becoming the Third Wave," *Ms.* January/February 1992.

Wandersee, Winifred D. *On the Move: American Women in the 1970s.* Boston: Twayne Publishers, 1988.

Winestine, Belle Fligelman. "Mother Was Shocked," *Montana: The Magazine of Western History.* Summer 1974. Vol. XXIV. No. 3.

A HISTORY OF THE
CONSUMER MOVEMENT

INTRODUCTION

Before 1800, most American households produced their own goods to meet nearly all their basic needs. As mass production technology improved, Americans began to buy more household goods than they produced at home, including food products such as flour, baking powder, chocolate, coffee, tea, oil and other staples.[1] This trend was spurred by the ability to manufacture inexpensively large quantities of household goods and distribute them over long distances and by increasing urbanization.[2] As this process took place, although consumers benefitted from less expensive, more abundant goods, problems also began to arise for consumers.

Mass production led to surges in supply or demand, more instability in the marketplace and new products on the market which often presented safety and health risks to consumers. Instability in the marketplace led to economic crises and uncompetitive practices which made it difficult for many firms to stay in business. The federal government responded by regulating the economy to maintain stability in the marketplace for such industries as railroads [and] banking and financial markets."[3] The government implemented these regulations to benefit business, but the promotion of stability also had benefits for consumers.

Adulteration of food and marketing of unsafe and ineffective drugs increased as the number of new consumer products on the market increased. Consumers organized campaigns which led the federal government to intervene in the economy, primarily to benefit consumers, with regulations designed to protect consumers from dangerous products and deceptive claims.

But government intervention in the economy is not always enough to ensure the protection or the interests of consumers. The agencies authorized to implement laws are subject to political manipulation and enforce regulations more stringently at some times than at others.[4] And laws to regulate competition in the marketplace or set standards for product safety do little to empower consumers "to initiate or challenge any of the numerous economic and safety rules regarding food, drugs, transportation, communications, housing, banking, insurance, energy, health and other services."[5]

Moreover, although Adam Smith wrote in *The Wealth of Nations*[6] in 1776 that "[c]onsumption is the sole end and purpose of production; and the interest of the producer ought to be attended to, only so far as it may be necessary for promoting that of the consumer,"[7] producers are motivated by profit and not by the interests of consumers. Although consumers often have significant choices among products offered by producers, consumers do not significantly influence what and when real choices are offered.[8]

To counter the ineffectiveness or unpredictability of government regulation and the profit motive of producers, consumers sometimes have banded together to gain autonomy in the marketplace through cooperatives, buying clubs and other forms of consumer empowerment.

ECONOMIC REGULATION

The increase in industrialization in the mid to late 19th century created problems for companies that often had a negative effect on consumers. Competition within some industries was so chaotic that no single firm could survive.[9] In response, large corporations joined together to create trusts with the "intent of controlling production, prices, and profits" in a particular industry, as did the Standard Oil Trust of the oil industry.[10] The trusts made it difficult for companies outside of the trust to compete in that particular industry. In both instances, consumers suffered from the instability of the market. Chaotic competition resulted in economic crises including depressions. And uncompetitive practices such as formation of trusts led to concentration of power that in many cases took away incentives, which in a competitive market would force producers to provide consumers with quality products at a low price.

To attempt to achieve some control of such economic abuses, government regulated business. These efforts were not on behalf of consumers. Rather they were efforts to facilitate free commerce.[11] In 1887, Congress created the Interstate Commerce Commission to regulate the railroad industry. The act was "the first comprehensive regulation of a particular industry ... and established the precedent of the independent regulatory commission."[12] And in 1890, Congress passed the Sherman Anti-Trust Act which declared trusts and other forms of monopolization illegal. But because the Act was weakly enforced, "the greatest wave of trust formation came in the two decades *after* its passage. By 1904, some 318 trusts were alleged to control two-fifths of the manufacturing assets in the United States."[13]

Congress created the Federal Trade Commission in 1914 to control unfair methods of competition such as monopolies or deceptive trade practices.[14] The FTC "was full of regulatory fervor during its 'youth,' but by the 1920s the commission was less inclined to interfere in all but the most extreme cases."[15]

EARLY CONSUMER ACTION

Before the turn of the century, consumers had few protections; in fact, individuals rarely thought of themselves as consumers. But the trend away from individual production of basic needs such as food and clothing and toward the industrial mass production of these needs left consumers vulnerable to unsafe and unhealthy products on the market. Women were most affected by the move to mass production because their role changed from producer to purchaser and because they made most of the decisions about what to buy and where to buy it. Women were the first to examine the problems, and to take action, on behalf of consumers.

In the early 1800s, cook books began to be published which covered many aspects of women's new role as purchaser. By the mid-1800s, guides to living within a particular income appeared. But women's magazines were most important in providing women with advice

about buying the new products on the market. Magazines including *The Delineator*, *Woman's Home Companion*, *Ladies Home Journal*, *Harper's Bazaar* and *Good Housekeeping* appeared in the 1870s and 1880s with domestic advice aimed at middle class housewives.[16]

As historian Peter Samson writes, "*Good Housekeeping* in particular, and women's magazines in general, successively assumed the task of 'consciousness raising' for the woman consumer. These magazines offered information about new products, recommended specific products and retailers and set standards for advertisers to ensure the reliability of the ads."[17] In 1894, *Ladies Home Journal* refused all advertisements disguised as reading material and established money back guarantees for products advertised in their pages.[18]

The women's magazines concerned themselves particularly with the issue of pure food.[19] As more and more people bought mass-produced goods instead of producing their own or buying from local merchants; adulteration — adding another substance to food, making it impure or of lesser quality — became widespread. Peter Samson writes, "Adulterants such as sand, saw dust, and other common substances [had] long been falsely represented as flour, coffee, tea, cocoa, and spices, while milk [was] mixed with water, and substitutes used for grain in beer and grapes in wine."[20] But more sophisticated means of adulteration became common as advances were made in chemistry, making it easier to hide the impurities from consumers.[21]

During the 19th century, few states had laws governing food purity and where laws did exist, officials rarely enforced them.[22] In response, citizens organized various kinds of activity around the issue of pure food to educate the public and advocate federal legislation. Women's magazines, food exhibits and magazines, public officials, women's clubs and muckraking journalists joined the campaign for pure food.

Much of the consumer advice of women's magazines centered on consumer information on adulterated food and on medical and chemical research on food. In addition, the magazines supported new laws to protect consumers from adulterated food and misleading claims. *Good Housekeeping* issued materials to its readers about pure food issues and how to influence legislators hoping to "inspire women consumers to stand up for their own rights and interests."[23] *Good Housekeeping* also established its own testing institute and awarded the "*Good Housekeeping* Standard of Excellence" to deserving brands. At least until the 1920s, the magazine was careful to avoid the influence of advertisers who might threaten to remove their ads to influence decisions.[24]

During the last two decades of the 19th century, public exhibitions of food products became popular, educating consumers about a variety of issues as well as ensuring that producers at least give thought to the interests of consumers. Although the food exhibitions, which resembled miniature world's fairs with thousands of people visiting elaborate food displays, accompanied by bands and orchestras, "were fundamentally commercial, they nonetheless marked a

significant chapter in the growth of consumer consciousness."[25]

In addition to the magazines devoted to women's issues, a number focused solely on food. *The Analyst*, published from 1885 to 1892, set up its own chemical laboratory to test products. Testing led *The Analyst* to uncover that condensed milk manufacturers were distributing deceptively sized cans. *The Analyst* also conducted an investigation into wholesale and retail costs, in an attempt to determine the cause of rising beef prices.[26]

THE CAMPAIGN FOR PURE FOOD LEGISLATION

By 1900, awareness was high among the general public about the issues of food purity.[27] But the campaign to pass federal legislation had just begun. One important advocate in the campaign for pure food legislation was Dr. Harvey W. Wiley, who became head of the Department of Agriculture's Bureau of

Patent Medicines, early 20th century.

Chemistry in 1883.[28] While at the Bureau of Chemistry, Wiley began investigating food purity and the use of chemical preservatives in food.

Wiley also gave his attention to the safety and effectiveness of drugs. Patent medicines were in widespread use at the time. These products made elaborate claims to cure illnesses from diabetes to cancer and often contained such drugs as "opium, morphine, heroin and cocaine."[29] Patent medicines, in addition to being ineffective, were often dangerous in that they were sometimes addictive.[30] Wiley issued reports urging federal laws to better protect the consumer from dangerous and adulterated foods and drugs. Wiley became a popular speaker at women's clubs, civic and business organizations.[31]

In 1903, Wiley formed a volunteer "poison squad" of young men in the Bureau of Chemistry who volunteered to participate in an experiment to test the effects of eating food treated with chemical preservatives.[32] For five years, the volunteers ate only food with measured amounts of preservatives including salicylic, sulphurous, and benzoic acids; borax; and formaldehyde. Wiley's experiments led him to recommend that use of chemical preservatives be limited and that producers prove the safety of their products and inform consumers, on product labels, of the use of any chemicals.[33]

Although some businesses supported Dr. Wiley's proposal for a federal law, whiskey distillers and patent medicine firms, who were the largest advertisers in the country, argued that the federal government had no business controlling what people eat, drink or use for medicine.[34]

It took the actions of consumers to generate public support and convince Congress to introduce and debate such regulation.[35] Food and Drug Administration historian Wallace F. Janssen writes, "[T]he tide was turned ... when the voteless but militant club women of the country rallied to the pure food cause."[36] Wiley himself gave credit to the women's groups for the success of the campaign for pure food legislation.[37]

Cartoon criticizing Patent medicine manufacturers, early 20th century.

The General Federation of Women's Clubs organized a Pure Food Committee in 1904 to generate public support for the proposed legislation. The Committee organized exhibits, petitions and speeches.[38] Professor of Home Economics Helen Sorenson wrote that "Even though women did not have the vote at that time, their work was of great importance."[39] The General Federation also joined with the National Consumers League, which advocated better conditions for workers, and the State Food Commissioners to organize the American Pure Food League to coordinate their efforts on pure food issues.[40]

Good Housekeeping launched a campaign in October of 1901 to encourage passage of federal legislation. The magazine prepared and distributed to subscribers a "pure food outfit" with a survey of the pure food issues and recommendations for influencing legislators.[41]

Social reforms proposed during the Progressive Reform era included support for pure food legislation. Although the Progressive agenda called for broad government and corporate reforms, its general aim was to ensure that the interests of "the people" were protected against "special" interests such as the patent medicine manufacturers.[42] Muckraking journalists were proponents of various Progressive causes and when journalist Upton Sinclair wrote about the meatpacking industry in Chicago, he gave new impetus to the campaign for pure food.

The legislation was stalled in early 1906 in the House of Representatives. Then Upton Sinclair's *The Jungle*[43] was published. Although Sinclair's novel was also a critique of capitalism and the conditions under which meatpackers worked and their families lived, the public responded in horror to the quality of meat they were buying.[44]

The following passage from *The Jungle* describes how spoiled ham was made into sausage:

> *There would be meat stored in great piles in rooms; and the water from leaky roofs would drip over it, and thousands of rats would race about on it. It was too dark in these storage places to see well, but a man could run his hand over piles of meat and sweep off handfuls of the dried dung of rats. These rats were nuisances, and the packers would put poisoned bread out for them, they would die, and then rats, bread, and meat would go into the hoppers together.*[45]

President Theodore Roosevelt capitalized on the public outcry and urged Congress to act.[46] On the same day in June of 1906, Congress passed both the Pure Food and Drug Act, which prohibited the sale of adulterated food and drugs and the use of false or misleading claims, and the Meat Inspection Act, which regulated conditions in the meatpacking industry. By January of 1907, 17 states had established food commissions.[47]

One significant change brought about by the new food and drug law was product labeling. Although few products were banned, the act did require that labels tell the truth about the product's contents. Labels that had previously served as advertising for the manufacturer were now more useful information to the consumer.[48]

After the new legislation was passed, women's groups and magazines continued their pure food work by educating the public and monitoring enforcement of the new laws. Leaders of the New York State Federation of Women's Clubs established the Daily Food Alliance, which from 1913 to 1916 pressed public officials to fulfill their responsibilities in carrying out the new laws. The Alliance worked for sanitary practices in food handling and honest labels, weights and measures.[49]

In addition, a number of newspapers regularly ran columns and published exposés on food adulteration issues. Alfred McCann, in 1913, published *Starving America*,[50] which documented widespread food adulteration. McCann continued to fight for reform by writing a regular column for the *New York Globe* where his investigations resulted in the arrest of more than 200 violators of the food law in just one year.[51]

The Bureau of Chemistry, of which Harvey Wiley was director, was authorized to carry out the new food and drug law. Wiley took an active role in enforcing the law in favor of the consumer by taking violators to court.[52] Partly because of his tough enforcement, the food industry responded by establishing powerful lobbying organizations to represent its interests.[53]

President Theodore Roosevelt then appointed a five-member board to review the decisions of the Bureau of Chemistry. The board was not part of the Pure Food and Drug Act, yet according to author Mark Nadel, "[T]he secretary of agriculture followed the board's advice in almost all conflicts with the Bureau of Chemistry."[54] Approximately two-thirds of Wiley's recommendations to prosecute violators of the act were overturned by the board.[55]

Wiley resigned in protest in 1912 and began to direct *Good Housekeeping*'s Bureau of Foods, Sanitation and Health. He wrote regular columns in the magazine and became "in effect, America's first professional consumer advocate."[56] Through his position at *Good Housekeeping*, he carried out his work for food and drug safety and purity.

Although *Good Housekeeping* played a role in enforcing the new act and continued to be involved in consumer affairs, by the 1920s, the magazine had lost much of its influence. The pressure of advertisers forced the magazine to ease its criteria for its seal of approval.[57]

INFLATION SPURS NEW CONSUMER ACTION

The years between 1910 and 1920 were marked with a surge in grassroots consumer activity centered primarily around the issue of inflation, which by 1909, had begun to rise rapidly. Government agencies conducted studies of the cost of living. The statistics they began to collect as a matter of course included how and what Americans bought and how much they earned. Public interest in the government studies was intense and "the rising cost of living was on everybody's lips."[58]

Consumers nationwide reacted to rising prices by launching independent boycotts of meat in early 1910. Inflation hit meat prices particularly hard and meat packers, as a result of the controversy around Upton Sinclair's book *The Jungle*, were distrusted by the public. The meat boycott in Cleveland, Ohio, organized by the Central Labor Union, was the most widely observed boycott in the country with a reported 100,000 Clevelanders signing a pledge not to eat meat for 30 days. And in Baltimore, Maryland, boycott organizers distributed 50,000 buttons with the slogan "I Don't Eat Meat. Do You?"[59]

Although unions were instrumental in organizing the boycotts, the boycotts appealed to all kinds of people. For example, two lawyers in Boston organized a No Meat club; in New York, the Women's Progressive League started a boycott and an artist organized the West-Side Anti-Meat League.[60]

The boycotts temporarily lowered the price of meat and were responsible for closing a few packing plants and retail meat markets, but their overall impact was minimal and short-lived. High prices led consumers to participate in the boycotts but a lack of organization and immediate gains led many consumers to give up too soon to have any real impact. Regardless of the outcome, the boycotts did set a precedent for independent consumer action.[61]

THE HOUSEWIVES LEAGUE

In 1911, housewives in New York City met informally to discuss prices at local groceries. They formed a new group, the Housewives League, which became an important force in the consumer movement. Members of the League agreed to shop only at stores which charged the lowest prices for given items, launched a successful boycott of butter in 1912 and encouraged the New York State legislature to pass legislation requiring packaged goods to carry labels specifying the weight or volume of the contents.[62]

The League's leader, Jeannie Dewey Heath, a full-time consumer advocate from 1911 until her death in 1932, traveled across the country giving lectures and organizing chapters of the League. Heath also petitioned and testified at hearings, and was appointed as a consumer representative, to committees of the federal and state governments.[63]

The League published the *Housewives League Magazine*, completely devoted to consumer issues. The Housewives League encouraged consumers to band together. At its height the League had 800,000 active members nationwide. The Housewives League did not significantly change economic policy, but the organization did give a voice to consumer concerns. Although government and business did not act on most of the League's concerns, they did begin to listen.[64]

Many watchdog advocacy groups faltered as the United States entered World War I. The federal government called on the Housewives League to change its focus to encourage conservation of food supplies to help the war effort. Furthermore, once inflation lessened and government responded to at least some of the pure food issues, many consumers saw less reason for activism.[65]

BUSINESS RESPONDS

Business, particularly retail stores, responded to the growing consumer awareness in a number of ways, including developing service programs such as allowing customers to return purchases for refund and consumer education in the form of pamphlets and demonstrations about products.[66] A group of business and advertising people formed the Better Business Bureau in 1916 to promote the cause of truth in advertising.[67]

These efforts were limited, however. Although the Better Business Bureau resolved that advertisers should not use paid testimonials in their ads, the Bureau lacked the power to enforce such resolutions and most advertisers continued to use paid testimonials. Many consumer advocates concluded that organization was the only way to affect significant change.[68]

CONSUMER EMPOWERMENT
THROUGH COOPERATIVES

Because government intervention in the economy on behalf of consumers remained limited, some consumers banded together to form cooperatives in an attempt to control at least some decisions about what is produced. A cooperative is a business owned and operated by the people who use it.[69] Profits are put back into the business and/or distributed to its members on the basis of how much each member participates.[70] Because members own and control the business, they not only benefit from using the cooperative to save money but also make decisions about how capital is spent and what products are purchased and sold. For example, cooperatives can buy and sell on the basis of "quality, safety, nutrition, warranty, durability" and "can refuse to stock products like tobacco or pesticides or foods with harmful additives in their stores."[71]

The concept of cooperatives was developed by Robert Owen of England in the early 1800s. Concerned about economic conditions for workers under the effects of the industrial revolution, Owen encouraged employees at his cotton mill to organize themselves to gain purchasing and producing power to fulfill their basic needs. The idea spread throughout England, but most cooperatives failed within a few years due to "poor management, insufficient capital and lack of dedication" among members.[72]

However, Owen's ideas were built upon by workers in Rochdale, England who formulated principles under which individual cooperative members became shareholders simply by buying goods at the cooperative. Any profits were distributed according to the amount purchased by each member.[73] In addition, the Rochdale Principles included membership open to everyone and a one person, one vote system.[74] This proved to be an effective and fair system which attracted and sustained members.[75]

The cooperative idea spread to the United States and during the 19th century, farmers and labor unions formed cooperatives to buy farm equipment and household goods collectively.[76] One of the first attempts at consumer cooperation was among urban, predominately middle class women in the late 1800s who organized cooperative kitchens and laundries in an effort to share the burden. Women created buying clubs to save money by making purchases together in large quantities. The feminist writer Charlotte Perkins Gilman encouraged the formation of cooperatives as a means to centralize "all household work in order to free women for the same kind of creative life that men led."[77] In 1907, Hyman Cohn organized a cooperative store in the Bronx and soon established the Cooperative League.[78] The rapidly increasing inflation in 1910 increased interest in forming consumer cooperatives.

Although many consumers were attracted to the cooperatives by lower prices, leaders of the new movement for consumer cooperatives (as had Robert Owen) advocated more than temporary relief from the high prices associated with inflation. They envisioned an economy in which only those goods the public wanted or needed would be produced and where consumers would have more voice in economic decisions. The leaders of the cooperative campaign developed an innovative theory of economics which for the first time considered, and promoted, the interests and role of consumers. These ideas of economic democracy influenced leaders of the consumer movement of the 1920s and 1930s.[79]

THE SECOND WAVE OF THE CONSUMER MOVEMENT

By 1925, changes in technology had once again significantly altered the ways Americans consumed. In 1907, only 8 percent of U.S. households had electricity; by 1925, the percentage was 53.2.[80] With electricity came dozens of new appliances including refrigerators, washing machines and vacuum cleaners.[81] The advertising industry, to sell an increasing amount of goods, encouraged consumers to buy products on the basis of style and color and status rather than buy for function, quality and price.[82] Consumer groups emerged to call attention to and question the tactics of advertisers and the nature of what was being produced as well as to empower consumers in the increasingly complex marketplace by providing product testing, analysis and information.

CONSUMERS RESEARCH

In 1927, Stuart Chase, an economist, and Frederick J. Schlink, an engineer, published a best-selling book called *Your Money's Worth*[83] which criticized American business, particularly advertising, from a consumer perspective. "The consumer movement, as the late 20th century knows it, was born on the day that *Your Money's Worth* was published in July, 1927," writes Peter Samson.[84]

Your Money's Worth explained the work of the federal government's National Bureau of Standards, where Schlink worked, which tested goods supplied to the U.S. government. Chase and Schlink concluded that the government, but not ordinary consumers, secured its money's worth because it collected and used information about products not accessible to consumers. The book described sales practices that kept consumers from obtaining information to help them make wise choices in the marketplace.[85]

Earlier critiques of advertising on behalf of consumers focused on the truth of the ads. The new criticism looked at the very nature of advertising, including the cost that advertising inevitably added to the price of goods as well as the psychological implications of manipulating people into buying things they otherwise would not buy.[86] "We are all Alices in a Wonderland of conflicting claims, bright promises, fancy packages, soaring words, and almost impenetrable ignorance," wrote Chase and Schlink.[87]

Your Money's Worth argued that slick advertising and lack of product information led consumers to buy products regardless of price or quality. The authors feared that these new sales practices would harm competition, traditionally based on consumers selecting products for price and quality.[88]

Other such sales practices included product differentiation (selling virtually the same product in different ways), attractive packaging, planned obsolescence (making products that would wear out in a short time), and lack of standardization (making it impossible for consumers to comparison shop).[89] Mainstream advertising had grown from basic product information to a more sophisticated lure.

Chase and Schlink urged consumers to "put pressure on retailers to carry the stock they desired; ... learn how to guard against short weight; [and] lobby for adequate protective legislation in matters of weights and measures and all other trade abuses."[90] To this end, Chase and Schlink founded Consumers Research and set up an independent testing laboratory. Subscriptions to their monthly newsletter, which reported the results of laboratory tests of various products, the *Consumer Bulletin*, helped finance the organization's operations.[91] To avoid any conflict with the interests of advertisers of products tested by the lab, the bulletin accepted no advertisements.[92]

Frederick J. Schlink and Consumers Research engineer Arthur Kallet wrote *100,000,000 Guinea Pigs: Dangers in Everyday Foods, Drugs and Cosmetics*[93] in 1933, which further fueled the movement for independent product testing. The best-seller "was an indictment of the way in which companies exposed unwitting consumers to untested new technologies. The metaphor of people as guinea pigs captured the feeling, fueled by the desperate conditions of the Great Depression, that consumers were at the mercy of larger forces."[94] Product testing gained in popularity but the economic conditions of the Depression led people to look to Consumers Research not only for product information. Many consumers called on Consumers Research to starting a political party, sell products under a consumer brand name and start a cooperative.[95]

CONSUMERS UNION

Internal disagreements developed within the Consumers Research organization, mostly between Frederick J. Schlink and the staff, who asked for shorter working hours and higher wages. When several employees applied to the American Federation of Labor to start a union, Schlink fired them. In response, employees launched a strike in September of 1935, demanding the fired workers be reinstated. When Arthur Kallet supported the strikers, he was dropped from the board of directors of Consumers Research.[96] Schlink refused attempts at arbitration.[97]

The striking workers eventually formed their own organization, Consumers Union (CU), in February of 1936 and appointed Arthur Kallet director.[98] In addition to testing and providing information about consumer products in a new magazine, the new organization pledged to report economic and medical issues as well as the "labor conditions under which such goods are produced and distributed."[99]

As a result of CU's criticism of brand-name products, more than 60 newspapers and magazines, to avoid offending the advertisers on which the newspapers and magazines depended, eventually refused to run advertisements for CU's magazine, *Consumer Reports.*[100] Other obstacles that CU faced include the publication of copy-cat magazines which analyzed products while accepting free samples of the products to test. In addition, at least partly at the instigation of opponents to the movement, the House Un-American Activities Committee investigated the consumer

movement beginning in 1938 to determine if consumer organizations were serving as Communist fronts. Consumers Union was acquitted of all such charges, but not until 1954.[101]

The Depression renewed interest in consumer cooperatives and President Franklin Roosevelt sent a commission to Europe in 1936 to study cooperatives there. The commission reported on the successes of consumer cooperation in England, Denmark, Finland and other countries. Americans learned of such achievements as those of the Swedish cooperatives which cut the price of rubber overshoes by one-half and of electric light bulbs by one-third.[102] Business opposition, however, prevented President Roosevelt from offering financial aid to cooperatives in the United States. Many of the cooperatives closed as small businesses developed rapidly in the late 1940s.[103]

The Rural Electrification Administration (REA) was created in 1935 by President Roosevelt to bring reasonably priced electricity to the nation's farms.[104] The private power industry was not willing to undertake rural electrification, so consumer-owned cooperatives with loans and technical assistance from the federal government emerged as an alternative solution.[105] From 1934 to 1941, the percentage of farms with electricity increased from 11 to 38 percent, although private power companies made up part of the increase.[106] The cooperatives still operate; as of 1985, more than 98 percent of the U.S. rural population belonged to the country's 985 rural electric cooperatives.[107]

THE CAMPAIGN FOR THE
1938 FOOD, DRUG AND COSMETIC ACT

By the 1930s, technological changes had brought new problems that the 1906 Pure Food and Drug Act did not cover.[108] The Act required only that information on a product be true, but did not require manufacturers to list anything more, such as contents or weight; false therapeutic claims for patent medicines were not covered and no standards existed by which to judge what constituted purity.[109] In 1933, after the election of President Franklin Roosevelt, his administration decided to push for changes in the 1906 law. By the time legislation passed in 1938, dozens of citizen groups had organized to rally support for the new provisions.[110]

The Food and Drug Administration (FDA), the successor of the Bureau of Chemistry, organized early support for stronger legislation. Ruth deForest Lamb, FDA's chief education officer, wrote *American Chamber of Horrors*,[111] documenting the hazardous foods and drugs still on the market in the United States. To demonstrate the need for stronger legislation, the FDA organized its "Chamber of Horrors," exhibit which displayed misbranded and adulterated products that the FDA could not prevent from being sold under existing law.[112]

Among the organizations most active in advocating consumer legislation were the American Home Economics Association, the National Congress of Parents and Teachers, the League of Women Voters and the American Association of University Women.[113] Organized club women, with representatives in Washington, DC, provided most of the support for rallying public opinion.[114] The women's groups generated public understanding of the proposed legislation, testified at hearings on the various proposals and were involved in the initial stages of drafting each of the proposed bills.[115]

Industry, strongly opposed to the first bill proposed in 1933, began to work to weaken various provisions. One strategy was to try to establish industry-sponsored women's clubs "to counteract the work of the autonomous women's groups who were determined to get real consumer protection."[116] Newspaper and magazine publishers, opposed to the bill because of its regulation of advertising, conducted an almost total blackout of news about the emerging legislation, preventing the public from learning about the debate.[117]

Business responded to the attacks on advertising by saying that advertising provided customers with more information than they would otherwise get and that it allowed businesses to create mass markets and increase the availability of goods.[118] The issue of regulation of advertising was resolved in 1938 when a separate measure, the Wheeler-Lea amendment to the Federal Trade Act, assigned responsibility for advertising to the Federal Trade Commission.[119]

The final impetus for passage of new food and drug legislation came in 1938 when a disaster was disclosed in which more than 100 people died from a poisonous "elixir of sulfanilamide."[120] The drug, which was never tested for safety, was not subject to any federal regulation.[121]

Congress passed the Food Drug and Cosmetic Act of 1938 authorizing the federal Food and Drug Administration to test the safety of new drugs before they are put on the market. The new law covered cosmetics in addition to food and drugs, required warning labels and ingredient listings on all drugs, required that drugs be proven safe before allowed on the market and gave the FDA power to obtain injunctions against the sale of products it found hazardous.[122]

During World War II, many consumer campaigns were put on hold and consumer advocates turned their attention to problems associated with the war.[123] For example, product testing by Consumers Union was interrupted because factories were producing war machinery instead of consumer goods such as washing machines and refrigerators. Furthermore, Consumers Union had difficulty buying sample products to test because of war-time rationing of consumer goods. However, Consumers Union joined other consumer groups in the federal government's conservation campaigns, publishing a weekly newsletter, *Bread and Butter*, "to help consumers keep track of wartime concerns such as price controls and the housing shortage."[124]

Esther Peterson, in her role as consumer advisor to the President, "symbolized government at its best and most humane, government devoted to improving the economic and social conditions of its citizens,"[125] wrote Rhoda Karpatkin, executive director of Consumers Union, when Peterson left her post as consumer advisor in 1981. Born in Provo, Utah, in 1906, Peterson credits her sense of commitment to progressive causes to her Mormon upbringing which encouraged unselfishness. Although the church also taught that the role of women was to marry and raise children, Peterson attended Brigham Young University where she was at the top of her class in physiology and chemistry. Discouraged from studying medicine due to her sex, Peterson decided to attend Columbia Teacher's College from which she graduated with a master's degree in physical education.[126]

© 1989 BEVERLY ORR

While working on her degree in New York City, Peterson was introduced to the world of progressive politics. Peterson attended political lectures by members of the labor movement. She recalls, "I had lived with people with closed, closed minds back in Utah, so it was a whole new experience for me. I began to read about the history of labor in Utah, which I had not known about. The whole thing began to piece together."[127]

After graduating in 1930, Peterson moved to Boston where she worked as a teacher and volunteered at the local chapter of the National Consumers League and at the YWCA's industrial department. At the YWCA she met with seamstresses from local mills and learned about their attempts to form a union in hopes of improving their oppressive working conditions and low wages.[128]

Peterson also taught at the Bryn Mawr Summer School for Women Workers where she met several leaders of the labor movement who offered her organizing jobs in New York. From the early 1930s to 1961, Peterson devoted her life to the labor movement, holding positions in the International Ladies Garment Workers Union, Amalgamated Clothing and Textile Workers and the American Federation of Labor - Congress of Industrial Organizations (AFL-CIO).[129]

Through her job as a lobbyist with the AFL-CIO in the late 1950s, Peterson met John F. Kennedy, then a U.S. Senator from Massachusetts. When Kennedy became President in 1961, he appointed Peterson director of the Department of Labor's Women's Bureau. When she accepted the job, she recalls, "[I]t seemed clear to me that the government needed to offer women more than mere tokens of recognition .... [W]e needed to call attention to the problem of the status of women in general."[130] One of the problems which women faced in the early 1960s was that their concerns were not taken seriously by those in power; as Peterson writes, "... feminism was commonly believed to be an antiquated, more-than-slightly ridiculous notion. Women who fought for women's rights routinely faced ridicule from the press and scorn from many in public office."[131]

As director of the Women's Bureau, Peterson was in a key role to address some of these inequalities. She convinced President Kennedy to allow her to organize the President's Commission on the Status of Women (PCSW), with Eleanor Roosevelt as chairperson. The Commission met between December 1961 and October 1963 and produced a report of findings and recommendations called *American Women*.[132] Describing the report years later, Peterson wrote, "Viewed from our current perspective, many of these proposals may appear moderate. Even so, not all of them have been realized."[133]

Many historians consider the Commission (and the establishment of state Status of Women Commissions across the country) and its report a major factor in the mobilization of women into a mass movement later in the 1960s. Peterson agrees, stating that it "created a medium through which the energy and outrage ... could be translated into constructive action."[134] A group of women who met through the PCSW decided to form the National Organization for Women in 1966. (For more on the role of the PCSW, see page 103).

"Others expanded on what Peterson had started with the commission, and Peterson shifted gears again and plunged into another fledgling area — consumer protection,"[135] writes Elliott Negin in *Public Citizen* magazine. Under President Lyndon Johnson, Peterson held two full-time jobs: assistant secretary of labor, a position to which Kennedy had promoted her, and the President's special assistant for consumer affairs, a position which Kennedy had promised her before his death. Her pro-consumer views angered business interests; the Advertising Federation of America, for example, labeled her "the most dangerous thing since Genghis Khan."[136] (One of her biggest critics, the Food and Marketing Institute, recognizing the value of Peterson's work, now honors consumer advocates with the Esther Peterson award.) But at the time, President Johnson, under political pressure, asked Peterson to step down and replaced her with Betty Furness, who, although many originally questioned her commitment to consumer protection, served an effective term under President Johnson.[137]

Ironically, Peterson's next career move caused some to question her commitment to the consumer.[138] She accepted the offer of the supermarket chain Giant Food Corporation to become its consumer advisor. During her stay there, Giant pioneered consumer protections now taken for granted, including open dating, unit pricing and nutritional and ingredient labeling on supermarket items. The reforms pleased consumers so much that business at Giant increased.[139]

When Jimmy Carter became President in 1977, Peterson resumed the position of director of the U.S. Office of Consumer Affairs. Carter assigned her the job of trying to win passage of a bill to create a new consumer protection agency to act on behalf of consumers in federal agencies and the courts. Big business lobbies fought a well-financed, aggressive campaign against the bill. The president of the Chamber of Commerce, Richard L. Lesher, ridiculed Peterson's forceful and spirited counterattack by paraphrasing Shakespeare's phrase "hell hath no fury like a woman scorned."[140] Peterson's protest, backed by women's groups, led to Lesher's retraction of the statement, but in February, 1978, the House of Representatives, in a close vote, rejected the consumer agency bill. Some of Peterson's supporters blamed the bill's defeat on Carter's lack of commitment and support.[141] Peterson explains the failure by saying, "We were a little David against a tremendous Goliath and I guess our little slingshot didn't matter much."[142]

Yet Peterson established significant reforms during her tenure at the U.S. Office of Consumer Affairs under President Carter in the areas of consumer complaint procedures, consumer education and petitioning other federal agencies to adopt better regulations. She also convinced Carter to reauthorize the Consumer Product Safety Commission despite Office of Management and Budget calls for its elimination. A final achievement set the tone for the next phase of her career: she convinced Carter, after two years of frustrating negotiations, to sign an executive order limiting the export of products that had been banned or restricted for use in the United States. The order also required manufacturers to submit warnings about product hazards to countries receiving hazardous goods from the United States. Carter signed the order less than a week before he left office, and the new President, Ronald Reagan, revoked it shortly after he took office.[143] The United Nations (UN) and countries all over the world actively support a ban on the export of hazardous products and the usefulness of warnings and restrictions has been demonstrated repeatedly.

Peterson's fight for the executive order affirmed her strong commitment to international consumer protection. After leaving the White House in 1981, Peterson joined the International Organization of Consumers Unions (IOCU) as its UN representative. She worked to encourage the UN to adopt voluntary international consumer protection guidelines, based largely on the consumer protection laws of the United States.[144] President Reagan opposed these international guidelines, calling them a "challenge to our free enterprise system" and "socialistic."[145] Peterson responds, "I have to laugh when I hear these charges. Because we're Socialist then, aren't we? We have these laws and regulations in our country...."[146] She explains U.S. opposition by saying, "The administration and business lobby groups just hope that none of our laws are established in other countries. They want to be able to exploit foreign markets unhindered."[147] Finally, after years of delay, the United States agreed to a watered down version of the guidelines, and the United Nations passed them in April 1985.[148]

Peterson turned her efforts to securing passage of a UN code of conduct for transnational corporations which would define the rights and responsibilities of transnational corporations in their international operations.[149] A revised set of guidelines passed at the 1992 UN session and was reported to the General Assembly. Peterson says the guidelines "will benefit the public in every country by setting up standards of decency, fair competition, fair market prices and greater honesty in the operation of businesses worldwide."[150] Peterson believes that consumers throughout the world will achieve effective protection only through a mass international consumer movement. She says, "I'm really concerned about the globalization of corporations. The consumer movement has got to become global too."[151]

CONSUMERS IN THE POST-WORLD WAR II ERA

From the end of World War II until the mid to late 1950s, little organized consumer activity took place. Consumer goods were available and consumers had money to buy them for the first time since before the Depression. In addition, the mood of the country supported a relaxation of government interference in the economy after the ordeals of the Depression and World War II were over.[152]

However, prices did rise considerably in the first few years after the war and the marketplace was inundated with new products and services including televisions, life insurance and credit cards.[153] Consumers around the country reacted to rising prices with buyers' strikes, but after "the shortages of the war years, consumers were eager to start spending their wartime savings and make up for past deprivation."[154] Consumers were relatively satisfied. In addition, the late 1940s and 1950s in general were not ripe for social protest, largely due to the chilling effects of McCarthyism.[155]

As consumers bought products not available during the war, they renewed their interest in the product testing of Consumers Union. The number of subscribers to *Consumer Reports* reached nearly 500,000 by 1950. In addition to product testing, CU represented consumers' interests before Congress on issues from watered ham to price fixing of drugs. CU also provided financial support to other consumer groups.[156]

THE THIRD WAVE OF THE CONSUMER MOVEMENT

By the late 1950s the mood of the country began to change. Michael Pertschuk, former director of the Federal Trade Commission, attributes the "growing public skepticism as to the morality of business" to a series of scandals, including criminal convictions of General Electric employees for price-fixing, anti-competitive practices in the drug industry, the thalidomide drug disaster and the aggressive marketing of cigarettes.[157]

In addition, two books published in the late 1950s contributed to a growing public awareness of both the methods and social effects of advertising. In 1957, Vance Packard published *The Hidden Persuaders*,[158] an indictment of "the advertising industry for using psychological techniques to manipulate consumers."[159] And in 1958, economist John Kenneth Galbraith wrote *The Affluent Society*,[160] in which he maintained that advertising, which encouraged the pursuit of private goods, led to an "unbalanced society" where public goods such as schools, museums and hospitals were undervalued.[161] These two books, although neither were written by consumer advocates, showed how little power consumers had relative to the power of business and gave credence to the argument to justify government involvement in the economy on behalf of consumers.

In 1957, Senator Estes Kefauver (D-TN) began hearings in Congress on the issues of monopoly power and price-fixing in the automobile, steel and drug industries and eventually arrived at the conclusion that, at least in the industries with most concentrated power, consumers were not being adequately protected. Kefauver concluded that the consumer suffered because certain industries held too much power and called for a Department of the Consumer and for stricter government regulation of the economy to ensure genuine competition.[162] Kefauver concluded that federal antitrust policy was not effective in regulating monopoly power and that the regulatory agencies were often more concerned with regulating "competition among firms within an industry than with regulating industry in the public interest."[163]

Kefauver introduced legislation in 1959 to encourage reductions in drug prices, but its chances of passage were slim.[164] The hearings, focusing on pricing and other economic factors in the drug industry with safety issues a secondary matter, continued through early 1962.[165]

Meanwhile, in March of 1962, President John Kennedy issued a "Consumers Bill of Rights" as part of a message to Congress urging it to strengthen consumer protection programs. The consumer rights included the right to safety, the right to be informed, the right to choose among a variety of products and services at competitive prices and the right to be heard in government formulation of consumer policy.[166] Kennedy did not urge approval of Kefauver's bill, although he mentioned several of its provisions.[167]

Kefauver's drug pricing bill was transferred to a different subcommittee in the Senate. The Kennedy Administration sent a much weaker drug bill, without the pricing provisions opposed by industry, to the House of Representatives in April 1962. Without Kefauver's participation, his bill was reworked in the Senate and the sections most disagreeable to industry were removed.[168]

Then another tragedy, similar to Upton Sinclair's exposé of the meatpacking industry in 1906 and the elixir of sulfanilamide tragedy in 1938, brought public attention to, and resulted in passage of legislation to further regulate, the safety and efficacy of prescription drugs. The drug thalidomide, a sedative, approved for use in Europe but not in the United States, was linked to severe deformities in infants whose mothers had taken the drug. *Washington Post* consumer reporter Morton Mintz, in a July 1962 front-page story, revealed that except for the efforts of FDA medical officer Dr. Frances O. Kelsey, thalidomide would have been on the market in the United States.[169] Stories about the thalidomide case appeared across the country with pictures of the affected children.[170] The narrowly averted disaster led to a public call for stricter regulation of drugs.[171]

The drug bill pending in both houses of Congress was strengthened as a result of the thalidomide story "so as to bring it closer to the form in which Kefauver had originally introduced it, with a notable exception. The changes pertained only to drug safety."[172] The drug pricing provisions were completely eliminated. The 1962 law, which amended the 1938 Food Drug and Cosmetic Act, requires that drugs be proven effective, as well as safe, before being placed on the market and requires drug manufacturers to warn of potential side effects on labels and in advertising. Despite delays in implementing some of the reforms, the 1962 Drug Amendments "led to a far safer and more accurately marketed drug supply in the United States."[173]

Several books published in the early 1960s also contributed to renewed interest in consumer issues.

Rachel Carson's *Silent Spring*[174] exposed the harmful effects of pesticides on the food chain and thus on human health. David Caplovitz's *The Poor Pay More*[175] documented the problems of low-income consumers and Jessica Mitford's *The American Way of Death*[176] uncovered abusive funeral sales practices.[177] Thus, as a result of a series of scandals, exposés and books and the widely publicized campaign for automobile safety, the public became more aware of the relationship between business and consumers and the stage was set for the third wave of the consumer movement.

THE CAMPAIGN FOR AUTOMOBILE SAFETY

Starting in 1956, Congress held hearings on automobile safety and in the next eight years passed three bills into law.[178] But the issue of auto safety in general received little attention until February of 1965, when Senator Abraham Ribicoff (D-CT) held hearings on traffic safety. Author Mark Nadel writes, "[T]he situation was structured to achieve publicity. The top officials of the auto industry were invited to testify. Like sheep to the slaughter, they came."[179] At the hearings, Senator Robert Kennedy (D-NY) pressured the president of General Motors to disclose how much of the company's profits were used to research and improve the safety of its vehicles.[180] GM's president disclosed that in 1964, the company, which made $1.7 billion in profits, spent only $1 million on safety research.[181]

In November of 1965, Ralph Nader published *Unsafe at Any Speed: The Designed-in Dangers of the American Automobile*,[182] an exposé that included the safety defects of General Motors' Chevrolet Corvair, "whose faulty rear suspension system made it possible to skid violently and roll over."[183] Nader charged that automobile companies designed their cars "for style, cost, performance and calculated obsolescence, but not — despite the 5 million reported accidents, nearly 40,000 fatalities, 110,000 permanent disabilities and 1.5 million injuries yearly — for safety."[184]

Unsafe at Any Speed challenged the auto industry's assertion that the cause of most auto accidents was the 'nut behind the wheel.' Rather, the inherent design deficiencies of automobiles were a major cause of auto crashes and casualties.[185] The book also described the "second collision," which happened after the initial crash, when occupants collided with the car's interior including "the spearlike steering column, exposed knobs and shattering glass."[186]

As former Federal Trade Commissioner Michael Pertschuk recounts, "When the automobile industry responded that it was the consumer's right to buy automobiles of any design and charged Nader with impeding freedom of choice, Nader wryly responded that it was admirable of the industry to defend that cherished civil liberty, 'the inalienable right to go through the windshield.'"[187] Nader called on the federal government to take responsibility for protecting consumers by mandating safety standards for automobiles.

In early 1966, President Lyndon Johnson's administration proposed a highway safety bill which consisted mostly of voluntary industry standards and which Ralph Nader called a "no-law law."[188] Then journalist James Ridgeway uncovered a General Motors investigation of Ralph Nader's private life. Alarmed by Nader's exposé, GM hired detectives to follow Nader in an attempt to find or possibly fabricate information that might undermine his credibility. The plan backfired.[189] The publicity surrounding the scandal put *Unsafe at Any Speed* on the bestseller list and made the public more aware of the arguments surrounding the auto safety issues.[190]

Senator Ribicoff convened hearings on the possible harassment of a witness (Nader had been scheduled to testify at congressional hearings on auto safety) and summoned James Roche, president of General Motors, to explain his company's harassment — and apologize to Nader.[191] Nader sued GM for invasion of privacy and "[a]fter adverse publicity, and fearing more of the same, GM agreed to give Nader $425,000 to drop his invasion of privacy suit. Nader used the money to bankroll literally dozens of consumer organizations."[192]

Public interest in auto safety was high and Congress soon passed the National Traffic and Motor Vehicle Safety Act of 1966 which provided for mandatory safety standards and a procedure for reporting of defects. For the first time, the automobile industry was subject to federal regulation.[193] Author Mark Nadel writes that "Most observers credit the GM investigation and resultant adverse publicity with being the key factor in passage of a stiff bill."[194] "The incident also served as a proof of a core Nader conviction: that one person, acting with intelligence and persistence, *can* make a difference — even if the target is the largest corporation in the world," writes David Bollier.[195]

The new law created the National Highway Traffic Safety Administration (NHTSA) with the authority to set safety standards for motor vehicles and to require auto manufacturers to notify owners of cars with safety defects.[196] In 1967, the first 30 safety standards were implemented, most designed to make car crashes less fatal. The standards included laminated windshields to prevent head and neck injury, collapsible steering columns to cushion trauma to the upper body, door locks designed to prevent occupants from flying out of the car in a crash and seat belts. Over the next 10 years, NHTSA issued tire safety standards, mandatory shoulder harnesses, head restraints, side-impact protections standards and new standards to protect fuel tanks from exploding in crashes.[197]

The success of auto safety reforms can be counted in statistics — over 200,000 lives saved and millions of injuries prevented between 1966 and 1991.[198] The efforts of Ralph Nader and other consumer advocates encouraged citizens to pay more attention to auto safety and forced the auto industry to make safety a higher priority.

CONSUMER ACTIONS OF THE 1960S AND 1970S

As a result of investigation of the role of business in price fixing of drugs and in automobile safety, the spotlight was once again on the consumer. Short-lived consumer boycotts erupted in 1966 and 1973. Citizens around the country set up new consumer groups at the local, state and national level and existing organizations were revitalized to launch various campaigns for consumer protection. New and existing consumer organizations focused on enforcement of existing laws and passage of new laws to regulate the economy and promote the health and safety of consumers. And citizens organized cooperatives, buying clubs and other forms of consumer empowerment.

In the fall of 1966, consumers across the country protested a sudden rise in supermarket prices through boycotts, demonstrations, and other actions.[199] The leaders and participants of the boycotts were mostly young women working at home and responsible for food shopping for their families. The participants perceived that higher food prices were at least in part caused by services such as trading stamps, games and contests which stores used to attract customers.[200] The protests originated in Denver, Colorado and quickly spread across the country as the media reported on the activities of various local groups.[201] The boycotts and protests had at least a short term effect: food prices fell approximately 2 percent partly due to the elimination of trading stamps and other games. However, the lower prices were not maintained.[202]

In 1973 when the price of meat skyrocketed, consumers across the country organized a one-week meat boycott by picketing supermarkets, organizing rallies, distributing leaflets and holding vegetarian recipe teach-ins. Boycott organizations formed in at least 37 states, where consumers met to discuss farm policy, agribusiness and consumer cooperatives. The boycott succeeded. Retail meat sales during the one-week boycott dropped by an estimated 50 to 80 percent.[203]

ECONOMIC REGULATION

In June of 1968, Ralph Nader gathered a group of young people to investigate the Federal Trade Commission, the federal agency charged with protecting consumers from shoddy products, fraudulent business practices and deceptive advertising. The report found the agency to be unresponsive to consumers and manipulated by commercial interests. Nader called on government to reform the regulatory agencies so that they work to foster genuine competition instead of protecting certain industries and to eliminate corporate welfare "both by cutting wasteful government subsidies to business and by reclaiming taxpayer-owned assets from private control."[204]

A special committee of the American Bar Association confirmed the findings of the exposé of the FTC,

"forcing President Nixon to appoint more vigorous leaders at the FTC. The exposé approach ... set a pattern for the consumer movement that continues today."[205] *Washington Post* reporter William Greider dubbed the young people coming to Washington "Nader's Raiders."[206] The students and recent college graduates went on to publish dozens of reports on government and corporate abuse, fraud and lethargy from the perspective of the average citizen.[207]

Most of industry strongly opposed Nader's proposals, but Edward B. Rust, then-president of the U.S. Chamber of Commerce admitted, "Business should be grateful for Ralph Nader. He is single-mindedly committed to making the free-enterprise system work as it's supposed to — to making marketplace realities of the very virtues that businessmen ascribe to the system."[208]

HEALTH AND SAFETY REGULATION

During the 1960s and 1970s, Congress and state legislatures passed dozens of consumer protection laws. Congress passed more than 25 consumer, environmental and other social regulatory laws between 1967 and 1973.[209] The new laws covered issues including dangerous toys, fair packaging and labeling, wholesome meat, product safety, flammable fabrics, consumer credit, poultry inspection and toxic substances.[210] By the 1970s, approximately 50 agencies and bureaus of the federal government included some functions affecting the consumer. And nearly every state and municipality had established some kind of consumer protection agency.[211]

Congress established the Consumer Product Safety Commission (CPSC) in 1972 as an independent regulatory agency to set standards of safety for many children's products including sleepwear, cribs and toys as well as other consumer products such as mattresses (for flammability). The CPSC has the authority to ban or recall certain dangerous products. Most states and cities established some kind of consumer office and most federal agencies have consumer offices as well.[212]

Consumer groups were instrumental in the success of many of these campaigns as well as in monitoring enforcement of the new laws. For example, the Center for Auto Safety, originally set up by Ralph Nader and Consumers Union, instigated recalls of unsafe automobiles, initiated class-action lawsuits against automakers and lobbied Congress for stiffer auto and highway safety protections. Some of the Center for Auto Safety's campaigns include: "Ford ambulances whose engines were catching on fire, power steering failures in GM cars, brake defects on Toyota Camrys, defective power windows in Jeep wagons that were strangling children, defective Ford Pinto gas tanks that could explode upon impact, and defective Firestone 500 radial tires that were linked to at least 50 deaths and several hundred injuries."[213]

Consumers Union established advocacy offices in Washington, DC, San Francisco and Austin, Texas in the 1970s and worked on issues including removal of lead from paint and utility rate setting.[214] CU continued its product testing which played an important role in publicizing automobile safety problems.[215] CU also provided grants to local consumer groups and played a role in the creation of the Consumer Federation of America (see below).[216]

Public Citizen was formed in 1971 by Ralph Nader as the umbrella organization under which Congress Watch, the Health Research Group, Litigation Group, Critical Mass and Buyers Up operate. Congress Watch launched dozens of legislative campaigns for government accountability including strengthening amendments to the Freedom of Information Act, campaign finance reform and ethics bills such as the Civil Service Reform Act of 1978 as well as consumer, environmental and worker safety issues.[217]

The Health Research Group's first campaign was a petition to the FDA in 1971 to request a ban on Red Dye No. 2, a food dye that can cause cancer. After a lengthy battle, FDA banned the dye five years later.[218] The Litigation Group filed dozens of lawsuits on behalf of the public, including 25 appeals that went before the Supreme Court. The issues they take on are diverse, including freedom of information, open government, union democracy, lawyers' ethics, food safety, occupational safety and health and the constitutional separation of powers.[219]

Local consumer groups also formed around the country, including San Francisco Consumer Action (SFCA), which was founded in 1971 by local volunteers working out of their homes.[220] In 1973, SFCA organized boycotts against high meat prices, started the California Food Action Campaign and presented testimony before congressional committees investigating corporate concentration in food industries.[221] In 1974, SFCA set up San Francisco Consumer Advocates to lobby for state consumer bills on issues such as rent control, collection agency practices, used-car warranties and drug labeling. Consumer Advocates also tallied the consumer voting records of California's U.S. Senators and Representatives.[222]

CONSUMER EMPOWERMENT

To empower themselves in the economy and in economic decision making, consumers went beyond government anti-trust enforcement and product safety and health laws. Consumers launched proposals for corporate democracy and alternative institutions such as buying clubs and group negotiating and complaint handling.

The Project on Corporate Responsibility advocated a larger voice for consumers, workers and shareholders in corporate policy making. Campaign GM worked to place public representatives on the GM Board of Directors. The project mobilized college students to pressure their schools to vote their GM stock proxies for 'social responsibility' resolutions — one of the earliest shareholder campaigns for corporate accountability.[223]

During the 1970s, thousands of informal food cooperatives, or buying clubs, were organized across the country by local residents who bought products and distributed them out of a member's home on a weekly or monthly basis.[224] By going directly to a producer or distributor, coops can buy at a discount of approximately 20 percent.[225] In addition to food cooperatives, consumers set up cooperatives to provide services such as child care, auto repair and legal services.[226]

Not only did these new cooperatives offer new services but they often were advocates for consumers as well. Many food coops consider social and environmental factors, such as offering food free of pesticides.[227] These consumer cooperatives initiated services subsequently adopted by supermarkets around the country such as unit pricing, developed by the Hyde Park Cooperative of Chicago, Illinois; open dating, stamping a date on packaged food to indicate the last day it should be sold; and nutritional labeling.[228] As of 1990, the National Cooperative Business Association (formerly the Cooperative League of the United States) represented 100 million members of over 45,000 cooperatives.[229]

Congress created the National Consumer Cooperative Bank in 1978 to make affordable loans to consumer and employee-owned cooperatives.[230] The Bank was not long underway when President Ronald Reagan took office and attacked the Bank. The Reagan Administration forced the Bank's Board of Directors to accept privatization of the Bank. The Bank dropped "consumer" from its title. The intention of Congress was to exclude cooperatives whose members are small businesses and to serve those cooperatives to which existing financial institutions would not offer credit.[231] However, the board of directors of the National Cooperative Bank (NCB) expanded the definition to include profit-oriented business cooperatives including True Value Hardware, FTD florist delivery service, Dunkin' Donuts and Kentucky Fried Chicken franchisees.[232] The orientation toward business cooperatives, which already had access to other sources of credit, came at the expense of cooperatives serving low-income people and start-up and student cooperatives.[233]

Buyers Up, a project of the consumer group Public Citizen launched in 1983, is a fuel-buying cooperative with approximately 7,000 members in the Washington, DC metropolitan area and another 2,300 in Baltimore, Maryland as of 1992. Buyers Up members purchase home heating oil as a group to negotiate for lower prices. The average savings are about 17 cents per gallon of heating oil, or $200 or more per year on individual home heating bills.[234] Through the Buyers Up office, consumers also have an outlet for complaint resolution and receive a newsletter full of advice for home energy efficiency. Fuel coops also operate in Connecticut, Massachusetts, New Jersey, New York, Pennsylvania and Rhode Island.

Another example of consumer buying power is the prescription drug discounts and group health insurance that the American Association of Retired Persons offers to its 20 million members over the age of 55.[235]

Citizen, consumer and labor organizations each pioneered forms of group negotiating. For example, these groups have negotiated with local cable companies to provide access and facilities for citizen use.[236] Some U.S. and Canadian cities have homeowner repair associations whose staffs prepare lists of approved contractors and handle homeowner complaints.[237] In addition, consumers in several states banded together in Citizen Utility Boards (CUBs) to negotiate with utility companies for lower utility rates. (For more on CUBs, see page 199).

In neighborhoods throughout the United States, community organizations negotiated with banks to reduce redlining practices. Redlining refers to the practice of drawing a red line around a particular community on a map and then limiting the availability of bank loans for any person residing within the red line, regardless of the qualifications of the individual.

When Gale Cincotta discovered that local banks were redlining her neighborhood, she organized her neighbors to challenge the banks. Borrowing the tactics of community organizer Saul Alinksy, Cincotta and her neighbors "disrupt[ed] business as usual by staging protests like taking up officers' time opening new accounts, then immediately closing them."[238]

In 1972, Cincotta helped create National People's Action (NPA), an umbrella organization for approximately 300 neighborhood groups. NPA successfully campaigned for passage of the federal Community Reinvestment Act which "requires that banks meet the credit needs of low- and moderate-income communities," and the Home Mortgage Disclosure Act which "mandates the release of information on where banks make home mortgages."[239]

Other consumers organized to negotiate as a group with corporations with which they had a complaint. For example, Diane Halferty organized Consumers Against General Motors (CAGM) to negotiate redress for complaints about certain GM cars.[240]

Citizens around the country also started hundreds of local consumer groups to handle individual consumer complaints, lobby for local consumer reform and educate the public.[241] Many operated on low budgets with volunteer help. The Consumers Education and Protection Association (CEPA) in Philadelphia was founded as a grass-roots consumer action group in 1966 with a largely lower-income, African American membership. CEPA helps individual consumers solve their own problems. Delegations of CEPA members first visit merchants to discuss the complaint and, if unresolved, then picket to apply further pressure.[242]

San Francisco Consumer Action (SFCA), originally set up to handle individual consumer complaints, grew into a larger, advocacy organization. Kay Pachtner, one of the volunteer founders, said, "We just dived in without knowing anything about the law or complaint handling. But we learned fast."[243]

In 1975, SFCA moved from volunteer staff taking on individual consumer complaints to consumer-run complaint resolution committees modeled after CEPA in Philadelphia.[244] SFCA decided that to be truly effective, it must move from handling individual complaints to working to prevent problems and find solutions that would protect all consumers.[245] SFCA continued public education efforts by publishing books and fact sheets, running its own radio talk show and producing public service announcements.[246]

THE CONSUMER MOVEMENT
AND THE CARTER ADMINISTRATION

When President Jimmy Carter took office in 1977, he appointed more than 60 consumer activists to various positions in his administration. Among those 60, Michael Pertschuk, a Senate committee staff director, was appointed chairman of the FTC; Susan King, of the National Committee for an Effective Congress, became commissioner of the Consumer Product Safety Commission; Joan Claybrook of Congress Watch was appointed administrator of the National Highway Traffic Safety Administration; and Carol Foreman, executive director of the Consumer Federation of America, became assistant secretary of Food and Consumer Services at the U.S. Department of Agriculture.[247]

These new government officials brought the consumer perspective to work for new innovations and better enforcement in their respective fields. For example, while Joan Claybrook was administrator of NHTSA, the agency "issued standards to improve frontal crash protection through installation of air bags and automatic belts; to improve the damage resistance of bumpers; prevent tampering with odometers; extend steering column protection to vans and light trucks; and improve seat belt comfort and convenience, among others."[248]

BUSINESS RESPONDS

The Chamber of Commerce formed a committee on consumer interests in the late 1960s.[249] And although some Chamber of Commerce members were genuinely interested in responding to consumer concerns, by the early 1970s, business began to fight back against the consumer influence in government decision making. In 1972, the chief executive officers (CEOs) of numerous corporations formed the Business Roundtable which "rapidly became both the preeminent lobbying institution and a symbol to all industry of the priority and legitimacy of political action by business."[250] The CEOs each made a personal commitment to engage in direct lobbying for business interests.[251]

The Chamber of Commerce revitalized its operations in the mid-1970s to embrace political action.[252] And throughout the 1970s, businesses formed hundreds of political action committees (PACs), and approximately 400 corporate headquarters moved to Washington, DC to better influence government policy making.[253]

With the election of President Ronald Reagan in 1980, the corporate representatives had a friend in the White House. President Reagan "stocked the government's regulatory agencies with industry representatives profoundly hostile to the laws they were supposed to administer."[254] Over the next several years, dozens of regulations were eliminated or relaxed. Various mandatory standards became voluntary guidelines without enforcement power. Enforcement of many of the regulations which remained was cut back as the number of staff and inspectors overseeing the laws was reduced and some of those remaining refused to prosecute clear violations.[255]

THE CAMPAIGN FOR A
CONSUMER PROTECTION AGENCY

During the 1970s, Congress proposed a federal consumer protection agency that would not enforce laws or make new regulations, but would ensure that consumers were represented in the decisions of other government agencies. The agency was nearly enacted in 1975 when both houses of Congress approved its creation but the bill died in the House-Senate conference committee when President Gerald Ford threatened to veto the measure.[256]

The proposal was again introduced in 1977, and because Jimmy Carter, who had stated his support of consumer issues, was President, passage seemed likely. Various consumer groups lobbied for the consumer agency and in 1978, Congress Watch launched a "Consumer Nickel Brigade." Hundreds of thousands of supporters of the new agency sent a nickel (the estimated cost to each taxpayer of the agency) to their representatives in Congress.[257]

However, industry strongly opposed the creation of the agency and organized a coalition of diverse business industries to lobby for its defeat.[258] In addition, President Carter "did not put the full force of his presidential prestige and power behind the legislation."[259] The bill was weakened considerably before reaching a vote but even then was narrowly defeated in the House of Representatives in February of 1978.[260]

A Harris poll, taken shortly after the agency's defeat, "showed that 58 percent of the public favor[ed] a federal agency to protect their consumer rights, with 28 percent opposed."[261] Although industry opposition certainly was the most important factor in its defeat, Michael Pertschuk writes that the proposed consumer agency "nevertheless suffered from an undertow of public disaffection with big government. The cause of generic consumer advocacy did not offer a manifest legal right or remedy for a specific consumer injury. The Consumer Protection Agency was manifestly more government; and what it would *do* was obscure."[262]

THE CONSUMER MOVEMENT IN THE 1990S

Consumer groups at the national, state and local levels continue to monitor government and business and to win protections for consumers. In addition, a number of public agencies, such as the New York City Department of Consumer Protection headed by former Nader associate Mark Green, take an active role in protecting consumer interests.

Consumer groups around the country are involved in a wide variety of issue areas including auto safety, health, insurance, credit, responsive government, corporate responsibility, citizen participation and education. The strategies used by these groups are also vary widely, from lobbying Congress and state legislatures, educating the public, resolving consumer complaints and involving citizens in the decision making process of government. For example, FairTest — the National Center for Fair and Open Testing, founded in 1985, "works to end the abuses, misuses and flaws of standardized testing."[263] The National Insurance Consumer Organization educates consumers on all aspects of buying insurance and advocates reform of unfair insurance industry practices and marketplace abuses.[264] Voter Revolt, with offices throughout California, works to expand the role and influence of citizens in lawmaking. Voter Revolt was instrumental in the passage of the 1988 ballot initiative to reform the insurance industry in California.[265] The Bankcard Holders of America educates the public about the use of credit, helps individual consumers resolve credit disputes and offers credit counseling.[266] The student-run Public Interest Research Groups also take an active role in consumer issues. (For more on the PIRGs, see pages 6-7).

The Center for Auto Safety continues to work to identify automobile defects, alert the public to such problems and press the NHTSA to take action. The Center for Science in the Public Interest (CSPI), founded by former Nader associates, works to educate the public and influence government and corporate policy with regard to issues of food safety and nutrition.[267] CSPI monitors the activities of the Food and Drug Administration, the Department of Agriculture and the Federal Trade Commission on issues such as nutritional labeling and advertising claims.[268]

Founded in 1967, the Consumer Federation of America (CFA) is a national federation of organizations with consumer interests, including labor unions, state and local consumer organizations, local consumer protection agencies, rural electric cooperatives, credit unions, the National Council of Senior Citizens and the National Consumers League.[269] CFA lobbies issues and serves as a clearinghouse and resource center to provide member organizations with information, technical assistance and financial support.[270] As of 1991, CFA included about 240 member organizations.

Consumers Union (CU) has tested in its laboratory a wide variety of consumer products and published the results in its monthly magazine, *Consumer Reports*, since 1936. In 1960, CU founded the International Organization of Consumers Unions (IOCU) to coordinate the efforts of consumer protection around the world. IOCU has developed from a clearinghouse on international consumer issues to a representative before various international bodies including the United Nations. IOCU was instrumental in the adoption of the United Nations Guidelines for Consumer Protection.[271]

By 1991, CU's product testing magazine, *Consumer Reports*, had a circulation of 4.8 million. CU also publishes a consumer magazine for young people, called *Zillions*, with 260,000 subscribers. As professor of consumer studies Robert Mayer writes, the information CU provides to its nearly five million subscribers "not only helps individual consumers get their money's worth in the marketplace but also provides consumer groups with ammunition in their attempts to pressure government entities and businesses."[272]

The National Consumers League was founded in 1899 to promote fair labor standards such as the minimum wage, restriction on child labor and workplace safety requirements.[273] The League sought to do this by informing consumers of their responsibility "for conditions under which goods are made and distributed."[274] League members, mostly women, organized to pressure retailers and promote fair working conditions by publishing "white lists" of factories with approved working conditions.[275] The NCL continues to work for fair labor standards in addition to food and drug safety, consumer information and health care issues.[276]

Public Citizen continues to advocate on behalf of the average citizen for greater protection of consumer interests as well as for government and corporate responsibility. Public Citizen has worked on dozens of issues including energy conservation, automotive fuel efficiency standards, air bags and nuclear safety.[277] Public Citizen was part of the campaign that resulted in the 1984 automatic crash protection standard, which requires new cars to have either an airbag or automatic seatbelts beginning in 1990. This standard alone is expected to save between 9,000 and 12,000 lives and 150,000 serious injuries a year.[278] As of 1991, Public Citizen had 100,000 members.

The Health Research Group works on food safety (food additives and dyes, vitamin-deficient infant formula), drug and medical device safety (bans on unsafe drugs and warning labels such as Reye's syndrome warnings on aspirin), women's health, preventive health care, consumer empowerment and the costs of health care.[279] And the Litigation Group continues to file lawsuits on behalf of "consumers harmed by cancer-causing food additives, workers exposed to toxic substances on the job, union members deprived of their rights by labor unions, citizens victimized by the legal profession's price-fixing and other anti-competitive practices and consumers recklessly exposed to the carcinogenic drug DES." The Litigation Group's lawsuits hold government and corporations accountable and to secure remedies not just for the individuals in the particular case but for all consumers, workers and citizens.[280]

San Francisco Consumer Action publishes *Consumer Action News* eight times a year and has a hotline for consumer complaints through which they refer consumers to an appropriate government agency or organization. Other consumer groups working at the state and local levels include the Florida Consumers Federation which works on energy issues, utility rate reform, tax reform, Medicaid coverage and toxic waste and the Virginia Citizens Consumer Council which surveys stores on business practices, prices, availability of merchandise and unsafe products and educates the public and represents consumer interests before legislative hearings.[281]

CONCLUSION

Before the turn of the century, consumers had few protections; in fact, individuals rarely thought of themselves as consumers. But organized campaigns to protect consumer interests and establish consumer rights resulted in federal and state laws, new regulatory agencies and consumer empowerment tools that have allowed consumers some access to economic decision making.

Writes David Bollier of the modern consumer movement, "The ultimate strength and staying power of the consumer movement stems from its status as more than an aggregation of bargain-minded consumers; it is a movement of *citizens* petitioning their government. They seek not just more equal buyer-seller relationships in the marketplace but a new role for citizens in the American constitutional system of self-governance."[282]

BIBLIOGRAPHY

America at Risk: A History of Consumer Protest. Film. Mount Vernon, NY: Consumers Union, 1984.

Angevine, Erma, ed. *Consumer Activists: They Made a Difference*. Mount Vernon, NY: Consumers Union Foundation, 1982.

Bollier, David and Joan Claybrook. *Freedom From Harm: The Civilizing Influence of Health, Safety and Environmental Regulation*. Washington, DC: Public Citizen and Democracy Project, 1986.

Bollier, David. *Citizen Action and Other Big Ideas: A History of Ralph Nader and the Modern Consumer Movement*. Washington, DC: Center for Study of Responsive Law, 1989.

Brennan, Shawn, ed. *Consumer Sourcebook: 1992-1993*. Seventh edition. Detroit: Gale Research, Inc., 1991.

Brobeck, Stephen J. *The Modern Consumer Movement: References and Resources*. Boston: G.K. Hall and Co., 1990.

Caplovitz, David. *The Poor Pay More*. New York: Free Press of Glencoe, 1963.

Carson, Rachel. *Silent Spring*. Boston: Houghton Mifflin, 1962.

Chase, Stuart and Frederick J. Schlink. *Your Money's Worth: A Study of the Waste of the Consumer Dollar*. New York: Macmillan, 1927.

Claybrook, Joan. *Retreat from Safety: Reagan's Attack on America's Health*. New York: Pantheon, 1984.

Claybrook, Joan. "Making a Difference: Celebrating 20 Years of Activism," *Public Citizen*. January/February 1991.

Collins, Jennifer. "Codifying Corporate Accountability," *Multinational Monitor*. June, 1990.

Cowan, Jessica, ed. *Good Works: A Guide to Careers in Social Change*. New York: Barricade Books, 1991.

Creighton, Lucy Black. *Pretenders to the Throne: The Consumer Movement in the United States*. Lexington, MA: D.C. Heath, 1976.

"50 Years Ago ...," *Consumer Reports*. January 1986.

"50 Years Ago: What Happened When Consumerism and Unionism, Two Great Social Movements of the 1930s, Collided,?" *Consumer Reports*. February 1986.

Finding Co-ops: A Resource Guide and Directory. Washington, DC: Cooperative Information Consortium, 1984.

Friedman, Monroe Peter. "The 1966 Consumer Protest as Seen by Its Leaders," *The Journal of Consumer Affairs*. Vol. 5, No. 1. Summer 1971.

Galbraith, John Kenneth. *The Affluent Society*. Boston: Houghton Mifflin, 1958.

Garland, Anne Witte. "Gale Cincotta," *Ms*. January 1986.

Haregot, Seyoum A. *The Failed Promise of the National Cooperative Bank*. Washington, DC: Center for Study of Responsive Law, 1989.

Herman, Thomas. "Betty Furness on Consumer Firing Line," *Wall Street Journal*, September 20, 1967.

Herrmann, Robert O., et al., "The Organization of the Consumer Movement: A Comparative Perspective," in E. Scott Maynes, ed. *The Frontier of Research in the*

Consumer Interest. Columbia, MO: American Council on Consumer Interests, 1988.

Herrmann, Robert O. "Consumerism: Its Goals, Organizations and Future," *Journal of Marketing*. Vol. 34. October 1970.

Herrmann, Robert O. "Consumer Protection: Yesterday, Today and Tomorrow," *Current History*. May 1980.

Janssen, Wallace F. "The Story of the Laws Behind the Labels," *FDA Consumer*. June 1981.

Kallet, Arthur and Frederick J. Schlink. *100,000,000 Guinea Pigs: Dangers in Everyday Foods, Drugs and Cosmetics*. New York: Vanguard Press, 1932.

Kramer, Nancy and Stephen A. Newman. *Getting What You Deserve: A Handbook for the Assertive Consumer*. Garden City, NY: Doubleday and Co., Inc., 1979.

Lamb, Ruth deForest. *American Chamber of Horrors: The Truth about Food and Drugs*. New York: Arno Press, 1976 [1936].

Mayer, Robert. *The Consumer Movement: Guardians of the Marketplace*. Boston: Twayne Publishers, 1989.

McCann, Alfred. *Starving America*. Cleveland, NY: F.M. Barton, 1913.

Mitford, Jessica. *The American Way of Death*. New York: Simon and Schuster, 1963.

Nadel, Mark V. *The Politics of Consumer Protection*. Indianapolis: Bobbs-Merrill, 1971.

Nader, Ralph. *Unsafe at Any Speed: The Designed-in Dangers of the American Automobile*. New York: Grossman, 1965.

Nader, Ralph. "The Consumer Movement Looks Ahead," in Alan Gartner, Colin Greer and Frank Riessman, eds. *Beyond Reagan: Alternatives for the '80s*. New York: Harper and Row, 1984.

National Cooperative Business Association 1990 Annual Report. Washington, DC: National Cooperative Business Association, 1990.

Negin, Elliott. "Esther Peterson: The Grande Dame of Consumerism," *Public Citizen*. Winter 1985.

Packard, Vance. *The Hidden Persuaders*. New York: D. McKay Co., 1957.

Pertschuk, Michael. *Revolt Against Regulation: The Rise and Pause of the Consumer Movement*. Berkeley: University of California Press, 1982.

Peterson, Esther. "Consumerism and International Markets," in Paul N. Bloom and Ruth Belk Smith, eds. *The Future of Consumerism*. Lexington, MA: Lexington Books, 1986.

Peterson, Esther. "The Kennedy Commission," In Irene Tinker, ed. *Women in Washington: Advocates for Public Policy*. Beverly Hills, CA: Sage Publications, 1983.

Rofsky, Mitchell. "Unfinished Business," in Ralph Nader Task Force on European Cooperatives. *Making Change?: Learning from Europe's Consumer Cooperatives*. Washington, DC: Center for Study of Responsive Law, 1985.

Samson, Peter Edward. "The Emergence of a Consumer Interest in America, 1870-1930." A dissertation submitted to the faculty of the division of the social sciences in candidacy for the degree of doctor of philosophy, Department of History. Chicago: University of Chicago, August 1980.

Silber, Norman I. *Test and Protest*. New York: Holmes and Meier, 1983.

Sinclair, Upton. *The Jungle*. New York: Doubleday, Page and Company, 1906.

Smith, Adam. *An Inquiry into the Nature and Causes of the Wealth of Nations*. Edwin Cannan, ed. Fifth edition abridged. New York: Random House, 1985 [1776].

Sorenson, Helen Laura. *The Consumer Movement: What It Is and What It Means*. New York: Arno Press, 1978 [1941].

United States President's Commission on the Status of Women. *American Women: The Report of the President's Commission on the Status of Women*. Washington, DC: Government Printing Office, 1963.

Wilson, Gregory and Elizabeth Brydolf. "Grass Roots Solutions: San Francisco Consumer Action," in Laura Nader, ed. *No Access to Law: Alternatives to the American Judicial System*. New York: Academic Press, 1980.

Woodstone, Arthur. "The Consumer Army: Rebels with a Cause," *Parade*. November 12, 1978.

A HISTORY OF THE
ENVIRONMENTAL MOVEMENT

INTRODUCTION

The modern movement to protect the environment has its roots in the conservation and preservation campaigns of the 19th century. These movements were concerned with managing the land to ensure continued resources and with saving the wilderness and its delicate ecosystem. The modern ecology and environmental movements are concerned with ensuring not only unlimited timber supplies or pristine wilderness but also clean drinking water, clean air to breathe and safe food to eat.

In the 1960s and 1970s, the environmental movement focused on pollution and campaigned for a regulatory framework to monitor and control pollution. By the 1980s, a new movement, focusing on toxic waste in communities set about to eliminate the source of toxic waste contamination threatening the health and environment of communities across the United States.

CONSERVATION AND PRESERVATION

Conservationism began in the late 1800s largely as a concern over the rapid depletion of the country's natural resources. "The natural world and its products were there to be used; the goal was wise management and, thereby, more effective use ... but more fundamental questions about industry itself and its products — including pollution — were rarely raised by conservationists," writes professor Robert Paehlke.[1]

Gifford Pinchot, a pioneer in the field of forest management, led the campaign to encourage wise use of natural resources, including timber and minerals.[2] Pinchot greatly influenced then-President Theodore Roosevelt, who embraced the growing conservation movement at a White House conference in 1908.[3] Roosevelt proclaimed:

We are coming to recognize as never before the right of the nation to guard its own future in the essential matter of natural resources. In the past we have admitted the right of the

individual to injure the future of the republic for its own present profit. The time has come for a change. As a people we have the right and the duty, second to none other but the right and duty of obeying the moral law, of requiring and doing justice, to protect ourselves and our children against wasteful development of our natural resources, whether that waste is caused by the actual destruction of such resources or by making them impossible of development hereafter.[4]

Roosevelt created the U.S. Forest Service and appointed Pinchot as the country's first chief forester. By 1909, the national forest system encompassed 148 million acres.[5]

Preservationists took the crusade further by urging preservation of nature from human exploitation, not as a "resource," but for its own sake. John Muir "campaigned tirelessly to save wilderness from the human effects of human activities, seeking to preserve it for itself and for quiet observation. ... Muir's perspective set him in opposition to the unfettered growth of the American economy, as the 'wise use' conservationists were not."[6] Muir and others founded the Sierra Club in 1892 to make the preservation cause more political and to save forever the wilderness of the Sierra Nevadas from human exploitation.[7] The Sierra Club today continues Muir's work across the country.

"The conservation/preservation split reflects far more than disagreement over humanity's responsibility toward the land: It is rooted in fundamentally different perceptions of humankind and nature," writes Peter Borrelli in *The Amicus Journal*.[8] Conservationists viewed the earth as there for the use of humanity while preservationists saw humanity as one part of nature. The debate, which still exists today, between conserving resources to ensure continued rapid economic growth and preservation as a means to protect the delicate ecosystem, was thus set.[9]

ECOLOGY

George Perkins Marsh laid the groundwork for much of the modern work on ecology, the interrelationship among all living things.[10] In *Man and Nature: Physical Geography as Modified by Human Action*,[11] published in 1864, Marsh evaluated "the unintended negative effects of human economic activities on the environment" long before the invention of the automobile or other modern sources of pollution.[12]

Ecologist Aldo Leopold drew on both Muir's political involvement and Marsh's work on ecology to publicize the intricate connection between nature and humanity.[13] Leopold applied his own observations and experience as a forester and wildlife manager to the science of ecology.[14] His book, *A Sand County Almanac*,[15] published in 1949, shortly after his death, eloquently explained the importance of the land, or nature, to the survival of humanity.

Leopold scientifically justified the principles of preservationism by applying ecology to the politics of land use decision making.[16] It was important not only to save wilderness for its own sake, as Muir advocated, but because the very survival of humanity depends upon it.[17] His "land ethic" required humans to acknowledge their relationship to the earth and act in accordance.[18] Leopold wrote: "Like winds and sunsets, wild things were taken for granted until progress began to do away with them. Now we face the question whether a still higher 'standard of living' is worth its cost in things natural, wild, and free. For us of the minority, the opportunity to see geese is more important than television ... ."[19]

THE CHEMICAL AGE AND ITS EFFECTS ON HEALTH AND THE ENVIRONMENT

World War II spurred the development of thousands of new chemicals.[20] During the war, the United States faced shortages of numerous goods previously imported from around the world and subsequently developed a number of synthetic materials as substitutes. For example, when silk from Asia was unavailable to make parachutes, synthetic fibers were developed to replace the silk. Plastics were developed to replace scarce metals unavailable for aircraft production.[21]

After the war, the chemical industry began "replacing wood and paper with plastic, cotton and wool with rayon and nylon, leather with vinyl, glass and steel with plastic [and] natural farming with chemical-intensive farming."[22] And under the "Atoms for Peace" program, nuclear electricity generators were built.[23]

These new technologies brought some important innovations, cheaper goods and greater convenience but also brought serious environmental and health problems. Pesticide use in the 1940s and 1950s killed a large proportion of the U.S. bird population. Chemical production facilities pollute streams, rivers and lakes with toxic discharges.[24] And nuclear facilities generate waste for which no safe method of disposal exists.

The chemical industry expanded at an exceptional rate. In 1940, approximately 2 billion pounds of synthetic organic chemicals and petrochemicals were produced in the United States. By 1988, that amount had grown to 214 billion pounds.[25]

"As the chemical industry expanded," writes Ron Brownstein, "no one in government seemed to be watching."[26] Few laws existed to require manufacturers to determine the effects of these new technologies on human health or the environment; for example, the effect of pesticides on people who eat the food on which pesticides are used or the effects to workers of daily exposure to chemicals in the workplace. What research was conducted of new chemicals usually focused on the acute dangers. The chronic effects and long-range consequences of the chemicals' use and disposal often were ignored and in some cases, covered up in the interest of short-term economic growth.[27] Professor Robert Paehlke writes that "It is all too common that the early findings of toxicologists and epidemiologists fail to provoke timely efforts to protect workers' health. Likewise, their data rarely finds its way into the public eye, and it is rarer still that their findings are considered in light of the effects of the substances they study upon the air, water, and population outside the factory."[28]

Many of the health and environmental effects of chemicals were not and still are not fully known. But connections between exposure to harmful substances in the workplace and worker health problems, the field of occupational health, were pioneered in the early 1700s by an Italian doctor, Bernardino Ramazzini.[29] Dr. Alice Hamilton, who pioneered the American occupational health field, described the devastating health effects of World War I munitions and chemical plants where new products were, in effect, tested not in laboratories but in factories on workers.[30] But not until the 1930s with the publication of two books, *100,000,000 Guinea Pigs*[31] and *American Chamber of Horrors*,[32] did public concern in the United States focus on connections between chemicals, such as lead and arsenic, and human health.[33] Public awareness of the effects of industrial pollution on human health was heightened due to two dramatic instances of deadly smog, in Donora, Pennsylvania in 1948 and again in London in 1952.[34]

But it was ecologist Rachel Carson's 1962 book, *Silent Spring*,[35] which woke the public to the extent to which chemicals, particularly pesticides, were pervasive in the environment and what that means for human health.[36] The title *Silent Spring* refers to the decline in bird populations in the United States due to increased pesticide use. Carson conveyed her findings "in language accessible to the educated public. Her style, a blend of scientific, political, and moral arguments, built upon the work of Aldo Leopold and became the hallmark of popular environmentalism," writes professor Robert Paehlke.[37]

In *Silent Spring*, Carson described an example of bioaccumulation — the buildup of toxic substances in the food chain — at Clear Lake, California where small amounts (.02 ppm) of the pesticide DDD were used to control gnats in the 1950s.[38] The pesticide moved through the food chain, from plankton to small fish to larger fish and finally to the grebes, or water birds. DDD accumulated in the grebes' fatty tissues at an average level of 1,600 ppm. At that level, the grebes died out in the Clear Lake region.[39] Although some scientists continued to argue that chemicals are harmless at small concentrations, Carson's findings created considerable controversy and public awareness and led the federal government to ban several toxic pesticides.[40]

Carson wrote in *Silent Spring*, "If the Bill of Rights contains no guarantee that a citizen shall be secure against lethal poisons distributed either by private individuals or by public officials, it is surely only because our forefathers, despite their considerable wisdom and foresight, could conceive of no such problem."[41]

The full health effects of exposure to chemicals and toxic pollution are still not known. People are exposed to pollution in a variety of ways, from workplace exposure to air pollution, water pollution, exposure to nuclear radiation and pesticides in the food chain. Scientists and doctors still do not know exactly how and why exposure to certain substances causes diseases such as cancer or heart disease and birth defects.[42]

By the 1960s, concern about the environment dramatically shifted from conservation and preservation to pollution and its consequences for human health and the environment. Numerous disasters, including the burning of the Cuyahoga River in Cleveland, Ohio in 1969;[43] an oil spill off the coast of Santa Barbara, California in 1969; meat and dairy products contaminated with the chemical PBB in Michigan in 1973; and the eutrophication or 'dying' of Lake Erie caused further public concern about pollution.[44]

CONCERN OVER RESOURCE DEPLETION

Concern about industrial pollution and its resultant health effects was joined by a concern for the rapid depletion of world resources, such as minerals and food. Numerous books and reports were published on the subject, leading to what critics called a doomsday syndrome.[45] Some environmentalists argued that the rapid depletion of resources was caused by overpopulation and thus could be remedied by controlling population. For example, Paul Ehrlich in his book *The Population Bomb*,[46] published in 1968, argued, "[T]he root cause of most environmental damage was excessive growth in human population. ... Either humanity changes its ways, or mass starvation is the price we will pay."[47]

Many environmentalists, notably biologist Barry Commoner, challenged Ehrlich's theories on population arguing that rather than population, it is society's harmful use of technology that accounts for the majority of environmental problems.[48] Commoner writes:

> The basic reasons for environmental degradation in the United States and all other industrialized countries since World War II are drastic changes in the technology of agricultural and industrial production and transportation: we now wash our clothes in detergents instead of soap; we drink beer out of throwaway bottles instead of returnable ones; we use man-made nitrogen fertilizer to grow food, instead of manure or crop rotation; we wear clothes made of synthetic fibers instead of cotton or wool; we drive heavy cars with high-powered, high-compression engines instead of lighter, low-powered low-compression pre-war types; we travel in airplanes and private cars and ship our freight by truck instead of the railroads or both.[49]

Amid the concerns about the rapid depletion of world resources came the energy crisis of 1973, "and the ensuing crisis mentality surrounding all energy sources."[50] When the price of oil skyrocketed, the United States adopted some energy conservation measures. These measures, including energy efficiency and renewable energy, reduced U.S. dependence on imported oil, at least temporarily. However, when the crisis lifted, the federal government abandoned many of these measures.[51] Many environmentalists see our energy gluttony and inefficiency as being at the heart of many of our most serious environmental problems. (For more on energy issues, see pages 197-201).

THE MODERN MOVEMENT

As a result of the heightened public awareness of environmental problems, thousands of people joined existing conservation and preservation groups.[52] And hundreds of new ecology or environmental groups appeared during the 1960s and 1970s.[53] Many environmental activists of the 1970s had previous experience in and borrowed tactics from the civil rights, anti-Vietnam War and student movements of the 1960s.[54] Many of these groups pressured Congress to protect the public by taking responsibility for pollution. Some groups worked for protection through the courts. Others took action in their local communities, starting recycling centers and community gardens.[55]

Enthusiasm for environmental issues culminated in the celebration of Earth Day on April 22, 1970. Wisconsin Senator Gaylord Nelson, an early anti-pollution advocate, authored the legislation that declared April 22nd as Earth Day.[56] College student Denis Hayes organized teach-ins on ecology issues on college campuses nationwide.[57] The idea expanded into a nationwide day of protests and demonstrations in which 20 million people participated to heighten awareness of environmental issues.[58] Celebrations included a plant-in at the University of Washington, organized to reclaim a wetland biology preserve which had been turned into a dump. Nearly 400 students and members of the faculty and the community planted pines, firs, willows and native shrubs.[59] "Earth Day in 1970 symbolized the fusing of traditional conservationism and preservationism with middle class, student and urban environmental concerns into the modern environmental movement," writes professor Victor Scheffer.[60]

Denis Hayes voiced the public mood behind the Earth Day effort: "We will not appeal any more to the conscience of institutions because institutions have no conscience. If we want them to do what is right, we must make them do what is right. We will use proxy fights, lawsuits, demonstrations, research, boycotts, ballots — whatever it takes. This may be our last chance. If environment is a fad, it's going to be our last fad."[61]

After Earth Day, groups of environmentalists around the country worked, using a variety of different methods including lobbying and litigation, to encourage solutions to environmental problems. For example, Environmental Action, which organized in 1970 to coordinate the celebrations for Earth Day, annually named its "Dirty Dozen" — the twelve members of Congress with the worst voting records on environmental issues.[62]

The student Public Interest Research Groups (PIRGs) initiated bottle and can recycling measures in various states across the country. In 1975, MASSPIRG gathered the 100,000 signatures needed to put a bottle-recycling bill on the ballot. Opponents of the proposed law, grocers, soft drink and liquor bottlers and distributors, spent over $2 million to lobby against it. The initiative was defeated at the polls by only 8/10 of 1 percent.[63]

MASSPIRG then went directly to the state legislature but again faced the opposition of powerful bottlers and distributors. MASSPIRG students held community meetings, spoke on radio programs and campaigned door-to-door to let residents know how successful the law had been in other states. By 1981, polls showed that 70 percent of Massachusetts residents supported the bottle bill. The legislature passed the bill, but the bill again went to a referendum, this time to override the legislature's passage of the bill. And in spite of the vast financial resources of the opposition, 59 percent of the votes cast supported the bottle bill, which went into effect in 1983.[64]

THE ENVIRONMENTAL CAMPAIGN MOVES TO THE COURTS AND LEGISLATURES

The heightened public awareness of the dangers to the environment and public health forced the federal government, in the early 1970s, to create a new regulatory system, including establishment of the Environmental Protection Agency and the Occupational Safety and Health Administration. As a result, gains were made in monitoring and guidelines were set for control and cleanup of pollution. Consequently, citizen environmental groups turned to the courts and the legislatures to monitor the government's progress and to continue to voice public concern for environmental issues.[65]

"It is through the courts that the environmental movement has achieved many of its victories (or avoided many possible losses) — defeating destructive projects, halting pollution, ensuring that the government does its job," writes Jon Naar.[66] Environmental groups often sue polluters to force them to comply with existing regulations or regulatory agencies to ensure that they enforce the law properly. Because regulatory agencies often do not have the funds to do everything Congress has instructed them to do, a

citizen suit often serves to set policy by requiring a reordering of priorities. Suits may stop or delay proposed construction or development projects by challenging the validity of permits or a company's ability to comply with standards. And environmental groups often are involved in court cases on the side of government regulators who are sued by a company denied a permit.[67]

In the early 1960s, the Scenic Hudson Preservation Conference, an environmental group, sued the Federal Power Commission[68] for allowing Consolidated Edison of New York to go ahead with plans to build a power plant at scenic Storm King Mountain on the Hudson River.[69] The Power Commission asked the court to dismiss the case because Scenic Hudson did not have an economic interest in the project. But the Court of Appeals for the Second Circuit ruled that Scenic Hudson should be allowed to bring suit because it did have an "aesthetic, conservational and recreational" interest in the area.[70] The idea of a noneconomic interest being sufficient to establish standing — the right to sue — was born.[71] The court also established that agencies must consider noneconomic factors, such as environmental damage, when licensing projects. The case is "generally credited with having given birth to environmental law."[72]

With their right to sue established, citizens could challenge environmental laws in court. With the dozens of laws that Congress subsequently passed, "the lawyers suddenly had a whole new arsenal of weapons. ... And from that period on, litigation would become one of the most important tools conservationists had at their disposal."[73]

Several organizations were founded during this time, including the Environmental Defense Fund (EDF) in 1967, the Natural Resources Defense Council (NRDC) in 1970 and the Sierra Club Legal Defense Fund in 1971.[74] Each has successfully used the courts as a tool in overseeing and enforcing existing environmental laws and regulations.

In 1969, Congress passed the National Environmental Policy Act (NEPA) which requires every federal agency to prepare an environmental impact statement

(EIS) to consider environmental factors in all decisions and to investigate alternatives that may be less damaging to the environment.[75] NEPA also established the Council on Environmental Quality to advise the President on environmental issues and monitor the EIS process.[76] In 1970, President Richard Nixon created the Environmental Protection Agency (EPA) to coordinate the environmental responsibilities of federal government agencies.[77]

The Clean Air Act of 1970 gave the EPA the power to set national air quality standards for pollutants that may endanger public health.[78] The Federal Water Pollution Control Act Amendments of 1972, or the Clean Water Act, required polluters to apply for permits regulating the kind and amount of allowable discharges and included a citizen suit provision under which citizens could sue polluters to force compliance with the law if state and federal officials did not.[79] The Clean Water Act is credited with saving up to $1 billion annually by preventing waterborne disease and up to $9.4 billion in increased recreational and property values.[80] In 1974, Congress passed the Safe Drinking Water Act to set health standards for toxic contaminants in drinking water systems.[81]

Congress amended the Federal Insecticide, Fungicide and Rodenticide Act (FIFRA) in 1964 to shift from the government to the manufacturer the burden of proving a chemical safe.[82] The stronger Federal Environmental Pesticide Control Act of 1972 required all manufacturers of pesticides to register their products with the EPA.[83] The Solid Waste Disposal Act of 1965 was passed to address the growing garbage disposal problem.[84] Five years later Congress passed the Resource Conservation and Recovery Act to encourage reuse and recycling.[85] Congress also passed legislation to protect wilderness and endangered species.[86]

The federal government rarely authorized funds adequate to carry out these legislative programs. And although the stated purpose of the National Environmental Policy Act of 1969 is "to prevent and eliminate damage to the environment,"[87] most of these legislative efforts focused on regulating and monitoring pollution rather than preventing or reducing pollution.

In 1971, a small group of environmentalists and peace activists set out from Vancouver in two boats called Greenpeace and Greenpeace, Too, for the Alaskan island of Amchitka. Their mission was to call attention to the dangers of ongoing underground nuclear testing conducted by the U.S. government. Calling themselves the Don't Make a Wave Committee — a reference to the possibility that the testing would generate tidal waves — the group never made it to Amchitka. But the action stirred public opinion and protests against the testing began to pour into Washington, DC. Within a year, the U.S. government halted the testing at Amchitka.[88]

The next year the group, under the name Greenpeace, decided to take on the French government which was conducting atmospheric tests of its nuclear weapons on the Pacific Ocean atoll of Mururoa. The group's sailboat, the Greenpeace III, was led by Canadian David McTaggart, later chairperson of Greenpeace International.[89] The activists prevented the French testing by refusing to leave the surrounding waters, despite constant harassment from French ships. McTaggart and his crew returned the following summer of 1973 to focus further attention on the French testing. This time the French boarded the Greenpeace boat and severely beat McTaggart and his crew. But the resultant public outcry led the French government to end atmospheric nuclear testing one year later, although it continued underground testing.[90]

Greenpeace next challenged the international whaling and sealing industries in an attempt to stop the killing of these animals for commercial purposes. Greenpeace activists confronted whaling ships from countries including the Soviet Union and Japan by sailing their small inflatable boats between huge whaling ships and their prey.[91] A Soviet whaling ship fired a harpoon over the heads of Greenpeace activists as they attempted to protect a whale under fire.[92]

Greenpeace also lobbied before the International Whaling Commission which eventually adopted an international moratorium on all commercial whaling that went into effect in 1986.[93] Greenpeace charges that commercial whale hunting continues under the guise of scientific research.[94] Thus, Greenpeace ships monitor compliance with the moratorium. However, the known annual harvest of whales, according to the *New York Times*, dropped from 25,000 in 1975 to 1,000 in 1988.[95]

Beginning in 1976, Greenpeace confronted seal hunters off the coast of Canada to draw attention to the annual slaughter of up to 200,000 whitecoat harp seal pups. Greenpeace activists shielded the pups from seal hunters and once again received world-wide attention which led to a dramatic drop in the demand for whitecoat seal pelts.[96] And the European Community banned the import of white seal fur products, further decreasing demand. Critics charged, however, that Greenpeace was not sensitive to the people who lost jobs as a result of the ban.[97]

In 1985, the Greenpeace flagship, Rainbow Warrior, was preparing for a protest journey to the French underground nuclear test site on Mururoa Atoll. On July 10, while the Rainbow Warrior was docked in New Zealand, two bombs exploded, sinking the ship and killing Greenpeace photographer Fernando Pereira.[98] Eventually, the French government was forced to take responsibility for the bombing. Greenpeace sued the French government and won $8 million in damages.[99]

Greenpeace continues to stage nonviolent direct actions around the world to call attention to a variety of issues including industrial pollution, ocean dumping of nuclear wastes and the international trade in

Greenpeace activists in Deepwater, NJ award Dupont a "Blue Ribbon" for producing the largest quantity of ozone-destroying CFCs per year.

© 1989 ROBERT VISSER/GREENPEACE

hazardous waste. The actions include sailing to Siberia to protest an illegal Soviet whaling station during which seven "activists were arrested and temporarily detained while others eluded pursuit to bring home documentary film of the incident; handcuffing themselves to toxic waste drums about to be dumped at sea; scuba-diving to plug the underwater discharge pipes of chemical polluters and parachuting off industrial smokestacks; scaling Mount Rushmore and the cliffs surrounding Niagara Falls and dangling off the Golden Gate bridge to protest various environmental and nuclear threats ..."[100]

Says Greenpeace USA director Peter Bahouth, "We are an activist organization that goes to the site of problems, whether it's Washington, DC, where certain policies are being made; or the ocean, where 35,000 miles of drift nets are dropped every evening, if it's a chemical company's pipe out the back of its factory, we'll be there. We want to go to where the problem is actually happening, show people what is going on and take some action."[101]

Another Greenpeace campaign focuses on the international hazardous waste trade. The U.S.-based chemical company American Cyanamid ships hazardous mercury sludge produced in New Jersey to South Africa for disposal or storage.[102] Greenpeace worked for an international ban on such trading which 82 countries — including every country in Africa except South Africa — around the world have signed.[103]

Greenpeace is working to connect the more than 8,000 grassroots groups around the United States fighting toxics in their communities, especially incinerators which burn toxic waste.[104] The goal of Greenpeace is to attack the root causes of toxics problems which it sees as "production technology choices being made by very small groups of people who care about the wrong things."[105] Says Peter Bahouth:

Decisions are affecting public health and are made in a very private way, with little thought as to the long-term implications. The big challenge is to figure out a way that we can affect those decisions so that people can become more involved. People will say, 'Wait a minute. We're not going to let a small group of businessmen make decisions which are affecting our health and our quality of life. ... Currently, chemicals are almost given a bill of rights; in other words, they are out there in the environment unless they are proven guilty, proven to be harmful. We should be saying that chemicals don't have rights, people have rights, and our right should be to a clean environment.[106]

Greenpeace has expanded to 23 countries and, with a fleet of seven ocean-going ships, works on 37 different campaign issues falling under the general categories of nuclear, toxics, ocean ecology or atmosphere and energy.[107] As of 1990, four million people worldwide were members of Greenpeace, two million of them in the United States.[108]

DISASTER SPURS GRASSROOTS CAMPAIGNS

Two events in the late 1970s, the accident at Three Mile Island nuclear power plant and the evacuation of hundreds of families from toxic waste-contaminated Love Canal, significantly changed the course of the environmental movement by focusing attention on the dangers of nuclear power and toxic waste to the environment and human health. Grassroots citizen movements emerged which involve communities around the country calling for an end to nuclear power and for prevention of and responsible disposal of toxic waste.

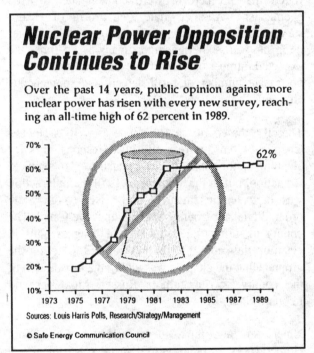

Nuclear Power Opposition Continues to Rise

Over the past 14 years, public opinion against more nuclear power has risen with every new survey, reaching an all-time high of 62 percent in 1989.

Sources: Louis Harris Polls, Research/Strategy/Management

© Safe Energy Communication Council

THREE MILE ISLAND
AND THE CAMPAIGN AGAINST NUCLEAR POWER

On March 28, 1979, one of the reactors at the Three Mile Island (TMI) nuclear facility outside of Harrisburg, Pennsylvania, experienced a partial melt-down, releasing unknown amounts of radiation into the surrounding atmosphere. Two days later, after company officials withheld information about the seriousness of the accident, state officials ordered the evacuation of pregnant women and children within a 5-mile radius of the plant. As many as 200,000 residents fled the area.[109]

The accident — the worst commercial nuclear accident in U.S. history — sparked widespread alarm over the dangers of nuclear power.[110] More than 90 consumer, labor, environmental, senior citizen, religious, minority and women's organizations formed the May 6 Coalition in response to the TMI accident to demand an end to the growing U.S. dependence on nuclear power. The coalition organized a march and rally in Washington, DC, in which an estimated 100,000 people participated. Another rally to protest nuclear power, which attracted 200,000 people, took place in September of 1979 in New York City.[111]

And on May 20, 1979, between 5,000 and 10,000 people participated in the "Women and Children" protest march to the Reading, Pennsylvania headquarters of Metropolitan-Edison (Met-Ed), the operators of the TMI plant.[112] The march marked the beginning of a long citizen struggle to win a thorough cleanup and compensation for health problems and to block the restart of the TMI facility.

More than 2,000 area residents filed suit against TMI's owners for cancers and other radiation-related health injuries. Many of the health effects from radiation exposure begin to show up 10 to 20 years after exposure. But in the year after the accident, one Pennsylvania Department of Health survey showed an abnormal number of babies born with serious thyroid problems.[113]

Little over a year after the accident, despite widespread community opposition, General Public Utilities, the parent company of TMI operator Met-Ed, vented radioactive gases directly into the atmosphere for 11 days. The action was later ruled illegal by the U.S. Court of Appeals for the District of Columbia. GPU then sent the first workers back into the plant to begin cleanup.[114] And in October, 1980, hearings began for restart of TMI-1, another reactor which had been shut down for refueling at the time of the accident.[115] Eventually, TMI's owner was convicted of falsifying and destroying safety data, which led to the 1979 accident.[116]

Citizen groups continued to protest, holding a rally on March 27, 1981 on the steps of the state capitol where protestors burned $47,500 worth of electric bills from Met-Ed, the operator of TMI.[117] The next day, 15,000 protestors from labor unions, environmental and safe energy groups and religious groups marched through Harrisburg marking the second anniversary of the accident.[118] Vickie DiSanto, a TMI area resident, said of the protests, "Nothing's going to make it worthwhile for us to have gone through it, but if we can keep anyone else from going through this same thing, it's going to mean something. It will ease the pain a little bit."[119]

Protests against nuclear power continued through the 1980s across the country. Every reactor ordered in the United States since 1973 has been canceled, and no new orders have been made since 1978.[120] The disaster called attention to the dangers of nuclear power to human health and the environment and raised questions about the role of government in promoting safe energy policies. Citizen groups around the country began to raise questions about the nuclear reactors in or nearby their communities: questions about disposal of radioactive wastes, evacuation plans in the event of a catastrophe, worker protection from excessive radiation exposure, incompetent plant workers and the possibility of terrorist attack.[121] A voter referendum campaign organized by citizens closed down the Rancho Seco plant in Sacramento, California in 1989.[122]

LOVE CANAL

The story of hazardous waste contamination at Love Canal in Niagara Falls, New York dates back to 1942, when the Hooker Chemical and Plastics Corporation drained Love Canal and buried hundreds of barrels of hazardous waste, containing 82 different chemical substances, among them an estimated 130 pounds of the highly toxic chemical dioxin.[123] Hooker later sold the land to the local Board of Education, which built an elementary school on top of the covered dump. The land was sold for only one dollar on the condition that Hooker be free from any future liability.[124]

Over time, the buried wastes leaked out of the barrels and began surfacing in the surrounding soil. The

chemicals caused a number of problems, including chemical burns and noxious odors.[125] In the mid-1970s, residents near the canal found a black oily substance in their basements. Concern from Love Canal residents prompted the local newspaper, the *Niagara Gazette*, to test the substance. The test revealed that the substance contained 15 organic chemicals, including three chlorinated hydrocarbons that are toxic by inhalation, ingestion and skin absorption.[126]

Eventually, in 1978, the New York State Department of Health surveyed the homes closest to the canal and found that 95 percent were contaminated by the chemicals.[127] Another State Department of Health survey concluded that "people living near the former dumpsite were experiencing as many as 3.5 times the expected number of miscarriages, as well as a disproportionate number of birth defects and spontaneous abortions."[128]

The city, the county and the state as well as Hooker Chemical Company refused to take responsibility for cleaning up the canal.[129] "Love Canal residents looked for action, but in the summer of 1978 the only action was bureaucratic finger-pointing. New York State ordered Niagara County to clean up Love Canal. The county in turn ordered the city of Niagara Falls to clean up the canal, but the city refused to act on the grounds that the cleanup was within the jurisdiction of the county," write authors Russell Mokhiber and Leonard Shen.[130]

Ninety percent of the residents formed the Love Canal Homeowners Association to demand government aid. They knocked on doors, gathered signatures on petitions, held public meetings, picketed and got arrested. In August of 1978, two years after the health effects were made public and after aggressive citizen organizing, the state Health Commissioner finally intervened, declared Love Canal an "official emergency" and advised pregnant women and children to move away immediately.[131]

Love Canal residents appealed to the federal government for help. In 1978, residents sent a telegram to President Jimmy Carter seeking federal funding for the evacuation of the remaining Love Canal families.

Carter declared a national emergency at Love Canal, and issued the first federal funds for a human-made disaster. Nearly 300 families were evacuated.[132]

But the problems continued for families living outside the evacuation area in homes located above old stream beds or dried-up ponds. These families reported high rates of miscarriages and birth defects as well as other illnesses. Residents, with the help of a cancer research scientist, surveyed homes and health problems and hypothesized that the chemicals were migrating through these previously wet areas of the canal. But once again the State Department of Health did not listen.[133]

Continued investigation uncovered additional underground dumpsites, waste dumped in the river and corresponding health effects. Lois Marie Gibbs and the Homeowners Association kept the issue in the public eye with meetings and protests. Finally, in November 1979, the state agreed to buy the homes of any remaining Love Canal residents who wished to leave. At the same time New York governor Hugh L. Carey announced plans to "revitalize" Love Canal by moving new families into the homes of those who had left. A few weeks later, the Love Canal Homeowners Association released a survey which found that of 15 pregnancies begun in the Love Canal area, only one ended in the birth of a healthy baby, four ended in miscarriages, two were stillborn and nine others were born with deformities.[134]

In May of 1980, the EPA released a study which "concluded that 11 of 36 Love Canal residents tested had suffered chromosomal damage — which could be a harbinger of future cancer, birth defects and other health problems."[135] The study came under attack and the EPA decided to wait to take further action until the study was reviewed. Residents demanded to be relocated. After the EPA continued to refuse to respond to the residents' requests, Lois Marie Gibbs, president of the Homeowners Association, temporarily held hostage two EPA officials to demand immediate evacuation.[136] Two days later another study was released indicating nerve damage among the remaining residents and President Carter declared a second federal emergency.[137]

In February of 1988, a U.S. District Court found Occidental Petroleum Corporation (Hooker Chemical's parent company) liable for cleaning up the Love Canal toxic waste dump in a suit the federal government brought in 1979.[138] Love Canal residents sued Hooker and settled in 1984 for $20 million.[139]

Congress responded to Love Canal and similar toxic dumpsites around the country by establishing the Comprehensive Environmental Response, Compensation and Liability Act of 1980. Better know as Superfund, this federal program was set up to administer $1.6 billion set aside to clean up the worst hazardous waste sites across the country. Superfund is financed with public funds and with funds from fines and taxes on polluting industries.[140] In 1980, the EPA estimated that more than 18,000 hazardous waste sites existed.[141] As of 1991, the sites on the EPA's national priority list — of the worst sites — numbered 1,245.[142]

THE ENVIRONMENTAL MOVEMENT ON THE DEFENSIVE

Despite growing concern for health and environmental risks, many segments of society continued to respond to environmental threats with what author Ron Brownstein calls the "macho of technology" — "the determined belief that the answer to any problem is the forceful development and marketing of more sophisticated, more elaborate technology; more singleminded application of American ingenuity without full consideration of its long-term impact on public health and the environment."[143]

In the late 1970s, business, particularly the heavily regulated chemical, oil refining and paper and wood products industries, organized a campaign to reverse the regulatory measures of the past decade.[144]

President Ronald Reagan took office in 1981 with an agenda to deregulate, arguing that environmental laws disrupt economic growth and create a large and unnecessary government bureaucracy. The Reagan administration made substantial cuts in the budgets of federal regulatory agencies. For example, in 1981 and 1982, the budget for EPA's four major programs (water, air, hazardous waste and pesticides) was cut by 30 percent.[145] Reagan fired the entire staff at the Council on Environmental Quality and cut its budget by 62 percent.[146]

While Reagan appointee Anne Gorsuch Burford was Administrator of EPA, dozens of regulations were revoked or delayed, while enforcement actions and litigation against polluters dropped by at least 70 percent.[147] Burford was forced to resign in March 1983. Eventually more than 20 Reagan-appointed EPA officials resigned after charges of unethical behavior or illegal activities.[148]

Much of the regulatory framework was weakened and enforcement made more difficult due to budget constraints. But overall, the size of the federal government grew during the Reagan administration as did the federal deficit. As Stewart Udall, Secretary of the Interior during the Kennedy administration and former member of Congress, stated in 1988, "History will confirm that Ronald Reagan's legacy created a massive fiscal debt restricting the options of his successors and of the American people for positive action on behalf of their air, water, and land."[149]

During the 1980s, many environmental groups worked to maintain the regulatory structure and also took many issues, for which the federal government no longer took responsibility, to the individual states. Meanwhile, people living in communities affected by pollution engaged in direct action campaigns, launching the toxics movement, to demand that government and industry ensure a safe and healthy environment.[150]

THE TOXICS MOVEMENT

A citizen movement grew out of the disaster at Love Canal. Communities across the country discovered their own hazardous waste problems: improperly stored or dumped chemicals surfacing in drinking water sources and in the soil, chemical exposure in the workplace and factories that produce chemicals and their by-products, polluting the air and water of surrounding communities.

The toxics movement differs significantly from the traditional environmental campaigns that primarily use the tactics of legislation and litigation to win environmental victories. The toxics movement consists of thousands of local, autonomous groups that work to clean up hazardous waste or block incinerators in their own communities. The local toxics groups are made up of people who live and work near hazardous waste sites and who are personally affected by the resulting contamination.[151]

Lois Marie Gibbs, president of the Love Canal Homeowners Association, founded the Citizen's Clearinghouse for Hazardous Waste (CCHW) in 1981 to assist other communities with toxic waste problems.[152] A leader in the toxics movement, CCHW provides technical assistance and training to encourage local community groups to take action for themselves. As of February 1991, of the groups following CCHW's advice, 99 percent had won their fights against proposed hazardous waste facilities.[153]

CCHW provides assistance to over 7,200 local citizen groups, with over a third of its membership in the South. CCHW places a special emphasis on outreach to underserved, low-income and minority communities and on including people from diverse backgrounds who want to have more control over decisions affecting their lives.[154] "CCHW stands for the rights of people to have control over their lives, to speak for themselves, and to have a meaningful role as equals in any and all decisions that will affect their lives, homes and families," writes former CCHW organizer Will Collette.[155]

During the 1980s, citizen toxics groups "defeated thousands of proposals for unsafe hazardous and solid waste facilities, including deep well injection systems, incinerators, landfills and sham recycling facilities."[156] In 1986, toxic waste initiatives put on the ballots by citizen groups in New York, New Jersey, California and Massachusetts all passed, authorizing significant increases in state environmental programs.[157] In every state, citizens are involved in campaigns to clean up Superfund sites and pressure industry to reduce its hazardous waste generation and emission. Citizens are participating in waste management planning, permit distribution and enforcement of regulations.[158]

In rural Warren, Massachusetts, a citizen group successfully defeated plans for a hazardous waste treatment plant in their community proposed by the IT Corporation. The group called itself StopIT.[159] In San Jose, California, the Silicon Valley Toxics Coalition convinced most of the local municipalities of Santa Clara County to pass ordinances that require "community access to information, special handling and storage procedures for acutely hazardous materials and emergency preparedness plans."[160] Other groups include the Clean Water Action Project which supports citizen activism around ground and surface water contamination in the Northeast, Citizens for a Better Environment which supports state toxic control legislation in California and the Midwest, Greenpeace and the student Public Interest Research Groups.

Local groups were instrumental in passage of the Superfund reauthorization bill in Congress in 1986. The National Toxics Campaign (NTC), which formed in 1983 as a coalition of nearly 300 citizen, church and labor groups, coordinated the activities of local groups organizing support for the reauthorization of Superfund. Local groups picketed and demonstrated in the home districts of Members of Congress who had not lent their support. And in the summer of 1986, the NTC organized the "Superdrive for Superfund," four truck caravans which collected contaminated water and soil samples from 200 toxic waste sites across the country and gathered two million signatures and delivered them to legislators in Washington.[161] "These truck caravans did much to galvanize local support and attract media attention to the need for congressional action," writes Kenneth Geiser.[162]

In 1986, Congress finally passed the $9 billion reauthorization, the Superfund Amendment and Reauthorization Act (SARA), the costliest piece of environmental legislation ever.[163] SARA established "a national public right to know about local chemical usage and releases" and established "community-by-community preparedness for chemical accidents."[164] Under Title III of SARA, companies must isclose information about the chemicals they use, store and emit at their facilities.[165]

Citizen toxics groups have formed successful coalitions of labor, community and religious groups.[166] When 340 members of the Oil, Chemical and Atomic Workers (OCAW) Local 4-620 in Geismar, Louisiana, were locked out during 1984 contract negotiations, the union members joined with local residents to wage a campaign against the BASF corporation which was endangering the lives of workers as well as polluting the community. Although BASF was the main target of the campaign, the coalition also challenged both the petrochemical industry in Louisiana and the state government on issues of environmental protection, workers health and safety and racial discrimination. The coalition succeeded in stopping the construction of a new BASF chemical facility at a site where the company had contaminated groundwater. OCAW won its five year fight with BASF in early 1990, signing a new 3-year contract.[167]

Also unique to the toxics movement is the democratic nature of the local organizations and the prevalence of women in leadership roles.[168] Says Theresa Freeman of Vermonters Organized for Cleanup of her work and the work of other women like her in the grassroots toxics movement, "We all have character traits that are similar. Traits like survival, determination, perseverance, equality. We're shaping a value system that doesn't exist and it's based on the fundamentals of democracy."[169]

Gary Cohen and John O'Connor of the National Toxics Campaign describe the goal of the toxics movement as fighting for environmental democracy, which they describe as follows:

> *If industry currently has the right to chemically trespass into our air, water, soil, food and bodies, then citizens must have the right to protect themselves, their neighborhood and their workplace. Specifically we must have the right to know what these chemicals are, how they affect our health, and what volume of waste is produced in relation to the volume of product. ... Citizens must have the right, moreover, to inspect the facilities, operations and processes that put poisons into the public air and waterways.*[170]

Many environmental organizations continue to advocate a strategy of negotiation and compromise about how much pollution is acceptable. The citizen toxic groups, however, are "demanding not that the dumping of hazardous waste be slowed down, but stopped; not that dioxin-producing incinerators be equipped with unworkable emission controls, but abandoned in favor of recycling."[171]

TOXICS REDUCTION AND PREVENTION

Citizen groups demanding that their communities be free of hazardous waste were quickly tagged by many in industry and government as having a "Not In My Backyard" (NIMBY) philosophy.[172] But most citizen toxics groups embrace a "Not in Anyone's Backyard" idea by working to reduce and prevent toxic problems.[173]

Reduction and prevention of toxics is part of a solution to the toxics problem that goes far beyond cleanup of existing dumpsites. Biologist Barry Commoner maintains that the regulatory approach (monitoring and controlling pollution) to environmental problems has largely failed. Significant progress is made only when pollutants are eliminated or significantly reduced at their source, before they are produced, rather than monitored and controlled after the pollutants are produced.[174]

For example, lead (which can cause serious health problems including mental retardation in children) emissions in the United States were reduced (not monitored or controlled) between 1975 and 1985 by 86 percent. As a result, the average lead levels in the blood of Americans decreased by 37 percent between 1976 and 1980.[175] By contrast, the United States has failed to reduce other air pollutant emissions, "which on the average, decreased by only 13.2 percent between 1975 and 1985."[176] Similarly, the pesticide DDT (which studies show causes cancers and interferes with the biochemistry of reproduction) was banned in 1972.[177] In birds tested between 1969 and 1975, the average DDT content decreased by 77 percent. And between 1970 and 1983, "average DDT levels in body fat in the American population decreased by 79 percent."[178]

To meet the goal of preventing toxic pollution, Barry Commoner recommends the following policy priorities: replace nonrenewable and nuclear energy with renewable energy sources, particularly solar; replace the chemically-based system of agriculture with organic farming; replace petrochemical products and processes with those more compatible with the environment; and replace dependence on cars and trucks with an expansion of railroads and mass transit systems.[179] According to Commoner, most of the technologies necessary to make these changes already exist but they must be integrated in to the overall system of production — no one technology alone can solve all environmental problems.[180]

To accomplish the changes outlined above, a number of environmental groups press the government to use its purchasing power to make environmentally-sound technologies profitable. For example, the federal government can stimulate the market for cars and trucks with smog-free engines.[181] And consumers play a role in stimulating pollution prevention. CCHW and NTC have organized nationwide campaigns to unite local groups to work to eliminate harmful products. In 1987, CCHW launched a boycott against McDonald's restaurants to force the fast food chain to stop using toxic polystyrene foam products. In November of 1990, McDonalds announced a phase out of polystyrene foam packaging.[182] (See page 256 for details on the McToxics fight). And the NTC convinced 1,200 supermarkets in North America to sign "Pesticide Reduction Agreements" promising to stop selling produce containing residues of cancer-causing pesticides by 1995.[183]

OTHER APPROACHES TO ENVIRONMENTAL SOLUTIONS

Bioregionalists look at the world in terms of ecologically defined regions rather than by political boundaries.[184] They call on people to take care of the bioregion in which they live by implementing "drastic changes in individual lifestyles which reject wasteful forms of consumption and embrace appropriate technology."[185] As of 1988, more than 100 bioregional groups existed from Oregon to Maine working on projects ranging "from the restoration of a salmon run in a northern California river to the preservation of family farms in Pennsylvania."[186]

Advocates of another approach, deep ecology, view human and nonhuman species "as having inherent and equal value, from which it follows that humans have no right to reduce the natural diversity of the earth."[187] Other environmental activists are working to win representation in legislative bodies by forming political parties. Particularly successful in Europe, Green Party candidates in Germany, Italy and England have won seats in their countries' parliaments.[188]

CONCLUSION

In the 1970s, public opinion polls showed that less than a majority of voters were concerned about the environment. By 1990, between two-thirds and four fifths of voters expressed strong concern about the environment. For example, the percentage of American voters very concerned about water pollution increased from 48 to 84 percent, from 1970 to 1990. In the late 1970s, only 27 percent of voters polled thought the government needed to do more to protect the environment. By 1990, that percentage had risen to 68 percent of American voters.[189]

One event that increased public concern was the Exxon oil spill in Prince William Sound, Alaska in 1989. "The *Exxon Valdez* oil spill galvanized voters' focus on corporations and the need for government action to regulate them, and has sharpened their negative assessment of the way both have responded to environmental problems," writes pollster Celinda Lake.[190] Thousands of individuals spontaneously boycotted Exxon products to protest the company's actions surrounding the spill.

The increase in public concern was also evidenced in the celebration of the 20th anniversary of Earth Day on April 22, 1990, in which an estimated 100 to 200 million people around the world participated.[191] Students in the United States were particularly active in the Earth Day celebrations holding "tree plantings, hikes, cleanups, outdoors fairs and special lectures and teach-ins" as well as initiating long-term projects such as recycling.[192]

With a public mandate to solve problems and with the pollution prevention strategies of the citizen toxics movement, environmental activists are well prepared to produce a new wave of victories for the environment and human health.

BIBLIOGRAPHY

"Action Line," *Everyone's Backyard*, January/February 1990, p. 15.

Allen, Durward L. "Leopold: The Founder," *American Forests*. September/October 1987.

"Bhopal on the Bayou," *Multinational Monitor*. January/February 1990.

Bollier, David. *Citizen Action and Other Big Ideas: A History of Ralph Nader and the Modern Consumer Movement*. Washington, DC: Center for Study of Responsive Law, 1989.

Bollier, David and Joan Claybrook. *Freedom From Harm: The Civilizing Influence of Health, Safety and Environmental Regulation*, Washington, DC: Public Citizen and Democracy Project, 1986.

Borrelli, Peter. "Environmentalism at a Crossroads: Reflections on the Old Old, New Old, Old New and New New Movements," *The Amicus Journal*. Summer 1987. Vol. 9. No. 3. First in a series.

Borrelli, Peter. "The Ecophilosophers: A Guide to Deep Ecologists, Bioregionalists, Greens and Others in Pursuit of Radical Change," *The Amicus Journal*. Spring 1988. Vol. 10, No. 2. Last in a series.

Carson, Rachel. *Silent Spring*. Greenwich, CT: Fawcett Publications, Inc., 1970 [1962].

Claybrook, Joan. *Retreat from Safety: Reagan's Attack on America's Health*. New York: Pantheon Books, 1984.

Cohen, Gary and John O'Connor, eds. *Fighting Toxics: A Manual for Protecting Your Family, Community and Workplace*. Washington, DC: Island Press, 1990.

Collette, Will. "Institutions: Citizen's Clearinghouse for Hazardous Wastes," *Environment*. Vol. 29. No. 9, November 1987.

Congressional Budget Office. "The Environmental Protection Agency: Overview of the Proposed 1984 Budget," April 1983.

Commoner, Barry. "A Reporter At Large: The Environment," *The New Yorker*. June 15, 1987.

Commoner, Barry. *Making Peace with the Planet*. New York: Pantheon Books, 1990.

Dolan, Maura and Larry B. Stammer. "200 Million Worldwide Pay Respect to Earth," *Los Angeles Times*. April 23, 1990.

Doroshow, Joanne. *A Decade of Delay, Deceit and Danger: Three Mile Island 1979-1989; A Retrospective*. Harrisburg, PA: Three Mile Island Alert, 1989.

Environmental Action. *Earth Day: The Beginning; A Guide for Survival*. New York: Arno Press and the New York Times, 1970.

Ehrlich, Paul R. *The Population Bomb*. New York: Ballantine Books, 1968.

Faber, Daniel and James O'Connor. "The Struggle for Nature: Environmental Crises and the Crisis of Environmentalism in the United States," *Capitalism, Nature, Socialism*. Summer 1989. No. 2.

Five Years of Progress: 1981-1986. Arlington, VA: Citizen's Clearinghouse for Hazardous Waste, 1986.

Flint, Anthony. "Environmental Movement Rekindles Student Activism on U.S. Campuses," *Boston Globe*. April 23, 1990.

Geiser, Kenneth. *One, Two, Many Environmentalists: The 1980s Transformation of the Environmental Movement*. Medford, MA: Department of Urban and Environmental Policy, Tufts University, 1987. Unpublished paper.

Gibbs, Lois Marie. "CCHW's 10th Anniversary: We've Come A Long Way," *Everyone's Backyard*. February, 1991.

Goldsteen, R.K. and John K. Schurr. *Demanding Democracy After Three Mile Island*. University of Florida Press, 1991.

"Greenpeace: An Antidote to Corporate Environmentalism, An Interview with Peter Bahouth," *Multinational Monitor*. March 1990.

Greenpeace ... For a Cleaner, Safer Earth. (Washington, DC: Greenpeace).

Griffin, Kelley. *More Action for a Change*. New York: Dembner Books, 1987.

Harwood, Michael. "Daredevils for the Environment," *The New York Times Magazine*. October 2, 1988.

Kallet, Arthur and Frederick J. Schlink. *100,000,000 Guinea Pigs: Dangers in Everyday Foods, Drugs and Cosmetics*. New York: Vanguard Press, 1932.

Lake, Celinda C. "The Environment: 20 Years After the First Earth Day," *The Polling Report*. April 9, 1990.

Lamb, Ruth deForest. *American Chamber of Horrors: The Truth about Food and Drugs*. New York: Arno Press, 1976 [1936].

Leopold, Aldo. *A Sand County Almanac and Sketches Here and There*. New York: Oxford University Press, 1964 [1949].

Leppzer, Robert, ed. *Voices from Three Mile Island: The People Speak Out*. Trumansburg, NY: Crossing Press, 1980.

Marsh, George Perkins. *Man and Nature: Physical Geography as Modified by Human Action*. Cambridge: Harvard University Press, 1965 [1864].

"McDonald's Surrenders," *Everyone's Backyard*, December 1990.

Naar, Jon. *Design for a Livable Planet: How You Can Help Clean Up the Environment*. New York: Harper and Row, Publishers, 1990.

Nader, Ralph, Ronald Brownstein and John Richard, eds. *Who's Poisoning America: Corporate Polluters and Their Victims in the Chemical Age*. San Francisco: Sierra Club Books, 1981.

Norton, Clark. "Green Giant," *The Washington Post Magazine*. September 3, 1989.

"Overhead Costs Spur Superfund Scrutiny," *Chicago Tribune*. October 3, 1991.

Paehlke, Robert C. *Environmentalism and the Future of Progressive Politics*. New Haven, CT: Yale University Press, 1989.

Russell, Dick. "The Monkeywrenchers: Whatever Happened to the Nice Little Old Lady in Tennis Shoes," *The Amicus Journal*. Fall 1987. Vol. 9. No. 4. Second in a series.

Russell, Dick. "Greenpeace: The Hippie Navy Gets Organized," *The Amicus Journal*. Summer 1984.

Scheffer, Victor B. *The Shaping of Environmentalism in America*. Seattle: University of Washington Press, 1991.

Stults, Karen. "Women Movers: Reflections on a Movement by Some of Its Leaders," *Everyone's Backyard*. Spring 1989.

Swanson, Stevenson and Casey Bukro. "Earth Day Festivities Remind Millions of Planet's Fragility," *Chicago Tribune*. April 23, 1990.

Turner, Tom. "The Legal Eagles," *The Amicus Journal*. Winter 1988. Vol. 10. No. 1. Third in a series.

Watkins, T.H. "Father of the Forests," *American Heritage*. February/March 1991. Volume 42. No. 1.

Wilkinson, Charles F. "Aldo Leopold and Western Water Law: Thinking Perpendicular to the Prior Appropriation Doctrine," *Land and Water Review*, University of Wyoming College of Law. Vol. XXVI. No. 1. 1989.

Zuckerman, Seth. "Environmentalism Turns 16: A Movement Takes Stock," *The Nation*. October 18, 1986.

Section Three

Techniques for Participation

Individual Action
Forming a Citizen Group
Public Education
Research
Direct Action
Citizen Lobbying
The Courts
Initiative and Referendum
Community Lawyer
Shareholder Activism
The Media
Fundraising

TECHNIQUES FOR PARTICIPATION

INTRODUCTION

"This country has more problems than it should tolerate and more solutions than it uses," writes Ralph Nader in the introduction to *Action for a Change: A Student's Manual for Public Interest Organizing.*[1] You will not need to look far in your school or community for problems that citizens can help solve. Instead of complaining that no one is doing anything, choose one problem or issue and get started. When setting long-range goals, try to imagine a model school, neighborhood or world. Then think of concrete ways to work toward those goals. Offer concrete solutions that attack the root of the problem.

Narrow down an issue to small goals attainable in a relatively brief period of time. For example, if you are concerned about the world's environment, start by initiating a school recycling drive. Once you have learned more about recycling and solid waste issues, promote recycling in the community and then lobby for local, state and federal solid waste policies that reflect your concerns.

Once you have chosen an issue and goals, decide whether to address the issue as an individual, join an organization which works on that issue or start your own group. Then plan a strategy and choose tactics to help reach your goals.

Discussed below are some of the many tactics and techniques that citizens have used throughout U.S. history to gain access to decision makers and to resolve community problems. You will not use all or even most of the tactics in one campaign, but wise choices will further your cause.

For example, in 1985, citizens in New York City organized to oppose a proposed garbage incinerator. First, 10,000 New Yorkers marched across the Brooklyn Bridge to show their opposition. The student-run New York Public Interest Research Group (NYPIRG) conducted a study of the environmental, health and financial consequences of the proposed incinerator. The report — which attracted media attention — offered an alternative in the form of a comprehensive recycling plan. Volunteers went door-to-door handing out leaflets to let others in the affected community know about the proposal and to urge them to call the mayor to voice their opposition to the proposed incinerator. More than 90 local groups formed a coalition to fight the incinerator. NYPIRG filed a lawsuit and the permit hearings for the incinerator were put on hold. NYPIRG and other groups lobbied the state legislature for a bill to support recycling. In January 1990, New York's new mayor, who pledged a two- to three-year moratorium on the incinerator, took office. Citizen groups continue to pressure the city for alternatives.[2]

INDIVIDUAL ACTION

Many of the techniques used to bring about change are most effective when carried out by groups of people, but individuals can use many tactics successfully. Individuals can take action by distributing pamphlets; attending and speaking at public meetings; gathering signatures for petitions; writing letters, making telephone calls or sending telegrams to government officials, the media and businesses; boycotting products or businesses; and employees can "blow the whistle" on unsafe or illegal situations.

Pamphleteering

One citizen who practices the philosophy that one person can make a difference is Charles L. Smith of Berkeley, California who educates the public by disseminating information through pamphlets. Charles Smith writes, "Pamphleteering is the personal use of the freedoms of speech and press ... It is an excellent system for introducing new ideas in an open society."[3] Smith writes that "pamphleteering has historically been used by persons who have sought to bring about change of intolerable situations," including Sam Adams, Thomas Paine and Margaret Sanger.[4]

Smith, who started pamphleteering in 1949, concentrates on issues which are not debated or discussed widely. He reads newspapers, magazines and journals, clipping articles about the many topics in which he is interested, such as parking and transportation problems, prison reform and drinking water quality. Acting as an individual, Smith passes on information to the citizens of Berkeley and surrounding communities which they are otherwise unlikely to receive. For example, when a nuclear power plant was proposed for Bodega Bay, California, in 1963, Smith took action by standing on a street corner wearing a sign which read "Bodega: 'Boom' or Bust?" and handing out informative flyers about the plant's economic and safety problems.[5]

Smith recommends that a pamphleteer create a flyer which is "authoritative, readable, reasonable, logical, concise and in general presentable and acceptable."[6] The flyer should not libel a person or organization. Next, a pamphleteer must create "a simple, readable sign (legible at a suitable distance) to be worn or displayed in a manner which predisposes passersby to accept your pamphlet."[7] Smith gives his pamphlets only to people who demonstrate curiosity or acceptance and therefore few people discard them.[8] Smith recommends distributing flyers on a street corner, or in other places where many potentially interested people may gather, such as conferences on related issues.[9]

Whistleblowing

Another individual action that courageous people take is whistleblowing — disclosing information about an illegal or dangerous action, usually in the workplace.[10] For example, in June of 1991, Linda Porter received the Cavallo Prize for Moral Courage which is awarded to individuals who "have chosen to speak out when it would have been far easier to have remained silent."[11] Porter, an employee of Brown and Root, Inc., a construction contractor at the Comanche Peak nuclear power plant in Texas, blew the whistle on worker health and safety violations she experienced at the plant.[12]

Porter began work at the plant in 1984 where her job was "to apply, strip and replace heavy paint coating on the plant structures."[13] Although her employer trained her in occupational safety, when Porter began to raise questions about the safety of crumbling concrete supports, "her concerns were met with ridicule ... [and] she and her crew were assigned to

the dirtiest and most difficult jobs."[14] Eventually, Porter was demoted and then fired. Within months, however, the company hired Porter back.

In 1987, Porter discovered that the coatings that she and other workers routinely used contained asbestos as well as several chemicals rated by government agencies as among the most dangerous for workers and the environment.[15] Not only Comanche Peak employees, but the entire community, were at risk because the plant dumped extra containers of coating in unlined pits near a recreational reservoir near the plant.[16]

Although Porter notified management of her findings and then reported them to the Nuclear Regulatory Commission and the Occupational Safety and Health Administration,[17] Brown and Root continued its intimidation tactics against Porter.[18] The company forced Porter and her crew to test the asbestos content of coatings applied to the walls of one room in the plant by sanding the coatings from the walls. The respirator Porter used to protect herself from the dust failed and she ingested large amounts of the dust through her nose and throat.[19] Porter continued to express safety concerns and was fired again.

The asbestos test left Porter with a myriad of health problems.[20] Despite her failing health, Porter stepped up her efforts to ensure that the plant management dealt with safety problems. Porter contacted the Government Accountability Project (GAP), a Washington, DC-based organization which provides legal assistance to "concerned citizens who witness dangerous, illegal or environmentally unsound practices in their workplaces and communities and choose to 'blow the whistle.'"[21] GAP is working with local groups in Texas "to ensure that the toxic chemicals are removed from unsafe landfills near the plant."[22]

As Porter continues her fight, she says, "What I'm seeking is for industry to understand that we're not going to be throwaway workers, and I want a message sent to regulators that they're not supposed to let this happen."[23]

After years of delay, Congress passed the Whistleblower Protection Act in 1989 to strengthen the government employees' code of ethics and give new protections to federal government whistleblowers, who often fear coming forward will cost them their job or their personal safety.[24]

FORMING A CITIZEN GROUP
AND RECRUITING SUPPORTERS

Individuals may find that joining with other people is more effective than working alone. Students may wish to start a new school organization, join an existing group or club or form a coalition of existing groups to work on a particular issue.

"There are several reasons why it is worth taking the time to organize a citizen action group," writes Mark Green in *Who Runs Congress?* "A group can commit more energy and resources than even the most dedicated individual. A group is more likely to have resources and endurance to carry a seemingly interminable project through to completion ..."[25]

A local group may want to affiliate with a national group or form a coalition with like-minded groups,[26] but if you decide to start a new group, advise Stephen Newman and Nancy Kramer in *Getting What You Deserve*, "There is no sure-fire, clear-cut blueprint for success; the goals, background and personalities of the founders will all determine the direction."[27]

Newman and Kramer instead offer the following tips:[28] Visit other groups to ask for advice and support; hold a meeting as soon as you have several people who are really interested in participating, not just joining. Start with a specific agenda for the meeting but let others contribute their ideas and suggestions; begin with one or two activities to avoid exhausting the group's energy; assign specific tasks to people, sharing responsibility and glory and; set small reachable goals.

Recruitment

Once an organization is formed, launch an education program to let the rest of the community know what the group is doing and to recruit members. When asked to join an organization, people naturally will want to know about the group's goals and tactics.

Talking with people face to face is the best way to involve them. To recruit members, citizen groups often go door-to-door (canvass) in the neighborhood affected by an issue, hold house meetings and speak at meetings of other community groups.[29] To recruit other students at school, ask for permission to speak to home room classes, hold an assembly or set up an information table in the cafeteria. Ask those interested for a small commitment, such as attending a meeting, writing a letter to a legislator or signing a petition.[30] Once members have been recruited, it is important to put them to work, letting them use their talents effectively to attack the goal from many angles.[31]

House meetings are a simple and effective way to recruit new members. Community organizer Fred Ross developed the house meeting method in the early 1950s as he organized Mexican American farm workers in Tustin, California, to fight segregated schools. Ross was struggling to find a way to bring people together when the farm workers suggested the idea.[32]

Ross asked those who were interested to invite their friends to small meetings at their homes to spread the word about issues and how they could become involved. Ross reached many people through these house meetings and successfully organized a voter registration drive that helped elect school board officials who ended school segregation in the area.[33]

Fred Ross taught the method to Cesar Chavez, president of the United Farm Workers (UFW).[34] When Chavez and Dolores Huerta, first vice-president of the UFW, began organizing farm workers, they used the house meeting method. Where other methods failed, with the house meetings, says Huerta, "[W]e were able to get together a thousand farm workers who were willing to put their names on the line and start paying their dues."[35]

Types of Citizen Groups

Three types of common citizen groups are the citizen lobby, the citizen coalition and community organization.[36]

Typically, a citizen lobby works to influence policy with a central office in Washington or the state capital and a network of citizens around the state or country ready to make phone calls, write letters, send telegrams and join together for demonstrations, visits to legislators and other actions at the capital.[37]

A coalition is a group of organizations working to pursue common interests.[38] Coalitions show the backing of a wide variety of groups on a particular issue.[39] And according to Marc Caplan in *A Citizens' Guide to Lobbying*, coalitions "pool the skills and resources of the groups involved, greatly increasing the resources that can be brought to bear on the issue."[40] One example of a coalition is the Citizen/Labor Energy Coalition, formed in 1977 by labor unions and citizen and environmental groups to work on energy issues by "developing policies that provide jobs, conservation, and price protection ..."[41] Often, coalitions are formed around a specific issue and disbanded when the issue is resolved.

Community organizing generally refers to people with common problems joining together to solve problems and to exercise power in the decisions that affect their lives. A community can be your class, school, neighborhood or town. Community organizer Lee Staples writes, "To solve problems, people need to get some control over the concrete circumstances of everyday life. Organizing seeks to do this. ... When people join together and organize, they increase their ability to get things done."[42]

Experienced organizers work to help people in communities learn the strength of their power and learn to participate in decision making processes. When people are organized, they are always a factor in the decisions that employers, government officials and landlords make every day and they do not need to depend only on a friendly lawyer or politician to take care of problems for them.[43]

Organizing has intangible as well as concrete benefits. People work together to make their community a better place to live and achieve a sense of satisfaction. As organizer Si Kahn writes, "People learn something new about themselves. They find dignity in place of mistreatment. They find self-respect instead of a lack of self-confidence. They begin to use more fully the skills and abilities that they possess: to work with other people, to influence, to speak up, to fight back."[44]

Community organizing uses many of the techniques described in this chapter. The techniques, however, are part of a long-term strategy to make citizens a permanent fixture in the community decision making process.

To build community support, organizers go door-to-door to identify interested people or issues of concern to the community, hold meetings and speak at community gatherings and religious groups to discuss issues and plan strategies.

One tactic community organizations use is the accountability session — meetings with elected officials at which members of the community can tell the official what they want done. Accountability sessions aim to work out agreements with officials at the meeting.[45]

The United States has a long history of community organizing; but Saul Alinsky, founder of the Industrial Areas Foundation in 1940, developed and refined community organizing as a technique and a profession.[46] Alinsky helped communities across the country organize themselves, trained other organizers and inspired the creation of dozens of new groups.[47] Harry Boyte writes in *The Backyard Revolution*, "Alinsky was extraordinarily creative in developing tactics and strategies for grassroots organizations. ... he urged tactics full of surprises, irreverence, drama and rapid change."[48]

One organization that built on the Alinsky model is National Peoples Action (NPA), a Chicago neighborhood group. When NPA discovered that local banks were redlining — a systematic refusal to approve loans for residents living within a particular area, despite individual qualifications — their neighborhood, they used Alinsky-style tactics to change the banks' practice.[49] Founder Gale Cincotta and her neighbors "disrupted business as usual by staging protests like taking up officers' time opening new accounts, then immediately closing them."[50] Since its founding in 1972, NPA has worked on issues including "housing, banking, energy costs, health care and military spending."[51] Hundreds of other community organizations, including the Association of Community Organizations for Reform Now (ACORN) and Citizen Action networks, are active across the country.

PUBLIC EDUCATION

Educating others about a particular issue is essential to mobilizing public support and the methods for doing so are limited only by the imagination. Public education methods include flyers, newsletters, reports, community hearings and video production. Many other techniques are also educational; for example, a picket informs the public about a complaint while pressuring its target.

Leaflets, Flyers, Posters and Bulletin Boards

Distributing leaflets and flyers helps to get a message to a large number of people quickly. Flyers are usually one page with a clear and concise message capable of attracting attention. Distribute flyers in areas where people congregate, including shopping malls and community gatherings, post them on bulletin boards and place them on car windshields.

Leaflets or flyers are a good way to publicize an event, such as a demonstration or fundraiser, briefly explain a group's views on an issue and recruit members to a campaign.[52] When publicizing an event, Nancy Brigham, in *How to Do Leaflets, Newsletters and Newspapers*, suggests including the following information on leaflets: what and where the event is; date and time; why it is important; who the sponsoring group is; who to contact; and a phone number to call.[53] Brigham also recommends that leaflets tackle one issue at a time, be specific, offer solutions when describing problems and be consistent in style so that people recognize flyers from your organization.[54]

Posters are more permanent announcements of meetings and actions than flyers and keep the issue in the eyes of the public.

A bulletin board is another way to let people know about current issues and activities. Writes Charles

Smith, "[A] good, well-operated bulletin board can make a community center into much more than just a gathering point. It can be a constant source of new or individual information..."[55]

Clearinghouses

A clearinghouse — a collection of information about specific issues — serves as a network to link individuals and groups with interests in common and to share information. The constituency may be the people of a single neighborhood or community, people or organizations across the country or international organizations.

Collecting information for a clearinghouse is an ongoing process. People contact clearinghouses looking for up-to-date as well as historical information. Clearinghouse operators organize the information in a filing cabinet or in a computer data base and provide information over the phone, by mail or via computer.

One example of a local clearinghouse is the Berkeley Information Network (BIN). Sponsored by the Berkeley, California public library, BIN provides community information and referrals at the library and over the telephone. The BIN maintains files with information on over 2,500 organizations, agencies and clubs which serve Berkeley residents.[56]

Newsletters

Newsletters educate and inform less active members of an organization or members who live away from the focus of the group's activities. Newsletters often contain updates on recent group actions, news related to the issues and opportunities for participation by less active members. Many citizen groups use newsletters to help maintain the solidarity and cohesion of a large organization, as well as to increase participation by members.

Newsletters can do a lot more than simply report a group's activities.[57] Nancy Brigham, in *How to Do Leaflets, Newsletters and Newspapers*, suggests reporting on important news that affects your readers but is not adequately covered by local newspapers or

TV news; covering the lives and activities of "ordinary" people in your neighborhood or town; reporting other group's activities as well as how they got started, their motivations and goals; and including a letters page to let readers voice their opinions about the newsletter or other relevant issues. A newsletter can be an important forum for the exchange of information and ideas.[58]

For an excellent guide to both the technical and substantive aspect of publishing a newsletter or newspaper, see Nancy Brigham's *How to Do Leaflets, Newsletters and Newspapers.*

Reports and Surveys

Citizen groups use reports and surveys to document evidence that a particular problem exists or is widespread and to offer the groups' solutions for change. A report can alert government officials, the media and the public to an issue and what can be done about it. Taping a video is another way to document problems, such as a busy intersection that needs a traffic light.

The United States Public Interest Research Group (U.S. PIRG) studies and reports on the correlation between the voting records of Members of Congress and the campaign contributions they accept. When U.S. PIRG compared campaign contributions from nuclear power industry political action committees (PACs) to congressional voting records on issues affecting the nuclear industry, they found "a link between PAC receipts and support of the nuclear industry's positions."[59] According to Gene Karpinski, executive director of U.S. PIRG, "It appears that the real reason for the contributions is to buy access and influence votes."[60] U.S. PIRG uses the PAC studies to advocate campaign finance reform.

Residents living near Love Canal in Niagara Falls, New York, after repeated attempts to convince government officials of the seriousness of residents' health problems related to exposure to toxic chemicals, conducted their own health survey. The Love Canal Homeowners Association surveyed women in the Love Canal area who had become pregnant in 1979.[61] Of the 15 pregnancies, only one resulted in a healthy baby; four ended in miscarriages, two infants

were stillborn and nine others, including a set of twins, were born with deformities.[62] The survey results were alarming and heightened the urgency in solving the problem.

Speakers' Bureaus

A speakers' bureau is a group of people ready and able to give speeches or conduct workshops on specific issues. The League of Women Voters selects members of its organization to form a speakers' bureau as a way of educating the public about issues of importance. Bureau speakers prepare speeches geared toward different listeners and contact other citizen groups, civic associations, schools and professional associations to offer their services at meetings and conferences.[63]

The Physicians for Social Responsibility (PSR), an organization of doctors dedicated to the prevention of nuclear war, the redirection of military spending to health care programs and environmental preservation, operates a speakers' bureau. PSR recruits doctors from its membership to speak about topics including the physician's role in preventing war, radioactive and toxic pollutants as well as health care reform. The PSR speakers' bureau adds new speaking topics as new issues of concern arise; for example, after the Chernobyl nuclear accident, bureau speakers addressed the effects of radiation on human health.[64]

Public Hearings, Candidates Nights and Film/Video Screenings

While official hearings are held at all levels of government and usually provide some measure of citizen participation, citizen groups often call their own hearings when the government, workplace or business refuses to include citizen points of view. For example, because the National Welfare Rights Organization (NWRO) anticipated they would not receive a fair hearing, they held their own hearing at the U.S. Capitol in November 1970 on a proposed welfare program. They scheduled the hearing two days before scheduled action by the Senate Finance Committee. Senator Fred Harris, a member of the Finance Committee, was so impressed by the hearing that he cast his vote in favor of the NWRO plan, giving it the vote needed to pass the committee.[65]

Hearings allow community members to ask questions and voice concerns to public or corporate officials and also can educate, publicize and establish an organization as a leading force on the issue.[66] Convincing potential participants to attend a hearing might be difficult. Yet Kim Bobo, et al., in *Organizing for Social Change*, point out that officials may find it difficult to explain a refusal to discuss issues with a large number of constituents.[67]

Other ideas for educating a local community include holding a candidates night to give the community an opportunity to ask candidates where they stand on certain issues,[68] conducting a teach-in and holding a community screening of a film or video that helps explain an issue. See the resources section for video ideas.

RESEARCH

Researching an issue will help identify the source of the problem, develop workable solutions and plan tactics for implementing solutions. Find out all you can about your issue and about potential opposition. Identify who is responsible for causing the problem and who has the authority to change it.[69] Also find out what is not known about a subject, for example the long-term health effects of a certain pollutant. Keep good records of information sources, including telephone calls, meetings, interviews and all written sources and, whenever possible, get statements in writing.[70] Clip newspaper and magazine articles related to your issue and keep them in a file.[71]

Background Research

Start at the library. Use newspaper and magazine articles for background on an issue and to decide where to go next in your research. The *Reader's Guide to Periodical Literature* indexes about 180 popular magazines but more than 50,000 magazines are published in the United States. Most libraries have specialized indexes for trade and professional journals from many different subjects and fields.[72] Try the *Alternative Press Index* for small political magazines

and newsletters. And the *Business Periodicals Index* is a good place to look for magazine articles on industry and particular corporations.

Most libraries have a number of directories of corporations including *Standard and Poor's Register of Executives and Directors, Moody's Manuals* and *Dun and Bradstreet's Million Dollar Directory* which list information on major corporations, including corporate officers, members of the boards of directors, financial information, subsidiaries and dates of annual meetings.[73]

Broadcast news programs also are indexed. Try the *Television News Index and Abstracts* which covers the national evening news as broadcast by ABC, CBS and NBC since 1972. *The McNeil-Lehrer Report* is a printed index to transcripts of all its programs, on microform from 1976 to the present.[74]

Consult the *United States Government Manual* to find out which agency or department of the federal government, if any, has the authority to change the situation, to research past and present policies and laws and to determine which agencies are responsible for regulating which industries. For local and state issues, call elected officials.

The federal government operates a depository library system that automatically sends the major documents the government publishes — bills, laws and agency journals and magazines — to the 1,400 participating libraries, including one in each congressional district.[75] More than two-thirds of the states operate a state documents depository system.[76] Copies of major state documents and publications are sent automatically to selected libraries around the state. The local library may have documents that are published locally, such as municipal budgets and committee reports.

Many libraries are beginning to subscribe to some of the thousands of computerized data bases which range from a computerized index to actual newspaper and magazine articles on line.[77] Searching a data base for information can save time but is generally expensive — from $35 to several hundred dollars per hour.[78] Some cities and states are computerizing files which are then available, 24 hours a day, to anyone with a personal computer and a modem.[79]

PeaceNet and EcoNet are non-profit computer networks run by the Institute for Global Communications that link groups around the world. You can find out what other groups are doing or make an announcement yourself using computer conferencing and electronic mail (e-mail).[80]

Other good sources of information include the local newspaper's files, community publications and personal contacts with people familiar with similar issues.[81] Use the resources in the back of this book to find citizen groups that work on issues of interest.

Right to Know

Citizen groups have fought to include "right to know" clauses in a number of federal and state laws to ensure citizen access to information about exposure to harmful substances.[82] In 1986, Congress passed the Emergency Planning and Community Right to Know Act which directs the Environmental Protection Agency (EPA) to compile an inventory of all chemical polluters (in 1987, more than 18,000 facilities and over 700 toxic chemicals) and make that information available to the public.[83] The citizen group OMB Watch publishes a guide to the law.[84]

In 1988, the EPA computerized the information, called the Toxic Release Inventory (TRI), through which citizens can find out what companies release what types of chemicals into their communities and in what quantities.[85] Access to the TRI computer database is available through the National Library of Medicine in Bethesda, Maryland.[86] Environmental activists around the country use the information to oppose toxic pollution in their communities.[87]

The Occupational Safety and Health Administration (OSHA) is the federal agency responsible for monitoring and enforcing laws and regulations that govern worker safety and health. OSHA covers only private industry, but some states have set up similar agencies to cover municipal and state workers.[88] Under the right to know "Hazard Communication" standard,

containers of hazardous chemicals must provide an immediate warning to workers; more detailed information on the chemical and its hazards must be made available on a material safety data sheet; and the employer must offer training to ensure that workers understand the labels and know how to handle hazardous substances safely.[89]

The Community Reinvestment Act requires banks to have a public file that describes how the bank plans to serve the community, including making loans to low-income people. Citizen groups often use this information to challenge whether banks are meeting this obligation.

Congress enacted the Freedom of Information Act (FOIA) in 1966 (strengthened in 1974) to give the public access to information held by the federal government. The FOIA requires the government to release any document, file or other record in the possession of any agency of the federal government, subject to nine specific exemptions. (See pages 219-226 for more information).

For more on researching legislators' backgrounds and voting records, see pages 185-196.

DIRECT ACTION

Direct actions "happen when a group of people takes collective action to confront a designated target with a set of specific demands. The group action involves people *directly* with the issue, using their numbers as a means of pressuring an opponent," writes community organizer Lee Staples.[90]

Boycott

"A boycott is an organized consumer refusal to buy a product or to buy from a particular seller," write Stephen Newman and Nancy Kramer in *Getting What You Deserve*.[91] The purpose of a boycott is to put economic pressure on a business to change a policy. Boycotts range from individual to international efforts to protest unfair or unethical practices of a company or organization.

"Because the average retail outlet depends on so many customers, it's often very difficult for people's organizations to really cut off very much of their trade," explains Si Kahn in *Organizing: A Guide for Grassroots Leaders*.[92] In addition, effective boycotts require significant amounts of time, energy and money. Most groups try to negotiate with the targeted business before launching a boycott. The legality of boycotts is also a factor to consider. Although the Supreme Court, in 1988, significantly expanded the right of unions to use secondary boycotts — those that affect the business of a company not involved in the main dispute — in general, legal boycotts must be directed at the business directly involved in the dispute.[93]

Despite the numerous obstacles, boycotts are often effective in pressuring a business to change its policies. Even if sales are affected only slightly, boycotts create negative publicity and the image of a business suffers. Boycotts were a popular tactic of American colonists who refused to buy numerous British goods to protest English policies the colonists thought unfair. In 1991, according to the Seattle-based Institute for Consumer Responsibility, groups throughout the United States were carrying out over 300 nationwide boycotts.[94]

An international boycott of the Swiss corporation Nestle, the world's largest seller of infant formula, organized by the Infant Formula Action Coalition (INFACT), began in 1977 to protest Nestle's aggressive promotion of its infant formula product to new mothers in developing countries.[95]

According to Nancy Gaschott of Action for Corporate Accountability (ACTION), "mothers — particularly in the developing countries — who don't have clean water and high incomes are not able to prepare feeding bottles safely. Mixed with bacteria-laden water and over-diluted to make it last longer, the expensive artificial milk becomes a daily dose of disease and malnutrition."[96] The United Nations estimates that one million infants die annually because they are bottle-fed rather than breast-fed.[97]

Used properly, with clean water and at the recommended doses, infant formula is a safe substitute for the small number of women who cannot breast-feed.

Yet for the majority of mothers, breast-feeding is not only cheaper, but is more beneficial for infants since it contains adequate nutrition as well as immunizing agents to protect against disease.[98]

To encourage the use of infant formula, its manufacturers provided hospitals with free samples of formula to give to mothers of newborns.[99] The mothers become dependent on the infant formula when their milk dries up and must continue to buy formula when the samples run out. In addition, infant formula manufacturers also hire "milk nurses" to visit mothers in maternity wards to promote bottle-feeding as better for the baby than breast-feeding.[100]

Citizen groups, concerned health workers and churches began in the early 1970s to pressure infant formula manufacturers to stop their aggressive promotion of bottle-feeding. Ten years later, various manufacturers did stop the most blatant forms of marketing but continued to distribute free samples.[101] Citizen groups responded with the Nestle boycott which "developed into one of the largest battles ever waged against corporate power by citizen groups, with over 100 organizations in some 65 countries joining in."[102]

Citizen groups also turned to the United Nations World Health Organization (WHO), which in 1981, passed the International Code of Marketing of Breastmilk Substitutes which prohibits certain sales tactics, including free hospital samples used as a sales inducement, and urged hospital health professionals to support breast-feeding.[103] The United States was the only country in the United Nations to vote against the Code.[104]

In 1984, INFACT ended the Nestle boycott when Nestle agreed to abide by the WHO Code. Critics of Nestle continued, however, to monitor Nestle's sales practices to ensure compliance measures were carried out.[105] In October 1988, ACTION announced a new boycott against Nestle and the American Home Products (AHP) corporation.[106] ACTION discovered that Nestle and AHP had violated the WHO International Code of Marketing of Breastmilk Substitutes by providing hospitals with free samples of infant formula. Shortly after the new boycott was launched, organizations in 20 countries lent their support.[107]

Picketing

Picketing — often used with other forms of direct action including boycotts and strikes — can be an effective way to publicize complaints and pressure a target to change its policies.

The first reported consumer picket, in New York City in 1934, involved a neighborhood group protesting a local bakery which raised the cost of its bread.[108] In the resulting court case, *Julie Baking Co., Inc.* v. *Graymond*, the court upheld the right to picket, with restrictions on the number of people and hours during which the group could protest.[109]

Specific laws regulating picketing include: at least one picketer must have a genuine dispute with the target of the picket; the picketers may not ask the business to do anything unlawful, or for the closing of the business; the picket must not contain false claims or exaggerations; the picketers may not use violence or abusive language, or create a disturbance; picketers may not prevent people from walking on the sidewalk or entering and leaving the store; and the location of the picketing or leafletting should be related to its purpose.[110] In addition, states or towns may require demonstrators to obtain a permit before picketing. The courts often overturn local ordinances restricting picketing.

Demonstrations/Protests

Protests, public demonstrations and marches can be effective on a mass scale or with only a small group of people. These types of protests increase public awareness and show public support for an issue. In one of the largest political demonstrations in U.S. history, 750,000 people gathered in New York City's Central Park in June of 1982 to support the citizen campaign for a freeze on nuclear weapons production.[111]

Protests or marches usually require a permit. The laws vary in different cities but the police department is a good place to begin a search for local requirements.

Strikes

In a strike, employees refuse to work, interrupting the normal flow of business at a workplace. Strikes, most commonly used as a bargaining weapon by labor unions, can persuade an employer to listen to employees since the company cannot produce without the workers.[112]

Until passage of the National Labor Relations Act of 1935, the right of workers to unionize was not recognized under federal law.[113] Workers used the strike to force employers to recognize the union as their bargaining representative.[114] Although the Taft-Hartley Act of 1947 placed significant restrictions on workers' right to strike, unions continue to use strikes to win wage increases, health and pension plans and improved working conditions.[115]

Different types of strikes include authorized strikes, those agreed upon by union officials or a majority of the union members. Wildcat strikes are called by a group of workers without official union support. Most strikes are walk-outs, when workers leave their jobs. A sit-down strike is when workers stop working but do not leave their place of employment. A sympathy strike is called by one union to support another union that is on strike. A jurisdictional strike results when two or more rival unions claim the right to work on the same job. A secondary strike occurs when workers call a work stoppage to try to force their employer to stop doing business with another employer who is involved in a labor dispute.[116]

When a strike begins, union members usually set up picket lines at the business' entrances. The purpose of the picket line is to explain why they are on strike, turn away other workers, discourage customers and to keep goods from being taken in or out of the building. Union members usually refuse to cross the picket line of another union.[117]

Nonviolent Civil Disobedience

Civil disobedience is the act of refusing to obey an existing law to protest the law or government policies or priorities. African Americans used nonviolent civil disobedience extensively during the Civil Rights movement to protest laws that segregated public facilities and that made it difficult or impossible to register and vote. Rosa Parks, secretary of the Alabama chapter of the National Association for the Advancement of Colored People, broke the law when she refused to give her seat on a Montgomery, Alabama bus to a white man. Parks' act of civil disobedience triggered the Montgomery bus boycott which succeeded in desegregating public buses in Montgomery.[118]

The sit-in is one type of nonviolent civil disobedience which students, beginning with a lunch counter sit-in in Greensboro, North Carolina in 1960, used to force more than 100 southern communities to end segregation in public places.[119]

Another type of civil disobedience is tax resistance — when people refuse to pay all or part of their income tax to protest government policies, usually those relating to issues of war and peace. Many tax resisters file their income tax forms with the Internal Revenue Service (IRS) every year and many enclose letters of protest instead of a check.[120] The IRS may respond by seizing bank accounts, pay checks and property, in addition to interest, to collect the tax owed.[121] But the thousands of resisters who withhold payment do so as a matter of conscience, not because of any proven effectiveness in changing policy.[122]

CITIZEN LOBBYING

Lobbying is the act of persuading legislators or other policy makers to change an existing law or policy, create a new one, or reject a change under consideration. The methods are basically the same whether trying to influence school administrators, city or county officials, state legislators or Members of Congress.

Decision makers are influenced by numerous factors including party affiliation, interests of campaign contributors, personal views and experience and public opinion. The job of the lobbyist is to find out which decision makers have not made up their minds or which can be persuaded to change them. Of course, other lobbyists will try to persuade the same legislators to vote the other way.

One of the more effective persuasion tactics citizen groups have is to show public support for a policy. Members of Congress, state legislators, city council members or school superintendents who want to be re-elected listen to their constituents. By showing that large numbers of constituents favor your bill or proposal, you can influence votes.

Public support, however, is rarely enough to pass legislation. An understanding of the legislative or decision making process as well as knowing who the key players are is essential to effective lobbying in Congress, state legislatures, county boards and city halls.

This section concentrates on the legislative process followed by Congress and most state legislatures, but much of the advice can be applied to city/county councils or school boards.

Identifying the Key Players

In a legislative campaign, start by identifying the most powerful legislators, including the chairs of committees and party leaders. Marc Caplan, in *A Citizens' Guide to Lobbying*, suggests that citizen lobbyists "[c]heck records of past legislative sessions, which may include transcripts of public hearings and floor debates, lists of bills and their sponsors, and records of votes. ... Read these to learn the key players and the lines of debate on each bill..."[123] See Activity One, How to Profile Your Member of Congress, for more on identifying legislators' motivations.

Because it is nearly impossible for a bill (a proposed law) to reach the full legislative body without first being considered in a relevant committee, the committee with jurisdiction over your issue plays an important role. Identify committee members, particularly the chairperson. Determine how each committee member has voted on similar issues. The committee staff are important contacts because they often specialize in particular issue areas, manage much of the information legislators receive, set priorities for issues, and can be instrumental in scheduling and providing access to important information.[124]

Become familiar with the various publications of the relevant governmental body that follow action in the current session. Most legislatures, for instance, publish a daily calendar of bills up for action in each house, a bulletin listing committee meetings, public hearings and other events and a journal recording activity from the day before.[125]

Writing a Bill and Finding a Sponsor

Ask legislators what laws exist or are under consideration dealing with the issue you want to solve. Ask which members of which committees and which agencies handle such laws.[126] Read copies of relevant laws, bills, resolutions and committee reports.[127]

If you determine that no bill exists to deal with your issue of concern, you can write your own. Writing a bill precisely is important. As Marc Caplan explains, "Shoddy draftsmanship gives opponents and potential supporters an easy excuse to oppose a bill, and gives you a reputation for carelessness."[128] A lawyer is valuable for writing legislation.[129]

Thorough research is essential. For whatever your proposal, whether a new federal law or a change in school policy, determine the immediate and future costs, how the funds will be provided, who benefits and why federal (or state or local) action is necessary.[130] The American Bar Association, the Council of State Governments and the American Law Institute publish collections of model legislation on various issues each year that may help you get started.[131] Contact other citizen groups that have succeeded in passing similar measures. For example, citizen groups have worked in many states to pass laws, which can be duplicated in your state, to require return deposits on bottles and cans. Citing successes from another state, city or school also gives the measure credibility.[132]

In the legislature, once the bill is written, a Member of Congress or state legislator must sponsor and introduce it. Your representative may not be the best person to introduce your bill. Rather, it is important to have someone who sits on the relevant committee introduce it. In addition, Mark Green in *Who Runs Congress?* advises to "beware of the token bill,"[133]

introduced by legislators to fulfill their responsibilities to constituents and then left to die without further attention from the legislator.

You need a sponsor who is committed and will work hard. The chairperson of the committee that will consider the bill is the best choice, but legislators who have sponsored similar bills or advocated similar issues are also a good choice.[134]

Introducing a bill in both houses of the legislature at the same time greatly speeds up the process since both houses must pass exactly the same bill. If the two houses end up with different versions, the bill must go to a conference committee, composed of members from each house to work out a compromise.[135]

Committee Hearings

Every bill is referred to an appropriate committee or subcommittee. Writes Marc Caplan, "This is the first hurdle for a bill. It is relatively simple for legislative leaders to kill a bill by referring it to a committee opposed to it."[136]

The committees hold hearings on most bills to gather information from different points of view. Mark Green advises that "Testimony is an important way to educate committee members, committee staff and the press. To ensure that your position gets a fair airing, you should help recruit relevant witnesses. ... You needn't be a professional 'expert' in order to testify effectively. Often personal experience and passion count far more than learning or polish."[137]

Testimony in these hearings needs to be in plain English, preferably spoken not read. Prepare to answer questions from opponents. Gimmicks or dramatic testimony from people affected personally by the issue often are successful in stressing a point, and capture the attention of the public and media. "During hearings on the coal mine health and safety bill, miners with severe black lung gripped the attention of [committee members] by showing how they collapsed from lack of breath after jumping up and down just a few times," writes Mark Green.[138] Testimony is recorded in the official transcript of the hearing, so prepare written copies for the record and to distribute to members of the committee and members of the press.[139]

Hearings are held at all levels of government as well as for school boards. Find out the procedure for participating in city/county council or school board hearings. If no such process exists, work to implement a mechanism that allows students to voice their concerns.

In the legislative process, the committee staff typically prepares a draft committee bill after the hearings. The committee meets in a mark-up session to go over the draft and propose amendments.[140] Mark-up sessions are where many details of bills are decided.[141] At this point the committee may vote on the bill, refer it to another committee, amend it to weaken its effect or ignore it.[142] If the vote is favorable, it goes before the full house of the legislature in which it was introduced.[143]

Once the bill reaches the floor, lobbyists attempt to persuade all legislators of the importance of the measure. Call legislators' offices to determine how they plan to vote, categorizing each as yes, no or undecided. Personally contact those who need persuading and call on the public to apply pressure as well. Ask sponsors and supporters to speak on the floor in support of the bill.[144]

Persuasion Tactics

In attempting to win votes, citizen groups use a variety of tactics to inform legislators and other decision makers as well as the public of the importance of proposed legislation. Legislators are most responsive when they know their constituents are following their actions on a particular issue. A citizen or student lobby must show that the public or the student body cares about and supports the proposed legislation or other policy change. Some common tactics include petitions, letter-writing campaigns, telegrams, telephone calls, personal visits with legislators and forming coalitions with other organizations.

"Legislators hear nothing from their constituents on the vast majority of bills. When they do get a few letters or telephone calls they take notice. Sometimes a handful of calls can change a vote. On a controversial issue, much more is needed," writes Marc Caplan.[145]

Legislators rarely read all the letters that come into their offices but most have their staff take a count to see where people stand.[146] The most effective letter-writing campaigns are those with large numbers of individually written letters rather than form letters.[147] Telegrams and telephone calls are particularly effective just before a vote. Legislators know constituents are watching their vote.[148]

Petitions, short, written statements of support, are most impressive when enough people have signed to show that more than a few people care about the issue and that the signatures represent an organized constituency. Signatures on petitions represent possible votes to decision makers. Common ways to gather signatures for petitions include canvassing door-to-door and setting up tables at shopping malls, supermarkets, schools or other heavily travelled areas.

Visiting a legislator, city official or school administrator gives citizen or student groups an opportunity to explain face to face the importance of their bill or proposal as well as the depth of support. Mark Green advises that "In personal lobbying it is also essential *to get exact commitments.*"[149] A legislator may fulfill a promise to vote "pro-education" only by voting yes on a weak bill after undermining stronger versions in the committee.[150]

Citizen lobbies form coalitions to increase their effectiveness. Coalitions often send letters to let decision makers know that groups have banded together in support of or opposition to a bill or policy.

After a Bill is Passed

The process is not over when a bill is passed. The executive may veto — except in North Carolina where the governor has no veto power — or refuse to spend all the money appropriated by the legislature.[151] And the agency responsible for carrying out the program may write ineffective regulations or simply may not enforce the law's provisions.[152] Citizen and student groups must monitor implementation of laws and policies and continue to pressure decision makers to ensure enforcement.

THE COURTS

Suits

Citizen groups, particularly in the civil rights and environmental movements, have won major victories through the courts. The courts are an important way to force the government to implement or enforce existing laws, to seek compensation for injury or harm and to obtain restraining orders.

Citizen groups frequently use litigation to force government agencies to take action when the agency is not enforcing a law, not acting within a prescribed time limit or in some other way not fulfilling its legal obligations. Since many federal agencies rarely have the funding required to enforce properly all the laws and regulations on the books, a lawsuit can help set priorities for government agencies by requiring them to choose one enforcement action over another.[153] Although many judges hesitate to change an agency's decision, if an agency decision appears to be arbitrary, or based on inadequate or inappropriate information, the court will often force the agency to adopt more appropriate action.[154]

A number of federal environmental laws contain specific provisions which allow citizens to sue when the law is not being enforced. These citizen suit provisions allow, for instance, any citizen to sue in federal court a polluter who is violating federal law or the terms of its permit. Citizens can sue the Environmental Protection Agency administrator for failing to enforce the law.[155]

A court will allow a suit only after the agency has taken final action and after administrative remedies are exhausted.[156] Many agencies have a hearing process to give the public an opportunity to voice disagreement with a decision or proposal. The hearing process is especially important in environmental issues where federal law requires companies to apply for permits before discharging pollutants.[157]

A class action suit is one in which a plaintiff (the person bringing the suit) represents a number of people charging the same or similar damage.[158] Such a suit is one way to win financial compensation for an injury or some other action from the offender. Often individuals cannot afford the cost and time to sue by themselves; class actions allows plaintiffs to pool their resources. In class action suits the courts generally require that all potential plaintiffs be notified.

Injunctions/Orders

Courts can issue emergency relief orders when a situation presents an immediate danger. Temporary restraining orders or preliminary injunctions are sought when clear and irreparable damage would occur without immediate court intervention.[159] The orders are issued for a period of a few days or until a hearing or trial can be scheduled.

Many factors apply in filing a suit. The injured person, the plaintiff, must have "standing" to sue — to have a sufficient interest or be directly affected by the problem in question. Cases must also be filed within the statute of limitations — the period of time during which a defendant, the person being sued, remains responsible for a problem. The statute of limitations is a particular problem in cases where health problems related to chemical exposure appear 20 to 30 years after the exposure.

Lawyers are usually necessary to carry out the technical aspects of the case.[160] To find a lawyer familiar with your type of case, talk with other organizations that have brought similar suits.[161] Public interest and advocacy groups may have lawyers interested in your case and some law schools have legal clinics to provide advice and handle cases at no charge.[162]

Bringing a case to court is a long and often expensive process. A lawsuit can take several years depending on the complexity of the case. In most lawsuits where money to compensate injured persons is sought, plaintiffs pay the lawyer nothing unless they receive money from the defendant. This form of payment is called a contingency fee. In a successful suit, the plaintiff pays the lawyer anywhere from 20 to 40 percent of the amount won.[163] In addition to attorneys fees, plaintiffs may be required to pay filing fees, photocopying, telephone bills and travel and fees for witnesses.[164] Some law firms that ordinarily charge high fees also take a few cases each year on a *pro bono* basis, or for the public good.[165]

In addition, free legal help for people who cannot afford to hire a lawyer may be available through legal aid and legal services, depending on the legal issue. Clients must have a low income. The offices are often so understaffed that they cannot handle all the cases that come to them.[166]

Small Claims Court

Small claims courts, which differ from state to state, are primarily an informal, simplified court procedure set up to enable people to collect small amounts of money in cases such as disputes between landlords and tenants, without hiring a lawyer.[167] The majority of plaintiffs win, but often do not receive all the money they request.[168]

People can take a case to small claims court after trying to resolve the problem in other ways, when they know who is responsible and when a dollar value, actual or estimated, can be put on their loss. The most frequent small claims court cases are those "compelling people to pay money agreed to in a contract and getting compensation for services performed ... ."[169]

To locate a small claims court, call the clerk or information office of any of the lower non-criminal courts.[170] Many courts as well as consumer agencies or groups issue materials which describe how the court works.[171] Before going to court to file a claim, the plaintiff must find the precise, legal name of the person or business involved in the dispute.[172] Most businesses and landlords must register with the government or file for a license to operate a business. Check with the county clerk, secretary of state, licensing boards and tax offices.[173]

Plaintiffs can sue for all expenses, within the court's limit, including transportation costs, phone bills and wages lost.[174] The court can decrease, but will never increase, the amount requested. The court will notify the defendant, who must appear in court or give up the right to have the case heard. Make sure all witnesses are present and, if necessary, get a subpoena ordering them to appear.[175] Prepare all records such as canceled checks or receipts, with a brief summary of any that are long or complex. Remember that at any time before the case, both parties can reach a compromise or settlement. If this happens, the settlement must be in writing and signed by both parties.[176]

Make sure to be on time for the trial, and have all the necessary papers. The average small claims case takes 20 minutes, so be concise.[177] Small claims court judges often help people to present their cases and may ask witnesses questions.[178] The court's decision will be given at the end of the trial or by mail within a few weeks.[179]

Winning plaintiffs often have trouble collecting on decisions in small claims court. Collection procedures vary, but generally require the plaintiff to make sure the judgment has been formally registered in the court's books. Then ask for help from a sheriff or marshal, who, with a court order, may seize a defendant's assets or wages to collect judgments.[180]

INITIATIVE AND REFERENDUM

The initiative/referendum process is the closest thing the United States has to direct democracy. Citizens enact or reject laws directly through the voting booth rather than through elected officials. David Schmidt, former director of the Initiative Resource Center, defines an initiative as a proposed new law initiated by citizens and placed on the ballot by a petition with the signatures of a specified number of voters.[181] In referendum, a law already approved by elected officials is then referred to the ballot either by citizen petition or by the officials.[182]

The initiative/referendum was a popular technique during the Populist farmers movement and the Progressive reform era. The state of Oregon adopted the initiative and referendum process in 1904 — second only to South Dakota in 1898 — and in the next 10 years passed initiatives to implement direct election of U.S. Senators, establish the nation's first presidential primary, eliminate the poll tax and extend the right to vote to women.[183] By the end of World War I, 20 state constitutions had adopted the initiative and referendum process.[184]

The initiative/referendum regained popularity in the 1970s and since then citizen groups have used the process to work on tax reform, environmental problems, voter registration reforms and to oppose nuclear power.[185] In 1977, a group of citizens campaigned to amend the U.S. Constitution to allow voters to pass laws nationally using the initiative, but the proposal died in both Senate and House committees.[186] Neither does the United States have a national referendum process.[187] Consequently, initiative and referendum issues must fall under state or local jurisdictions.

Citizen groups turn to initiatives when state legislators or city officials refuse to respond to an issue, despite public opinion. Even defeated initiatives, as well as those that never reach the ballot, have spurred state legislatures to take action on issues which concern the public.[188]

The following state constitutions allow for voter initiatives: Alaska, Arizona, Arkansas, California, Colorado, Florida, Idaho, Illinois, Maine, Michigan, Missouri, Massachusetts, Montana, Nebraska, Nevada, North Dakota, Ohio, Oklahoma, Oregon, South Dakota, Utah, Washington and Wyoming. Of these only Florida and Illinois do not have referendum provisions. New Mexico and Maryland have statewide provisions for referenda, but not initiatives.[189]

When an individual or group of citizens decide that a new law is needed and their elected officials are unlikely to pass it, they may consider an initiative campaign. Citizens first need to consult with their representative at the state or local level about bills dealing with the issue. If no bills are currently under consideration, a group of citizens may ask that one be introduced. When all possibility of passing a bill through elected officials is exhausted, citizens can start the initiative process.

Citizen sponsors research the state or local requirements for initiative petitions. The rules concerning the number of signatures and deadlines for submitting initiatives vary according to jurisdiction. Consult the city or town clerk or registrar of voters for local rules. For a statewide petition, contact the secretary of state.[190]

Sponsors need to determine the exact wording of the new law, with the assistance of lawyers or legislators.[191] Then the petition drive needs to be planned. The most effective petition drive strategy divides the total number of signatures required into manageable segments, either per volunteer, per month or per week.[192] Groups need to obtain at least 25 percent more than the legal minimum to have a cushion of extra signatures because officials will invalidate any illegible names or names of people not registered to vote in the jurisdiction.[193]

In most jurisdictions sponsors are required to submit their petition to election officials before they start collecting signatures. After the petition has been circulated, sponsors submit the completed petition to election officials for verification, and keep a receipt and photocopies of each petition in case they are lost by officials.[194]

COMMUNITY LAWYER

The residents of Winchester, also known as Winsted, Connecticut have a community lawyer to help them exercise their rights and strengthen their involvement in the governance of their community. The lawyer serves as a watchdog and representative of citizen interests at public meetings, helps citizens to find the proper channels through which to make grievances known, refers citizens to useful sources of information, provides assistance with the technical aspects of introducing legislative initiatives to deal with specific concerns and advocates on their behalf, *pro bono*, on issues of community-wide significance.[195]

Charlene LaVoie, the Winchester, Connecticut Community Lawyer (CL), drafted an ordinance to ban polystyrene foam food containers in Winchester. Despite strong opposition from plastics manufacturers and users, the town passed the ordinance, joining a growing number of communities across the country.[196]

The Community Lawyer has written pamphlets for citizens on freedom of information laws, the right of initiative, home rule and the local government to demystify the local and state government process.[197] LaVoie writes, "[P]articipatory government is not an efficient or tidy mode of governing. It requires that people assert their rights and accept their responsibilities as citizens. The CL Project is one step toward strengthening the process and practice of self government."[198]

SHAREHOLDER ACTIVISM

Shareholder activism consists of filing shareholder resolutions and lobbying shareholders to vote in support of the resolutions; divesting of stock in unethical corporations; and investing in socially responsible enterprises. These techniques can generate publicity, educate corporate executives as well as the public and shape the activities of corporations.[199]

Public corporations, those that sell stock to the public, hold annual meetings of shareholders to discuss the company's direction and to elect a new board of directors. Shareholders may vote on board nominees as well as any resolutions dealing with company policy, including those proposed by shareholders.

Shareholders may file resolutions to be considered at the annual meeting. The federal Securities and Exchange Commission (SEC) oversees shareholder interaction with companies. The SEC has specific procedural requirements for shareholder resolutions.[200]

Since the management of a corporation generally controls a majority of the stock through proxies, it is nearly impossible to pass a shareholder resolution. About a third of the resolutions are never voted on because the company makes some concession on the issue and the resolution is withdrawn.[201] The purpose of most shareholder resolutions is to create publicity about corporate policy that would outrage the public enough to pressure legislators and corporate management to change policy.[202]

Shareholder activism techniques were first developed by community organizer Saul Alinsky who, in 1966, convinced the owners of 39,000 shares of Eastman Kodak to vote in opposition to the management's

record in hiring minorities.[203] Eventually, the company agreed to implement a minority hiring program.

The success of the South Africa divestment campaign is one example of effective shareholder activism. Throughout the 1970s and 1980s, a wide variety of religious, student and citizen groups waged a campaign to force U.S. corporations to stop doing business in South Africa. Citizen groups filed shareholder resolutions and convinced large investors, including the State of California, the Smithsonian Institution, the cities of Washington, DC and Philadelphia and hundreds of churches, foundations and state and city pension funds, to divest — sell their stock — in companies that continued to operate in South Africa.[204] Students at more than 140 U.S. universities convinced their schools to adopt some divestment policy toward South Africa.[205] Although the shareholder campaigns do not fully account for the divestment trend, between 1985 and 1988, 172 U.S. companies ended their direct investment in South Africa.[206]

Many individual citizens as well as institutional investors such as union pension funds are investing their money in ethical or socially responsible companies which allows investors to dictate the terms of their investments.[207]

THE MEDIA:
CITIZEN ACCESS TO
NEWSPAPERS, TELEVISION AND RADIO

Letters to the editor. Americans read the letters to the editor column more frequently than anything else on the editorial page.[208] Letters are therefore an extremely effective way to air different points of view on an issue. Of course, newspapers do not print every letter received, but many papers tabulate letters for in-house opinion surveys.[209]

To increase the chances that the paper prints your letter, follow these guidelines:

■ Keep it short and on target to avoid having it edited. Newspapers will cut a long letter down to 250-350 words or less.

■ Avoid flowery language and unnecessary lead-ins such as "I'm sure everyone would agree with me that..."

■ Make reference to a recent editorial column or news story that prompted your letter.[210]

■ Send an original, neat, handwritten, or preferably typed, letter. Newspapers reject photocopied letters but may print letters from an organized letter-writing campaign if each letter is original.[211]

Opposite Editorials (Op-Eds). In addition to letters, papers run opinion columns on either the editorial or Op-Ed (opposite editorial) pages, or frequently both. The writers are generally nationally syndicated columnists and little space may be given to articles on local matters written by local citizens. Ask your paper what their policy is concerning opinion columns submitted by local citizens.

Citizen response to editorials. Radio and television stations often broadcast editorials.[212] Although radio and television stations no longer are required to present differing points of view (the Federal Communications Commission abolished the Fairness Doctrine in 1987), many do welcome responses from citizens. This is an excellent way to explain your view on an issue without any interruption or editing by a reporter or news editor.[213]

WRC-TV Channel Four in Washington, DC, airs station editorials and responses from the community on controversial community issues. WRC-TV also airs "Your Turn," an opportunity for citizens to address the community about issues they choose. Challenge your local stations to adopt similar opportunities for citizen access.[214]

Feature stories in print or on television. Feature stories are best suited to a description of an interesting personality, or a special activity. If your group has a good subject for a feature story, let the appropriate news person know.[215]

Editorial endorsements. The editorial support of the local newspaper can carry tremendous weight for a particular issue or for your organization. Present your case to the editor. If the local paper thinks your

proposal is a good one or that your actions are constructive, it is harder for others in the community to attack you as irresponsible without somehow implying that the paper also is wrong.[216]

Weekly columns. While it is somewhat difficult to break into a daily paper, weekly papers, especially local shopper papers, are a good place to start for a column by you or your organization. Daily papers may be willing to run a well-written guest column occasionally.[217]

Call-in shows. Many radio stations have talk lines, where listeners may call in and discuss a variety of issues. Calling in your views on an issue can do much to broaden public awareness, reaching thousands of people.[218]

Guest shows. Guest shows and panel shows on local radio and television stations are important vehicles for reaching large numbers of people. It is often difficult to arrange a booking on one of these shows, but the more you and your issues are publicized, the more likely your request will be granted. Make sure that the people who select interviewees or panelists know who you represent and the importance of what you and your group are doing.[219]

Public service announcements (PSAs), community billboards. Many radio and television stations air public service announcements. This is free time but is reserved for announcement of events and meetings or for public service information. It cannot be used to denounce a legislator, advocate legislation or otherwise express an opinion.[220]

Call local television and radio stations to find out their procedures for accepting PSAs, including the standard length of their PSAs, whether they prefer a written script or a prepared tape and the deadline for submission.[221]

News Releases. Use news (or press) releases to announce events that are newsworthy, but that would not receive coverage without a release. Write press releases in a clear, concise news style. Write the release as you would like to see it appear in the paper. Read the paper closely and write your ideal story so it sounds like one of the articles your have just read. That means you or your group should be referred to in the third person, for example, "Students for the Environment announced today..." To express an opinion, use direct quotations and identify the sources.[222]

Make the major point of the story clearly and directly in the first paragraph.[223] Follow, for the rest of the release, the inverted pyramid style: the most vital information at the beginning of the release, with subsequent paragraphs arranged in order of declining importance.[224] Newspaper writers use this style to

allow editors to cut the story from the bottom, leaving the most important information.[225] Include a brief description of the group.[226]

Start the release with the group's name, address and telephone number at the top of the page or use official stationery.[227] In addition, at the top of the release, include the name of a specific person who can answer questions. Use a headline, just like a newspaper story. For releases of more than one page, write "MORE" at the end of each page except the last.[228] On the last page, type "###" under the final paragraph to signify the end of the release.[229]

Students for the Environment
Central High School
Anytown, USA
Tel: (000) 555-1111

NEWS RELEASE

FOR RELEASE: CONTACT: Jane Doe
January 2, 1992 10:00 A.M.   Tel: 555-1111

Students Find Central High School Wasting Energy

Student environmentalists conducted an energy wastehunt at Central High School in Anytown and found wasteful energy practices. "Central High School is throwing taxpayer money out the window as well as disregarding the environmental costs of wasting energy," said Jane Doe, president of Students for the Environment, the group that conducted the survey.

The wastehunt found the following: students in classrooms on the west side of the building open windows in cold weather due to a malfunctioning thermostat that causes too much heat in those class- rooms; the heating and air conditioning equipment has not been serviced in three years; and dirty, dusty lighting fixtures inhibit all the light from getting through.

"The changes we are proposing cost little and the potential savings on energy bills are big," said Doe.

The group asked the school administration to implement the following changes: replace the thermostat in the west wing of the building; implement regular servicing of heating and cooling equipment, including cleaning and replacing filters; clean lighting fixtures; consider buying a heat pump to help the furnace operate more efficiently (heat pumps can cut electricity use by 30 to 40 percent according to the Department of Energy); and establish a student energy patrol to continue monitoring wasteful energy practices.

Students for the Environment plans to track Central High School's utility bills over the next few months to measure savings from the changes.

Students for the Environment, formed in 1991, is a group of 300 students at Central High School who have joined together to promote energy efficiency, recycling and other environmental issues.

###

See the sample release and keep the following in mind:[230]

■ If you live in a city with two newspapers, try to divide releases evenly between morning and afternoon to avoid offending either group of newspapers.

■ Less official news happens on weekends and holidays than during the work week. Delivering on Thursday or Friday for release on weekends or holidays is sometimes a good way to ensure more coverage. Monday morning papers are especially in need of news since few staff people collect news over the weekend.

■ Take advantage of seasonal lulls — during the summer or around holidays. Of course, the audience can be smaller too.

■ Wednesday papers usually carry a great deal of advertising — mainly supermarket ads. More ads mean more pages and usually more space for news.

■ Do not assume special knowledge on the part of the press. While members of the press may be able to grasp your issues and arguments better than the general public, they are seldom experts on all the issues they cover.

News Conferences. Use news conferences for events which are urgent and important. News conferences are particularly important for radio and television and serve several purposes: initiating a major project; announcing conclusions of a study, exposing injustices, or calling for a ban on a harmful product.[231]

However, limit news conferences to important statements or events. The quickest way to diminish your overall press coverage, especially with radio and television reporters, is to call news conferences too often.[232]

The key to a successful conference is careful planning so that everything runs smoothly. Form is often as important as content in communicating with the public.[233] For example, be sure that the podium and microphone are the correct height for the speaker, and that all electronic equipment is in proper working order.

Here are a few specific things to keep in mind when planning a news conference:[234]

■ Prepare and rehearse the conference thoroughly, ahead of time.

■ The day before your conference, issue an editor's advisory over the local wire services — Associated Press (AP) and United Press International (UPI) — announcing the time and place of the conference and the general topic. To issue the advisory, call your local AP and UPI offices and say that you have an item to be listed in their day book. Keep the advisory short. Mentioning visuals is especially important to attract television cameras. Include a telephone number and the name of a person to call for additional information. But do not go into too great detail about your announcements or subject matter to avoid giving away the main news of the conference.

■ Call radio and television stations early on the morning of the conference as a reminder. Talk with the assignment editor or news director. Give the pertinent data and do a brief selling job.

■ Send both the newspaper's assignment editor and the reporter covering your issue an advisory several days before the conference and call them again the day before the conference. Point out any scheduled visual event so they can send a photographer.

■ Make the location for the conference as easily accessible as possible. If the location has to be out of the way, include directions with your editor's advisory or phone calls.

■ If the location is outside, have an alternative indoor site in case of bad weather. Make your decision to move the conference in time to give the press adequate notice.

■ Most news conferences consist of a statement from the speaker followed by questions from the press.

■ Deliver copies of any materials to be distributed at the conference to the wire services a few hours before the conference. Local wire service bureaus usually do not cover news conferences because of insufficient staff. Most radio stations and many local newspapers get their news from the wire services so be sure that the wire services receive all materials released. "Embargo," or hold for release, the material until the start of the news conference.

■ Have your release ready to hand out at the conference. Make the beginning of the release the major point of your conference, not the fact that you are having a conference.

Media events. Use media events to dramatize a point that otherwise would not receive attention. Media events with a large number of people or a degree of flamboyance are often most effective. Some common media events include pickets, marches, rallies and displays. Also, many citizen groups have developed creative media events which depend less on volume and more on uniqueness.[235] For example, when Public Citizen was lobbying Congress for airbag safety protections in cars, Public Citizen president Joan Claybrook arranged to have crash-damaged cars parked next to the U.S. Capitol. The owners of the cars who survived the crashes — only because the cars had been equipped with experimental air bags — stood nearby.[236]

Radio audios. Suggestions for handling radio audios:[237]

■ Ask for the newsroom, identify yourself and your group, and say you have a news story. If no one is available in the newsroom, leave a message and continue to call back periodically.

■ Prepare a summary of the news release. Have an outline of important points before you.

■ Be prepared to answer typical questions, such as "What is the significance of this survey?" or "What does your group want public officials to do?"

■ When the station is taping, the phone will sound as if it is dead except for the "beep" some stations use when recording.

■ If you make a factual error, tell the interviewer; it is easy to retape and much better than putting a mistake on the air. Remember also that pauses and stumbling can be edited out.

■ Finally, if the interviewer says something quite inaccurate, do not hesitate to break in and make a correction. Remember that most interviewers are trying to cooperate with you to produce a good story.

Basics For Better Coverage

To use the news media effectively and maximize your coverage, Marc Caplan suggests the following:[238]

■ Your story must be action-oriented and timely. Something must happen — something that will interest the public.

■ If you want television coverage, make your story visual.

■ Include a positive call for action. An approach that consists of attacking without ever advancing some positive action is not popular.

■ The various media face different time constraints. Reporters for afternoon papers may need material by 8:30 a.m. to make the first edition. Television people often need their information by 3:00 p.m. for the evening news. Learn the deadlines for papers and broadcasts, and consider these deadlines when you release a story.

■ Prepare a standard press list, including national, state and local newspapers, wire services, radio and television stations and relevant magazines. Include the name of the editor or news director for each, along with other contacts, such as reporters or people who might have a special interest in your story. Also include editorial writers on the list. Make up address labels and photocopy them to save the time of typing envelopes each time you do a release.

■ Deliver releases by hand to local news outlets. When the release is dropped off in person instead of relying on mail delivery, better coverage is often the result if you have an opportunity to talk to an editor or reporter and explain the importance of your story.

■ Whenever you put out a report longer than a few pages or longer than 10 minutes' reading, issue a brief summary as well as the press release.

■ Joint or coalition releases are another way to maximize coverage of your issue. Ask other groups to endorse your position either one at a time or simultaneously. Discretion is advisable here; you may not want to be associated with every organization.

FUNDRAISING

From a school club to a nationwide citizen group, almost all organizations need money to carry out their programs and activities. Fundraising options include: dues, pledges, door-to-door canvassing, direct mail, payroll deductions, special events, grants and selling newsletters, products or services.

Dues produce a dependable income for programs.[239] Joan Flanagan, author of *The Grassroots Guide to Fundraising*, suggests that to set up a dues rate, figure out how much money is needed for a program and then divide by the number of people who will realistically buy memberships.[240] This should approximate the amount a membership should cost. Many groups offer memberships which vary according to income to allow more people to join. For example, many group provide lower rates for senior citizens, students and others who live on a fixed income.[241]

Pledges provide the opportunity to spread a donation over a period of time. For example, a contributor may give $10 per month for 12 months instead of giving $120 up front. Pledges offer flexibility for those on limited incomes who still want to give large contributions.[242]

Door-to-door canvassing is the most labor-intensive form of fundraising, but can also produce the highest profits for the organization.[243] The work is difficult so usually canvassers are paid by either commission or salary. Groups that are well-known or located in a large city often use a professional canvassing program; smaller communities groups often canvass with volunteers. Canvassing also provides instant feedback on public opinion about your projects.[244]

Direct mail — sending an appeal to prospective donors or members through the mail — is expensive and usually results in only a small percentage of responses. However, if appeals are sent to enough people even a small percentage can result in many new dues-paying members. Direct mail expenses include postage, stationery and envelopes. Special postage rates exist for groups with non-profit status.[245]

Newsletters are an effective way to tell people about activities and specific programs as well as bring in money from subscription charges and advertisements.[246]

Special events — speakers bureaus, dances, potluck dinners, holiday or seasonal carnivals and raffles — are an important way to build community support and involvement as well as raise money.[247] Operating a business such as a thrift shop or used book store or providing a service are also good ways to raise money.[248]

The Buffalo, New York affiliate of Women's Action for Nuclear Disarmament (WAND) organizes a "Mums for Moms" flower sale every Mother's Day. The flowers come with a peace message and information about the organization. WAND has a kit to help other groups organize similar sales.[249]

Grants

Pursuing a grant from either the government, foundations or corporations is a highly competitive way to raise funds. In addition, grantmakers may impose restrictions on how the money can be used, seriously inhibiting the freedom of the organization to make its own decisions. Many foundations are willing to provide start-up or seed money with the understanding that the group will become self-sufficient.[250] Thoroughly research funding sources to determine the conditions for grants; many give only within a specific geographical or issue area. To locate foundations, contact the Foundation Center with collections of materials in over 100 U.S. cities and/or consult the *Grant Seekers Guide*.[251]

Many citizen groups apply to the Internal Revenue Service (IRS) for tax-exempt status. To qualify under Internal Revenue Code Section 501(c)(3) for tax-exempt status, an organization must be a "nonprofit corporation, unincorporated association, or trust which engages in educational, religious, scientific or other charitable activities."[252] Such organizations may accept contributions from individuals and corporations, which are deductible from the donor's federal income tax. Organizations with 501(c)(3) status may accept funding from foundations. Lobbying activities of 501(c)(3) organizations are restricted and such organizations may not engage in partisan political campaign activities. State laws governing nonprofit organizations vary.[253]

An organization that qualifies for tax-exempt status under the Internal Revenue Code Section 501(c)(4) must be "designed to develop and implement programs for the promotion of 'social welfare.'"[254] While 501(c)(4) organizations are exempt from paying federal taxes, contributors and members may not deduct contributions and/or dues from their own federal income tax. A 501(c)(4) organization is not limited in its lobbying activities, may advocate a point of view on controversial issues and may engage in limited political campaign activities.[255]

Writing a Grant Proposal

Although the requirements for each foundation and government agency vary widely, the following guidelines from Norman Kiritz in *The Rich Get Richer and the Poor Write Proposals*, are a good starting point for writing a grant proposal.[256]

Begin with a clear, concise summary to describe the group, the scope of its project and the projected costs. Grantmakers appreciate proposal summaries.[257]

Follow the summary with an introduction to establish the organization's history, credibility, uniqueness, significant accomplishments and organizational goals.[258] Follow the introduction with a problem statement or assessment of need. Establish the program objectives. Describe the project's goals and how the project will accomplish its goals.[259]

Include a detailed budget. Ask for a specific amount of money. Establish that once the grant ends the group will be able to continue the program without the funding source.[260]

After sending the proposal, follow-up with a phone call. Ask whether the foundation received the proposal, if they have any questions or need additional materials.[261]

BIBLIOGRAPHY

Angiolillo, Paul and Aaron Bernstein. "The Secondary Boycott Gets a Second Wind," *Business Week*. June 27, 1988.

Ayvazian, Andrea. "No Payment Enclosed: Why I Resist War Taxes," *The Progressive*. April 1989.

Berkeley Information Network fact sheet. Berkeley, CA: Berkeley Public Library, 1991.

Bobo, Kim, Jackie Kendall and Steve Max of the Midwest Academy. *Organizing for Social Change: A Manual for Activists in the 1990s*. Washington, DC: Seven Locks Press, 1991.

Bollier, David. *Citizen Action and Other Big Ideas: A History of Ralph Nader and the Modern Consumer Movement*. Washington, DC: Center for Study of Responsive Law, 1989.

Boyte, Harry C. *The Backyard Revolution: Understanding the New Citizen Movement*. Philadelphia: Temple University Press, 1980.

Brigham, Nancy with Maria Catalfio and Dick Cluster. *How To Do Leaflets, Newsletters and Newspapers*. Detroit: PEP Publishers, 1991.

Caplan, Marc. *A Citizens' Guide to Lobbying*. New York: Dembner Books, 1983.

Cohen, Gary and John O'Connor. *Fighting Toxics: A Manual for Protecting Your Family, Community and Workplace*. Washington DC: Island Press, 1990.

Democracy by Initiative: Shaping California's Fourth Branch of Government - Report and Recommendations of the California Commission on Campaign Financing. Los Angeles, CA: Center for Responsive Government, 1992.

Engdahl, Don. "Pamphleteer Stalks Bodega Bay A-Plant," *Santa Rosa Press Democrat.* September 5, 1963.

Flanagan, Joan. *The Grass Roots Fundraising Book: How to Raise Money in Your Community.* Chicago: Contemporary Books, Inc., 1982.

Garland, Anne Witte. "Gale Cincotta," *Ms.* January 1986.

Gaschott, Nancy. "Babies at Risk: Infant Formula Still Takes Its Toll," *Multinational Monitor.* October 1986.

"The Good, the Bad and the Miscreant," *Multinational Monitor.* December 1988.

Going to Court in the Public Interest: A Guide for Community Groups. Washington, DC: League of Women Voters Education Fund, 1983.

Green, Mark. *Who Runs Congress?* Fourth edition. New York: Dell Publishing Co., 1984.

Huerta, Dolores. "Reflections on the UFW Experience," *The Center Magazine.* July/August 1985.

Kahn, Si. *Organizing: A Guide for Grassroots Leaders.* Revised edition. Silver Spring, MD: National Association of Social Workers, 1991.

Kelsey, Janet and Don Wiener. "The Citizen/Labor Energy Coalition," *Social Policy.* Spring 1983.

Kiritz, Norman J. "Program Planning and Proposal Writing," in Nancy Mitiguy, ed. *The Rich Get Richer and the Poor Write Proposals.* Amherst, MA: University of Massachusetts Citizen Involvement Training Project, 1978.

Lasson, Kenneth and the Public Citizen Litigation Group. *Representing Yourself: What You Can Do Without a Lawyer.* Washington, DC: Public Citizen, 1983.

LaVoie, Charlene. *The Community Lawyer Project.* Winchester, CT: Community Lawyer, September 1991.

Lewis, Barbara A. *The Kid's Guide to Social Action: How to Solve the Social Problems You Choose — And Turn Creative Thinking into Positive Action.* Minneapolis: Free Spirit Publishing, 1991.

Mokhiber, Russell and Leonard Shen. "Love Canal," in Ralph Nader, Ronald Brownstein and John Richard, eds., *Who's Poisoning America?: Corporate Polluters and their Victims in the Chemical Age.* San Francisco: Sierra Club Books, 1981.

Mokhiber, Russell. "Infant Formula: Hawking Disaster in the Third World," *Multinational Monitor.* April 1987.

Mother's Day for Peace Action Kit. Arlington, MA: Women's Action for Nuclear Disarmament.

Naar, Jon. *Design for a Livable Planet: How You Can Help Clean Up the Environment.* New York: Harper and Row Publishers, 1990.

Nader, Ralph and Steven Gold. "Letters to the Editor: How About a Little Down-Home *Glasnost?*," *Columbia Journalism Review.* September/October 1988.

Nader, Ralph and Donald Ross. *Action for a Change: A Student's Manual for Public Interest Organizing.* Revised edition. New York: Grossman Publishers, 1972.

"Nestle: The Boycott's Back," *Multinational Monitor.* September 1988.

Newman, Stephen A. and Nancy Kramer. *Getting What You Deserve: A Handbook for the Assertive Consumer.* Garden City, NY: Doubleday and Co. Inc., 1979.

Non-Profit Organizations, Public Policy and the Political Process: A Guide to the Internal Revenue Code and Federal Election Campaign Act. Washington, DC: Perkins Coie, 1987.

"Nuclear Power Industry PACs Gave Over $25 Million to Congressional Candidates, 1981-1988; Key Nuclear Licensing Vote Coming Up in House," press release. Washington, DC: United States Public Interest Research Group, September, 1989.

Schmidt, David D. "Government by the People: Voters Are Writing New Laws Through Initiative and Referendum," *Public Citizen.* June 1986.

Schmidt, David D. *Citizen Lawmakers: The Ballot Initiative Revolution.* Philadelphia: Temple University Press, 1989.

The Shareholder Proposal Process: A Step-by-Step Guide to Shareholder Activism for Individuals and Institutions. Washington, DC: United Shareholders Association, 1987.

Shellow, Jill R. and Nancy C. Stella, eds. *Grant Seekers Guide*. Third edition. Mt. Kisco, NY: Moyer Bell Limited, 1989.

Sitkoff, Harvard. *The Struggle for Black Equality: 1954-1980*. New York: Hill and Wang, 1981.

Smith, Charles L. *The Hobby of Pamphleteering*. Berkeley, CA: Charles L. Smith, 1962, revised 1989.

Smith, Charles L. *Uses of a Clearinghouse: Mutual Self-Help in Any Organization*. Berkeley, CA: Charles L. Smith, 1989.

Speaking Out: Setting Up a Speaker's Bureau. Washington, DC: League of Women Voters of the United States, 1977.

Staples, Lee, ed. *Roots to Power: A Manual for Grassroots Organizing*. New York: Praeger, 1984.

"The Struggle for Worker Safety," *Bridging the Gap*, Fall 1991.

Summa, John. "Killing Them Sweetly," *Multinational Monitor*. November 1988.

Ullmann, John and Jan Colbert and the Investigative Reporters and Editors, Inc., eds. *The Reporter's Handbook: An Investigator's Guide to Documents and Techniques*. Second edition. New York: St. Martin's Press, 1991.

Using Community Right to Know: A Guide to a New Federal Law. Washington, DC: OMB Watch, 1988.

"Voice of Conscience: An Interview with Timothy Smith," *Multinational Monitor*. December 1988.

Welsh, Heidi J. "Shareholder Activism," *Multinational Monitor*. December 1988.

World Book Encyclopedia, No. 18. Chicago: World Book, Inc., 1989.

Section Four

Student Activities

Profiling Members of Congress
Energy Wastehunt
Toy Safety Survey
Freedom of Information Act
Voter Participation Profile
Disability Access Survey
Green Consumer
Jury Representativeness Survey
Time Dollar
Evaluating Television News

ACTIVITY ONE:
PROFILING MEMBERS OF CONGRESS

INTRODUCTION

Over 200 college students working for the Congress Project developed detailed profiles of every Member of Congress in the summer of 1972. This activity is based on those profiles but can easily be adapted for state legislators. Profiling Members of Congress or state legislators gives students a firsthand look at many important factors — performance, vision, biases, obligations and conflicts of interest — which may influence the actions of officeholders. By distributing profiles throughout the community, students can help educate the voters while learning about the political process.

As part of the profile, or as a separate project, students can develop, in chart form, a Voting Record Scorecard. Consumer, environmental, labor and other groups use scorecards to identify those Members of Congress with particularly good or bad voting records on legislation of interest to their group. For example, the Environmental Action developed a "Dirty Dozen" list of the Members of Congress who had, in their view, the worst voting records on environmental issues. Environmental Action distributes their list nationwide to members, other interest groups and the media. Scorecards are also useful for providing information to voters at election time.

HOW TO DEVELOP A CONGRESSIONAL PROFILE

I. DECIDE WHO TO PROFILE

Depending on available time and how the information will be used, students can choose to profile: 1) their state's two U.S. Senators, 2) their U.S. Representative, 3) the full congressional delegation from the students' state or 4) members of a particular congressional or legislative committee considering legislation of interest to the students. Profiling numerous legislators allows for comparison of voting records, campaign contributions and other factors of interest to constituents.

II. INFORMATION TO INCLUDE

Choose some or all of the following:

A. BACKGROUND OF THE MEMBER OF CONGRESS

Write a brief biography including legislators' education, family history, party affiliation, previous occupations, organizational memberships, voting record on specific issues, number of terms in office and the committees and subcommittees on which the legislator serves. Contact legislators' Washington, DC or district offices for biographical information and consult the resources section.

B. FACTS ABOUT THE CONGRESSIONAL DISTRICT(S)

Include data about the districts' population, minority representation, percentage of population in urban, rural and metropolitan areas, median age, median income, education, occupations and economy.

C. SPONSORSHIP OF LEGISLATION

Legislation introduced by legislators is often dictated by the committees on which they sit. But legislators can sign on as co-sponsors to any bill under consideration. Sponsorship indicates the types of issues a legislator considers important.

D. VOTING RECORD

A voting scorecard can be part of the profile or a separate project. Scorecards can compare votes on numerous issues by all Members of Congress from a state or votes by all Members of Congress on one or two pieces of legislation. Scorecards can also tally votes by all committee members on specific legislation or votes by all state legislators.

1. Choose the issue areas for which you want to list voting records. These could include: environmental

and consumer issues, educational issues, campaign finance reform, civil rights, labor, taxes, defense spending, pay raises for Senators and Representatives, increase in the minimum wage and immigration quotas and restrictions.

2. Develop a list of legislation to include in the voting record scorecard. Read some of the scorecards developed by interest and lobby groups listed in the resources section for an overview of what legislation these groups consider important and for ideas about format (notice how concise they can be graphically). Contact the committees in both Houses of Congress which are responsible for the chosen issue areas.

3. Because issues and legislation are most often quite complex, include a short narrative about each piece of legislation in the Scorecard, so those reading it will understand exactly what a yes or no vote on the bill meant.

4. Include the frequency with which legislators vote and how often they vote with their party. *Congressional Quarterly* tabulates both of these statistics for a variety of issues.

5. Few Members of Congress provide their voting records for an entire year or session on request to constituents. They may offer instead their record on particular votes.

E. INNOVATIVE WORK/VIEWS ON IMPORTANT ISSUES

Some legislators are unusually persistent or creative in attracting attention to problems or issues they consider particularly important, and in trying to pass legislation to address those problems. For example, former Wisconsin Senator William Proxmire gave his monthly Golden Fleece award to "the biggest example of ridiculous, ironic or wasteful government spending."[1]

Try to arrange interviews with the legislators to be profiled to discover which issues interest them. Use the sample questions on page 195 as a starting point for developing your own questions. Call the legislators' state or district offices to find out when they will each be in their home districts. Other sources of information include staff members, former opponents, reporters and lobbyists. Review legislators' press releases and newsletters as well as newspaper and magazine articles and any published works by the legislators.

F. MEDIA COVERAGE

Over several months, track coverage of legislators by local newspapers, TV and radio for general information for the profile as well as to determine how often the legislators receive coverage. Check to see if the legislators are covered in national news magazines like *Time*, *Newsweek*, or *U.S. News and World Report* or "national" papers like the *Wall Street Journal*, *Washington Post*, *New York Times* or *Los Angeles Times*. Also check coverage in smaller circulation publications such as newsletters and journals.

Review press releases from the legislators' offices to see if the newspaper articles and TV and radio stories simply duplicate the press releases or are produced independently by the media. While reviewing press releases, make notes by subject area to determine whether or not the legislators' voting records are consistent with information released to the press.

G. CAMPAIGN FINANCE

A survey of campaign contributions can reveal candidates' allegiances and obligations. As journalist Penny Loeb writes in the *Reporter's Handbook*, "[I]t's not enough just to list who gives what to which candidate or what investments a candidate has. The real story is why a person or business gives something to a candidate - and what they get in return."[2]

Nearly every candidate must engage in raising some campaign funds. Campaign funding sources, when compared to the legislators' voting records and committee assignments, can identify potential conflicts of interest. Be careful not to jump to conclusions but rather raise questions about the potential for a conflict.

Candidates for Congress (and President) are required to report all contributions of $200 or more from individuals and all size contributions from political action committees (PACs) and political party committees as well as any bank loan.[3] PACs and political parties are also required to report when and where they spend money. Thus, you can research all the contributions to a particular candidate's campaign or all the candidates to whom a PAC or party gave funds.

The Federal Elections Commission (FEC) keeps records for all federal campaigns. Microfilm cartridges, which are the official FEC record, contain information dating back to the 1972 elections. Computer indexes provide detailed campaign finance information beginning with the 1977-78 election cycle. Most computer record printouts are free to students.

For a detailed pamphlet listing available FEC records, write or call for a free copy of *Using FEC Campaign Information*. See the resources section for the FEC's address and toll-free telephone number.

Common Cause and Public Citizen's Congress Watch both publish studies and reports on PAC contributions, personal financial holdings, honoraria and proposals for campaign finance reform. See the resources section.

Laws on campaign finance disclosure for state and local elections vary from state to state. Contact the state board of elections for particular information.

CAMPAIGN FINANCE: AN OVERVIEW

The cost of running a campaign for public office — especially for Congress — is growing rapidly. The average cost in 1990 of winning a seat in the U.S. Senate was nearly $4 million, more than six times what it cost in 1976.[4] The increased cost is due largely to increases in the cost of television and radio advertising as well as postage rates. The amount of money needed is so high that Members of Congress must spend a large amount of their time in office raising money for the next election. For example, a member of the House has to raise an average of $17,000 a month during a two-year term and Senators must raise almost $56,000 per month during a six-year term.[5]

The high costs of campaigns also discourage potential candidates from entering a race since incumbents find it easier to raise money. As a result, 98 percent of House incumbents who sought reelection in 1988 won their races.[6] This contributes to a lack of diversity in Congress. For example, women and minorities are under-represented. After the 1988 election, out of 535 Members of Congress, only 30 were female — 28 Representatives and two Senators.[7] And only 24 African Americans, 11 Latino and 7 Asian American lawmakers were Members of Congress.[8]

The high cost of running for federal office places an enormous burden on elected officials to avoid being influenced in the way they vote by the organizations and individuals financing their campaigns. In voting studies on dozens of different issues, votes correspond to the interests of campaign contributors with disquieting frequency. For example, the United States Public Interest Research Group (U.S. PIRG) studied the votes on key nuclear safety issues by members of the House Energy and Commerce Committee and the Senate Energy and Natural Resources Committee. Of the committee members who received more than $50,000 from nuclear industry political action committees (PACs) during the period from January 1981 to December 1986, 88 percent voted in favor of the nuclear industry's position on key committee votes including votes on limiting the industry's liability for nuclear accidents.[9]

As Kathleen Welch, a former lobbyist with U.S. PIRG, writes, "Rather than representing the constituents who voted for them, Members of Congress seem to be in the business of raising money, assuring reelection, and representing the concerns of the special interests who line their campaign coffers."[10]

Current Financing Strategies

Most Members of Congress — at least those without the financial means themselves — finance their campaigns with money from political action committees (PACs), from individual contributors and to a lesser extent, from "soft money" spending on behalf of candidates.

A PAC is a group of like-minded people — employees of corporations, members of trade associations, labor unions or ideological groups — who raise funds among themselves to give to candidates collectively rather than as individuals.[11] PACs pool the money and contribute it to federal candidates in large amounts — up to a ceiling of $5,000 per candidate for primary campaigns and $5,000 for general campaigns.[12] PACs thus have the ability to aggregate both money and influence over candidates. The PACs, including a Realtors' PAC, Doctors' PAC, Teachers' PAC, Auto Workers' PAC, Automobile Dealers' PAC, Bankers' PAC and Home Builders' PAC, to name a few, send special interest signals of great clarity. By gaining a disproportionate degree of influence with Members of Congress, special interest PAC contributions undermine the one person - one vote principle of democracy.[13]

PACs representing diverse interests including labor, corporations and trade associations attempt to help candidates win elections. Although business PACs outspend labor PACs nearly three to one, most PACs have several characteristics in common.[14] PACs favor incumbents, who have a much greater chance of winning an election. PACs also favor Members of Congress who are committee chairs and who sit on the "money" committees — the House Ways and Means, House Appropriations, Senate Finance and Senate Appropriations Committees — and are therefore in the best position to benefit a PAC's constituencies. In addition, PACs often combine to support the same candidates — the winners. PACs give money to unopposed and highly popular candidates and to both candidates in some contests. Moreover, after an election in which they have backed a loser, PACs often make contributions to the winner.[15]

Campaign finance law limits the amount of money an individual can contribute to a federal candidate to $1,000 for each primary and $1,000 for each general election.[16] "Soft money" refers to legal methods of skirting the spirit of campaign finance reforms limiting individual contributions. Under a 1979 change in the federal election law, individuals can bypass the limit on individual contributions by contributing instead to a candidate's political party. The amount an individual can contribute to a party is not subject to

disclosure or spending ceiling provisions. The party can then spend the money on party-building activities such as paying for expenses of local party campaign headquarters, thus freeing more of a candidate's money for expenses directly related to the campaign.[17]

In addition, individuals can spend an unlimited amount on behalf of candidates, as long as the money does not go directly to the candidate or the campaign.[18] These "independent" funders are free to go on the offensive against other candidates by sponsoring television ads, for example, which have contributed to a rise in negative campaigning.[19]

Another soft money tactic — bundling — involves PACs which collect checks from individuals made out to the candidate, send the checks to the candidate in a bundle, skirting the PAC spending limit since the checks are made out to the candidate not to the PAC. In addition, an individual can give a tax-deductible gift to a charitable foundation set up by the candidate, which is supposed to be nonpolitical, but often blurs the line.[20]

History of Campaign Finance Reform

The influence of campaign contributions has been an issue in federal politics at least since the 1830s. The Civil Service Reform Act of 1883 ended the practice of soliciting campaign contributions from civil servants in Washington who owed their jobs to political appointments.[21] The Tilman Act of 1907 prohibited corporations and national banks from making money contributions to candidates for federal office, although other types of political expenditures, including individual contributions, were not prohibited.[22] Congress passed the Corrupt Practices Act of 1925 to require candidates to report receipts and expenditures, but the Act rarely was enforced.[23]

The next substantial reform of the campaign finance system was the enactment of the Federal Election Campaign Act of 1971, which extended the scope of congressional regulation beyond the general election to include primaries, caucuses and conventions.[24] The Act strengthened disclosure requirements for federal election campaigns and required that information be made available to the public as well as codified rules regulating the use of corporate and union treasuries to establish separate funds to make campaign contributions. These rules permitted corporations to collect "voluntary" contributions from their employees to advance partisan political views, thus officially recognizing the existence of PACs. The changes established equal treatment for corporations and labor organizations, but excluded (until 1974) entities with government contracts.[25]

The Federal Election Campaign Act of 1974 "was a direct outgrowth of the Watergate scandal and a public shocked at the volume of large secret gifts to Richard Nixon's Committee to Reelect the President," writes Mark Green in *Who Runs Congress?*.[26] The Act created the Federal Elections Commission (FEC) to administer revised disclosure provisions, to compel campaign committees to report contributions and to investigate suspected violations of law. The 1974 Act established public funding of presidential campaigns by providing matching funds — public funds to match every dollar candidates raise themselves — for presidential primaries. The Act created full public funding of general elections by creating the income tax check off which allows taxpayers to decide if they want one dollar of their taxes to go to the fund.[27]

The 1974 Act placed limits on the amount an individual, special interest group or PAC could contribute; limited the overall amount a candidate could spend; and limited the amount candidates could spend of their own money. The Act also repealed the rule which had prohibited corporations with government contracts from creating PACs.[28] After repeal of the rule which had limited the formation of PACs, the number of labor PACs grew 75 percent in the next nine years, business PACs 1,750 percent.[29] And between 1974 and 1988, the number of PACs grew from approximately 608 to 4,828.[30]

The Supreme Court struck down, on First Amendment grounds, both the limit on the total amount candidates could spend and the limits on candidates' use of personal funds. The case, *Buckley* v. *Valeo*, challenged the 1974 Federal Election Campaign Act on the grounds that limiting the use of money for political purposes was an unconstitutional restriction of free speech, since all meaningful political communication requires the use of money.[31]

Proposals for Further Reform

The following are some of the reforms proposed for lessening the effect of campaign finance on the democratic process:

- Public financing of congressional elections — Under this plan, Senate and House candidates who agreed to specified campaign spending limits would become eligible for public funding, or matching public funds, which would come from a voluntary income tax checkoff system. The advantages of public financing include reducing dependence on PACs and lessening the advantage of incumbents.[32]

- Provide candidates with free TV and radio time, financed by using the surplus from the presidential election taxpayer check-off, to lower the cost of running a campaign.[33]

- Require broadcasters to provide candidates with air time at cost as a condition of license granting and renewal.[34]

- Prohibit all PAC contributions to federal candidates — to deprive groups of the power to aggregate money and hand it out to candidates.[35]

- Limit the total amount of PAC contributions candidates accept per election.[36]

- Abolish subsidized PACs but permit voluntary PACs. Prohibit corporations and unions from using their general treasury funds to set up PACs, but continue to allow PACs that raise the start-up funds from individual contributions.[37]

- Amend the Constitution to enable Congress and the states to "enact laws regulating the amounts of contributions and expenditures intended to affect elections."[38]

- Ban contributions to congressional candidates from persons who are not entitled to vote for them, those who do not live in the candidate's district for the House or do not live in the candidate's state for the Senate.[39]

■ Regulate "soft money" independent expenditures by requiring that independently financed advertising prominently identify the source of its funding and by providing public funding to general election candidates against whom independent spending efforts are directed.[40]

■ Increase tax credits to encourage individual citizens to contribute to candidates.[41]

H. Factors Affecting Election/ Re-election of Legislators

Did the legislator use any unusual campaign techniques, or stress one or two specific issues? Did they align with their political party on all important issues, or take a different stand on one or more? Did the legislator have the support of particular interest groups?

A legislator's brochures, pamphlets, newsletters, posters, media ads and statements are useful to determine a campaign's focus. Also try to speak to the legislator's Press Aide. And during an election campaign, attend a rally or event for the candidate.

I. Personal Finances

Personal finances may create conflicts of interest. When reviewing personal financial information, note any connections with corporations, banks or interest groups. Then compare these connections with committees on which the legislator sits, legislation introduced and voting records. Identify any potential areas of conflict of interest.

The Ethics in Government Act of 1978 requires limited disclosure of information concerning personal finances. Members of the House of Representatives must list all business and professional income of more than $100 or stocks worth over $1000. Senators must disclose all speaking fees and must disclose income from honoraria, dividends, interest, rent, capital gains, trusts, estates and other sources; gifts of transporta-

tion, lodging, food or entertainment; reimbursements; property; liabilities and other financial information; non-governmental positions; agreements for future employment or continuation of payments or benefits; and "blind-trust" financial arrangements. Various minimum or maximum amounts govern what must be reported.

The reports filed by each Representative and each Senator are due on May 15th of each year and are released to the public on June 14th. Reports for the House of Representatives are available at the Office of Records and Registration, 1036 Longworth House Office Building, Washington, DC 20515. Senate reports are available at the Office of Public Records, 232 Hart Senate Office Building, Washington, DC 20510. Individual copies of Senate reports, but not the House, are available through the mail from the above address for a copying charge of 20 cents a page.

The reports are also on file at the office of each state's Secretary of State for all members of that state's congressional delegation and for each of the state's two U.S. Senators. Reports for the House of Representatives, but not the Senate, are available at all Federal Depository Libraries.

Members of Congress are required to report other expenditures including mass mailings, foreign gifts received, foreign travel and conflict of interest statements for outside business or employment activity. This information is available in the following two reports:

Report of the Secretary of the Senate - published twice a year - Secretary of the Senate, 5208 U.S. Capitol Building, Washington, DC 20510. Available free of charge.

Report of the Clerk of the House - published twice a year - Clerk of the House, H-105 U.S. Capitol Building, Washington, DC 20515. Available free of charge.

In addition, Public Citizen's Congress Watch publishes a report on publicly, as well as privately, funded travel expenditures of Members of Congress.

III. RESOURCES

Contacting Members of Congress

Address for members of the U.S. House of Representatives:

The Honorable _____
U.S. House of Representatives
Washington, DC 20515

Address for U.S. Senators:

The Honorable _____
U.S. Senate
Washington, DC 20510

Background on Members of Congress

Some of these directories may be in your public or university library:

Congressional Directory — Published annually by the Superintendent of Documents, U.S. Government Printing Office, Washington, DC 20402-9325. $15. Contains biographical information on Members of Congress, lists committee assignments and staff and names federal agency officials.

Who's Who in Congress — Published annually by Congressional Quarterly, 1414 22nd Street, NW, Washington, DC 20037. $7.95. A pocket-sized guide to Congress including biographical data, phone numbers, staff, committee assignments, election results, CQ's vote studies (frequency of voting and percentage of votes aligned with Representative's party and with the President), rankings from four interest groups, votes on selected key votes (with an explanation of why votes were chosen).

Politics in America — Published annually by Congressional Quarterly, 1414 22nd Street, NW, Washington, DC 20037. $39.95. Detailed profiles of all Members of Congress, election results, campaign finance data, interest group ratings, CQ's voting studies.

Congressional Yellowbook — Published quarterly by the Monitor Publishing Company, 104 Fifth Avenue, 2nd floor, New York, NY 10011. $175 yearly subscription includes four editions. Brief biographical information on each Member of Congress, staff, committee and subcommittee assignments, leadership positions and membership in official groups and informal caucuses.

State Yellow Book — Published twice a year by the Monitor Publishing Company, 104 Fifth Avenue, 2nd floor, New York, NY 10011. $150 yearly subscription includes two volumes. Directory of executive and legislative branches of all 50 states, the District of Columbia and the four insular U.S. territories including demographics, history, state maps and geographical information; economic and education data; and sources for obtaining public records.

Congressional Staff Directory — Published twice a year by Staff Directories, Ltd. P.O. Box 62, Mount Vernon, VA 22121. $59. Includes biographies of all Members of Congress as well as their key staff and committees, subcommittees.

Almanac of American Politics — Published every two years by the *National Journal*, 1730 M Street, NW, Washington, DC 20036. $44.95. Contains biographical information on Members of Congress and state governors; and statistical information on their records, states and districts.

Information on Congressional Districts

Congressional District Atlas — Published every two years by the U.S. Government Printing Office, Washington, DC 20402. $33. Contains maps of districts, counties and municipalities and statistical information about these areas.

Congressional Districts Wall Map — Published occasionally by the Superintendent of Documents, Bureau of the Census, DPD, Public Unit, 1201 E. 10th Street, Jeffersonville, IN 47132. The 1987 map is available for $4.75.

Congress Poster — Published by Congressional Quarterly, 1414 22nd Street, NW, Washington, DC 20037. $14.95. The map shows congressional districts, including every senator and representative and party affiliation as of the November, 1990 elections.

Congressional Districts in the 1990s — Published by Congressional Quarterly, 1414 22nd Street, NW, Washington, DC 20037. Check with CQ for price. Contains complete demographic and political profiles of all 435 congressional districts. Updated after census data is available at the turn of each decade.

Information on Legislation

Congressional documents such as bills, committee reports, presidential messages to Congress, resolutions and public laws may be obtained free by writing the offices listed below. Include bill number or clear document reference and a self-addressed label.

House Document Room, U.S. House of Representatives, 2nd and D Streets, SW, B-18, Washington, DC 20515.

Senate Document Room, Hart Building, Washington, DC 20510-7106.

Committee Documents may be obtained free of charge by writing to your congressional representative or to the relevant committee (at the address listed above for Members of Congress). Such documents include: legislative calendars of committee activity, listing every bill referred to the committee and what action has been taken; listings of all recent committee documents, including hearings (with transcripts of witness testimony) and committee reports on legislation and special studies; committee rules.

Congressional Record — Published each day Congress is in session by the U.S. Government Printing Office, Superintendent of Documents, Washington, DC 20402. Yearly subscription, $225 (paper); $118 (microfiche); $1.50 per issue. Contains all legislative activity for that particular day, floor debate and votes, bills introduced, committee reports filed, schedules of committee hearings, speeches, etc.

LEGIS — This legislative information service by phone will provide a list of all legislation sponsored by any Member of Congress during the current or past session of Congress. They will send a printout with the information at no cost. Clerk of the House, Office of Legislative Information, House Office Building Annex 2, 3rd and D Streets, SW, Room 696, Washington, DC 20515. (202) 225-1772.

Congressional Quarterly Almanac — Published annually by Congressional Quarterly, 1414 22nd Street, NW, Washington, DC 20027. $195. Contains a summary, organized by topic, of all legislative activity for the previous session. A particularly good source for interpreting legislation.

Congressional Quarterly Weekly Report — Published weekly (when Congress is in session) by Congressional Quarterly, 1414 22nd Street, NW, Washington, DC 20037. Provides information on congressional activities, progress of major bills, voting and activities of legislators, news events affecting Congress and background on issues.

Congressional Roll Call — Published at the end of each session of Congress by Congressional Quarterly, 1414 22nd Street, NW, Washington, DC 20037. $19.95. Includes a chronology and analysis of all House and Senate roll call votes.

Congressional Index Service (CIS) — Published monthly, with quarterly and annual cumulative volumes, by the CIS, 4520 East-West Highway, Suite 800, Bethesda, MD 20814. Indexes congressional publications since 1970 and includes summaries of hearings, reports, committee prints and other congressional documents and provides an index by subject, author, witness, etc.

"SCORECARDS" DEVELOPED BY VARIOUS INTEREST GROUPS

The following groups rate the Members of Congress according to their voting records on specific issues of interest to them and develop "Scorecards" or Voting Record Reports with that information. They will give you some good ideas regarding information to include and format. Most copies are free.

American Conservative Union
(conservative issues/$2.00)
38 Ivy Street SE
Washington, DC 20003

American Federation of Labor/Congress
of Industrial Organizations AFL-CIO
(economic/labor issues)
815 16th Street NW
Washington, DC 20006

Americans for Democratic Action
(liberal issues/$5.00)
1511 K Street NW, Suite 941
Washington, DC 20005

Children's Defense Fund (children's issues)
122 C Street NW
Washington, DC 20006

Common Cause (good government issues)
2030 M Street NW
Washington, DC 20036

Congressional Quarterly (major issues)
1414 22nd Street NW
Washington, DC 20037

Consumer Federation of America
 (consumer issues/$10.00)
1424 16th Street NW
Washington, DC 20036

Environmental Action (environmental issues)
6930 Carrol Avenue, Suite 600
Takoma Park, MD 20912

Friends Committee on National Legislation
(peace issues)
245 2nd Street NE
Washington, DC 20002

Leadership Conference on Civil Rights
(civil rights issues)
2027 Massachusetts Avenue NW
Washington, DC 20036

League of Conservation Voters
(environmental issues/$3.00)
1150 Connecticut Avenue NW
Washington, DC 20036

National Association for the Advancement of Colored
People (African American issues)
1025 Vermont Avenue NW
Washington, DC 20036

National Council of Senior Citizens (seniors issues)
1511 K Street NW
Washington, DC 20005

National Education Association
(education/teachers' issues)
1201 16th Street NW
Washington, DC 20036

National Farmers Union (agricultural issues)
600 Maryland Avenue SE
Washington, DC 20024

National Women's Political Caucus (women's issues)
1275 K Street NW, Suite #750
Washington, DC 20005

Public Citizen's Congress Watch
(consumer issues/$5.00)
215 Pennsylvania Avenue SE
Washington, DC 20003

U.S. Chamber of Commerce
(business and industry issues)
1615 H Street NW
Washington, DC 20062

INFORMATION ON CAMPAIGN FINANCE AND PACs

Federal Election Commission, Public Records Office, 999 E Street, NW, Washington, DC 20463. Toll free number: (800) 424-9530.

The FEC provides various educational services free of charge, including audio-visual materials, publications, speakers and a toll-free phone number. Publications include:

Using FEC Campaign Finance Information, 1988.

Supporting Federal Candidates: A Guide for Citizens, 1987.

The Federal Election Commission: The First 10 Years, 1975-1985.

Common Cause, 2030 M Street NW, Washington, DC 20036. Publishes a bi-monthly magazine; in-depth studies on PAC receipts; periodic bulletins and fact sheets on federal as well as state campaign finance issues and a questionnaire for congressional candidates on campaign finance issues. Membership in Common Cause, which includes a subscription to the magazine, is $20/year, $10 for students.

Public Citizen's Congress Watch, 215 Pennsylvania Avenue SE, Washington, DC 20003. Publishes periodic PAC studies and congressional travel expenditure surveys. Membership in Public Citizen, 2000 P Street NW, Washington, DC 20036, which includes a subscription to the bi-monthly magazine *Public Citizen*, is $20/year.

Green, Mark, et al. *Who Runs Congress?* Fourth edition. New York: Dell Publishing Co., 1984. Introduction by Ralph Nader. A citizen's guide to who owns, influences and rules Congress with a primer for taking on Congress. Available from the Center for Study of Responsive Law, P.O. Box 19367, Washington, DC 20036. $3.95 plus postage.

Makinson, Larry. *Open Secrets: The Dollar Power of PACS in Congress.* 1990. Published by Congressional Quarterly, 1414 22nd Street NW, Washington, DC 20037. $120. Describes, and provides some analysis of, the major PAC contributions of all Members of Congress.

Makinson, Larry. *The Price of Admission.* 1989. Published by the Center for Responsive Politics, 1320 19th Street NW, Suite M1, Washington, DC 20036. $19.95. Provides general information on campaign spending during the 1988 elections.

SAMPLE QUESTIONS TO ASK MEMBERS OF CONGRESS

1. What do you regard as the three most innovative actions you have taken as a Member of Congress?

2. What pieces of legislation that you have introduced or co-sponsored in this Congress do you most want to see enacted and why?

3. The referendum allows citizens to express their views on specific issues. Do you favor a national referendum? If so, do you favor a binding or non-binding referendum? What issues do you think should be placed on a national referendum ballot?

4. The initiative allows citizens, through the petitioning process, to place proposals for legislation on the ballot. Do you favor a national initiative and what issues would you recommend be placed on a national initiative ballot? If you do not favor the initiative, why not?

5. What new tools would you give citizens, both individually and as a group, to assist them in overseeing the activities of Members of Congress and congressional committees and to have more influence over Congress outside of partisan party politics?

6. What methods or practices do you recommend for making citizens' complaints to Members of Congress more meaningful in terms of institutional reform — such as pooling letters for analysis of patterns of abuse?

7. What would you identify as the most important omissions or lost opportunities in this Congress?

8. What subsidies for business in the current budget would you recommend be eliminated?

9. Which federal agencies do you think should have their budgets increased and which ones should have their budgets decreased?

10. What are the three most important changes you would make in the regulatory agencies and why? What would this accomplish?

11. Which rules of Congress do you think are most in need of amendment, and how would you change them?

12. Which factors most influence your votes in Committee and on the floor?

13. Which congressional lobby is the most effective and why?

14. Do you believe Members of Congress should have to disclose all aspects of their personal wealth and financial interests?

15. Do you think that a Member of Congress should not vote on matters that directly affect substantial holdings of that legislator?

16. Do you favor rotation of congressional committee assignments every six or eight years to avoid stagnation and ingrained relationships between legislators and special interests?

17. Do you publish complete tabulations of your floor and committee voting and attendance records for your constituents on request?

18. What changes would you make in the present system of campaign financing?

19. Do you think Members of Congress pay excessive attention, in the form of staff and office budget, to the servicing of individual constituent complaints at the expense of their legislative functions?

20. Would you favor the creation of a congressional "ombudsman"? Would one such positions be sufficient to cut through executive branch red tape?

21. Is Congress ineffective with so many overlapping subcommittees and full committees? If so, why are they not reduced in number?

22. Do you think Members of Congress are paid excessively high salaries and benefits? Would you be in favor of another pay raise or a pay cut?

23. Do you think that citizens should be given more facilities and rights to organize themselves better as taxpayers, consumers and workers so as to better inform, mobilize and improve the performance of the various agencies and programs of the federal government? (e.g. ratepayers, taxpayers vis-à-vis subsidies and taxpayer assets, workers for job safety, depositors vis-à-vis banks and savings and loans).

BIBLIOGRAPHY

Background Information on Campaign Finance Reform and Honoraria: U.S. Senate. Fact sheet. Washington, DC: Common Cause, Fall 1990.

Green, Mark, et al. *Who Runs Congress?* Fourth edition. New York: Dell Publishing Co., 1984.

If You Care About the Voice of Minorities in American Politics, You Should Care About Campaign Finance Reform. Fact sheet. Washington, DC: Public Citizen, 1990.

If You Care About the Voice of Women in American Politics, You Should Care About Campaign Finance Reform. Fact sheet. Washington, DC: Public Citizen's Congress Watch, 1990.

Makinson, Larry. *The Price of Admission: An Illustrated Atlas of Campaign Spending in the 1988 Congressional Elections.* Washington, DC: Center for Responsive Politics, 1989.

Monk, Catherine. *Ralph Nader's Congress Project Profile Kit.* Washington, DC: Center for Study of Responsive Law, 1981.

"Nuclear Power Industry PACS Gave Over $17 Million to Congressional Candidates; Key Nuclear Safety Vote Scheduled in House July 29," press release. Washington, DC: United States Public Interest Research Group, July 25, 1987.

Public Citizen Policy Paper on Campaign Finance Reform. Washington, DC: Public Citizen's Congress Watch.

"Reagan's Inaugural Festivities Win Proxmire's Fleece Award," Reuters Ltd. wire service, March 31, 1987.

Stern, Philip M. *The Best Congress Money Can Buy.* New York: Pantheon Books, 1988.

Stone, Mary N. *Facts on PACs: Political Action Committees and American Campaign Finance.* Washington, DC: League of Women Voters Education Fund, 1984.

Ullmann, John and Jan Colbert, eds. *Reporter's Handbook: An Investigator's Guide to Documents and Techniques.* Second edition. New York: St. Martin's Press, 1991.

Using FEC Campaign Finance Information. Washington, DC: Federal Elections Commission, 1988.

We the People For Public Funding: Questions and Answers on Public Funding of Congressional Campaigns. Washington, DC: Public Citizen's Congress Watch.

Welch, Kathleen A. "Democracy for Sale: The Need for Campaign Finance Reform," *In the Public Interest.* Spring 1990.

ACTIVITY TWO:
ENERGY WASTEHUNT

I. INTRODUCTION

Energy efficiency means adopting "technologies that use less energy to achieve the same results."[1] For example, efficient light bulbs produce the same intensity of light as other bulbs but use less electricity and last longer, and fuel efficient cars use less gasoline to travel the same distance. Energy efficiency does not mean adjusting the thermostat to uncomfortable levels that are too cold in winter and too hot in summer. Instead, studies show that significant reductions in energy use are feasible without affecting the quality of life.[2]

Energy efficiency has played an important part in reducing overall energy use in the United States since the energy crises of the 1970s, when gasoline shortages and high gasoline prices forced the country to rethink how it uses and wastes energy.[3] At that time, the federal government adopted a national energy strategy which included funding for research and development of energy efficient technologies and development of alternative energy sources including solar energy.[4]

The conservation efforts begun in the 1970s are now saving the United States more than 13 million barrels of oil per day.[5] Without these efforts, given energy use at 1973 levels, it would require 35 percent more fuel each day to enjoy the current standard of living in the United States.[6]

Considerable potential exists for increased energy efficiency. For example, a 1989 study by the American Council for an Energy-Efficient Economy shows that cost-effective energy efficiency improvements, using currently available technologies, can reduce projected annual energy use by almost 20 percent by the year 2000 and save $75 billion a year.[7]

However, as the energy crises of the 1970s passed and gasoline prices fell, the federal government abandoned many efficiency programs and cut funding for research and development of renewable energy sources by 82 percent between 1981 and 1989.[8] Despite the lack of government funding, technologies were developed and improved in the 1980s. By 1988, renewable energy, principally hydropower and biomass, provided 7.6 percent of U.S. energy, more than nuclear power.[9] Furthermore, the cost of these clean, renewable sources is expected to continue to fall in the 1990s.[10]

This activity discusses current energy sources and some alternatives, including energy efficiency. By conducting an energy wastehunt to identify wasteful uses of energy in the school and by implementing various efficiency techniques, students can help their school save money on utility bills. For example, students in Washington, DC, who regularly patrol their schools to check for energy waste, saved their school over $43,000 in energy bills. (See their story on pages 5-6).

II. ENERGY USE IN THE UNITED STATES

The United States relies on nonrenewable, finite natural resources including oil, coal, natural gas and uranium to produce the energy needed in every aspect of our lives. All of these energy sources will eventually run out. For example, oil, which provides 30 percent of the world's energy, is expected to run dry in about 50 years.[11] In addition, even if supplies were plentiful for centuries, all of these nonrenewable energy sources cause serious environmental damage, including air pollution, acid rain and greenhouse gas emissions which cause global warming.[12]

Reliance on oil requires continued exploration for new sources, leading oil companies to exploit untouched wilderness. Transportation of oil supplies on the oceans has led to oil spills — including the Exxon Valdez spill at Prince William Sound, Alaska in 1989 — which have damaged marine life and contaminated virtually every body of sea water in the world.[13] Reliance on oil imported from the Middle East continues to shape our relationship with that area of the world.

Coal-burning plants, without proper scrubbing devices, produce polluted air which contributes heavily to the acid rain phenomenon and global warming.[14]

Nuclear energy poses a threat of enormous environmental and health consequences in the event of accidents such as those at Three Mile Island and Chernobyl. Nuclear power plants produce radioactive waste that will continue to be harmful for thousands of years and create controversy over where to store it. Furthermore, the long-term damage of radiation to human health, such as cancer or genetic damage, is not fully known.[15] Nuclear power is more expensive to generate than power from fossil fuels, energy efficiency and many sources of renewable energy.[16]

III. SOLUTIONS: RENEWABLE ENERGY AND ENERGY EFFICIENCY

A combination of energy efficient technologies and various renewable energy sources can address many of the problems associated with reliance on oil, coal and nuclear power. Neither increased efficiency nor one single source of renewable energy can replace dependence on oil, coal and nuclear power. But together these sources can significantly reduce pollution, reduce dependence on foreign oil and lengthen the amount of time before nonrenewables run out. Existing government spending on oil exploration and nuclear research could be redirected to building more efficient factories and automobiles and to researching solar energy and other renewable technologies.

A. RENEWABLE ENERGY SOURCES

Renewable energy sources — which come from unlimited resources and include solar, wind, hydroelectric and geothermal power and biomass — produce little or no pollution. A 1989 Union of Concerned Scientists report maintains that renewable energy technology could supply 50 percent of U.S. energy by 2020 and, in the short term, 15 percent of U.S. energy needs by 2000.[17] Renewable sources provided 17 percent of the world's energy in 1988.[18]

Solar Energy

Solar technologies include active and passive solar systems, photovoltaics and solar-thermal technology. Active solar systems collect energy from the sun to heat space or water directly in a house or other building. Passive solar systems employ design techniques which use the sun's energy for heating, cooling and lighting.[19] Approximately 200,000 residential passive solar buildings, which obtain 30 to 40 percent of their energy from the sun, were built in the United States between 1975 and 1985.[20]

Photovoltaic cells produce electric current directly from the sun's rays. Solar thermal plants use large mirrors to focus the sun's energy on a liquid which is then used to produce steam to create electricity. Seven solar thermal plants operating in California together produce over 200 megawatts of power, enough for about 100,000 homes.[21] And, according to the Department of Energy, if the newer technologies are developed and deployed, new houses could derive 80 percent of their heating and 60 percent of their cooling from solar energy.[22]

Wind Power

Wind power is used in California where 18,000 wind turbines generate enough electric power to serve approximately 300,000 homes at a price competitive with conventional sources of power.[23]

Hydroelectric Power

Hydroelectric power — which converts the kinetic energy of flowing water into mechanical power or electricity — is currently the most widely used renewable energy source, providing 13 percent of total U.S. electricity.[24] Large hydroelectric plants often cause environmental problems including flooding, erosion and destruction of wildlife. But small and medium sized projects can avoid these problems.[25]

Geothermal Power

Geothermal power — which uses heat beneath the earth's crust to spin turbines — emits little carbon dioxide, a greenhouse gas, and supplies 7 percent of California's electric power.[26]

Biomass and Biofuels

Biomass — which includes wood, wood wastes and agricultural wastes, alcohol fuels derived from grains and other plant matter, and methane — accounts for 4 to 5 percent of U.S. primary energy consumption.[27]

Biofuels, such as ethanol and methanol, provide liquid energy for transportation. Some biofuels have their own problems. For example, methanol produces the suspected carcinogen, formaldehyde. But the cleaner corn-based ethanol was used as a gasoline additive to reduce harmful emissions in approximately 8 percent of all the automotive fuel burned in 1988.[28]

Hydrogen fuel, produced by using solar energy to split water particles, is a promising renewable energy source which is still in the stages of research and development but is currently used as a major fuel to power the space shuttle.[29]

B. ENERGY EFFICIENCY METHODS: DOING MORE WITH LESS

Energy efficiency is the fastest-growing, most abundant, least polluting and lowest-cost energy resource available in the United States.[30]

Cogeneration

Cogeneration uses energy that would otherwise be wasted by capturing energy used to produce electricity and using it again for heating, refrigerating or manufacturing processes rather than discarding it into the air. Thus, both electricity and heat are produced using the same fuel. For example, a utility plant that produces only electricity is about 32 percent efficient, but with cogeneration reusing the same fuel, the plant can approach 80 percent efficiency.[31]

Cogeneration is also useful in individual buildings or factories which can produce their own electricity as well as provide heating or cooling. By the end of 1988, cogeneration was producing about 4 percent of the U.S. electricity supply at costs usually lower than those of conventional power and could supply as much power as 100 nuclear plants by the year 2000.[32]

Utility Companies

To avoid the cost of building new power plants, many electric utility companies have begun to adopt energy efficiency measures. Utilities have monopolies on energy production in their local markets which guarantee a certain demand. When demand goes up as the population increases, utilities eventually have to build costly new power plants. If the utility employs energy efficiency measures at its power plants and encourages its consumers to use energy more efficiently, the energy saved can supply the new consumers and the utility will not need to build a new power plants.[33]

Around the country, environmental groups have won court orders requiring public utilities to adopt and encourage efficiency measures. For example, in California, when a court order forced the Pacific Gas and Electric Company to spend $250 million to save energy, the utility avoided spending seven times that amount on additional but unneeded energy supplies.[34]

One way for citizens to have more control over the way public utilities are regulated is to form a Citizen Utility Board (CUB). Citizens in several states (Wisconsin, Illinois, Oregon and New York) have banded together to form CUBs to strengthen their ability to participate in and challenge the rate setting and decision making processes.

CUBs operate by inserting a flyer in official government mailings (with the sanction of the state legislature) offering citizens the opportunity to band together to represent themselves. Small membership fees are pooled to hire a permanent staff to represent ratepayers before all branches of government, including the state public utility commission, on utility matters affecting them. This idea costs the taxpayer nothing and does not create another government agency.[35]

Fuel Efficiency

Motor vehicles, a major source of air pollution, consume over 60 percent of the oil used in the United States.[36] Increasing automobile fuel efficiency reduces oil consumption and cuts carbon dioxide emissions. Technology exists to manufacture new cars with an average fuel economy of at least 45 miles-per-gallon by the year 2000.[37]

Between 1975 and 1985, the average fuel economy of new cars and light trucks increased by more than 66 percent. By 1985, the country was saving over 2.4 million barrels of oil per day, or 60 percent of U.S. oil imports.[38]

Industrial efficiency

Energy efficiency in U.S. industry improved significantly between 1973 and 1988. But U.S. industry is still significantly less energy-efficient than its Japanese and European competitors which use less than half the energy per unit of industrial output. Japanese industry has reduced its energy intensity at nearly twice the rate of U.S. industry.[39] Our federal government cut support for development of industrial efficiency methods by almost 60 percent between 1981 and 1989.[40]

Several methods of energy efficiency are readily available for industrial applications. Using more efficient electric motors is one way to eliminate industrial energy waste.[41] In addition, using recycled materials to produce steel, aluminum and glass saves energy and reduces waste streams. For example, recycled aluminum requires 95 percent less energy than producing aluminum from raw materials, and recycled paper requires 64 percent less energy than making paper from virgin wood pulp.[42]

Design Methods and Technologies for Buildings and Appliances

Innovations in design techniques since the 1970s have increased the energy efficiency of new buildings as well as appliances. Energy saving design technologies include improved insulation and other building materials, employment of solar designs which make use of natural lighting and new lighting technologies including compact fluorescents.

Many of these design innovations can adapt or retrofit older houses and buildings. For example, energy use fell by an average of 25 percent in a study of 40,000 houses that were retrofitted with energy efficient technologies.[43]

Insulation

Superinsulated houses and buildings use large amounts of insulation in walls and ceilings, double- or triple-pane windows and ventilation systems to maintain indoor air quality, and recover heat from the air exhaust. Superinsulated houses can cost-effectively reduce heating fuel needs by more than 75 percent. The initial costs, however, are high and, as a result, less than 1 percent of new houses today are superinsulated.[44] Federal, state and local governments can solve this problem by tightening the building codes

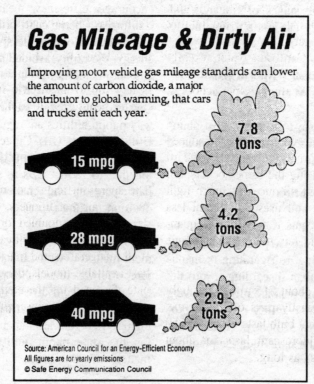

Gas Mileage & Dirty Air

Improving motor vehicle gas mileage standards can lower the amount of carbon dioxide, a major contributor to global warming, that cars and trucks emit each year.

15 mpg — 7.8 tons

28 mpg — 4.2 tons

40 mpg — 2.9 tons

Source: American Council for an Energy-Efficient Economy
All figures are for yearly emissions
© Safe Energy Communication Council

and by offering incentives to builders through interest deductions for efficiency investments.[45]

Windows are a major source of energy loss, since conventional glass allows heat to pass through easily. About 4 percent of total U.S. energy leaks through windows.[46] Substitutes include double- or triple-pane windows and low emissivity (Low-E) superwindows which are coated with heat-reflective film to insulate 4 to 5 times better than double-glazed windows.[47]

Lighting

Lighting accounts for approximately 20 percent of the electricity generated in the United States and accounts for 25 percent or more if the energy used by air conditioning and ventilation systems to remove heat generated by lighting is included. About half of the air conditioning use in a typical office building is to take away the heat from inefficient lighting.[48]

Energy efficient lighting systems — which can cut energy use by as much as 75 percent — include compact fluorescent bulbs, solid-state electronic ballasts that can reduce power use by 20 to 35 percent compared with conventional ballasts, design features which make optimum use of natural light and lighting controls that automatically turn lights off when they are not needed.[49] Schools in California which recently switched to new fluorescent lighting systems are saving from $4000 to $12,000 annually per school in electric bills.[50]

High-efficiency compact fluorescent bulbs, introduced in the early 1980s, can readily replace standard incandescent light bulbs, using the same sockets. An 18-watt compact fluorescent produces as much light as a 75-watt incandescent and uses 75 percent less energy.[51] Compact fluorescents run at high frequencies, without flickering and humming like old-style fluorescents.[52]

Compact fluorescents cost about $15 to $18 per light bulb. But the investment easily pays off over time. For example, an incandescent bulb lasts for about 750 hours while a compact fluorescent lasts for about 10,000 hours, thirteen times as long.[53]

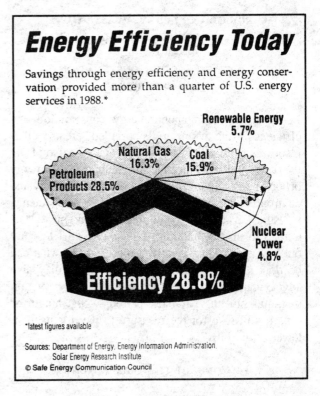

Energy Efficiency Today

Savings through energy efficiency and energy conservation provided more than a quarter of U.S. energy services in 1988.*

Renewable Energy 5.7%

Natural Gas 16.3%

Coal 15.9%

Petroleum Products 28.5%

Nuclear Power 4.8%

Efficiency 28.8%

*latest figures available

Sources: Department of Energy, Energy Information Administration.
Solar Energy Research Institute
© Safe Energy Communication Council

Heating and air conditioning equipment

Technological advances have succeeded both in producing equipment that is more energy efficient and in developing ways to adapt/retrofit existing systems to increase energy efficiency. For example, adding a heat pump to an electric furnace can cut electricity use for heating by 30 to 40 percent.[54]

Appliances

The energy efficiency of major electrical appliances such as air conditioners, refrigerators and clothes dryers can be doubled or tripled with technology either existing today or available by the mid-1990s.[55] If all refrigerators and freezers were as efficient as the best available models, the energy saved would eliminate the need for the equivalent of 15 large, 1,000 megawatt nuclear power plants.[56]

CONDUCT AN ENERGY "WASTE HUNT" IN YOUR SCHOOL

I. STUDY ENERGY CONSERVATION AND EFFICIENCY

Learn all you can about energy conservation and efficiency using the materials provided here as well as resources from your community. Invite a person from the local utility company, the state or city energy office or from a citizen group working on energy and environmental issues to address the class on efficiency measures. Many utility companies now have staff trained to inspect buildings with a checklist to point out how energy is currently being used and what can be done to use it more efficiently. They may also advise you on the costs of the suggested conservation measures and the pay-back period — the length of time it will take for the measure to pay for itself in lower utility bills.

II. CONDUCT THE WASTE HUNT

Work with school maintenance personnel to investigate areas of the school where energy is wasted and can be conserved. (Use the checklist beginning on page 203). The checklist is divided into two categories: 1) technologies that your school could adopt to save energy and 2) maintenance and use (items you can check on an occasional and regular basis and that cost little or nothing to implement).

III. MAKE AND IMPLEMENT RECOMMENDATIONS

Identify ways in which your school is wasting energy and recommend more efficient solutions. Categorize the various efficiency measures by cost and energy savings. Some measures — such as turning off the lights — cost nothing. Other measures require an initial cost but will pay for themselves over time.

Work out an implementation plan with school administrators that will fit into the school's short-term and long-term budget.

Organize a student Energy Patrol to monitor the school building on a regular basis.

Once you have implemented some of the efficiency methods, track the school's utility bills over the next few months to estimate savings. Turn your data into a story for the school newspaper and/or produce and distribute a fact sheet to let other students know about your project. Announce your survey results to the community. (See the sample news release on page 176).

ENERGY CONSERVATION SURVEY FOR SCHOOLS

A. HEATING, AIR CONDITIONING AND VENTILATION

Heating, cooling and ventilation account for 59.2 percent of energy use in U.S. commercial buildings including schools according to the U.S. Department of Energy.[57] Efficiency methods and technologies can significantly reduce the amount of energy needed to adequately heat and cool buildings. Check for the following:

Technologies	Yes	No
• Does the furnace use a heat pump?	☐	☐
• Do doors and windows have adequate weatherstripping and caulking?	☐	☐
• Are there storm doors and windows throughout the building?	☐	☐
• Are there shades or blinds on windows to control the amount of sun entering the building, to help decrease demand on the air conditioning system?	☐	☐
• Is there at least 6" of insulation in the walls?	☐	☐
• Is there at least 4" of insulation in the ceilings?	☐	☐
• Is there at least 3' of insulation under the floors?	☐	☐
• Are the air ducts insulated?	☐	☐
• Are the hot water heater and hot water and steam pipes insulated?	☐	☐
• Are there automatic clock devices on thermostats so systems are turned off when not needed?	☐	☐
• Are thermostats located away from sources of outside air?	☐	☐
• Are there separate thermostat controls in areas used only during certain hours, for example, in the cafeteria or conference rooms?	☐	☐
• Radiators can be made more efficient by using reflectors, heat reflecting panels made from insulating material and covered by metal foil, which are easy to make.		

Maintenance and Use	Yes	No
• Are heating and cooling equipment regularly serviced, including cleaning and changing filters annually or semi-annually?	☐	☐
• Are ducts and pipes checked for leaks at least once a year?	☐	☐
• Are there any broken or cracked windows allowing heated or cooled air to escape?	☐	☐
• Check electric sockets and walls, floors and windows for cracks and openings where air can escape.	☐	☐
• Are windows and doors kept closed when the heating or cooling system is in use?	☐	☐
• Are window shades open on sunny days in the winter to let in the light and heat of the sun?	☐	☐
• Are air vents (or radiators) unblocked to permit maximum air flow?	☐	☐
• Are rooms not in use closed off?	☐	☐

B. Lighting

Lighting accounts for 25 percent of energy use in commercial buildings.[58] Implementing energy efficient lighting systems can greatly reduce energy use.

Technologies	Yes	No
• Are there separate light switches for separate areas of the building?	☐	☐
• Is fluorescent overhead lighting used instead of incandescent lighting?	☐	☐
• Has the local electric utility company evaluated the lighting system to determine how it can be made more energy efficient?	☐	☐

Maintenance and Use	Yes	No
• Is lighting in areas of the building used only during part of the day turned off when those areas are not in use?	☐	☐
• Is lighting turned off where sunlight provides sufficient illumination?	☐	☐
• Make sure windows and lighting fixtures are clean to maximize natural daylight and the output of light bulbs.	☐	☐

C. Hot Water

The energy used to heat water accounts for approximately 5.6 percent of energy use in commercial buildings, according to the U.S. Department of Energy.[59]

Technologies	Yes	No
• Is the hot water storage tank insulated?	☐	☐
• Is the hot water heater insulated?	☐	☐
• Has consideration been given to installation of a solar hot water heater?	☐	☐
• Are water control or aerator devices which can cut water flow by 50 percent in use on faucets?	☐	☐
• Are toilet dams used to cut down on water use in bathrooms?	☐	☐

Maintenance and Use	Yes	No
• Is hot water set at or below 120 degrees except for use in dishwashers for which the temperature should be at least 140 degrees?	☐	☐
• Are any of the faucets in the cafeteria or bathrooms leaking?	☐	☐

BIBLIOGRAPHY

Abrahamson, Dean and Peter Ciborowski. "Harvest of Sand: Agriculture's Future in a Changing Climate," The Amicus Journal, Spring 1984, Vol. 5. No. 4.

Bell, Thomas. "Schools Put Power in Students' Hands: Energy Patrols Boost Morale, Lower Utility Bills," *Washington Post*. February 7, 1991.

Bollier, David. *Citizen Action and Other Big Ideas: A History of Ralph Nader and the Modern Consumer Movement*. Washington, DC: Center for Study of Responsive Law, 1989.

Brower, Michael. *Cool Energy: The Renewable Solution to Global Warming*. Washington, DC: Union of Concerned Scientists, 1989.

Byrne, Jeanne. *Myth Busters #5: Renewable Energy*. Washington, DC: Safe Energy Communication Council, 1990.

Corson, Walter H., ed. *The Global Ecology Handbook: What You Can Do about the Environmental Crisis*. Boston: Beacon Press, 1990.

Fedoruk, Nicholas. *Myth Busters #6: Energy Efficiency*. Washington, DC: Safe Energy Communications Council, 1990.

Fischer, Michael. "Oil At Any Cost?," *World Link*. July/August 1989.

Flavin, Christopher and Rick Piltz with Chris Nichols. *Sustainable Energy*. Washington, DC: Renew America, 1989.

Flavin, Christopher. *Worldwatch Paper 91: Slowing Global Warming: A Worldwide Strategy*. Washington, DC: Worldwatch Institute, 1989.

Geller, Howard. *Energy Efficiency Paper No. 2: National Energy Efficiency Platform: Description and Potential Impacts*. Washington, DC: American Council for an Energy-Efficient Economy, 1989.

Geller, Howard. *Residential Equipment Efficiency: A State of the Art Review*. Washington, DC: American Council for an Energy-Efficient Economy, 1988.

International Energy Annual. Washington, DC: U.S. Department of Energy, Energy Information Administration, 1991.

Manning-Anderson, Joanne. *For the People*. Reading, MA: Addison-Wesley, 1976.

Naar, Jon. *Design for a Livable Planet: How You Can Help Clean Up the Environment*. New York: Harper and Row Publishers, 1990.

Tips for Energy Savers. Washington, DC: U.S. Department of Energy.

ACTIVITY THREE:
TOY SAFETY SURVEY

INTRODUCTION

Toys can bring months or years of entertainment and learning experiences to a child. Unfortunately, some toys might instead bring injury or death. Despite the efforts of consumer groups and the government, dangerous toys continue to be available to unsuspecting consumers. Toys can strangle, choke, blind, cut or burn the children playing with them.

The Consumer Product Safety Commission (CPSC) — the federal agency responsible for setting and enforcing toy safety regulations — reported 33 children died in toy related accidents between January 1989 and September 1990. Twenty of the 33 reported deaths were caused by choking — involving balloons, balls, marbles and small parts of toys. Five deaths involved toy chests, five involved riding toys and three were from strangulation on straps of different types.[1] And approximately 148,000 children were treated for injuries related to toys.[2] However, because the data are based solely on injuries and deaths reported to hospital emergency rooms, many consumer groups believe that actual numbers of toy-related injuries and deaths are much higher.[3]

One way to protect children from becoming victims of hazardous toys is to survey local stores for dangerous toys and make the information available to the public and the agencies charged with toy regulation. For many years, national consumer groups such as Americans for Democratic Action (ADA) and college-based Public Interest Research Groups (PIRGs) have done just that. As a result, consumers hear more about hazardous toys, and the government has used the information to set new safety standards and recall toys violating existing standards.

Such surveys should be done every year, by as many groups, in as many areas as possible. Many consumers never question the safety of toys before they buy. The publicity generated by a survey for dangerous toys can alert them to the problem in general, as well as to specific toys or types of toys to avoid. Students will provide a valuable community service, while learning organizing skills.

FEDERAL TOY SAFETY REGULATION AND ENFORCEMENT

The CPSC has issued mandatory safety specifications for toys. Toys which fail to meet these specifications may not be legally sold in stores. Some specifications apply to certain toys, such as lawn darts and toy caps and guns (toy-specific regulation) and others apply to the hazard a toy can present to a child, such as lead paint on a toy (hazard-specific regulation). The CPSC does not examine or test each toy for safety before it can be sold, but instead relies on manufacturers to make sure their toys meet the following CPSC specifications:[4]

Small Parts: CPSC regulations ban small parts in toys intended for children under the age of three years to protect children from choking on, gagging on, or swallowing them. A number of toys are exempt from this standard. (See page 216).

Sharp Points and Edges: Toys with sharp edges may not be marketed to children under eight years of age. Manufacturers must follow CPSC specifications to ensure that toys intended for those under eight years of age do not have sharp points or sharp glass or metal edges.

Electrically Operated Toys: Safety specifications for electrically operated toys and children's products are designed to prevent electric shock and burn injuries which could result from poorly constructed electrical toys. Electrically operated toys must be age-labeled for children over eight years old only.

Pacifiers and Rattles: The regulations state that pacifiers and rattles must be large enough so that they cannot become lodged in an infant's throat. They must also be constructed so that they will not separate into small pieces.

Lawn Darts: The CPSC banned most types of lawn darts in 1988 because they present a significant risk of skull puncture wounds. Before 1988, an average of 670 people were injured every year and three children died in accidents involving lawn darts.

Clacker Balls: Clacker balls consist of two plastic balls connected by a cord which can be "clacked" together by a rhythmic motion of the hand. These toys must be manufactured so that the plastic balls will not shatter or fly off the ends of the cord.

Toy Caps and Guns: To prevent hearing damage, the CPSC has limited the noise that toy caps and guns may make to 138 decibels.

Lead in Paint: To prevent lead poisoning, the amount of lead in paint used on toys and other childrens' articles is limited to less than 0.06 percent.

Aluminized Polyester Film Kites: The CPSC has banned these kites because they can become entangled in powerlines and cause electric shock or electrocution.

Toxics in Art Supplies: To protect children and adults from toxic chemicals used in common art and craft materials, federal law requires informational labeling on art and craft materials containing toxic chemicals. The regulations also restrict the use of the most hazardous of the products in school classrooms.

Toys with Hazardous Chemicals: The Federal Hazardous Substances Act prohibits the use of poisonous and otherwise harmful chemicals in toys and other articles intended for use by children. Products designed for older children, such as chemistry sets, model rockets and airplane sets, which must have dangerous chemicals, may be sold if accompanied by instructions and warnings.

If the CPSC identifies a toy — through its own limited toy surveying, a consumer group survey or after a child is injured — which violates the specifications, it can require the manufacturer to correct all future production or it can ban future sale of the toy. If the CPSC determines that the toy presents a substantial product hazard, it can recall it. Because of inadequate enforcement, however, banned and recalled toys often remain on store shelves. For example, after the Indoor Gym House of Creative Playthings, Inc. caused the strangulation deaths of two children, the CPSC recalled the product. But, by this time, 400,000

of the toys had been distributed and less than half were returned.[5]

For hazards beyond those covered by the CPSC, the manufacturers themselves decide which toys will be tested, develop standards for testing and pay for what testing is conducted. Companies often contract with independent testing laboratories to test their toys for them. These laboratories offer their own seals of approval or other certifications (not endorsed by the CPSC), which manufacturers then use to promote customer confidence. If the article passes the tests, the toymakers may use the results for product promotion, but manufacturers and testers do not have to disclose any failures to the public.[6]

The Toy Manufacturers of America (TMA), an industry association, has its own set of safety standards for toy makers, but these are voluntary, not mandatory standards. Furthermore, not all toy manufacturers belong to the association, including hundreds of makers of imported toys.[7]

TMA's voluntary standards include age labeling, which is a statement on the package of the age at which the manufacturer determines children can safely play with the toy. However, age labels can be confusing to consumers because recommendations are not consistent among manufacturers and rarely explain the risks posed by any particular toy, whether or not it is used by children within the suggested age range. Furthermore, many consumers believe the labels refer to mental ability needed to play with the toy, not its hazards.[8]

Even with federal and state toy safety laws and TMA standards, dangerous toys remain in many stores. More than 150,000 different kinds of toys are available in thousands of stores across the United States, making enforcement of existing regulations difficult.[9] Despite more toys on the market, the federal government has reduced funding for the CPSC. The CPSC had 13 regional offices when it was created in 1972. By 1989, the number of offices had been cut to three. In addition to enforcement problems, the federal government has taken little action to identify additional hazardous toys and ban them.[10]

Consumer groups have used toy survey data to lobby Congress, the CPSC and state legislatures to restore funding for toy safety enforcement and strengthen recall notification procedures. Consumer groups also call for increased regulation, including consistent age labeling, standards for crib toys, labels warning of choking hazards of balloons and marbles and increased dimensions of the test tube used for small parts (a number of children under age three die each year from choking on toys that are just a little bigger than the test cylinder).[11]

HOW TO CONDUCT A DANGEROUS TOY SURVEY

Conducting a dangerous toy survey can involve the following steps:

▪ Find out if a group in your area has done a dangerous toy survey in the last year or two. If you live in one of the states where the PIRG has done such a survey, contact them to combine your efforts with their project. This will provide you with the coordinating help of an experienced group, and will give them a broader-based, more comprehensive survey. Also check with your city, county and state Consumer Affairs Office or Health Department and local newspapers or television stations to find out if any other group has undertaken such a survey in or near your city.

Or, contact one of the local or national groups that conduct annual toy surveys to obtain their list of dangerous toys identified in stores. Instead of making the safety determinations yourself, use another group's list of dangerous toys to survey local stores for those particular hazards. Also contact the CPSC for a list of any recently recalled toys to make sure toy stores have taken those toys off the shelves.

▪ Research state toy safety standards. If they differ significantly from the federal regulations, add them to your survey. Find out who enforces state laws, if any, and where the closest office of the CPSC is located. Speak with them to find out what enforcement or surveying activities they have done in the last year.

▪ Raise money for project expenses. If at all possible, purchase each type of toy identified as dangerous, to re-test it away from the store and to have it available for a press conference or interviews with the press. Refer to the Techniques chapter for fundraising ideas.

▪ Decide what types of dangerous toys to survey.

The CPSC regulations for several of these toy hazards include specific testing procedures aimed at manufacturers. These procedures are complicated and expensive (with the exception of the small parts test) to conduct, making it impractical for students to test for those types of toy hazards.

Small Parts

The test for the small-parts hazard is simple, effective and inexpensive. If a toy, or a part of a toy, fits fully, without compressing it, into a truncated right cylinder testing tube with a diameter of 1.25 inches and a depth ranging from 1.00 to 2.25 inches, the toy or toy part fails the test because it is too small and can cause choking in children three years or younger.[12]

Toys usually fail the small parts tests in one of the following ways: 1) the toy has small parts as packaged; 2) small parts break off when the toy is dropped or pulled under normal wear and tear.[13] (See page 216 for a store checklist of toys covered under the small parts regulation). Students can easily conduct the small parts cylinder test and the tube is inexpensive to purchase. See the resources section to order the "No-Choke Test Tube."

Toys with Sharp Points or Edges

Testing to determine whether toys violate the CPSC testing procedures for sharp points and glass or metal edges is complicated and expensive. However, you could include this category in your survey with the intention of identifying only toys that present a blatant hazard. For example, Oregon PIRG surveyors found a toy tool box, marketed for children under 8, that contained a saw with serrated edges and a sharp point. The box was not marked with a "conspicuous, legible and visible" warning about the "functional" sharp edge; therefore, the toy clearly violated the regulations.[14] Report any such obvious violations of the sharp points and edges labeling standard.

Crib Toys

Although crib toys that pose a strangulation risk to infants are not covered by a CPSC standard, they do fall under a voluntary manufacturers' labeling standard. If you want to include them in your toy survey, simply keep alert for very obvious violations, for example, crib toys that are attached from one side of the crib to the other, such as crib "gyms" or "exercisers." When an infant is old enough to pull up or sit up, at the age of five months or older, they can pull themselves over the apparatus and then fall or pull down on it and strangle. If a toy is made to hang across the crib in this way, the voluntary standard is a label on both the packaging and the item warning about the hazard to infants over the age of five months and advising that the item be removed from the crib at that time.[15]

■ Decide which stores to survey. In addition to toy stores, try to include stores with toy sections such as department stores, large drug stores, hobby stores and novelty stores. The number of students participating in the project will determine the number of stores surveyed.

■ Develop a time line for the survey. Because so many toys are purchased for Hanukkah and Christmas, late November is an ideal time to release toy survey results. That is the time that both the ADA and PIRGs have chosen. To be ready with results at that time, begin planning in September and surveying in October. A wall calendar plotting the project week-by-week will help you stay organized.

■ Assign surveyors to stores

Assign teams of two surveyors each to cover either a small store or a section of a large store. If more than one team is sent to a store, give each team certain categories of toys to investigate, to avoid confusion or duplication of effort. Make all arrangements for dates to survey and for transportation for the surveyors to and from the stores.

Use the forms at the end of this project to make store assignments and record data on hazardous toys. Also use the checklist to avoid confusion about regulations while at the store.

Surveyors should be forewarned that they may not find any dangerous toys at the store(s) they survey. Although they may at first feel disappointed by this, at second thought they might be happy and relieved. If your entire survey turns up no dangerous toys, which is unlikely, you can still issue a report and a guide to shopping for safe toys.

■ Conduct the surveys

If possible, a few coordinators should be available by phone while surveyors are at stores, to answer questions that might arise during the store surveying.

Examine the toys slowly and methodically, taking care not to disturb shoppers and to attract as little attention as possible. Check for posted notices of toys recalled by the CPSC.

If questioned by a store employee, briefly explain about the toy survey and how it will help consumers and stores by identifying any dangerous toys that violate federal safety standards and, therefore, should be taken off the shelves. Very few groups doing this survey have encountered any real hostility from, or problems with, store managers. However, if you are asked to leave the store, do so and immediately report the incident to the project coordinator, who can then call the store to legitimize the surveyors. If the store refuses to cooperate, include this information in your final report.

■ Compile Survey Data; Write Final Report and Press Release

Begin compiling the survey data as soon as forms from each store are returned by surveyors. Identify toys to be purchased for a re-test, and begin re-testing during the last week of surveying. Use the toy purchase form at the end of the project to return to the stores to purchase particular toys. If you do not have enough money to purchase one of each toy identified as hazardous, send a second team to re-test the toy.

Compile results, identifying all dangerous toys found and all the stores selling those toys. Then make a list, indicating all the dangerous toys found at each store.

After completing the final report, summarize the most important points in a press release. Contact the local newspapers and television and radio stations. Remember you want to inform consumers about the toy safety issue in general and about your survey results specifically.

If you found dangerous toys in any stores, you might want to announce the survey with a press conference in addition to a release. Demonstrate why the toy is dangerous and how you tested it; that kind of visual approach may attract TV coverage and photographers from newspapers. (Refer to pages 173-179 for specifics about media coverage).

■ Follow up on results of survey

Present your survey data and research to the CPSC or state legislature in support of strengthened toy safety standards.

Consider sharing your survey results and toy safety expertise with young children by speaking to classes or after-school programs at elementary schools. For an excellent guide to teaching younger children about toy safety, consult *Toys, You and the Real World*, a curriculum (listed in the bibliography) developed by attorney and toy safety advocate Edward Swartz.

TOY SAFETY SURVEY TEAMS AND STORE ASSIGNMENTS

Surveyor _____   Surveyor _____

Phone # _____   Phone # _____

Address _____   Address _____

_____   _____

Stores and Address To Be Surveyed:

1. _____

   _____

2. _____

   _____

3. _____

   _____

4. _____

   _____

DANGEROUS TOY(S) IDENTIFIED DURING SURVEY

Use One Form For Each Dangerous Toy

Surveyor _____   Surveyor _____

Address _____   Address _____

_____   _____

Date of Survey _____

Store Name _____

Address _____

Name of Toy _____

Manufacturer _____

Address _____

Price _____

Description
of toy _____

_____

Description
of hazard _____

_____

_____

_____

_____

_____

TOY PURCHASE FORM

Surveyor _____   Phone # _____

Surveyor _____   Phone # _____

Date _____

Store Name _____

Address _____

Toy Name _____

Manufacturer _____

Address _____

Price of Toy _____

Toy Description
_____
_____
_____
_____

Describe Hazard
_____
_____
_____
_____

STORE CHECKLIST FOR TOY SAFETY SURVEY

The following are broad categories of toys intended for children under the age of three and subject to the small parts requirement:
- Toys with an age label recommending them for children under the age of three.
- Toys described as infant, baby, or toddler toys on the package.
- The toys listed below, which are specifically mentioned in the small parts section of the federal regulation, in 16 Code of Federal Regulations, Section 1501.2.:
  ➤ Squeeze toys
  ➤ Teethers
  ➤ Crib exercisers
  ➤ Crib gyms
  ➤ Crib mobiles
  ➤ Other toys or articles intended to be affixed to a crib, stroller, playpen or baby carriage
  ➤ Pull and push toys
  ➤ Pounding toys
  ➤ Blocks and stacking sets
  ➤ Bathtub, wading pool and sand toys
  ➤ Rocking, spring and stick horses and other figures
  ➤ Chime and musical balls and carousels
  ➤ Jack-in-the-boxes
  ➤ Stuffed, plush and flocked animals and other figures
  ➤ Preschool toys, games and puzzles intended for use by children under 3
  ➤ Riding toys intended for use by children under 3
  ➤ Infant and juvenile furniture articles which are intended for use by children under 3 such as cribs, playpens, baby bouncers and walkers, strollers and carriages
  ➤ Dolls which are intended for use by children under 3 such as baby dolls, rag dolls and bean bag dolls
  ➤ Toy cars, trucks and other vehicles intended for use by children under 3
  ➤ In addition, such articles include any other toys or articles which are intended, marketed or labeled to be entrusted to or used by children under 3 years of age.

The following toys are specifically EXEMPTED from the small parts regulation:
  ➤ Balloons
  ➤ Books and other articles made of paper
  ➤ Writing materials such as crayons, chalk, pencils, and pens
  ➤ Children's clothing and accessories, such as shoe lace holders and buttons
  ➤ Grooming, feeding, and hygiene products, such as diaper pins and clips, barrettes, toothbrushes, drinking glasses, dishes and eating utensils
  ➤ Phonograph records
  ➤ Modeling clay and similar products
  ➤ Fingerpaints, watercolors, and other paint sets
  ➤ Rattles (as defined at 16 CFR 1510.2); and Pacifiers (as defined at 16 CFR 1511.2(a)).

BIBLIOGRAPHY

The 1989 Toy Report. Washington, DC: Americans for Democratic Action, Consumer Affairs Committee, 1989.

Citron, Ellen. *Trouble in Toyland: Unsafe Toys in Massachusetts*. Boston: Massachusetts Public Interest Research Group, 1990.

Play It Safe! A brochure/poster published by the American Trial Lawyers Association and the Johns Hopkins Injury Prevention Center. Send a self-addressed, stamped envelope to Play It Safe!, P.O. Box 3717, Washington, DC 20007.

Sikes, Lucinda. *Trouble in Toyland: Unsafe Toys in the United States*. Washington, DC: U.S. Public Interest Research Group, 1990.

Stubenvoll, Jon. *The 1990 Dangerous Dozen: Unsafe Toys*. Portland: Oregon State Public Interest Research Group, 1990.

Stubenvoll, Jon. *Student Guide to Toy Safety Project* (Portland: Oregon State Public Interest Research Group, 1990

Swartz, Edward. *Toys That Don't Care*. Boston: Gambit, Inc., 1971.

Swartz, Edward. *Toys That Kill*. NY: Vintage Books, 1986.

Swartz, Edward. *Toys, You and the Real World: Critical Thinking and Participation Skills for Young Consumers*. Boston: Freedom Trail Communications, Inc., 1989. Curriculum for elementary students, available in English and Spanish.

Toy Safety for Consumers. Portland, OR: Oregon State Public Interest Research Group.

"Toys," *Buyer's Market*. Volume 3. No. 9. November 1987.

Which Toy for Which Child: A Consumer's Guide for Selecting Suitable Toys, Ages Birth Through Five. Washington, DC: Consumer Product Safety Commission, 1988.

No-Choke Test Tube available from:
Toys to Grow On
P.O. Box 17
Long Beach, CA 90801

ORGANIZATIONS

U.S. Consumer Product Safety Commission
Washington, DC 20207
   Hotline for consumer complaints and recall information: (800) 638-2772

Americans for Democratic Action
1511 K Street NW, Suite 941
Washington, DC 20002

Michelle Snow Foundation
3569 Paine Drive
Riverside, CA 92503
   Founded by David Snow, whose seven-year-old daughter died from a lawn dart injury. Snow worked to ban lawn darts and actively campaigns against other toy safety hazards.

World Against Toys Causing Harm (WATCH)
10 Marshall Street
Boston, MA 02108

Public Interest Research Groups that conduct annual toy surveys:

California PIRG (CALPIRG)
1147 S. Robertson Boulevard #203
Los Angeles, CA 90035

Connecticut PIRG (ConnPIRG)
219 Park Road 2nd floor
W. Hartford, CT 06119

Florida PIRG (FPIRG)
308 E. Park Avenue Suite 213
Tallahassee, FL 32301

Illinois PIRG
205 S. State Street Suite 1400
Chicago, IL 60604

Massachusetts PIRG (MASSPIRG)
29 Temple Place
Boston, MA 02111

New Jersey PIRG (NJPIRG)
103 Bayard Street
New Brunswick, NJ 08901

Ohio PIRG (OPIRG)
2084 1/2 N. High Street
Columbus, OH 43201

Oregon PIRG (OSPIRG)
1536 SE 11th Street
Portland, OR 97214

Pennsylvania PIRG (PennPIRG)
3507 Lancaster Avenue
Philadelphia, PA 19104

U.S. PIRG
215 Pennsylvania Avenue, SE
Washington, DC 20003

ACTIVITY FOUR:
USING THE FREEDOM OF
INFORMATION ACT

I. INTRODUCTION

At its core, participatory democracy decries locked files and closed doors. Good citizens study their governors, challenge the decisions they make and petition or vote for change when change is needed. But no citizen can carry out these responsibilities when government is secret. Tapping Officials' Secrets[1]

The Freedom of Information Act (FOIA) is a powerful tool for citizens monitoring the activities of government or business. Because of the FOIA, most government information is readily available to those who seek it. Citizen groups, journalists and scholars have used the Freedom of Information Act to "uncover hundreds of cases of government waste and fraud, unsafe environmental practices, dangerous consumer products, unethical behavior and assorted wrongdoing" such as "the dangerous defects in Firestone 500 steel-belted radial tires and the exploding gas tanks of Ford Pintos."[2]

Examples of citizen groups using the FOIA to monitor government activity include U.S. Department of Agriculture meat inspection reports obtained by the consumer group Public Citizen "which confirmed the existence of unhealthy conditions in meat packing facilities and inspectors' failures to report deficiencies."[3] Public Citizen's Critical Mass Energy Project uses the FOIA to compile a comprehensive annual list of safety "mishaps" which occur at the nation's nuclear power plants. (Nearly 3,000 occurred in 1987.)[4] And the citizen group Common Cause acquired information from the Defense Department showing that 10 corporations with major government contracts had billed more than $2 million in lobbying expenses to the taxpayers.[5]

This activity introduces the FOIA to students and gives them an opportunity to practice using this tool by requesting and reviewing information held by the Federal Bureau of Investigation (FBI). FBI files are of particular interest because the agency has collected information on a variety of people and events discussed in the movement history chapters of this book.

II. THE FREEDOM OF INFORMATION ACT: A TOOL FOR OPEN GOVERNMENT

To demonstrate the degree of secrecy within federal government agencies, Rep. John E. Moss of California held congressional hearings from 1955 to 1966. Moss, as a Member of Congress, often found it difficult to convince the executive branch to share information with Congress. As a result of these hearings, Congress enacted the Freedom of Information Act (FOIA) in 1966 to give the public access to information collected and held by the federal government.[6]

The FOIA guarantees the right to request and receive any document, file or other record — including papers, reports, letters, films, computer tapes, photographs and sound recordings — in the possession of any agency of the federal government, subject to nine specific exceptions. (See page 226).[7] The FOIA also authorized information requesters to sue in federal court to force federal agencies to comply with the Act.[8]

Many federal agencies quickly found ways to subvert the new law by delaying their responses to requests, charging high fees for searching for and copying records and interpreting broadly the exemptions to the Act.[9] Citizen groups lobbied Congress for a stronger law which was passed in 1974. The FOIA amendments imposed response deadlines, a waiver of search and copying fees for information to be used in the public benefit and narrower definitions as to what records are exempt from the Act.[10]

A number of additional tools have opened up the affairs of government to the public. These include the 1972 Federal Advisory Committee Act which the consumer movement rallied to pass and which set uniform ground rules for the conduct of the government's 1,439 advisory committees to prevent political manipulations of technical expertise. The Act, as amended in 1975, requires that meetings be open to the public, that records be kept and made available to the public and that representation on committees be balanced and open to public scrutiny.[11] Another information tool is the Privacy Act of 1974 which protects the public from misuse and disclosure of personal information that might be disclosed under the FOIA. Under the Privacy Act, individuals have a right of access to their own files, except those from law enforcement agencies and the Central Intelligence Agency.[12] Other information tools won by citizen campaigns include public access to presidential records; right-to-know laws directing the Environmental Protection Agency and the Occupational Safety and Health Administration to disclose to the public toxic hazards to which residents and workers are exposed; whistleblower rights; and the discovery process during product liability litigation.[13]

II. USING THE FREEDOM OF INFORMATION ACT

The FOIA applies to every agency, department, regulatory commission, government controlled corporation and other establishments within the federal executive branch. The FOIA also applies to the Executive Office of the President and the Office of Management and Budget, but not to the President or the President's immediate staff. The Act does not apply to everything that receives federal funding, or to Congress, the federal courts, private corporations or federally funded state agencies.[14]

Any individual — including all U.S. citizens as well as foreign nationals — can make a request under the FOIA. Or, the request can be made in the name of a corporation, partnership or other entity, including a citizen group or press organization.[15]

Although the federal FOIA does not apply to state government agencies, all 50 states and the District of Columbia have their own laws on access to state agency information.[16] These rules vary considerably from state to state, but most state open government laws provide access to autopsy reports, police reports and election records.

Much information from the federal government can be acquired through informal means. An agency's public information, press or FOIA officer may provide the information without a formal FOIA request. If an informal request fails, begin the process of applying formally for the information.[17] A FOIA request must be in writing. Consult the sample FOIA request letter on page 224.

Determine exactly the information you want and which agency has it. You do not need to identify a specific document by name or title, but you must provide a description reasonable enough to allow a government employee familiar with an agency's files to locate the records you want.[18]

Each federal agency has a FOIA officer responsible for handling information requests. Large agencies may have FOIA officers in various subdivisions. If you know exactly which subdivision has the information, send your request to its FOIA officer. If not, the FOIA officer of the agency will forward it to the appropriate office.[19]

State that the request is being made pursuant to the FOIA (5 U.S.C. Sec. 552). Write "Freedom of Information Request" on the envelope and on the letter. If possible, send the request via registered mail, return receipt requested. Keep a photocopy of your letter and your receipt.[20]

The law sets specific deadlines for replying to FOIA requests: 10 working days for the initial request and 20 working days for the administrative appeal. Certain agencies chronically fail to meet the Act's time requirements due to inadequate staff and resources. The FBI often takes six to twelve months or longer to process a request fully; other agencies that have long delays include the CIA and the State and Justice Departments. According to the FOI Service Center, the courts are often reluctant to strictly enforce the FOIA's time limits as long as agencies are processing requests diligently and in a reasonable manner.[21]

Agencies may charge "reasonable" fees for the direct costs of searching for and copying the requested records, but different fees are charged according to the category or status of the requestor. A noncommercial status applies to students and provides for two hours of free document search time and free duplication of 100 pages. Copies over 100 pages generally cost from 10 to 25 cents per page.[22] Request to be notified by phone or through the mail if the pages exceed the first free 100 pages.

If your request is partially or entirely denied, you have the right to appeal the decision. A FOIA appeal can be filed by a simple letter. See page 225 for a sample appeal letter. You also have the option to appeal if your request is granted but the fees are too high. If 10 business days have passed since the agency received your request and you still have not received a reply from the agency, you also have the right of appeal.[23]

A CASE STUDY:
THE FEDERAL BUREAU OF INVESTIGATION (FBI)

The Federal Bureau of Investigation (FBI), a division of the U.S. Department of Justice, is authorized to investigate all violations of federal law except those specifically assigned to other agencies. The FBI investigates organized crime, white-collar crime, foreign counterintelligence, terrorism, drugs and violent crimes as well as bank robberies, kidnapings and civil rights violations.[24]

The FBI also has a long history of gathering intelligence on the activities of domestic political organizations. Much of this investigative work, particularly under the administration of J. Edgar Hoover, FBI Director from 1924 to 1972, was conducted without the knowledge or permission of the President or the U.S. Attorney General, who are supposed to direct the actions of the agency.[25] Between 1956 and 1971, Hoover conducted counter-intelligence programs (COINTELPRO) — involving wire-taps and break-ins — against the Communist Party, the Socialist Work-

ers Party, the women's liberation movement, anti-Vietnam War groups, black nationalist groups and white hate groups. A reporter with NBC news used information obtained from a FOIA request to confirm the existence of the COINTELPRO operation, which was formally terminated only after this disclosure.[26]

In 1976, the U.S. Senate's Select Committee to Study Governmental Operations with Respect to Intelligence Activities (the Church committee) detailed "how heavily the FBI and the CIA were involved in watching, reporting on and occasionally disrupting Americans peacefully exercising their constitutional rights."[27] Legislation was proposed, but not passed, in 1977 to curtail FBI authority to investigate domestic political groups. Many of the abuses have disappeared since Hoover's departure. Still, from 1983 to 1985, the FBI investigated the Committee in Solidarity with the People of El Salvador (CISPES) and agents interviewed American schoolchildren who wrote letters to Soviet President Mikhail Gorbachev.[28]

Choosing a Topic

The FBI has a preprocessed list (available free from the address below) of frequently requested topics already collected from their files. Since no time is required to search for the materials, the files on this list can be obtained relatively quickly. However, these files generally contain thousands of pages — too much to read through and too expensive for the purpose of this project.

Listed below are summaries of some of the information in seven of the files on the FBI's preprocessed list to help you be specific about what you want. If you choose from this list, be as specific as possible. To reduce the number of pages requested (100 pages are free with additional pages costing 10 to 25 cents each), narrow your request to certain dates or geographic areas.

Parts of the file may be blacked out because the subject referred to is still living, or the information may refer to his or her private life. Access to these files is also open to the public by appointment at the FBI office in Washington, DC.

Direct your requests to: FBI, J. Edgar Hoover Building, FOIA Officer, 10th and Pennsylvania Avenue, NW, Washington, DC 20535.

SUMMARIES OF SEVEN FILES
SELECTED FROM THE PREPROCESSED LIST

Jane Addams - Addams was a leader in the settlement house movement as well as a founder of the Women's International League for Peace and Freedom (WILPF) in the early 1900s.

The 188-page file has more information about WILPF than Jane Addams, including: a 4/25/24 memorandum covering the history and actions of WILPF, numerous WILPF documents from early conferences and speeches by important members, reports on WILPF leaders and memoranda to FBI Director Hoover on the history of the group.

The Highlander School - The Highlander School conducted seminars and workshops on citizen organizing primarily during the 1940s and 1950s.

The 1,107-page file includes: a report dated 4/24/41 on the school's activities and teachers, articles from local newspapers about the school and letters from citizens complaining about the activities of the school.

A. Philip Randolph - Randolph was monitored by the FBI because of his continued protests against the federal government's treatment of African Americans.

The 767-page file includes: a four-page letter dated 2/18/43 concerning Randolph's trip to Oklahoma City which discusses Randolph's plans for the March on Washington movement; an 18-page report dated 6/2/44 which discusses Randolph's personal history, activities and speeches; and an 11-page document dated 10/18/63 which offers another FBI history of Randolph and his activities.

Student Nonviolent Coordinating Committee - SNCC was a student group instrumental in many of the struggles of the Civil Rights movement.

The 2,887-page file includes: an August 1967 68-page report on SNCC; information on SNCC leaders

including Stokely Carmichael and H. Rap Brown; reports on local SNCC activities in major cities around the country, most of which are under or around 100 pages and include:

Section 3	Baltimore
Section 4	Boston
Section 5	Buffalo
Section 6	Chicago
Section 7	Cincinnati
Section 8	Cleveland
Section 9	Dallas
Section 10	Detroit
Section 11	Houston
Section 12	Indianapolis
Section 13	Los Angeles
Section 14	New York
Section 15	Portland
Section 16	San Francisco
Section 17	Seattle
Section 18	Washington, D.C.
Section 19	Springfield

Clergy and Laity Concerned About Vietnam (CALC) - CALC held numerous protests against U.S. involvement in Vietnam and against the draft.

This 1,699-page file includes: a six-page teletype dated 2/14/69 which describes a CALC conference concerning the Vietnam war and a six-page report dated 2/19/68 which discusses CALC's protests against the draft.

American Indian Movement (AIM) - AIM protested the government's treatment of Native Americans.

The 17,722-page file includes: a four-page report dated 1/9/73 about an AIM meeting in Duluth, MN; an eight-page report dated 1/31/73 on Dennis Banks and AIM's conflicts with local authorities; reports on AIM activity on the Trail of Broken Treaties; reports on AIM occupation of the Bureau of Indian Affairs; and reports on the actions of AIM leaders Russell Means and Dennis Banks.

COINTELPRO New Left - This file contains information on Students for a Democratic Society (SDS) — a student group opposed to the Vietnam War — and its chapters on college campuses around the country.

The 6,244-page file includes: a 12-page report dated 9/9/69 on student leader Jerry Rubin; a two-page report dated 10/9/68 on FBI action against the New Left; a three-page report dated 7/5/68 on 12 steps the FBI must take to combat the New Left; reports on SDS activities around the country; a two-page memorandum dated 1/19/70 on FBI efforts to intimidate a member of the Weatherman faction of SDS; and a two-page memorandum dated 12/30/69 on potential and pending counterintelligence action.

Sample FOIA Request Letter[29]

Your Address
Daytime Phone
Date

Freedom of Information Office
Agency
Address

Re: FOIA Request

Dear FOIA Officer:

Pursuant to the federal Freedom of Information Act, 5 U.S.C. S 552, I request access to and copies of all records pertaining to (here, clearly describe what you want. Include identifying material, such as names, places and the period of time about which you are inquiring. If you think they will help to explain what you are looking for, attach news clips, reports and other documents describing the subject of your research.)

I am requesting these records in a non-commercial capacity as a high school student for a school project studying access to government information. The non-commercial capacity allows for two hours of free search time and free duplication of 100 pages.
If any expenses in excess of the above would be incurred in connection with this request, please contact me before any such charges are incurred.

If my request is denied in whole or part, I ask that you justify all deletions by reference to specific exemptions of the act. I reserve the right to appeal your decision to withhold any information.

I will expect a response within 10 business days after receipt, as the statute requires.

Thank you for your assistance.

Sincerely,

Your Name

Sample FOIA Appeal Letter

Your Address
Daytime Phone
Date

Agency Administrator
Agency
Address

Re: Freedom of Information Appeal

Dear Administrator:

This is an appeal under the Freedom of Information Act, 5 U.S.C. S 552. On (date), I made a FOIA request to your agency for (brief description of what you requested). On (date), your agency denied my request on the grounds that (state the reasons given by the agency). Copies of my request and the denial are enclosed.

(Or when the agency delays) It has been ___ business days since my request was received by your agency. This period clearly exceeds the 10 days provided by the statute, thus I deem my request denied. Copies of my correspondence and the postal form showing receipt by your office are enclosed.

The information which I have requested is clearly releasable under the FOIA and, in my opinion, may not validly be protected by any of the Act's exemptions.

(Here, address why you think their justification for a specific exemption is incorrect. Add that the request is part of a legitimate school project.)

I trust that upon reconsideration, you will reverse the decision denying me access to this material and grant my original request.

As I have made this request in a non-commercial capacity and this information is of timely value, I would appreciate your expediting the consideration of my appeal in every way possible. In any case, I will expect to receive your decision within 20 business days, as required by the statute.

Thank you for your assistance.

Sincerely,

Your Name

FOIA EXEMPTIONS:[30]

1) National security information;

2) Internal agency rules - exempts rules and practices of agency personnel that are "predominately internal" and where disclosure serves no substantial public interest;

3) Information exempted by another federal statute - honors mandatory non-disclosure provisions in other laws, e.g., laws governing income tax returns and completed census bureau forms;

4) Trade secrets - commercial or financial information, disclosure of which would cause substantial competitive injury to the submitter;

5) Internal agency memorandum - protects information about an agency's decision making process;

6) Personal privacy information;

7) Investigatory records - protects information compiled for law enforcement purposes, disclosure of which could reasonably interfere with enforcement proceedings or identify a confidential source; and

8) and 9) Other exemptions - two special-interest exemptions related to banking and oil well information which are not relevant to most applications of the Act.

BIBLIOGRAPHY

Bollier, David. *Citizen Action and Other Big Ideas: A History of Ralph Nader and the Modern Consumer Movement*. Washington, DC: Center for Study of Responsive Law, 1991.

English, Elaine P. *How to Use the Federal FOI Act*, Fifth edition. Washington, DC: The FOI Service Center, 1985.

FBI FOIPA Section Preprocessed List: Compiled As Of 2/22/91. Washington, DC: Federal Bureau of Investigation, 1991.

Federal Bureau of Investigation Facts and History. Washington, DC: U.S. Department of Justice, 1990.

The Freedom of Information Act: A User's Guide. Washington, DC: The Freedom of Information Clearinghouse, 1989.

Moore, W. John. "Old Ghosts, Future Shock," *National Journal*. December 30, 1989.

Pogrebin, Letty Cottin. "Have You Ever Supported Equal Pay, Child Care or Women's Groups?: The FBI Was Watching You" *Ms*. June 1977.

Tapping Officials' Secrets. Washington, DC: Reporters Committee for Freedom of the Press, 1989.

Theoharis, Athan G. "FBI Surveillance During the Cold War Years: A Constitutional Crisis," *The Public Historian*. Winter 1981.

ACTIVITY FIVE:
A COMMUNITY PROFILE OF
VOTER PARTICIPATION

INTRODUCTION

Voting is one way citizens can have a say in the decisions that affect their lives — decisions about jobs, school budgets, health care, the environment, minimum wage, housing, crime and safety. But every year fewer and fewer Americans — especially young Americans — go to the polls. In the 1988 elections for President, only 57.4 percent of the voting age population reported casting a vote according to a survey conducted by the U.S. Bureau of the Census. According to tabulated votes cast for President, only 50 percent of the population voted. Even fewer Americans vote in non-presidential elections.[1]

Many reasons are cited for the lack of participation, including powerlessness, apathy and cynicism. But one important factor may be the various institutional barriers to registration and voting that discourage many people from making the effort. For example, in a 1983 comparison of voter participation, the United States ranked 23rd of 24 democratic countries with only 53 percent of the population voting.[2] However, when participation among registered voters is compared, the United States ranked 11th of the 24 countries with 87 percent of registered voters voting.[3] The United States is the only major democracy where the government does not assume responsibility for helping citizens cope with voter registration procedures.[4] When people are registered they vote, but structural restrictions in the United States often keep people from registering.

Many segments of U.S. society are under-represented in the electorate, including people with low incomes and little education as well as young people and minorities. Only 36 percent of eligible 18 to 24-year-olds voted in the 1988 presidential election.[5] Of 3.6 million eligible African American voters in that age group, only 1.2 million, or 35 percent, voted in 1988. And of 2.7 million Latinos in that age group, only

447,000, or 17 percent voted.[6] However, 75 percent of the 18 to 24-year-olds, who registered, did vote in the 1988 election.[7]

Non-voters could have played significant roles in past elections. For example, polls in 1980 showed that voters favored Ronald Reagan 52 to 38 percent over Jimmy Carter, while non-voters favored Carter 51 to 37 percent over Reagan.[8]

The purpose of this project is to study patterns of voter registration and participation in your community to identify possible institutional barriers that cause low voter participation among voters of different age groups, races, education levels and geographic locations. Profiling these patterns will help identify some of the barriers to full participation in your community. Students will complete the profile by making recommendations to their community to improve voter participation.

STUDENTS REGISTERING STUDENTS

Several innovative programs around the country are encouraging voter participation among young people. Programs in both Los Angeles, California and Dade County, Florida have brought voter registration to high schools. Students who are 18 years old, or who will turn 18 by the next election, can register to vote in their social studies classes. In 1990, in Dade County, 98 percent of eligible students registered.[9]

And in New York City, a coalition of three groups working to increase voter participation — People For the American Way, 100% Vote/Human Serve and the New York Public Interest Research Group (NYPIRG) — has found that the most effective way to register high school students to vote is for students to register one another. The coalition's project — Youth Vote '91: Register the Power — helps high schools design and implement voter registration and education programs and publishes a student guide to registering classmates.

Students in the New York program do more than distribute registration forms. They engage their classmates in discussions about the history of the right to vote in the United States and the importance of the youth vote, stressing the influence that their votes can have on issues such as college tuition, taxes, the drinking age, minimum wage and the draft.[10]

The students then answer questions about the registration forms and encourage their classmates to learn more about the candidates and issues of importance in the upcoming election. The project, as of 1991, had trained more than 100 student registrars and registered 3,000 students.[11] Students registered through the program are checked against eligibility lists — which are made available only to school administrators — so that school officials can track the rate of registration.

People for the American Way is working to implement similar programs across the country. Their *First Vote* teaching unit and video on registration and voting are aimed at stimulating discussion in senior high school social studies courses.[12]

Before beginning this project, students may want to participate in a community voter registration drive or register other students at school. This will introduce students to the voter registration procedures in their communities.

HISTORY OF BARRIERS TO VOTING

Throughout the history of the United States, restrictions on voting have excluded large segments of the population, including women, African Americans and illiterate and non-English speaking people. African American men; women and young people aged 18 to 21 won the right to vote after the Fourteenth, Nineteenth and Twenty-sixth Amendments to the U.S. Constitution were ratified.

Although African American men won the right to vote after the Civil War and began to participate in the electoral system in large numbers during Reconstruc-

tion, in the 1880s many southern states began to implement laws, including poll taxes and literacy tests, that eventually disenfranchised approximately three-quarters of the population, black and white.[13] For example, in 1877, Georgia implemented a poll tax, requiring voters to pay a fee to vote. In 1882, South Carolina, followed by Florida in 1889, adopted an "eight-box" law, which required voters to deposit separate ballots in each of the boxes marked for different candidates, making it virtually impossible for illiterate people to master the practice. Many southern states allowed local election officers to decide which potential voters were qualified. This flexibility was instrumental in keeping African Americans and low-income white people from voting.[14]

Mississippi's 1890 literacy test and $2 poll tax drove voter participation down to 17 percent by 1900.[15] In South Carolina in 1880; 83.7 percent of the eligible population voted, in 1900, 18 percent.[16] Southern states were not alone. Eleven states in the North and the West imposed literacy requirements between 1890 and 1926.[17]

Literacy tests, "good character" clauses which allowed exceptions for voters who could understand some portion of the state constitution and "grandfather" clauses which exempted white people whose grandfathers voted or fought for the South during the Civil War, technically allowed low-income white people to vote.[18] However, many, unwilling to risk the humiliation of failing a voting test, still did not vote.[19]

The Voting Rights Act of 1965 eliminated state restrictions on the right to vote. The Act says "No voting qualification or prerequisite to vote or standard practice or procedure shall be imposed or applied ... in a manner which results in a denial or abridgement of the right of any citizen of the United States to vote on account of race or color."[20]

CURRENT BARRIERS TO VOTER PARTICIPATION

While literacy tests and poll taxes were largely eliminated with the Voting Rights Act of 1965, a number of barriers continue to restrict voter registration around the country.

The practice of voter registration, compiling a list of eligible voters, became common as populations grew and voter fraud by political parties increased. Where it was used, voter registration decreased voter participation by approximately 30 percent in the early 1900s.[21] By 1929, all but three states — Arkansas, Indiana and Texas — had registration requirements and those three soon followed.[22]

A number of registration procedures, which differ from state to state, make registration difficult or at least inconvenient. For example, the New York City Board of Elections discards registration forms written in pencil, forms signed only on one side and forms with middle initial or with Mr. or Ms. written only on one side of the form.[23]

In addition, some states with post card registration do not have forms readily available and limit the number of forms that registrars — people designated to register voters — can take out of the elections office at one time.[24] West Virginia requires every registrant to appear before a notary public, which creates problems for voter registration campaign efforts.[25] In states without mail registration, many boards of election refuse to deputize campaign volunteers.[26]

To keep voter registration lists up-to-date, many state and local governments purge their lists periodically. The purpose of purging is to keep people from fraudulently voting in the name of someone who has moved or died.[27] However, purging also removes the names of voters who have not voted in a certain number of elections.[28]

PROPOSALS FOR REFORM

Removing the barriers that make it difficult or inconvenient to register can greatly increase voter registration and participation. Proposals for reform include election-day registration, elimination of purging, mail-in registration and motor-voter registration.

Election Day Registration

One way to increase voter registration is to allow people to register to vote on election day. North Dakota has required no voter registration since 1951

and three states — Maine, Minnesota and Wisconsin — allow registration on election day.[29] The turnout of the voting age population in these four states is approximately 12 percentage points higher than the national average.[30] Minnesota estimates that election day registration accounts for 5 to 10 percent of voter turnout.[31] Of same-day registrants in Minnesota, approximately 30 percent are not new voters, but simply people who have changed address.[32]

Elimination of Purging

Purging voter registration lists penalizes registered voters who have not been to the polls in a specified number of years. To keep the lists up-to-date, state and local governments can modify their lists using death notices from the coroner's office and change of address notifications from the driver's license bureau or other government agencies.[33] In addition, a voter whose name has been purged could still vote, using a challenged ballot, one that is verified and then counted after the election. The challenged ballot is used as a fraud prevention measure in states with same-day or no registration.[34]

Mail-In Voter Registration

Twenty-six states and Washington, DC currently allow all eligible citizens (without specifying a reason) to register by mail.[35] Mail-in registration makes it easier for everyone to register, particularly those who are unable to go to an office to register because of work conflicts, disability or age.

Mail-in registration programs involve distributing voter registration forms at public agencies, including libraries. Citizens can mail the forms to the registration office, eliminating the need to register in person. Mail-in registration is cost-effective; states using the system estimate production costs of one to two cents per form and many states have developed partnerships in which private organizations and corporations absorb the costs of printing and distributing the forms. Mail-in registration has not been linked to any increases in fraud.[36]

Mail-in registration has succeeded in increasing registration in several areas. For example, Ohio improved its national ranking in voter turnout from 25th to 15th after implementing an aggressive mail registration program.[37] Texas registered 1.5 million new voters through the state's "Voter '88" program, of which mail-in registration was a key component.[38]

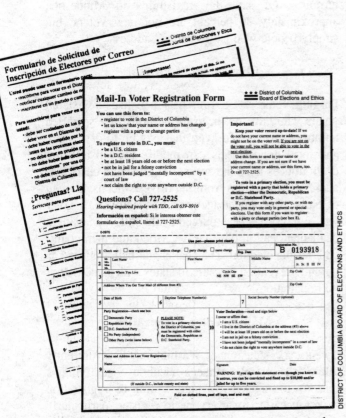

Mail-in Voter Registration Forms in Spanish and English.

Motor-Voter Registration

Motor-voter registration allows citizens to register to vote when applying for or renewing their drivers' licenses. More than 20 states make voter registration forms available at motor vehicle departments, and 15 states and Washington, DC require the motor vehicle department to transfer completed registration forms to the elections office.[39]

The most effective programs are staff-active, when the citizen is asked directly, "Would you like to register to vote here today?"[40] When clerks in North Carolina began asking people if they would like to register to vote, completed forms increased from approximately eight to more than 100 per day.[41]

A passive motor-voter system exists when citizens are notified indirectly, usually by public notice, that they may request and obtain a voter registration form.[42] Other states make registration postcards available at motor vehicle departments. But if prospective voters must mail the form or personally deliver it to the elections office, the system is not a motor-voter program.[43]

Many states can transfer all the information, except an original signature, by computer. If citizens have the opportunity to renew drivers' licenses by mail, the system also can allow for voter registration. Between May 1989 and January 1991, 44.8 percent of all new registrations in the District of Columbia were generated by the motor-voter program.[44] Voter registration can take place in other public agencies in addition to the motor vehicle department. As of 1991, 12 states had expanded the location of registration forms to agencies of welfare, health and unemployment.[45]

VOTER REGISTRATION AND PARTICIPATION SURVEY

I. COLLECTION OF REGISTRATION AND PARTICIPATION DATA

By collecting the data listed below, students will identify barriers in their communities to full voter participation. Included are data from Washington, DC to give you some concrete examples of one city's voter registration and participation profile.

Local organizations working on voter registration may have collected some of the information this profile requires. If not, these groups may offer guidance in your search and will have general information on voting and registration barriers in your area. Find out if citizen groups or the state or local government have proposed and/or implemented any changes recently to improve voter participation.

The local board of elections will have most of the information necessary for completing a profile. The board is often located in city hall or the police station. Some of the data will not be available. Always ask where you might find additional information and follow every possible lead. Make special note of all statistics not available or outdated; this will be a part of your evaluation of the registration process.

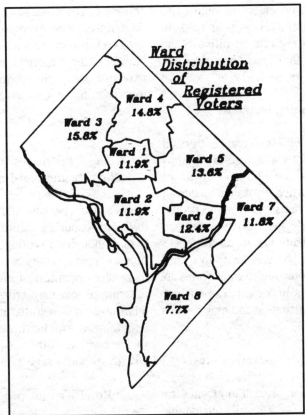

Distribution of Registered Voters Among Wards of the District of Columbia.

A. REGISTRATION PROCEDURES

The information listed below will help you evaluate the current registration process in your community.

District Maps

Draw maps of your districts (they will differ for each house of the state legislature and for the U.S. congressional districts). Include surrounding districts. This visual picture will help you understand the area to be profiled and target your constituency.

District Ranking

Find out how your state ranks in percentage of registered voters nationwide and how your district ranks within the state.

Deadline for eligibility in the next election or primary

Registration deadlines are usually 10 to 30 days before the election. For many voters, unaware of the deadline, this is a significant barrier. In Washington, DC, voters must register 30 days before the election to be eligible for that election. Only three states — Maine, Minnesota and Wisconsin — allow registration the same day as an election. North Dakota requires no registration.[46]

Location and operating hours of registration sites

Requiring registration at one or a few central offices can create transportation problems in both rural and urban areas. Find out if public transportation is available and how much it costs. In addition, registration offices often are open only during the same hours people work, making it inconvenient to register to vote. Indicate the registration sites on your map. In Washington, DC, the main registration office is the District Board of Elections and Ethics, open Monday through Friday from 8:30 a.m. to 4:30 p.m.

Optional registration methods

Mail-in registration allows a citizen to register through the mail. Many states do not allow mail-in registration, creating problems for those who have difficulty getting to the registration office, or doing so during business hours. Motor-voter registration allows people to register when they renew their driver's license. Motor-voter, however, is likely not to reach people with low-incomes since they are less likely to own a car. Therefore, access to voter registration forms in other government agencies is important. The District of Columbia uses mail-in registration and motor-voter registration.

Location of temporary registration sites

Many states set up temporary registration sites to reach additional voters. Find out if restrictions on the location of temporary sites exist. If your state provides for temporary or branch registration sites, check if they are located in high volume sites like welfare, food stamp and unemployment offices. Place these temporary registration sites on your map. Washington, DC, does not have temporary registration sites but mail-in registration applications are available in public libraries, police stations and fire stations.

State and local rules for deputization of registrars

Registrars are people authorized to register voters. Local rules making deputization more difficult will thus deter individuals and organizations from conducting voter registration drives. In Washington, DC, no restrictions apply to becoming a registrar; anyone can use the mail-in registration application to register voters.

Restrictions on registrars

Numerous court cases have ruled illegal both limits on the number of forms registrars can take to temporary sites and restrictions on access to high volume areas. However, these barriers, although not official policy, may still occur. No apparent rules exist in Washington, DC that could adversely affect a registration drive.

Provisions for registering illiterate and non-English speaking people

Non-English speakers and illiterate people may have difficulty obtaining information about voter registration. Although the Voting Rights Act of 1965 banned literacy tests, complicated registration forms can themselves be a test of literacy. In Washington, DC, illiterate people may bring a friend, or the registrars themselves will help the individual fill out the form. People who are homeless may register through a shelter because of the need for a mailing address. The District provides registration forms in Spanish.

Provisions for people with disabilities

People with physical or mental disabilities as well as elderly people may find registration restrictions a problem. Inaccessibility of registration forms and sites as well as a lack of sensitive assistance exclude many people with disabilities from full electoral participation. In Washington, DC, elderly and disabled voters can register entirely through the mail, never having to leave their homes.

High School registration

Do local high schools make special efforts to encourage first-time voters to participate? Is high-school registration available? (See pages 227-228 for details on model programs).

Students

College students who attend school away from home may find it difficult to register to vote or to determine where they are eligible to register and vote. College towns may discourage voter registration by students, even though students live in their college community most of the year and have an interest in what happens there.[47]

Public education programs

Are there telephone information lines to answer questions about voting procedures? Are registration sites and deadlines well publicized in the community?

Purging practices

Is the voter registration list purged frequently? Do the purges result in eligible voters being dropped from the lists? In September 1982, Washington, DC conducted a purge to eliminate out-dated records and inaccurate data. In the following primary, 20,000 voters cast challenged ballots when their names did not appear on the precinct voter lists. The District responded with a mail canvass on odd-numbered years designed to verify residences and a purge of inactive voters if they have not voted in the past four years.

Other local restrictions

Declaring party affiliation at the time of registration, restricting distribution of registration forms and requiring witnesses for registration are all barriers to registration. Some states require registration for each federal, state and local election.[48] Washington, DC has a single registration for all elections. Witnesses are not required for registration.

B. VOTER TURNOUT

As important as factors affecting registration are factors that affect voting. Collection of the data listed below will help you evaluate your community's voter turnout.

Election calendar

Obtain a calendar that lists dates for all general, primary and special elections. For example, primary elections in Washington, DC are held on the first Monday in September and general elections are held in November. In Washington, DC, only voters registered for a particular party can vote in that party's primary, but some states do allow voters to cross over to vote in another party's primary.

Transportation to polling places

Either the local government or private organizations such as churches and civic groups may provide transportation to polls, candidate debates or town meetings. For many people a convenient community bus or van often encourages voting or attendance at important meetings. The Washington, DC government does not sponsor an organized transportation system to and from the polls. The District does, however, have a good public transportation system and religious groups are active in transporting their members to the polls.

Local voter information programs

What opportunities are offered by other groups in your community for voters to meet with candidates for public office? Do business associations, community groups, unions or PTAs sponsor such forums? Are the forums nonpartisan? Are they equally accessible to working and non-working voters, suburban and city citizens? Citizens of Washington, DC won the right to vote for President in 1964 and won limited home rule (allowing election of a mayor, city council and school board) in 1973.[49] Although District residents elect a non-voting delegate to Congress, they have no voting representatives in Congress and no state governor or legislators. Therefore local elections — for mayor, city council and board of education — are of great importance. Various organizations hold debates and forums before elections.

Voter information provided by the media

The media have an obligation to inform the public about upcoming elections. Do the media offer full and accurate coverage of candidates' views and important community issues? Do newspapers carry simple explanations of ballot questions? Do the local media sponsor candidate forums on radio or TV? Review local newspapers' coverage for the month before the last election. Washington, DC has two major daily newspapers and several local television stations which cover local elections.

Hours and location of the polls

Are the polls open before and after normal working hours? Are the polls located in places that are convenient for all members of the district? In Washington, DC, 140 precincts each have their own polling sites which are open from 7 a.m. to 8 p.m.

Ballots in languages other than English

Are foreign language ballots available, or provisions made for those who do not speak English? Washington, DC, with a substantial Spanish-speaking population, provides ballots in Spanish.

Provisions for illiterate voters

How do poll supervisors deal with those who are illiterate? Is the alternative procedure degrading or humiliating? In Washington, DC, volunteers at the polls will help an illiterate person vote or that voter may bring a friend with whom they may feel more comfortable.

Provisions for voters with disabilities

Are parking and special assistance provided for people with disabilities? In Washington, DC, elderly and disabled voters have access to ramps, special parking places, wheel chair voting booths and curbside assistance. People with other disabilities, such as sight impairments, can bring someone with them for assistance.

Absentee ballots (ease or difficulty obtaining)

Many people, including students and travelers, are away from their district on election day. Are absentee ballots convenient? In Washington, DC, absentee voters accounted for 1.8 percent of the votes in the November 6, 1990 election. Voters must request an absentee ballot at least seven days before the election.

C. Statistics About Registration and Voting

Registration and voting statistics for your community will help identify areas where improvement in voter participation is needed. The local board of elections and secretary of state are the most likely sources for this information. Some examples from Washington, DC data are included. Collect the following information:

1. Statistics on population broken down by age, race and income.

Table 1—1988 Population of Washington, DC by Age and Race[50]

Age	15-24	25-34	35-44	45-54	55-64	65+	Total
Black/Other	77,000	83,700	58,200	46,800	48,100	47,900	361,700
White	22,500	42,100	32,800	15,500	14,900	29,200	157,000
Total	**99,500**	**125,800**	**91,000**	**62,300**	**63,000**	**77,100**	**518,700**

Table 2—1988 Population of Washington, DC by Ward, Race and Income

Ward	1	2	3	4	5	6	7	8	**Total**
% Black/Other	75	52	11	88	90	79	96	91	**73**
% White	25	48	89	12	10	21	4	9	**27**
Average Income (in thousands)	19	23	38	24	20	22	18	17	**23**

Table 3—1990 Washington, DC Population by Ward and Race[51]

Ward	Black	White	**	Asian	Latino	Other	18+
1	45,151	24,211	283	1,739	14,002	8,295	65,781
2	34,739	40,851	243	3,705	5,635	2,100	72,320
3	4,782	73,602	124	3,478	5,383	1,218	73,071
4	66,561	9,230	226	594	3,735	1,814	64,324
5	67,401	6,539	153	432	1,273	529	59,373
6	51,509	18,174	163	555	1,170	368	57,458
7	67,123	1,698	144	111	542	236	51,617
8	62,438	5,362	130	550	970	389	45,864
Total	**399,604**	**179,667**	**1,466**	**11,214**	**32,710**	**14,949**	**489,808**

** American Indian, Eskimo, Aleut

2. Compute the following three percentages:

   a. $\dfrac{\text{Number of registered voters}}{\text{Voting age population}}$ = % of eligible voters who are registered

   b. $\dfrac{\text{Number of people voting}}{\text{Number of registered voters}}$ = % registered voters who voted

   c. $\dfrac{\text{Number of people voting}}{\text{Voting age population}}$ = % of eligible voters who voted

Table 4—Washington DC Registration and Voting in November 1990 Election[52]

   a. $\dfrac{\text{308,105 registered voters}}{\text{466,000 voting age population}}$ = 66% (% of eligible voters who are registered)

   b. $\dfrac{\text{171,677 people voting}}{\text{308,105 registered voters}}$ = 55.7% (% registered voters who voted)

   c. $\dfrac{\text{171,677 people voting}}{\text{466,000 voting age population}}$ = 36.8% (% of eligible voters who voted)

3. Break down the above statistics by race, age, income, geographic location and non-English speakers.

4. What percentage of voting-age citizens vote, in presidential elections?
Non-presidential elections?
Primary elections?
Special elections and referenda?
Are there differences by precinct?
What percentage of residents have declared political party affiliations?

Table 5—Voting and Registration in Washington, DC by Ward[53]

Wards	1	2	3	4	5	6	7	8	Average
% registered*	66	60	74	71	68	71	65	57	67
% registered who voted~	51	52	65	62	57	54	56	42	56
% of eligible population who voted~	33	31	48	44	38	38	36	24	37
% of all voters who were male**	42	44	40	38	37	41	35	33	39
% of all voters who were female**	58	57	60	62	63	59	65	67	61

* As of December 1990
** 1988 presidential Election
~ 11/6/90 election

Table 6—Washington, DC Registration Statistics as of November, 1988[54]

Age	18-24	25-34	35-44	45-54	55-64	65+
% of eligible voters who were registered	43.8	58.3	76.1	68.2	51.6	54.8

5. Chart these basic statistics for the last five to 10 elections, making note of any trends that have developed. Note similarities and differences in the turnout on issues related to local, state and national elections.

II. ANALYSIS AND RECOMMENDATIONS

A. ALTERNATIVE REGISTRATION PROVISIONS

Consider the registration provisions described on pages 229-230 when making recommendations for your community.

B. ANALYSIS OF COLLECTED DATA

Evaluate the collected data to identify clearly areas where voter participation could be improved. For example, based on the data collected on Washington, DC, we reached the following conclusions and recommendations:

Registration

1. Although mail-in voter registration forms are available in police stations, fire stations, public libraries and the DC Board of Elections and Ethics, forms are not available in other public agencies (such as welfare, health, unemployment compensation, utilities, tax and other public assistance offices) where lower income voters could be reached.

2. A primary barrier to registration in Washington, DC is the requirement that voters register at least 30 days before an election. Election-day registration would remedy this problem. Elections officials often cite the possibility of fraud as a reason not to use election day registration, a problem which is worsened when the population is transient. However, the Washington, DC wards with the lowest voter registration percentages represent a population that is not transient.

3. Washington, DC adopted pro-active motor-voter registration in 1989, with a voter registration form attached to the drivers license renewal form. Since its adoption, motor-voter registration has accounted for 44.8 percent of new registrations, and 35.2 percent of total voter registration transactions.

Voter participation

1. As of December 1990, 66.7 percent of eligible Washington, DC residents were registered to vote. This number varies within the eight wards that divide the city from 56.8 percent to 74.4 percent, indicating that significant improvement could be made in effectively recruiting voters from all areas of the city.

2. The predominantly low-income 8th ward has the lowest percentage of registered voters. The more affluent wards have the highest percentages of registered voters. Those residents of the 8th ward who are registered vote at the lowest level. Of the total voting age population, only 24 percent of 8th ward residents voted, or only half of the 48 percent turnout from the affluent 3rd ward. This indicates a serious problem in reaching out to low-income voters.

3. Registration among 18 to 24-year-olds is 43.8 percent, approximately 8 percent lower than the next age group. Although consistent with the rest of the country, the low percentage reflects the lack of an active registration program designed to attract young voters.

4. Statistics from the same years were not always available for this report, creating some problems in drawing conclusions. Additional statistics, including a breakdown of registered voters by age, would help in drawing stronger conclusions within each ward. The Washington, DC government needs to produce current statistics and data.

5. The District needs to make registration and voting more accessible to all segments of the population. The division between the more affluent Ward 3 and the low-income Ward 8 represents the sharp contrast in voting power within the District. Election-day registration and expansion of the location of mail-in registration ballots to all public agencies are obvious recommendations. Younger voters need to be reached in school to increase their registration levels.

C. IMPLEMENTATION AND ACTION

Find out the approximate costs of implementing your recommendations. Publicize your findings and ask for a response from your local state legislator, urging action on the recommendations of the report. Contact groups already working on the issues and work together to stimulate a community response to your recommendations by presenting the report to the local media, through press releases and news conferences.

ORGANIZATIONS

Center for Policy Alternatives
2000 Florida Avenue, NW
Washington, DC 20009

District of Columbia Board of Elections and Ethics
District Building, Room 4
1350 Pennsylvania Avenue, NW
Washington, DC 20004-3084

National Association of Secretaries of State
30 East Broad Street, 14th floor
Columbus, OH 43266-0418

ORGANIZATIONS WORKING ON
LOCAL VOTER REGISTRATION

A. Philip Randolph Institute
1444 I Street, NW, 3rd Floor
Washington, DC 20005

This non-partisan voter registration and education organization works through African American trade unions to register minorities. This group is designed to connect the labor movement with African Americans working in low-income communities nationwide.

League of Rural Voters
232 Third Avenue North, Suite 300
Minneapolis, MN 55401

The League of Rural Voters attempts to educate those in rural America to become more active in the political process. LRV conducted Rural Voter '88, a nationally coordinated drive to bring informed rural voters to the polls on election day.

League of Women Voters
1730 M Street, NW
Washington, DC 20036

A nonpartisan political organization that encourages the informed and active participation of voters in the 1200 local and state leagues around the country. Its bimonthly magazine *The National Voter* reports on how voters can be more effective.

Midwest Voter Registration
431 S. Dearborn, Suite 1103
Chicago, IL 60605

Midwest Voter coordinates efforts throughout the Midwest, primarily in Illinois and Indiana to increase voter registration in all communities. They work with deputized registrars to target communities for registration.

National Association for the Advancement of Colored People
4805 Mt. Hope Drive
Baltimore, MD 21215-3297

The NAACP works on the voter education and registration of minority voters in various capacities within its 2,200 offices nationwide.

National Coalition on Black Voter Participation
1629 K Street, NW, Suite 801
Washington, DC 20006

The National Coalition's principle goal is to increase minority participation through voter registration and education. Among other activities, they conduct Operation Big Vote in over 70 communities in 29 states around the country.

National Urban League, Inc.
500 E. 62nd Street
New York, NY 10021

The Urban League's 113 affiliates in 34 states work with African Americans and other minorities to increase opportunity through voter registration.

New York Public Interest Group (NYPIRG)
9 Murray Street
New York, NY 10007

NYPIRG is a student-directed organization working on environmental, consumer and social justice issues.

100% Vote/Human Serve
622 West 113th Street, Room 410
New York, NY 10025

100% Vote/Human Serve is a national voter registration reform organization which is advocating automatic registration when citizens apply for government services.

People For The American Way
2000 M Street, NW, Suite 400
Washington, DC 20016

This non-partisan organization is working on a voting project attempting to increase registration and advocate legislation designed to reduce registration barriers.

Project Vote
1424 16th Street, NW, Suite 101
Washington, DC 20036

This non-partisan group works primarily with low-income and minority voters through education and voter registration. Project Vote has video tape training to help organize registration volunteers.

Southwest Voter Registration Education Project
403 E. Commerce, Suite 220
San Antonio, TX 78205

The SVREP is a non-partisan organization committed to increasing the participation of Latino communities. The organization, since 1974, has conducted over 1,150 voter registration and voter education campaigns in California, Arizona, New Mexico, Colorado, Texas, Oklahoma, Utah, Nevada, Idaho, Montana, Wyoming and South Dakota.

BIBLIOGRAPHY

Creating the Opportunity: How Voting Laws Affect Voter Turnout. Washington, DC: The Committee for the Study of the American Electorate, 1987.

District of Columbia General Election: Final and Complete Election Results. Washington, DC: DC Board of Elections and Ethics, 1990.

Election Day Registration. Washington, DC: Center for Policy Alternatives, 1990.

First Vote: A Teaching Unit on Registration and Voting. Curriculum and video. Washington, DC: People for the American Way.

How to Organize and Implement a Successful Non-Partisan Voter Participation Campaign. Washington, DC: National Coalition on Black Voter Participation, Operation Big Vote, 1983.

Jackson, Charlene and Rebecca Hoffman. *Youth Vote '91: Register the Power, Student Guide to Registering Classmates*. New York, NY: New York Public Interest Research Group, 1991.

Mail-In Voter Registration. Fact sheet. Washington, DC: Center for Policy Alternatives, 1990.

Making a Difference: A Voters Service/Citizen Information Handbook. Washington, DC: League of Women Voters, 1978.

Monthly Report of Voter Registration Statistics for the period ending December 31, 1990. Washington, DC: DC Board of Elections and Ethics, 1990.

"Motor Voter" Facts and Figures. Washington, DC: DC Board of Elections and Ethics, January 1991.

Motor Voter Registration. Fact sheet. Washington, DC: Center for Policy Alternatives, 1990.

Piven, Frances Fox and Richard A. Cloward. *Why Americans Don't Vote*. New York: Pantheon Books, 1988.

Report of the Task Force on Barriers to Voting. Columbus, OH: National Association of Secretaries of State, 1987.

Renewing the Promise: The 20th Anniversary of the 18-Year-Old Vote. Washington, DC: People for the American Way, 1991.

States with Motor Voter and Other Agency-Based Voter Registration Programs. New York: 100% Vote/Human Serve, 1991.

U.S. Department of Commerce - Bureau of the Census. *Voting and Registration in the Election of November 1988*. Washington, DC: Government Printing Office, October 1989.

Voting in the District of Columbia: Development, Current Trends and Progress in Administration. Washington, DC: DC Board of Elections and Ethics, 1988.

Youth Vote '91: Register the Power Fact sheet. New York: Youth Vote '91, 1991.

ACTIVITY SIX:
ACCESS FOR
PEOPLE WITH DISABILITIES

I. INTRODUCTION

People with physical and mental disabilities encounter barriers in many aspects of their daily lives, including education, employment and housing. These barriers rob the 43 million Americans who have some type of physical or mental disability of many of their rights by denying them full access to society.[1] It is not only physical barriers, such as buildings inaccessible to people using wheelchairs, but psychological barriers — those in people's minds — that limit opportunities. These barriers take many forms, including "inaccessible buildings and telecommunications, unusable transportation vehicles, denial of job opportunities, segregated schooling, placement into institutions, lack of necessary support services and social isolation."[2]

Intolerant attitudes and misunderstanding of the nature of disabilities are prevalent in our society. One way to overcome barriers is to avoid segregation of people with disabilities. Everyone — disabled and nondisabled — benefits from having contact with people from many walks of life. Many schools have developed innovative special education programs to remedy past patterns of segregation.

In addition to the psychological barriers that other people impose on them, people with physical disabilities encounter numerous physical barriers. For most people, stairs do not cause a problem, nor do narrow doorways or elevator buttons marked simply with a number. But they can prevent thousands of people from doing many of the things that others take for granted. The design of buildings and transportation systems can make it much more difficult or impossible for people with disabilities to work, travel, attend school, go to a movie or do other routine things.[3]

This project will help students identify some of the physical barriers that people with certain types of disabilities encounter as well as some changes that

society can make to ensure the rights of disabled people.

II. DISABILITY RIGHTS ACTIVISM

"Like racial minorities, women, and gays, people with disabilities have been the target of systematic discrimination in this country ranging from exclusion due to lack of simple physical access to outright prejudice," writes Mary Johnson, editor of *The Disability Rag.*[4] Since the mid-1970s, a disability rights movement has fought in the courts and legislatures, as well as through direct action, to secure access and protection from discrimination.[5] Disability rights activists have won campaigns to change building codes to require barrier-free access, to equip city buses with wheelchair lifts and to be included in laws that prohibit employment discrimination.[6]

In 1973, disability rights activists staged a sit-in at the Lincoln Memorial to protest discrimination against disabled people.[7] Congress responded by passing the Rehabilitation Act of 1973 to require federal contractors to take affirmative action in the employment of qualified disabled employees. The Rehabilitation Act also requires that programs and activities which receive federal funding, including some public schools, be physically accessible to disabled people (see below).[8]

Disability rights organizations such as the Americans Disabled for Accessible Public Transportation (ADAPT) used tactics of civil disobedience in their campaigns to win access to public transportation in cities around the country.[9] For example, in St. Louis, Missouri, 41 members of ADAPT were jailed overnight for blocking entrances to a conference of the American Public Transportation Association which opposed equipping city buses with wheelchair lifts because of the cost. Other organizations, such as the Eastern Paralyzed Veterans Association (EPVA), won access to public transportation through the courts. The

EPVA won a court order in February 1988 requiring the city of Philadelphia to make some subway stations accessible and won a six-year campaign to require New York City to spend $40 million on elevators at key subway stops.[10]

Disability rights activists succeeded in lobbying Congress to pass the Americans With Disabilities Act (ADA) of 1990 which extends to disabled Americans the same protections against discrimination that women and African Americans won in the 1960s and 1970s. For example, the ADA prohibits discrimination against disabled people by employers with 15 or more workers and requires employers to make "reasonable accommodation" to their employees' disabilities.[11] The Act also requires most public accommodations to be physically accessible to disabled people (see below).

III. PHYSICAL BARRIERS CAUSED BY BUILDING DESIGN

People who use wheelchairs, people with sight and hearing impairments and people with a variety of other conditions that cause them to require assistance with walking encounter numerous physical barriers in buildings. The problems of accessibility are different for each of these groups.

For example, people with hearing impairments need visual alarms that flash when a fire alarm goes off. People with sight impairments need signs, symbols and warning devices designed with raised or indented characters or symbols, including braille or alphabet characters placed next to elevator buttons. Maps or signs with directions need to include raised characters or a tape with audio directions.

For people who use a wheelchair, the following design changes can improve access to buildings: parking spaces close to entrances of buildings; ramps leading into buildings; hallways and doorways wide enough to accommodate a wheelchair; telephones, elevator buttons and sinks low enough to be used by someone who is not standing; and handrails and grab bars at showers, tubs and toilets. None of these items is a luxury. They are essential if everyone is to have an equal opportunity to participate in our society.

IV. MAKING BUILDINGS MORE ACCESSIBLE

A. LAWS AND STANDARDS ON ACCESS FOR PEOPLE WITH DISABILITIES

Congress enacted the Architectural Barriers Act (ABA) in 1968 to ensure that buildings and facilities which are designed, constructed, altered or leased by or on behalf of the federal government are accessible (can be approached, entered and used by physically disabled people).[12] Included in this category are federal office buildings and facilities, all military facilities including housing, all post offices, Veterans Administration hospitals and other hospitals built with federal money, all public housing and other federally-funded housing.

The Rehabilitation Act of 1973 requires the buildings and facilities, including public schools, libraries and transportation programs, that provide federally-funded programs and activities must be accessible, even if it requires architectural modifications.[13] All such buildings must meet specific federal accessibility standards which cover parking lots, pathways, drinking fountains, telephones, ramps, stairs, entrances, doors, gates, lobbies, hallways, elevators, assembly rooms and bathrooms.

The federal agencies responsible for setting the standards for building compliance under the ABA and the Rehabilitation Act produced the Uniform Federal Accessibility Standards (UFAS) in 1984. The UFAS are based on standards developed by the American National Standards Institute (ANSI), a non-governmental organization which developed accessibility standards for buildings based on the recommendations of disabled people, rehabilitation specialists, architects, builders and manufacturers.[14]

The UFAS, which apply to any facility covered by the ABA and Section 504 of the Rehabilitation Act of 1973, include requirements for adaptations to make buildings accessible to those who use wheelchairs and for people with sight and hearing impairments.[15] Congress, in the Rehabilitation Act of 1973, created the Architectural and Transportation Barriers Compliance Board (ATBCB) to ensure compliance with the standards outlined in the ABA and the 1973 Act.[16]

The ATBCB investigates complaints about noncompliance, issues orders to enforce compliance with the ABA and provides technical assistance to the public about removing physical barriers.[17]

The Americans with Disabilities Act of 1990 extends to state and local governments and the private sector the requirements established in the 1973 Rehabilitation Act.[18] The ADA requires public accommodations such as restaurants, hotels, theaters, shopping centers and malls, retail stores, museums, libraries, parks, private schools, day care centers and other similar places to be accessible. The law requires these public accommodations to remove physical barriers or provide alternative methods of service (if easily accomplished without much expense).[19]

B. SURVEYING FOR ACCESSIBILITY

The survey form presented below was adapted from a survey checklist developed by the ATBCB to check for compliance with the UFAS, a survey form developed by the Fairfax County Schools in Virginia for use specifically in surveying schools and a survey developed by Professor Douglas Prillaman for a course at the College of William and Mary.

The ATBCB survey form is too comprehensive to include in full here. However, most sections relevant to schools are included. The purpose of this student survey is not to make absolute determinations about compliance with federal, state or local laws. Rather, conducting the survey will give you a general idea about how accessible your school is when looked at in the light of federal standards. Some items may seem too specific until you think about exactly why they are needed.

The survey will also encourage students to think about the many barriers people with disabilities face every day. Students can also use the information to observe buildings and facilities in the community.

Before you begin the survey, check with local and state agencies which set building standards and codes to find out what, if any, accessibility standards they set. Review their survey forms and compare them to

this one. State and local laws must be at least as stringent as federal law.

1. Conduct the Survey

Notify the school administration and maintenance staff that you will be conducting a survey. If the group of students interested in conducting the survey is large, it may be useful to divide into teams, each surveying different sections of the school. Make copies of the survey form and bring a clipboard, pen or pencil and a measuring tape. When completing the survey form, if you cannot determine whether or not the element complies, indicate this with a question mark. If the element does not exist, mark it "N/A" (not applicable).

2. Survey Results

You may find that your school has done all, or almost all, of the things necessary to make the school accessible to people with disabilities. If not, bring the problems to the attention of school administrators and ask what they are prepared to do to make the needed improvements.

If school administrators are unwilling or unable to act on their own, you may want to present a report to the school board with your findings and recommendations or consider other ways to make the accessibility issue a priority.

3. Follow-Up Ideas

Survey other schools in your district or other buildings covered by federal, state or local accessibility standards. The full federal survey for the Uniform Accessibility Standards is available from the Architectural and Transportation Barriers Compliance Board. You may also file a formal, written complaint with the ATBCB to charge that a building or facility is inaccessible.

Contact local groups working on disability rights issues and ask them if you can assist them with surveying or other efforts.

ACCESSIBILITY SURVEY FORM

Building Name and Address:

_____

_____

Surveyor's Name:

_____

Date of Survey:

_____

Parking Accessibility	Yes	No
1. Are accessible parking spaces the closest spaces to the building's accessible entrances?	☐	☐
2. Are parking spaces clearly marked as reserved for people with disabilities?	☐	☐
3. Is the disability head-in parking space 13' wide if single, or 21' wide if double?	☐	☐
4. Does the disability parking space have an aisle running along the side of the space with room for a wheelchair?	☐	☐
5. Is a curb ramp easily accessible from the parking space?	☐	☐
6. Are the required number of accessible spaces provided? (See chart at end of survey)	☐	☐

Walkway Accessibility	Yes	No
1. Is slope of walkway gentle?	☐	☐
2. Is walkway free of curbs and steps?	☐	☐
3. Is walkway made of solid materials, not gravel or widely-spaced flagstones?	☐	☐
4. Are there leveled, ramped walkways or curb ramps from the parking lot to the entrances of the building?	☐	☐
5. Are walkways or paths at least 4' wide?	☐	☐

Entryway

	Yes	No
1. Is the accessible entrance to the building not a service entrance unless the only entrance to the building is a service entrance?	☐	☐
2. Are access-ramps at least 36" wide?	☐	☐
3. Is the slope, if any, gentle?	☐	☐
4. Do ramps longer than 30' have turns with a level platform of 5' square?	☐	☐
5. Do ramps longer than 6' have handrails on both sides, 30" to 34" above finished surface?	☐	☐
6. Do entrance platforms, ramps and walkways have non-slip surfaces?	☐	☐
7. Within the boundaries of the site, is the accessible entrance connected by an accessible route to existing public transportation stops, accessible parking and passenger loading zones, and to public streets or sidewalks?	☐	☐

Doorways

	Yes	No
1. Is door threshold no higher than 1/2"?	☐	☐
2. Is door at least 32" wide?	☐	☐
3. Can doors be opened and closed with one hand?	☐	☐
4. Does door close slowly enough to allow a person with a disability to use it?	☐	☐
5. If turnstiles or revolving doors are used on an accessible route, is there an accessible gate or door?	☐	☐

Hallways

	Yes	No
1. Are hallways wide enough to manipulate a wheelchair; (exit halls 6' minimum, service corridors 3' minimum)?	☐	☐
2. Are floors of non-slip material?	☐	☐
3. Are fixtures fire extinguishers, fire alarms & light switches a maximum 4' above the floor?	☐	☐
4. Are room numbers raised or engraved to be accessible to those with sight impairments? Are they on, or next to, the door on the door handle side? Are they set between 36" and 60" high?	☐ ☐	☐ ☐
5. Are the lights on the fire alarms designed to blink if the alarm goes off?		

Auditorium

	Yes	No
1. Is auditorium accessible from main level hallway, a ramp or an elevator?	☐	☐
2. Is the stage accessible from main level hallway, a ramp or elevator?	☐	☐
3. Is there a spectator section for wheelchairs? State location or a plan for accommodating wheelchairs.	☐	☐

_____

_____

	Yes	No
Is seating in places other than in aisles or in front of first row?	☐	☐
Are there a variety of choices/locations for wheelchair seating?	☐	☐
Does seating allow wheelchair user to sit next to companions?	☐	☐
Does seating adjoin an accessible route that also serves as an emergency exit?	☐	☐
4. If the assembly area has an audio-amplification system, is there a listening system for persons with severe hearing loss?	☐	☐

Library

	Yes	No
1. Is library accessible from main level hallway, a ramp or elevator?	☐	☐
2. Are card catalogs 54" or less from the floor?	☐	☐
3. Is equipment like microfilm machines and computers on low, accessible tables?	☐	☐
4. Are at least 5 percent of the tables and carrels accessible to people using wheelchairs, and do they have at least a 27" knee clearance?	☐	☐

Gymnasium

	Yes	No
1. Is gymnasium accessible from main level hallway, a ramp or elevator?	☐	☐
2. Is there a spectator section for wheelchairs? State location or plan for accommodating wheelchairs.	☐	☐

_____

_____

	Yes	No
3. Are male and female locker rooms accessible from main level hallway, a ramp or elevator?	☐	☐
4. Is there an accessible changing area which includes locker(s) at appropriate height (between 9" and 54"), unobstructed aisle space for lockers and changing benches wide enough for safe transfers from wheelchairs?	☐	☐

5. Do shower facilities have grab bars, a seat and a hand-held shower head?
   (See Restroom section for restroom access in locker room.) □ □

Cafeteria   Yes   No

1. Is cafeteria accessible from main level hallway, a ramp or elevator? □ □
2. Is the width of the food service line a minimum of 36" wide? □ □
3. Is the turn in the food service line a minimum of 36" wide? □ □
4. Are tray slides mounted no higher than 34" above the floor? □ □
5. Are utensils, trays and condiments placed no higher than 54" from the floor? □ □

Water Fountains   Yes   No

1. Is there one accessible water fountain on each floor? □ □
2. Do water fountains have clear knee space between bottom of basin and floor
   which is 27" high? □ □
3. Are controls and spouts in front or side-mounted near front edge? □ □
4. Is fountain spout no more than 36" from floor? (30" in elementary schools) □ □

Public Telephones   Yes   No

1. Is there at least one public telephone in each telephone group, with 30" x 45"
   clear floor space in front of it? □ □
2. Is the highest operable part of the telephone no more than 48" (front reach)
   or 54" (side reach)? □ □
3. Are phone books also within these reach ranges? □ □
4. Is there an amplification system for hearing impaired people available
   on one phone? (It is usually a button that you press to increase the volume) □ □

Stairs (for access for the visually impaired)   Yes   No

1. Is each step no higher than 7"? □ □
2. Are stair treads no less than 11" wide? □ □
3. Does the top of the step stick out more than 1-1/2"? □ □
4. Are there handrails on both sides of stairs? □ □
5. Is inside handrail continuous? □ □
6. Does handrail continue at least 12" beyond top/bottom of stairway? □ □

Elevator(s)

	Yes	No
1. Does elevator have at least 4'3" x 5'8" floor space (minimum)?	☐	☐
2. Is the highest button on the inside and outside controls no higher that 42"? (36" to top button for elementary schools)	☐	☐
3. Are the controls labeled in braille?	☐	☐
4. Do controls have light and tone signals for visually and hearing impaired people?	☐	☐
5. Does elevator floor meet the building floor with no more than a 1/2" step-up?	☐	☐
6. Are building levels not served by the elevator served by a ramp or lift device?	☐	☐

Playing Fields/Stadium

	Yes	No
1. Are there leveled, ramp walkways or curb ramps from building to fields and stadium?	☐	☐
Football Field	☐	☐
Baseball Field	☐	☐
Tennis Courts	☐	☐
Other Field(s)	☐	☐
2. Are leveled, ramped walkways or curb ramps from parking lot to play fields or stadium?	☐	☐
Football Field	☐	☐
Baseball Field	☐	☐
Tennis Courts	☐	☐
Other Field(s)	☐	☐
3. Are parking spaces reserved for people with physical disabilities within 200' of these fields, the gym, etc.?	☐	☐
4. Do restrooms meet accessibility standards? (see Restrooms section)	☐	☐
5. Are the bleachers accessible, and can a wheelchair user sit next to companions in the bleachers?	☐	☐

Restroom Accessibility

	Yes	No
1. Are restrooms on accessible routes?	☐	☐
2. Is threshold of the door 1/2" or lower?	☐	☐
3. Does restroom have turning space of 5' x 5' for wheelchairs?	☐	☐
4. Is light switch no higher than 48" from floor?	☐	☐

Toilet Area

	Yes	No
1. Is the accessible toilet stall at least 56" by 60" wide?	☐	☐

2. If door swings in, is there 5' x 5' clear space between the door and toilet? ☐ ☐
3. Is the door 32" wide? ☐ ☐
4. Are toilet seats 17" to 19" from floor? (15" for children's facilities) ☐ ☐
5. Is toilet paper dispenser mounted between 19" and 32" above finished floor? ☐ ☐
6. Are there grab-bars? ☐ ☐
7. Does men's room have a urinal with opening at 19" above floor? ☐ ☐

Sinks   Yes   No

1. Does sink have at least 27" of knee clearance? ☐ ☐
2. Are bottoms of soap dispensers no more than 38" from floor? ☐ ☐
3. Are towel dispensers mounted no higher than 40"? ☐ ☐
4. Are trash cans accessible or are disposal units mounted no higher than 34" from floor? ☐ ☐
5. Is one mirror mounted no higher than 40" from the floor? ☐ ☐
6. Is there space in front of the sink at least 30" x 48"? ☐ ☐
7. Are faucets equipped with 4" wrist handles? ☐ ☐

Classrooms   Yes   No

1. Is level space provided? ☐ ☐
2. Are 1 percent of the stations accessible? ☐ ☐

Requirements for Parking Lots

Total Parking in Lot   Required Minimum Number of Accessible Spaces
1 to 25 1
26 to 50 2
51 to 75 3
76 to 100 4
101 to 150 5
151 to 200 6
201 to 300 7
301 to 400 8
401 to 500 9
501 to 1000 ....2 percent of total
1001 and over ....20 + 1 for each 100 over 1000

Source: UFAS Accessibility Checklist (Washington, DC: U.S. Architectural and Transportation Compliance Board, 1990).

ORGANIZATIONS

American Council for the Blind
1155 15th Street, NW
Washington, DC 20005

American Foundation for the Blind
1615 M Street, NW, Suite 250
Washington, DC 20036

Disability Rights Education and Defense Fund
2212 6th Street
Berkeley, CA 94710

National Center for Law and the Deaf
Gallaudet College
7th Street and Florida Avenue, NE
Washington, DC 20002

National Council on Independent Living
RCIL, Troy Atrium
4th and Broadway
Troy, NY 12180

National Disability Action Center
2021 L Street, NW Suite 800
Washington, DC 20036

The National Federation of the Blind
1800 Johnson Street
Baltimore, MD 21230

The Paralyzed Veterans of America
801 18th Street, NW
Washington, DC 20036

U.S. Architectural and Transportation Barriers
Compliance Board
111 18th Street, NW Suite 501
Washington, DC 20036-3894

World Institute on Disability
510 16th Street
Oakland, CA 94612

BIBLIOGRAPHY

Access America: The Architectural Barriers Act and You. Washington, DC: U.S. Architectural and Transportation Barriers Compliance Board.

Americans with Disabilities Act Fact Sheet. Washington, DC: U.S. Architectural and Transportation Barriers Compliance Board, 1990.

Bruck, Lilly. *Access: The Guide to a Better Life for Disabled Americans.* Orangeburg, NY: Consumers Union, 1978.

School Survey for Accessibility. McLean, VA: Fairfax County School Board, 1990.

Golden, Marilyn. "Not on the Front Page," *The East Bay Guardian*, June 1991.

Glastris, Paul. "The Mixed Blessing of a Movement," *U.S. News and World Report.* September 18, 1989.

Goldman, Charles D. "Right of Way: The Americans with Disabilities Act," *The Washington Lawyer.* March/April 1991.

Johnson, Mary. "Disabled Americans Push for Access," *The Progressive.* August 1991.

Kleinfield, Sonny. "The Handicapped: Hidden No Longer," *Atlantic Monthly.* December 1977.

Shapiro, Joseph P. "Liberation Day for the Disabled," *U.S. News and World Report.* September 18, 1989.

Uniform Federal Accessibility Standards. Washington, DC: General Services Administration, Dept. of Defense, Dept. of Housing and Urban Development, U.S. Postal Service, 1988.

UFAS Accessibility Checklist. Washington, DC: U.S. Architectural and Transportation Barriers Compliance Board, 1990.

Weber, Joseph. "The Last 'Minority' Fights For Its Rights: The Disabled are battling prejudice with '60s-style activism," *Business Week.* June 6, 1988.

ACTIVITY SEVEN:
MAKE YOUR SCHOOL
A GREEN CONSUMER

Activity Seven contains three projects to help students develop ecological habits that will continue to bear fruit in their adult lives. Students learn about some of the ways schools can change their buying habits to do less damage to the environment by conducting a school purchasing survey and by eliminating polystyrene foam products. And students learn about both the role of recycling in solving the problem of solid waste disposal and how to set up a recycling program to meet the needs of their school or community.

INTRODUCTION: WHAT IS GREEN CONSUMING?

Green consuming means basing individual decisions about what to buy on concerns about the environment. A 1989 market research poll found that 89 percent of Americans are concerned about the impact on the environment of the products they purchase, more than half say they decline to buy certain products out of concern for the environment, and 78 percent would pay more for a product packaged with recyclable or biodegradable materials.[1]

Green consuming is also a marketing strategy that many companies use to sell products to consumers who are increasingly concerned about the environment. Some of the advertising claims and "green" labels are misleading. For example, federal regulations allow paper products to carry the "recycled" label when they include just 40 percent recycled content. In addition, that portion may consist mostly of paper left over from production processes, not paper that has been used and then recycled.[2]

Choosing one product over another is only one factor in minimizing individual impact on the environment. Another consideration is the quantity of products used and thrown away. Companies trying to sell products are unlikely to remind you, the buyer, that part of the solution to pollution is buying fewer products. One way to reduce the quantity of throwaway products is

to cut down on unnecessary packaging. According to the Environmental Protection Agency, packaging accounts for 32 percent of the municipal solid waste stream by weight.[3] Eliminating unnecessary packaging can help to solve the solid waste problem.

In addition, changes in individual buying patterns can address only part of the problem since individuals are limited by the kinds of products available to buy. An individual who wants to cut down on air pollution by using more energy-efficient transportation is limited by the community's choices on mass transit systems and by auto manufacturers' decisions on how fuel-efficient they build cars. Despite the limits, individual actions are an important way citizens can tell government and business that they want the root causes of pollution eliminated.

To help build the market for recycled products, Congress passed the Resource Conservation and Recovery Act in 1976 which requires the federal government to purchase products, when possible, made from recovered — reusable or recycled — materials.[4] For example, if the U.S. government, the largest single consumer of paper in the world, buys only recycled paper products, manufacturers have an incentive to make them. However, the Environmental Protection Agency only began implementing the law with some force in 1986.[5]

SOLID WASTE: A GROWING PROBLEM

Although the United States has only 5 percent of the world's population, it produces 25 percent of its pollutants and 30 percent of its garbage.[6] An average U.S. citizen generates four to six pounds of municipal solid waste — waste from households, institutions and businesses — every day. Annually, this adds up to 179 to 268 million tons of municipal solid waste.[7] As the amount of garbage Americans produce grows, the problem of disposal grows as well.

Municipal solid waste is made up of the following materials:[8]

	By Weight	By Volume
paper and paperboard	40.0%	34.1%
yard wastes	17.6%	10.3%
metals	8.5%	12.1%
glass	7.0%	2.0%
plastics	8.0%	19.9%
food wastes	7.4%	3.3%
other	11.6%	18.4%

CURRENT APPROACHES TO SOLID WASTE DISPOSAL

In the United States, 80 percent of municipal solid waste goes to landfills, 10 percent is incinerated and 10 percent is recycled. An undetermined amount of waste is dumped illegally into the ocean or on land.[9]

Landfills present serious environmental problems and they are filling up fast. In 1978, the United States had about 20,000 landfills. By 1988, the number had dropped to about 6,000.[10] Although laws exist to minimize the health and environmental hazards of landfills, in 1988, municipal landfills accounted for 21 percent of the sites on EPA's Superfund list of the nation's worst toxic waste problems.[11] Wastes seep underground, pollute groundwater and can contaminate drinking water supplies. Faced with diminishing landfill space, some communities are sending their wastes to other states and some have shipped waste to other countries.[12]

Incineration refers to a complex process of burning trash. Some incinerators, called waste-to-energy or resource recovery plants, can generate steam and/or electrical energy.[13] However, incinerators are expensive to build and maintain, and the toxic ash — left over after burning — still has to be buried in landfills. Incinerators pollute by releasing metals, acid gases, carbon monoxide and dioxins into the air. Also, drinking water is susceptible to contamination if toxic ash seeps into groundwater.[14]

Incinerators and large-scale recycling programs compete for the same materials, such as paper, which are easy to recycle, but also easy to burn. Local governments often make legal agreements with incinerator operators which require that most of the area's trash will be burned, to guarantee enough business for the incinerator company. This effectively puts a limit on the amount of waste a community can recycle.[15]

Community groups around the country have successfully defeated proposals for incinerators in their communities in favor of source reduction and recycling.[16]

WASTE MANAGEMENT SOLUTIONS FOR THE LONG TERM

New approaches are essential to avoid being buried under our garbage. The economic and environmental pressures of waste disposal have forced state and local governments around the country to adopt waste management programs which include long-term planning for community waste disposal needs and a system which combines source reduction, reuse and recycling to minimize costs and maximize health and environmental protection.

SOURCE REDUCTION AND REUSE

If waste is not created, it presents no disposal problem. Source reduction involves designing, manufacturing and using products with fewer and less toxic raw materials, that are durable and reusable, easy to repair and to recycle.[17] For example, refillable ball point pens last for many years, while their disposable counterparts are thrown away after only a few months.

Recycling

Recycling cuts down on the amount of trash sent to landfills, slows down depletion of natural resources, saves energy and cuts down on air and water pollution.[18] Recycling one print run of a Sunday edition of the *New York Times* would save 75,000 trees.[19]

As of 1988, the United States recycled only 10 percent of its municipal solid waste, according to the

Environmental Protection Agency.[20] The potential exists, however, to recycle much more. Some communities in Europe, Asia and North America have overall recycling rates as high as 65 percent.[21]

Return Deposit Legislation

As of 1990, nine states had laws requiring return deposits on beverage containers to encourage recycling.[22] Customers pay an extra five to ten cents per bottle, and upon returning the bottle, they get their money back. In its first two years of operation, New York's bottle law saved $50 to $100 million in energy costs, $50 million in cleanup expenditures and $19 million in solid waste disposal, while increasing employment by nearly 4,000 jobs.[23]

Before passage of New York's 1983 bottle bill, according to the New York State Department of Environmental Conservation, only 4 percent of glass, 1 percent of plastic and 15 percent of aluminum was removed from the waste stream for recycling. By 1986, 80 percent of glass, 50 percent of plastic and 60 percent of aluminum was removed for recycling.[24]

I. GREEN CONSUMING — SCHOOL PURCHASING SURVEY

A. PURCHASING PROCESS

Find out how purchasing decisions are made for your school. Most likely, much of the purchasing is done for the entire school district or, for some products, for the entire state. Approximately 25 states have laws mandating use of state funds to procure items made from recycled materials.[25] The aim of this policy is to create demand for recycled products by using the leverage of government contracting. Changing the buying patterns for the school district or state will have a much larger effect than changes made at just one school.

Work with the school personnel responsible for procurement, or buying, for the school. Find out what restrictions are in place on buying decisions and what the procedure is for making most purchases. Generally, a bidding process will be quite specific. Purchasing decisions are probably made by more than one person,

for example, one for the cafeteria and another for the office and teachers may make some purchasing decisions themselves.

GOVERNMENT PURCHASING PROJECT

Federal, state and local governments in the United States spend nearly one trillion dollars a year for goods and services, amounting to nearly 20 percent of the Gross National Product.[26] Government purchases include cars, paper, appliances, light bulbs, fuel, cleaners and health insurance.[27] Because the government is such a big consumer, its buying decisions can encourage business to develop and manufacture products that are safe, environmentally friendly and energy efficient.

Writes Eleanor Lewis, director of the Government Purchasing Project, "Government orders can help create the volume needed to lower prices for new technologies and products due to economies of scale."[28] For example, in the early 1980s, consumer groups persuaded the General Services Administration (GSA) to place an order for airbag-equipped cars for government use. Ford Motor Company filled the GSA order with 5,000 airbag-equipped Ford Tempos and soon offered airbags as an option on two of its models available to the general public. Other auto companies soon followed.[29]

The Washington-based Government Purchasing Project (GPP) lobbies the government to use its purchasing power to promote recycling, energy efficiency and pollution prevention. The GPP operates an Energy Efficiency Clearinghouse for government officials responsible for purchasing. The Clearinghouse also offers suggestions for interested citizens who wish to influence government purchasing decisions.

B. CONDUCT A REDUCE, REUSE, RECYCLE SURVEY

Divide your survey by category of product. For example, look at all products purchased for cleaning and pest control, for the cafeteria and for the office and classrooms. Evaluate the products your school purchases by asking the following questions:

- Is the product necessary?
- Can the product be reused?
- Can the product be recycled given recycling opportunities currently available to your school?
- Is the product made from recycled materials?
- How is the product packaged? Can the product be bought in bulk to cut down on packaging?
- Does the product contain toxic ingredients?
- Is the product energy efficient?

C. EVALUATING PRODUCTS AND ALTERNATIVES

Once you have surveyed the purchases your school makes, evaluate where changes can be made. For example, toxic cleaning products can be replaced with non-petroleum based soaps or, for washing windows, a mixture of vinegar and water. The cafeteria can purchase organic (grown without the use of pesticides) fruits and vegetables and can reduce packaging by buying items in bulk. The administrative office can buy recycled paper products. And the chemistry lab can implement a microscale system to reduce the amount of harmful chemicals used in student chemistry experiments.

Use the resources section to gather more information on safe, non-toxic products. Research alternatives and make recommendations regarding cost, quality and availability. When evaluating alternatives, consider the following:

Plastics

Plastics are made from non-renewable, petroleum-based chemicals, many of which are highly toxic and result "in hazardous wastes, toxic air emission, and discharges of toxic effluence into waterways."[30] The use of toxic chemicals in the production of plastics also can be harmful to the workers who make them and the people who live near plastics factories.[31]

According to Environmental Action, a grassroots environmental group, the single largest use of plastics is packaging, accounting for one-fourth of all plastics produced, or 12 billion pounds of plastic each year.[32] More and more products are packaged with non-recyclable plastic. For example, the Quaker Oats Company added a plastic bottom and lid to its container which had been all-cardboard for 80 years.[33]

Although plastics make up 7 percent of municipal trash by weight, they account for 30 percent of the volume in landfills.[34] Incineration of plastics produces toxic gases.[35] As of 1990, only 2 percent of plastics were recycled, some of which were used to make heavy plastic items such as park benches and fence posts.[36] The many different kinds of plastic make it necessary to separate before recycling. And some products, made with multiple layers of plastics and paper, are nearly impossible to recycle.[37]

Made of
Recycled Materials

Made of
Recyclable Materials

ENVIRONMENTAL PROTECTION AGENCY

"Recyclable" Labels

The label "recycled" means that a product is made from (at least in part) already used materials. The "recyclable" label means that the product can be recycled, if the consumer chooses to do so and if a recycling center for that material is available to the consumer. The recyclable label does not necessarily mean that the product already has been recycled.[38] The symbols for recycled and recyclable materials are shown above.

Biodegradability

Some manufacturers claim that their plastic products, for example, trash bags, are biodegradable and therefore less harmful to the environment than non-biodegradable plastics. But Environmental Action and other citizen groups have called these claims a "hoax."[39] And a study commissioned by Greenpeace and conducted by the Center for the Biology of Natural Systems, *Breaking Down the Degradable Plastics Scam*, analyzed the claims of manufacturers of so-called biodegradable plastics and determined that none of these major manufacturers could support their claims.[40] According to Greenpeace, the only true biodegradable plastics are those made from natural polymers such as PHBV, which is produced by bacteria, and cellophane, which is made of cellulose produced by plants. These products are not in general commercial use because they are too expensive or have been replaced by mass-produced plastics. Cellophane has the additional drawback of releasing toxins during manufacture.[41]

Furthermore, most waste is buried deep inside landfills where degradation is slowed due to the lack of oxygen. Even newspapers fail to degrade in many landfills.[42]

D. IMPLEMENT THE RECOMMENDATIONS

Meet with purchasing personnel to develop an implementation plan. Once your school has changed certain buying patterns, inform students and faculty, the community and your elected officials about your project. Encourage other schools in your district and in your state to implement the same changes.

Write to the manufacturers of the products your school discontinues to let them know why you have stopped purchasing their products. Also write to the companies that manufacture the replacement products to encourage them to continue or improve their manufacturing and packaging processes.

Consider establishing a school recycling program, a compost pile for yard and cafeteria waste and an organic garden to further contribute to making your school more environmentally sound.

II. TARGETING POLYSTYRENE FOAM (STYROFOAM) PRODUCTS

Eliminating polystyrene foam products (commonly called Styrofoam, the trade name used by Dow Chemical) from your school is a good way to begin a green consumer campaign. Schools across the country as well as religious and citizen groups have successfully campaigned to replace polystyrene foam with more environmentally-friendly products. Use the information below about the hazards of polystyrene products to justify the switch. (See the story of the campaign at West Milford High School in New Jersey on pages 7-8).

The Citizen's Clearinghouse for Hazardous Waste (CCHW) launched a nationwide campaign in August 1987 to encourage McDonald's restaurants to stop using its polystyrene foam packages. Through CCHW's "Operation Send It Back," thousands of people sent the fast food restaurant's polystyrene clamshells to McDonald's headquarters. CCHW chose McDonald's because the restaurant accounted for such a large amount (approximately 10 percent) of polystyrene foam use in the United States.[43] Local environmental, school and citizen groups around the country boycotted and picketed their McDonald's restaurants and campaigned for local ordinances to ban polystyrene foam products.[44]

In November 1990, McDonald's announced they would begin phasing-out use of their polystyrene foam clamshells — but not polystyrene foam coffee cups — used at their U.S. restaurants in 60 days. Other fast food restaurants quickly followed with similar plans. The McDonald's plan replaces foam packaging with a plasticized paper that is not recyclable. However, the restaurant said the switch away from the bulky polystyrene foam would result in a 90 percent reduction in the volume of solid waste McDonald's generates.[45]

While targeting McDonald's, CCHW and other groups worked to ban polystyrene foam as well as other plastics packaging in their schools and communities. More than 100 cities and towns across the country proposed laws curbing the use of plastic food packaging. Some of the cities that banned polystyrene foam include Hamden, Connecticut; Portland, Oregon; Minneapolis and St. Paul, Minnesota; and Newark, New Jersey.[46]

A. DEFINITION

Polystyrene foam is a petroleum-based product composed of the chemical polystyrene which is either mixed with liquid CFC or pentane and placed in a mold or is injected into the mold with CFC or pentane gas. In the mold, polystyrene expands into the foam material used for disposable cups, plates, packaging material and egg cartons.[47]

B. PRODUCTION

Production of polystyrene foam products is hazardous both to the environment and to worker health and safety. Polystyrene production uses petroleum, a dwindling, non-renewable energy source, and results in toxic waste. The Environmental Protection Agency has ranked styrene and benzene (both polystyrene ingredients) among the top six chemicals whose production creates the most hazardous wastes.[48]

One of two chemicals, chlorofluorocarbons (CFCs) or pentane, is used to give polystyrene foam its puffy consistency. The use of CFCs contributes to the destruction of the ozone layer of the atmosphere.[49] Although industry has announced a phase-out of CFCs in polystyrene foam production, a replacement gas, CFC-22 or HCFC, also damages the atmospheric ozone, though to a lesser extent.[50] Production of polystyrene foam using pentane contributes to air pollution.[51]

The use of pentane, a flammable substance, also adds the risk of explosion in the workplace. On July 5, 1990, 17 workers were killed in an explosion at Arco's polystyrene plant in Channelview, Texas.[52] And chemicals, including styrene and pentane, used in the production of polystyrene foam can cause the following occupational health hazards: eye and nose irritation, headaches, fatigue, muscular weakness, inflammation of the liver, skin disease and, in severe cases, death.[53]

C. HEALTH EFFECTS OF POLYSTYRENE FOAM USE

A 1988 study, published by the Foundation for Advancements in Science and Education, revealed that styrene was found in human fatty tissue with a frequency of 100 percent. The study cited the use of "styrene-based disposable cups" as a possible common source of styrene contamination in humans.[54]

Because styrene is soluble in oil and ethanol, substances commonly found in foods and alcoholic beverages, consumers can ingest styrene when using polystyrene foam cups for certain food and drink. Styrene is toxic to humans, attacking the central and peripheral nervous systems. And although evidence exists that styrene causes cancer in animals, it has not yet been proven to cause cancer in humans.[55]

D. DISPOSAL

In addition to hazards associated with its production and use, polystyrene foam takes up valuable landfill space, poses a litter problem, takes hundreds of years to degrade and is a threat to wildlife when they ingest it.[56]

Polystyrene foam manufacturers have made attempts to recycle a small proportion of their products. Recycled foam can be used to make products such as cafeteria trays, trash containers, insulation and packaging materials, none of which can be recycled again.[57] However, because polystyrene foam is inexpensive to manufacture, the costs of transporting and collecting the used foam outweigh the benefits of recycling it. So industry groups have subsidized recycling programs to create a market for the recycled foam. And because what little polystyrene is collected and recycled is not used to make new burger boxes, a continuous demand for nonrecycled polystyrene foam exists.[58] Furthermore, recycling does not eliminate the environmental and health hazards associated with polystyrene production or use.

E. ALTERNATIVES

Alternatives to polystyrene foam products are readily available. Durable, reusable items, including ceramic cups and plates are the best alternative. Recycled paper and other biodegradables are also available.[59]

III. RECYCLING PROGRAMS FOR STUDENTS

Students in schools around the country have success-fully implemented recycling projects from a one-time aluminum can drive to a business that raises $40,000 a year. Five different approaches to school-based recycling programs are described in this section.[60] Students are encouraged to select a program to fit the needs of their school and/or community. Efforts to reduce the use of certain products and reuse others can be made a part of several of the following recy-cling programs.

A. ANALYZE THE COMMUNITY AND SCHOOL WASTE STREAMS

Obtain data from the local Sanitation, Public Works or Environmental Resources Department to determine the characteristics of municipal solid waste in your community. Analyze the types of waste that make up the community solid waste stream. Determine how solid waste is managed in your community, including what percentage goes to landfills, incineration and recycling. Find out if your community ships its garbage to other states.

Analyze the school waste stream by conducting a survey of products bought for the school. Determining what is thrown away can be done by determining what is bought in the first place. Meet with school personnel responsible for buying products for building maintenance, the cafeteria, administrative offices and classrooms to find out what products are purchased regularly for the school. You do not have to rummage through trash cans to determine how many aluminum cans the cafeteria buys, and throws away, each day.

B. RESEARCH STATE AND LOCAL WASTE MANAGEMENT LAWS AND PROGRAMS

Find out about recycling programs in your communi-ty, who operates them and what items are included. Recycling may be mandated by the state or local government or may be completely operated by private businesses or community groups.

Obtain copies of any city, county or state laws on recycling or solid waste disposal plans. Check require-ments against actual implementation and find out what percentage of the community participates. Contact the government officials in charge of enforc-ing the laws and write a summary of their activities, rating their effectiveness. Find out if it is possible for the community to recycle more of the waste stream than is mandated by law. For private recycling pro-grams, obtain information about the convenience of drop off centers, operating hours, and other pertinent information.

C. CHOOSE A RECYCLING PROGRAM

Each of the programs described below requires different amounts of time and energy and depends on the types of recyclables appropriately included and the space available for storage of recyclables at the school. Whether community recycling programs exist, and what kinds, will also affect your choice. Students are encouraged to select one program to fit the needs of their school and/or community. Consult the EPA's *School Recycling Programs: A Handbook for Educa-tors*, on which the following ideas are based.

Materials used at school

Organize an on-going recycling program for materials used and thrown away at school. If your community has a recycling program and the school does not yet participate, organize your program to work with the community program.

One-time recycling for materials from home

Organize a one-time or occasional recycling drive for recyclables from home, including aluminum cans, newspapers and glass bottles. Arrange for a private recycling company to pick them up from the school or arrange for volunteers to transport the materials to a community-run recycling center or collection site or to a private recycling company.

This project is necessary, of course, only if your community has no recycling program for residences. Or you can organize for collection of items not included in the community program, provided you find a market for the recyclables first. For instance, if the community program does not accept telephone books, organize an annual drive to collect out-of-date phone books and ask the telephone company to help find a recycler. Midlothian Middle School in Richmond, Virginia holds an annual aluminum can drive which in 1987 raised more than $2,000 for the school's science department.[61]

Ongoing recycling for materials from home

Another option involves setting up a permanent, in-school collection center for recyclables generated at home. If your community has a curbside recycling program or a drop-off center, this project would apply only to recyclable items not included in the community program and for which a market is readily available.

This type of program requires that the school provide a storage space for the collected recyclables. Berkeley Elementary School in Williamsburg, Virginia, converted an old storage shed into a collection site for aluminum cans brought in from the community.[62] Arrange to have the recyclables collected from the school fairly frequently either by volunteers who will take them to recycling centers in nearby communities or by a private company which will buy or accept the materials.

An in-school, long-term recycling program requires careful planning and the continuous involvement of students and school staff. At the same time it offers students an invaluable experience in organizing and managing a project and an opportunity to see the results of efforts on a daily or weekly basis.

Establish an ongoing account with a local recycling center

Another option is to arrange a program through a local recycling center. Students and parents bring their recyclables directly to the center at their convenience. If the recycling center is private and pays for recyclables, your school can set up an account with the center so that payments for materials brought in by students and their families are directly credited to your school.

This option does not require you to set up storage space or handle recyclables at school. It is important, however, to provide a base at school for the recycling drive. Classroom activities and school publicity will reinforce recycling lessons and increase participation. If the school informs the community of its drive, residents may donate recyclables at the center for the school account.

Set up a community collection point at school

This option entails setting up a collection center at your school that the entire community can use. Since schools often serve as focal points for local residents, they can be ideal drop-off points for recycling. Mercer Island High School in Mercer Island, Washington, has run a community recycling program since 1975 which accepts paper, glass, aluminum and tin cans and newspapers. As of 1990, the program served 21,000 residents and raised $40,000 a year. Students staff and manage the recycling center and the money raised pays their part-time salaries. The recycling effort also pays for student activities, environmental speakers, trips, projects and student scholarships.[63]

Identify a storage facility at the school where individuals can drop off their recyclables in an easily accessible place, such as a parking lot. Either arrange for pickup of the collected items or enlist school and community members to transport the collected materials to a recycling company. Since this program directly involves the community and depends on the support of its residents, it will be important to reach these people in your publicity efforts.

D. FIND A MARKET

If no city, county or state recycling program exists, you will have to find companies to take or buy the recyclable items. Some products, such as high grade paper, are frequently in demand. For others, including newspapers, it may be more difficult to find a market. Check the yellow pages for private companies to whom you can sell or give the materials. Look under such headings as "recycling", "waste paper", "scrap" or "junk."

For aluminum cans check with local stores that sell canned beverages. The aluminum industry encourages recycling programs, so many stores participate in the programs and collect and pay for used cans.

E. DECIDE WHAT MATERIALS TO INCLUDE

Materials commonly included in recycling programs are aluminum cans (soda and beverage cans); bi-metal cans (made of aluminum and tin or steel and tin and used for packaging food, fruit, vegetables and juice); paper, including newspaper, high quality paper and corrugated cardboard; glass bottles and jars; and yard refuse. Base your decisions on the information you have gathered about recycling programs in your community as well as the available market.

Before you decide to recycle an item, first determine if it can be replaced with a durable, reusable product. For example, if teachers use polystyrene foam or paper cups for coffee or tea, replace them with reusable cups instead of recycling the paper or polystyrene foam. Students in West Milford, New Jersey replaced environmentally damaging polystyrene foam cafeteria trays with paper ones until they found out that washable reusable trays were less expensive in the long run.

If the school has much yard waste — grass clippings and leaves — a simple and cost-effective way to recycle them is to create a compost pile. The resulting material can be used for mulch at the school or in community gardens. Food waste from the cafeteria also can be composted.

F. COORDINATE WITH COMMUNITY RECYCLING PROGRAMS

Identify other organizations in the community that regularly recycle. If an existing volunteer group conducts a recycling drive, avoid competing with its efforts. The group may depend on its program for funding sources and enough garbage most likely exists for everyone to recycle.

G. WORK OUT A BUDGET

Setting up any recycling program will involve some costs, however, these costs can often be recovered from the operation of the program. Find out if your school budget can cover the costs of launching the program. If no school start-up funds are available, investigate other possible sources of funding, such as the PTA, service clubs, civic organizations and local businesses.

H. ESTABLISH A COLLECTION AND STORAGE SYSTEM

Contact the local health or public works department to find out about local ordinances that may apply to school recycling programs. Contact fire marshals regarding safe storage procedures and regulations if you are considering an in-school program. For example, if you are considering recycling paper, ask if any specific storage requirements must be followed to prevent fire hazards.

To keep the program running efficiently, your collection system needs to be as simple and organized as possible. Depending on the type of program you have chosen, designate deposit locations, either within or outside your school. Acquire, label and place appropriate containers for the collected recyclables.

If storing recyclables at school, provide ample storage space, preferably with truck access. Use a shed, garage, or even a receptacle specially designed for your type of recyclable(s). For example, some glass recyclers use an igloo structure and aluminum can recyclers often provide special dumpster storage bins. Students can crush cans before they are stored, so they will take up less space.

Materials also need to be separated properly. For example, newspaper often needs to be separated from magazines and other glossy paper. Newspaper, high grade paper (letter paper and photocopying paper) and boxes are processed separately and must be sorted separately. Glass containers usually are processed by color — clear, brown and green — and must be sorted that way. Follow carefully the requirements of the community program or private company with whom you deposit the recyclables.

I. EDUCATE THE SCHOOL AND THE COMMUNITY ABOUT THE PROGRAM

Publicity is essential to the success of any recycling program. Announce your plans to the community if you are planning one of the programs that include outside involvement. Send press releases to newspapers and radio stations, and place announcements in weekly shopper guides, on local bulletin boards and in newsletters to help inform the surrounding community. States and communities may be willing to be partners in promoting your school recycling program, so check with municipal or state officials about special publications they have developed about recycling.

At a regular school assembly or a meeting called especially for this purpose, describe to students and staff how the program will run and what they can do to participate. If you cannot make arrangements for a large meeting, hand out flyers and hold small class discussions. Display examples of recyclables and storage containers. To make sure that the recycling program does not interfere with class schedules or create conflicts, schedule a regular time for collection.

BIBLIOGRAPHY

Characterization of Municipal Solid Waste In the United States: 1990 Update. Washington, DC: U.S. Environmental Protection Agency, 1990.

Corson, Walter H. *The Global Ecology Handbook: What You Can Do About the Environmental Crisis*. Boston: Beacon Press, 1990.

Dadd, Debra Lynn and Andre Carothers. "A Bill of Goods?: Green Consuming in Perspective," *Greenpeace*. May/June 1990.

Dumanoski, Dianne. "McDonald's to Banish Foam Boxes," *The Boston Globe*. November 2, 1990.

Facts to Act On: Are Styrene Food and Beverage Containers a Health Hazard? Washington, DC: Institute for Local Self-Reliance, 1990. Release #5.

"Is Styrofoam Clean?," *Everyone's Backyard*. Citizen's Clearinghouse for Hazardous Waste. December 1990.

Let's Reduce and Recycle: Curriculum for Solid Waste Act Awareness. Washington, DC: Environmental Protection Agency, 1990.

Lipsett, Brian. "Plastics Industry Grasps for Straws," *Everyone's Backyard*. Citizen's Clearinghouse for Hazardous Waste. January/February 1990.

"McDonald's Surrenders," *Everyone's Backyard*. December 1990.

Naar, Jon. *Design For a Livable Planet: How You Can Help Clean Up the Environment*. New York: Harper and Row Publishers, 1990.

Nader, Ralph. "Big Consumer," *Mother Jones*. November/December 1990.

Nader, Ralph, Eleanor J. Lewis and Eric Weltman of the Government Purchasing Project. Testimony before the Subcommittee on Oversight of Government Management of the Senate Governmental Affairs Committee. November 8, 1991.

Nonhazardous Waste: State Management of Municipal Landfills and Landfill Expansions. Washington, DC: General Accounting Office, 1989.

Packaging: Solid Waste Action Paper #2. Washington, DC: Environmental Action Foundation, 1990.

Pardue, Leslie. "Biodegradable Plastics: A Contradiction in Terms?" *E Magazine*. April 1990.

"Plastic Pollution: Front-End and Back," *Environmental Action*. July/August 1988.

"Plastics in Packaging," *Environmental Action*. July/August 1988.

Pollock, Cynthia. *Mining Urban Wastes: The Potential for Recycling*. Washington, DC: Worldwatch Institute, 1987.

Pollock, Cynthia, "Realizing Recycling's Potential," *State of the World*. Washington, DC: Worldwatch Institute, 1988.

Polystyrene - Styrofoam Fact Sheet. Barre, VT: Vermonters Organized for Cleanup, 1988.

Rifkin, Jeremy, ed. *The Green Lifestyle Handbook: 1001 Ways You Can Heal the Earth*. New York: Henry Holt and Co., 1990.

School Recycling Programs: A Handbook for Educators. Washington, DC: U.S. Environmental Protection Agency, 1990.

Science or PR?: Solid Waste Action Paper #1. Washington, DC: Environmental Action Foundation, 1990.

Styrofoam Fact Sheet. Falls Church, VA: Citizen's Clearinghouse for Hazardous Waste, 1988.

"Styrofoam Wars: Stamping Out Toxic Food Packaging," *E Magazine*. April 1990.

Waste: Choices for Communities. Washington, DC: Concern, Inc., 1988.

ACTIVITY EIGHT:
A STUDY OF REPRESENTATIVENESS IN THE JURY SELECTION PROCESS

INTRODUCTION

Members of the rap music group *2 Live Crew* were arrested and charged with violating Florida obscenity laws in June 1991, in Fort Lauderdale, Florida after they performed songs from an album that a Federal judge previously had declared obscene. The group's lawyer, Bruce Rogow, argued that his clients could not receive a fair trial with a jury chosen only from the list of registered voters, which is the method of jury selection in Florida courts. Since young people and minorities register to vote at a much lower rate than other segments of the population, Rogow maintained that a jury selected from registered voters could not represent a true cross-section of the community, which U.S. law requires.[1]

Rogow argued that a representative jury was especially important in this case because the obscenity charge required the jury to apply "community standards" in deciding what is obscene. Rogow suggested that potential jurors also be selected from drivers license lists to reach more African Americans and young people. As jury selection progressed, the presiding judge decided to select the jury from a larger number of people than usual. However, only three African Americans were among the 70 prospective jurors called, and one was excused.[2]

Trial by jury is a cornerstone of our democratic legal system. To be most effective, the jury must be representative of the community. Writes Paul Hudson in *Young People Not Welcome*, "[W]ithout this representative cross-section on a jury, justice will be determined by the few instead of by the entire community in the manner it was intended."[3] The exclusion of groups of people, for example young people or minority groups (as in the case of *2 Live Crew*), can alienate these groups from the legal and judicial systems and can "lead to a further erosion of respect for the judicial system and the law in general."[4]

The purpose of this activity is to learn about the history and functions of the jury system and to survey your community's jury selection process. If the current selection system does not produce a representative cross-section of potential jurors, students can recommend changes for their community. Students might want to start by observing a jury trial, sitting in on an orientation session for jurors or asking the court's representative to speak with students. The survey is based on a study conducted by college students working with New York Public Interest Research Group (NYPIRG).

HISTORY OF THE JURY SYSTEM

The modern jury can be traced back to the Middle Ages when a jury was essentially a group of witnesses, usually neighbors of the defendant (the person accused of the crime). By the mid-18th century, juries acted only as judges of the facts, not witnesses themselves, much like today's jury.[5]

American colonists were subject to English law which included the right to trial by jury in most cases. The jury provided a safeguard for colonists charged with political crimes. For example, in 1670, William Penn was charged with illegal speech and assembly. Most colonists believed that Penn was charged because the King of England did not like his religious beliefs (Penn was a Quaker). The colonial jury found Penn not guilty, although the court threatened and eventually fined and punished the jurors (members of the jury).[6]

As tensions grew between the colonies and England, the King increasingly restricted the colonists' right to jury trial, using instead judges appointed by the King to decide court cases. In 1765, England passed the Stamp Act which placed a duty or tax on all legal documents, newspapers, pamphlets, college degrees and other documents.[7] The colonists strongly objected to passage of the Act, partly because the admiralty courts, which operated without juries, were given jurisdiction to enforce the Act.[8] In 1776, in the Declaration of Independence, American colonists listed among their grievances with England "depriving us, in many cases, the benefits of trial by jury."[9]

As the drafters of the federal and state constitutions for the new nation set about their work, they emphasized the importance of the jury trial. Article Three of the U.S. Constitution guarantees the right to trial by jury in criminal cases (those in which the government prosecutes an individual for breaking the law). But the Constitution did not include the right to trial by jury in civil cases (those in which one individual sues another for injury or damage). Civil juries were not included at least in part because Federalists, like Alexander Hamilton, believed that civil jury practice varied too widely from state to state to be included in the federal constitution. Furthermore, the framers did not include any other individual liberties (later added in the Bill of Rights) in the body of the Constitution.[10]

Lack of the civil jury as well as other individual liberties caused a controversy between Federalists and Anti-Federalists over whether or not to adopt the Constitution. Hamilton wrote that the Constitution's drafters did not mean to exclude the civil jury, rather that the individual states could best define that right in their state constitutions.[11] Eventually, in 1791, the controversy led to adoption of the Bill of Rights, the first 10 amendments to the Constitution. The Sixth Amendment reaffirms the right to trial by jury in criminal cases and the Seventh Amendment guarantees that right in civil jury trials.[12]

Juries originally consisted of 12 jurors and required a unanimous verdict. In the early 1970s, the Supreme Court upheld the legality of six-person juries and non-unanimous verdicts in civil cases.[13] Studies have shown that these measures have not saved time or money, the reasons for which they were adopted. Instead, smaller juries are less representative of the community and non-unanimous verdicts allow jurors to pay less attention to minority or dissenting views.[14]

Although the principle of trial by jury was considered of utmost importance by the authors of the Constitu-

tion, they were not equally concerned that the jury be representative of the community or even consist of the accused's true peers. Racial minorities, particularly African Americans, women and people under the age of 21 were excluded consistently from jury service, as they were from most rights of citizenship which applied only to white male property owners over the age of 21.

In 1965, the Supreme Court ruled unconstitutional a practice of systematic exclusion of members of one race from a jury pool.[15] And in 1975, the Court ruled that Louisiana's practice of excluding women from juries was not legal.[16] Congress passed the Jury Selection and Service Act of 1968 to ensure that all citizens with cases before federal courts have the right to juries selected at random from a fair cross-section of the community and that no citizen can be excluded from jury service on account of race, color, religion, sex, national origin or economic status.[17] Although Congress and the courts have ruled illegal the most blatant forms of discrimination, the jury selections process may still result in a less than representative jury panel.

Jury service is a mandatory civic duty; it is illegal in most jurisdictions to fail to respond to a summons for jury duty.[18] While many citizens called for jury duty ask to be excused for a variety of reasons, those who do serve are glad they did. The Center for Jury Studies of the National Center for State Courts interviewed jurors after trial and found that 90 percent of them viewed the experience favorably.[19]

FUNCTIONS AND IMPORTANCE OF THE JURY SYSTEM

A jury reflects the attitudes and mores of the community from which it is drawn. It lives only for the day and does justice according to its lights. The group of 12 who are drawn to hear a case, makes the decision and melts away. It is not present the next day to be criticized. It is the one governmental agency that has no ambition. It is as human as the people who make it up. It is sometimes the victim of passions. But it also takes the sharp edges off a law and uses conscience to ame-

liorate a hardship. Since it is of and from the community, it gives the law an acceptance which verdicts of judges could not do.[20]

So wrote the late U.S. Supreme Court Justice William O. Douglas about the important functions of the jury in a democracy. Jury trials serve as the conscience of the community, as a check on official power, as a means of disclosure of information to the public and as an opportunity for citizens to participate directly in the implementation of the laws of their country.

Juries bring the conscience of the community, reflecting its values and standards, to the legal system. For example, juries sometimes "bend" the law to achieve justice in individual cases, a function of juries the Supreme Court has repeatedly upheld. Jury nullification results when juries reach verdicts which do not follow the law the judge says is governing. Northern juries often "bent" the law to acquit (find not guilty) abolitionists who, in helping slaves escape, were charged with violating fugitive slave laws.[21]

The Supreme Court has recognized in numerous decisions that an important function of the jury system is to act as a check on official power.[22] Instead of a decision being made by one person, a judge, who could be biased, prejudiced or politically motivated, jury decisions are made by a group of citizens from the community. And because juries meet in secret and only temporarily, juries find it less difficult than a judge to make unpopular decisions, further ensuring that power is not abused.

In civil cases where citizens seek compensation for injury or harm (personal injury suits), the jury plays a powerful role in deterring future unsafe practices. Author Joanne Doroshow writes, "It is well recognized that automobile and other product manufacturers, hospitals, pharmaceutical companies and other defendants in personal injury actions have redesigned products, improved medical care and taken other steps to improve or save lives following jury trials and verdicts."[23]

In personal injury suits involving corporate negligence or wrongdoing, jury trials can result in large money awards to victims. But jurors are not only compensat-

ing victims, they are sending a message to wrongdoers that certain types of conduct will not be tolerated in the community.[24] For example, the foreman of the Houston, Texas jury which assessed $10.53 billion against Texaco for improperly interfering with a merger between Pennzoil Co. and Getty Oil, said, "We wanted to send a message to corporate America that they can't get away with this type of action and not be punished."[25] Because corporations cannot predict the amount of money a jury might award in the event of wrongdoing, it is in the interest of the corporation to change its behavior. It is the unpredictability of jury awards that serves to deter corporate wrongdoing.[26]

Disclosure of information during a personal injury trial can inform millions of people through the mass media of important information about specific dangerous products, unsafe workplaces and other wrongdoing.[27]

But 90 percent of civil trials are not personal injury suits and U.S. citizens rely on the civil jury system to decide all kinds of cases such as violations of civil rights.[28]

Jury duty gives citizens an opportunity to participate in government. Deciding matters of law by jury also makes the law of the people, because the people have a role in applying it.[29] Author Marlene Adler Marks writes in *The Suing of America*, "The use of lawsuits is an affirmation that the individual can fight against big corporations, the government, his own employer, the faceless bureaucracies that rule his life — that he has equal power against his adversaries through the courts."[30]

CRITICISMS OF THE JURY SYSTEM

Most criticism of the jury system has focused on the civil jury. Critics of the civil jury system argue that jurors cannot understand complex cases, that jury verdicts are arbitrary and based on emotions and that jury trials are too inefficient and costly.[31] But as the Supreme Court has upheld, and as constitutional scholar Charles Wolfram writes, the nation's founders "were not arguing for the institution of civil jury trial in the belief that jury trials were short, inexpensive, decorous and productive of the same decisions that judges sitting without juries would produce. The inconveniences of jury trial were accepted precisely because in important instances, through its ability to disregard substantive rules of laws, the jury would reach a result that the judge either could not or would not reach."[32] Furthermore, numerous studies refute these criticisms.

Professors Valerie P. Hans and Neil Vidmar find that juror incompetence is rare. Instead, because jurors can pool their collective memories, they can remember far more than one person alone.[33] And jury scholars Harry Kalven and Hans Zeisel found "much evidence that most people, once actually serving in a trial, become highly serious and responsible toward their task and toward the joint effort to deliberate through to a verdict."[34] Furthermore, judges can assist juries in understanding complex cases by allowing them to take notes on testimony and allowing them to ask questions as the case proceeds.[35]

Joanne Doroshow writes in *Safeguarding a Pillar of Democracy*, "[D]espite some administrative burdens associated with juries, the frustrations of some jurors and the occasional unsound jury verdict, the consensus among judges, lawyers and jurors themselves is that the system works extremely well. Jurors, representative members of the community randomly chosen to sit in judgment of others, deliberate carefully, render competent and just verdicts, and then fade anonymously back into the community."[36]

Critics argue jurors allow emotions and sentimentality to enter their decisions, resulting in unjust monetary awards in personal injury suits.[37] Many studies refute this charge.[38] Moreover, jury verdicts have remained stable in constant dollars since the late 1950s.[39] Furthermore, large awards (such as over one million dollars) are infrequent and are often reduced by the court.[40]

Another criticism of the jury system is that it contributes to delay in the justice system since jury selection can add two or more days to trial time. According to 1980 statistics, 77 percent of non-jury trials were completed in three days or less, compared to 60 percent of jury trials. But again, speed was not the reason given by the nation's founders for insisting on the right to trial by jury.[41]

A coalition of corporate lobbies and insurance companies launched advertising campaigns during the 1980s to advocate weakening the civil jury system "to prevent consumers from obtaining jury verdicts against corporations that place dangerous products in the marketplace or workplace."[42] One court considered these ads "jury tampering" because the ads "might convince some jurors to arbitrarily reduce personal injury awards."[43]

However, corporate lobbies and insurance companies advocate a number of measures to weaken civil juries. These include caps on the amount of money a jury may award, restrictions and limits on the amount of punitive damages a jury may award, limits on lawyers' contingency fees (when lawyers collect a percentage of the award upon winning the case) which provides many victims with access to civil jury trials, mandatory mediation before or in place of a jury trial and product liability legislation to protect manufacturers from liability from injuries caused by unsafe products.[44]

JURY SELECTION PROCESSES

The process for selecting jurors and methods of serving varies from state to state and jurisdiction to jurisdiction. Generally, the courts choose a list or lists of citizens in the area and send out questionnaires to eliminate wrong addresses and people who cannot serve because of their health, the nature of their job, criminal record or some other factor determined by the court. The names left on the list are called the jury pool. The courts then choose a random sample of names from the jury pool to summon for jury service.

Once jurors are called to serve, they undergo a final process, called *voir dire*, in which they are questioned to determine if they have a personal interest in the case or have beliefs or prejudices that would make them biased and therefore unfit to serve (challenge for cause). The lawyers in the case may also make peremptory challenges (eliminate a number of potential jurors for no reason).[45]

Selection of the Source List(s)

Historically, voter lists have been the main source of names used to call citizens for jury duty. However, courts that use only the voter list are likely to exclude a large number of young people, low-income people, minority groups and many others who register to vote at lower rates than other segments of the population.[46] For example, a 1976 NYPIRG study of the Broome County, New York jury selection process, which used only the voter registration list, found that the average juror was 10.4 years older than the average Broome County citizen eligible for jury service.[47] (See the tables on page 271).

Reliance on voter registration lists often excludes college students, who have voting residences in other counties.[48] College students are not selected at their permanent homes where they register to vote because they do not meet residency requirements and are not selected at school because they are not registered to vote there.

Today, in addition to voter lists, many state and local courts use drivers license lists, city directories, telephone books, local census lists and lists of real property and income taxpayers, welfare recipients, high school graduates, naturalized citizens, hunting licenses, utility customers and dog licenses.[49] The federal census, tax and social security lists are not available by law.[50] Some lists can produce unexpected results. For example, when a Kansas court used the state census list, a dog was summoned for jury duty because the census taker had used names from mailboxes.[51]

Officials may argue that using more than one list is too expensive and that combining lists is difficult. However, lists can be combined by computer easily and at relatively little cost.[52] As of 1986, nine states used merged voters and drivers lists statewide. These two lists are merged with some other list in three more states and courts in nine other states use some combination of lists.[53]

In general, the addition of the drivers list helps to ensure that young people and minorities are included,

because in most jurisdictions, more people are licensed to drive than are registered to vote.[54]

A 1990 study found that 45 percent of adults in the United States had been summoned for jury duty at least once, up from 35 percent in 1984.[55] The increase is attributed to the increasing use of drivers and other lists in selecting the jury pool and the adoption of the one day/one trial system which allows jurors to fulfill their jury duty obligation in one day, if not assigned to a trial, or for the length of the trial. According to the National Center for State Courts, approximately 22 percent of all jurisdictions in the United States have adopted this rule.[56] The use of more than one list also helps ensure that people will not avoid registering to vote to avoid serving jury duty.[57]

To accurately reflect the community, a source list should be both representative and inclusive. "Inclusiveness refers to the percentage of the population that is on the lists. If all eligible citizens are on the list, the list is totally inclusive ... Representativeness is the degree to which a less than fully inclusive list mirrors the characteristics of the total population," write G. Thomas Munsterman and Janice T. Munsterman of the National Center for State Courts.[58]

The use of more than one list does not automatically guarantee a representative or inclusive source list. Increasing inclusiveness can sometimes make a list less representative.[59] For example, if the court uses the list of local property owners, it may exclude the same groups excluded by the voter list, resulting in a jury pool less representative than using only the voter list.[60] The National Center for State Courts' standards suggest that "officials responsible for preparing the source list are strongly encouraged to make it as inclusive as possible given financial and statutory limitations."[61]

Other Factors Affecting Representative Juries

Once the source lists(s) is chosen, "the processes of summoning, qualification and excusal can undo the benefits provided by the use of multiple lists."[62] The jury will be less representative if the source list(s) is inaccurate, with a large number of wrong names and addresses, if the court allows a large number of excusals from jury service and if the court does not enforce summons calling potential jurors to serve.[63] Furthermore, the jury pool (the names from which potential jurors are drawn) must be updated frequently to accurately reflect new residents.[64]

A number of other factors can contribute to a lack of a representative cross-section of the community ending up in the jury pool. These factors include lack of child care facilities, a low or nonexistent jury stipend and lack of or low transportation reimbursement. No child care facilities or compensation can act to exclude women with young families.[65] Lack of transportation reimbursement makes jury service difficult or impossible for potential jurors without private automobile transportation.[66]

Many people cannot afford to serve if their employer does not pay their salary while they are on jury duty.[67] Jury stipends are often so small that employed persons find jury service a serious financial hardship, unless their employer pays their regular salary. Most large businesses pay their employee's regular salary during jury service; however, self-employed persons, small businesspersons, hourly wage earners and others cannot make up their lost income.[68]

Direct discrimination in jury selection based on occupation or economic class is unconstitutional.[69] However, the NYPIRG study found that the employees of certain corporations were greatly over-represented on the jury panels in proportion to their representation in the jury-age population.[70] In Broome County those corporations over-represented generally have policies to encourage jury service and continue to pay employees' full salary while they serve as jurors.[71] Consequently, people who did not work for one of these corporations were under-represented on the jury panels.

CONDUCTING THE STUDY

Do jury selection practices in your community underrepresent any segment of the population? Typically, young people, students, persons not employed by large companies and non-voters do not serve on juries in proportion to their numbers in the community. The purpose of this survey is to determine if a statistical disparity exists between the representation of various groups in the population and their representation on jury panels and to determine how the jury selection process results in such disparities.

The NYPIRG study, on which this survey is based, found that in Broome County, New York, jury selection practices which use only the voter list and update the jury pool infrequently gave "strong preference to persons between 50 and 60 years of age, men, long-standing residents and persons employed in salaried positions for certain large business corporations."[72]

A. DETERMINE THE JURY SELECTION PROCESS FOR YOUR COMMUNITY

Find out who administers the jury selection process in your area. This office is typically called the jury commissioner. Determine what state, county or city requirements apply to the court's responsibility for selecting jurors. NYPIRG researchers found most of the data for their study by sending a questionnaire (see below for a sample questionnaire) and interviewing the jury commissioner as well as consulting population statistics.

Check your library for *Population and Housing Characteristics*, published by the Bureau of the Census of the Department of Commerce, which gives a breakdown of the population of every county in a state by age, sex and race. Statistics for each state are in a separate volume and are updated every 10 years to reflect new census data. Individual volumes can be purchased from the Government Printing Office in Washington, DC.

Describe each step of the jury selection process in your community (up to the stage where potential jurors are called for a specific trial). The steps generally include: 1) selection of a source list(s); 2) mailing of questionnaires to determine who on the source list(s) is not eligible for jury service (in general, a juror must be a U.S. citizen, a resident of the court's jurisdiction, 18 years of age, able to read and write English and have no felony or serious misdemeanor conviction); 3) random selection of names for specific trial terms; 4) summons to appear at the courthouse; and 5) excusal or disqualification from jury service.[73]

B. SURVEY LOCAL BUSINESSES TO DETERMINE COMPENSATION PRACTICES FOR EMPLOYEES SERVING JURY DUTY

In the NYPIRG study, the student researchers telephoned each of the major employers in the area to find out their policies on compensating employees serving jury duty. Include the school system in your survey to find out what compensation is available for teachers and principals. This information will help determine if workers who are compensated are over-represented and workers who are not compensated by their employers are under-represented in the makeup of the community's juries. Also ask each business how many people it employs so you can compare the representation of various-sized businesses in the community to their representation on jury panels.

C. COMPARE DATA TO POPULATION STATISTICS

Compare and correlate data obtained from the jury commissioner with population statistics to determine the representation of the following factors on jury panels and in the general population: age, gender, occupation, education, geographic area, income and place of employment. Chart the data in tables as indicated in the examples from the NYPIRG study on pages 271.

The NYPIRG study found that young people (aged 18 to 30) made up 29 percent of the jury-age population, but only 7 percent of the jury panelists. The 51 to 60 age group, only 17 percent of the jury-age population, made up 35 percent of those serving on juries.[74]

If your survey uncovers disparities in representation of certain groups in the population, the next step is to determine what aspect of the jury selection process results in the disparity. Examine the source list(s), the frequency with which the source list(s) is updated, the potential juror questionnaire, the summons enforcement practices, the method of excusal, the stipend for lost income, compensation for transportation expenses and the availability of child care.

To test the source list for inclusiveness, compare it to population figures of the jurisdiction for the appropriate age groups.[75] Be aware, however, that the list(s) may include people who have moved or list names more than once.[76] Thus the number of names on such a list does not necessarily mean it is inclusive. The number of names on a source list can even exceed the number of persons living in the jurisdiction.[77]

RESULTS AND RECOMMENDATIONS

Find out who has the authority to change the jury selection process, for example, the city council, the jury board or the state legislature. No one list or combination of lists will serve all needs, therefore each community must determine for itself what is the best means for achieving inclusiveness and representativeness.[78] The National Center for State Courts has written standards to assist courts in ensuring that the selection process is inclusive and representative.[79]

Make recommendations based on the needs of your community. Propose specific changes. Call on local employers to support the jury system by compensating their employees serving jury duty. The NYPIRG study made the following recommendations:[80]

1. Expansion of the jury pool using source lists other than the voting list, in which younger persons, students, lower income and minority groups are greatly under-represented, could eliminate a major source of discrimination.

2. Raising jury stipends would allow citizens who do not work for a large corporation or are not independently wealthy to serve on a jury.

3. Provide jurors with transportation expenses.

4. Child care or day care reimbursement for jurors with young children would allow more young women to serve on juries.

5. The Jury Commissioner should encourage students and all eligible persons to serve on juries. Likewise, the Commissioner should stop employers, teachers, school administrators and others from discouraging

jury service. This is particularly important for groups such as students, who have generally been excluded from jury service in the past.

6. Reducing the number of jurors excused from jury duty would increase the pool from which jurors are selected. The Jury Commissioner should revise rules for excusing jurors to eliminate excusals for reasons of inconvenience.

7. The jury pool should be updated frequently and names of jurors who have already served should not be placed back in the jury pool immediately.

You might also want to consider the following:

8. Ask local officials to declare a "Jury Appreciation Week" to give recognition to the importance of jury service. Contact the American Board of Trial Advocates for more information.[81]

9. If your area does not use the one day/one trial method of jury service or does not allow jurors to call in each day to determine whether or not they need to be present; ask local officials to implement these methods.

10. If a low percentage of those summoned for jury service report to the court, ask local officials to review summons enforcement.

Table I. Broome County Jury Panel Statistics, 1974[82]

Age of Panel	No. of Jurors	Percentage of Panel
21-30	42	2%
31-40	148	7%
41-50	543	29%
51-60	718	38%
61-70	425	23%
Total	**1,876**	**99%**

Average Age 53.1 years old

Table II. Broome County Census Statistics, 1970

Age	No. of People	Percentage of Population
21-30	29,277	24%
31-40	23,964	19%
41-50	27,237	22%
51-60	24,003	19%
61-70	17, 045	14%
Total	**121,526**	**98%**

Average Age 42.7 years old
Note: 18-20 year-olds were not eligible for service at the time of selection of these panels.

Table III. Jury Panel by Age and Sex, 1974

	Males		Females	
Age	No. of People	% of Panel	No. of People	% of Panel
21-30	26	1.3%	16	.8%
31-40	103	5.5%	45	2.3%
41-50	324	17.2%	219	11.6%
51-60	383	20.5%	335	17.8%
61-70	220	11.7%	205	10.7%
Total	**1,056**	**56.2%**	**820**	**43.2%**

Table IV. Population by Age and Sex, 1970

	Males		Females	
Age	No. of People	% of Popul.	No. of People	% of Popul.
21-30	13,849	11.4%	15,428	12.6%
31-40	11,761	9.7%	12,203	10.0%
41-50	13,055	10.7%	14,182	11.6%
51-60	1139	89.3%	12,605	10.7%
61-70	7,531	6.2%	9,514	7.8%
Total	**57,594**	**47.3%**	**63,932**	**52.7%**

QUESTIONNAIRE FOR JURY COMMISSIONER

➤ What type of source list(s) is used; for example, voter registration, drivers license?

_____

➤ How often is the source list(s) updated?

_____

➤ How are names randomly selected from the source list(s)?

_____

➤ What is the response rate to jury questionnaires and how are the returned questionnaires processed?

_____

_____

➤ What questions are asked on the questionnaire that might exclude potential jurors, for example, residency, citizenship, age, criminal record?

_____

_____

➤ How can people be excused from jury service and what proportion are excused?

_____

➤ What compensation, if any, does the court offer for transportation and lost pay?

_____

➤ What is the demographic breakdown of members of jury panels, in percentages of jurors according to age, gender, occupation, place of employment, education level, income and race?

_____

_____

➤ Do procedures exist to ensure that jurors do not serve too often?

_____

BIBLIOGRAPHY

Doroshow, Joanne. *Safeguarding a Pillar of Democracy: A Proposal for a National Association of Civil Jurors.* Washington, DC: Center for Study of Responsive Law, 1992.

Hudson, Paul. *Young People Not Welcome: A Study of Discrimination in Broome County's Jury Selection Process.* New York: New York Public Interest Research Group, 1976.

Munsterman, G. Thomas and Janice T. Munsterman. "The Search for Jury Representativeness," *The Justice System Journal.* Vol. 11. No. 1. 1986.

The Official American Board of Trial Advocates Handbook for Planning City Tour Bill of Rights/Jury Appreciation Ceremonies Encino, CA: American Board of Trial Advocates, 1992.

Rimer, Sara. "Rap Group's Lawyer Challenges Selection of Jury," *The New York Times.* October 11, 1991.

Standards Relating to Juror Use and Management. Williamsburg, VA: National Center for State Courts, 1982.

ACTIVITY NINE: TIME DOLLARS

INTRODUCTION

Activity nine introduces the innovative concept of Time Dollars, or service credits, created by Dr. Edgar Cahn. A Time Dollar — one hour of your time exchanged for one hour of someone else's time — allows people to provide and receive needed services while creating a sense of community. A Time Dollar program can be set up using existing institutions or organizations as a base. For example, Time Dollar programs could transform neighborhood schools into centers of community activity where people of all ages receive and provide services. Or an existing organization within the school, such as Junior Achievement (a program involving thousands of students who run their own businesses), could serve as a base for students to provide community services such as an errand service or a visiting singing group for the elderly. The possibilities are limited only by your imagination.

This activity is excerpted from the book *Time Dollars: The New Currency That Enables Americans to Turn Their Hidden Resource — Time — Into Personal Security and Community Renewal* by Edgar Cahn and Jonathan Rowe.

WHAT ARE TIME DOLLARS AND HOW DO THEY WORK?

The Time Dollar is a currency that literally turns time into money. If you serve in a Time Dollar program, you earn credits for the time you spend helping other members. One hour of service earns you one credit — a service credit (or a Time Dollar). With that credit, you can "buy" an hour of a particular service that you need. If you don't need all the credits you earn, you can save them up. Or you can donate them to someone you know. Or you can give them back to the "bank," so that the people who run the program can make sure the members with the severest needs get all the help they require.

Time Dollar programs have grown up in all shapes and sizes, from the small program in a senior citizens building to a coalition of over half-a-dozen major organizations operating at over 30 different program sites. They all have one thing in common, however — a commitment to transform a group of strangers into a community.

Time Dollars embody the concept of reciprocal exchange: You help me and I'll help you. It's how healthy communities used to operate, before the money-driven market separated the realm of work from that of community. In the early settlements, neighbors had to help one another because there was no other way to survive. The barn raising, the harvesting of neighbors' fields, the quilting bees, and "breaking out" bees to open snow-blocked roads — these were not just nostalgic Currier and Ives conceits. They were daily necessities of frontier life.

Unlike traditional volunteer programs, Time Dollar programs recognize that people who need help, can often help others, too — just in different ways. Time Dollars take away the stigma of charity. Members who receive help are undertaking an obligation to repay the help if they can. Even housebound seniors can help another member, if only through "telephone reassurance" — a simple phone call to chat and make sure things are okay.

Resistance to accepting "charity" reflects more than stubborn pride. It reflects a basic need: the need to be needed, to give to others, to be valued. This need, rarely recognized by our traditional systems of caring for the elderly, shines through with amazing clarity when service credit volunteers are at work.

"People always tell you to call if ever you need help," says one Washington, D.C. service credit volunteer. "But then they'll be busy, or you just don't feel right disturbing them. I don't like to ask anybody for anything. But when I broke my hip and had to go to the hospital, I called and got someone to drive me home with the credits I had earned. I don't like to spend them much, though. It's like a last resort."

In many volunteer programs, volunteers are thought of as "extras." In the Time Dollar program, volunteers are part of the formal structure. This is one of the reasons that the drop-out rate for Time Dollar programs has been in the vicinity of 3 percent, as opposed to the roughly 40 percent drop-out rate for conventional volunteer programs.

There are now about 3,000 service credit volunteers at work in this country, in nine states and the District of Columbia. They are providing about 15,000 hours of service a month. Most of them are people over 60, but some are younger, including high school students.

As part of the Miami, Florida, Time Dollar program, students at Florida Memorial College broke ground so that senior citizens could plant vegetable or flower gardens. The students even built boxes on legs so that the seniors could garden without bending over. At the same time, the college needed dorm monitors, and day care for faculty kids. Students needed a home away from home. Soon, the planning committee held a test run that yielded vegetable gardens for the elderly and a Thanksgiving day turkey dinner for out-of-state college students. Other seniors in the Miami Time Dollar program tutor elementary school students.

In Washington, DC, high school students are using service credits to satisfy a community service requirement for graduation. At other Time Dollar programs, high school students are mowing lawns or painting houses for senior citizens, for example, and contributing their credits to other seniors who need them.

If governments and institutions ever embrace the concept of Time Dollars, the whole arena of public service can become a kind of bustling enterprise zone. Teenagers who earn credits helping seniors, for example, might use them to pay tuition at public colleges. Public housing tenants could use Time Dollars to pay part of their rents. People could defray part of their medical bills through Time Dollars earned by helping other sick people. Citizens could

pay part of their local property taxes in Time Dollars, so they'd lend a hand as well as just passing a buck.

STARTING A TIME DOLLAR PROGRAM

Starting a Time Dollar program in many ways is like starting a business. You need to decide what services you want to offer, who will provide them, who your customers will be, and how you will reach them. You need to develop a strategy to recruit your work force. You need a marketing plan to attract organizations and institutions that may need your services for their clients or members. And you have to worry about paying for things like rent, phone bills, photocopying, and the cost of whatever core administrative staff is needed to manage the enterprise.

The only thing you don't have to worry about is finding money to pay your "workers"; they earn Time Dollars. Most of them do, at least. You may have to secure the services of someone who has to be paid in dollars for at least part of his or her time. But more about that later.

I. PLANNING AND ORGANIZING THE PROGRAM

There are six steps to be completed here before your concept can become a reality.

Identify needs you will meet, the services you will provide and those you will serve.

No doubt you already have some idea of the particular need or social problem you want to address. That may mean more than you think it does. It means you suspect that a significant part of the need can be dealt with by peers or family or friends or neighbors provided their time can be mobilized on a sustained basis.

It means something else: You have an intuitive, gut sense of what you personally want to be involved in. Time Dollars will enable you to make a difference if you are willing to make the commitment yourself. So now you know what your "mission" is. The question is: How do you accomplish it?

You must now ask what these people who work with you will want to buy with those Time Dollars. If you produce child day care and they want child day care for themselves as well, then you need only produce that one service. If you produce home care for the elderly or transportation or translation services and that is what they will want, you need go no further. But if you think they will be more willing to help you if they can use the Time Dollars to purchase a different kind of service, then you have to find a way to make that happen. You can either add that second service to what your program provides or you can search for another person or group or organization to do so. Possibly you will be able to buy the services in exchange for what you produce.

Assess Your Community's Need

Several groups meeting over a period of months asked themselves two questions: What do people need? What kinds of services would people want to buy with the Time Dollars they earn? They came up with the three categories below. The list also serves as a practical guide in choosing areas of service to pursue.

It was understood that it would take several years before all of these services could actually become available. But it was useful to make projections because people could see how, over time, their Time Dollars would become more useful.

Services to Elderly	Services to Children	Educational Services
Adult day care	After-school day	Arts & Crafts
Advocacy	care	Certificate
Companionship	Babysitting	programs
Escort	Child development	Citizenship
Excursions	Home visiting	Entitlements
Gardening	Latch key	Entrepreneurial/
Home repairs	Preschool	management
Homemaker services	Prenatal	Establishing a day-care
Letter writing	School support services:	business
Light housekeeping	Cafeteria aide	Exercise classes
Meal Preparation	Classroom aide	First Aid
Pet care	Library aide	Literacy/English
Post-hospital	Monitor	Literacy/Spanish
discharge	Teacher's aide	Parenting classes
Reading	Tutor	Sewing classes
Religious	Sick-baby daycare	Special courses
Visitations	for working parents	Avocational
Respite Care		Continuing
Shopping		Education
Telephone		Weekend Institutes
assurance		Teen pregnancy
Translation		
Transportation		
Typing		

Intergenerational exchanges are clearly the next frontier for Time Dollars. Many elderly don't want to work with other elderly people; they want to pass on their affection and their traditions to the young. The need for affordable child day care is critical and growing. The synergy is there. It is bound to happen. The potential for home-based day care rather than care rendered at a center is great.

This table not only helps you decide what to produce, but it suggests what other services should be produced elsewhere so your "workers" can spend the Time Dollars they earn on something they really need or want. There may be some exciting possibilities you overlooked. Think about it. Brainstorm with others. Work with other groups. Trust your collective judgment.

A word of caution: Start with a limited range of services (two or three) that you are relatively sure you can deliver. That way people come to know the program, rely on it, and can identify it with a particular need. Do *not* try to launch an all-purpose, social service barter system to provide every conceivable kind of service and meet every conceivable kind of need. It won't work. You can't mount 15 new lines of service at the same time.

Choosing and Securing a Base

The base of operations depends on what you want to do. For example, you could operate it out of your own home or apartment if you plan to provide a neighbor-to-neighbor type service. But there are reasons why you might prefer to set up elsewhere.

Logistics

Time Dollar programs recruit volunteers, receive requests for service, match volunteers and recipients, keep track of hours, provide some form of quality control. All of this requires logistical support. Organizations and institutions normally have certain built-in capacities: phones, office space, staff, recognition, and record-keeping ability. They can usually provide support with little or no additional cost. Your own school or place of employment, worship or social activity may be just such a base.

Constituency-Orientation

Organizations normally are built around a mission. They have a client base, a membership, and a constituency that can be tapped. Congregations have elderly members; senior centers serve meals and provide services to the elderly; senior housing complexes have a built-in pool of volunteers and recipients; hospitals often discharge elderly patients who need a variety of non-medical support services. Securing an organizational base greatly facilitates the job of recruiting volunteers and generating requests for service.

Philosophy

Time Dollar programs are more than a service delivery system; they are a vehicle for recreating a sense of community. They tend to have names like Friend-to-Friend or Member-to-Member. No matter how long we live in one place or how close we live to one another, we often live as strangers. If you choose an organization as a base, you will be increasing the rewards and benefits of being associated with that institution. Creating a Time Dollar program means increasing the ways in which people can relate to each other. The base can be almost anywhere: a religious congregation, a veterans organization, a senior center, a community college, a community-oriented public school, a membership club or a block association. Time Dollar programs rebuild community. They tend to spin off efforts and activities for which people do not earn Time Dollars, like crime watch programs, food banks and informal neighbor-watching-out-for-neighbor systems. Here are some options and considerations when choosing the organizational base.

Start with One Organization or a Coalition?

Most of the original Time Dollar programs started by finding one organization with the interest, capability and energy to make a program work. In Miami, however, the organizers decided to create a coalition (they called it a consortium) in order to involve organizations from diverse ethnic groups, with sufficient geographic spread to offer county-wide coverage. The coalition method was slower getting off the ground but has proven to be more successful at pulling in other organizations because no one group "owned" the program.

In another community, some 19 organizations have banded together because they knew that, in combination, they had the clout to secure a grant from the local community foundation. They chose this route even though they were already in competition with each other on separate grant applications!

Which route should you take? The choices are not mutually exclusive. Follow whatever strategy will tap the most energy fastest. The depth of commitment and excitement from the leadership or from a particularly energetic staff member can make all the difference in launching a successful program. Enthusiasm and energy are major considerations. Hopefully, there will be several sources. If only one group is ready, go with it. But do what you can to keep the door open. And involve enough other groups in the planning that they can come into the program when they are ready or when resources permit. A successful program generates imitation; other organizations want to join or set up their own.

What organizations might be sponsors?

Organizations now sponsoring Time Dollar programs include a non-profit community hospital, a health maintenance organization, a community college, a senior center network, a state social service agency, various churches and a community-oriented primary care clinic. It is important to appreciate that they are involved in a way that advances their own institutional mission. In securing a sponsor or base, you would do well to think through ways in which *your* vision of a Time Dollar program could advance the institution's own agenda and mission. Sometimes the incentives are intangible; sometimes they are very tangible.

For example, community-oriented non-profit hospitals are sponsors because they want to say to their patients: "We care about you *after* you leave the hospital." That is good business because it fills hospital beds. It also makes it possible to discharge patients who don't need hospital-level care, yet must have some support system when they return home. That can help cost-containment efforts that in turn affect hospital finances. And many schools recognize that service to the community is an important aspect of their students' education.

Whatever their particular reasons for sponsoring a Time Dollar program, organizations of all kinds find that launching one gives their members something to be proud of and enhances their image in the community. So consider all possible organizations: retiree associations, chambers of commerce, veterans associations, condominium and tenants associations, unions, fraternal organizations.

Build Around Strengths

In picking a base, the basic principle is: build around its strengths. First, get the support of the leadership. That may mean key board members; it may mean the executive director. Someone at the top must share your vision and must believe that Time Dollars offer a special opportunity for the organization to fulfill its mission. If no one of influence believes that, if you feel you are just being tolerated, this may be the wrong "home" for the program.

Second, some institutions and agencies have "captive" memberships: senior housing projects where tenants meet regularly, congregate meal sites, patient discharge units in hospitals which arrange services for patients going home, congregations or student bodies. The program's design for recruitment and for identifying service recipients should "piggyback" on those internal features.

Third, structure your program around the natural flow of the organization by recruiting as the base organization communicates with its members or clients. For example, a health clinic may remind people about their appointments and can also inquire if the patient needs a ride or can give a ride to someone else in return for Time Dollars.

If a "regular" fails to show up for several days at a congregate meal site, the staff finds a Time Dollar member who is a neighbor to look in on him or her and deliver a meal. If expectant mothers tend to drop out of pre-natal programs, one program will offer them an incentive to finish in the form of a "free" grandmother (earning Time Dollars) to help with the newborn.

A word of caution: If you find that the "base" you chose already has a volunteer program, avoid conflict or competition. Schools, hospitals, churches and synagogues all have volunteer organizations. That's great. They can still add a Time Dollar program. But in trying to persuade them to do so, do not denigrate volunteer programs. They fill a real need and they provide special, meaningful opportunities for people to serve. There are few enough people who give selflessly; the last thing you want to do is put them down.

If there is a volunteer coordinator, he or she may feel threatened by a Time Dollar program. It is a whole new undertaking. She may feel overwhelmed by the number of tasks entailed. The coordinator of a hospital volunteer program who was very interested suddenly became concerned about whether starting a Time Dollar program meant that she would now have to pay Time Dollars to the volunteers who run the gift shop and to the candy-stripers who visit each patient daily and wheel in a cart with magazines and candy.

The following suggestions may prove useful:

• Distinguish volunteer programs which operate within an institution, augmenting that institution's staff capacity (like volunteers running the gift shop), from Time Dollar programs which tend to give one-on-one service in people's homes or in settings where volunteers have not been heavily used before.

• Time Dollar programs should *add* to the programs and resources of an institution, not substitute for existing volunteer programs. For example, a Time Dollar program might enable an institution to stay open nights and weekends or take on additional service components. Your best bet is to start by making the Time Dollar program separate. Do not try to incorporate it in any ongoing volunteer program, at least in the beginning.

• Retain flexibility on whether existing volunteer programs should be included in the Time Dollar program. Make the decision on a case-by-case basis and avoid making *any* decision until you have contacted people in ongoing programs and had the benefit of their experience and intuition in sorting out the pros and cons.

Establishing Basic Policies and Procedures For the Program

Establishing policies and procedures couldn't be simpler. This is because a procedure manual has already been developed as part of the Compleat Time Dollars Kit. Familiarize yourself with the procedure manual, then put it aside until a problem arises. Check the manual for guidance and modify it as experience dictates.

If you become part of a coalition, you have to work out certain administrative, fiscal and governance issues. Who will be fiscal agent for the coalition? Where will records be kept? Above all, what mutual obligations do each of the coalition members have to each other for Time Dollars earned by individuals associated with one group or another? Details have to be worked out in advance; for example, can one organization gain access to the membership lists of another in order to fill an urgent need for a volunteer?

It is best to work out such issues in advance to avoid any charges that one group is "raiding" another for volunteers.

Finding a Coordinator (or Director) and Establishing Basic Staffing Pattern

These are among the most critical decisions you will make in establishing a Time Dollar unit, so choose carefully. The choices you make could be the difference between success and failure. Here are some tips to follow.

Choosing a Director

The best programs have people with a kind of contagious warmth and enthusiasm that makes others feel welcome and appreciated. They are excited by the idea of the mission and by its potential. They do not need to be professionals. They *do* need to be self-starters who are not easily discouraged, who have lots of energy and a warm smile of approval always ready. They do not need to be extroverts; they can be low-key and modest.

Those who have this kind of "people touch" are often reluctant to spend time at record keeping. They are fantastic at making presentations, recruiting, responding to phone calls and hand tooling assignments that match just the right volunteer with the right recipient of service. It is best to make full use of those talents. However, there must be a clear understanding that the director is responsible for seeing to it that somehow the hours get recorded and the volunteers get their monthly or quarterly bank statements.

Building a Staff

There are three standard possibilities here: full-time, part-time, and volunteer staff. One way or another, some mix of these is needed to make sure that everything that needs to be done, is done. At least one program is being run almost entirely by volunteer staff who earn Time Dollars for the time they spend running it. Many other Time Dollar programs rely on member volunteers as part-time staff. Naturally, the more all-volunteer the staff is, the cheaper the program is to run.

281

The decision as to which mix to use depends on the answers to three questions. First, how much are people associated with this organization — you, for example — willing to do? Second, how much will others do to help you? Third, how much can this organization pay to have the work done?

Increasingly, programs are turning to a federal agency, ACTION, which operates a program called VISTA (Volunteers In Service To America). This program provides stipends of approximately $410 per month for "full time" volunteers. Miami uses 12 VISTA positions to recruit, match providers and recipients, make presentations and oversee the 32 locations out of which the program runs. The St. Louis program run by Grace Hill Neighborhood Services has received several VISTA slots. Centro San Vicente in El Paso, Texas, has been awarded six VISTAs who will coordinate the transportation element of each of the Time Dollar initiatives they are launching.

Such VISTA grants can be renewed for up to four years. Until longer-term funding strategies are implemented, this support is proving helpful. (A copy of one of the funded VISTA applications is available as part of the Compleat Time Dollar Kit).

There is a tendency to feel that a program has to have paid, professional staff to be effective. Most Time Dollar programs have at least one paid staff person as director. Those running Time Dollar programs really are candidates for burn-out because they are totally committed to what they are doing but they give so much of themselves. That means that over the long haul, you need to plan for some fund raising strategy that will provide pay for at least the core staff.

Whether you have paid staff or not, you have to divide up some of the responsibilities. If you rely primarily on volunteer staff, you probably have to start with a core group of committed individuals, parsing out tasks to other members as the program grows.

While you can run a program with only one person, it's a good idea to have a back-up in the wings. This not only gives the main person help and relief, but it gives the program room to grow.

Several programs have steering committees made up of staff, members, and funding sources. These committees generally set broad policy for the program, such as whom the program will serve, who is eligible to earn credits, and who is eligible to spend them, and consider whether any major new initiative is to be launched.

Record Keeping to Run a Time Dollar Program

There are three basic kinds of record keeping.

Bank Records: This credit-and-debit system records credits earned, credits spent, and credits given away.

Volunteer Assignments: Someone has to search the pool of volunteers to find someone available nearby, willing to do needed tasks and, if necessary, able to negotiate steps or speak a language other than English or drive at night or tolerate being in the same room with a smoker. A tentative match has to be made, then confirmed with both parties.

A Quality Control System: Put this in place early to track performance, provide follow-up, check on whether things are going well, and deal with complaints.

At first, some people thought that a computer was essential to these tasks. It turns out that one can make do with a regular index card file though it gets more cumbersome as the numbers pass 50. Records do have to be kept. Volunteers have to be matched. A small program can be run out of a shoe box. And even with large programs, it turns out that there are two ways to create one.

BIG = BIG
or: SMALL + SMALL + SMALL = BIG

Time Dollar programs are not intended to create an impersonal monolithic army of volunteers to be "matched" by some form of computer dating service. The program directors who are most effective get involved personally in the matching process, to make sure that helpers and recipients will get along, at least, and possibly even bond as friends.

Computer programs can match people by ZIP code, task, availability, experience, and so forth. They are helpful in narrowing the list of candidates, but this is less critical than the personal touch, particularly when programs are getting off the ground.

The need for a computer grows as the program grows in size and when there is staff turnover. New staff have to make matches among people they don't know. Here, the computer can help greatly.

Eventually, computer programs will assume a more important role as the numbers get more massive and as people start spending more credits than in the beginning. Computer programs can be particularly helpful in making sure that volunteers whom a program director might not know personally get assignments. There is a natural tendency to keep using the volunteers who have proven reliable. A computer program will help identify members who have not had an assignment recently, an essential factor in keeping effective, enthusiastic volunteers.

Everyone knows tales of woe about the early efforts to develop a user-friendly, yet powerful, computer program. Now you can set a program with screens in English and Spanish that requires no computer expertise, can be used on any IBM-type computer, and keeps the records, helps with matching, tracks assignments, and generates reports. The program and forms are available as part of the Compleat Time Dollar Kit.

Preparing Your Budget

How much does it cost to operate a Time Dollar program? The cost of Time Dollar programs varies depending on whether administrative staff is paid or volunteer, paid staff is full-time or part-time, volunteer insurance is required, and office or meeting space has to be rented. Although no program has yet succeeded in being self-sustaining (no outside support), some programs have come very close and have a lot of ideas about how to get closer still.

In the years 1985 through 1987, it took investments of between $60,000 and $100,000 to launch the first Time Dollar programs in Washington, D.C. and Missouri. In 1988, the State of Michigan's success proved you could start a program with grants ranging from $10,000 to $20,000.

Today, it should be possible for anyone with access to *Time Dollars: The New Currency That Enables Americans to Turn Their Hidden Resource — Time — Into Personal Security and Community Renewal* by Edgar Cahn and Jonathan Rowe to launch a program for $100 or so, if they are prepared to work full-time (and over-time) without compensation (and maybe even wangle help from their friends). Access to a personal computer makes things considerably simpler — but is not essential.

Of course, you really do have to have some things before you can start a Time Dollar program. You can buy them, find someone to donate them, or donate them yourself. The process of preparing your budget starts with thinking through how you're going to obtain basic resources including office space; a place to meet, train and socialize; staff; phone and answering machine; office furniture; supplies; a brochure; membership and credit/debit forms; photocopying/printing; volunteer insurance; refreshments, special events, awards, certificates; reimbursement of travel expenses; and a computer and printer (optional).

The budget items listed below can add up to a lot or almost nothing depending on how formal you make them. While you need the various plans listed, they might consist of only a few handwritten pages, costing nothing more than the paper they're written on. Even the kits and materials listed can be fairly informal, although they should be neatly typewritten.

- Plan for recruiting/servicing members & membership kit
- Volunteer training materials
- Fund-raising plan and materials
- Publicity plan and press kit
- Administrative policy and procedures manual

Once you've worked through what you need to start your Time Dollar program, you can start writing up how much you expect each of the things to cost.

II. How to Launch the New Currency

Now you're ready to blast off and put your good intentions into practice — help the elderly to go shopping, provide child care for working mothers, see that the sick have transportation to the doctor, and more. But first, there are some things you have to do. Fortunately, many others have done these already so you can profit from their groundwork to save time and effort.

Developing an informational package

Such a package should contain a brochure, a one-page hand-out, a set of questions and answers, one or two newspaper or magazine articles so that people know that the idea has been tried elsewhere and has worked. Samples of these materials are included in the book *Time Dollars*.

Your brochure can be as simple or fancy as you want to make it. If you have access to a computer with a word-processing program and laser printer, you can usually make a brochure at very low cost. If you have access to a photocopier as well, you can make a lot of brochures for next to nothing. If you're not up for creating a brochure, a one page hand-out will do. A brochure needs to contain answers to these questions:

- What is the program's name?
- What are Time Dollars?
- Why are Time Dollars important?
- What does the program do?
- What services does it provide?
- Why is this program important?
- Who can join?
- Why should I join?
- If I want to join, whom should I call? Where should I go? What can I expect?

As soon as you can, you should add testimonials from members of your program who have received help and from others who have provided service. Eventually you will want to incorporate these testimonials into the brochure itself but until you do, just print them on a separate sheet of paper and tuck them into the brochure. Remember, people are often convinced by testimonials even when they're not convinced by your assertions, no matter how eloquent. After all, you're selling something. Testimonials are proof that what you're selling is worth buying into.

Developing a "sales pitch" or presentation

There are some basic points you will want to get across in talking to groups and individuals. Your own personal enthusiasm is more important than any specific information you want to convey. When you're trying to recruit volunteers into the program, the last thing you want to say is that they should earn Time Dollars against the day they need them. People don't want to think about that grim possibility, especially seniors, and they certainly don't want to join a program where that's what people are thinking about. As Terrie Raphael, director of the ElderPlan program observed, the insurance industry discovered long ago that they had to sell "life insurance, not death insurance."

It's the same with Time Dollar programs. You have to sell people on the personal satisfaction, the sense of being needed and the new friends they make in helping others. People want to build networks and they want to cease being afraid of strangers. They want to be less alone, and they want to know that they have something to offer that others value and need. And they will like the idea of being part of the wave of the future, especially when it means recapturing the best of their past. These inducements, coupled with human interest stories and personal testimonials, are most effective.

A 10-minute video introduced by Ralph Nader and shown on network TV is available as part of the Compleat Time Dollar Kit. It explains the idea, shows several programs in action, gives people a feel for how a program actually works. It helps to break the ice and generate discussion.

Deciding on the Source and Number of Recruits

Think small: Five or seven is more than enough. You and a friend ought to be able to drag that many acquaintances in to get things going. From that point on, it gets easier and easier because they give testimonials and you use what they are doing to give examples to others to get them interested. Here, the choice of a base or site may be essential. One announcement at a meal site for seniors is likely to net you more than you can handle, particularly if a staff person or the head of the organization introduces you and "endorses" the idea. Make sure you can give them an assignment within two to three days. "Use them or lose them" is really true about volunteers. In identifying the initial volunteers, take advantage of the base you have selected and the tips on how to build a program around the "natural flow" of the organization.

Identifying and Securing Service Recipients

This particular task is more difficult than most people think. It is critical that you not underestimate the difficulty. First, people generally don't like to accept charity. Even though Time Dollar programs are self-help programs, not charity, you have to convince them of that. Second, people might need help, but that doesn't mean they'll ask for it. Frequently, they equate asking for help with begging on street corners. Third, people are afraid to invite strangers into their homes. They are warned by their neighbors and children not to open their door to strangers, and with good reason, considering some of the scams that have been perpetrated in recent years. So be prepared to demonstrate to both the prospective member and his or her family and friends that your program is legitimate, and that the volunteers coming to the recipient's home are trustworthy.

It may help to explain to the person receiving help that he or she has something to offer to the program and that, as soon as possible, you will expect her to be earning Time Dollars. Even if she is still confined to bed, she can be part of the Telephone Assurance pool that makes contact with other members and checks to see if a service performed was satisfactory.

That makes clear to people that you don't view them merely as charity cases.

Your best bet is to identify one or two organizations or agency staff who always need help for a client and who can virtually guarantee to deliver some requests for assistance on an ongoing basis. Be creative in identifying these organizations. For instance:

■ Make a pitch to organizations that provide home-delivered meals; they have a built-in list of people who need companionship, grocery shopping, and light meal preparation.

■ Talk to hospital discharge planners; they know the recently discharged patients who require non-medical support beyond what insurance covers.

■ Organizations to which elderly and disabled people travel could use a transportation service.

■ Pre-natal care centers could use a "grandmother service" to help mothers with new-born infants.

■ Hospice always needs more volunteers. And even though Hospice has intensive training requirements for those volunteers who work most closely with the family, they often need a volunteer who will just take the kids to the zoo, or do some shopping.

The point to remember is this: we are a society where many who need help are reluctant to ask for it. Channels for seeking help informally have disappeared for many. So be prepared to invest extra time in generating requests for help.

Arranging Insurance for the Givers and Recipients

It is essential to carry insurance that will cover any injury to a Time Dollar volunteer or to a person receiving help from a volunteer. Accidents happen; people get hurt and you don't want anybody to be worse off for having participated in the program. A special insurance program for volunteers has been offered for over 20 years by CIMA (Corporate Insurance Management), 216 Payton Street, Alexandria, VA 22314. Phone: (703) 739-9300. The annual premiums are phenomenally low; $3 per year (personal liability $.50, accident insurance: $2.50) buys $1 million in coverage for injury to the volunteer or the recipient. An additional $3 buys excess automobile coverage for volunteers using their cars. The carrier is INA (Insurance Company of North America). In some states, volunteers to state agencies are covered by worker's compensation; Pacific Presbyterian Hospital covers all of its volunteers with worker's compensation but does not require that the organizations in its Time Dollar coalition do likewise. Check out the applicable law. But regardless, get the private insurance.

Arranging for Media Coverage

Sometimes editors actually read press releases and make assignments. More often, releases get thrown away. Make some personal phone calls to local reporters and editors. Contact them early and provide regular updates as the program gets off the ground. Also, try to get a public service announcement on the radio. Ideally, you want a story that simultaneously announces the start of the program and describes one or two of the first assignments that members are carrying out. That, in turn, becomes part of your hand-out packet at meetings and for new volunteers. Local TV news likes this kind of story: Producers can film at their convenience and use it as "filler" on a slow day. A story about a new Time Dollar program has the feel of a "hard" news event which stays current for days if not weeks.

Conducting Training and Making Assignments

You will need a packet of orientation materials and forms. The orientation materials include a statement of rights and responsibilities, a summary of dos and don'ts and a code of ethics for members.

Training: What Works Best

All programs provide some kind of basic orientation. They need to gather information on new members, to introduce them in greater depth to the Time Dollar concept, and to provide a briefing on the code of ethics and dos and don'ts. The "don'ts" are important:

don't try to lift someone; don't administer medication. (People trying to be helpful can sometime exceed their own physical capability and their own knowledge without realizing it.) Beyond that initial orientation, programs differ greatly in their approach.

Some provide a great deal of training. Most directors have found that training turns off many volunteers because they have already helped out neighbors or raised children or done the things they will be asked to do in the program. So, effective programs disguise the training by incorporating it into regular social events and gatherings. Pot luck lunches where volunteers engage in joint problem solving are an example. They stimulate insights, identify resources and options and create a new kind of social setting for volunteers. This kind of informal exchange is probably the best kind of training, particularly when a resource person is available. A team approach where volunteers are paired for an assignment provides a kind of safety margin for the service recipient; supervision, back-up calls, and spot checks provide additional margins of safety during on-the-job training.

Other programs insist on training because they want Time Dollars to provide a new opportunity for life-long learning and for the acquisition of new skills. Participants in ElderPlan's peer counseling program take real pride in counseling skills. All programs seem enthusiastic about providing a kind of continuing education on subjects of interest to members — such as sessions on financial planning, entitlements, insurance, etc. If you build in substantial training, award certificates. If it can be done in a community college setting, so much the better.

The principal conclusion is: don't be doctrinaire about the need for training. If people like it, if it builds morale and a sense of family, that's great. If it turns people off and they tend to drop out, then cut the training and get them involved, preferably teamed up with a more experienced volunteer at first.

III. How to Sustain the Bank

Before you even get started, people often ask how you plan to survive over the long haul. They wonder what will happen after the initial funding gives out, or who will carry it if you should disappear. There *are* answers — even though there are no guarantees.

Time Dollars are a new idea. The very *worst* that can happen is that some people will help some other people and feel proud that they did so. And some people will get help they would have missed, and they won't feel they were begging for it or taking it from someone else who needed it more. Those are not exactly terrible things even if the program "fails" and dies. The "downside," the so-called worst case scenario, is better than doing nothing.

The upside is really exhilarating. If the program succeeds, then new possibilities open up in virtually every sphere of social activity. Where we count upon the student, the patient, the family, the neighborhood and the community to carry part of the load, there is a new way of rewarding and stimulating that effort without vast increases in taxes or expenditures. Time Dollar programs hold out the possibility of tapping a vast reserve of human energy and hope that neither the market economy nor appeals to volunteerism nor threats of being "terminated" from some program have been able to touch. Time Dollars give your organization a chance to get in on the ground floor, to be innovators and social entrepreneurs.

So don't get defensive. The worst that can happen is good. The best that can happen is that we can begin to dream and hope and trust again. That's worth some effort and even some risk. Now for the more concrete answers.

Long Range Program Developments

Programs have to take root and grow. Increased self-sufficiency is a radical notion in an economy built on specialization and mutual dependence.

How to Generate Reciprocity

Many social service agencies are funded to provide free services. Some organizations like health clinics and child day care programs are required or obliged to charge a fee but have flexibility to set up a sliding-fee scale based on ability to pay. Such agencies are

typically overwhelmed. The people they help almost invariably come with a bundle of problems unrelated to what the agency does or outside the scope of the agency's sphere of operations. Time Dollars offer a way to turn the time of clients into a resource with which to address those problems. Any agency that gives free or subsidized service should give serious consideration to charging a fee to be paid ·in Time Dollars by those whom they help. There are two reasons.

First, charging a fee to be paid in service transforms the helping relationship from one of subordination between professional and client (with the taint of charity) to one of reciprocity. It assumes that the person being helped has something of value to give to others.

Second, enlisting clients as part of a mutual help network enables the agency to mobilize resources that its clients desperately need, often as much as anything the agency itself can provide. If every agency giving away services could use those services as a catalyst to create a resource bank of people prepared to do anything from baby sitting to engaging in a neighborhood crime watch program, then many of the problems that bear on the agency's mission can be addressed. People who are isolated need a way to create informal support networks. Providing services for a Time Dollar fee can trigger the creation of such networks. That may actually rebuild community and create a sense of extended family with the capacity to address problems far more effectively than any single-purpose agency.

In addition, that one Time Dollar fee will trigger more service when the client helps another person, then that person in turn can be asked to "pay back" with Time Dollars for the help received. That turns the efforts of paid staff into a chain reaction that just keeps going. There will be exceptions of course: people who can genuinely not pay back. Yet, even in such cases, there are often family or friends or fellow members of a congregation who will happily pay back. Even bedridden people can be part of a telephone visiting program.

The presumption ought to be that everyone has something to give. If we act as if we believe it, we will find out that faith is vindicated. If we act as if people are worthless and simply manipulating the system, they will probably confirm our worst fears. So set the right tone. A Time Dollar fee-for-service policy can trigger major social change.

Employee Time Dollar Programs

Except for the once-a-year United Way drive, employees rarely have reason to give thought, as employees, to finding ways to do community service as an extension of their employment.

Why not institute a Time Dollar program as an option for every employee at every work site? Participation should *never* be imposed as an obligation. But employers could make participation easy and even attractive by offering Time Dollar volunteers the opportunity to participate in a variety of programs such as flex time, on-site day care and special health packages.

There is no reason why the employer and the employees cannot seize the opportunity to convert their work site into a base from which to build community, neighborliness and a sense of extended family. And there is no reason why every employer should not endeavor to convert an agency, corporation, or institution into a good citizen contributing tangibly to the civic health of a community.

Long-Term Financial Survival

We can anticipate that the short- to middle-term survival of some programs will depend upon creative fundraising that runs the gamut from bake sales to creative grantsmanship of the most sophisticated kind. This will be coupled with efforts to get private sector contributions where philanthropy might have a positive effect on business. Thus, banks and other businesses are an obvious starting point. Studies indicate that they lose a considerable number of employee days because a work force composed largely of women is struggling to cope with child care and parent care problems, often simultaneously.

Three basic strategies have emerged to generate long-term revenue streams necessary to support Time Dollar programs.

Institutionalizing the Program

Grants are great but they provide only short-term funding. Where it is clear that a Time Dollar program generates net revenue or reduces significant costs to an institution, then it is worthwhile for that institution or organization to absorb the cost as part of its basic operating budget. That means the program's survival is no longer contingent on hustling short term support.

The Miami program, for example, has generated numerous referrals to South Shore Hospital and resulted in billings to government Medicare and Medicaid programs estimated to be in excess of $1 million. The Greater Southeast Community Hospital in Washington, DC, has used its Time Dollar program as part of an advertising campaign to project its image in the community as a leader in health care. ElderPlan uses its Eldercare program as a selling point to seniors in a hotly competitive market for Health Maintenance Organizations. If Time Dollar programs could reduce maintenance and security costs in housing projects or improve student performance in schools — to give just two examples — that would make the case for building in administrative costs into the core operating budget of those institutions.

Servathon: Using Time Dollar Volunteers To Raise Cash Dollars

All of us have heard of walkathons: friends, merchants and employers pledge a certain amount to charity for each mile a participant walks. That often gets hundreds and even thousands of people out walking as a way of raising money for a good cause. Why not adapt the basic concept to Time Dollars? Why not solicit pledges of $1 for each hour of service that people provide through the program. The arithmetic is simple: 100 Time Dollar volunteers averaging four hours per week for 50 weeks would generate 20,000 hours a year. Multiply that by $1 an hour and the organization could raise $20,000 by helping others while its members earned Time Dollars for themselves.

If the organization needed start-up funds, it could ask for an advance on the first quarter of the money in order to hire the coordinator and get the program launched. The understanding would be that it could not get the next installment until volunteers had generated enough hours to "earn" the first installment.

A variation would be to sign up two organizations willing to provide matching grants of 50 cents per hour of service (or 4 organizations at 25 cents, and so on) if the program meets its stated goal.

Legislative or Public Sector Support

During the next two to five years, ongoing programs of any magnitude will require a funding source for both the core operation and for expansion and innovation.

Here, the public sector can play a critical role; given budget constraints, government at every level will want Time Dollar programs to succeed and to expand. Legislators will be interested as a way to address constituent problems without spending lots of money. The chief executive — governor, mayor, and perhaps even the White House — wants to find ways to meet need that are cost effective. However, heads of agencies with jurisdiction over the problem will not always be enthusiastic. By and large, they desperately need increases in appropriations just to avoid imposing cutbacks. They will give a polite audience and appear to be very interested but unless they are peculiarly innovative or mavericks, they will tend, regardless of party or ideology, to regard Time Dollars as a very mixed blessing indeed.

Approaches to the public sector include funding through an agency dealing with elderly, youth or welfare problems; VISTA volunteer grants; and legislation to establish a Time Dollar program.

RESOURCES

Cahn, Edgar and Jonathan Rowe. *Time Dollars: The New Currency That Enables Americans to Turn Their Hidden Resource — Time — Into Personal Security and Community Renewal.* Emmaus, PA: Rodale Press, 1992.

Cahn, Edgar. *The Compleat Time Dollar Kit.* Washington, DC: Essential Information, 1991.

Contains *How to Grow Time Dollars* — a full manual ($15); a systems and procedure manual available as hard copy or on Word Perfect 5.0 disk ($10); grantsmanship manual ($15); 10-minute video ($12); a computer program with forms for keeping records, making and tracking assignments, and compiling reports ($45). Compleat Kit: $78.75.

Order from Essential Information, P.O. Box 19405, Washington, DC 20036.

Below is a list of names and places to contact for further information about service credit programs.

Dr. Edgar S. Cahn
5500 39th Street, NW
Washington, DC 20015
Tel: (202) 483-0549
FAX: (202) 462-6261

Service Credit programs now operating:

California
Janeane Randolph
Volunteer Exchange Program (VIP)
30th Street Senior Services
Pacific Presbyterian Medical Center
225 30th Street
San Francisco, CA 94131
(415) 550-2260

Connecticut
Betty Barath
Janna Deveny
Project Independence
74 West Main Street
Norwich, CT 06360
(203) 886-0677

Florida

Anna Miyares
Executive Director, Time Dollar Inc.
of Greater Miami
P.O. Box 415157
Miami Beach, FL 33141-5157
(305) 866-5758

Massachusetts

Lavado Bryan
Director, VITA
Kit Clark Senior House
1500 Dorchester Avenue
Dorchester, MA 02122
(617) 825-5000

Missouri

Richard Gram
Betty Marver
Time Dollar Exchange
Grace Hill Neighborhood Services, Inc.
2600 Hadley Street
St. Louis, MO 63106
(314) 241-2200

Norma Hasselman
Joanne Polowy
State of Missouri Older Volunteer Service Bank
933 Leslie Boulevard
Jefferson City, MO 65101
(314) 751-3082

New York

Dr. Terrie Raphael, Director
Mashi Blech, Manager of Volunteer Programs
Member-to-Member
Elderplan, Inc.
1276 50th Street
Brooklyn, NY 11219
(718) 438-1593

Oklahoma

Rita Ulman
Life, Inc.
3200 NW 48th Street, Suite 100
Oklahoma City, OK 73112
(405) 236-0277

Texas

Pat MacMaster
Director, SAVE
Family Service of San Antonio
230 Pereida Street
San Antonio, TX 78210
(512) 226-3391

Washington, DC

Zefferine Wheeler
Coordinator, Pastoral Care
Greater Southeast Center for the Aging
1380 Southern Avenue, SE
Washington, DC 20032
(202) 563-8100 x 51

ACTIVITY TEN:
EVALUATING
LOCAL TELEVISION NEWS

INTRODUCTION

Public access to information is vital to a democracy. The public depends on the news media to produce the information they need to make informed decisions. How can citizens ensure that the media fulfill their responsibilities? Newspapers, protected by the First Amendment, are free from any government regulation.* In contrast, because the public airwaves are a public commonwealth under federal law, the government puts certain restrictions on television broadcasters to protect the right of the public to receive information. Citizens have an important role to play in overseeing the effectiveness of the media, in holding them accountable not only for the stories they do cover, but for the ones they do not. This activity discusses some of the issues that affect the ability of the media to perform their important function of informing the public and provides students with one way to evaluate local news broadcasts and to suggest improvements.

IMPORTANCE OF THE MEDIA

The media play an important role in a democracy by serving as a check on political and economic power. A democratic society functions best when publishers, broadcasters, editors and reporters question the current state of affairs, including illuminating the character and actions of persons in power. Ideally, the media are the public's eyes and ears: skeptical, suspicious and demanding or airing answers on every subject of concern to society.

The nation's founders recognized that access to information, data and opinions from many different sources is necessary if citizens are to make decisions about society's problems and elect representatives in an informed and intelligent manner. To protect the public's right to information, the founders wrote the First Amendment to the U.S. Constitution which states: "Congress shall make no law ... abridging the freedom of speech, or of the press."

The authors of the First Amendment were most concerned about protecting both citizens and the press from government censorship, which they had experienced under the rule of the King of England. Thus the First Amendment prohibits the government from censoring the press — radio, television, newspapers and magazines — and the speech of individual citizens.

But in the early days of the nation, citizens had access to the means of communication, in the form of handbills and pamphlets and through town meetings. With the development and growth of radio (and later television), government censorship was no longer the only major threat to citizen access to the means of communication and information.[1] Today, the First Amendment rights of the public to free speech are most restricted by a lack of access to the airwaves or the electronic mass media.

The public owns the airwaves; like parks, streets and waterways, the airwaves are to be used for the benefit of everyone. But since there are far more people

---

* This activity addresses the influence of television as a source of news. Newspapers are, of course, important as well. For an excellent guide to evaluating local newspaper performance, see the listing under David Bollier in the bibliography.

interested in using the airwaves than there are available channels, Congress passed the Communications Act of 1934 to regulate the airwaves and to create the Federal Communications Commission (FCC). Congress decided to allow businesses to use the public's airwaves for commercial profit.[2] In other countries, including England, the government controls at least part of the airwaves and funds educational and information programming.

The FCC grants television broadcasters exclusive five-year, renewable licenses (seven years for radio licenses) to use the airwaves. In return, Congress requires broadcast license holders to use the airwaves in the "public interest, convenience and necessity."[3] The FCC issued a number of regulations to ensure that the airwaves not be monopolized by one viewpoint or one type of programming and to promote the public's First Amendment right to contrasting views "from as many divergent sources as possible."[4]

The government decided to issue such broadcasting licenses on a local basis, believing that local business ownership of stations would ensure the best response to the unique needs of the community. As public trustees, broadcasters are supposed to discover and fulfill the needs and interests of the station's service area, given its unique population and problems, including the public's need for information. These considerations, and the promotion of diversity of both station ownership and programming, became known as the "public interest standard" by which the FCC judged station operation.[5]

To further the public interest standard the FCC required broadcasters to show certain amounts of all kinds of programming: children's programming, religious programs, educational programs, political broadcasts, news, local and national public affairs and weather reports as well as entertainment programming. In addition, the FCC required broadcasters to make equal opportunities available to all political candidates to purchase airtime.[6]

DEREGULATION OF THE AIRWAVES

It is clear to us that the idea of diversity of viewpoints from antagonistic sources is at the heart of the commission's licensing responsibility. If our democratic society is to function, nothing can be more important than insuring that there is a free flow of information from as many divergent sources as possible.
Federal Communications Commission, 1975.[7]

So spoke the FCC in 1975. But during the 1980s, the FCC, under direction of President Ronald Reagan's appointees, abolished television programming regulations which affirmatively promoted the use of the airwaves in the interest of the public.[8]

In 1982, the FCC abolished a rule that had forbidden broadcasters from selling stations within less than three years of their acquisition. In the four years after the rule was abolished, the number of television stations sold annually (after being held less than two years) increased by almost eight times, raising serious questions as to whether license holders could meet their public interest obligations.[9]

In 1984, the FCC also eliminated limits on time devoted to commercials per hour. The limits had required that broadcasters air no more than 16 minutes per hour of commercials. Since the FCC lifted the regulation, program-length commercials have become numerous.[10]

The FCC no longer requires broadcasters to interview representatives of the community or to study community problems and air relevant programming. Since deregulation, all the networks and most of their affiliates have made dramatic cutbacks in their news departments, including elimination of network documentary units, reduction of local public affairs staff and decreases in public affairs programming.[11]

Until the 1980s, the FCC promoted diversity of program sources, or diverse station ownership, with rules prohibiting any party from owning or controlling more than one radio or television station in the same community. The FCC also limited the number of stations a business could own nationwide to seven AM radio, seven FM radio and seven television stations.[12] Under deregulation during the 1980s, however, the FCC increased the number of stations any single party could own from seven to 12 of each type (AM, FM and television stations) so long as any one company does not reach more than 25 percent of the national audience.[13]

In 1984, the FCC eliminated the 5-5-10 guideline which required broadcasters to air at least 5 percent local, 5 percent informational (news and public affairs) and 10 percent non-entertainment programming between 6 a.m. and midnight. The guideline was designed to ensure that broadcasters air alternative and public interest programs (in addition to entertainment and commercials) and to increase the likelihood that the programming interests of all citizens in the community would be met. In eliminating the regulation, the FCC argued that a "free market" and competition could best assure that broadcasters operate in the public interest.[14]

Before 1984, any station not meeting the 5-5-10 guideline at the time of license renewal was subject to review by the FCC to determine if the station's owner was using the airwaves solely for profitable entertainment and commercials while neglecting to air alternative programming and public interest programs dealing with important and controversial issues or community problems.[15]

In 1987, the FCC repealed the Fairness Doctrine, which was the public's primary right of access to the airwaves. The doctrine required broadcasters to air important and controversial topics of public concern while providing a fair presentation of contrasting views.[16] Groups of all political persuasions used the doctrine to ensure fair coverage of many issues.[17] Attorney John Banzhaf, in 1969, asked the FCC to require broadcasters to inform the audiences about the harmful effects of cigarette smoking if they aired advertisements from cigarette manufacturers. As a result, the tobacco industry eventually withdrew all cigarette ads from the airwaves.[18] Ralph Nader and Claire Riley write that, "Without the Fairness Doctrine, citizens actually have substantially less leverage to ensure that broadcasters provide balanced coverage of controversial issues."[19]

The FCC abolished the Fairness Doctrine on the grounds that the rule made broadcasters less likely to air controversial programs for fear that lawsuits would arise charging a station was unfair. As a result, the FCC concluded that the Fairness Doctrine was responsible for hindering the amount of public affairs programming on the airwaves. It further concluded that an unregulated free market, without a Fairness Doctrine, would increase the amount of programming devoted to controversial issues of public importance.[20]

A study by Essential Information, however, shows that between 1979 and 1988, television broadcasters aired 51 percent less public affairs programming between 6 a.m. and midnight on commercial television in the markets studied. The study also found that broadcasters aired 39 percent less local public affairs programming.[21] Thus, the FCC's theory that market forces propel broadcasters to air public interest programming has not borne out.[22]

Critics of deregulation have called on the FCC to reinstate the rules that promoted use of the airwaves in the public interest.[23]

CABLE

Although, like broadcasters who use the public's airwaves, cable companies use the public's streets to lay their wires and have monopolies on delivering service to residents in cities, few restrictions apply to the cable industry regarding protection of the public's First Amendment right to free speech.

Congress deregulated the cable industry in 1984 by prohibiting local governments from regulating cable television rates. But after the legislation's provisions went into effect in 1986, cable rates rose sharply. And between 1990 and 1992, cable rates climbed twice as fast as the rate of inflation.[24] In response to consumer outrage over rising cable rates, Congress, in the late

1980s, began to consider proposals to return control of cable prices to local governments and to promote competition among local cable monopolies.[25]

HOW WELL DO BROADCASTERS SERVE THE PUBLIC?

Although the reversal of these regulations has taken away at least part of the media's mandate to serve the public, Americans need access to more information and news about their world than ever before. How well do broadcasters fill that need? Critics point to a number of instances where the media are late covering or pay little attention to some issues while completely ignoring others.

When the media do cover important issues, they often cover them late. Writes Morton Mintz, "Was it news that the air we breathe was being poisoned by the exhausts of tens of millions of motor vehicles? In most cities the press paid no serious attention until the poisoning was far advanced."[26]

Media messages have a profound effect; subjects treated briefly or superficially have little effect on public consciousness, while stories frequently repeated and analyzed to form a coherent picture create priorities in the general public and in the government.[27] For example, between 1939 and 1945, a number of articles appeared in U.S. newspapers about Nazi atrocities against Jewish people in Germany. The articles were placed on the back pages however, and few people took notice.[28]

When journalist Kirk Johnson contrasted over 3,000 news stories in Boston's largest newspapers, television and radio stations with black-owned newspapers and radio, he found dramatic differences in the coverage of African Americans. Most of the stories in the major media covered crime or violence.[29] In contrast, in the black-owned media, "57 percent of the stories ... suggested a black community thirsty for educational advancement and entrepreneurial achievement ... Many of these stories went unreported by the major media."[30]

Other important news stories are ignored. For example, all the major U.S. newspapers and the three television network nightly newscasts chose to cover, in a positive light, a series of Soviet coal miners' strikes staged over an eight-day period in the summer of 1989. In September 1989, a six-month United Mine Workers of America strike against a coal company over pension and health benefits climaxed in a dramatic four-day takeover of a coal plant in Virginia. Although this was the first major worker occupation of a U.S. plant since 1937, the *New York Times* and the three networks ignored the story.[31]

Furthermore, the media decide which voices will or will not be heard. A study of 40 months of the ABC news program *Nightline*, by the media watch organization Fairness and Accuracy in Reporting (FAIR), is a case in point. FAIR found that of the 19 American guests who appeared more than five times on the show, all were men and all but two were white.[32] Only 10.3 percent of the show's guests were female. Of the 20 most frequent guests, none were women.[33]

The study also found that "representatives of civic and community organizations, popular social movements [and] minority communities" are absent from the list of guests which usually favors "government spokespeople, assorted 'experts,' and journalists."[34] For example, on programs dealing with economic issues, "corporate representatives outnumbered labor spokespeople seven-to-one."[35] Ted Koppel, host of *Nightline*, responded that the FAIR study was "missing the larger point. Ours is a news program. It is not meant to be a forum to give all divergent views in the United States equal access. When we are covering the news, we try to go to the people involved in the news."[36] But what is "news" is determined by media companies such as ABC.

Nightline is not alone in underrepresenting the views of women and minorities as well as other voices. According to Susan J. Douglas of FAIR, "female 'experts' are interviewed for the nightly news when the topic is abortion, child-care or affirmative action; but when the topic is war, foreign policy or national purpose, female voices are ignored."[37] Another study, published in the magazine *Mother Jones*, "found that the 10 individuals who appeared most frequently as analysts on CBS, ABC and NBC nightly news (some as many as 58 times in two years) were all men."[38]

In addition, the voices of women and minorities are often underrepresented not only in the content, but in the reporting of news. A 1990 study by the Women, Men and Media Project found that only 15 percent of correspondents on the commercial networks, ABC, CBS and NBC, were female. And another study at Southern Illinois University found that of the 100 mostly frequently seen correspondents on the networks in 1989, only eight were women.[39]

Although nearly 25 percent of U.S. citizens are African American, Latino, Asian or Native American, minorities made up only 8 percent of news employees at commercial radio stations and 16 percent at commercial television stations.[40] Says columnist Clarence Page, "I think it hurts the [coverage] as far as having sensitivity during the day to what issues are important in the black community and also what issues are developing in the black community, and the Hispanic community too."[41]

FACTORS CONTRIBUTING TO LACK OF DIVERSITY AND OVERALL QUALITY OF MEDIA COVERAGE

Media critic Ben Bagdikian, professor at the University of California at Berkeley, cites three factors — concentration of ownership, corporate control and cross-ownership of media outlets — which contribute to the lack of diversity and affect the overall quality of the information the public receives.

Concentration of Ownership

"Never in history have so many people been informed of important public events by so few," writes author James Donahue.[42] As of 1990, approximately 1,700 daily newspapers, 11,000 magazines, 9,000 radio and 1,000 television stations, 2,500 book publishers and seven movie studios — a total of 25,000 media outlets — operated in the United States.[43] Yet, the majority of these outlets are owned by just 23 different companies (down from 46 in 1981).[44]

Ben Bagdikian, in *The Media Monopoly*, writes that "centralized control over information, whether governmental or private, is incompatible with freedom. Modern democracies need a choice of politics and ideas, and that choice requires access to truly diverse

and competing sources of news, literature, entertainment, and popular culture."[45]

Corporate Ownership of Media

Media outlets are commercial, for-profit businesses. A company that makes decisions based on maximizing profits may not fulfill its First Amendment responsibility to serve the public.[46] For example, in 1966, the CBS television network refused to cancel a rerun of "I Love Lucy" for a crucial Senate hearing on the Vietnam War. CBS News president Fred Friendly resigned over the decision; CBS told him that shareholders would not tolerate the loss of revenue from the delayed episode.[47]

Critics argue that because advertisers only want to reach those segments of the public who spend the most money on their products, broadcasters who rely on advertising money will choose programs that appeal primarily to those people. This often excludes children, the elderly and American families who fall below the income level targeted by advertisers.[48] Thus the specific needs of smaller, less profitable audiences, including minorities will not be met. In addition, corporate owners will not want to risk antagonizing advertisers by showing a program that would make certain segments of the population angry or upset.[49]

Businesses are more likely to cover business issues in a favorable light and downplay news that concerns the outside community but is unfavorable to their own company. FAIR conducted a study in 1990 to analyze newspaper and television coverage of labor issues which concluded that "the lives of 100 million working people — those who make the U.S. economy and society run — are being routinely ignored, marginalized or inaccurately portrayed in the media."[50] According to the study, little more than two percent of the total air time of the network evening news was given over to issues involving labor, including childcare, the minimum wage and worker safety and health. However, reporting on business and economics received twice that amount of air time.[51]

At the least, corporations routinely seek to avoid embarrassing publicity and seek to maximize sympathetic public opinion and favorable government policies.[52] These large and powerful corporate interests are no longer outsiders; they own the communication systems that are supposed to be the independent watchdogs of government and other powerful institutions in society.[53]

Cross-Ownership of Media

These few media competitors often own other types of media (cross-ownership) and cannot adequately oversee the actions of each other. According to Ben Bagdikian, "In the past, each medium used to act like a watchdog over the behavior of the competing media. The newspaper industry watched magazines and both kept a public eye on the broadcasting industry."[54] But now, for example, the Washington Post Company owns the *Washington Post* newspaper, *Newsweek* magazine and several television stations.

Effects of the Lack of Diversity

Without competition, in the form of a large number of different types of media owners who offer diverse opinions and information on many topics, democracy is weakened. Other media voices do exist outside of the control of the large companies, and they are important, but their weak voices tend to be drowned out by the widespread, powerful mass media.[55]

Bagdikian writes that the "primary danger of excessive media power is ... promoting the politics and economics of the corporate world."[56] Media owners are corporations that are also defense contractors, manufacturers of electronics and owners of insurance and banking interests. These interests and the interest of the public right to know are continually in conflict.[57]

Without the ability to exchange ideas and receive information from many diverse sources through the media, citizens are forced to rely on a small number of large corporations for their impressions of society, politics, the arts and the public itself.[58]

WHAT CITIZENS CAN DO ABOUT BROADCASTING QUALITY

Letters of Complaint/Petition to Deny

Citizens can send letters of complaint to both the local TV station and to the FCC, which will keep the complaint on file and consider it when the station's license comes up for renewal. Citizens also can challenge renewal of a broadcaster's license with a petition to deny, which informs the FCC that citizens for whom the broadcaster acts as a trustee are not satisfied with the broadcaster's performance.[59] However, these efforts historically have had minimal effect.

Audience Network

Congress held hearings in May 1991 to explore the creation of an Audience Network — a national voluntary membership institution of viewers and listeners — that could serve as the audience's 'community intelligence.' The group's primary organizing and educating tool would be air time. Congress would grant the democratically operated group 60 minutes of time on each commercial radio and television station each day during prime time (television) and drive time (radio). Audience Network could agree with the stations to exchange these time slots for others whenever necessary to serve better the membership and the needs of the public. In addition, Audience Network could sell a limited amount of its daily air time to the stations to raise more funds for its activities. By granting Audience Network the right to prime time, Congress gives the organization effective bargaining power vis-à-vis the stations.[60]

During its time slot, the Audience Network would air a variety of cultural, political, entertainment, scientific or other programs that it produced or obtained. Major abuses which are not publicized for years on commercial media would receive prompter attention free of the constraints of corporate advertisers. It would periodically inform the public about the organization's activities and discuss media reform issues. With its financial resources, and its access to airtime, Audience Network, at both local and national studio levels, could also provide central production facilities and act as a time broker for other non-profit groups that wished to produce and air quality programs.[61]

Audience Network would represent the interests of its members before the FCC, the courts and Congress itself — wherever broadcasting policy is being made. Any citizen age sixteen and over could become a member of Audience Network by contributing a modest amount, say $10 annually, to the organization. The fee could be waived for those unable to pay. Members' contributions would constitute Audience Network's consistent source of funding; the group would require no expenditure of tax dollars.[62]

Viewers and listeners need not be told that the only alternative to their dislike of programs is to turn off their sets. The choices could be far more numerous, more affirmative or initiatory, and the difference among programs more genuine. Audience Network would provide a flow of ideas and imagination, for a change, *from* the people of this country *to* the people of this country through their communication network. The Audience Network, in short, could serve as a self-funded, independent, ongoing communications link between viewers and listeners.[63]

Cable Access

While cable does not yet reach the number of people broadcast television does, it is an important media outlet. To promote diversity of viewpoints and programming, cities often require cable companies to include certain access channels on their cable systems. A wide variety of programs are aired on public access time, from election night programs to showcases of local sports talent to documentaries on historic places in the community to cultural activities of ethnic groups. Each of the three types of access — public, educational and government (PEG) — may have a separate channel or all may share one channel on the cable system.[64]

A nonprofit corporation or department in the municipality is usually set up to manage the access operation, or the cable company or local library organizes the effort. In most cities with access channels, the public has the opportunity to be trained in video production and can prepare video programming which is shown on the reserved access channels. Limited funding can come from a number of sources, such as the cable company, municipality or community entity.[65]

Cable Consumer Action Groups

Another way to promote citizen participation in cable is to set up cable consumer action groups (CCAGs). CCAGs are patterned on Citizen Utility Boards (CUBs), democratically-governed advocacy groups that utility ratepayers organize to gain representation in utility decision making. (See page 199). CCAGs would require cable television companies to insert a notice in customer billing envelopes inviting cable viewers to join a viewer-controlled and viewer-funded cable group. The group would not be connected to cable companies or the government in any way and would represent the concerns of cable television viewers before government agencies. For example, consumer complaints about cable rate increases could be addressed before government regulatory agencies.[66]

HOW TO CONDUCT A SURVEY OF LOCAL NEWS PROGRAMMING

I. INTRODUCTION

The transcript of a half-hour television news broadcast would fill approximately two pages of an ordinary newspaper.[67] That is not much space in which to cover all the important issues vital to the community. Yet approximately 70 percent of Americans report that they get most of their news about the world from television.[68] Television stations, which use the public's airwaves, have an obligation to serve the community.

How well do the local television news programs meet their obligation to the community? Citizens should become active watchdogs of their local television station because it is important that the public have confidence in the media and share its commitment to press freedom. This activity will help students evaluate their community's local television news programs to determine how well they serve the public. By evaluating the content of news broadcasts over a two-month period, students can assess stations' performance and recommend improvements.

II. METHODOLOGY

A. CHOOSE A COMPOSITE WEEK

Instead of evaluating the television news for seven days in a one-week period, choosing seven days over a two-month period will likely result in a better representation of each of the news programs. To select a random sample of broadcasts to make up a typical one-week period, write down the day and date of every day in the two-month period on separate slips of paper. Draw the slips from a hat until you pick all seven days of the week, three from one month, four from the other.

B. TAPE THE NEWS SHOWS

For each day in the composite week, tape the local evening news show of each station in your area that airs one. Choose the most-watched half-hour or hour of each show. By taping the programs, you can stop and start the tape to evaluate the content more easily. If your community has three stations that produce news shows nightly, by the end of the two-month period you will have 21 separate news broadcasts recorded and ready to evaluate.

C. TIME AND CATEGORIZE EACH NEWS STORY

As you watch each recorded broadcast, write down the topic and record the length in minutes of each story. Also record the amount of time dedicated to commercials. Set up categories for the kinds of stories covered in the news broadcasts. As you categorize, discuss each story. Decide for yourselves how well each story serves the needs of the community. Suggested categories are:

■ **Critical issues** — Include in this category stories of critical importance to the public, for example, reporting on health care issues such as AIDS or information to help voters make informed decisions. Also include investigative pieces which go beyond reporting the basic facts of an event to attempt to draw larger meanings, including the causes and solutions to problems. Do the stories consider how events affect all segments of the community, for example, how business issues affect workers and consumers, not just investors? Do reports of national stories such as consumer fraud or hazards offer a local follow-up?

■ **Crisis reporting** — This category covers reports on fires, crime and other crises. Are such stories reported with analysis as to why the crisis took place? For example, when the stations report on the latest fatal car wreck do they attempt any in-depth analysis of highway or auto safety standards for the state or area and do they identify the make and model routinely? Do they interview community leaders who might have solutions to on-going problems of which that day's crisis is only a symptom? Are all parts of the city or county adequately covered?

■ **Entertainment/Fluff** — Which stories serve primarily as entertainment? Do the anchors spend time talking among themselves or interviewing their own reporters when they could be covering more news?

■ **Information** — Include stories in this category that offer pertinent information to the community such as weather forecasts and sports information. Do the sports stories cover female sports as well as male? Are the weather forecasts too long and over-reported?

D. EVALUATE AND COMPARE THE CONTENT

Count the number of stories in each category for each station. Compare time devoted to commercials among the various stations. Learn more about each station, including the following:

■ Find out who owns each television station in your community and if each owner is located primarily in your community. The FCC can tell you who holds the broadcast license for each station. Find out if the owners have other business interests that could cause conflicts of interest.
■ Find out how many investigative reporters each station has. Does it have a reporter assigned to cover consumer, environmental and community issues full-time?
■ Compare the number of female and minority reporters, anchors and producers at each station.
■ Do the stations air editorials? If so, do they provide time for responses and guest editorials?

E. RECOMMENDATIONS

Evaluate your data to determine which news show gave the best serious coverage during the composite week. Write a brief report showing the results and explaining your methodology. Explain that the survey is an attempt to evaluate how well the broadcasters are using the public's airwaves. Make recommendations to each of the stations on how you think they could improve coverage, such as assigning reporters to particular issue areas or offering analysis from leaders of community groups. Announce your findings to the community. (See pages 173-179 for guidelines to using the media).

Organizations

Fairness and Accuracy in Reporting
130 W. 25th Street
New York, NY 10001

Federal Communications Commission
1919 M Street, NW
Washington, DC 20554

BIBLIOGRAPHY

Action Kit. Washington, DC: Citizens for the Cable Consumer Participation Amendment, 1992.

Andrews, Edmund L. "Deeply Divided House Panel Backs Limits on Cable Rates," *The New York Times*. April 9, 1992.

Bagdikian, Ben H. *The Media Monopoly*. Third edition. Boston: Beacon Press, 1990.

Bagdikian, Ben H. "The Media Brokers: Concentration and Ownership of the Press," *Multinational Monitor*. September 1987.

Bollier, David. *How to Appraise and Improve Your Daily Newspaper*. Washington, DC: Center for Study of Responsive Law, 1980.

Camire, Dennis. "Senate OKs Cable Bill, Passage in House Likely," Gannett News Service, January 31, 1992.

Donahue, James. *Shortchanging the Viewers: Broadcasters' Neglect of Public Interest Programming*. Washington, DC: Essential Information, 1989.

Donahue, James. *Audience Network Action Kit*. Washington, DC: Audience Network Action Project, 1991.

Douglas, Susan J. "The Representation of Women in the News Media," *Extra!* March/April 1991.

Hoynes, William and David Croteau. *Are You On the Nightline Guest List?: An Analysis of 40 Months of Nightline Programming*. New York: Fairness and Accuracy in Reporting, 1989.

Knaus, Holley. "Labor's Press," *Multinational Monitor*. November 1990.

Lee, Martin A. and Norman Solomon. *Unreliable Sources: A Guide to Detecting Bias in News Media*. New York: Carol Publishing Group, 1990.

Mintz, Morton and Jerry S. Cohen. *Power, Inc.: Public and Private Rulers and How to Make Them Accountable*. New York: Viking Press, 1976.

Nader, Ralph. Testimony Before the House Subcommittee on Telecommunications and Finance of the House Committee on Energy and Commerce. May 13, 1991.

Nader, Ralph and Claire Riley. "Oh, Say Can You See: A Broadcast Network for the Audience," *The Journal of Law and Politics*. Vol. V. No. 1. Fall 1988.

Southworth, Judy. "Women Media Workers: No Room at the Top," *Extra!* March/April 1991.

Tasini, Jonathan. *Lost in the Margins: Labor and the Media*. New York: Fairness and Accuracy in Reporting, 1990.

"Television," *Buyer's Market*. December 1987. Vol. 3. No. 10.

75 IDEAS FOR STUDENT ACTIVITIES

INTRODUCTION

Listed below are 75 ideas, arranged in 10 different categories, for student activities. These suggestions should help facilitate discussion about projects students may wish to take on in their school or community.

ENVIRONMENT AND ENERGY

■ Waste disposal
Investigate community waste disposal program, including plans for future landfills or incinerators.

■ Drinking water
Investigate quality of school drinking water at the source and at the tap, checking for lead, contaminants and toxins.

■ Indoor air pollution audit
Check school for indoor pollution including asbestos, radon, formaldehyde, hazardous cleaning supplies, pesticides, etc.

■ Alternative energy sources/group buying
Study energy use, residential and commercial, survey community for support of a buying group for home heating oil.

■ Lifeline Utility Rate Proposal
Propose to provide electricity for citizens' basic needs — lighting, cooking and refrigeration — at an affordable rate by lobbying the legislature or public service commission.

■ Residential hazardous waste cleanup day
Set up days for proper collection of hazardous waste, including paints, cleaning supplies, motor oil, etc.

■ Car pool/commuter services
Survey existing services and needs in your community.

■ Guide to cloth diaper services and stores
Survey your community for services and distribute a guide to hospitals, baby stores, etc.

■ Service station recycling
Publish a guide to service stations which recycle motor oil, batteries and/or old tires.

■ High Occupancy Vehicle (HOV) lanes
Urge your state legislature to establish HOV lanes to encourage carpooling.

■ Pesticide spraying
Use right-to-know laws to determine chemicals used by lawn-care and extermination companies. Urge your community government to pass an ordinance requiring notices to be posted for pesticide spraying.

■ Pollution streamwalk
Monitor the discharge of industrial pollution into streams and rivers, report the conditions of waterways to state and local environmental protection agencies.

■ Emergency evacuation/response plans
Evaluate state and local response plans in the event of a nuclear accident or hazardous waste transportation accident, including evacuation, hospital and emergency services readiness.

■ Right-to-Know
Exercise right-to-know laws to discover pollutants emitted by local industry.

■ Nuclear plants
Check how a local nuclear plant disposes of waste, especially low-level waste.

THE WORKPLACE

- Occupational health and safety

Survey workplaces for compliance with Occupational Safety and Health Administration (OSHA) standards; request federal inspection in the event of violation of a standard, imminent danger and/or presence of a "recognized hazard."

- Noise pollution

Survey workplaces for excessive noise levels, interview workers regarding hearing loss or related problems, request federal OSHA inspection for violation of noise standards, arrange for non-company health specialists to tour the workplace and to test workers for hearing loss.

- Child care

Write a guide to child care availability and quality; survey daycare centers, private providers, company programs for services, costs, violations, etc.

- Pension funds

Evaluate a company's pension plan to find out how well it serves employees and how and where the funds are invested.

- Employment discrimination

Compare employment agency responses between men and women, whites and minorities of equal qualification.

- Job market guide

Produce a guide for high school seniors to the local job market. Check each employer's compliance with workplace safety rules, availability of pension fund, sex or race discrimination, environmental record, consumer protests.

HOUSING

- Homelessness

Conduct a study of local homeless problem and policies.

- Community development grants

Investigate allotment of community development grants.

- Landlord/tenant guide

Write a guide to local landlord/tenant regulations.

GOVERNMENT

- Procurement policy

Study local government procurement policies to check for life-cycle efficiency, compliance with "bad-boy" laws and environmentally sound products.

- Tax study

Study collection and distribution of local taxes.

- Property tax assessment

Check to see if standards for property tax assessments are the same from one neighborhood to another. Compare standards for homeowners to those for owners of other types of property.

- Tax projects

Reform inequities by releasing a report to the public and state attorney general, file a class-action suit, picket or demonstrate outside businesses getting tax breaks, campaign to vote out of office assessors or other elected officials who refuse to reform, convince a state representative to hold hearings on tax abuses.

- Initiative campaign

Lobby for the initiative process in states where it does not exist.

- Government inspection programs

Collect data on present government inspection programs including percentage of locations inspected, number of inspectors in the field, frequency of inspections (required v. actual), qualifications of inspectors, training programs, surprise or planned inspections, length of each inspection, procedures for violations, penalties, follow-up inspections, results to public and employees.

■ Government agency or department profile

Study a government agency or department, including how it was set up, its authority, annual reports, studies, personnel; interview present and past personnel, recommend reforms.

■ Small claims court

Evaluate small claims court to determining accessibility by interviewing clerks, judges, examining court records. Publish a guidebook to make the process more accessible.

■ Legislation watch

Monitor progress of bills in state legislature or issue before city council or board of education.

■ Candidate/Issue debate

Sponsor a debate among candidates or elected officials and groups opposing local policies.

■ City council guide

Write a how-to guide on drafting, proposing and passing a bill in City Council.

■ Public documents guide

Write a guide to access to public documents, such as drivers and marriage licenses, building permits.

■ Smoking ordinances

Analyze how much smoking in public places is permitted and work for a town ordinance to protect nonsmokers.

CONSUMER

■ Organic produce guide

Survey shoppers to show willingness to buy organically-grown (pesticide-free) produce to persuade grocery stores to sell organic produce. Produce a guide to stores selling organic produce, reporting on source and availability and verification method. List and detail dangers of pesticides on other foods sold in supermarkets.

■ Market basket survey

Survey supermarkets to compare prices and availability of basic items; compare different branches of the same supermarket to see if prices differ according to the community.

■ Prescription drug price disclosure survey

Survey pharmacies to compare brand name and generic drug prices. Work to repeal anti-substitution laws as well as anti-advertising provisions or test pharmacy compliance with existing disclosure laws.

■ Advertised specials survey

Survey supermarkets and pharmacies for compliance with Federal Trade Commission regulations regarding advertised specials, including availability, price, condition of product and sales tactics.

■ Meat survey

Survey supermarkets for fraud in meat packaging: marking a package at a higher weight than it contains and/or selling meat with more than the allowed amount of fat and/or mislabeling to indicate lower fat content than the package contains.

■ Open Dating survey

Survey supermarkets for compliance with open dating code including which products are to be dated, type of open dating to be used, how and where the product is to be stamped and any explanatory phrases to be used. If the community does not have an open dating regulation, survey shoppers to show support and need.

■ Fraudulent repair practices

Survey repair shops. Use a product in need of repair to test their honesty and competence. Follow up with programs to license repair shops or pressure businesses.

■ Bank survey

Survey banks and savings and loans for least expensive credit sources, compare interest rates, automatic teller machine (ATM) and credit charges as well as other services and fees. Check for compliance with Truth in Lending law which requires that all interest rates be quoted according to the annual percentage rate of interest.

■ Savings and Loans

Study an S&L's investment policies: investment criteria, where most investment is made and whether the association has a commitment to social action.

■ Buyers action center and/or Automobile safety and complaint center

Form a buyers action center to protect consumers' rights in the marketplace via consumer education programs and consumer complaint resolution.

■ Green grocery

Encourage supermarkets to sell produce without wrapping it in plastic, to provide paper bags, recycling bins and bulk foods.

■ Highway safety

Survey local highway hazards.

■ Airbags

Survey local car dealers which sell airbag-equipped cars to determine ease in buying such a car.

■ All-Terrain Vehicles (ATVs)

Survey local stores to determine compliance with age restrictions in selling ATVs.

■ Tanning salons

Survey tanning salons for compliance with regulations requiring warning labels on every machine.

■ Dry cleaners

Survey dry cleaners to uncover discrimination against women by charging higher prices for women's clothing than men's.

■ Billboards

Survey billboards to determine if alcohol and tobacco ads are aimed at minority communities.

MEDIA

■ Newspaper/TV news survey

Monitor local news outlets for editorial content and determine the number of reporters/pages/time per topic.

■ Letters to the editor

Determine the letter to the editor policy of local newspapers.

■ Public access survey

Survey public access channels to evaluate outreach, accessibility, content and who uses them.

■ Public affairs survey

Survey local TV stations for amount of public affairs programming.

■ "No TV Week"

Conduct a community-wide "No TV Week" to demonstrate influence of television and to encourage other activities such as reading.

HEALTH CARE

■ Consumer directory of doctors

Provide consumers with basic information about educational credentials, availability, fees and services.

■ Nursing home care

Survey nursing homes' licenses and federal inspection reports for compliance.

■ Access to hospitals

Survey access to hospitals as required under the Hill-Burton Act.

■ Hospital projects

1) Prepare a shopper's guide to hospitals describing facilities, employment practices, services and costs including increases in cost over previous ten-year period;

2) Investigate hospitals' Boards of Trustees to determine adequacy of consumer/patient/employee representation, potential conflict of interest;

3) Survey hospital emergency services, including ambulance service and emergency rooms;

4) Participate in the hospital inspection and accreditation process.

CRIME

- Incarceration study

  Investigate rates of and alternatives to incarceration.

- Crime prevention

  Study methods of crime prevention.

- Domestic violence

  Conduct a survey of domestic violence.

- Crime study

  Profile nature of crime in your community.

SCHOOLS

- Sex discrimination survey

  Survey the public school system for unequal expenditures on and discrimination in male and female physical education and extracurricular activities and discrimination in textbooks, library books and school activities such as hall patrols, safety squads and promotion of teachers.

- School lunch program evaluation

  Evaluate school lunch and vending machine foods for nutritional content and additives/preservatives. Urge the adoption of healthy meals and snacks.

- Chemistry Lab

  Evaluate toxic and hazardous materials used in school chemistry labs; adopt microscale chemistry techniques to reduce exposure.

- Tracking

  Analyze school tracking system for possible discrimination by counting the number of minorities and women in upper level v. lower level, determine at what age and grade level tracking begins.

BUSINESS

- Industrial revenue bonds

  Investigate Industrial revenue bonds and job creation.

- Federal contractor discrimination

  Investigate companies or universities with federal contracts over $50,000 which are required to practice affirmative action — compare before and after employment figures to determine the company's progress.

- Corporate taxes

  1) Survey companies for illegal tax avoidance, for example, not listing improvements or additions, removing property from jurisdiction, over-depreciation and delinquency;

  2) Investigate legal methods of avoiding paying a fair share, for example, low-tax zones, special districts, industrial development bonds and exemptions and tax abatement.

- Interlocking directorates

  Investigate relationships among directors and board members of major businesses, especially banks and utilities.

RESOURCES

GENERAL

Cowan, Jessica, ed. *Good Works: A Guide to Careers in Social Change*. New York: Barricade Books, 1991. A directory of over 800 citizen organizations throughout the United States.

CHILDREN'S ORGANIZATIONS

Advocates for Children of New York, Inc.
24-16 Bridge Plaza South
Long Island City, NY 11101
    Works to protect educational entitlements and due process rights of disadvantaged public school children in New York City.

Children Now
926 J Street, Suite 413
Sacramento, CA 95814
    Combines policy analysis, outreach, implementation and advocacy strategies to improve the lives of children and their families. Publishes the annual *Report Card '90* grading the condition of California's children.

Children's Defense Fund
122 C Street, NW
Washington, DC 20001
    Conducts research and advocacy on behalf of poor, minority and disabled children. Publishes *Adolescent Pregnancy Prevention Clearinghouse* six times a year and *Children's Defense Fund Reports* monthly.

Books, Reports, Pamphlets

A Children's Defense Budget. Reports on the status of U.S. children and the developments and trends shaping their condition. Washington, DC: Children's Defense Fund. $13.95.

Children's Defense Fund's Nonpartisan Congressional Voting Record. Washington, DC: Children's Defense Fund. $3.50.

CITIZENSHIP/LEGAL EDUCATION ORGANIZATIONS

American Bar Association
750 North Lake Shore Drive
Chicago, Illinois 60611
    The American Bar Association is a nonprofit, independent national research institute committed to basic research on law and legal institutions. Publishes law-related educational materials.

Center for Civic Education
5146 Douglas Fir Road
Calabasas, CA 91302
    Works to improve educational resources and curricula for civics education. Publishes *Center Correspondent* quarterly.

Close Up Foundation
44 Canal Center Plaza
Alexandria, VA 22314
    A nonpartisan educational foundation promoting citizen involvement in government.

Constitutional Rights Foundation (CRF)
601 South Kingsley Drive
Los Angeles, CA 90005
    Publishes *School Youth Service Network*, a quarterly newsletter that reports on youth service projects around the country and the progress of state-wide community service programs.

Council for the Advancement of Citizenship
44 Canal Center Plaza
Alexandria, VA 22314
    Works to promote informed, responsible citizenship education through clearinghouse services, publications and reports. Publishes *Citizenship Education News* quarterly.

National Institute for Citizen Education in the Law
711 G Street, SE
Washington, DC 20003
    Educates citizens on the law and the U.S. legal system.

Books, Reports, Pamphlets

American Bar Association Catalog. Chicago: American Bar Association. Catalog of books, periodicals, pamphlets and audiovisual materials published or endorsed by the American Bar Association.

CIVITAS: A Framework for Civic Education. Calabasas, CA: Center for Civic Education, 1991.

Excel in Civics: Lessons in Citizenship. Saint Paul: West Publishing, 1985. A teacher's manual is available.

Great Trials in American History: Civil War to the Present. Saint Paul: West Publishing, 1985. For grades 8-12. 15 crucial trials in historical, social and legal context. A teacher's manual is available.

Law and the Consumer. Washington, DC: National Institute for Citizen Education in the Law, 1982. For grades 9-12 to teach consumer education, home economics and family living. A teacher's manual is available.

Street Law Mock Trial Manual. Washington, DC: National Institute for Citizen Education in the Law, 1984. For grades 7-12. Six optional mock trials on civil, criminal and constitutional issues.

CIVIL RIGHTS/CIVIL LIBERTIES ORGANIZATIONS

American-Arab Anti-Discrimination Committee
4201 Connecticut Avenue, NW, Suite 500
Washington, DC 20008
Works to combat anti-Arab stereotyping, defamation and discrimination and to promote a better understanding of the cultural heritage of Arab Americans.

American Civil Liberties Union
132 W. 43 Street, Second floor
New York, NY 10036
Works to protect and expand the rights and liberties of U.S. citizens and to defend the U.S. Constitution through litigation.

Human Rights Campaign Fund
1012 14th Street, NW, Suite 607
Washington, DC 20005
Works to mobilize grassroots support for, and educate and lobby legislators for lesbian and gay rights. Publishes *Momentum* quarterly.

Lambda Legal Defense and Education Fund, Inc.
666 Broadway 12th floor
New York, NY 10012
Pursues test-case litigation, nationwide, in areas of concern to gay men and lesbians. Publishes *AIDS Update* 6 times a year and *Lambda Update* 3 times a year.

Leadership Conference on Civil Rights
2027 Massachusetts Avenue, NW
Washington, DC 20036

Mexican American Legal Defense and Educational Fund (MALDEF)
634 South Spring Street, 11th Floor
Los Angeles, CA 90014
Works to protect the civil rights of Hispanic Americans through class action litigation, advocacy and community education. Publishes *MALDEF Newsletter* 3 times a year.

National Association for the Advancement of Colored People (NAACP)
4805 Mt. Hope Drive
Baltimore, MD 21215-3297
Works to ensure the political, educational, social and economic equality of African Americans primarily through litigation and lobbying. Publishes *CRISIS Magazine* monthly.

National Gay and Lesbian Task Force
1517 U Street, NW
Washington, DC 20009
Uses lobbying and citizen organizing to work for gay and lesbian civil rights and a responsive federal AIDS policy. Publishes annual *Gay Violence and Victimization Report* and *Task Force Report*, a quarterly newsletter.

National Indian Education Association
1819 H Street, NW, Suite 800
Washington, DC 20006
Helps Native American and Alaskan Native students keep traditional tribal values while learning to be productive citizens in an increasingly technological world.

National Rainbow Coalition
P.O. Box 27385
Washington, DC 20005
Works to empower, to advocate, to persuade and to build consensus in areas of civil rights, religious, labor, government, education, business and academia, the environment and health care.

National Urban League
500 East 62nd Street
New York, NY 10021
     Works to promote educational attainment, employment and economic self-sufficiency for African Americans.

Native American Rights Fund
1506 Broadway
Boulder, CO 80302-6296
     Works on issues related to the preservation of tribal existence, protection of tribal natural resources, promotion of human rights, government accountability and the development of Indian law.

Operation PUSH (People United to Serve Humanity)
950 E. 50th Street
Chicago, IL 60615
     Works to revitalize African American communities.

Puerto Rican Legal Defense and Education Fund
99 Hudson Street 14th Floor
New York, NY 10013
     Works to protect Puerto Ricans and other Latinos in areas such as education, fair housing, employment discrimination, voting rights and health care.

Southern Christian Leadership Conference
334 Auburn Avenue, NE
Atlanta, GA 30312
     Works to provide moral and spiritual leadership in the struggle against racial oppression. Publishes *SCLC Magazine* 4 to 6 times a year.

Southern Poverty Law Center
400 Washington Avenue
Montgomery, Alabama 36104
     Operates the Klanwatch Project to monitor the activities of, and file suit against, illegal white supremacist activities. Publishes *Teaching Tolerance*, a biannual publication to help teachers promote racial and religious tolerance in the classroom.

Books, Reports, Pamphlets

The Rights of Aliens and Refugees. Carbondale, IL: Southern Illinois University Press, American Civil Liberties Union, 1990.

The Rights of Authors and Artists. New York: Bantam Books, American Civil Liberties Union, 1984.

The Rights of Crime Victims. New York: Bantam Books, American Civil Liberties Union, 1985.

The Rights of Employees. New York: Bantam Books, American Civil Liberties Union, 1984.

The Rights of Gay People. New York: Bantam Books, American Civil Liberties Union, 1983.

The Rights of Older Persons. Carbondale, IL: Southern Illinois University Press, American Civil Liberties Union, 1989.

The Rights of Patients. Carbondale, IL: Southern Illinois University Press, American Civil Liberties Union, 1989.

The Rights of Prisoners. Carbondale, IL: Southern Illinois University Press, American Civil Liberties Union, 1988.

The Rights of Single People. New York: Bantam Books, American Civil Liberties Union, 1985.

The Rights of Students. Carbondale, IL: Southern Illinois University Press, American Civil Liberties Union, 1988.

The Rights of Teachers. New York: Bantam Books, American Civil Liberties Union, 1984.

The Rights of Women. New York: Bantam Books, American Civil Liberties Union, 1984.

The Rights of Young People. New York: Bantam Books, American Civil Liberties Union, 1985.

Your Right to Government Information. New York: Bantam Books, American Civil Liberties Union, 1985.

Your Right to Privacy. Carbondale, IL: Southern Illinois University Press, American Civil Liberties Union, 1990.

Seeger, Pete and Bob Reiser. *Everybody Says Freedom*. New Market, TN: Highlander, 1989. A portrait of the music of the Civil Rights movement. $19.

Teaching Tolerance. Montgomery, AL: Southern Poverty Law Center, 1991. A free, biannual publication for teachers dedicated to promoting racial and religious tolerance.

COMMUNITY LAWYER

Charlene LaVoie
P.O. Box 1044
Winchester, CT 06098

COMMUNITY ORGANIZING ORGANIZATIONS

Association of Community Organizations for Reform Now (ACORN)
845 Flatbush Avenue
Brooklyn, NY 11226
(718) 693-6700
     With offices in several cities, organizes people in low income communities to work on campaigns involving such issues as housing, banking and education.

Citizen Action
1300 Connecticut Avenue, NW, Suite 401
Washington, DC 20036
     A national citizen's political organization dedicated to increasing citizen participation in economic and political decision making. Publishes *Citizen Action News* quarterly.

Midwest Academy
225 West Ohio Street, Suite 250
Chicago, IL 60610
     Works to help low and moderate income people to win benefits and empower themselves to build a more just society.

National Association of Neighborhoods
1651 Fuller Street, NW
Washington, DC 20009
     Consists of over 2,000 community groups and small businesses working to promote social and economic development. Publishes *NAN Bulletin* quarterly.

National Peoples Action
810 N. Milwaukee Avenue
Chicago, IL 60622
     A nationwide network of grassroots community activists who work on a variety of issues.

Books, Reports, Pamphlets

Alinsky, Saul. *Reveille for Radicals*. New York: Vintage Books, 1969.

Alinsky, Saul. *Rules for Radicals*. New York: Random House, 1971.

Bobo, Tim, Jackie Kendal and Steve Max. *Midwest Academy Organizing Manual: Organizing for Social Change*. Chicago: Seven Locks Press, 1991.

Booth, Heather, Harry Boyte and Steve Max. *Citizen Action and the New American Populism*. Philadelphia: Temple University Press, 1986.

Boyte, Harry C. *Commonwealth*. New York: The Free Press, 1989.

Boyte, Harry C. *The Backyard Revolution*. Philadelphia: Temple University Press, 1980.

Boyte, Harry C. *Community is Possible*. New York: Harper and Row, 1984.

Fink, Leon. *The Radical Vision of Saul Alinsky*. Mahway, Paulist Press, 1984.

Fisher, Robert. *Let the People Decide: Neighborhood Organizing in America*. Boston: G.K. Hall, 1984.

Freeman, Jo, ed., *Social Movements of the Sixties and Seventies*. New York: Longman, 1983.

Horwitt, Sanford D. *Let Them Call Me Rebel: Saul Alinsky — His Life and Legacy*. New York: Alfred A. Knopf, Inc., 1989.

Slayton, Robert. *Back of the Yards: The Making of a Local Democracy*. Chicago: University of Chicago Press, 1986.

CONSUMER/CORPORATE ACCOUNTABILITY ORGANIZATIONS

Action for Corporate Accountability
129 Church Street
New Haven, CT 06510
     Alerts the public and takes action to stop corporate practices which cause infant death and disease. Conducts a boycott of Nestle and American Home Products for violations of international infant formula standards.

American Association of Retired Persons
601 E Street, NW
Washington, DC 20049
     Serves the needs and interests of retired persons through legislative advocacy, research, informative programs and community services.

Bankcard Holders of America
560 Herndon Parkway, Suite 120
Herndon, VA 22070

Educates the public about the wise and careful use of credit.

Buyers Up
P.O. Box 53005
Washington, DC 20009

A membership organization dedicated to saving people money through group purchases of heating oil and energy services.

Center for Auto Safety
2001 S Street, NW, Suite 410
Washington, DC 20009

Conducts research and advocacy on highway safety, vehicle safety, economy and reliability and informs citizens of consumer transportation issues.

Center for the Study of Commercialism
1875 Connecticut Avenue NW, Suite 300
Washington, DC 20009-5728

Researches, documents, publicizes and opposes the excessive intrusion of commercial interests in society.

Citizen Utility Board Organizing Project
P.O. Box 19312
Washington, DC 20036

Assists in organizing state-wide groups to represent utility consumers before rate-making boards, the courts and the legislature.

Consumer Action
116 New Montgomery Street, Suite 223
San Francisco, CA 94105

Works to educate and advise the public through a telephone consumer line, publications and public hearings. Publishes *The CA Newsletter* 8 times a year.

Consumer Federation of America
1424 16th Street, NW, Suite 604
Washington, DC 20036

An advocacy, education and membership organization which works to advance pro-consumer policy before Congress, regulatory agencies and the courts. Publishes *CFAnews* 8 times a year.

Consumers Union of the United States, Inc.
101 Truman Avenue
Yonkers, NY 10703-1057

Provides consumers with information and advice on goods, services, health and personal finance and a variety of other consumer issues. Publishes *Consumer Reports* monthly.

Co-op America
2100 M Street, NW, Suite 310
Washington, DC 20036

Promotes consumer cooperatives and educates consumers and businesses on socially responsible buying and investing. Publishes *Co-op America Quarterly* and *Boycott Action News* (BAN) quarterly.

FairTest
National Center for Fair and Open Testing
342 Broadway
Cambridge, MA 02139

Works to end the abuses, misuses and flaws of standardized testing.

Florida Consumers Federation
937 Belvedere Road
West Palm Beach, FL 33405

Provides public education, lobbies government on energy issues, utility rate reform and tax reform.

Government Purchasing Project
P.O. Box 19367
Washington, DC 20036

Promotes government purchase and use of energy-efficient and environmentally sound technologies and products.

INFACT
256 Hanover Street, Third Floor
Boston, MA 02113

Works on international campaigns to stop the abuses of transnational corporations that endanger the health and survival of people around the world.

Institute for Consumer Responsibility (ICR)
6506 28th Avenue, NE
Seattle, WA 98115

Educates citizens to exercise direct control over corporations by using the boycott for social change. Publishes *National Boycott News*.

Interfaith Center on Corporate Responsibility (ICCR)
475 Riverside Drive, Room 566
New York, NY 10115-0050

Helps members work as institutional investors to hold corporations socially accountable. Publishes *The Corporate Examiner* 10 times a year.

National Consumers League
815 15th Street, NW, Suite 928
Washington, DC 20005

Conducts research, education and advocacy to represent and inform consumers and workers. Publishes *NCL Bulletin* bimonthly.

National Family Farm Coalition
80 F Street, NW, Suite 714
Washington, DC 20001

Works for progressive agriculture policy reforms to strengthen family farm-based sustainable agriculture.

National Insurance Consumer Organization
121 Payne Street
Alexandria, VA 22314

Educates consumers on all aspects of buying insurance and serves as a consumer advocate on public policy matters.

Public Citizen
2000 P Street, NW
Washington, DC 20036

An umbrella organization for Buyers Up, Litigation Group, Health Research Group and Congress Watch which works to protect and promote the rights of consumers and citizens.

United Shareholders Association
1667 K Street, NW, Suite 770
Washington, DC 20006

A grassroots advocacy organization which promotes shareholders' rights and greater accountability of management to shareholders.

United States Public Interest Research Group
215 Pennsylvania Avenue, SE
Washington, DC 20003

The national lobbying office for state PIRGs, focuses on environmental and consumer protection and energy and government reform. Publishes *Citizen Agenda* quarterly.

Virginia Citizens Consumer Council
1611 S. Walter Reed Drive, Room 107
Arlington, VA 22204

Promotes and represents the rights and general interests of consumers.

Voter Revolt
3325 Wilshire Boulevard, Suite 550
Los Angeles, CA 90010

Works to change the role and influence of citizens in lawmaking by advocating reform measures of critical concern to Californians.

Books, Reports, Pamphlets

ATM Fees Go Up, Up, Up! Washington, DC: U.S.PIRG, 1991. $5.

Braiman-Lipson, J. and D.F. Raub. *Toy Buying Guide.* Fairfield, OH: Consumer Reports, 1988. Information on the educational and play value, safety and durability of 400 popular toys for children 5 to 14 years of age. Sections on toys for infant and special-needs children. $6.95.

Consumer Guide to Advertising. Washington, DC: American Association of Retired Persons. Guide to recognizing deceptive advertising. $17.50.

Indecent Exposure: Consumers Getting "Burned" by Tanning Salons. Washington, DC: U.S.PIRG, 1991. Documents the failure of tanning salon operators to comply with federal law designed to warn consumers of hazards associated with tanning machines. $6.

Is That Traveling Sales Job For You?. Washington, DC: National Consumers League, 1989. Helps young adults avoid exploitative situations, suggests questions to ask during interviews, outlines guidelines for ethical salespeople and gives warning signs of a dishonest company. $1.

Mierzwinski, Ed and Lucinda Sikes. *The Big Book Of PIRG Consumer Projects.* Washington, DC: U.S.PIRG, 1990. Contains citizen projects to improve communities including consumer credit, defective cars and auto safety, food safety, generic drugs, environmental impact, consumer rip-offs, insurance, supermarket pricing, utility complaints and better government.

Not a Pretty Picture: Toxics in Art Supplies in Washington, D.C. Area Public Schools. Washington, DC: U.S.PIRG, 1986. $5.

Selling America's Kids: Commercial Pressures on Kids of the 90s. Mount Vernon, NY: Consumers Union Education Services, 1990.

CRIME ORGANIZATIONS

National Crime Prevention Council
733 15th Street, NW, Suite 540
Washington, DC 20005

National Crime Prevention Council and National Institute for Citizen Education in the Law publish educational materials on crime prevention programs.

EDUCATION ORGANIZATIONS

Council on Interracial Books for Children
1841 Broadway
New York, NY 10023

Develops teaching and training materials designed to reduce racism and sexism in school and society. Catalog: *Resources to Counter Racism, Sexism and Other Forms of Bias in School and Society.*

FairTest
National Center for Fair & Open Testing
342 Broadway
Cambridge, MA 02139-1802

Works to eliminate the biases and inadequacies of national tests at all grade levels. Publishes *Fairtest Examiner* quarterly.

Highlander Education and Research Center
Route 3, Box 370
New Market, TN 37820

Provides educational programs aimed at sustaining and aiding emergent community leadership in Appalachia and the South.

LULAC National Educational Service Centers
777 North Capitol Street, NE, Suite 305
Washington, DC 20002

Works with business and government to improve the educational conditions of the Latino community in the United States. Publishes *Opportunity to Lead* 3 times a year.

National Council for History Education, Inc.
26915 Westwood Road, Suite A-2
Westlake, OH 44145-4656

Promotes the importance of history in school and society. Publishes *History Matters!* ten times a year.

National Issues Forums
100 Commons Road
Dayton, OH 45459

Holds public forums around the country aimed at increasing citizen discussion and cultivating the arts of public debate about the issues of the day.

People For the American Way
2000 M Street, NW, Suite 400
Washington, DC 20036

Promotes constitutional liberties such as First Amendment rights and the right to privacy and civil rights, through education, advocacy and litigation.

Project Public Life
Hubert H. Humphrey Institute of Public Affairs
301 19th Avenue South
Minneapolis, MN 55455

Works to stimulate discussion on public decision making and has a program of citizen education in the use of power, judgment, imagination and reflection on experience.

Study Circle Resource Center
Route 169, Box 203
Pomfret, CT 06258

Publishes course material and articles for small group discussions around issues and themes of democracy and citizenship.

Women's Educational Equity Act Publishing Center
Education Development Center, Inc.
55 Chapel Street
Newton, MA 02160

Books, Reports, Pamphlets

The Adventures of a Radical Hillbilly. New Market, TN: Highlander, 1981. Bill Moyers interviews Myles Horton about his life, his philosophy of education and Highlander. $15.

Attacks on the Freedom to Learn: The 1988-1989 Report. Washington, DC: People for the American Way. A detailed state-by-state listing of censorship attempts and other challenges to public schools. $7.95.

Beckwith, Barbara, John Weiss and Bob Schaeffer. *Standing Up to The SAT.* Cambridge, MA: National Center for Fair & Open Testing. $6.95. Demystifies the SAT and offers successful strategies for taking it.

Boyte, Harry C. and Kathryn Stoff-Hoff. *Doing Politics: A Study Circle in Citizen Action.* Minneapolis: Project Public Life, 1991.

A Consumer's Guide to Biology Textbooks. Washington, DC: People for the American Way, 1989. $9.95.

Democracy's Next Generation. Washington, DC: People for the American Way, 1990. A study of more than 1,000 young people aged 15-24 and 400 social studies teachers; explores the attitudes and values of today's youth concerning citizenship, civic participation, voting, politics and government. $10.95.

The Highlander Folk School: A History of its Major Programs 1932-1961. New Market, TN: Highlander. $30.

Horne, Gerald, ed. *Thinking and Rethinking U.S. History.* New York: Council on Interracial Books for Children. 1991. Reviews leading U.S. history textbooks and points out discriminatory histories that exclude the experiences of minorities.

Jackdaws: Primary Source Portfolios. Amawalk, NY: Jackdaw Publications, 1991. A catalog of primary source duplications about the American Revolution, the U.S. Constitution, Voting Rights for African Americans, Japanese-American internment, Woman Suffrage, populism, child labor and others.

Looking at History: A Review of Major U.S. History Textbooks. Washington, DC: People for the American Way. $10.95.

Making the Rules: A Guidebook for Young People Who Intend to Make a Difference. Minneapolis: Project Public Life, 1991.

Protecting the Freedom to Learn: A Citizen's Guide. Washington, DC: People for the American Way, 1990. $5.95.

Resources for Educational Equity. Newton, MA: Women's Educational Equity Act Publishing Center, 1992. Free catalog describes over 250 nonsexist, multicultural materials designed for teachers and others.

Teaching Today's Constitution. Culver City: Social Studies School Service. Organized lesson plans explain step-by-step how to conduct a mock trial, opinion polls, small project groups and other teaching activities for direct student participation. $17.95.

We the People: A Review of U.S. Government and Civics Textbooks. Washington, DC: People for the American Way, 1987. $9.95.

ELDERLY ORGANIZATIONS

American Association of Retired Persons
601 E Street, NW
Washington, DC 20049
    Serves the needs and interests of retired persons through legislative advocacy, research, information programs and community services.

Gray Panthers
3700 Chestnut Street
Philadelphia, PA 19104
    An inter-generational organization working to combat age discrimination.

National Council of Senior Citizens
1331 F Street, NW
Washington, DC 20004-1171
    Advocates on behalf of senior citizens.

Books, Reports, Pamphlets

Establishing a Nursing Home Community Council. Washington, DC: American Association of Retired Persons. $1.

Preparing a Directory of Long-Term Care Services. Washington, DC: American Association of Retired Persons, 1986.

ENVIRONMENTAL ORGANIZATIONS

Acid Rain Foundation
1410 Varsity Drive
Raleigh, NC 27606
    Provides educational materials on acid rain for grades K-12.

Bio-Integral Resource Center
Box 7414
Berkeley, CA 94707
    Provides information on the least toxic methods of managing pests.

California Rural Legal Assistance Foundation/ Earth Island Institute
2111 Mission Street, Suite 401
San Francisco, CA 94110
    Publishes *Race, Poverty & the Environment*, a quarterly newsletter that combines social and environmental justice.

Center for the Biology of Natural Systems
Queens College, City University of New York
Flushing, NY 11367

Researches municipal solid waste disposal, renewable energy and other environmental issues.

Central States Education Center
809 South Fifth
Champaign, IL 61820

Helps citizen groups work to protect their local environment by offering technical assistance on waste issues.

Citizen's Clearinghouse for Hazardous Wastes (CCHW)
119 Rowell Court, P.O. Box 6806
Falls Church, VA 22040

Works to help local groups form and fight dumps, incinerators, toxic discharges, military waste and other toxic polluters. Publishes *Everyone's Backyard* bimonthly.

Clean Water Action Project
317 Pennsylvania Avenue, SE
Washington, DC 20003

Works for clean and safe water, controlling toxic chemicals and the protection of natural resources.

Concern, Inc.
1794 Columbia Road, NW
Washington, DC 20009

Provides environmental information and guidelines for community action.

Council on Economic Priorities
30 Irving Place
New York, NY 10003

Works to enhance corporate performance in the areas of military spending, energy, the environment and fair employment practices.

Council on the Environment of New York City (CENYC)
51 Chambers Street, Room 228
New York, NY 10007

Works to promote environmental awareness among New Yorkers and to develop solutions to environmental problems.

Earthwise Consumer
Box 1506
Mill Valley, CA 94942

Publishes consumer information on environmentally sound products. Publishes *The Earthwise Consumer* 8 times a year.

Ecology Center
2530 San Pablo Avenue
Berkeley, CA 94702

Provides information on recycling, ecology, nature, environment, gardening and farming.

Environmental Action Coalition
625 Broadway, 2nd Floor
New York, NY 10012

Works on solid waste, urban forestry, water use and environmental education issues.

Environmental Action Foundation
6930 Carroll Avenue, Suite 600
Takoma Park, MD 20912

Works on issues such as acid rain, plastics, solid waste and toxics through research, public education, organizing, advocacy and legal action. Publishes *Environmental Action Magazine* and *Powerline* bimonthly and *Wastelines* quarterly.

Environmental Defense Fund
257 Park Avenue South
New York, NY 10010

Links science, economics and law to create economically viable solutions to environmental problems.

Environmental Health Watch
4115 Bridge Avenue, Suite 104
Cleveland, OH 44113

An information center on hazardous materials in the home and community, designed to educate the public on the health effects of dangerous toxics.

Friends of the Earth
218 D Street, SE
Washington, DC 20003

Works with hundreds of grassroots groups working on issues ranging from groundwater protection and agricultural biotechnology to preventing toxic chemical accidents.

Global Tomorrow Coalition
1325 G Street, NW, Suite 915
Washington, DC 20005-3104

Works to build U.S. leadership on long-term, interrelated trends in environment, population and resource use.

Greenpeace
1436 U Street, NW
Washington, DC 20009

Conducts campaigns on toxic waste elimination, nuclear disarmament, protection of marine mammals and alternatives to environmentally destructive energy consumption. Publishes *Greenpeace Magazine* bimonthly.

Household Hazardous Waste Project
901 S. National, Box 108
Springfield, MO 65804
Provides training, educational and organizing materials for their clearinghouse and referral service, answering questions regarding household hazardous materials.

INFORM, Inc.
381 Park Avenue South
New York, NY 10016
Researches such issues as hazardous waste reduction, garbage management, air pollution and land and water conservation. Publishes *INFORM Reports* quarterly.

Institute for Environmental Education
32000 Chagrin Boulevard
Cleveland, OH 44124
Provides a year-long environmental studies program.

Institute for Local Self-Reliance
2435 18th Street, NW
Washington, DC 20009
Encourages cities to pursue local self-reliance as a development strategy, combining local political authority and modern technology to become more independent.

Kids Against Pollution
Tenakill High School
275 High Street
Closter, NJ 07624
Anti-pollution organization run by and for students.

National Coalition Against the Misuse of Pesticides
701 E Street, SE, Suite 200
Washington, DC 20003
NCAMP researches and publishes information on alternatives to pesticides. Publishes *Pesticides and You* 5 times a year.

National Library of Medicine
U.S. Department of Health and Human Services
TRI Representative
8600 Rockville Pike
Bethesda, MD 20894
Manages the TOXNET system which included the Toxic Release Inventory database.

National Recycling Coalition, Inc.
1101 30th Street, NW, Suite 305
Washington, DC 20007
Association of professional recyclers, environmental groups and individuals; promotes recycling, provides technical assistance and information on recycling. Publishes *The NRC Connection* quarterly.

National Toxics Campaign
1168 Commonwealth Avenue
Boston, MA 02134
Works to implement citizen-based preventive solutions to toxic and environmental problems. Publishes *Toxic Times: Right-to-Know News* quarterly.

National Wildlife Federation
1400 16th Street, NW
Washington, DC 20036
Promotes the wise use of natural resources and the protection of the global environment. Publishes *Cool it! Connection* quarterly.

Natural Resources Defense Council
122 E 42nd Street, 45th Floor
New York, NY 10168
Works to protect America's endangered natural resources by monitoring and working with government agencies, scientific research, litigation and citizen education.

Nature Conservancy
1815 North Lynn Street
Arlington, VA 22209
International environmental organization dedicated to the preservation of global diversity. (rare plants, animals and natural communities)

New York Public Interest Research Group (NYPIRG)
9 Murray Street
New York, NY 10007
A student-run, state-wide, environmental and consumer organization working on solid waste issues, nuclear power and incinerators.

Nuclear Information and Resource Service
1424 16th Street, NW, Suite 601
Washington, DC 20036
A national clearinghouse and networking center on nuclear power issues. Publishes *Groundswell* quarterly.

OMB Watch
2001 O Street, NW
Washington, DC 20036
Monitors the Office of Management and Budget, the largest unit within the Executive Office of the President. Provides citizen education on related legislative and administrative issues. Publishes a guide to the federal community right-to-know law.

P3 Foundation Inc.
P.O. Box 52
Montgomery, VT 05470

Publishes *P3, The Earth-based Magazine for Kids* monthly, which explains environmental issues to children and provides suggestions for individual action.

Rainforest Action Network
301 Broadway, Suite A
San Francisco, CA 94133

Coordinates environmental and human rights organizations on major campaigns to protect the rainforests.

Renew America
1400 16th Street, NW, Suite 710
Washington, DC 20036

An environmental education organization researching positive local, state and national policies and programs designed to protect and enhance the environment.

Rocky Mountain Institute (RMI)
1739 Snowmass Creek Road
Old Snowmass, CO 81654

Researches energy, water, agriculture, economic renewal and global energy issues to encourage an efficient and sustainable use of resources as a path to global security.

Safe Energy Communication Council (SECC)
1717 Massachusetts Avenue, NW, Suite LL215
Washington, DC 20036

A national coalition of environmental, energy and media groups working to increase public awareness on energy efficiency and renewable energy.

Save What's Left
Coral Springs High School
7201 West Sample Road
Coral Springs, FL 33065

A worldwide network of high school students working on a variety of environmental issues.

Sierra Club
730 Polk Street
San Francisco, CA 94109

Works on enforcement of the Clean Air Act, preserving national parks and forests, global warming and international development lending reform.

Student Conservation Association, Inc.
P.O. Box 550
Charlestown, NH 03603

Helps students find programs and internships in the conservation field.

Student Environmental Action Coalition
P.O. Box 1168
University of North Carolina
Chapel Hill, NC 27514

An alliance of student environmental organizations which acts as a clearinghouse of information and facilitates the sharing of knowledge and experience necessary to successfully achieve a healthy planet.

Union of Concerned Scientists
26 Church Street
Cambridge, MA 02238

A nonprofit organization of nearly 100,000 scientists and other citizens concerned about the impact of advanced technology, including nuclear power on society.

United States Public Interest Research Group (U.S. PIRG)
215 Pennsylvania Avenue, SE
Washington, DC 20003

The national lobbying office for state PIRGs, student-run organizations working on environmental protection, consumer protection and government reform.

World Resources Institute
1709 New York Avenue, NW
Washington, DC 20036

Works to provide accurate information about global resources and environmental conditions, analyze emerging issues and develop creative and workable policy responses.

World Wildlife Fund
1250 24th Street, NW
Washington, DC 20037

Provides information on protection of endangered wildlife, wetlands, rain forests in Asia, Latin America and Africa.

Worldwatch Institute
1776 Massachusetts Avenue, NW
Washington, DC 20036-1904

Works to alert policymakers and the public about emerging global trends in the management of natural and human resources. Publishes *Worldwatch* bimonthly.

Zero Population Growth
1400 16th Street, NW, Suite 320
Washington, DC 20036

Publishes a variety of information on population problems and issues. Publishes *The ZPG Reporter* bimonthly.

Books, Reports, Pamphlets

Energy Efficiency/Renewable Energy

Acid Rain and Electricity Conservation. Takoma Park, MD: Environmental Action Foundation, 1987. $20.

Alternative Budget for Energy Conservation. Takoma Park, MD: Environmental Action Foundation, 1990. $10.

Alternative Energy Packet. Washington, DC: Nuclear Information and Resource Service. $5.

Fact Packets on Energy Issues: Global Warming; Effects of Electric and Magnetic Fields from Transmission Lines; State Least-Cost Electricity Planning; Making Your Home Energy Efficient. Takoma Park, MD: Environmental Action Foundation. $4 each.

MYTHBusters #3: Foreign Oil Dependence. Washington, DC: Safe Energy Communication Council. $3.

MYTHBusters #5: Renewable Energy. Washington, DC: Safe Energy Communication Council. $3.

MYTHBusters #6: Energy Efficiency. Washington, DC: Safe Energy Communication Council. $3.

Pollock, Cynthia. *Renewable Energy: Today's Contribution, Tomorrow's Promise.* Washington, DC: Worldwatch Institute, 1988. $5.

Renewables Are Ready: A Guide to Teaching Renewable Energy in Junior and Senior High School Classrooms. Cambridge, MA: Union of Concerned Scientists, 1991. Contains experiments, simulations and other activities to teach about renewable energy. $5. Ten or more copies, $3. each.

Simpson, Walter. *Recipe for an Effective Campus Energy Conservation Program.* Cambridge: Union of Concerned Scientists, 1991. Describes energy conservation experiences at SUNY Buffalo, where utility bills were reduced by approximately $3 million a year. Provides practical, common-sense guidelines for establishing similar programs at other universities and large institutions. $2.

Global Warming

A Consumer's Guide to Protecting the Ozone Layer. Boston: National Toxics Campaign. $1.50.

Global Warming and The Car. Takoma Park, MD: Environmental Action Foundation. $.20.

Global Warming and Energy Choices. Washington, DC: Concern, Inc., 1991. $4.

Global Warming Packet. Washington, DC: Nuclear Information and Resource Service. $5.

Global Warming: The Greenpeace Report. New York: Oxford University Press, 1990.

Global Warming: A Primer. Washington, DC: Zero Population Growth. 1990.

Lyman, Grancesca, et al. *The Greenhouse Trap: What We're Doing to the Atmosphere and How We Can Slow Global Warming.* Washington, DC: World Resources Institute, 1991. $9.95.

MYTHBusters #4: The Greenhouse Effect. Washington, DC: Safe Energy Communication Council. $3.

Green Consumer

Be an Environmentally Alert Consumer. Washington, DC: Environmental Protection Agency, 1990.

Guide to Hazardous Products Around the Home. Springfield, MO: Household Hazardous Waste Project.

Healthy House Catalog: National Directory of Indoor Pollution Resources. Cleveland: Environmental Health Watch and the Housing Resource Center, 1990.

Shopping for a Better World. New York: Council on Economic Priorities. $5.95. Ratings of hundreds of supermarket items.

Nuclear Issues

BRC ("Below Regulatory Concern" Radioactive Waste) Packet. Washington, DC: Nuclear Information and Resource Service. $7.

Greenpeace Book of the Nuclear Age. New York: Random House, 1989.

MYTHBusters #2: Nuclear Waste Disposal. Washington, DC: Safe Energy Communication Council. $3.

NIRS Factsheets (Nuclear Waste, Nuclear Dangers, Nuclear Accidents, Emergency Planning, Low Level Waste, Energy Efficiency, Solar Energy, Renewable Energy.) Washington, DC: Nuclear Information and Resource Service. $.10 each.

Radiation and Health Packet. Washington, DC: Nuclear Information and Resource Service. $5.

Teachers Resource Guide. Washington, DC: Nuclear Information and Resource Service. Includes annotated listings of books, films, videotapes and other materials suitable for secondary school classroom use on nuclear power and weapons. $7.50.

Packaging and Plastics

Breaking Down the Degradable Plastics Scam. Washington, DC: Greenpeace USA, 1990. $5.

Degradable Plastics Boycott Kit. Takoma Park, MD: Environmental Action Foundation. $3.

Plagued by Packaging: A Consumer Guide to Excess Packaging and Disposable Waste Problems. New York: New York Public Interest Research Group, Inc., 1990.

Plastics: America's Packaging Dilemma. New York: Environmental Action Coalition, 1990. $12.50.

Wirka, Jeanne. *Wrapped in Plastics.* Takoma Park, MD: Environmental Action Foundation, 1990. $10.

Pesticides

Citizen's Guide to Pesticides. Washington, DC: Environmental Protection Agency, 1990.

Fact Packet on Pesticides. Takoma Park, MD: Environmental Action Foundation, 1990. $3.

Pest Control Without Toxic Chemicals. Washington, DC: National Coalition Against the Misuse of Pesticides, 1989. $.50.

Pesticide Safety Myths and Fact. Washington, DC: National Coalition Against the Misuse of Pesticides, 1989. $.50.

Pesticides in Food: What the Public Needs to Know. Washington, DC: Natural Resources Defense Council. $7.50.

Pesticides & Your Fruits and Vegetables. Washington, DC: National Coalition Against the Misuse of Pesticides, 1989. $.50.

A Practical Strategy to Reduce Dangerous Pesticides in Our Food and Environment. Boston: National Toxics Campaign. An organizing kit for citizens who want to get their supermarkets to sign the Pesticide Reduction Agreement. $10.

Taking Action to Control Pesticides and Promote Alternatives. Washington, DC: National Coalition Against the Misuse of Pesticides, 1989. $3.

Population

Ehrlich, Paul and Anne Ehrlich. *The Population Explosion.* New York: Simon and Schuster, 1990.

Facts Sheets. Washington, DC: Zero Population Growth.

For Earth's Sake Teaching Kit. Washington, DC: Zero Population Growth, 1990. $24.95.

Global 2000 Countdown Kit. Washington, DC: Zero Population Growth, 1991. $19.95.

The Population Challenge. Washington, DC: Zero Population Growth, 1985. Contains facts and a broad overview of the influences and effects of population on the environment, the economy and other world issues.

USA by Numbers Teaching Kit. Washington, DC: Zero Population Growth, 1989. $19.95.

World Population. Washington, DC: Zero Population Growth. $29.95. Video.

Zero Population Growth Education Catalog. Washington, DC: Zero Population Growth, 1990.

Rainforests

Cowell, Adrian. *The Decade of Destruction.* New York: Henry Holt, 1990.

Craighead, Jean. *The Tropical Rain Forest.* Washington, DC: Island Press. 1990.

Education Kit: Vanishing Rainforest. Washington, DC: World Wildlife Fund. $20.

Goodland, Robert, ed. *Race to Save the Tropics.* Washington, DC: Island Press, 1990.

Head, Suzanne and Robert Heinzman. *Lessons of the Rainforest.* San Francisco: Sierra Club, 1990.

Lewis, Scott. *The Rainforest Book: How You Can Save the World's Rainforests*. Washington, DC: Living Planet Press, 1990. $5.95.

Miller, Kenton and Laura Tangley. *Trees of Life: Protecting Tropical Forests and Their Biological Wealth*. Boston: Beacon Press, 1991.

Rainforest Action Guide. San Francisco: Rainforest Action Network, 1990. Contains information on rainforests and lists other publications for further reading.

Teacher's Guide: Rainforests: Tropical Treasures (Nature Scope, vol. 16). Washington, DC: National Wildlife Federation. $9.50.

Teacher's Resource Guide: Rainforests-A Teacher's Resource Guide. San Francisco: Rainforest Action Network. $5.

Wilson, E.O. *Biodiversity*. Boston: National Academy Press, 1988.

Workshops and materials: Tropical Rainforest Education Program. San Francisco: Tropical Rainforest Education Program.

Recycling/Solid Waste

The Burning Question: Garbage Incineration Versus Total Recycling in New York City. New York: NYPIRG, 1986.

Backyard Composting. Berkeley, CA: Ecology Center.

Cohen, N., M. Herz and J. Rustin. *Coming Full Circle: Successful Recycling Today*. New York: Environmental Defense Fund, 1988. $20.

Deciding Where It's Going To Go: A Simulation of a Landfill Siting/Solid Waste Management Hearing. Washington State University, Department of Ecology.

Household Wastes: Issues and Opportunities. Washington, DC: Concern, Inc., 1989. $4.

Let's Reduce and Recycle: Curriculum for Solid Waste Awareness. Washington, DC: Environmental Protection Agency, 1990.

Pollock, Cynthia. *Mining Urban Wastes: The Potential for Recycling*. Washington, DC: Worldwatch Institute, 1987. $5.

Once Is Not Enough: A Citizen's Recycling Manual. Boston: National Toxics Campaign. Outlines the scope of solid waste problems and offers practical organizing approaches to recycling and composting. $3.

Recycling Paper Facts and Figures Fact Sheet. Washington, DC: National Recycling Coalition.

Recycling Works!: State and Local Solutions to Solid Waste Management Problems. Washington, DC: Environmental Protection Agency, Office of Solid Waste, 1989.

Seldman, Neil. *An Environmental Review of Incineration Technologies*. Washington, DC: Institute for Local Self-Reliance, 1986.

Solid Waste Action Guidebook. Falls Church, VA: Citizen's Clearinghouse for Hazardous Wastes. 1987. A tactical manual for grassroots action on municipal waste. $8.98.

The Solid Waste Dilemma: An Agenda for Action. Washington, DC: U.S. Environmental Protection Agency, Office of Solid Waste, 1990.

Waste Away: Information and Activities for Investigating Trash Problems and Solutions. Woodstock, VT: Vermont Institute of Natural Science, 1989.

Waste: Choices for Communities. Washington, DC: Concern, Inc., 1988. $4.

What About Waste? Lansing, MI: Michigan Department of Natural Resources.

Toxic Waste

A Citizen's Toxic Waste Audit Manual. Washington, DC: Greenpeace USA, 1990. $20.

Cohen, Gary and John O'Conner, eds. *Fighting Toxics: A Manual for Protecting Your Family, Community and Workplace*. Washington, DC: Island Press, 1990.

Superfund Scorecard. Washington, DC: U.S.PIRG, 1986. $2.

Toxic Prevention: A Citizen's Platform. Boston: National Toxics Campaign. $3.50.

Toxics Use Reduction: From Pollution Control to Pollution Prevention. Boston: National Toxics Campaign, 1989.

Using Community Right to Know: A Guide to a New Federal Law. Washington, DC: OMB Watch, 1988.

Using Your Right-To-Know: Dealing With Operating Facilities. Falls Church, VA: Citizen's Clearinghouse For Hazardous Waste. 1989. How to find out about toxic chemicals in your community and what you can do. $9.95.

Water Pollution

America's Water Crisis...Fact?...or Fiction?. Boston: National Toxics Campaign. $1.

A Consumer's Guide to Protecting Your Drinking Water. Boston: National Toxics Campaign. This brochure addresses water contamination, water filters and bottled water. $4.

Drinking Water. Washington, DC: Concern, Inc., 1991. $4.

Groundwater. Washington, DC: Concern, Inc., 1989. $4.

Lead And Your Drinking Water. Washington, DC: Environmental Protection Agency, 1987.

Testing for Toxics: A Guide to Investigating Drinking Water Quality. Washington, DC: U.S.PIRG, 1986. Provides step-by-step guide for activists to document the quality of their drinking water. $5.

General

1987-89 State of the States. Washington, DC: Renew America, 1989.

Caplan, Ruth. *Our Earth, Ourselves*. New York: Bantam Books, 1990.

The Citizen Health Survey. Boston: National Toxics Campaign. Survey that citizens can use to document health problems in their community. $8.50.

Corporate Campaigns: How to Research a Campaign. Boston: National Toxics Campaign. A primer for citizen campaigns that aim to influence the way corporations do business. $4.50.

Corson, Walter H. *The Global Ecology Handbook: What You Can Do About the Environmental Crisis*. Global Tomorrow Coalition. Boston: Beacon Press, 1990.

Empowering Ourselves: Women and Toxics Organizing. Falls Church, VA: Citizen's Clearinghouse For Hazardous Wastes, 1989. $6.95.

Environmental Backgrounder. Washington, DC: Environmental Protection Agency, 1989. Topics available: wetlands, ozone, carbon monoxide, radon, asbestos, acid rain, etc.

Gibbs, Lois Marie. *Love Canal: My Story*. Falls Church, VA: Citizen's Clearinghouse for Hazardous Wastes. The inside story of the first toxic fight solved by organizing.

Global ReLeaf Action Guide. Washington, DC: The American Forestry Association, 1991. $1.50.

History of the Grassroots Movement for Environmental Justice. Falls Church, VA: Citizen's Clearinghouse for Hazardous Wastes, Inc. 1986. First detailed history of the Grassroots Movement for Environmental Justice. $8.50.

Individual Actions: To Conserve Our Planets' Resources. Takoma Park, MD: Environmental Action, 1990.

Making Polluters Pay: A Citizen's Guide to Legal Actions and Organizing. Takoma Park, MD: Environmental Action Foundation, 1986. $15.

MYTHBusters #1: Demand Forecasting. Washington, DC: Safe Energy Communication Council. $.25.

Naar, Jon. *Design for a Livable Planet: How You Can Help Clean Up The Environment*. New York: Harper and Row Publishers, 1990.

The Neighborhood Inspection. Boston: National Toxics Campaign. $7.

Organizing to Win. Boston: National Toxics Campaign. A guide to organizing in your community. $5.50.

Pollution Prevention Action Plan. Washington, DC: Sponsored by Citizen's Clearinghouse for Hazardous Waste, Clean Water Action, Greenpeace, National Toxics Campaign, U.S. Public Interest Research Group, 1990.

Researching and Obtaining Information. Boston: National Toxics Campaign.

DeVeney, Charles. *Save What's Left: Centuries to Create, Seconds To Destroy*. Coral Springs, FL: Save What's Left, 1991. The organizing manual for Save What's Left environmental clubs.

Seventh Generation, Catalog. Colchester, VT 05446. An environmentally aware mail order company with a large selection of fluorescent lamps.

Brown, Lester, et al. *State of the World 1991*. Washington, DC: Worldwatch Institute, 1991. $19.95 (hardback) $10.95 (paperback).

Understanding Environmental Health Risks and Reducing Exposure. Washington, DC: Environmental Protection Agency, 1990.

What Chemicals Each Industry Uses: A Sourcebook for Citizens. Environmental Research Foundation, 1988.

Will A Health Survey Work for You?. Falls Church, VA: Citizen's Clearinghouse for Hazardous Wastes, Inc. 1984. $8.95.

Curricula

A Curriculum Activities Guide to Water Pollution Equipment and Environmental Studies, Volumes I & II. Cleveland: Institute for Environmental Education. $34.

A Curriculum Activities Guide to Water Pollution Equipment and Environmental Studies, Volume III. Cleveland: Institute for Environmental Education. $17.

A Curriculum Activities Guide to Solid Waste Environmental Studies, Volume IV. Cleveland: Institute for Environmental Education. $17.

A Directory of Selected Environmental Education Materials. Washington, DC: World Resources Institute, 1988.

Educator's Earthday Sourcebook Grades K-6. Washington, DC: Environmental Protection Agency, 1990.

Educator's Earthday Sourcebook Grades 7-12. Washington, DC: Environmental Protection Agency, 1990.

Environmental Education Materials For Teachers and Young People (Grades K-12). Washington, DC: Environmental Protection Agency, 1988.

An Environmental Guide for Teachers. Cleveland: Institute for Environmental Education. $17.

A Guide to Recycling and Environmental Education Material. Washington, DC: Institute for Local Self-Reliance, 1990. A bibliography of curricula on environmental and recycling topics.

Here Today Here Tomorrow. Trenton: New Jersey Department of Environmental Protection, 1989.

How to Plan A Conservation Education Program. Washington, DC: World Resources Institute, 1990.

Lingenfelter, Jan. *A-Way With Waste: A Curriculum for Schools*. Redmond, WA: Washington State University, 1985.

Recycle Today! Educational Materials for Grades K-12. Washington, DC: Environmental Protection Agency, 1990.

Recycling Study Guide. Madison: Wisconsin Department of Natural Resources.

School Recycling Programs: A Handbook for Educators. Washington, DC: Environmental Protection Agency, 1990.

A School-based Waste Minimization and Education Program Resource Manual, Volume IX. Cleveland: Institute for Environmental Education. $24.

Teacher's Guide to World Resources 1990-91. Washington, DC: World Resources Institute. Step-by-step lesson plans and teaching strategies on global warming; deforestation and biodiversity; oceans and coasts; population, poverty and land degradation; air and water pollution; and natural resources economics. $5.

Training Student Organizers Curriculum. New York: Council on the Environment of New York City, 1990.

FUNDRAISING

Foundation Center
79 Fifth Avenue
New York, NY 10003
(800) 424-9836

GOOD GOVERNMENT ORGANIZATIONS

Americans for Democratic Action
1511 K Street, NW, Suite 941
Washington, DC 20005
Conducts education and lobbying and supports political candidates in support of issues such as health care, family/medical leave, civil rights.

Resources

Citizen Action
1120 19th Street, NW Suite 630
Washington, DC 20036
A national political organization attempting to increase citizen participation and offer alternatives in health care, environmental and economic issues. Publishes *Citizen Action News* quarterly.

Citizens for Tax Justice
1311 L Street, NW, Suite 400
Washington, DC 20005
Works to give citizens a voice in the development of tax laws at the local, state and national levels. CTJ believes people should be taxed based upon their ability to pay.

Common Cause
2030 M Street, NW
Washington, DC 20036
A nonpartisan citizen group that works to improve government operations through standards of ethics, civil rights and campaign finance reform. Publishes *Common Cause Magazine* bimonthly.

Connecticut Citizen Action Group
2074 Park Street
Hartford, CT 06106
A citizen group which organizes Connecticut citizens to address issues and work toward specific objectives, such as the passage of global warming legislation. Also works on public education and coalition building.

Council of State Governments
444 N. Capitol Street, NW Suite 201
Washington, DC 20001
Works with the executive and legislative branches of state governments to provide a forum for information exchange and to supply research and communications services.

Government Accountability Project
810 First Street, NE, Suite 630
Washington, DC 20002
Provides legal information and support to whistleblowers (employees who report on the illegal, corrupt or wasteful practices of their employers). Runs EPA Watch to monitor activities of the Environmental Protection Agency. Publishes *Bridging the GAP* quarterly.

League of Women Voters
1730 M Street, NW
Washington, DC 20036
The League is a nonpartisan political group working to improve citizen participation in government through voter registration and public debates.

OMB Watch
1731 Connecticut Avenue, NW
Washington, DC 20009
Monitors the Office of Management and Budget, the largest unit within the Executive Office of the President. Provides citizen education on related legislative and administrative issues.

United States Public Interest Research Group (U.S. PIRG)
215 Pennsylvania Avenue, SE
Washington, DC 20003
The national lobbying office for state PIRGs, student-run organizations working on environmental protection, consumer protection and government reform. Publishes *Citizen Agenda* quarterly.

Books, Reports, Pamphlets

A Grassroots Lobbying Handbook for Local League Activists. Washington, DC: League of Women Voters.

Anatomy of a Hearing. Washington, DC: League of Women Voters of the United States, 1972. $1.

How to Watch a Debate. Washington, DC: League of Women Voters, 1986. $.75. Targeted to high school students. Includes advice on what to watch and listen for in candidate debates at any level of government.

Know Your Community. Washington, DC: League of Women Voters, 1972. $1.75. Guide to help citizens and organizations interested in change take a good look at the existing structure and functions of their local government.

Know Your County. Washington, DC: League of Women Voters, 1974. $1.25. Outline for making a complete survey of the structure and functions of county government.

Know Your Schools. Washington, DC: League of Women Voters, 1974. $1.50. Outline to help citizens analyze their school's organization, operation, financing and education programs.

Glazer, Myron and Penina Glazer. *The Whistleblowers.* Available from the Government Accountability Project.

Using Community Right to Know: A Guide to a New Federal Law. Washington, DC: OMB Watch, 1988.

323

HEALTH/NUTRITION ORGANIZATIONS

Action on Smoking and Health (ASH)
2013 H Street, NW
Washington, DC 20006

Takes legal action for non-smokers' rights and has petitioned government agencies to limit smoking and make sure rules are enforced.

Americans for Safe Food
1875 Connecticut Avenue, NW, Suite 300
Washington, DC 20009-5728

A national coalition of consumer, environmental and other organizations working to increase the availability of safer foods through the reduction of pesticides, animal drugs and other synthetic agricultural chemicals.

Center For Science in the Public Interest (CSPI)
1875 Connecticut Avenue, NW, Suite 300
Washington, DC 20009

Researches, educates and advocates on nutrition, diet, food safety, alcohol and related health issues. Publishes *Nutrition Action Healthletter* ten times a year.

Center for Study of Responsive Law
P.O. Box 19367
Washington, DC 20036

Publishes a variety of consumer-related materials.

Community Nutrition Institute
2001 S Street, NW, Suite 530
Washington, DC 20009

Works as a public advocate for safe food and health policies by reporting on research and policy developments. Publishes *Nutrition Week* weekly.

Public Citizen Health Research Group
2000 P Street, NW, Suite 700
Washington, DC 20036

Works to protect the public's health by monitoring the work of the medical establishment, drug industry and health-related regulatory industries. Publishes *Health Letter* monthly.

Public Voice for Food and Health Policy
1001 Connecticut Avenue, NW, Suite 522
Washington, DC 20036

Works to increase citizen input on food and health issues including federal fish inspection, stronger pesticide regulation and women's health issues. Publishes *Action Alert* quarterly and *Advocacy Update* monthly.

Books, Reports, Pamphlets

Brody, Jane. *Jane Brody's Nutrition Book.* New York: New York Times Books, 1981.

Citizens' Action Handbook on Alcohol and Tobacco Billboard Advertising. Washington, DC: Center for Science in the Public Interest. An activists manual. $6.95.

Eating Clean: Overcoming Food Hazards. Washington, DC: Center for Study of Responsive Law, 1989. A collection of various sources of issues on food. $8.

How to Develop a Home Delivered Meals Program. Washington, DC: Community Nutrition Institute, 1980. $20.

Jacobson, Michael and Paula Klevan Zeller. *Eat, Think and Be Healthy!.* Washington, DC: Center for Science in the Public Interest, 1987. Guaranteed to appeal to kids' imagination and sense of fun — while teaching them the basics of good nutrition. 56 activities include many illustrations and handouts. $8.95.

Organic Food Mail-Order Suppliers. Washington, DC: Americans for Safe Food, 1989. State-by-state directory of growers and distributors of organic foods. $1.50.

Organizing for Better School Food. Washington, DC: Center for Science in the Public Interest. An activist's manual for improving school food service programs. $7.

White Paper on School-Lunch Nutrition. Washington, DC: Center for Science in the Public Interest. Recommends a number of changes in school-lunch programs to improve overall nutritional quality. $5.

HUMAN RIGHTS ORGANIZATIONS

Amnesty International USA
322 Eighth Avenue
New York, NY 10001

An independent worldwide movement working for the release of all prisoners of conscience, fair and prompt trials for political prisoners and an end to torture and executions. Publishes *Amnesty Action* bimonthly and *Student Action* monthly for high school and college students.

Center for Constitutional Rights
666 Broadway, 7th Floor
New York, NY 10012

A national public interest law firm working for constitutional and human rights under the Constitution and international human rights laws.

Cultural Survival
53 Church Street
Cambridge, MA 02138

Advocates for the rights of indigenous peoples around the globe and works to protect those people from government and corporate oppression. Publishes *Cultural Survival Quarterly*.

Books, Reports, Pamphlets

ABC of Human Rights. New York: United Nations Publications. $3.

Amnesty International Handbook. New York: Amnesty International USA, 1984. A basic reference manual for members and individuals interested in group work, campaigns, policies, working rules and the structure of the organization. $5.

The Human Rights Library: Amnesty International. New York: Amnesty International USA. Catalog of Amnesty International's work and concerns in more than 133 countries.

Torture by Governments. New York: Amnesty International, 1984. A seven-part educational guide for high school students addressing the pertinent aspects of torture, including why governments torture, the effects of torture on the victims, the mentality of the torturer and how concerned individuals can help eradicate torture. $3.95

Universal Declaration of Human Rights. New York: United Nations Publications. $1.

Wilson, James. *The Original Americans: U.S. Indians*. Cambridge: Cultural Survival, 1986. $6.

You Could Be Arrested. New York: Amnesty International, 1988. Introductory video about Amnesty International for high school students. Includes interviews with former prisoners of conscience, high school group members and rock musicians involved in the human rights movement. $20.

HUNGER AND POVERTY ORGANIZATIONS

Bread for the World
802 Rhode Island Avenue, NE
Washington, DC 20018

A nationwide Christian movement that lobbies the nation's decision-makers, seeking solutions to world hunger. Publishes *Current Bread for the World Newsletter* 10 times a year.

Coalition for the Homeless
2824 Sherman Avenue, NW
Washington, DC 20001

Operates temporary homes and shelters to help the homeless regain self-sufficiency and return to independent living.

Community for Creative Nonviolence (CCNV)
425 Second Street, NW
Washington, DC 20001

Provides direct services to homeless people and works to change U.S. homeless policy.

Food Research and Action Center (FRAC)
1319 F Street, NW
Washington, DC 20004

A legal, research and advocacy center working to end hunger and malnutrition in the United States. Publishes *Foodlines: A Chronicle of Hunger and Poverty in America* bimonthly.

Habitat for Humanity
121 Habitat Street
Americus, Georgia 31709-3498

Works to end poverty and housing shortages worldwide, largely through volunteer labor.

Housing Now
425 Second Street, NW
Washington, DC 20001

A coalition of more than 100 national and local groups working for affordable housing for all Americans.

Institute for Food and Development Policy/Food First
145 Ninth Street
San Francisco, CA 94103.

Works to educate citizens on the root causes of and solutions to hunger and poverty. Publishes *Food First News* quarterly.

National Coalition for the Homeless
1621 Connecticut Avenue, NW, Suite 400
Washington, DC 20009

A federation of individuals, agencies and organizations working to secure rights, services and housing for the homeless. Publishes *Safety Network* monthly.

National Student Campaign Against Hunger And Homelessness
29 Temple Place, Fifth Floor
Boston, MA 02111

Puts student concerns into action by providing immediate relief to the hungry and homeless with long-term solutions. Publishes *Students Making a Difference* quarterly.

Oxfam America
115 Broadway
Boston, MA 02116

Oxfam helps to fund locally-generated grassroots development work in 32 countries.

Books, Reports, Pamphlets

A Chance to Survive: A Study Course on Child Health. Washington, DC: Bread for the World, 1989. Includes slides. $5.

Collins, Joseph and Frances Moore Lappe. *Food First: Beyond the Myth of Scarcity*. San Francisco: Institute for Food and Development Policy. $4.95.

Fighting Hunger: A Guide for Development of Community Action Projects. Washington, DC: League of Women Voters, 1990. Designed to provide volunteers with basic information for local efforts to fight hunger. Includes case studies of successful League projects, with contacts for more information. $5.

Food As a Weapon Study Kit. Washington, DC: Bread for the World, 1991. $2.

FRAC's Guide to the Food Stamp Program. Washington, DC: Food Research and Action Center.

Fruits of Our Labor: A Reader on Work in the United States. Washington, DC: Bread for the World, 1988. $3.

Fuel for Excellence: FRAC's Guide to School Breakfast Expansion. Washington, DC: Food Research & Action Center, 1990. $10.

Housing and Homelessness: A Teaching Guide. Washington, DC: Housing Now, 1989.

Hunger 1990: Study Aid. Washington, DC: Bread for the World, 1990. $1.50.

The Hunger Cleanup Manual. Boston: The National Student Campaign Against Hunger and Homelessness.

Hunger in a Land of Plenty: A Study Action Guide. Washington, DC: Bread for the World, 1985. $2.50.

Hunger in America. Washington, DC: Food Research & Action Center, 1988. A 17-minute educational slide show, offering a clear and informative presentation of the causes of hunger and different advocacy for improved food programs. $75.

Hunger Myths and Facts. San Francisco: Institute for Food and Development Policy. $2.

In a World of Abundance, Why Hunger?. Boston: Oxfam America.

Lappe, Frances Moore. *Diet for a Small Planet*. San Francisco: Institute for Food and Development Policy, 1991. $3.95.

Poverty in United States Information Packet. Washington, DC: Food Research & Action Center, 1991. $2.

The Relationship Between Nutrition and Learning. Washington, DC: Food Research & Action Center, 1989. $7.

Setting a New Course: Expanding Collegiate Curricula to Incorporate the Study of Hunger and Homelessness. Boston: The National Student Campaign Against Hunger and Homelessness, 1990. $5.

Simon, Arthur. *Bread for the World*. Washington, DC: Bread for the World, 1984. $5.95.

Williams, Sonja. *Exploding the Hunger Myths: A High School Curriculum*. San Francisco: Institute for Food and Development Policy. $15.

LABOR ORGANIZATIONS

American Federation of Labor and Congress of Industrial Organizations (AFL-CIO)
815 16th Street, NW
Washington, DC 20006

A national federation of unions which works to promote and foster union organizing campaigns and worker rights.

Coalition of Labor Union Women (CLUW)
15 Union Square
New York, NY 10003

Works to promote women's issues in the labor movement and increase the number of women in union leadership. Publishes *CLUW News* bimonthly.

Labor Notes
7435 Michigan Avenue
Detroit, MI 48210

Publishes *Labor Notes,* a monthly magazine of issues pertaining to unions in America.

Labor Party Advocates
P.O. Box 1510
Highland Park, NJ 08904

Advocates a more worker-oriented political agenda and mobilizes support for a labor party. Publishes *Labor Party Advocates Newsletter* bimonthly.

Midwest Center for Labor Research
3411 West Diversey, Room 10
Chicago, IL 60647

A nonprofit consulting group, offering a wide variety of economic development services, specializing in maintaining industrial employment.

Mujer Obrera
1113 E. Yardell
El Paso, TX 79902

Takes direct action against the sweatshop conditions in the sewing industry on the U.S.-Mexico border.

National Safe Workplace Institute
122 S. Michigan Avenue, Suite 1450
Chicago, IL 60603

Examines government and corporate policies and programs to advance safety and health in the workplace.

New Directions
P.O. Box 6876
St. Louis, MO 63144

Works for internal democracy and accountability to the membership of the United Auto Workers.

9 To 5, National Association of Working Women
614 Superior Avenue, NW
Cleveland, OH 44113

9 to 5 works to win better pay, rights and respect on the job for women through organizing, advocacy and public education. Publishes *9 to 5 Newsletter* 10 times a year.

Teamsters for a Democratic Union
Box 10128
Detroit, MI 48210

Works to bring greater internal democracy to the Teamsters Union.

Tsongas Industrial History Center
Boott Mill Foot of John Street
Lowell, MA 01852

United Farm Workers
P.O. Box 62
Keene, CA 93531

Works to end the exploitation of farm workers, promote the availability of safe and affordable food, ban the use of dangerous pesticides and challenge the strong influence of agribusiness in state and national government.

United Postal Workers Union
WestConn Area Local
P.O. Box 3885
Danbury, CT 06813

Books, Reports, Pamphlets

Green, Hardy. *On Strike at Hormel: The Struggle For A Democratic Labor Movement*. Philadelphia: Temple University Press, 1990.

How Schools Are Teaching About Labor: A Collection of Guidelines & Lesson Plans. Washington, DC: AFL-CIO, 1988.

Labor/Working Class Bibliography. Danbury, CT: WestConn Local, American Postal Workers Union, 1990. Bibliography of more than 600 titles compiled for high school teachers and students.

Labotz, Dan. *Rank-and-File Rebellion: Teamsters for a Democratic Union*. New York: Verso Press, 1990.

Perry, Joan. *Ten Hour Movement: Labor Protests in Lowell in the mid-19th Century*. Lowell, MA: Tsongas Industrial History Center, 1989.

Whose Business Is It Anyway?. Washington, DC: National Consumers League. A national opinion survey on workplace decisions and employee privacy. $10.

MEDIA/COMMUNICATIONS/INFORMATION ORGANIZATIONS

Action for Children's Television
20 University Road
Cambridge, MA 02138

Works to encourage diversity in children's TV, to discourage commercialization of children's programming and to eliminate deceptive advertising aimed at young viewers.

Center for Investigative Reporting
530 Howard Street, 2nd Floor
San Francisco, CA 94105-3007

Works to train journalists in investigative reporting, serve as a base for investigative journalists and help educate the public.

Center for the Study of Commercialism
1875 Connecticut Avenue, NW, Suite 300
Washington, DC 20009

Researches, publicizes and opposes the invasion of commercial interests into practically every corner of society. Helps immunize citizens against the siege of advertising.

Children's Express
245 Seventh Avenue, 5th Floor
New York, NY 10001-7302

A news service covering children's issues, reported by children and edited by teenagers.

The Counter-Propaganda Press
Box 365
Park Forest, IL 60466

Publishes books on advertising that affects children in school and at home.

FAIR (Fairness & Accuracy in Reporting)
130 West 25th Street
New York, NY 10001

A national media watch group focusing on the narrow corporate ownership of the press and its insensitivity to women, labor and minorities. Publishes *Extra!* 8 times a year.

Institute for Global Communications
18 DeBoom Street
San Francisco, CA 94107
(415) 442-0220

Operates ECONet and PeaceNet, electronic communications networks for organizations and individuals involved in environmental, disarmament, social justice and peace issues.

Media Access Project
2000 M Street, NW, Suite 400
Washington, DC 20036

A public interest law firm working to protect access to information for the listening and viewing public.

Media Watch
1803 Mission Street, Suite 7
Santa Cruz, CA 95060

Publishes *Media Watch*, a quarterly newsletter dedicated to improving the image of women in the media.

Telecommunications Research & Action Center (TRAC)
P.O. Box 12038
Washington, DC 20005

Represents consumer interests in telecommunications, cable and telephone regulatory reform.

Books, Reports, Pamphlets

All the Usual Suspects: The McNeil/Lehrer NewsHour. New York: Fairness & Accuracy in Reporting, 1990.

Are You On The Nightline Guest List? New York: Fairness & Accuracy in Reporting, 1989.

Brigham, Nancy with Maria Catalfio and Dick Cluster. *How to Do Leaflets, Newsletters & Newspapers.* Detroit: PEP Publishers, 1991. 1-800-289-0963.

Children's Express: How to Do It. New York: Children's Express. Shows how to set up a news service reported and edited by students, covering children's issues.

Community Cable for and by Children: An ACT Handbook. Cambridge: Action for Children's Television, 1983. $5.

Dictating Content: How Advertising Pressures Can Corrupt a Free Press. Washington, DC: Center for the Study of Commercialism, 1992. Documents how the fear of advertiser pressure has caused editors and reporters to censor information. $10.

How to Be Heard. New York: Children's Express.

How to Plan and Print Your Own Newspaper. New York: Children's Express.

Listen To Us! New York: Children's Express.

Lost in the Margins: Labor and the Media. New York: Fairness & Accuracy in Reporting, 1990.

The Media and Children's Issues. New York: Children's Express.

Media Skills Manual. Washington, DC: Safe Energy Communication Council. $17.50.

Rank, Hugh. *The Pitch: How to Analyze Ads: A Simple 1-2-3-4-5 Way to Understand the Basic Pattern of Persuasion in Advertising.* Park Forest, IL: The Counter-Propaganda Press, 1991.

TV News & Children. Cambridge: Action for Children's Television, 1987. $5.

328

TV-Smart Kids Need Savvy Parents. New York: E.P. Dutton, 1986.

PEACE ORGANIZATIONS

American Friends Service Committee (AFSC)
1501 Cherry Street
Philadelphia, PA 19102
   Carries out programs of service, development, justice and peace to bring about social improvement.

Center for Common Security
P.O. Box 275
Williamstown, MA 01267
   A student-based, student-run organization that has initiated courses on issues of student leadership and nonviolent alternatives at Williams College and other colleges around the country.

Center for Defense Information
1500 Massachusetts Avenue, NW
Washington, DC 20005
   Opposes excessive expenditures for weapons and policies that increase the danger of nuclear war and believes that strong social, economic, political and military components contribute equally to the nation's security. Publishes *Defense Monitor* 10 times a year.

Children's Campaign for Nuclear Disarmament
14 Everit Street
New Haven, CT 06511
   Run by youth aged 18 and younger dedicated to ending the arms race.

Conscience and Military Tax Campaign
4534 1/2 University Way, NE, Suite 204
Seattle, WA 98105
   Organizes public events concerning the war tax and offers counseling and workshops on how to resist the war tax. Publishes *Conscience* quarterly.

Consortium on Peace Research, Education and Development (COPRED)
Center of Conflict Resolution
George Mason University
4400 University Drive
Fairfax, VA 22030
   Publishes materials on peace and peace education.

Educators for Social Responsibility
23 Garden Street
Cambridge, MA 02138
   Comprised of teachers, administrators, parents and other concerned citizens working to help students understand issues such as U.S.-Soviet relations, the spread of nuclear weapons and the need for conflict resolution and negotiation. Publishes *Forum* twice a year.

Fellowship of Reconciliation (FOR)
Box 271, 523 North Broadway
Nyack, NY 10960
   Works on peace and human rights issues focusing on racial and economic justice, nonviolence resolution and global disarmament. Publishes *Fellowship* 8 times a year.

National Campaign for a Peace Tax Fund
2121 Decatur Place, NW
Washington, DC 20008
   Works for legislation that would allow persons opposed to war to have the military portion of their taxes go into a trust fund for projects that enhance peace.

National Peace Institute Foundation
110 Maryland Avenue, NE
Washington, DC 20002
   A non-governmental group concerned with the development of the U.S. Institute of Peace, peace education, conflict resolution, the United Nations and the Alliance for Our Common Future. Publishes *Peace Reporter* quarterly.

Neighbor to Neighbor (N2N)
2601 Mission Street, Room 400
San Francisco, CA 94110
   A national grassroots organization working to end U.S. intervention in Central America and to achieve a foreign policy based on true democratic ideals.

Peace Education Resource Center
2437 North Grant Boulevard
Milwaukee, WI 53210
   Publishes curriculum materials on peace issues for schools, churches, synagogues and communities.

People's Anti-War Mobilization
P.O. Box 1819
Madison Square Station
New York, NY 10010
   High school and college students who oppose war, racism, discrimination and imperialism.

Physicians for Social Responsibility
1000 16th Street, NW, Suite 810
Washington, DC 20036
(202) 785-3777

Nationwide organization of physicians and others whose main goal is nuclear disarmament. The organization also works on shifting federal budget priorities away from military spending and toward spending on basic human needs such as housing, education and health care, and on environmental effects on health, such as the effects of toxic pollution.

SANE/FREEZE: Campaign for Global Security
1819 H Street, NW, Suite 1000
Washington, DC 20006

A grassroots national group working to reverse the arms race, abolish nuclear weapons and achieve world peace and justice. Publishes *SANE/FREEZE Focus* quarterly.

Union of Concerned Scientists
26 Church Street
Cambridge, MA 02238

An organization of scientists concerned about the impact of advanced technology on society, including peace issues.

War Resisters League
339 Lafayette Street
New York, NY 10012

Helps provide educational information on peace and war resistance through a variety of publications. Publishes *The Nonviolent Activist* 8 times a year.

Women's Action for Nuclear Disarmament
P.O. Box B
Arlington, MA 02174

Works to increase women's political power and to eliminate weapons of mass destruction and redirect military resources to human and environmental needs.

Women's International League for Peace and Freedom
1213 Race Street
Philadelphia, PA 19107-1671

Works to achieve social, political, economic and psychological conditions to ensure peace and freedom throughout the world.

World Federalist Association
418 7th Street, SE
Washington, DC 20003

Attempts to abolish war and preserve a livable world through a just and enforceable World Law.

Books, Reports, Pamphlets

The ABCs of the United Nations. Philadelphia: Women's International League for Peace and Freedom. Highlights the history, achievements and structure of the United Nations. $.25.

Alternatives to Violence: A Manual for Teaching Peacemaking to Youth and Adults. Fairfax, VA: Consortium on Peace Research, Education and Development, 1985. Twenty 45-minute units designed to increase understanding of the sources of violence and nonviolent alternatives and to develop skills in nonviolent methods of conflict resolution. $7.95.

Caldicott, Helen. *Missile Envy: The Arms Race and Nuclear War*. Washington, DC: Women's Action for Nuclear Disarmament Education Fund. $2.50.

Choices: A Unit on Conflict and Nuclear War. Cambridge: Union of Concerned Scientists, 1989. A junior-high school curriculum. $9.95.

Holmes, Robert L. *Nonviolence in Theory and Practice*. Belmont, CA: Wadsworth Publishing.

Chester, Isabelle. *Listen to Women for a Change*. Philadelphia: Women's International League for Peace and Freedom. Life experiences of women around the world working for social change. $4.

Midgley, Jane. *Women's Budget, 4th Edition*. Philadelphia: Women's International League for Peace and Freedom. Emphasizes the costs of intervention and the impact of U.S. budget priorities on people of color and women.

Peace Resource Center Catalog. Wilmington: Peace Resource Center. A catalog of peace resources, books and films.

Peace Education Packet. Fairfax, VA: Consortium on Peace Research, Education and Development, 1982. Includes booklets, pamphlets, newsletters, flyers and catalogs, covering a variety of issues, teaching styles and strategies of peace education, provides a general overview of resources available for peace educators. $10.75.

Peace and Peacemaking: Book Lists for Pre-K through 12. Fairfax, VA: Consortium on Peace Research, Education and Development, 1982. $1.25.

People Have Rights!: They Have Responsibilities, Too. Fairfax, VA: Consortium on Peace Research, Education and Development, 1982. Includes booklets, pamphlets, newsletters, flyers and catalogs covering a variety of issues, teaching styles and strategies of peace educators. $10.75.

Reardon, Betty. *Comprehensive Peace Education.* Educators for Social Responsibility. $14.

War Resisters League Literature List. New York: War Resisters League. Includes publications on a variety of issues including peace, disarmament and conscientious objection.

STUDENT/YOUTH SERVICE ORGANIZATIONS

Campus Outreach Opportunity League (COOL)
386 McNeal Hall
University of Minnesota
St. Paul, MN 55108
Facilitates student involvement in community problem-solving efforts, provides organizing resources and training and publishes a newsletter.

Creating Our Future
398 North Ferndale
Mill Valley, CA 94941
A youth leadership network organization of high school environmentalists.

National Association of Secondary School Principals
1904 Association Drive
Reston, VA 22091
Publishes *The Student Council Advisor* and formed the American Student Council Association to help schools establish student councils.

National Student Campaign Against Hunger And Homelessness
29 Temple Place, Fifth Floor
Boston, MA 02111
Puts student concerns into action by providing immediate relief to the hungry and homeless and long-term solutions. Publishes *Students Making a Difference* quarterly.

United States Public Interest Research Group
215 Pennsylvania Avenue, SE
Washington, DC 20003
The national lobbying office for student-run state PIRGs, focuses on environmental and consumer protection and energy and government reform. Publishes *Citizen Agenda* quarterly.

United States Student Association (USSA)
1012 14th Street, NW, Suite 207
Washington, DC 20005
Works for student empowerment by lobbying Congress and training students around the country in direct action organizing. Publishes *Legislative Update* bi-weekly during the congressional session.

Youth Action
2335 18th Street, NW
Washington, DC 20009
Works with young people ages 14 to 25, encouraging them to address social, economic and environmental issues which affect them and their communities. Publishes *The Noise!* quarterly.

Youth Service America
1319 F Street, NW, Suite 900
Washington, DC 20004
Runs the *Youth Volunteer Corps of America* which involves students from age 12 to 18 in intensive team service projects that are sponsored and managed by local nonprofit and community serving organizations.

Books, Reports, Pamphlets

Democracy at Risk: An Analysis of the High Incidence of Non-Voting Among America's Youth. Washington, DC: Youth Action, 1988.

Lewis, Barbara A. *The Kid's Guide to Social Action: How to Solve the Social Problems You Choose — And Turn Creative Thinking Into Positive Action.* Minneapolis: Free Spirit Publishing, 1991. (800) 735-7323.

Rose, Jean B. *The Connection Dimension: Strategies for bringing your community together.* Scotia-Glenville Schools, Scotia, NY 12302, 1989.

Sterner, William. *The Student Council Advisor.* Reston, VA: National Association of Secondary School Principals, 1979.

WOMEN'S ORGANIZATIONS

Center for Women Policy Studies
2000 P Street, NW, Suite 508
Washington, DC 20036
Policy, research, development and advocacy programs concentrate on educational equity, work and family issues and reproductive rights and health.

Fund for the Feminist Majority
1600 Wilson Boulevard, Suite 704
Arlington, VA 22209
　　Works to eliminate sex discrimination and to promote equality, reproductive rights and a feminist agenda through research, lobbying, litigation, direct action and public education. Publishes *Feminist Majority Report* bimonthly.

Glenhurst Publications Inc.
Central Community Center
6300 Walker Street
St. Louis Park, MN 55416
　　Publishes books, videos and manuals tracing the lives of important women in the United States as well as the rest of the world.

Institute for Women's Policy Research
1400 20th Street, NW Suite 104
Washington, DC 20036
　　Conducts feminist-oriented research for policymakers, legislators and women's advocacy organizations.

National Abortion Rights Action League
1101 14th Street, NW
Washington, DC 20005
　　Works to guarantee every woman the right to choose and obtain a legal abortion. Publishes *Campus Newsletter* quarterly.

National Black Women's Health Project
1237 Abernathy Boulevard
Atlanta, GA 30310
　　Works to define, promote and maintain the physical, mental and emotional well-being of black women.

National Clearinghouse on Marital and Date Rape
2325 Oak
Berkeley, CA 94708
　　Provides current information on legislation, litigation and attitudes condoning the targeting of women and children for abuse.

National Coalition Against Domestic Violence
1012 14th Street, NW, Suite 807
Washington, DC 20005
　　A national group of grassroots shelter and service programs for battered women providing technical assistance and training to end personal and societal violence against women and children. Publishes *The Voice* 3 times a year.

National Congress of Neighborhood Women
249 Manhattan Avenue
Brooklyn, NY 11211
　　Works to strengthen women's leadership roles in neighborhoods by giving support, information, training and recognition for their work.

National Organization for Women
1000 16th Street, NW Suite 700
Washington, DC 20036
　　Works for legal, political, social and economic change in society to bring women into participation in the mainstream of American society.

National Woman's Party
144 Constitution Avenue, NE
Washington, DC 20002
　　Works for passage of the Equal Rights Amendment to the U.S. Constitution.

National Women's Health Network
1325 G Street, NW
Washington, DC 20005
　　Advocates for better health policies for women and provides information to individual women to enable them to have more control over health decisions.

National Women's History Project
7738 Bell Road
Windsor, CA 95492-8515
　　Publishes books, videos and classroom materials on women's history.

National Women's Political Caucus
1275 K Street, NW, Suite 750
Washington, DC 20005
　　Works to elect and appoint women to public office while promoting economic freedom, reproductive freedom and equal rights for women. Publishes *Women's Political Times* quarterly.

Older Women's League (OWL)
730 11th Street, NW, Suite 300
Washington, DC 20001
　　A grassroots group working on health care, employment, care giving, pension and other issues affecting midlife to older women. Publishes *OWL Observer* bimonthly.

Planned Parenthood Federation of America, Inc.
810 Seventh Avenue
New York, NY 10019

Works for reproductive health services and education dedicated to each individual's right to an independent decision about having children.

Wider Opportunities for Women (WOW)
1325 G Street, NW, Lower Level
Washington, DC 20005-3104

Works with economically disadvantaged women to help them achieve economic independence and equality. Publishes *Women At Work* twice a year.

Women's Legal Defense Fund
1875 Connecticut Avenue, NW Suite 710
Washington, DC 20009

Conducts lobbying, litigation and community organizing to achieve equality for women by working on issues including family and medical leave, affirmative action, sexual harassment and wage discrimination. Publishes *WLDF News* twice a year.

Books, Reports, Pamphlets

1990-91 Women's History Catalog. Windsor: National Women's History Project, 1991.

Burgoa, Carol and Barbara Tomin. *A Multi-Cultural Women's History Elementary Curriculum Unit*. Windsor, CA: National Women's History Project, 1987.

Campus Activist Materials. Washington, DC: National Abortion Rights Action League.

Eisenberg, Bonnie. *Woman Suffrage Movement 1848-1920*. Windsor, CA: National Women's History Project, 1985.

Garland, Anne Witte. *Women Activists: Challenging the Abuse of Power*. New York: The Feminist Press, 1988.

The Glenhurst Collection of Women's History and Culture. St. Louis Park, MN: Glenhurst Publications Inc., 1990.

MacGregor, Molly Murphy. *Women and the Constitution Curriculum Unit*. Windsor, CA: National Women's History Project, 1988.

Mounting a Prenatal Care Campaign in Your Community. Washington, DC: Children's Defense Fund, 1986. $5.95.

Pay Equity: Issues & Answers. Washington, DC: League of Women Voters, 1986.

Planned Parenthood Resource Catalog for Educators and Health Care Professionals. New York: Planned Parenthood Federation of America, Inc. A guide to parenthood, sexuality and reproductive health care.

Tillet, Rebecca. *How to Change the World: A Woman's Guide to Grassroots Lobbying*. Washington, DC: National Women's Political Caucus, 1991.

Women's History Curriculum Guide. Windsor, CA: National Women's History Project.

U.S. GOVERNMENT AGENCIES

Consumer Product Safety Commission (CPSC)
5401 Westbard Avenue
Bethesda, MD 20207

Responsible for protecting the public against "unreasonable" risks of injury associated with consumer products, assisting consumers in evaluating the safety of consumer products, developing uniform safety standards for consumer products and promoting research and investigation into causes and prevention of product-related injuries.

Council on Environmental Quality (CEQ)
722 Jackson Place, NW
Washington, DC 20503

Responsible for advising and assisting the U.S. President on environmental programs and policies.

Department of Agriculture (USDA)
14th and Independence Avenue, SW
Washington, DC 20250

Responsible for encouraging proper management and conservation of U.S. natural resources, management of the National Forest System, rural development and protecting consumers by inspecting the meat and poultry industry.

Department of Commerce
Bureau of the Census
Washington, DC 20233

Conducts the national census to determine congressional representation. Also generates data to aid in government decisions regarding demographics and economic policy.

Department of Education
400 Maryland Avenue, SW
Washington, DC 20202

Responsible for ensuring access to equal educational opportunity, assisting state and local school systems and promoting educational improvements.

Department of Health and Human Services (HHS)
200 Independence Avenue, SW
Washington, DC 20585

Responsible for administering U.S. welfare and Social Security programs, U.S. Medicare and Medicaid programs and other human service and health programs.

Department of Labor
200 Constitution Avenue, NW
Washington, DC 20210

Responsible for fostering, promoting and developing the welfare of U.S. wage earners. Also responsible for improving working conditions and opportunities for profitable employment. Administers federal labor laws guaranteeing workers' rights.

Environmental Protection Agency (EPA)
401 M Street, SW
Washington, DC 20460

Responsible for enforcement of federal environmental law. Publishes *EPA Journal* bimonthly.

Federal Communications Commission (FCC)
Consumer Assistance Division, Room 254
1919 M Street, NW
Washington, DC 20554

Charged with regulating interstate and international communications by radio, television, wire, satellite and cable.

Federal Information Center
P.O. Box 600
Cumberland, MD 21502

Staff answers questions about how the federal government works.

Federal Trade Commission (FTC)
Bureau of Consumer Protection
Office of Consumer/Business Education
Washington, DC 20580

Responsible for regulation of interstate commerce and protecting public from false and deceptive advertising. Publishes materials on a number of consumer issues, including shopping by mail or phone, warranties, telemarketing and health care.

Food and Drug Administration (FDA)
5600 Fishers Lane, #1471
Rockville, MD 20857

Responsible for protecting citizens from hazardous foods, drugs and cosmetics.

General Accounting Office (GAO)
441 G Street, NW
Washington, DC 20548
To request reports or receive monthly listings of reports:
P.O. Box 6015, Gaithersburg, MD 20077

Charged with helping Congress in its oversight of federal programs. Reviews federal programs and operations and makes recommendations to Congress and agency officials to improve operations and make programs more efficient.

National Institutes of Health (NIH)
9000 Rockville Pike #344
Bethesda, MD 20892

Responsible for supporting and conducting biomedical research, disseminating information to health professionals and the public and supporting research training.

National Library of Medicine
U.S. Department of Health and Human Services
TRI Representative
8600 Rockville Pike
Bethesda, MD 20894

Manages the TOXNET system which includes the Toxic Release Inventory database.

Nuclear Regulatory Commission (NRC)
1717 H Street, NW
Washington, DC 20555

Responsible for licensing and inspecting nuclear facilities and investigating cases involving exposure of workers to unsafe working conditions.

Occupational Safety and Health Administration (OSHA)
United States Department of Labor, OSHA, N3647
200 Constitution Avenue, NW
Washington, DC 20210

Charged with regulating safety and health in the workplace.

Securities and Exchange Commission (SEC)
450 5th Street, NW
Washington, DC 20549

Charged with regulating public companies, investment companies and other businesses to protect investors. Regulates business operations and requires filing of disclosure statements.

Books, Reports, Pamphlets

Facts for Young Consumers. Washington, DC: Federal Trade Commission. 1990. This pamphlet has consumer advice on buying a used car, buying by mail, warranties, credit laws, eyeglass prescriptions, indoor tanning, sunscreens and health and beauty products.

Composition of Foods Agriculture Handbook #8. Washington, DC: U.S. Government Printing Office.

Diet, Nutrition and Cancer Prevention: The Good News. Bethesda, MD: National Institutes of Health, 1987. Helps select, prepare and serve healthier foods. Includes a list of high-fiber and low-fat foods.

Dietary Guidelines for Americans-Avoid Too Much Sodium. Washington, DC: Department of Agriculture, 1986. One of a series of dietary bulletins with tips on sodium in the diet, a guide to the sodium content of foods, estimating the amount of sodium in the diet and suggestions on how to avoid too much sodium.

Discovering Vegetables: The Nutrition Education Guidebook for School Food Service Managers and Cooperators, For Use With Children Ages 5 Through 8. Washington, DC: Superintendent of Documents, 1975. $2.75.

Food Additives. Washington, DC: Food and Drug Administration, 1982. Why chemicals are added to foods and how additive use is regulated.

A Word About Low-Sodium Diets. Washington, DC: Food and Drug Administration, 1984. Includes recipes for salt substitutes.

CONTESTS AND PROGRAMS

Citizen Bee
The Close Up Foundation
44 Canal Center Plaza
Alexandria, VA 22314

Winners receive certificates, prizes, media recognition, all-expense-paid travel to Washington, DC and an educational bonus. The champion is awarded a cash prize for post-secondary education. Deadline is December 15.

Civic Achievement Award Program
The Close Up Foundation
44 Canal Center Plaza
Alexandria, VA 22314

Civics award for students in grades five through eight.

Future Problem Solving Program
115 Main Street, Box 98
Aberdeen, NC 28315

Sponsors an annual awards competition for Community Problem Solving/Future Problem Solving. Individual state deadlines for FPSP. Winners go to national competition. March 31 deadline.

The Giraffe Project
P.O. Box 759
Langley, WA 98260

Recognizes courage of individuals of all ages who "stick their necks out" for others. May deadline. Also offers training in community action.

Model United Nations
485 Fifth Avenue
New York, NY 10017

Over 60,000 high school and college students participate in the model U.N. annually. Students assume the roles of "ambassadors" to the U.N.; debate the current issues on the U.N.'s agenda; research the countries they represent, organize positions, prepare policy papers, draft resolutions and practice rules of procedure.

National Wildlife Federation
National Conservation Awards Program
1400 16th Street, NW
Washington, DC 20036-2266

Annual awards for contributions to the environment. Awards statuette of the whooping crane and expense-paid trip to receive the award.

President's Environmental Youth Awards
401 M Street, SW
Washington, DC 20460

Ten regional winners receive expense-paid trip to Washington, DC to receive annual awards for contributions to the environment. July 31 deadline.

Thomas Jefferson Forum, Inc.
131 State Street, Suite 305
Boston, MA 02109

Assists faculty coordinators at participating schools with the recruitment, placement, supervision and assessment of student volunteers while also working with students to develop leadership skills through service.

United Nations Environment Program
Information and Public Affairs
P.O. Box 30552
Nairobi, Kenya

The program recognizes environmental contributions by youth with Global 500 Awards.

Yoshiyama Award
P.O. Box 19247
Washington, DC 20036

Awards $5,000 to 6-8 high school seniors for extraordinary community service.

VIDEO

KIDSNET
6856 Eastern Avenue, NW, Suite 208
Washington, DC 20012

An electronic database clearinghouse that provides in-depth information, including more than 20,000 educational video and audio sources and current public, commercial and cable television programming for children. The database can be searched by grade level, subject area or special needs. For those without a computer and modem, the service can be used via telephone.

Franco, Debra. *Alternative Visions: Distributing Independent Media in a Home Video World.* This book discusses the problems of independent video distribution by looking at case studies. Available from Foundation for Independent Video and Film, 625 Broadway, New York, NY 10012, $12.95.

FILM AND VIDEO PRODUCERS AND DISTRIBUTORS

Action for Children's Television
20 University Road
Cambridge, MA 02138

Catalog of ACT videos. $1.

American Social History Project
Hunter College
695 Park Avenue, Room 340 North
New York, NY 10021

Produced and distributes *Who Built America?* a series of seven half-hour videos which present a social history of the United States from the American Revolution to the Civil War. Accompanied by viewer guides, teacher handbook.

Asian Cinevision
32 East Broadway
New York, NY 10002

The Asian American Media Reference Guide. Directory of more than 500 Asian American audio-visual programs.

Bullfrog Films
Oley, PA 19547

Distributes film and video on environmental issues.

California Newsreel
149 Ninth Street, #420
San Francisco, CA 94103

Berkeley In The Sixties. 1990.

Cambridge Documentary Films, Inc.
P.O. Box 385
Cambridge, MA 02139

Eugene Debs & The American Movement. A biographical documentary of working people during the turbulent rise of capitalism in the United States.

Still Killing Us Softly: Advertising's Image of Women. Thirty minute film about advertising's continuing assault on the self-images of women, men and children.

Center for Defense Information
1500 Massachusetts Avenue, NW
Washington, DC 20005

America's Defense Monitor. Half-hour videotapes with discussion guides and up-to-date suggestions for further reading. $25.

Churchill Films
12210 Nebraska Avenue
Los Angeles, CA 90025

Distributes more than 400 videos and films for young people, with a special emphasis on health issues.

Cinema Guild
1697 Broadway, Suite 803
New York, NY 10019

Distributes over 400 social documentaries.

Direct Cinema Limited
P.O. Box 669799
Los Angeles, CA 90069

Distributes 350 social documentaries.

Educational Film and Video Project
5332 College Avenue, Suite 101
Oakland, CA 94618

Produces and distributes film and video about the nuclear arms race, U.S. policy in Central America and the global environment.

Educational Video Center
60 East 13th Street
New York, NY 10003

Teaches inner-city youth to produce video documentaries on relevant issues.

Empowerment Project
1653 18th Street, Suite 3
Santa Monica, CA 90404

Produced and distributes *Coverup:Behind the Iran-Contra Affair* and *The Panama Deception*.

Filmmakers Library
124 East 40th Street, Suite 901
New York, NY 11016

Distributes independent film and video to educators.

Films Incorporated
5547 N. Ravenswood Avenue
Chicago, IL 60640-1199

Alice Walker. The video profiles the author of the Pulitzer Prize-winning novel *The Color Purple*, tracing Walker's deep sense of personal mission and strong sense of self that helped her to triumph over her humble beginnings as the eighth child of a Georgia sharecropper.

Gloria Steinem. Profiles a leader of the women's rights movement and founder of *Ms. magazine*.

First Run/Icarus Films
200 Park Avenue South, Suite 1319
New York, NY 10003

Born in Flames. 1983. A futuristic tale of feminist turmoil that is still brewing years after a "peaceful" social revolution.

Bread and Roses Too. A film that underscores the role labor unions can play in the lives of working men and women.

Fundi: The Story of Ella Baker. Joanne Grant. 1986. A highlight of the turbulent years of the 1960's with the viewing of history from the story of Ella Baker.

I am somebody. 1970. When 400 poorly paid black women hospital workers in Charleston, South Carolina, went on strike in 1969 to demand union recognition and an increase in their hourly wage, they soon found that they were confronting not only their employers, but also the National Guard and the power of the State government.

The War at Home. Barry A. Brown and Glenn Silber. 1979. Highlights the Vietnam struggle on the home front with interviews of students, community leaders and Vietnam veterans.

Greenpeace
1436 U Street, NW
Washington, DC 20009

Before It's Too Late. Highlights six communities around the country fighting to shut down or prevent the construction of facilities that produce toxic waste. $19.95.

Greenpeace's Greatest Hits. A 60 minute film that portrays Greenpeace's major campaigns from 1971-88. $29.95.

Highlander Education and Research Center
Route 3, Box 370
New Market, TN 37820

You Got to Move. A documentary about personal and social transformation. The film shows how Tennessee's legendary Highlander Folk School and other individuals worked for civil, environmental and women's rights in the South.

INFACT
256 Hanover Street, Third Floor
Boston, MA 02113

Deadly Deception: General Electric, Nuclear Weapons & Our Environment. A half-hour Academy Award-winning video by Debra Chasnoff.

Intermedia
1600 Dexter Avenue, North
Seattle, WA 98109

Distributes educational film and video for young people.

Media Network
39 W. 14th Street, Suite 403
New York, NY 10011

Images of Color. Catalog of more than 80 films, videotapes and slideshows on issues affecting Asian, African, Latino and Native American communities $11.50 institutions and organizations. $6.50 individuals.

In Her Own Image: Films and Videos Empowering Women for the Future. Catalog of over 80 films and videos by and about women. $11.50.

Safe Planet: The Guide to Environmental Film and Video. The guide evaluates more than 80 films and videos for use by educators and others. The topics include hazardous waste, recycling, global warming, work place hazards and many others. $11.50 institutions/organizations. $7.50 individuals.

Seeing through AIDS. Catalog of more than 80 titles addressing AIDS and AIDS related issues, including women and AIDS, youth AIDS activism, etc. $11.50 institutions and organizations. $6.50 individuals.

Museum of the American Indian
Film and Video Center
3753 Broadway at 155th Street
New York, NY 10032
    Native Americans on Film and Video. Catalog of media by and about Native Americans.

New Day Films
121 W. 27th Street
New York, NY 10001
    Union Maids, 1976.

People for the American Way
2000 M Street, NW, Suite 400
Washington, DC 20036
    Censorship in Our Schools: Hawkins County, TN. A video about a schoolhouse in a small rural community that became a censorship battleground when religious fundamentalists moved to ban an established reading series, VHS or 3/4". $20.

Third World Newsreel
335 W. 38th Street, 5th floor
New York, NY 10018
    Produces and distributes video on international and domestic social issues.

Warner Brothers Home Video
    Roger and Me. Written and directed by Michael Moore. A docu-comedy of what happened to the community of Flint, Michigan (home of the Flint sit-down strike) during the 1980s as General Motors closed auto factories, laid off workers and moved their jobs overseas.

William Greaves Productions, Inc.
230 W. 55th Street, #26D
New York, NY 10019
    Ida B. Wells: A Passion for Justice.

Women Make Movies
225 Lafayette Street
New York, NY 10012
    Produces and distributes film and video by and about women.

NOTES

PREFACE

[1] *Democracy's Next Generation: A Study of Youth and Teachers* (Washington, DC: People for the American Way, 1989), p. 12.

[2] *Democracy's Next Generation*, p. 15.

[3] *Democracy's Next Generation*, p. 15.

[4] *Democracy's Next Generation*, p. 144.

[5] *Democracy's Next Generation*, pp. 18-19.

[6] Si Kahn, *Organizing: A Guide for Grassroots Leaders*, Revised edition (Silver Spring, MD: National Association of Social Workers, 1991), p. 14.

[7] Kahn, p. 15.

[8] Lawrence Goodwyn, "Organizing Democracy: The Limits of Theory and Practice," *democracy*, January 1981, p. 49.

[9] Goodwyn, p. 46.

PROFILES OF STUDENTS IN ACTION

[1] James Ridgeway and Dan Bischoff, "Fighting Ronald McToxic: Children Lead a Crusade Against the Clown and His Clamshells," *Village Voice*, Vol. XXXV, No. 24, June 12, 1990, p. 33.

[2] Stuart Taylor, Jr., "Court, 5-3, Widens Power of Schools to Act as Censors," *The New York Times*, January 14, 1988, p. A1.

[3] Robert Kelly, "Pupils Putting Funds Where Forests Are," *St. Louis Post-Dispatch*.

[4] Charles DeVeney, *Save What's Left: Centuries to Create, Seconds to Destroy* (Coral Springs, FL: Save What's Left, 1991), p. 5.

[5] DeVeney, p. 6.

[6] DeVeney, p. 6.

[7] DeVeney, p. 7.

[8] Naftali Bendavid, "It's Not Easy Being Green, But Push by Broward Students Takes Root," *The Miami Herald*, April, 21 1991, p. 1; DeVeney, p. 7.

[9] Bendavid, p. 14A.

[10] Bendavid, p. 14A.

[11] Bendavid, p. 14A; correspondence with Save What's Left, May 1991.

[12] Bendavid, p. 14A.

[13] Gary Curreri, "Students do Speaking for Trees," *Coral Springs News*, October 24, 1990, p. 1A.

[14] Larry Kahn, "Dispute Continues Over Protest," *Coral Springs Forum*, November 15, 1990.

[15] DeVeney, p. 6.

[16] Chuck Clark, "The Fourth 'R: 'Recycling Finds Niche in School Curriculums as Teen Activists Rally Behind the Environment," Fort Lauderdale *Sun-Sentinel*, January 20, 1991, p. B1.

[17] Lynne Henderson, "Commissioners Delay Approval of Tree Ordinance Modifications," *Coral Springs News*, November 14, 1990, p. 8A.

[18] Clark, p. B1.

[19] "TV Trouble at North High," *Zillions*, April/May 1991, p. 31.

[20] John Murray, "TV in the Classroom: News or Nikes?," *Extra!* September/October 1991, p. 6.

[21] "TV Trouble," p. 31.

[22] "TV Trouble," p. 31.

[23] Associated Press, October 22, 1990.

[24] "TV Trouble," p. 31.

[25] Murray, p. 6.

[26] Michelle Healy, "Despite Static, Channel One Has Strong First Year," *USA Today*, March 5, 1991, p. 4D.

[27] Healy, p. 4D.

[28] Murray, p. 6.

[29] Murray, p. 6.

[30] Murray, p. 6.

[31] Healy, p. 4D.

[32] "TV Trouble," p. 31.

[33] "TV Trouble," p. 31.

[34] "TV Trouble," pp. 31-32.

[35] Correspondence with North High School, March 1991.

[36] Associated Press, October 22, 1990.

[37] "TV Trouble," p. 32.

[38] "TV Trouble," p. 32.

[39] Thomas Bell, "Schools Put Power in Students' Hands: Energy Patrols Boost Morale, Lower Utility Bills," *The Washington Post*, February 7, 1991, p. J1.

[40] Bell, p. J1.

[41] Bell, p. J1.

[42] Conversation with Lilly Lewis, March 1991.

[43] Conversation with Barry Sprague, March 1991.

[44] Conversation with Barry Sprague, March 1991.

[45] Conversation with Barry Sprague, March 1991.

[46] Kelley Griffin, *More Action for a Change* (New York: Dembner Books, 1987), pp. 135-144.

[47] As quoted in Griffin, p. 139.

[48] As quoted in Griffin, p. 139.

[49] Griffin, pp. 135-144.

[50] As quoted in Griffin, pp. 142, 143.

[51] Griffin, pp. xi, xii.

[52] Griffin, p. 14.

[53] Griffin, pp. 19-20.

[54] Griffin, pp. 19-20.

[55] Griffin, pp. 33-38.

[56] Ralph Nader, Introduction to Griffin, p. xvii.

[57] George James, "Pupil Starts A Revolution of Her Own: Ban Plastics," *The New York Times*, April 28, 1989, p. B1; Ridgeway and Bischoff, p. 29.

[58] James, pp. B1, B4.

[59] James, p. B4.

[60] James, p. B4.

[61] James, p. B4.

[62] Katherine Hutt, "Drastic Plastic: West Milford Kids 'Recruit' Dr. Ruth," The North Jersey *Herald and News*, June 8, 1989, p. A4.

[63] James, p. B4.

[64] Hutt, pp. A-1, A-4.

[65] Ridgeway and Bischoff, p. 29.

[66] Correspondence with West Milford High School Environmental Club, May 1991.

[67] As quoted in "Young Take Environmental Concern to United Nations," *The Sussex Herald.* May 2, 1989.

[68] Ralph Nader, Introduction to Claire Townsend, *Old Age: The Last Segregation* (New York: Bantam Books, 1971), p. ix.

[69] Ralph Nader introduction to Townsend, pp. x-xi.

[70] Townsend, pp. xvi-xvii.

[71] Townsend, p. xvi.

[72] Townsend, p. xvi.

[73] Townsend, p. xv.

[74] Townsend, p. 157.

[75] George Lardner, Jr., "Nursing Home Conditions Hit By Nader Unit," *The Washington Post*, December 18, 1970, p. A2.

[76] Townsend, p. xvii.

[77] Lardner, p. A2.

[78] Barbara A. Lewis, *The Kid's Guide to Social Action: How to Solve the Social Problems You Choose -- And Turn Creative Thinking into Positive Action* (Minneapolis: Free Spirit Publishing, 1991), p. 7.

[79] Lewis, p. 7.

[80] Lewis, p. 7.

[81] Lewis, p. 7.

[82] Lewis, p. 8.

[83] Lewis, pp. 8-9.

[84] Lewis, p. 10.

[85] Lewis, p. 10.

[86] Lewis, p. 10.

[87] Lewis, p. 11.

[88] Lewis, p. 11.

INTRODUCTION

[1] Howard Zinn, *A People's History of the United States* (New York: Harper and Row, 1980), p. 8.

[2] Zinn, p. 8.

[3] *We the People: A Review of U.S. Government and Civics Textbooks* (Washington, DC: People for the American Way, 1987), p. ii.

[4] *We the People*, p. ii.

[5] *We the People*, p. i.

CIVIL RIGHTS MOVEMENT

[1] Stokely Carmichael and Charles V. Hamilton, *Black Power* (New York: Vintage Books, 1967), p. 25.

[2] Howard Zinn, *A People's History of the United States* (New York: Harper and Row, 1980), p. 25.

[3] Zinn, p. 23.

[4] Zinn, p. 32.

[5] Richard Kluger, *Simple Justice* (New York: Vintage Books, 1975), p. 27; William H. Harris, *The Harder We Run: Black Workers Since the Civil War* (New York: Oxford University Press, 1982), p. 8; Zinn, p. 168.

[6] Leon F. Litwack, *North of Slavery: The Negro in the Free States 1790-1860* (Chicago: University of Chicago Press, 1961), pp. 14-15.

[7] Kluger, p. 35.

[8] Leon F. Litwack, *Been in the Storm So Long: The Aftermath of Slavery* (New York: Alfred A. Knopf, 1979), p. 16.

[9] Zinn, p. 32.

[10] Zinn, p. 180.

[11] Zinn, p. 175.

[12] Zinn, p. 176.

[13] Zinn, p. 179.

[14] Zinn, p. 179.

[15] Zinn, p. 171.

[16] Zinn, p. 187.

[17] Carmichael and Hamilton, p. 25.

[18] Carmichael and Hamilton, p. 25.

[19] Zinn, p. 435.

[20] Zinn, pp. 193-195.

[21] Henry Hampton and Steve Fayer, *Voices of Freedom: An Oral History of the Civil Rights Movement From the 1950s Through the 1980s* (New York: Bantam Books, 1990), p. xxiii.

[22] Harvard Sitkoff, *The Struggle for Black Equality: 1954-1980* (New York: Hill and Wang, 1981), p. 4.

[23] Harris, p. 8.

[24] Kluger, pp. 59-60.

[25] Juan Williams, *Eyes on the Prize: America's Civil Rights Years, 1954-1965* (New York: Viking, 1987), p. 10.

[26] Williams, *Eyes on the Prize*, p. 10.

[27] Kluger, p. 72.

[28] Kluger, p. 73.

[29] Williams, *Eyes on the Prize*, p. 9.

[30] Aldon D. Morris, *The Origins of the Civil Rights Movement: Black Communities Organizing for Change* (New York: The Free Press, 1984), p. 2.

[31] Hampton and Fayer, p. xxiii.

[32] Harris, pp. 8-9.

[33] Harris, pp. 10-13.

[34] Harris, pp. 52-53.

[35] Harris, pp. 26, 53-55, 61.

[36] Harris, pp. 42-44.

[37] Harris, pp. 19, 25-26.

[38] Harris, p. 37.

[39] Harris, Chapter 4.

[40] Dorothy Sterling, *Black Foremothers: Three Lives* (New York: Feminist Press, 1988), p. 77.

[41] Ellen Cantarow with Susan Gushee O'Malley and Sharon Hartman Strom, *Moving the Mountain: Women Working for Social Change* (Old Westbury, NY: The Feminist Press, 1980), p. xxxi.

[42] Cantarow, *et al.*, pp. xxxi-xxxii.

[43] Kluger, p. 68.

[44] Mary White Ovington, *How the National Association for the Advancement of Colored People Began* pamphlet (Washington, DC: NAACP, originally published in 1914).

[45] Sterling, pp. 104-105.

[46] *75th Annual Conference Program* (New York: National Urban League, 1985.

[47] Lawrence W. Levine, "Marcus Garvey's Moment," *The New Republic*, October 29, 1984, p. 26.

[48] E. David Cronon, *Black Moses: The Story of Marcus Garvey and the Universal Negro Improvement Association* (Madison: The University of Wisconsin Press, 1981 [1955]), p. 184.

[49] Cronon, p. 16; Levine, p. 29.

[50] Levine, p. 26.

[51] Levine, p. 29.

[52] Levine, p. 29.

[53] Cronon, p. 144; Levine, p. 29.

[54] Carmichael and Hamilton, p. 27; Harris, pp. 54-55.

[55] Claudia Koonz, "The Auxiliary of Hate," *The New York Times Book Review*, January 5, 1992, p. 22.

[56] Zinn, p. 435.

[57] Langston Hughes, *Langston Hughes Reader* (New York: George Braziller, Inc. 1958), p. 123.

[58] Harris, pp. 97-98, 100.

[59] Harris, p. 101.

[60] Harris, pp. 98-99; see also Nate Shaw with Theodore Rosengarten, *All God's Dangers* (New York: Vintage Books, 1984).

[61] Harris, p. 104.

[62] Harris, p. 105.

[63] Harris, p. 107.

[64] Harris, p. 122.

[65] Harris, p. 116.

[66] Harris, pp. 115-116.

[67] Fred Powledge, *Free at Last? The Civil Rights Movement and the People Who Made It* (Boston: Little, Brown, 1991), pp. 25, 28.

[68] Harris, p. 117.

[69] Harris, p. 113.

[70] Harris, p. 125.

[71] See Winthrop D. Jordan and Leon F. Litwack, *The United States.* Seventh Combined Edition (Englewood Cliffs, NJ: Prentice Hall, 1991), p. 710; Harris, p. 113.

[72] Hampton and Fayer, p. xxv.

[73] Sitkoff, p. 16.

[74] Zinn, p. 440.

[75] Sitkoff, p. 19.

[76] Williams, *Eyes on the Prize*, p. 2.

[77] *Journal of Negro Education*, Volume IV, Number 3, Summer 1935, as cited in Kluger, p. 169.

[78] Williams, *Eyes on the Prize*, p. 10.

[79] Williams, *Eyes on the Prize*, pp. 10-11.

[80] Williams, *Eyes on the Prize*, p. 11.

[81] Kluger, pp. 192-3.

[82] Juan Williams, "Marshall's Law," In *Eight Men and a Lady: Profiles of the Justices of the Supreme Court* (Bethesda, MD: National Press, 1990), p. 124.

[83] Williams, *Eyes on the Prize*, pp. 14-15.

[84] Kluger, p. 291.

[85] Kluger, pp. 293-294.

[86] Williams, *Eyes on the Prize*, p. 19.

[87] Kluger, p. 459.

[88] Kluger, pp. 459-460.

[89] Kluger, p. 466.

[90] Kluger, pp. 468-469.

[91] Kluger, pp. 470-471.

[92] Kluger, p. 476.

[93] Kluger, pp. 476-478; Williams, *Eyes on the Prize*, p. 27.

[94] Sitkoff, p. 20.

[95] Williams, *Eyes on the Prize*, p. 31.

[96] Kluger, p. 553.

[97] Kluger, p. 562.

[98] Williams, *Eyes on the Prize*, p. 31.

[99] Lisa Aldred, *Thurgood Marshall: Supreme Court Justice* (New York: Chelsea House Publishers, 1990), p. 18.

[100] Williams, "Marshall's Law," p. 129.

[101] Williams, *Eyes on the Prize*, p. 34.

[102] Williams, "Marshall's Law," p. 131.

[103] Kluger, p. 720.

[104] J. Harvie Wilkinson III, *From Brown to Bakke: The Supreme Court and School Integration: 1954-1978* (Oxford: Oxford University Press, 1979), pp. 78, 82.

[105] Williams, "Marshall's Law," p. 131.

[106] Williams, *Eyes on the Prize*, pp. 92-94.

[107] Williams, *Eyes on the Prize*, p. 93.

[108] Williams, *Eyes on the Prize*, p. 96.

[109] Williams, *Eyes on the Prize*, pp. 99-100.

[110] Williams, *Eyes on the Prize*, pp. 100-101; Hampton and Fayer, p. 36.

[111] Leon Friedman, ed., *The Civil Rights Reader* (New York: Walker and Company, 1968), pp. 164-165.

[112] Hampton and Fayer, pp. 46-47.

[113] Hampton and Fayer, p. 47.

[114] Hampton and Fayer, p. 48.

[115] Williams, *Eyes on the Prize*, p. 118.

[116] Williams, "Marshall's Law," p. 133.

[117] Williams, "Marshall's Law," pp. 133-4.

[118] Williams, "Marshall's Law," p. 118.

[119] Williams, "Marshall's Law," p. 119.

[120] Williams, "Marshall's Law," p. 120.

[121] Williams, "Marshall's Law," pp. 120-121.

[122] Williams, "Marshall's Law," p. 121.

[123] Williams, "Marshall's Law," p. 122.

[124] Williams, "Marshall's Law," p. 125.

[125] Williams, "Marshall's Law," p. 125.

[126] Williams, "Marshall's Law," pp. 127-128.

[127] Williams, "Marshall's Law," p. 116.

[128] Aldred, p. 118.

[129] Aldred, p. 120.

[130] Williams, "Marshall's Law," pp. 141-2.

[131] Williams, "Marshall's Law," p. 140.

[132] Quoted in Williams, "Marshall's Law," p. 117.

[133] Dominic J. Capeci, Jr., "From Harlem to Montgomery: The Bus Boycotts And Leadership of Adam Clayton Powell, Jr. and Martin Luther King, Jr.," *The Historian: A Journal of History*, Vol. 41, No. 4, August 1979, pp. 721-737.

[134] Hampton and Fayer, p. 18.

[135] Williams, *Eyes on the Prize*, p. 63.

[136] Zinn, p. 242.

[137] Howell Raines, *My Soul is Rested: The Story of the Civil Rights Movement in the Deep South* (New York: Penguin, 1977), pp. 41, 44.

[138] Sitkoff, p. 43.

[139] Hampton and Fayer, p. 22; Williams, *Eyes on the Prize*, p. 61.

[140] Williams, *Eyes on the Prize*, pp. 69, 72.

[141] Friedman, p. 38.

[142] Friedman, p. 38.

[143] Williams, *Eyes on the Prize*, p. 73; Hampton and Fayer, pp. 23-34.

[144] Friedman, p. 39.

[145] Zinn, p. 442.

[146] Williams, *Eyes on the Prize*, p. 85.; Hampton and Fayer, p. 28; Zinn, p. 442.

[147] Hampton and Fayer, p. 30.

[148] Hampton and Fayer, pp. 31-32.

[149] Williams, *Eyes on the Prize*, pp. 87-88.

[150] Williams, *Eyes on the Prize*, p. 88.

[151] Williams, *Eyes on the Prize*, p. 89.

[152] Friedman, p. 40.

[153] Williams, *Eyes on the Prize*, p. 88.

[154] Williams, *Eyes on the Prize*, p. 87-89.

[155] Morris, p. 126.

[156] Friedman, pp. 231-233; Kluger, p. 754.

[157] Sitkoff, p. 84.

[158] Thomas Rose and John Greenya, *Black Leaders: Then and Now* (Garrett Park, MD: Garrett Park Press, 1984), p. 11.

[159] Rose and Greenya, p. 12.

[160] Zinn, p. 444.

[161] Zinn, p. 444.

[162] Sitkoff, p. 81.

[163] Clayborne Carson, *In Struggle: SNCC and the Black Awakening of the 1960s* (Cambridge: Harvard University Press, 1981), p. 11.

[164] Rose and Greenya, p. 15.

[165] Rose and Greenya, p. 15.

[166] Carson, p. 22.

[167] Rose and Greenya, p. 15.

[168] Rose and Greenya, p. 16.

[169] Rose and Greenya, pp. 17,18.

[170] Raines, p. 86.

[171] Rose and Greenya, p. 20.

[172] Raines, pp. 89-90.

[173] Rose and Greenya, p. 21.

[174] Cantarow, p. 83.

[175] Carson, p. 20.

[176] Raines, pp. 101-102.

[177] James Forman, *The Making of Black Revolutionaries* (Washington, DC: Open Hand Publishing, Inc., 1985), p. 217.

[178] Ella Baker reporting in the *South Patriot*, May 1960, as quoted in Forman, p. 218.

[179] Carson, p. 30.

[180] Carson, p. 30.

[181] Sitkoff, p. 87.

[182] Forman, p. 215.

[183] Cantarow, pp. 54, 62; Mary King, *Freedom Song: A Personal Story of the 1960s Civil Rights Movement* (New York: William Morrow and Company, Inc., 1987), p. 42.

[184] Carson, p. 20.

[185] Cantarow, p. 63.

[186] Cantarow, p. 63.

[187] Cantarow, p. 54.

[188] Gerda Lerner, ed., *Black Women in White America: A Documentary History* (New York: Pantheon Books, 1972), p. 347.

[189] King, p. 282.

[190] King, p. 282.

[191] Lerner, p. 351.

[192] Cantarow, p. 82.

[193] Cantarow, pp. 89-91.

[194] Lerner, p. 346.

[195] Sitkoff, p. 97.

[196] Hampton and Fayer, p. 74.

[197] Hampton and Fayer, p. 74; Sitkoff, p. 99; Williams, *Eyes on the Prize*, p. 145.

[198] Sitkoff, p. 97; Raines, p. 110.

[199] Hampton and Fayer, p. 75.

[200] Sitkoff, p. 100; Raines, pp. 110-111.

[201] Hampton and Fayer, p. 77.

[202] Hampton and Fayer, p. 78.

[203] Hampton and Fayer, p. 79.

[204] Hampton and Fayer, pp. 79, 81.

[205] Hampton and Fayer, p. 82.

[206] Hampton and Fayer, p. 83.

[207] Hampton and Fayer, pp. 83-84.

[208] Hampton and Fayer, pp. 85-86, 89.

[209] Sitkoff, pp. 104-105.

[210] Williams, *Eyes on the Prize*, p. 155.

[211] Carson, p. 36.

[212] Sitkoff, p. 108; Williams, *Eyes on the Prize*, p. 158.

[213] Williams, *Eyes on the Prize*, pp. 158-159; Sitkoff, p. 110; Zinn, p. 445.

[214] Sitkoff, p. 112.

[215] Sitkoff, p. 110.

[216] Sitkoff, pp. 114-115.

[217] Sitkoff, pp. 114-116.

[218] Cantarow, p. 87.

[219] Raines, pp. 233-234.

[220] Friedman, pp. 167-173.

[221] Raines, pp. 234-235.

[222] Sitkoff, p. 116.

[223] Sitkoff, pp. 116-117.

[224] Sitkoff, pp. 117-118; Williams, *Eyes on the Prize*, p. 213.

[225] Raines, pp. 230-231.

[226] Hampton and Fayer, pp. 98-99, 104.

[227] Hampton and Fayer, p. 147.

[228] Hampton and Fayer, pp. 148-149.

[229] Hampton and Fayer, p. 149.

[230] Hampton and Fayer, p. 150.

[231] Hampton and Fayer, pp. 6, 151, 154-155.

[232] Hampton and Fayer, p. 181.

[233] Hampton and Fayer, p. 181.

[234] Sitkoff, p. 156.

[235] Hampton and Fayer, p. 124.

[236] Hampton and Fayer, pp. 124-125.

[237] Hampton and Fayer, p. 125.

[238] Hampton and Fayer, p. 128.

[239] Hampton and Fayer, pp. 127, 129, 131, 133.

[240] Hampton and Fayer, p. 133.

[241] Hampton and Fayer, p. 134.

[242] Hampton and Fayer, p. 137.

[243] Sitkoff, pp. 159-165.

[244] Sitkoff, pp. 159-165.

[245] Sitkoff, pp. 161, 165.

[246] Sitkoff, p. 165.

[247] Zinn, p. 449.

[248] Hampton and Fayer, p. 171.

[249] Sitkoff, pp. 170-171.

[250] Hampton and Fayer, p. 185; Sitkoff, pp. 170-171.

[251] Sitkoff, p. 172.

[252] Williams, *Eyes on the Prize*, pp. 230-231; Sitkoff, p. 175.

[253] Hampton and Fayer, p. 195.

[254] Hampton and Fayer, p. 195; Raines, p. 289.

[255] Raines, pp. 249-255.

[256] Williams, *Eyes on the Prize*, p. 233, Hampton and Fayer p. 185.

[257] Carson, p. 123; Williams, *Eyes on the Prize*, pp. 242-243.

[258] Sitkoff, p. 181.

[259] Sitkoff, pp. 184-185; Carson p. 127.

[260] Cantarow, p. 91.

[261] Hampton and Fayer, p. 213.

[262] Hampton and Fayer, p. 214.

[263] Hampton and Fayer, p. 213.

[264] Hampton and Fayer, pp. 214-215; Sitkoff, p. 188.

[265] Hampton and Fayer, pp. 222-223; Williams, *Eyes on the Prize*, p. 265.

[266] Hampton and Fayer, pp. 226-227, 229; Sitkoff, pp. 189-190; Williams, *Eyes on the Prize*, p. 273.

[267] Sitkoff, p. 190.

[268] Hampton and Fayer, pp. 229-230.

[269] Hampton and Fayer, pp. 231-232.

[270] Hampton and Fayer, p. 234.

[271] Hampton and Fayer, pp. 236, 238; Williams, *Eyes on the Prize*, pp. 282-283.

[272] Raines, p. 221.

[273] Hampton and Fayer, p. 272; Friedman, p. 260.

[274] Sitkoff, p. 228.

[275] Hampton and Fayer, pp. 241-242.

[276] Hampton and Fayer, pp. 242-243.

[277] Hampton and Fayer, p. 243; "Black Muslims: From Fringe to Bedrock," *U.S. News and World Report*, Vol. 109, No. 14, October 8, 1990, p. 71.

[278] Sitkoff, p. 153.

[279] Hampton and Fayer, pp. 241-242; King, p. 288.

[280] Hampton and Fayer, pp. 254-255.

[281] Hampton and Fayer, p. 243.

[282] Hampton and Fayer, p. 260.

[283] Hampton and Fayer, p. 244.

[284] Hampton and Fayer, pp. 258-259.

[285] Hampton and Fayer, p. 244.

[286] Hampton and Fayer, pp. 249.

[287] Alex Haley, *The Autobiography of Malcolm X* (New York: Grove Press, 1965).

[288] Sitkoff, p. 211.

[289] "Black Muslims: From Fringe to Bedrock," p. 71.

[290] Hampton and Fayer, p. 268.

[291] Hampton and Fayer, pp. 267-270.

[292] Hampton and Fayer, p. 272.

[293] Hampton and Fayer, p. 272.

[294] Hampton and Fayer, p. 272.

295 Hampton and Fayer, pp. 272-275.

296 Hampton and Fayer, p. 275; Charles E. Fager, *Selma, 1965* (New York: Charles Scribner's Sons, 1974), p. 206.

297 Hampton and Fayer, p. 277.

298 Hampton and Fayer, pp. 277-279.

299 Hampton and Fayer, p. 279.

300 Zinn, p. 448.

301 Hampton and Fayer, p. 279.

302 Hampton and Fayer, pp. 279-280.

303 Hampton and Fayer, pp. 280-281.

304 Hampton and Fayer, p. 289.

305 Hampton and Fayer, p. 290.

306 Hampton and Fayer, p. 294.

307 Hampton and Fayer, p. 294.

308 Hampton and Fayer, p. 297-298.

309 Hampton and Fayer, pp. 352-353.

310 Hampton and Fayer, pp. 350, 354.

311 Hampton and Fayer, p. 350.

312 Hampton and Fayer, p. 353.

313 Hampton and Fayer, pp. 355-356.

314 Hampton and Fayer, p. 359.

315 Hampton and Fayer, pp. 372, 512.

316 Hampton and Fayer, pp. 511-512.

317 Judith Clavir Albert and Stewart Edward Albert, eds., *The Sixties Papers: Documents of a Rebellious Decade* (New York: Praeger, 1984), p. 27.

318 Zinn, p. 455.

319 Sitkoff, pp. 200-201.

320 Kluger, p. 762.

321 Sitkoff, p. 206.

322 Sitkoff, pp. 204-205.

323 Sitkoff, p. 205.

324 Herbert Aptheker, *Afro American History: The Modern Era* (Secaucus, NJ: The Citadel Press, 1971), pp. 246, 249-253.

325 Cited in Harris, p. 152.

326 Sitkoff, pp. 202, 205, 234.

327 Zinn, p. 453.

328 Zinn, p. 453.

329 Hampton and Fayer, p. 298.

330 Zinn, p. 453.

331 Kluger, p. 762.

332 Sitkoff, p. 222.

333 Sitkoff, pp. 222-223.

334 Wilkinson, pp. 78, 116; Hampton and Fayer, p. 587.

335 Kluger, p. 768.

336 Kluger, p. 768.

337 Kluger, p. 772.

338 Sitkoff, p. 227.

339 Sitkoff, p. 225.

340 Sitkoff, pp. 225-226.

341 Sitkoff, p. 227.

342 Hampton and Fayer, p. 660; Ralph G. Neas, "The Civil Rights Legacy of the Reagan Years," *USA Today: The Magazine of the American Scene*. Society for the Advancement of Education, Vol. 118, No. 2538, March 1990, p. 17; Jordan and Litwack, p. 867.

343 Neas, p. 16.

344 Neas, p. 17.

345 Neas, p. 18.

346 Neas, p. 18.

347 *Justice for Wards Cove Workers Act* (Washington, DC: Leadership Conference on Civil Rights), p. 3.

348 Janet Dewart, ed., *State of Black America 1989* (New York: The National Urban League, 1989), p. 113.

349 Dewart, p. 114; Bureau of the Census of the Economics and Statistics Administration of the U.S. Department of Commerce, 1990 Census - Advance Copy.

350 Dewart, p. 9.

351 Dewart, p. 12.

352 Dewart, p. 31.

353 Dewart, p. 18.

354 Dewart, p. 70.

355 Dewart, p. 71.

356 Dewart, p. 72.

357 *Civil Rights Monitor* (Washington, DC: Leadership Conference Education Fund, Summer 1991), p. 7.

358 *Civil Rights Monitor* (Washington, DC: Leadership Education Fund, Fall 1990), p. 2.

359 *Civil Rights Monitor* (Washington, DC: Leadership Conference Education Fund, Fall 1990), p. 2.

360 *Civil Rights Monitor* (Washington, DC: Leadership Conference Education Fund, Summer 1991), p. 8.

361 "End of the Quota Non-Issue?" *New York Times*, April 24, 1991, p. A24.

362 Interview with Andrew Goldfarb of the Leadership Conference on Civil Rights, November 26, 1991.

363 *Civil Rights Monitor* (Washington, DC: Leadership Conference Education Fund, Summer 1991), p. 2.

364 Ann Devroy, "President Signs Civil Rights Bill," *Washington Post*, November 22, 1991, p. A1.

365 Devroy, p. A1.

366 Devroy, p. A14.

367 Salim Muwakkil, "Black Leaders Favor 'Self-Help' Over Integration," *In These Times*, October 10-16, 1990, p. 2.

368 Muwakkil, "Black Leaders Favor," p. 2.

369 Neas, p. 18.

370 Salim Muwakkil, "An Organized PUSH for Black Participation," *In These Times*, September 12-18, 1990, p. 7.

371 Muwakkil, "An Organized PUSH," p. 7.

372 Muwakkil, "An Organized PUSH," p. 7.

373 Muwakkil, "An Organized PUSH," p. 7.

374 Muwakkil, "An Organized PUSH," p. 7.

[375] Pat Redmond, "Women of Color Set Agenda," *New Directions for Women*, September 1990, pp. 1, 8.

[376] Dewart, p. 185.

LABOR MOVEMENT

[1] Alfred F. Young, "Revolutionary Mechanics," in Paul Buhle and Alan Dawley, eds., *Working for Democracy: American Workers from the Revolution to the Present* (Urbana: University of Illinois Press, 1985), p. 2; American Social History Project, under the direction of Herbert G. Gutman, *Who Built America?: Working People and the Nation's Economy, Politics, Culture and Society.* Volume I (New York: Pantheon, 1989), p. 240.

[2] Eleanor Flexner, *Century of Struggle: The Women's Rights Movement in the United States* (Cambridge, MA: The Belknap Press of Harvard University Press, 1975), p. 9.

[3] As cited in Young, p. 3.

[4] Young, pp. 3-4.

[5] Leon Litwack, *The American Labor Movement* (Englewood Cliffs, NJ: Prentice Hall, Inc., 1962), p. 7.

[6] Franklin Rosemont, "Workingmen's Parties," in Buhle and Dawley, p. 12.

[7] Rosemont, p. 11.

[8] Howard Zinn, *A People's History of the United States* (New York: Harper and Row Publishers, 1980), pp. 216-127.

[9] Sara M. Evans and Harry C. Boyte, *Free Spaces: The Sources of Democratic Change in America* (New York: Harper and Row Publishers, 1986), p. 116.

[10] Rosemont, p. 14.

[11] Rosemont, pp. 15-16.

[12] Gus Tyler, *The Labor Revolution: Trade Unions in a New America* (New York: The Viking Press, 1967 [1966]), p. 62.

[13] American Social History Project, p. 327.

[14] Rosemont, p. 14.

[15] Rosemont, p. 14.

[16] Rosemont, p. 15.

[17] Rosemont, p. 14.

[18] Adrian A. Paradis, *Labor in Action: The Story of the American Labor Movement* (New York: Julian Messner, 1975 [1963]), pp. 25-26.

[19] Rosemont, p. 13.

[20] Rosemont, pp. 16-18.

[21] Rosemont, p. 18.

[22] American Social History Project, p. 332.

[23] *A Short History of American Labor* (Washington, DC: AFL-CIO, 1981), p. 4.

[24] Douglas L. Leslie, *Labor Law in a Nutshell* (St. Paul, MN: West Publishing, Co., 1986), p. 2.

[25] Flexner, p. 24.

[26] Flexner, p. 53.

[27] Flexner, p. 53.

[28] Evans and Boyte, p. 117; Flexner, pp. 55-57; Zinn, p. 223.

[29] Flexner, pp. 57-58.

[30] Flexner, p. 58.

[31] Flexner, pp. 59-60; Zinn, p. 225.

[32] As quoted in Zinn, p. 225.

[33] Rosemont, p. 11.

[34] Zinn, p. 225.

[35] American Social History Project, pp. 354-358.

[36] Zinn, p. 222.

[37] American Social History Project, pp. 354-358.

[38] American Social History Project, p. 360.

[39] American Social History Project, p. 362.

[40] Eric Foner, "Workers and Slavery," in Buhle and Dawley, p. 22.

[41] American Social History Project, p. 362.

[42] Foner, "Workers and Slavery," p. 22; American Social History Project, p. 363.

[43] Foner, pp. 22-23.

[44] Zinn, p. 230.

[45] Zinn, pp. 230-232.

[46] Zinn, p. 228; Foner, p. 27.

[47] Alan Dawley, "Paths to Power after the Civil War," in Buhle and Dawley, p. 41.

[48] Litwack, pp. 83-87.

[49] Harvey Wasserman, *Harvey Wasserman's History of the United States* (New York: Four Wall Eight Windows, 1988), pp. 115, 118; American Social History Project, p. 546.

[50] Zinn, p. 237.

[51] Zinn, pp. 239-240.

[52] American Social History Project, pp. 553-558.

[53] Dawley, p. 44; American Social History Project, pp. 553, 558.

[54] Herbert G. Gutman, "The Worker's Search for Power: Labor in the Gilded Age," in Wayne Morgan, ed., *The Gilded Age* (Syracuse, NY: Syracuse University Press, 1963), p. 40.

[55] Gutman, p. 41.

[56] Gutman, pp. 41, 44-45.

[57] Gutman, pp. 41-44.

[58] Gutman, pp. 45-46.

[59] Gutman, pp. 47-52.

[60] Gutman, pp. 47-52.

[61] Gutman, p. 68.

[62] Wasserman, p. 118.

[63] Nell Irvin Painter, "Black Workers from Reconstruction to the Great Depression," in Buhle and Dawley, p. 65.

[64] Dawley, p. 42.

[65] Wasserman, p. 118.

[66] Dawley, p. 45.

[67] Dawley, p. 45.

[68] Wasserman, pp. 119-120.

[69] Wasserman, p. 120; *A Short History of American Labor*, pp. 4-5.

[70] Wasserman, pp. 121-122; Staughton Lynd, ed., *American Labor Radicalism: Testimonies and Interpretations* (New York: John Wiley and Sons, 1973), p. 3.

[71] Zinn, p. 321.

[72] Lynd, p. 3.

[73] Wasserman, p. 122.

[74] Wasserman, p. 144.

[75] Wasserman, p. 144; Painter, p. 69.

[76] Zinn, p. 272; Lynd, p. 3.

[77] Zinn, p. 273; Wasserman, p. 135.

[78] Zinn, p. 273.

[79] Wasserman, p. 130.

[80] Zinn, p. 274; Wasserman, pp. 130-131.

[81] Zinn, p. 273, 274-275.

[82] Zinn, p. 275; Wasserman, pp. 135, 137.

[83] Wasserman, pp. 134-137; Zinn, p. 275.

[84] Edward Bellamy, *Looking Backward: 2000-1887* (Boston: Houghton-Mifflin, 1966 [1887]).

[85] Zinn, p. 258.

[86] Zinn, pp. 258-259.

[87] Zinn, p. 346.

[88] Wasserman, pp. 137-143.

[89] Wasserman, pp. 140-141.

[90] Zinn, p. 322; Wasserman, p. 147.

[91] Zinn, p. 322; Wasserman, p. 147.

[92] Wasserman, p. 151.

[93] Wasserman, pp. 151, 154.

[94] Paul Buhle, "Socialists and Wobblies," in Buhle and Dawley, p. 58; Zinn, p. 327.

[95] Zinn, p. 327-328; Buhle, p. 59.

[96] Zinn, p. 329.

[97] Buhle, p. 58.

[98] Zinn, p. 324.

[99] Wasserman, pp. 152, 165; Zinn, p. 326.

[100] Wasserman, p. 152.

[101] Wasserman, pp. 150-151.

[102] Zinn, p. 341.

[103] Flexner, p. 205.

[104] Flexner, pp. 213, 214, 253.

[105] Flexner, p. 220.

[106] Flexner, p. 248.

[107] Flexner, pp. 248-251; Zinn, p. 318.

[108] Flexner, pp. 251-252.

[109] Flexner, p. 255.

[110] Joseph Gustaitis, "Mary Harris Jones: The Most Dangerous Woman in America," *American History Illustrated*, January 1988, p. 22.

[111] Alden Whitman, ed., *American Reformers* (New York: H.W. Wilson Company, 1985), p. 483.

[112] Whitman, p. 483.

[113] Priscilla Long, *Mother Jones, Woman Organizer and Her Relations With Miner's Wives, Working Women and the Suffrage Movement* (Boston: South End Press, 1976), p. 4.

[114] Long, p. 4.

[115] Whitman, p. 484.

[116] Long, p. 6.

[117] As quoted in Eve Merriam, ed., *Growing Up Female: Ten Lives* (Garden City, NY: Doubleday, 1971), p. 219.

[118] Whitman, p. 484.

[119] As quoted in Merriam, p. 221.

[120] As quoted in Merriam, p. 223.

[121] As quoted in Merriam, p. 226.

[122] As quoted in Whitman, p. 484.

[123] Wasserman, p. 166.

[124] Zinn, p. 356.

[125] Zinn, pp. 358-359.

[126] Zinn, pp. 363-364.

[127] See Paul Buhle, "Socialists and Wobblies," in Buhle and Dawley, p. 59.

[128] Buhle, p. 59.

[129] Buhle, p. 60.

[130] Zinn, pp. 316-317.

[131] David Montgomery, *Worker's Control in America* (Cambridge: Cambridge University Press, 1979), p. 3.

[132] Montgomery, *Worker's Control in America*, p. 4.

[133] Montgomery, *Worker's Control in America*, p. 4.

[134] David Montgomery, "The Farmer-Labor Party," in Buhle and Dawley, p. 73.

[135] Montgomery, "The Farmer-Labor Party," p. 74.

[136] Montgomery, "The Farmer-Labor Party," pp. 76-77, 79.

[137] Montgomery, "The Farmer-Labor Party," p. 78.

[138] Montgomery, "The Farmer-Labor Party," pp. 80-81.

[139] William H. Harris, *The Harder We Run: Black Workers Since the Civil War* (New York: Oxford University Press, 1982), pp. 20, 60.

[140] Harris, pp. 59-60.

[141] Harris, pp. 78-79.

[142] Harris, pp. 79- 81.

[143] Harris, pp. 79-80.

[144] Harris, pp. 83-84, 86.

[145] Harris, p. 81; Painter, p. 70.

[146] Harris, pp. 77-78, 82-83.

[147] Harris, pp. 88-89, 92.

[148] Harris, pp. 92-93.

[149] Painter, pp. 69-70.

[150] Painter, p. 71.

[151] Zinn, p. 376.

[152] James R. Green, "Labor and the New Deal," in Buhle and Dawley, p. 84.

[153] See *A Short History of Labor*, p. 12.

[154] Zinn, p. 373.

[155] Zinn, pp. 377-378.

[156] Zinn, p. 378.

[157] Zinn, p. 385.

[158] Zinn, p. 385.

[159] Alice Lynd and Staughton Lynd, eds., *Rank and File: Personal Histories by Working-Class Organizers* (New York: Monthly Review Press, 1988 [1981]), p. 71.

[160] Lynd and Lynd, p. 71.

[161] Zinn, p. 383.

[162] Green, p. 84; Zinn, p. 383.

[163] Zinn, p. 386.

[164] Zinn, p. 386.

[165] Green, p. 86.

[166] Kim Moody, *An Injury to All: The Decline of American Unionism* (New York: Verso, 1988), p. 17.

[167] Zinn, pp. 386-387.

[168] Green, pp. 87-90; Zinn. pp. 386, 392; See *A Short History of American Labor*, p. 12.

[169] Zinn, p. 383.

[170] Green, p. 87.

[171] Zinn, pp. 392.

[172] Zinn, p. 392.

[173] Zinn, pp. 392-393.

[174] Zinn, pp. 392-393.

[175] Zinn, pp. 393-394.

[176] Zinn, p. 390; *A Short History of American Labor*, p. 13.

[177] Richard Thomas, "Blacks and the CIO," in Buhle and Dawley, p. 94; see Zinn, p. 396.

[178] Thomas, p. 94.

[179] Barbara S. Griffith, *The Crisis of American Labor: Operation Dixie and the Defeat of the CIO* (Philadelphia: Temple University Press, 1988), pp. 9-10.

[180] Zinn, p. 390; Lynd, p. 49.

[181] Zinn, pp. 390-391.

[182] Evans and Boyte, p. 143.

[183] Zinn, p. 391.

[184] Evans and Boyte, p. 144.

[185] Zinn, p. 391.

[186] Evans and Boyte, p. 144.

[187] Zinn, p. 391.

[188] Evans and Boyte, p. 144.

[189] Evans and Boyte, pp. 143-144.

[190] Henry Kraus, *The Many and the Few: A Chronicle of the Dynamic Auto Workers* (Los Angeles: The Plantin Press, 1947), pp. 286-293, as cited in Lynd, p. 63.

[191] Zinn, p. 391.

[192] Griffith, p. 8.

[193] Moody, p. 19.

[194] Moody, p. xv.

[195] Zinn, p. 393.

[196] Moody, p. 30.

[197] Zinn, p. 393.

[198] Moody, p. 19.

[199] George Lipsitz, "Labor and the Cold War," in Buhle and Dawley, p. 112.

[200] Moody, p. 29.

[201] Lipsitz, p. 112.

[202] Moody, p. 31.

[203] Zinn, pp. 408-409.

[204] Griffith, p. 13.

[205] Lipsitz, p. 104.

[206] Zinn, p. 409; Lipsitz, pp. 103-105.

[207] Lipsitz, p. 107.

[208] Moody, pp. 26-27.

[209] Marty Jezer, *The Dark Ages: Life in the United States 1945-1960* (Boston: South End Press, 1982), p. 208.

[210] Jezer, pp. 208-209.

[211] Jezer, pp. 208-209.

[212] Jezer, pp. 208-209.

[213] Moody, pp. 26-27.

[214] Lipsitz, pp. 107-108; Jezer, pp. 211-212.

[215] Moody, pp. 38-39.

[216] Zinn, pp. 417-426.

[217] Lipsitz, pp. 108-112.

[218] Jezer, p. 83.

[219] Jezer, p. 213.

[220] Jezer, p. 211-213.

[221] Moody, p. 36.

[222] Moody, pp. 37-38.

[223] Lipsitz, p. 112.

[224] Lipsitz, p. 112.

[225] Jezer, pp. 213-214.

[226] Jezer, p. 218.

[227] Thomas, pp. 96-99.

[228] Thomas, pp. 99-100.

[229] Richard Thomas, "Blacks and the CIO," in Buhle and Dawley, eds., *Working for Democracy*, p. 100.

[230] J. Craig Jenkins and Charles Perrow, "Insurgency of the Powerless: Farm Worker Movements (1946-1972)," *American Sociological Review*, April 1977, Vol. 42, No. 2, pp. 249, 252.

[231] Jacques E. Levy, *Cesar Chavez: Autobiography of La Causa* (New York: W.W. Norton and Company, Inc., 1975), pp. 72-75.

[232] Cesar Chavez, "The Organizer's Tale," in Staughton Lynd, ed., *American Labor Radicalism: Testimonies and Interpretations* (New York: John Wiley and Sons, Inc., 1973), pp. 138, 141.

[233] Evans and Boyte, p. 146.

[234] Chavez, p. 141; Jenkins and Perrow, p. 263.

[235] Chavez, p. 142.

[236] Chavez, pp. 142-143.

[237] Jenkins and Perrow, p. 263; Evans and Boyte, p. 146; Dolores Huerta, "Reflections on the UFW Experience," *The Center Magazine*, July/August 1985, p. 3.

[238] Jenkins and Perrow, p. 263.

[239] Chavez, pp. 144-145.

[240] Jenkins and Perrow, p. 264; Harry Bernstein, "La Causa Lives: 26 Years of Cesar Chavez and the UFW," *Christianity and Crisis*, Vol. 48, No. 2, February 15, 1988, p. 35.

[241] Huerta, p. 5.

[242] Bernstein, p. 35.

[243] Jenkins and Perrow, p. 264.

[244] Jenkins and Perrow, p. 263.

[245] "For 35 Days, Water ...," *Food and Justice*, September 1988, p. 4.

[246] Bernstein, p. 35.

[247] Jenkins and Perrow, pp. 265-266.

[248] Bernstein, p. 35.

[249] *Straight Talk on the Fresh Grape Boycott*. Flyer. (Delano, CA: National Farm Worker Ministry).

[250] Jenkins and Perrow, p. 263.

[251] Bernstein, p. 35.

[252] Richard Steven Street, "The Lettuce Strike Story: UFW's March for Justice," *The Nation*, January 19, 1980, p. 45; Bernstein, p. 36.

[253] Bernstein, p. 36.

[254] Street, p. 46.

[255] Bernstein, p. 36.

[256] Bernstein, p. 36.

[257] Bernstein, pp. 36-37.

[258] Chavez, pp. 146-147.

[259] Moody, p. 11; "Corporate Campaigns," *Multinational Monitor*, March 15, 1986, p. 3.

[260] Montgomery, *Workers' Control in America*, p. 6; Lynd, p. 7.

[261] Curtis Seltzer, *Fire in the Hole: Miners and Managers in the American Coal Industry* (Lexington: The University Press of Kentucky, 1989), pp. 93, 94.

[262] Seltzer, p. 93.

[263] Robert Coles and Harry Huge, "Black Lung: Mining as a Way of Death," *The New Republic*, January 25, 1969, p. 18.

[264] Ralph Nader, "They're Still Breathing," *The New Republic*, February 3, 1968, p. 15.

[265] Bill Worthington, Lee Smith and Ed Ryan, "Miners for Democracy," in Lynd and Lynd, p. 281.

[266] Coles and Huge, p. 19.

[267] Seltzer, p. 95.

[268] Seltzer, p. 95.

[269] Robert G. Sherrill, "West Virginia Miracle: The Black Lung Rebellion," *The Nation*, April 28, 1969, p. 531.

[270] Sherrill, p. 531.

[271] Seltzer, p. 98.

[272] "The Boys Who Got Excited," *The New Republic*, March 22, 1969, p. 7.

[273] Sherrill, p. 529.

[274] Ralph Nader, "Aftermath to Murder: Yablonski's Unfinished Business," *The Nation*, January 26, 1970, p. 70.

[275] Sherrill, p. 529.

[276] "The Boys Who Got Excited," p. 7.

[277] Seltzer, p. 97.

[278] Stephen Cupps, "Coal Mines: Death By Runaround," *The Nation*, August 31, 1970, p. 146; David Bollier and Joan Claybrook, *Freedom from Harm: the Civilizing Influence of Health, Safety and Environmental Regulation* (Washington, DC: Public Citizen and Democracy Project, 1986), p. 288.

[279] Seltzer, p. 101.

[280] Cupps, pp. 146, 148.

[281] Robert Cassidy, "Appalachian Coal Miners: Life and Death Underground," *The New Republic*, December 12, 1970, p. 13.

[282] Cassidy, p. 13.

[283] Cassidy, p. 13.

[284] Nader, "Aftermath to Murder: Yablonski's Unfinished Business," p. 70.

[285] Nader, "Aftermath to Murder: Yablonski's Unfinished Business," p. 70.

[286] "Death of a Rebel," *Newsweek*, January 19, 1970, p. 22.

[287] Moody, pp. 88-89.

[288] Moody, p. 141.

[289] Robert Weissman, "Replacing the Union: Business's Labor Offensive," *Multinational Monitor*, April 1991, p. 12.

[290] Weissman, pp. 10-12.

[291] Moody, p. 303; Bureau of Labor Statistics, U.S. Department of Labor, 1992.

[292] Michael Moore, "Made in Mexico: Reagan Administration Encourages U.S. Businesses to Move Jobs South of the Border," *Multinational Monitor*, February 1987, p. 3.

[293] Tom Barry, ed. *Mexico: A Country Guide* (Albuquerque: Inter-Hemisphere Education Resource Center, 1992).

[294] "Corporate Campaigns," p. 3.

[295] Ray Rogers, "How to Confront Corporations," *Business and Society Review*, Vol. 38, 1981, p. 60.

[296] "Corporate Campaigns," p. 3.

[297] Rogers, pp. 60-64.

[298] "Concessions and Convictions: Striking Meatpackers Face-Off Against the UFCW and Hormel," *Multinational Monitor*, March 15, 1986, p. 4.

[299] "Bhopal on the Bayou," *Multinational Monitor*, January/February 1990, p. 5.

[300] Sidney Lens, "Labor and Capital Today and Tomorrow," in Buhle and Dawley, p. 141; Moody, pp. 296-302.

[301] Michael Merrill, "Why There Will Be a U.S. Labor Party by the Year 2000," *Social Policy*, Spring 1990, pp. 51-53.

[302] As cited in Merrill, p. 45.

[303] Moody, pp. 229-236; "New Directions for the UAW: An Interview with Jerry Tucker," *Multinational Monitor*, January/February 1990, p. 27.

[304] Debbie Nathan, "Garment Workers: The Long, Last Strike," *Ms.*, July/August 1991, p. 100.

[305] Barbara Mayer Wertheimer, "Women Workers," in Buhle and Dawley, pp. 119-120.

[306] Wertheimer, p. 122.

[307] Moody, p. 4; Bureau of Labor Statistics, U.S. Department of Labor, 1992.

[308] As quoted in Moody, p. 239.

WOMEN'S RIGHTS MOVEMENT

[1] Sara M. Evans, *Born for Liberty: A History of Women in America* (New York: The Free Press, 1989), p. 22.

[2] Eleanor Flexner, *Century of Struggle: The Woman's Rights Movement in the United States*, Revised edition (Cambridge, MA: The Belknap Press of Harvard University Press, 1975 [1959]), p. 8; Evans, pp. 22-23.

[3] Flexner, p. 5; Evans, pp. 28, 42.

[4] Flexner, pp. 33-34, 44, 86.

[5] Flexner, p. 7.

[6] Evans, p. 22; Flexner, p. 7.

[7] Flexner, p. 8.

[8] Evans, pp. 9-12, 18-19.

[9] Flexner, pp. 9-12.

[10] Flexner, p. 15.

[11] Flexner, p. 15.

[12] Flexner, p. 23.

[13] Eleanor Flexner, pp. 23-24, quoting Jean-Jacques Rousseau, *Emile or A Treatise on Education*, ed. W.H. Payne (New York: 1906), p. 263.

[14] Evans, p. 58.

[15] Evans, pp. 57-58.

[16] Flexner, p. 23.

[17] Evans, p. 58; Flexner, pp. 15-18; 24-25.

[18] Flexner, pp. 25-26.

[19] Flexner, pp. 27-36.

[20] Flexner, p. 37.

[21] Flexner, p. 37.

[22] Flexner, p. 38.

[23] Flexner, p. 39.

[24] Flexner, p. 39.

[25] Evans, p. 72.

[26] Harriet A. Jacobs, *Incidents in the Life of a Slave Girl, Written by Herself* (Cambridge, MA: Harvard University Press, 1987 [1861]), p. 77.

[27] Jacobs, p. 1.

[28] Evans, pp. 74-75.

[29] Flexner, pp. 42-45.

[30] Flexner, pp. 45-46.

[31] Flexner, p. 46.

[32] Flexner, pp. 47-48.

[33] Flexner, pp. 50-51.

[34] Flexner, pp. 71-72.

[35] Flexner, p. 71; Evans, p. 81.

[36] Beth Millstein Kava and Jeanne Bodin, *We, the American Women: A Documentary History*, Revised edition (Chicago: Science Research Associates, Inc., 1983 [1977]), p. 98.

[37] As quoted in Ellen Carol DuBois, *Feminism and Suffrage: The Emergence of an Independent Women's Movement in America 1848-1869* (Ithaca, NY: Cornell University Press, 1978), p. 33.

[38] Flexner, p. vii.

[39] Flexner, p. 74.

[40] Kava and Bodin, p. 98.

[41] Flexner, pp. 74-77.

[42] Flexner, p. 77.

[43] Evans, pp. 101-102.

[44] Flexner, p. 81.

[45] Evans, p. 104.

[46] Flexner, p. 83.

[47] Flexner, p. 8.

[48] Kava and Bodin, pp. 98, 100.

[49] Flexner, pp. 85-88.

[50] Kava and Bodin, pp. 99-100.

[51] Evans, p. 103.

[52] DuBois, *Feminism and Suffrage*, p. 26.

[53] DuBois, *Feminism and Suffrage*, pp. 25-26.

[54] DuBois, *Feminism and Suffrage*, p. 26; Ellen Carol DuBois, ed., *Elizabeth Cady Stanton, Susan B. Anthony: Correspondence, Writings, Speeches* (New York: Schocken Books, 1981), pp. 58-59.

[55] DuBois, *Feminism and Suffrage*, p. 30.

[56] Mari Jo Buhle and Paul Buhle, eds., *The Concise History of Woman Suffrage: Selections from the Classic Work of Stanton, Anthony, Gage and Harper* (Urbana: University of Illinois Press, 1978), pp. 159-160.

[57] Flexner, pp. 109-111.

[58] Flexner, p. 146.

[59] Flexner, p. 148.

[60] Flexner, p. 146.

[61] Flexner, pp. 146-147.

[62] Flexner, p. 148.

[63] Flexner, pp. 150-151.

[64] Evans, pp. 122-123.

[65] Flexner, p. 155.

[66] Flexner, pp. 155-156; Evans, p. 123.

[67] Flexner, pp. 167-168.

[68] Kava and Bodin, pp. 175-176.

[69] Flexner, pp. 171-172.

[70] Flexner, p. 172.

[71] Kava and Bodin, p. 175.

[72] Flexner, p. 178.

[73] Flexner, pp. 155-156.

[74] Flexner, pp. 178, 179, 228.

[75] Kava and Bodin, p. 65.

[76] Flexner, p. 164.

[77] Flexner, p. 164.

[78] Flexner, pp. 180-181.

[79] Steven M. Buechler, *Women's Movements in the United States: Woman Suffrage, Equal Rights and Beyond* (New Brunswick, NJ: Rutgers University Press, 1990), p. 53.

[80] Evans, p. 153.

81 Elizabeth Cady Stanton, *The Woman's Bible* (New York: European Publishing Co., 1892-1898).

82 Flexner, p. 226.

83 Flexner, pp. 226-227.

84 Evans, p. 153.

85 Flexner, pp. 228, 244.

86 Flexner, pp. 246-247.

87 Marianna W. Davis, ed., *Contributions of Black Women to America*, Volume II (Columbia, SC: Kenday Press, 1981), pp. 101-102.

88 Davis, p. 101.

89 Buechler, p. 145.

90 Evans, p. 156.

91 Davis, pp. 100-101.

92 Flexner, p. 247.

93 Flexner, p. 256.

94 Flexner, pp. 256-258.

95 As quoted in Flexner, p. 258.

96 Flexner, p. 260.

97 Flexner, p. 261.

98 Kava and Bodin, p. 178.

99 Evans, p. 167.

100 Flexner, pp. 263-265.

101 Flexner, p. 265.

102 Flexner, p. 268.

103 Flexner, p. 271.

104 Flexner, p. 272.

105 Kava and Bodin, p. 179.

106 Evans, p. 166.

107 Flexner, pp. 273-274.

108 Flexner, pp. 275-276.

109 Flexner, p. 278.

110 Flexner, p. 278.

111 Flexner, p. 277.

112 Flexner, pp. 279-280.

113 Flexner, pp. 286-287.

114 Flexner, pp. 292-293.

115 Flexner, p. 294.

116 Flexner, pp. 294-295.

117 Flexner, p. 295.

118 Kava and Bodin, p. 182.

119 Flexner, p. 295.

120 Flexner, p. 297.

121 Flexner, pp. 282-283, 288-291, 294, 296.

122 Flexner, p. 301.

123 Flexner, pp. 301-302; 323.

124 Flexner, pp. 323-324.

125 Flexner, p. 327.

126 Gerda Lerner, *The Woman in American History* (Menlo Park, CA: Addison-Wesley Publishing Company, 1971), p. 171; Anne F. Scott and Andrew M. Scott, "One Half the People: The Fight for Woman Suffrage" in Linda K. Kerber and Jane Sherron DeHart, eds., *Women's America: Refocusing the Past*, Third edition (New York: Oxford University Press, 1991), p. 338.

127 Flexner, pp. 328-329.

128 Kava and Bodin, p. 183.

129 As quoted in Carol McCulley and Diana Morley, *Jeannette Rankin: First Woman in Congress* (Windsor, CA: National Women's History Project, 1989), p. 15.

130 Belle Fligelman Winestine, "Mother Was Shocked," *Montana: The Magazine of Western History*. Summer 1974, Vol. XXIV, No. 3, p. 76.

131 McCulley and Morley, pp. 5, 8-10.

132 Winestine, p. 72; McCulley and Morley, p. 12.

133 Winestine, p. 73.

134 McCulley and Morley, p. 12.

135 Winestine, p. 74.

136 McCulley and Morley, p. 13.

137 McCulley and Morley, p. 13; Norma Smith, "The Woman Who Said No to War: A Day in the Life of Jeannette Rankin," *Ms.*, March 1986, p. 88.

138 Winestine, p. 74.

139 As quoted in Winestine, p. 75.

140 Winestine, p. 74.

141 Smith, p. 88.

142 Winestine, p. 74.

143 Winestine, p. 75.

144 McCulley and Morley, p. 16.

145 As quoted in Smith, p. 88.

146 Smith, p. 89.

147 McCulley and Morley, p. 16; "Sharp Tongue at 91: Across 9 Decades: Jeannette Rankin," *SRS News*, January 1970, p. 13.

148 Winestine, p. 78; McCulley and Morley, p. 17.

149 McCulley and Morley, pp. 17-18, 20.

150 McCulley and Morley, pp. 18-19.

151 McCulley and Morley, p. 18.

152 As quoted in McCulley and Morley, pp. 17-18.

153 McCulley and Morley, p. 19.

154 Winestine, p. 78; McCulley and Morley, p. 19.

155 As quoted in McCulley and Morley, p. 20.

156 Smith, p. 86.

157 McCulley and Morley, pp. 5, 20-21; Judy Flander, "Jeannette Rankin Meets Her 'Crush' -- Mr. Nader," Washington, DC *Evening Star and Daily News*, September 2, 1972.

158 McCulley and Morley, p. 20.

159 McCulley and Morley, p. 21.

160 As quoted in Flander, Washington, DC *Evening Star and Daily News*, September 2, 1972.

161 Flander, Washington, DC *Evening Star and Daily News*, September 2, 1972.

[162] Evans, p. 187.

[163] Evans, pp. 187-188.

[164] Evans, p. 189.

[165] Evans, p. 189.

[166] Harrison, p. 143.

[167] Flexner, p. 338.

[168] Evans, pp. 160-161, 182.

[169] Evans, p. 176.

[170] Kava and Bodin, p. 203.

[171] Evans, pp. 161, 175.

[172] Dorothy M. Brown, *Setting a Course: American Women in the 1920s* (Boston: Twayne Publishers, 1987), p. 133.

[173] Brown, p. 150.

[174] Brown, pp. 151-154.

[175] Brown, p. 95.

[176] Evans, p. 182.

[177] Brown, p. 95.

[178] Evans, pp. 182-183; Brown, p. 85.

[179] Brown, pp. 84, 111.

[180] Brown, pp. 94, 110.

[181] Cynthia Harrison, *On Account of Sex: The Politics of Women's Issues 1945-1968* (Berkeley: University of California Press, 1988), pp. 7-8.

[182] Flexner, p. 220.

[183] Harrison, p. 8.

[184] Harrison, pp. 8-9.

[185] Evans, p. 193.

[186] Evans, p. 187.

[187] Evans, p. 187.

[188] Evans, p. 193.

[189] Harrison, p. 9.

[190] Evans, p. 193.

[191] Leila J. Rupp and Verta Taylor, *Survival in the Doldrums: The American Women's Rights Movement, 1945 to the 1960s* (New York: Oxford University, 1987), p. 25.

[192] Rupp and Taylor, p. 6; Harrison, pp. 10-11.

[193] Evans, p. 201.

[194] Kava and Bodin, p. 228.

[195] Evans, pp. 202-203.

[196] Kava and Bodin, p. 228.

[197] Evans, p. 199.

[198] Susan M. Hartmann, *The Home Front and Beyond: American Women in the 1940s* (Boston: Twayne Publishers, 1982), p. 55.

[199] Kava and Bodin, p. 182.

[200] Hartmann, p. 55.

[201] Miriam Frank, Marilyn Ziebarth and Connie Field, *The Life and Times of Rosie the Riveter: The Story of 3 Million Working Women During World War II*, Educator's edition (Emeryville, CA: Clarity Educational Productions, 1982), p. 17.

[202] Evans, p. 222; Frank, et al, p. 92.

[203] Evans, p. 222.

[204] Connie Field, producer and director, *The Life and Times of Rosie the Riveter* (film) (Emeryville, CA: Clarity Educational Productions, 1980).

[205] Eva Lapin, *Mothers in Overalls* (pamphlet) (New York: Workers Library Publishers, 1943), p. 6.

[206] Frank, et al, p. 13.

[207] Hartmann, p. 79.

[208] Harrison, p. 3.

[209] Hartmann, p. 57.

[210] Evans, pp. 223-224.

[211] D'Ann Campbell, *Women at War with America: Private Lives in a Patriotic Era* (Cambridge, MA: Harvard University Press, 1984), p. 147.

[212] Hartmann, pp. 60-61.

[213] Hartmann, p. 57.

[214] Hartmann, p. 57.

[215] Hartmann, p. 61.

[216] Hartmann, p. 66.

[217] Frank, et al, pp. 35-36.

[218] Evans, p. 223.

[219] Frank, et al., p. 84.

[220] Frank, et al, pp. 13, 16.

[221] Frank, et al, p. 13.

[222] Frank, et al, p. 51.

[223] Teresa Amott and Julie Matthaei, *Race, Gender, and Work: A Multicultural Economic History of Women in the United States* (Boston: South End Press, 1991), p. 173; Evans, pp. 223, 225.

[224] Frank, et al, p. 53.

[225] Amott and Matthaei, p. 228.

[226] Amott and Matthaei, pp. 228-230.

[227] Evans, p. 230; Frank, et al, p. 19.

[228] Evans, p. 231.

[229] Evans, pp. 231, 232.

[230] Amott and Matthaei, p. 173.

[231] Frank, et al, p. 94; "Give Back Their Jobs," *Woman's Home Companion*, October 1943, p. 6.

[232] Frank, et al, p. 94.

[233] Betty Friedan, *The Feminine Mystique* (New York: Laurel Books, 1973 [1963]), p. 14.

[234] Marynia L. Foot Farnham and Ferdinand Lundberg, *Modern Woman: The Lost Sex* (New York: Harper and Brothers, 1947).

[235] Frank, et al, p. 95; Rupp and Taylor, p. 19.

[236] Friedan, p. 11.

[237] Friedan, p. 12.

[238] Rupp and Taylor, p. 12.

[239] Rupp and Taylor, p. 13.

[240] Rupp and Taylor, p. 15.

[241] Rupp and Taylor, p. 15.

[242] Evans, pp. 251-252.

[243] Rupp and Taylor, p. 19.

[244] Rupp and Taylor, p. 18.

[245] Harrison, pp. 3, 7.

[246] Harrison, pp. 16-17.

[247] Harrison, p. 16.

[248] Harrison, p. 16.

[249] Harrison, p. 19.

[250] Harrison, pp. 17, 19-20.

[251] Harrison, pp. 18, 41, 44-45.

[252] Harrison, p. 22.

[253] Harrison, p. 23.

[254] Harrison, p. 23.

[255] Harrison, p. 45.

[256] Rupp and Taylor, p. 20.

[257] Harrison, pp. 23, 45-50.

[258] Evans, p. 265.

[259] Evans, pp. 265-266.

[260] Evans, pp. 264-267.

[261] Friedan, p. 345.

[262] Marcia Cohen, *The Sisterhood: The Inside Story of the Women's Movement and the Leaders Who Made It Happen* (New York: Fawcett Columbine, 1988), pp. 92, 94-95.

[263] Friedan, p. 351.

[264] Friedan, p. 330.

[265] Cohen, p. 96.

[266] Cohen, p. 99.

[267] Friedan, p. 14.

[268] United States President's Commission on the Status of Women, *American Women: The Report of the President's Commission on the Status of Women* (Washington, DC: Government Printing Office, 1963).

[269] Harrison, pp. 113-114; Evans, p. 274-275.

[270] Evans, p. 275; Harrison, pp. 111-113.

[271] Harrison, p. 89.

[272] Evans, p. 265.

[273] Harrison, p. 92.

[274] Harrison, pp. 94-95.

[275] Harrison, pp. 97-100.

[276] Harrison, p. 104.

[277] Harrison, pp. 104-105.

[278] Harrison, p. 176.

[279] Harrison, p. 176.

[280] Harrison, pp. 177-178.

[281] Martha Griffiths, *New York Times* Oral History Program - Former Members of Congress. Number 32: Martha W. Griffiths, Member of Congress from Michigan, 1955-1975, Appendix One, pp. 3, 7, 4.

[282] Griffiths, Appendix One, p. 6.

[283] Harrison, p. 179.

[284] Griffiths, Appendix One, p. 11; Harrison, p. 181.

[285] Harrison, pp. 179-181.

[286] Griffiths, p. 75.

[287] Susan Deller Ross and Ann Barcher, *The Rights of Women: The Basic ACLU Guide to a Woman's Rights* (Toronto: Bantam Books, 1984), p. 29.

[288] Evans, p. 272.

[289] Evans, p. 272.

[290] As quoted in Friedan, p. 368.

[291] Harrison, pp. 187-191.

[292] Griffiths, Appendix One, p. 19; Harrison, p. 191.

[293] Harrison, p. 191; Cohen, p. 132.

[294] Harrison, p. 191.

[295] Cohen, pp. 132-133.

[296] Evans, p. 277.

[297] Evans, p. 277.

[298] Cohen, p. 139; Harrison, p. 204.

[299] Friedan, p. 373.

[300] Cohen, p. 140.

[301] Cohen, p. 140.

[302] Harrison, p. 204.

[303] Cohen, pp. 139, 206.

[304] Griffiths, Appendix One, pp. 29-30.

[305] Harrison, p. 204.

[306] Evans, p. 278.

[307] Evans, p. 278.

[308] Harrison, p. 205.

[309] Evans, p. 280.

[310] Evans, p. 281.

[311] Robin Morgan, ed., *Sisterhood is Powerful: An Anthology of Writings from the Women's Liberation Movement* (New York: Vintage Books, 1970), p. xxiii.

[312] Cohen, p. 123.

[313] Evans, p. 282.

[314] Evans, p. 279.

[315] Alice Echols, *Daring to Be Bad: Radical Feminism in America, 1967-1975* (Minneapolis: University of Minnesota Press, 1989), p. 139.

[316] Echols, p. 15.

[317] Echols, pp. 3-4.

[318] Ellen Willis, Foreword to Echols, pp. ix-x.

[319] Willis, Foreword to Echols, p. vii.

[320] Cohen, p. 178.

[321] Willis, Foreword to Echols, p. x.

[322] Evans, p. 283.

[323] Evans, p. 288.

[324] Evans, p. 288.

[325] Evans, p. 288; Echols, p. 4.

[326] Evans, p. 288.

[327] Friedan, pp. 375-376.

[328] Friedan, p. 376.

[329] As quoted in Cohen, p. 287.

[330] Winifred D. Wandersee, *On the Move: American Women in the 1970s* (Boston: Twayne Publishers, 1988), p. 177.

[331] Wandersee, p. 177.

[332] *Congressional Record*, August 10, 1970: 28004.

[333] Cohen, pp. 245, 340; Wandersee, pp. 177, 178, 198.

[334] Evans, p. 291.

[335] Friedan, p. 377.

[336] Friedan, p. 377.

[337] Evans, p. 291.

[338] Cohen, pp. 325-329.

[339] Cohen, pp. 270, 393.

[340] Evans, pp. 291-292.

[341] Wandersee, pp. 91-92.

[342] Wandersee, p. 93.

[343] Evans, p. 293.

[344] Evans, p. 300.

[345] Evans, p. 300.

[346] Echols, p. 291.

[347] As quoted in Echols, p. 32.

[348] Echols, p. 32; Cohen, pp. 270-271.

[349] Frances M. Beal, "Double Jeopardy: To Be Black and Female," in Morgan, ed., *Sisterhood is Powerful*, p. 384.

[350] Echols, pp. 32, 293, 295.

[351] Susan Faludi, *Backlash: The Undeclared War Against American Women* (New York: Crown Publishing, Inc., 1991), p. xviii.

[352] Evans, p. 304.

[353] Evans, p. 301.

[354] Wandersee, p. 198.

[355] Griffiths, pp. 104-105.

[356] Evans, p. 305.

[357] Faludi, p. 412.

[358] Faludi, p. 412.

[359] Evans, p. 305; Faludi, p. 412.

[360] Karen Houppert, "Wildflowers Among the Ivy: New Campus Radicals," *Ms.* September/October 1991, p. 53.

[361] Houppert, p. 54.

[362] Diana M. Pearce, "The Feminization of Poverty: Women, Work and Welfare," *Urban and Social Change Review*, Winter-Spring 1978, p. 28.

[363] Pearce, pp. 29-35.

[364] Donna Milgram, "Passing the NEW Act," *Women at Work* (Washington, DC: National Commission on Working Women and the Women's Work Force Network of Wider Opportunities for Women, Fall/Winter 1991/1992), p. 3.

[365] "Women, Work and Family" Fact sheet (Washington, DC: National Commission on Working Women of Wider Opportunities for Women, November 1991).

[366] "Employment Rights Project for Women of Color" (Washington, DC: Women's Legal Defense Fund).

[367] Steven Pressman. "The Feminization of Poverty: Causes and Remedies," *Challenge.* March/April 1988, p. 57

[368] Faludi, p. xvii.

[369] "About WOW" Fact sheet (Washington, DC: Wider Opportunities for Women, 1991).

[370] "Employment Rights Project for Women of Color" (Washington, DC: Women's Legal Defense Fund).

[371] Faludi, p. xvii.

[372] Faludi, pp. xvi, 369.

[373] Faludi, p. 369.

[374] Faludi, p. xix.

[375] Houppert, pp. 54-58.

[376] Faludi, p. 364.

[377] Faludi, p. xiii.

[378] Faludi, p. xiii.

[379] "Backgrounder on the National Women's Political Caucus" Fact sheet (Washington, DC: National Women's Political Caucus, October 1991).

[380] "Feminist Majority Campaign for Gender Balance Laws" Fact sheet (Arlington, VA: Fund for the Feminist Majority, 1991).

[381] "Feminist Majority Campaign for Gender Balance Laws" Fact sheet (Arlington, VA: Fund for the Feminist Majority, 1991).

[382] Ellie Smeal, "Why I Support a New Party," *Ms.* January/February 1991, pp. 72-73.

[383] Interview with Sharon Griffiths of the National Woman's Party, November 27, 1991.

[384] Faludi, p. 76; Nancy Gibbs, "The War Against Feminism," *Newsweek*, March 9, 1992, pp. 50-56.

[385] In reference to a third wave, see Rebecca Walker, "Becoming the Third Wave," *Ms.* January/February 1992, pp. 39-41.

CONSUMER MOVEMENT

[1] Peter Edward Samson, "The Emergence of a Consumer Interest in America, 1870-1930" A dissertation submitted to the faculty of the division of the social sciences in candidacy for the degree of doctor of philosophy, Department of History (Chicago: University of Chicago, August 1980), p. 47.

[2] Robert Mayer, *The Consumer Movement: Guardians of the Marketplace* (Boston: Twayne Publishers, 1989), p. 12.

[3] David Bollier and Joan Claybrook, *Freedom From Harm: The Civilizing Influence of Health, Safety and Environmental Regulation* (Washington, DC: Public Citizen and the Democracy Project, 1986), p. 2, footnote.

[4] Ralph Nader, "The Consumer Movement Looks Ahead," in Alan Gartner, Colin Greer and Frank Riessman, eds., *Beyond Reagan: Alternatives for the '80s* (New York: Harper and Row Publishers, 1984), p. 271.

[5] Nader, p. 272.

[6] Adam Smith, *An Inquiry into the Nature and Causes of tne Wealth of Nations*, Edwin Cannan, ed. Fifth edition abridged (New York: Random House, 1985 [1776]).

[7] Adam Smith, *An Inquiry into the Nature and Causes of the Wealth of Nations* (New York: The Modern Library, 1937 [1776]), p. 625, as cited in Samson, p. 5.

[8] Lucy Black Creighton, *Pretenders to the Throne: The Consumer Movement in the United States* (Lexington, MA: D.C. Heath, 1976), p. 5.

[9] Mayer, p. 14.

[10] Mayer, p. 15.

[11] Mayer, p. 16.

[12] Mark V. Nadel, *The Politics of Consumer Protection* (Indianapolis: Bobbs-Merrill, 1971), p. 6.

[13] Mayer, p. 16.

[14] Nadel, p. 26, quoting *United States Government Organization Manual -- 1970-1971* (Washington, DC: 1970), p. 440.

[15] Nadel, p. 26.

[16] Samson, pp. 8-13.

[17] Samson, pp. 17-18.

[18] Samson, p. 23.

[19] Samson, p. 28.

[20] Samson, p. 48.

[21] Samson, p. 49.

[22] Samson, p. 73.

[23] Samson, p. 28.

[24] Samson, pp. 28, 36.

[25] Samson, pp. 65, 67, 70.

[26] Samson, pp. 56-58.

[27] Samson, p. 54.

[28] Wallace F. Janssen, "The Story of the Laws Behind the Labels," *FDA Consumer*, June 1981, pp. 33-35.

[29] Janssen, p. 35.

[30] Mayer, pp. 14-15.

[31] Janssen, p. 35.

[32] Janssen, p. 35.

[33] Janssen, p. 36.

[34] Janssen, p. 35.

[35] Mayer, p. 16.

[36] Janssen, p. 35.

[37] Janssen, p. 35.

[38] Helen Laura Sorenson, *The Consumer Movement: What It Is and What It Means* (New York: Arno Press, 1978 [1941]), p. 7.

[39] Sorenson, p. 7.

[40] Sorenson, p. 7.

[41] Samson, p. 28.

[42] Mayer, p. 18.

[43] Upton Sinclair, *The Jungle* (New York: Doubleday, Page and Company, 1906).

[44] Nadel, p. 11.

[45] As quoted in Mayer, p. 18.

[46] Nadel, pp. 11-12.

[47] Samson, p. 78.

[48] Samson, p. 81.

[49] Samson, p. 98.

[50] Alfred McCann, *Starving America* (Cleveland, NY: F.M. Barton, 1913).

[51] Samson, p. 94.

[52] Janssen, p. 35; Samson, p. 31.

[53] Samson, p. 31.

[54] Nadel, p. 24.

[55] Nadel, p. 24.

[56] Nadel, p. 24; Samson, p. 32.

[57] Samson, pp. 30, 36.

[58] Samson, pp. 112, 118.

[59] Samson, pp. 149-150.

[60] Samson, p. 150.

[61] Samson, pp. 151-152.

[62] Samson, p. 159.

[63] Samson, p. 158.

[64] Samson, pp. 162-165, 172.

[65] Samson, pp. 175, 180, 181.

[66] Samson, pp. 195-199, 222-227.

[67] Samson, p. 242.

[68] Samson, pp. 236, 249, 250, 254, 255.

[69] *Finding Co-ops: A Resource Guide and Directory* (Washington, DC: Cooperative Information Consortium, 1984), p. 11.

[70] *Finding Co-ops*, p. 14.

[71] Ralph Nader, as quoted in David Bollier, *Citizen Action and Other Big Ideas: A History of Ralph Nader and the Modern Consumer Movement* (Washington, DC: Center for Study of Responsive Law, 1989), p. 19.

[72] Samson, pp. 266-267.

[73] Samson, p. 267.

[74] Sorenson, p. 141.

[75] Samson, p. 267.

[76] Samson, p. 268-269.

[77] Samson, p. 155.

[78] Samson, p. 276.

[79] Samson, pp. 276-278, 283.

[80] Mayer, p. 19.

[81] Mayer, p. 19.

[82] Mayer, pp. 19-20.

[83] Stuart Chase and F. J. Schlink, *Your Money's Worth: A Study of the Waste of the Consumer Dollar* (New York: Macmillan, 1927).

[84] Samson, p. 288.

[85] Creighton, p. 20.

[86] Samson, p. 306.

[87] As quoted in Creighton, p. 19.

[88] Samson, p. 307.

[89] Mayer, p. 20.

[90] Samson, p. 313.

[91] Creighton, p. 20.

[92] "50 Years Ago...," *Consumer Reports*, January 1986, p. 10.

[93] Arthur Kallet and Frederick J. Schlink, *100,000,000 Guinea Pigs: Dangers in Everyday Foods, Drugs and Cosmetics* (New York: Vanguard Press, 1932).

[94] As quoted in Mayer, p. 21.

[95] "50 Years Ago...," p. 10.

[96] "50 Years Ago...," p. 10.

[97] "50 Years Ago... What Happened When Consumerism and Unionism, Two Great Social Movements of the 1930s, Collided?," *Consumer Reports*, February 1986, p. 76.

[98] "50 Years Ago...," p. 10.

[99] "50 Years Ago ... What Happened When Consumerism and Unionism, Two Great Social Movements of the 1930s, Collided?," p. 76.

[100] "50 Years Ago ... What Happened When Consumerism and Unionism, Two Great Social Movements of the 1930s, Collided?," p. 78.

[101] "50 Years Ago ... What Happened When Consumerism and Unionism, Two Great Social Movements of the 1930s, Collided?," pp. 78-79.

[102] Sorenson, p. 138.

[103] Mitchell Rofsky, "Unfinished Business," in Ralph Nader Task Force on European Cooperatives, *Making Change?: Learning from Europe's Consumer Cooperatives* (Washington, DC: Center for Study of Responsive Law, 1985), p. 201.

[104] Mayer, p. 23.

[105] Mayer, p. 23.

[106] Mayer, p. 24.

[107] Rofsky, p. 218.

[108] Janssen, p. 37.

[109] Janssen, p. 37.

[110] Janssen, p. 37.

[111] Ruth deForest Lamb, *American Chamber of Horrors: The Truth about Food and Drugs* (New York: Arno Press, 1976 [1936]).

[112] Sorenson, p. 12.

[113] Sorenson, pp. 13, 86, 97.

[114] Janssen, p. 37.

[115] Sorenson, p. 13.

[116] Sorenson, pp. 12, 13.

[117] Nadel, p. 17.

[118] Creighton, p. 28.

[119] Nadel, p. 18.

[120] Janssen, p. 39.

[121] Nadel, p. 18.

[122] Nadel, p. 19.

[123] Creighton, p. 30.

[124] "50 Years Ago ... What Happened When Consumerism and Unionism, Two Great Social Movements of the 1930s, Collided?," p. 79.

[125] As quoted in Elliott Negin, "Esther Peterson: The Grand Dame of Consumerism," *Public Citizen*, Winter 1985, p. 20.

[126] Negin, p. 17.

[127] Negin, p. 17.

[128] Negin, p. 17.

[129] Negin, p. 17.

[130] Esther Peterson, "The Kennedy Commission," in Irene Tinker, ed., *Women in Washington: Advocates for Public Policy* (Beverly Hills, CA: Sage Publications, 1983), pp. 22-23.

[131] Peterson, "The Kennedy Commission," p. 21.

[132] United States President's Commission on the Status of Women, *American Women: The Report of the President's Commission on the Status of Women* (Washington, DC: Government Printing Office, 1963).

[133] Peterson, "The Kennedy Commission," p. 28.

[134] Peterson, "The Kennedy Commission," p. 33.

[135] Negin, p. 19.

[136] Negin, p. 19.

[137] Thomas Herman, "Betty Furness on Consumer Firing Line," *Wall Street Journal*, September 20, 1967, p. 18.

[138] Negin, p. 19.

[139] Negin, p. 19.

[140] Negin, p. 20.

[141] Negin, p. 20.

[142] Negin, p. 20.

[143] Negin, p. 20.

[144] Esther Peterson, "Consumerism and International Markets," in Paul N. Bloom and Ruth Belk Smith, eds., *The Future of Consumerism* (Lexington, MA: Lexington Books, 1986), p. 181.

[145] Negin, p. 21.

[146] Negin, p. 21.

[147] Negin, p. 21.

[148] Peterson, "Consumerism and International Markets," p. 180.

[149] Jennifer Collins, "Codifying Corporate Accountability," *Multinational Monitor*, June 1990, p. 16.

[150] Collins, p. 18.

[151] Negin, p. 21.

[152] Creighton, p. 31.

[153] Mayer, p. 25.

[154] Creighton, p. 32; Mayer, p. 25.

[155] Mayer, p. 25.

[156] "50 Years Ago ... What Happened When Consumerism and Unionism, Two Great Social Movements of the 1930s, Collided?," p. 79.

[157] Michael Pertschuk, *Revolt Against Regulation: The Rise and Pause of the Consumer Movement* (Berkeley: University of California Press, 1982), p. 14.

[158] Vance Packard, *The Hidden Persuaders* (New York: D. McKay Co., 1957).

[159] Mayer, p. 26.

[160] John Kenneth Galbraith, *The Affluent Society* (Boston: Houghton Mifflin, 1958).

[161] Mayer, p. 26.

[162] Creighton, p. 34; Nadel, p. 122.

[163] Creighton, p. 34.

[164] Mayer, p. 27.

[165] Nadel, p. 123.

[166] Mayer, p. 27.

[167] Nadel, p. 124.

[168] Nadel, pp. 124-125.

169 Janssen, p. 44; Mayer, p. 27; Nadel, pp. 127-128.

170 Mayer, pp. 94-95.

171 Creighton, p. 34.

172 Nadel, p. 129.

173 Bollier and Claybrook, p. 31.

174 Rachel Carson, *Silent Spring* (Boston: Houghton Mifflin, 1962).

175 David Caplovitz, *The Poor Pay More* (New York: Free Press of Glencoe, 1963).

176 Jessica Mitford, *The American Way of Death* (New York: Simon and Schuster, 1963).

177 Mayer, p. 26.

178 Nadel, p. 138.

179 Nadel, p. 139.

180 Creighton, p. 52.

181 Bollier, p. 3.

182 Ralph Nader, *Unsafe at Any Speed: The Designed-in Dangers of the American Automobile* (New York: Grossman, 1965).

183 Bollier, p. 2.

184 As quoted in Bollier, p. 2.

185 Bollier, pp. 2, 3.

186 Bollier, pp. 2, 3.

187 Pertschuk, p. 41.

188 Nadel, p. 140.

189 Bollier, p. 3.

190 Nadel, p. 141.

191 Bollier, p. 3.

192 Mayer, p. 42.

193 Nadel, p. 143.

194 Nadel, p. 141.

195 Bollier, p. 3.

196 Bollier, p. 53.

197 Bollier, p. 53.

198 Ralph Nader, May, 1992.

199 Monroe Peter Friedman, "The 1966 Consumer Protest as Seen by Its Leaders," *The Journal of Consumer Affairs*, Vol. 5, No.1, Summer 1971, p. 1.

200 Friedman, p. 13.

201 Friedman, p. 19.

202 Friedman, p. 20.

203 Nancy Kramer and Stephen A. Newman, *Getting What You Deserve: A Handbook for the Assertive Consumer* (Garden City, NY: Doubleday and Co. Inc., 1979), p. 303.

204 Bollier, p. 11.

205 Mayer, p. 95.

206 Bollier, p. 6.

207 Bollier, p. 7.

208 Speech before National Association of Life Insurance Underwriters Convention, Chicago, IL, September 18, 1973, as quoted in Pertschuk, p. 16.

209 Pertschuk, p. 5.

210 Mayer, p. 29.

211 Samson, p. 328.

212 Mayer, p. 29.

213 Bollier, p. 55.

214 "50 Years Ago ... What Happened When Consumerism and Unionism, Two Great Social Movements of the 1930s, Collided?," p. 79.

215 Mayer, p. 43.

216 Robert O. Herrmann, et al., "The Organization of the Consumer Movement: A Comparative Perspective," in E. Scott Maynes, ed. *The Frontier of Research in the Consumer Interest* (Columbia, MO: American Council on Consumer Interests, 1988), p. 483.

217 Bollier, p. 28.

218 Bollier, p. 76.

219 Bollier, p. 65.

220 Gregory Wilson and Elizabeth Brydolf, "Grass Roots Solutions: San Francisco Consumer Action," in Laura Nader, ed. *No Access to Law: Alternatives to the American Judicial System* (New York: Academic Press, 1980), p. 417.

221 Wilson and Brydolf, p. 431.

222 Wilson and Brydolf, p. 431.

223 Bollier, pp. 7, 8.

224 Rofsky, p. 203.

225 Nader, p. 280.

226 *Finding Co-ops*, p. 14.

227 Rofsky, p. 204.

228 Rofsky, p. 204.

229 *National Cooperative Business Association 1990 Annual Report* (Washington, DC: National Cooperative Business Association, 1990), p. 4.

230 Ralph Nader, Foreword to Seyoum Haregot, *The Failed Promise of the National Cooperative Bank* (Washington, DC: Center for Study of Responsive Law, 1989), p. 4.

231 Seyoum Haregot, *The Failed Promise of the National Cooperative Bank* (Washington, DC: Center for Study of Responsive Law, 1989), pp. 5, 18.

232 Haregot, pp. 12-19.

233 Haregot, p. 47.

234 Bollier, p. 21.

235 Nader, p. 280.

236 Nader, p. 271.

237 Nader, p. 282.

238 Anne Witte Garland, "Gale Cincotta," *Ms.*, January 1986, p. 51.

239 Garland, p. 103.

240 Nader, pp. 280-281.

241 Herrmann, et al., "The Organizations...," p. 475.

242 Herrmann, et al., "The Organizations...," p. 475.

243 Wilson and Brydolf, p. 418.

244 Wilson and Brydolf, p. 419.

245 Wilson and Brydolf, p. 458.

246 Wilson and Brydolf, p. 457.

247 Bollier, p. 29.

248 Bollier, p. 54.

[249] Pertschuk, p. 16.

[250] Pertschuk, p. 57.

[251] Pertschuk, p. 57.

[252] Pertschuk, p. 57.

[253] Bollier, p. 29.

[254] Bollier, p. 30.

[255] See Joan Claybrook, *Retreat from Safety: Reagan's Attack on America's Health* (New York: Pantheon, 1984).

[256] Mayer, pp. 79-80.

[257] Mayer, p. 80; Bollier, p. 30.

[258] Mayer, pp. 79-80.

[259] Bollier, p. 30.

[260] Arthur Woodstone, "The Consumer Army: Rebels With a Cause," *Parade*, November 12, 1978.

[261] Woodstone.

[262] Pertschuk, p. 123.

[263] Correspondence with FairTest, June 1992.

[264] Shawn Brennan, ed., *Consumer Sourcebook: 1992-1993*, Seventh edition (Detroit: Gale Research, Inc., 1991), p. 343.

[265] Jessica Cowan, ed., *Good Works: A Guide to Careers in Social Change*, (New York: Barricade Books, 1991) p. 353.

[266] Brennan, p. 192.

[267] Mayer, p. 44.

[268] Mayer, p. 44.

[269] Robert O. Herrmann, "Consumerism: Its Goals, Organizations and Future," *Journal of Marketing*, Vol. 34, October 1970, p. 58; Mayer, p. 43.

[270] Mayer, p. 43.

[271] Herrmann, et al., p. 483.

[272] Mayer, p. 43.

[273] Mayer, pp. 45-46.

[274] Sorenson, p. 125.

[275] Sorenson, p. 126.

[276] Mayer, pp. 45-46.

[277] Joan Claybrook, "Making a Difference: Celebrating 20 Years of Activism," *Public Citizen*, January/February 1991, p. 26.

[278] Bollier, p. 54.

[279] Bollier, pp. 76-84.

[280] Bollier, pp. 65, 66.

[281] Brennan, pp. 429, 512.

[282] Bollier, p. 22.

ENVIRONMENTAL MOVEMENT

[1] Robert C. Paehlke, *Environmentalism and the Future of Progressive Politics* (New Haven, CT: Yale University Press, 1989), p. 15.

[2] T.H. Watkins, "Father of the Forests," *American Heritage*, February/March 1991. Volume 42, No. 1, pp. 86-98.

[3] Peter Borrelli, "The Ecophilosophers: A Guide to Deep Ecologists, Bioregionalists, Greens and Others in Pursuit of Radical Change," *The Amicus Journal*. Spring 1988. Vol. 10, No. 2. Last in a series, p. 31.

[4] As quoted in Borrelli, "The Ecophilosophers," p. 31.

[5] Watkins, pp. 91-92.

[6] Paehlke, pp. 16-17.

[7] Watkins, pp. 92-93.

[8] Borrelli, "The Ecophilosophers," p. 32.

[9] Borrelli, "The Ecophilosophers," pp. 31-32.

[10] Paehlke, p. 15.

[11] George Perkins Marsh, *Man and Nature: Physical Geography as Modified by Human Action* (Cambridge: Harvard University Press, 1965 [1864]).

[12] Paehlke, p. 15.

[13] Paehlke, p. 18.

[14] Charles F. Wilkinson, "Aldo Leopold and Western Water Law: Thinking Perpendicular to the Prior Appropriation Doctrine," *Land and Water Review*, University of Wyoming College of Law, Vol. XXVI, No. 1, 1989, p. 20.

[15] Aldo Leopold, *A Sand County Almanac and Sketches Here and There* (New York: Oxford University Press, 1964 [1949]).

[16] Wilkinson, p. 19.

[17] Paehlke, p. 18.

[18] Wilkinson, p. 21.

[19] As quoted in Durward L. Allen, "Leopold: The Founder," *American Forests*, September/October 1987, p. 27.

[20] Ronald Brownstein, "The Toxic Tragedy," in Ralph Nader, Ronald Brownstein and John Richard, eds., *Who's Poisoning America: Corporate Polluters and Their Victims in the Chemical Age* (San Francisco: Sierra Club Books, 1981), p. 5.

[21] Gary Cohen and John O'Connor, eds., *Fighting Toxics: A Manual for Protecting Your Family, Community and Workplace* (Washington, DC: Island Press, 1990), p. 15.

[22] Cohen and O'Connor, p. 16.

[23] Brownstein, p. 5.

[24] Cohen and O'Connor, p. 16.

[25] Cohen and O'Connor, p. 270, citing *Chemical Engineering News*, May 1989.

[26] Brownstein, p. 5.

[27] Brownstein, p. 5.

[28] Paehlke, p. 25.

[29] Paehlke, p. 24.

[30] Paehlke, p. 27.

[31] Arthur Kallet and Frederick J. Schlink, *100,000,000 Guinea Pigs: Dangers in Everyday Foods, Drugs and Cosmetics* (New York: Vanguard Press, 1932).

[32] Ruth deForest Lamb, *American Chamber of Horrors: The Truth about Food and Drugs* (New York: Arno Press, 1976 [1936]).

[33] Paehlke, p. 27.

[34] Paehlke, p. 29; Brownstein, p. 8.

[35] Rachel Carson, *Silent Spring* (Boston: Houghton Mifflin, 1962).

[36] Paehlke, p. 28.

[37] Paehlke, p. 28.

[38] Rachel Carson, *Silent Spring* (Greenwich, CT: Fawcett Publications, Inc., 1970 [1962]), p. 51.

[39] Carson, pp. 51-52.

[40] Paehlke, p. 29.

[41] Carson, p. 22.

[42] Brownstein, pp 10-31; Cohen and O'Connor, p. 13.

[43] David Bollier and Joan Claybrook, *Freedom From Harm: The Civilizing Influence of Health, Safety and Environmental Regulation* (Washington, DC: Public Citizen and Democracy Project, 1986), p. 118.

[44] Victor B. Scheffer, *The Shaping of Environmentalism in America*, (Seattle: University of Washington Press, 1991), p. 6; Ellen E. Grzech, "PBB," in Nader, et al., pp. 60-84; Barry Commoner, "A Reporter At Large: The Environment," *The New Yorker*, June 15, 1987, p. 51.

[45] Scheffer, p. 11.

[46] Paul R. Ehrlich, *The Population Bomb* (New York: Ballantine Books, 1968).

[47] Paehlke, p. 55.

[48] Paehlke, pp. 58-59.

[49] As quoted in Paehlke, pp. 58-59.

[50] Paehlke, pp. 53, 76.

[51] Paehlke, pp. 103-104.

[52] Kenneth Geiser, *One, Two, Many Environmentalists: The 1980s Transformation of the Environmental Movement* (Medford, MA: Department of Urban and Environmental Policy, Tufts University, 1987), p. 8.

[53] Scheffer, pp. 113-114.

[54] Geiser, p. 7.

[55] Scheffer, p. 123.

[56] Peter Borrelli, "Environmentalism at a Crossroads: Reflections on the Old Old, New Old, Old New and New New Movements," *The Amicus Journal*, Summer 1987, Vol. 9, No. 3, First in a series, p. 24.

[57] Borrelli, "Environmentalism at a Crossroads," p. 26.

[58] Scheffer, p. 125.

[59] Scheffer, p. 125.

[60] Daniel Faber and James O'Connor, "The Struggle for Nature: Environmental Crises and the Crisis of Environmentalism in the United States," *Capitalism, Nature, Socialism*, Summer 1989, No. 2, p. 15.

[61] Environmental Action, *Earth Day: The Beginning; A Guide to Survival* (New York: Arno Press and the New York Times, 1970) p. xvii, as quoted in Scheffer, p. 125.

[62] Scheffer, p. 139.

[63] Kelley Griffin, *More Action for a Change* (New York: Dembner Books, 1987), pp. 40-41.

[64] Griffin, pp. 41-43.

[65] Faber and O'Connor, p. 29.

[66] Jon Naar, *Design for a Livable Planet: How You Can Help Clean Up the Environment* (New York: Harper and Row, Publishers, 1990), pp. 247-248.

[67] Naar, pp. 247-251.

[68] *Scenic Hudson Preservation Conference* v. *Federal Power Commission* (Storm King I) 354 F.2nd 608, (1965).

[69] Tom Turner, "The Legal Eagles," *The Amicus Journal*, Winter 1988, Vol. 10, No. 1, Third in a series, p. 26.

[70] Turner, p. 26.

[71] Turner, p. 26.

[72] Turner, p. 25.

[73] Turner, p. 26.

[74] Scheffer, pp. 138-139.

[75] Turner, p. 27.

[76] Turner, p. 27.

[77] Turner, p. 27.

[78] Bollier and Claybrook, p. 283.

[79] Bollier and Claybrook, pp. 132, 285.

[80] Scheffer, p. 150.

[81] Bollier and Claybrook, p. 286..

[82] Scheffer, p. 151.

[83] Bollier and Claybrook, p. 276.

[84] Bollier and Claybrook, p. 286; Scheffer, p. 152.

[85] Bollier and Claybrook, p. 287; Scheffer, p. 152.

[86] Scheffer, pp. 158-162.

[87] Barry Commoner, *Making Peace With the Planet* (New York: Pantheon Books, 1990), p. 170.

[88] Michael Harwood, "Daredevils for the Environment," *The New York Times Magazine*, October 2, 1988.

[89] Harwood, "Daredevils for the Environment."

[90] Harwood, "Daredevils for the Environment."

[91] Clark Norton, "Green Giant," *The Washington Post Magazine*. September 3, 1989, p. 26.

[92] Harwood, "Daredevils for the Environment."

[93] Dick Russell. "The Monkeywrenchers: Whatever Happened to the Nice Little Old Lady in Tennis Shoes," *The Amicus Journal*, Fall 1987, Vol. 9, No. 4, Second in a series, p. 22.

[94] *Greenpeace ... For a Cleaner, Safer Earth* (Washington, DC: Greenpeace).

[95] Harwood, "Daredevils for the Environment."

[96] *Greenpeace ... For a Cleaner, Safer Earth.*

[97] Harwood, "Daredevils for the Environment;" Norton, p. 36.

[98] Norton, p. 25.

[99] Norton, p. 26.

[100] Norton, p. 25.

[101] "Greenpeace: An Antidote to Corporate Environmentalism, An Interview with Peter Bahouth," *Multinational Monitor*, March 1990, p. 26.

[102] "Greenpeace: An Antidote to Corporate Environmentalism," p. 28.

[103] "Greenpeace: An Antidote to Corporate Environmentalism," pp. 26-27.

[104] "Greenpeace: An Antidote to Corporate Environmentalism," p. 27.

[105] "Greenpeace: An Antidote to Corporate Environmentalism," p. 27.

[106] "Greenpeace: An Antidote to Corporate Environmentalism," p. 27.

[107] "Greenpeace: An Antidote to Corporate Environmentalism," p. 26.

[108] "Greenpeace: An Antidote to Corporate Environmentalism," p. 26.

[109] Joanne Doroshow, *A Decade of Delay, Deceit and Danger: Three Mile Island 1979-1989; A Retrospective* (Harrisburg, PA: Three Mile Island Alert, 1989), pp. 2-3.

[110] Doroshow, p. 2.

[111] Doroshow, pp. 5-6.

[112] Doroshow, p. 4.

[113] Doroshow, pp. 6-8.

[114] Doroshow, pp. 2, 8.

[115] Doroshow, p. 9.

[116] Doroshow, p. 29.

[117] Doroshow, p. 10.

[118] Doroshow, p. 11.

[119] Robert Leppzer, ed., *Voices from Three Mile Island: The People Speak Out* (Trumansburg, NY: Crossing Press, 1980), p. 86.

[120] Doroshow, p. 29.

[121] David Bollier, *Citizen Action and Other Big Ideas: A History of Ralph Nader and the Modern Consumer Movement* (Washington, DC: Center for Study of Responsive Law, 1989), p. 45.

[122] Bollier, p. 46.

[123] Russell Mokhiber and Leonard Shen, "Love Canal," in Nader, et al., pp. 270-272.

[124] Mokhiber and Shen, pp. 274-275.

[125] Mokhiber and Shen, p. 273.

[126] Mokhiber and Shen, p. 279.

[127] Mokhiber and Shen, p. 281.

[128] Mokhiber and Shen, p. 282.

[129] Mokhiber and Shen, p. 283.

[130] Mokhiber and Shen, p. 284.

[131] Mokhiber and Shen, p. 285.

[132] Mokhiber and Shen, pp. 285-286.

[133] Mokhiber and Shen, pp. 287-288.

[134] Mokhiber and Shen, pp. 289-296.

[135] Mokhiber and Shen, p. 297.

[136] Mokhiber and Shen, p. 297.

[137] Mokhiber and Shen, p. 297.

[138] United Press International, February 24, 1988.

[139] Mokhiber and Shen, p. 275.

[140] Mokhiber and Shen, p. 301.

[141] Scheffer, p. 153.

[142] "Overhead Costs Spur Superfund Scrutiny," *Chicago Tribune*, October 3, 1991, p. C8.

[143] Brownstein, p. 50.

[144] Faber and O'Connor, p. 23.

[145] Congressional Budget Office, "The Environmental Protection Agency: Overview of the Proposed 1984 Budget," April 1983, p. 3 as cited in Joan Claybrook, *Retreat from Safety: Reagan's Attack on America's Health* (New York: Pantheon Books, 1984), p. 122.

[146] Faber and O'Connor, p. 24; Commoner, "A Reporter at Large," p. 46.

[147] Bollier and Claybrook, p. 97.

[148] Bollier and Claybrook, p. 98.

[149] Scheffer, p. 179.

[150] Commoner, "A Reporter at Large," pp. 67-68.

[151] Geiser, pp. 2-3.

[152] Will Collette, "Institutions: Citizen's Clearinghouse for Hazardous Wastes," *Environment*, Vol. 29, No. 9, November 1987, p. 44.

[153] Lois Marie Gibbs, "CCHW's 10th Anniversary: We've Come A Long Way," *Everyone's Backyard*, February 1991, p. 4.

[154] Gibbs, p. 2; Collette, p. 44.

[155] Collette, p. 45.

[156] Gibbs, p. 4.

[157] Geiser, p. 1.

[158] Cohen and O'Connor, p. 4.

[159] Geiser, p. 5.

[160] Geiser, p. 5.

[161] Cohen and O'Connor, p. 7.

[162] Geiser, p. 6.

[163] Geiser, p. 1.

[164] Cohen and O'Connor, p. 168.

[165] Cohen and O'Connor, p. 80.

[166] Geiser, pp. 16-17.

[167] "Action Line," *Everyone's Backyard*, January/February 1990, p. 15; "Bhopal on the Bayou," *Multinational Monitor*, January/February, 1990, p. 5.

[168] Karen Stults, "Women Movers: Reflections on a Movement By Some of Its Leaders," *Everyone's Backyard*, Spring 1989, p. 1.

[169] Stults, p. 1.

[170] Cohen and O'Connor, p. 23.

[171] Commoner, *Making Peace with the Planet*, p. 179.

[172] *Five Years of Progress: 1981-1986* (Arlington, VA: Citizen's Clearinghouse for Hazardous Waste, 1986), p. 20.

[173] Seth Zuckerman, "Environmentalism Turns 16: A Movement Takes Stock," *The Nation*, October 18, 1986, p. 369.

[174] Commoner, "A Reporter at Large," p. 51.

[175] Commoner, "A Reporter at Large," p. 47.

[176] Commoner, "A Reporter at Large," p. 47.

[177] Commoner, "A Reporter at Large," p. 52.

[178] Commoner, "A Reporter at Large," p. 52.

[179] Commoner, *Making Peace with the Planet*, p. 175.

[180] Commoner, *Making Peace with the Planet*, pp. 196-197.

[181] Commoner, *Making Peace with the Planet*, pp. 205-207.

[182] "McDonald's Surrenders," *Everyone's Backyard*, December 1990, p. 2.

[183] Cohen and O'Connor, p. 8.

[184] Commoner, *Making Peace With the Planet*, pp. 171-172.

[185] Faber and O'Connor, p. 32.

[186] Borelli, "The Ecophilosophers," p. 34; Zuckerman, p. 370.

[187] Borelli, "The Ecophilosophers," p. 32.

[188] Borelli, "The Ecophilosophers," p. 36.

[189] Celinda C. Lake, "The Environment: 20 Years After the First Earth Day," *The Polling Report*, April 9, 1990, p. 6.

[190] Lake, p. 6.

[191] Stevenson Swanson and Casey Bukro, "Earth Day Festivities Remind Millions of Planet's Fragility," *Chicago Tribune*, April 23, 1990, p. C1; Maura Dolan and Larry B. Stammer, "200 Million Worldwide Pay Respect to Earth," *Los Angeles Times*, April 23, 1990, p. A1.

[192] Anthony Flint, "Environmental Movement Rekindles Student Activism on U.S. Campuses," *Boston Globe*, April 23, 1990, p. 17p.

TECHNIQUES

[1] Ralph Nader and Donald Ross, *Action for a Change: A Student's Manual for Public Interest Organizing*. Revised edition (New York: Grossman Publishers, 1972), p. 3.

[2] Jon Naar, *Design for a Livable Planet: How You Can Help Clean Up the Environment* (New York: Harper and Row, 1990), pp. 274, 275.

[3] Charles L. Smith, *The Hobby of Pamphleteering* (Berkeley, CA: Charles L. Smith, 1962, revised 1989).

[4] Smith, *The Hobby of Pamphleteering*.

[5] Don Engdahl, "Pamphleteer Stalks Bodega Bay A-Plant," *Santa Rosa Press Democrat*, September 5, 1963, p. 22.

[6] Smith, *The Hobby of Pamphleteering*.

[7] Smith, *The Hobby of Pamphleteering*.

[8] Smith, *The Hobby of Pamphleteering*.

[9] Smith, *The Hobby of Pamphleteering*.

[10] David Bollier, *Citizen Action and Other Big Ideas: A History of Ralph Nader and the Modern Consumer Movement* (Washington, DC: Center for Study of Responsive Law, 1989), pp. 39-40.

[11] "The Struggle for Worker Safety," *Bridging the GAP*, Fall 1991, p. 2.

[12] "The Struggle for Worker Safety," p. 1.

[13] "The Struggle for Worker Safety," p. 1.

[14] "The Struggle for Worker Safety," p. 1.

[15] "The Struggle for Worker Safety," p. 1.

[16] "The Struggle for Worker Safety," p. 2.

[17] "The Struggle for Worker Safety," p. 2.

[18] "The Struggle for Worker Safety," p. 2.

[19] "The Struggle for Worker Safety," p. 2.

[20] "The Struggle for Worker Safety," p. 2.

[21] "The Struggle for Worker Safety," p. 2.

[22] "The Struggle for Worker Safety," p. 2.

[23] "The Struggle for Worker Safety," p. 2.

[24] Bollier, p. 40.

[25] Mark Green, *Who Runs Congress?* Fourth edition (New York: Dell Publishing Co., Inc., 1984), p. 377.

[26] Green, p. 378.

[27] Stephen A. Newman and Nancy Kramer, *Getting What You Deserve: A Handbook for the Assertive Consumer* (Garden City, NY: Doubleday and Co., Inc., 1979), p. 293.

[28] Newman and Kramer, pp. 293-294.

[29] Marc Caplan, *A Citizens' Guide to Lobbying* (New York: Dembner Books, 1983), p. 65.

[30] Si Kahn, *Organizing: A Guide for Grassroots Leaders*. Revised edition (Silver Spring, MD: National Association of Social Workers, 1991), p. 104.

[31] Kahn, pp. 108-9, 110.

[32] Dolores Huerta, "Reflections on the UFW Experience," *The Center Magazine*, July/August 1985, p. 2.

[33] Huerta, p. 2.

[34] Huerta, p. 2.

[35] Huerta, pp. 2-3.

[36] Caplan, p. 62.

[37] Caplan, p. 63.

[38] Caplan, p. 71.

[39] Caplan, p. 71.

[40] Caplan, p. 71.

[41] Janet Kelsey and Don Wiener, "The Citizen/Labor Energy Coalition," *Social Policy*, Spring 1983, p. 16.

[42] Lee Staples, ed., *Roots to Power: A Manual for Grassroots Organizing* (New York: Praeger, 1984), p. 1.

[43] Staples, pp. 4-6.

[44] Kahn, p. 10.

[45] Kim Bobo, Jackie Kendall and Steve Max of the Midwest Academy, *Organizing for Social Change: A Manual for Activists in the 1990s* (Washington, DC: Seven Locks Press, 1991), p. 29.

[46] Harry C. Boyte, *The Backyard Revolution: Understanding the New Citizen Movement* (Philadelphia: Temple University Press, 1980), pp. 49-50.

[47] Boyte, p. 50.

[48] Boyte, p. 51.

[49] Anne Witte Garland, "Gale Cincotta" *Ms.*, January 1986, p. 51.

[50] Garland, p. 51.

[51] Garland, p. 101.

[52] Nancy Brigham with Maria Catalfio and Dick Cluster, *How to Do Leaflets, Newsletters and Newspapers* (Detroit: PEP Publishers, 1991), pp. 9-10.

[53] Brigham, p. 9.

[54] Brigham, pp. 10-11.

[55] Charles L. Smith, *Uses of a Clearinghouse: Mutual Self-Help in Any Organization* (Berkeley, CA: Charles L. Smith, 1989).

[56] *Berkeley Information Network* fact sheet (Berkeley, CA: Berkeley Public Library, 1991).

[57] Brigham, p. 19.

[58] Brigham, p. 19.

[59] "Nuclear Power Industry PACS Gave Over $25 Million to Congressional Candidates, 1981-1988; Key Nuclear Licensing Vote Coming Up in House," press release (Washington, DC: United States Public Interest Research Group, September 15, 1989), p. 1.

[60] "Nuclear Power Industry PACs Gave Over ...," p. 2.

[61] Russell Mokhiber and Leonard Shen, "Love Canal," in Ralph Nader, Ronald Brownstein and John Richard, eds., *Who's Poisoning America?: Corporate Polluters and their Victims in the Chemical Age* (San Francisco: Sierra Club Books, 1981), p. 296.

[62] Mokhiber and Shen, p. 296, citing Love Canal Homeowners Association "Pregnancy Outcome Study."

[63] *Speaking Out: Setting Up a Speaker's Bureau* (Washington, DC: League of Women Voters of the United States, 1977).

[64] Interview with Bj King-Taylor of Physicians for Social Responsibility, November, 1991.

[65] Green, p. 392.

[66] Bobo et al., p. 29.

[67] Bobo, et al., p. 36.

[68] Bobo et al., p. 13.

[69] Will Collette, "Research for Organizing," in Lee Staples, ed., *Roots to Power: A Manual for Grassroots Organizing* (New York: Praeger, 1984), p. 144.

[70] Collette, p. 148.

[71] Collette, p. 149.

[72] John Ullmann, Jan Colbert and the Investigative Reporters and Editors Inc., eds., *The Reporter's Handbook: An Investigator's Guide to Documents and Techniques*. Second edition (New York: St. Martin's Press, 1991), p. 43.

[73] Bobo, et al., p. 172.

[74] Ullmann and Colbert, p. 44.

[75] Ullmann and Colbert, p. 30.

[76] Ullmann and Colbert, p. 35.

[77] Bobo, et al., p. 173.

[78] Ullmann and Colbert, p. 46.

[79] Ullmann and Colbert, p. 47.

[80] Brigham, p. 89.

[81] Caplan, p. 27.

[82] Bollier, p. 37.

[83] Bollier, p. 37.

[84] *Using Community Right to Know: A Guide to a New Federal Law* (Washington, DC: OMB Watch, 1988).

[85] Bollier, p. 37.

[86] National Library of Medicine, U.S. Department of Health and Human Services, TRI Representative, 8600 Rockville Pike, Bethesda, MD 20894.

[87] Bollier, p. 38.

[88] Ullmann and Colbert, p. 269.

[89] Ullmann and Colbert, p. 289.

[90] Staples, p. 3.

[91] Newman and Kramer, p. 307.

[92] Kahn, pp. 174-175.

[93] Paul Angiolillo and Aaron Bernstein, "The Secondary Boycott Gets a Second Wind," *Business Week*, June 27, 1988, p. 82.

[94] Interview with the Institute for Consumer Responsibility, December 1991.

[95] Russell Mokhiber, "Infant Formula: Hawking Disaster in the Third World," *Multinational Monitor*, April 1987, p. 21.

[96] Nancy Gaschott, "Babies at Risk: Infant Formula Still Takes Its Toll," *Multinational Monitor*, October 1986, p. 11.

[97] Gaschott, p. 11.

[98] Mokhiber, "Infant Formula: Hawking Disaster in the Third World," p. 20.

[99] Gaschott, p. 12.

[100] Mokhiber, "Infant Formula: Hawking Disaster in the Third World," p. 20.

[101] Gaschott, p. 11.

[102] John Summa, "Killing Them Sweetly," *Multinational Monitor*, November 1988, p. 28.

[103] Gaschott, p. 11.

[104] Gaschott, p. 11.

[105] Gaschott, p. 11.

[106] "Nestle: The Boycott's Back," *Multinational Monitor*, September 1988, p. 4.

[107] "Nestle: The Boycott's Back," p. 4.

[108] Newman and Kramer, p. 306.

[109] Newman and Kramer, p. 306.

[110] Newman and Kramer, pp. 305-306.

[111] Green, p. 364.

[112] Kahn, p. 247.

[113] Kahn, p. 247.

[114] Kahn, p. 247.

[115] *World Book Encyclopedia*, No. 18 (Chicago: World Book, Inc., 1989), p. 929.

[116] *World Book Encyclopedia*, p. 929.

[117] *World Book Encyclopedia*, p. 930.

[118] Harvard Sitkoff, *The Struggle for Black Equality: 1954-1980* (New York: Hill and Wang, 1981), pp. 41-58.

[119] Sitkoff, p. 81.

[120] Andrea Ayvazian, "No Payment Enclosed: Why I Resist War Taxes," *The Progressive*, April 1989, p. 19.

[121] Ayvazian, p. 20.

[122] Ayvazian, p. 21.

[123] Caplan, p. 33.

[124] Caplan, p. 120.

[125] Caplan, p. 38.

[126] Green, p. 372.

[127] Green, p. 373.

[128] Caplan, p. 31.

[129] Caplan, p. 32.

[130] Green, p. 374.

[131] Caplan, p. 32.

[132] Caplan, p. 27.

[133] Green, p. 382.

[134] Caplan, pp. 42-43.

[135] Caplan, p. 40.

[136] Caplan, p. 39.

[137] Green, pp. 383-384.

138 Green, p. 384.

139 Caplan, p. 138.

140 Green, p. 384.

141 Green, p. 384.

142 Caplan, p. 39.

143 Green, p. 383.

144 Caplan, pp. 153-166.

145 Caplan, p. 58.

146 Green, p. 387.

147 Green, p. 387.

148 Green, p. 387.

149 Green, p. 386.

150 Green, p. 386.

151 Caplan, pp. 175, 176.

152 Green, p. 391.

153 Naar, p. 251.

154 Gary Cohen and John O'Connor, *Fighting Toxics: A Manual for Protecting Your Family, Community and Workplace* (Washington, DC: Island Press, 1990), pp. 217-220.

155 Naar, p. 247.

156 Cohen and O'Connor, p. 221.

157 Naar, p. 247.

158 Newman and Kramer, p. 279.

159 Cohen and O'Connor, p. 228.

160 *Going to Court in the Public Interest: A Guide for Community Groups* (Washington, DC: League of Women Voters Education Fund, 1983), p. 5.

161 *Going to Court in the Public Interest*, p. 4.

162 Cohen and O'Connor, p. 212.

163 Cohen and O'Connor, p. 212.

164 *Going to Court in the Public Interest*, p. 3.

165 *Going to Court in the Public Interest*, p. 3.

166 Newman and Kramer, p. 275.

167 Newman and Kramer, p. 281.

168 Newman and Kramer, p. 281.

169 Kenneth Lasson and the Public Citizen Litigation Group, *Representing Yourself: What You Can Do Without a Lawyer* (Washington, DC: Public Citizen, 1983), p. 136.

170 Newman and Kramer, p. 281.

171 Newman and Kramer, pp. 281-282.

172 Lasson, p. 139.

173 Lasson, p. 140.

174 Newman and Kramer, p. 282.

175 Newman and Kramer, pp. 282-283.

176 Newman and Kramer, p. 283.

177 Newman and Kramer, p. 284.

178 Newman and Kramer, p. 284.

179 Newman and Kramer, p. 285.

180 Newman and Kramer, p. 285.

181 David D. Schmidt, "Government by the People: Voters Are Writing New Laws Through Initiative and Referendum," *Public Citizen*, June 1986, p. 12.

182 Schmidt, "Government by the People," p. 12.

183 Schmidt, "Government by the People," p. 14.

184 Schmidt, "Government by the People," p. 14.

185 Schmidt, "Government by the People," p. 15.

186 Schmidt, "Government by the People," p. 15.

187 Schmidt, "Government by the People," p. 19.

188 Schmidt, "Government by the People," p. 15.

189 Schmidt, "Government by the People," p. 14.

190 David D. Schmidt, *Citizen Lawmakers: The Ballot Initiative Revolution* (Philadelphia: Temple University Press, 1989), pp. 191-192.

191 Schmidt, *Citizen Lawmakers*, p. 193.

192 Schmidt, *Citizen Lawmakers*, p. 196.

193 Schmidt, *Citizen Lawmakers*, p. 192.

194 Schmidt, *Citizen Lawmakers*, p. 200.

195 Charlene LaVoie, *The Community Lawyer Project* (Winchester, CT: Community Lawyer, September 1991), p. 2.

196 LaVoie, p. 4.

197 LaVoie, p. 5.

198 LaVoie, p. 6.

199 Heidi J. Welsh, "Shareholder Activism," *Multinational Monitor*, December 1988, pp. 9-10.

200 *The Shareholder Proposal Process: A Step-by-Step Guide to Shareholder Activism for Individuals and Institutions* (Washington, DC: United Shareholders Association, 1987).

201 "Voice of Conscience: An Interview with Timothy Smith," *Multinational Monitor*, December 1988, p. 21.

202 Welsh, pp. 9-10.

203 Welsh, p. 9.

204 "Voice of Conscience," p. 21.

205 Welsh, p. 10.

206 Welsh, p. 11.

207 "The Good, the Bad and the Miscreant," *Multinational Monitor*, December 1988, p. 5.

208 Ralph Nader and Steven Gold, "Letters to the Editor: How About a Little Down-Home *Glasnost*?" *Columbia Journalism Review*, September/October 1988, p. 53.

209 Nader and Gold, p. 54.

210 Caplan, p. 84.

211 Caplan, p. 84.

212 Caplan, p. 85.

213 Caplan, p. 85.

214 Telephone conversation with Angela Owens, editorial director, WRC-TV, May 1992.

215 Caplan, p. 84.

216 Caplan, p. 85.

217 Caplan, p. 86.

218 Caplan, p. 86.

[219] Caplan, p. 86.

[220] Caplan, p. 87.

[221] Caplan, pp. 86-87.

[222] Caplan, p. 92.

[223] Caplan, p. 92.

[224] Caplan, p. 92.

[225] Caplan, p. 92.

[226] Caplan, p. 93.

[227] Caplan, p. 93.

[228] Caplan, p. 93.

[229] Caplan, p. 93.

[230] Caplan, pp. 90-91.

[231] Caplan, p. 93.

[232] Caplan, p. 93.

[233] Caplan, p. 94.

[234] Caplan, pp. 94-96.

[235] Bobo, et al., p. 28.

[236] Bollier, p. 28.

[237] Caplan, p. 97.

[238] Caplan, pp. 88, 98-101.

[239] Joan Flanagan, *The Grass Roots Fundraising Book: How to Raise Money in Your Community* (Chicago: Contemporary Books, Inc., 1982), p. 49.

[240] Flanagan, p. 53.

[241] Flanagan, p. 56.

[242] Flanagan, pp. 66-67.

[243] Flanagan, p. 84.

[244] Flanagan, pp. 84-85.

[245] Flanagan, pp. 91-92.

[246] Flanagan, p. 101.

[247] Flanagan, p. 141-142.

[248] Flanagan, pp. 130-136.

[249] Bobo et al., p. 181.

[250] Bobo, et al., p. 177.

[251] The Foundation Center, 79 Fifth Avenue, New York, NY 10003. Telephone (800) 424-9836; Jill R. Shellow and Nancy C. Stella, eds., *Grant Seekers Guide*. Third edition (Mt. Kisco, NY: Moyer Bell Limited, 1989).

[252] *Non-Profit Organizations, Public Policy and the Political Process: A Guide to the Internal Revenue Code and Federal Election Campaign Act* (Washington, DC: Perkins Coie, 1987), p. 3.

[253] *Non-Profit Organizations*, p. 3.

[254] *Non-Profit Organizations*, p. 23.

[255] *Non-Profit Organizations*, p. 23.

[256] Norman J. Kiritz, "Program Planning and Proposal Writing," in Nancy Mitiguy, ed., *The Rich Get Richer and the Poor Write Proposals* (Amherst, MA: University of Massachusetts Citizen Involvement Training Project, 1978), p. 43.

[257] Kiritz, p. 43.

[258] Kiritz, p. 44.

[259] Kiritz, pp. 44-46.

[260] Kiritz, p. 48.

[261] Kiritz, p. 59.

PROFILING MEMBERS OF CONGRESS

[1] "Reagan's Inaugural Festivities Win Proxmire's Fleece Award," Reuters Ltd. wire service, March 31, 1987.

[2] Penny Loeb, "Investigating Politicians," in John Ullmann and Jan Colbert, eds., *The Reporter's Handbook: An Investigator's Guide to Documents and Techniques*, Second edition (New York: St. Martin's Press, 1991), p. 148.

[3] Loeb, p. 149.

[4] *Background Information on Campaign Finance Reform and Honoraria: U.S. Senate*, Fact sheet (Washington, DC: Common Cause, Fall 1990).

[5] Kathleen A. Welch, "Democracy for Sale: The Need for Campaign Finance Reform," *In the Public Interest*, Spring 1990, p. 35.

[6] *We the People For Public Funding: Questions and Answers on Public Funding of Congressional Campaigns* (Washington, DC: Public Citizen's Congress Watch).

[7] *If You Care About the Voice of Women in American Politics, You Should Care About Campaign Finance Reform*, Fact sheet (Washington, DC: Public Citizen's Congress Watch, 1990).

[8] *If You Care About the Voice of Minorities in American Politics, You Should Care About Campaign Finance Reform*, Fact sheet (Washington, DC: Public Citizen, 1990).

[9] "Nuclear Power Industry PACS Gave Over $17 Million to Congressional Candidates; Key Nuclear Safety Vote Scheduled in House July 29," press release (Washington, DC: United States Public Interest Research Group, July 25, 1987), p. 2.

[10] Welch, p. 35.

[11] Mark Green, et al., *Who Runs Congress?* Fourth edition (New York: Dell Publishing Co., 1984), p. 29.

[12] Green, p. 29.

[13] Welch, p. 32.

[14] Philip M. Stern, *The Best Congress Money Can Buy* (New York: Pantheon Books, 1988), p. 24; Green, p. 31.

[15] Stern, pp. 6, 21, 31; Green, p. 31.

[16] Green, p. 52.

[17] Stern, p. 163.

[18] Stern, p. 165.

[19] Stern, pp. 168-169.

[20] Stern, p. 170.

[21] Welch, p. 32.

[22] Welch, p. 32.

[23] Green, p. 49.

[24] Green, p. 50.

[25] Green, pp. 50-52.

[26] Green, p. 52.

[27] Green, p. 52.

[28] Green, pp. 52-53.

[29] Green, p. 54.

[30] Larry Makinson, *The Price of Admission: An Illustrated Atlas of Campaign Spending in the 1988 Congressional Elections* (Washington, DC: Center for Study of Responsive Politics, 1989), p. 14. as cited in Welch, p. 33.

[31] Green, p. 52.

[32] *Public Citizen Policy Paper on Campaign Finance Reform* (Washington, DC: Public Citizen's Congress Watch) and Green, p. 55; Stern, p. 180; Welch, p. 39 citing Common Cause president, Fred Wertheimer.

[33] Green, p. 55.

[34] Green, p. 56.

[35] Stern, p. 182.

[36] Green, p. 55.

[37] Green, p. 56.

[38] Green, p. 56.

[39] Stern, p. 183.

[40] Stern, p. 189.

[41] Green, p. 55.

ENERGY WASTEHUNT

[1] Nicholas Fedoruk, *MythBusters #6: Energy Efficiency* (Washington, DC: Safe Energy Communication Council, 1990), p. 1.

[2] Dean Abrahamson and Peter Ciborowski, "Harvest of Sand: Agriculture's Future in a Changing Climate," *The Amicus Journal*, Spring 1984, Vol. 5, No. 4, p. 43.

[3] Fedoruk, p. 2.

[4] Michael Fischer, executive director of the Sierra Club, quoting a Lawrence Livermore Laboratory report, in "Oil at Any Cost?," *World Link*, July/August 1989, p. 9.

[5] Fischer, p. 9.

[6] Fischer, p. 9.

[7] Howard Geller, *Energy Efficiency Paper No. 2: National Energy Efficiency Platform: Description and Potential Impacts* (Washington, DC: American Council for an Energy-Efficient Economy, 1989), pp. 10-11 as cited in Fedoruk, p. 4.

[8] Christopher Flavin and Rick Piltz with Chris Nichols, *Sustainable Energy* (Washington, DC: Renew America, 1989), p. 5.

[9] Flavin and Piltz, p. 5.

[10] Jeanne Byrne, *Myth Busters #5: Renewable Energy* (Washington, DC: Safe Energy Communication Council, 1990), p. 6.

[11] Jon Naar, *Design for a Livable Planet: How You Can Help Clean Up the Environment* (New York: Harper and Row Publishers, 1990), p. 190.

[12] Naar, pp. 189-190.

[13] Naar, pp. 63-64, 190.

[14] Byrne, p. 1.

[15] Naar, pp. 153-166.

[16] Flavin and Piltz, p. 4.

[17] Brower, Michael, *Cool Energy: The Renewable Solution to Global Warming* (Washington, DC: Union of Concerned Scientists, 1989).

[18] Christopher Flavin, *Worldwatch Paper 91: Slowing Global Warming: A Worldwide Strategy* (Washington, DC: Worldwatch Institute, October 1989), p. 33 as cited in Byrne, p. 1.

[19] Byrne, pp. 2-3.

[20] Flavin and Piltz, p. 13.

[21] Naar, p. 204.

[22] *National Solar Buildings Technology Program, Five Year Research Plan, 1989-1993* (Washington, DC: U.S. Department of Energy) as quoted in Flavin and Piltz, p. 14.

[23] Robert Lynette, *Wind Energy Systems* (Washington, DC: report to Forum on Renewable Energy and Climate Change, 1989) as cited in Naar, p. 199.

[24] Naar, p. 196.

[25] Naar, pp. 196-197.

[26] *The Potential of Renewable Energy: An Interlaboratory Analytic Paper*, Solar Energy Research Institute, et al., September 1989, p. A-23, as cited in Byrne, p. 4.

[27] Brower, p. 53 as cited in Byrne, p. 3.

[28] *The Potential of Renewable Energy: An Interlaboratory Analytic Paper*, Solar Energy Research Institute, et al., September 1989, p. A-76, as cited in Byrne, p. 4.

[29] Byrne, p. 5.

[30] Fedoruk, p. 1.

[31] Walter H. Corson, ed., *Global Ecology Handbook: What You Can Do About the Environmental Crisis* (Boston: Beacon Press, 1990), p. 205.

[32] Naar, p. 193.

[33] Naar, pp. 193, 195.

[34] Naar, p. 193.

[35] David Bollier, *Citizen Action and Other Big Ideas: A History of Ralph Nader and the Modern Consumer Movement* (Washington, DC: Center for Study of Responsive Law, 1989), p. 21.

[36] Naar, p. 195.

[37] Flavin and Piltz, p. 43.

[38] Fischer, p. 9.

[39] Flavin and Piltz, p. 18.

[40] Flavin and Piltz, p. 20.

[41] Flavin and Piltz, p. 19.

[42] Flavin and Piltz, p. 20.

[43] Flavin and Piltz, p. 13.

[44] Flavin and Piltz, p. 13.

[45] Flavin and Piltz, p. 43.

[46] Flavin and Piltz, p. 13.

[47] Naar, p. 217.

[48] Amory B. Lovins, *The State of the Art: Space Cooling* (Old Snowmass, CO: Rocky Mountain Institute, 1986) pp. 35-36, as cited in Flavin and Piltz, p. 15.

[49] Flavin and Piltz, p. 16.

[50] Conversation with commercial energy auditor Carl Anderson, Pacific Gas and Electric Co., San Diego, CA.

[51] Flavin and Piltz, p. 16.

[52] Flavin and Piltz, p. 16.

[53] Flavin and Piltz, p. 16.

[54] *Tips for Energy Savers* (Washington, DC: U.S. Department of Energy) p. 5.

55 Howard Geller, *Residential Energy Efficiency: A State of the Art Review* (Washington, DC: American Council for an Energy-Efficient Economy, 1988) as cited in Fedoruk, p. 5.

56 Fedoruk, p. 5 based on data in Howard Geller, *Residential Equipment Efficiency: A State of the Art Review.*

57 Flavin and Piltz, p. 14.

58 Flavin and Piltz, p. 14.

59 Flavin and Piltz, p. 14.

TOY SAFETY SURVEY

1 As cited in Jon Stubenvoll, *The 1990 Dangerous Dozen: Unsafe Toys* (Portland: Oregon State Public Interest Research Group, 1990), p. 6.

2 As cited in Stubenvoll, *1990 Dangerous Dozen*, p. 8.

3 Stubenvoll, *1990 Dangerous Dozen*, pp. 4, 6.

4 Stubenvoll, *1990 Dangerous Dozen*, pp. 9-12; Lucinda Sikes, *Trouble in Toyland: Unsafe Toys in the United States* (Washington, DC: U.S. Public Interest Research Group, 1990), p. 2; *Toy Safety for Consumers* (Portland: Oregon State Public Interest Research Group), p. 6.

5 "Toys," *Buyer's Market.* Vol. 3, No. 9, November 1987, p. 3.

6 "Toys," p. 2.

7 *Toy Safety for Consumers*, p. 6.

8 "Toys," p. 3.

9 Stubenvoll, *1990 Dangerous Dozen*, p. 12.

10 Stubenvoll, *1990 Dangerous Dozen*, p. 12.

11 Stubenvoll, *1990 Dangerous Dozen*, pp. 9, 21; Sikes, p. 17; Ellen Citron, *Trouble in Toyland: Unsafe Toys in Massachusetts* (Boston: Massachusetts Public Interest Research Group, 1990), pp. 19-20.

12 Stubenvoll, *1990 Dangerous Dozen*, p. 9.

13 Jon Stubenvoll, *Student Guide to Toy Safety Project* (Portland: Oregon State Public Interest Research Group, 1990), p. 13.

14 Stubenvoll, *1990 Dangerous Dozen*, p. 11.

15 Sikes, pp. 6-7.

FREEDOM OF INFORMATION ACT

1 *Tapping Officials' Secrets* (Washington, DC: Reporter's Committee for Freedom of the Press, 1989), p. i.

2 David Bollier, *Citizen Action and Other Big Ideas: A History of Ralph Nader and the Modern Consumer Movement* (Washington, DC: Center for Study of Responsive Law, 1991), p. 39.

3 Bollier, p. 42.

4 Bollier, p. 39.

5 Elaine P. English, *How to Use the Federal FOI Act*, Fifth edition (Washington, DC: The FOI Service Center, 1985), p. 2.

6 Bollier, p. 40.

7 *The Freedom of Information Act: A User's Guide* (Washington, DC: The Freedom of Information Clearinghouse, 1989); English, p. 3.

8 Bollier, p. 40.

9 Bollier, p. 40.

10 Bollier, pp. 40-41.

11 Bollier, p. 43.

12 *The Freedom of Information Act: A User's Guide.*

13 Bollier, pp. 44-45.

14 English, p. 3.

15 English, p. 4.

16 *The Freedom of Information Act: A User's Guide.*

17 English, p. 5.

18 *The Freedom of Information Act: A User's Guide.*

19 English, p. 5.

20 English, p. 5.

21 English, p. 7.

22 *The Freedom of Information Act: A User's Guide.*

23 *The Freedom of Information Act: A User's Guide.*

24 *Federal Bureau of Investigation Facts and History* (Washington, DC: U.S. Department of Justice, 1990), p. 1.

25 Athan G. Theoharis, "FBI Surveillance During the Cold War Years: A Constitutional Crisis," *The Public Historian*, Winter 1981, p. 10.

26 Theoharis, p. 13; Bollier, p. 39.

27 Leon Friedman, in Letty Cottin Pogrebin, "Have You Ever Supported Equal Pay, Child Care or Women's Groups?: The FBI Was Watching You," *Ms.*, June 1977, p. 42.

28 John W. Moore, "Old Ghosts, Future Shock," *National Journal*, December 30, 1989, p. 3105.

29 Both the request and appeal letters are based on samples in English, pp. 20-21; and *The Freedom of Information Act: A User's Guide.*

30 As listed in *The Freedom of Information Act: A User's Guide.*

VOTER PARTICIPATION PROFILE

1 U.S. Department of Commerce - Bureau of the Census, *Voting and Registration in the Election of November 1988* (Washington, DC: Government Printing Office, October 1989), p. 1 (fn), p. 2 (Table A).

2 Frances Fox Piven and Richard A. Cloward, *Why Americans Don't Vote* (New York: Pantheon Books, 1988), p. 5.

3 Piven and Cloward, p. 19.

4 Piven and Cloward, p. 17.

5 *Voting and Registration in the Election of November 1988*, p. 2, Table A.

6 *Voting and Registration in the Election of November 1988*, p. 6, Table F.

7 *Voting and Registration in the Election of November 1988*, p. 13, Table 1.

8 Piven and Cloward, p. 12.

9 *Renewing the Promise: The 20th Anniversary of the 18-Year-Old Vote* (Washington, DC: People for the American Way, 1991), p. 16.

10 Charlene Jackson and Rebecca Hoffman, *Youth Vote '91: Register the Power, Student Guide to Registering Classmates* (New York: New York Public Interest Research Group, 1991).

11 *Youth Vote '91: Register the Power* Fact sheet (New York: Youth Vote '91, 1991).

[12] *First Vote: A Teaching Unit on Registration and Voting,* Curriculum and video (Washington, DC: People for the American Way).

[13] Piven and Cloward, p. 80.

[14] Piven and Cloward, p. 81.

[15] Piven and Cloward, p. 82.

[16] Piven and Cloward, p. 84.

[17] Piven and Cloward, p. 87.

[18] Piven and Cloward, p. 83.

[19] Piven and Cloward, p. 83.

[20] 42 U.S.C. Section 1973(a)(1982), as cited in Piven and Cloward, pp. 276-277.

[21] Piven and Cloward, p. 94.

[22] Piven and Cloward, p. 88.

[23] Piven and Cloward, p. 179.

[24] Piven and Cloward, p. 196.

[25] Piven and Cloward, p. 196.

[26] Piven and Cloward, p. 197.

[27] *Creating the Opportunity: How Voting Laws Affect Voter Turnout* (Washington, DC: The Committee for the Study of the American Electorate, 1987), p 12.

[28] *Report of the Task Force on Barriers to Voting,* (Columbus, OH: National Association of Secretaries of State, 1987), p. 15.

[29] *Election Day Registration* (Washington, DC: Center for Policy Alternatives, 1990), p.1.

[30] *Report of the Task Force on Barriers to Voting,* p. 14.

[31] *Election Day Registration,* p. 2.

[32] *Election Day Registration,* p. 2.

[33] *Creating the Opportunity,* p. 18.

[34] *Report of the Task Force on Barriers to Voting,* p. 14.

[35] *Mail-In Voter Registration* Fact sheet (Washington, DC: Center for Policy Alternatives, 1990), p. 1.

[36] *Mail-In Voter Registration,* p. 3.

[37] *Mail-In Voter Registration,* p. 1.

[38] *Mail-In Voter Registration,* p. 1.

[39] *Motor Voter Registration* Fact sheet (Washington, DC: Center for Policy Alternatives, 1990), p. 1.

[40] *Motor Voter Registration,* p. 1.

[41] *Motor Voter Registration,* p. 1.

[42] *Motor Voter Registration,* p. 1.

[43] *Motor Voter Registration,* p. 1.

[44] *"Motor Voter" Facts and Figures* (Washington, DC: D.C. Board of Elections and Ethics, January 1991).

[45] *States With Motor Voter and Other Agency-Based Voter Registration Programs* (New York: 100% Vote/Human Serve, 1991).

[46] *Election Day Registration,* p. 2.

[47] *Report of the Task Force on Barriers to Voting,* p. 4.

[48] *Report of the Task Force on Barriers to Voting,* p. 8.

[49] *Voting in the District of Columbia: Development, Current Trends and Progress in Administration* (Washington, DC: DC Board of Elections and Ethics, 1988), p. 1.

[50] "Estimated Population of the District of Columbia By Age, Race and Sex," (Washington, DC: DC Office of Planning, 1988).

[51] "1990: Population and Housing Units by 1982 Ward," (Washington, DC: DC Office of Planning, 1991).

[52] *District of Columbia General Election: Final and Complete Election Results* (Washington, DC: DC Board of Elections and Ethics, 1990); *Monthly Report of Voter Registration Statistics for the period ending December 31, 1990* (Washington, DC: DC Board of Elections and Ethics, 1990).

[53] *Monthly Report of Voter Registration Statistics*; *District of Columbia General Election: Final and Complete Election Results*; *A Statistical View of the DC Voter Roll - As of March 31, 1990* (Washington, DC: DC Board of Elections and Ethics, 1990), p. 7.

[54] *Voting in the District of Columbia,* p. 12.

DISABILITY ACCESS SURVEY

[1] U.S. Bureau of the Census figure as cited in Mary Johnson, "Disabled Americans Push for Access," *The Progressive,* August 1991, p. 21.

[2] Marilyn Golden, "Not on the Front Page," *The East Bay Guardian,* June 1991.

[3] *Access America: The Architectural Barriers Act and You* (Washington, DC: U.S. Architectural and Transportation Barriers Compliance Board), p. 1.

[4] Johnson, p. 21.

[5] Johnson, p. 21.

[6] Johnson, p. 21.

[7] Sonny Kleinfield, "The Handicapped: Hidden No Longer," *Atlantic Monthly,* December 1977, p. 87.

[8] Charles D. Goldman, "Right of Way: The Americans with Disabilities Act," *The Washington Lawyer,* March/April 1991, p. 36; *UFAS Accessibility Checklist* (Washington, DC: U.S. Architectural and Transportation Barriers Compliance Board, 1990), p. 4.

[9] Joseph P. Shapiro, "Liberation Day for the Disabled," *U.S. News and World Report,* September 18, 1989, p. 20.

[10] Joseph Weber, "The Last 'Minority' Fights For Its Rights: The Disabled are battling prejudice with '60s-style activism," *Business Week,* June 6, 1988, p. 140.

[11] Johnson, p. 21.

[12] *Uniform Federal Accessibility Standards* (Washington, DC: General Services Administration, Dept. of Defense, Dept. of Housing and Urban Development, U.S. Postal Service, 1988), p. 3; *UFAS Accessibility Checklist,* p. 4.

[13] *UFAS Accessibility Checklist,* p. 4.

[14] *Uniform Federal Accessibility Standards,* p. 1.

[15] *UFAS Accessibility Checklist,* p. 4.

[16] *Uniform Federal Accessibility Standards,* p. 1.

[17] *Access America,* p. 4.

[18] Johnson, p. 21.

[19] *Americans with Disabilities Act Fact Sheet* (Washington, DC: U.S. Architectural and Transportation Barriers Compliance Board, 1990). p. 3.

GREEN CONSUMER

[1] Michael Peters Group survey quoted in Debra Lynn Dadd and Andre Carothers, "A Bill of Goods?: Green Consuming in Perspective," *Greenpeace*, May/June 1990, p. 8.

[2] Dadd and Carothers, p. 10.

[3] *Packaging: Solid Waste Action Paper #2* (Washington, DC: Environmental Action Foundation, 1990).

[4] Cynthia Pollock, *Mining Urban Wastes: The Potential for Recycling* (Washington, DC: Worldwatch Institute, 1987), p. 43.

[5] Pollock, *Mining Urban Wastes*, p. 43.

[6] Jeremy Rifkin, ed., *The Green Lifestyle Handbook: 1001 Ways You Can Heal the Earth* (New York: Henry Holt and Co., 1990), p. 53.

[7] *Waste: Choices for Communities* (Washington, DC: Concern, Inc., 1988), p. 2.

[8] *Characterization of Municipal Waste in the United States: 1990 Update* (Washington, DC: U.S. Environmental Protection Agency, 1990), pp. ES-5 and ES-8.

[9] *Waste: Choices for Communities*, p. 2.

[10] Walter H. Corson, *The Global Ecology Handbook: What You Can Do About the Environmental Crisis* (Boston: Beacon Press, 1990), p. 266.

[11] *Nonhazardous Waste: State Management of Municipal Landfills and Landfill Expansions* (Washington, DC: General Accounting Office, 1989), p. 2.

[12] *Waste: Choices for Communities*, p. 4.

[13] *Waste: Choices for Communities*, p. 4.

[14] Jon Naar, *Design for a Livable Planet: How You Can Help Clean Up the Environment* (New York: Harper and Row Publishers, 1990), p. 13; *Waste: Choices for Communities*, p. 5.

[15] Naar, p. 13; *Waste: Choices for Communities*, p. 5.

[16] Naar, p. 14.

[17] Corson, pp. 277, 279.

[18] Naar, p. 14.

[19] Pollock, *Mining Urban Wastes*, p. 22.

[20] *Waste: Choices for Communities*, p. 2.

[21] Naar, p. 15.

[22] Naar, p. 19.

[23] Cynthia Pollock, "Realizing Recycling's Potential," *State of the World* (Washington, DC: Worldwatch Institute, 1988), pp. 107-108 as quoted in Naar, pp. 19-20.

[24] *Waste: Choices for Communities*, p. 13.

[25] Naar, p. 243.

[26] National Institute of Government Purchasing, Inc., Falls Church, Virginia, 1990, as cited in Ralph Nader, Eleanor J. Lewis and Eric Weltman of the Government Purchasing Project, Testimony before the Subcommittee on Oversight of Government Management of the Senate Governmental Affairs Committee, November 8, 1991, p. 1.

[27] Ralph Nader, "Big Consumer," *Mother Jones*, November/December 1990, p. 21.

[28] Nader, et al., Testimony before the Subcommittee on Oversight of Government Management, p. 1.

[29] Nader, "Big Consumer," p. 21.

[30] "Plastic Pollution: Front-End and Back," *Environmental Action*, July/August 1988, p. 19.

[31] "Plastic Pollution," p. 19.

[32] "Plastics in Packaging," *Environmental Action*, July/August 1988, p. 18.

[33] *Packaging: Solid Waste Action Paper #2*, pp. 1-2.

[34] Myra Klockenbrink, "Plastics Industry, Under Pressure, Begins to Invest in Recycling," *New York Times*, August 30, 1988, as quoted in Naar, p. 21.

[35] *Waste: Choices for Communities*, p. 7.

[36] Naar, pp. 21, 23.

[37] *Waste: Choices for Communities*, p. 8; "Packaging: Solid Waste Action Paper #2, p. 2.

[38] *Let's Reduce and Recycle: Curriculum for Solid Waste Awareness* (Washington, DC: U.S. Environmental Protection Agency, 1990), p. 89.

[39] *Packaging: Solid Waste Action Paper #2*, p. 2.

[40] Dadd and Carothers, p. 11.

[41] Dadd and Carothers, p. 11.

[42] Leslie Pardue, "Biodegradable Plastics: A Contradiction in Terms?" *E Magazine*, April 1990, p. 52.

[43] "Styrofoam Wars: Stamping Out Toxic Food Packaging," *E Magazine*, April 1990, p. 24; Dianne Dumanoski, "McDonald's to Banish Foam Boxes," *The Boston Globe*, November 2, 1990.

[44] "McDonald's Surrenders," *Everyone's Backyard*, December 1990, pp. 2-3.

[45] "McDonald's Surrenders," pp. 2-3; Dumanoski, Metro, p. 1.

[46] "Styrofoam Wars," p. 24.

[47] *Styrofoam Fact Sheet* (Falls Church, VA: Citizen's Clearinghouse for Hazardous Waste, 1988).

[48] *Polystyrene - Styrofoam Fact Sheet* (Barre, VT: Vermonters Organized for Clean-Up, 1988).

[49] *Polystyrene - Styrofoam Fact Sheet*.

[50] "Styrofoam Wars," p. 24.

[51] *Polystyrene - Styrofoam Fact Sheet*.

[52] "Is Styrofoam Clean?," *Everyone's Backyard*, Citizen's Clearinghouse for Hazardous Waste, December 1990, p. 19.

[53] *Styrofoam Fact Sheet*.

[54] *Facts To Act On: Are Styrene Food and Beverage Containers a Health Hazard?* (Washington, DC: Institute for Local Self-Reliance, 1990) Release #5.

[55] *Facts To Act On: Are Styrene Food and Beverage Containers a Health Hazard?*

[56] *Styrofoam Fact Sheet*.

[57] "Styrofoam Wars," p. 24.

[58] *Packaging: Solid Waste Action Paper #2*, p. 2.

[59] *Styrofoam Fact Sheet*.

[60] Based on *School Recycling Programs: A Handbook for Educators* (Washington, DC: U.S. Environmental Protection Agency, 1990).

[61] *School Recycling Programs*, p. 4.

[62] *School Recycling Programs*, p. 5.

[63] *School Recycling Programs*, p. 9.

JURY REPRESENTATIVENESS SURVEY

[1] Sara Rimer, "Rap Group's Lawyer Challenges Selection of Jury," *The New York Times*, October 11, 1991, p. A16.

[2] Rimer, p. A16.

[3] Paul Hudson, *Young People Not Welcome: A Study of Discrimination in Broome County's Jury Selection Process* (New York: New York Public Interest Research Group, 1976), p. 1.

[4] Hudson, p. 25.

[5] Joanne Doroshow, *Safeguarding a Pillar of Democracy: A Proposal for a National Association of Civil Jurors* (Center for Study of Responsive Law, 1992), pp. 4-5.

[6] Doroshow, pp. 5-6.

[7] Doroshow, p. 6.

[8] Doroshow, p. 6.

[9] As quoted in Doroshow, p. 7.

[10] Doroshow, pp. 7-8.

[11] Doroshow, p. 8.

[12] Doroshow, p. 9.

[13] Doroshow, p. 10.

[14] Doroshow, p. 10.

[15] *Swain* v. *Alabama*, 380 U.S. 202 (1965), as cited in Doroshow, p. 12.

[16] *Taylor* v. *Louisiana*, 419 U.S. 522 (1975), as cited in Doroshow, p. 12.

[17] Doroshow, p. 12.

[18] Doroshow, p. 14.

[19] G. Thomas Munsterman and Janice Munsterman, *Survey of Jurors in Selected Pennsylvania Courts* (Williamsburg, VA: Center for Jury Studies, National Center for State Courts, 1983), as cited in Doroshow, p. 15.

[20] As quoted in Doroshow, pp. 19-20.

[21] Doroshow, pp. 17-18.

[22] Doroshow, p. 17.

[23] Doroshow, p. 22.

[24] Doroshow, p. 21.

[25] As quoted in Doroshow, p. 21.

[26] Doroshow, p. 21.

[27] Doroshow, p. 22.

[28] Doroshow, pp. 26-27.

[29] Doroshow, p. 15.

[30] As cited in Doroshow, p. 27.

[31] Doroshow, p. 30.

[32] Charles W. Wolfram, "The Constitutional History of the Seventh Amendment," *Minnesota Law Review*, Vol. 57, 1973, p. 671, as quoted in Doroshow, p. 30.

[33] Doroshow, p. 31.

[34] As quoted in Doroshow, p. 31.

[35] Doroshow, p. 32.

[36] Doroshow, p. 1.

[37] Doroshow, pp. 35-36.

[38] Doroshow, p. 35-36, citing *Product Liability: Verdicts and Case Resolution in Five States* (Washington, DC: General Accounting Office, 1989) and John Guinther, *The Jury in America* (1988).

[39] Doroshow, pp. 35-36.

[40] Doroshow, p. 36.

[41] Doroshow, pp. 36-37.

[42] Doroshow, pp. 26, 38.

[43] Doroshow, p. 39.

[44] Doroshow, pp. 46-52.

[45] Doroshow, p. 14.

[46] Hudson, p. 13.

[47] Hudson, p. 2.

[48] Hudson, p. 13.

[49] G. Thomas Munsterman and Janice T. Munsterman, "The Search for Jury Representativeness," *The Justice System Journal*, Vol. 11, No. 1, 1986, p. 65.

[50] Munsterman and Munsterman, "The Search for Jury Representativeness," p. 65.

[51] Munsterman and Munsterman, "The Search for Jury Representativeness," p. 66.

[52] *Standards Relating to Juror Use and Management*, (Williamsburg, VA: National Center for State Courts, 1982), p. 27.

[53] Munsterman and Munsterman, "The Search for Jury Representativeness," p. 66.

[54] Munsterman and Munsterman, "The Search for Jury Representativeness," p. 71; *Standards Relating to Juror Use and Management*, p. 26.

[55] As cited in Doroshow, p. 13.

[56] As cited in Doroshow, p. 13.

[57] Munsterman and Munsterman, "The Search for Jury Representativeness," p. 65.

[58] Munsterman and Munsterman, "The Search for Jury Representativeness," p. 62.

[59] *Standards Relating to Juror Use and Management*, p. 25.

[60] *Standards Relating to Juror Use and Management*, p. 25.

[61] *Standards Relating to Juror Use and Management*, p. 25.

[62] Munsterman and Munsterman, "The Search for Jury Representativeness," p. 74.

[63] Munsterman and Munsterman, "The Search for Jury Representativeness," p. 73.

[64] Hudson, p. 2.

[65] Hudson, p. 3.

[66] Hudson, p. 3.

[67] Doroshow, pp. 12-13.

[68] Hudson, p. 3.

[69] *Thiel* v. *So. Pac. RR*, 328 U.S. 217 (1946), as cited in Hudson, p. 17.

[70] Hudson, p. 17.

[71] Hudson, p. 18.

[72] Hudson, p. 2.

[73] Hudson, p. 12.

[74] Hudson, p. 13.

[75] Munsterman and Munsterman, "The Search for Jury Representativeness," p. 63.

[76] Munsterman and Munsterman, "The Search for Jury Representativeness," p. 63.

[77] Munsterman and Munsterman, "The Search for Jury Representativeness," p. 63.

[78] Munsterman and Munsterman, "The Search for Jury Representativeness," p. 76.

[79] Munsterman and Munsterman, "The Search for Jury Representativeness," p. 62.

[80] Hudson, pp. 21-24.

[81] *The Official American Board of Trial Advocates Handbook for Planning City Tour Bill of Rights/Jury Appreciation Ceremonies* (Encino, CA: American Board of Trial Advocates, 1992).

[82] Tables are from Paul Hudson, *Young People Not Welcome: A Study of Discrimination in Broome County's Jury Selection Process* (New York: New York Public Interest Research Group, 1976), pp. 28-29.

EVALUATING TELEVISION NEWS

[1] Ralph Nader and Claire Riley, "Oh, Say Can You See: A Broadcast Network for the Audience," *The Journal of Law and Politics*, Vol. V, No. 1, Fall 1988, p. 10.

[2] Nader and Riley, pp. 2-17.

[3] Federal Communications Act of 1934 47 U.S.C. 301-399 (1982) as cited in Nader and Riley, p. 2, fn 2.

[4] *Second Report and Order*, 50 FCC 2d 1046 (1975) as cited in James Donahue, *Shortchanging the Viewers: Broadcasters' Neglect of Public Interest Programming* (Washington, DC: Essential Information, 1989), p. 3.

[5] Nader and Riley, p. 24.

[6] Nader and Riley, pp. 31-33.

[7] *Second Report and Order*, 50 FCC 2d 1046 (1975), as cited in Donahue, *Shortchanging the Viewers*, p. 3.

[8] Nader and Riley, pp. 37-38.

[9] Ralph Nader, Testimony before the House Subcommittee on Telecommunications and Finance of the House Committee on Energy and Commerce, May 13, 1991, p. 4.

[10] Nader, Testimony, p. 5.

[11] Nader, Testimony, p. 6.

[12] Nader and Riley, p. 35.

[13] Nader and Riley, p. 35.

[14] Donahue, *Shortchanging the Viewers*, p. 1.

[15] Donahue, *Shortchanging the Viewers*, pp. 3-4.

[16] Donahue, *Shortchanging the Viewers*, p. 1.

[17] Nader and Riley, p. 28.

[18] "Television," *Buyer's Market*, Vol. 3, No. 10, December 1987, p. 5.

[19] Nader and Riley, p. 30.

[20] Donahue, *Shortchanging the Viewers*, p. 1.

[21] Donahue, *Shortchanging the Viewers*, p. 1.

[22] Donahue, *Shortchanging the Viewers*, p. 1.

[23] Donahue, *Shortchanging the Viewers*, p. 2.

[24] Edmund L. Andrews, "Deeply Divided House Panel Backs Limits on Cable Rates," *The New York Times*, April 9, 1992, p. D4.

[25] Andrews, p. D4; Dennis Camire, "Senate OKs Cable Bill, Passage in House Likely," Gannett News Service, January 31, 1992.

[26] Morton Mintz and Jerry S. Cohen, *Power, Inc.: Public and Private Rulers and How to Make Them Accountable* (New York: Viking Press, 1976), pp. 423, 436.

[27] Ben H. Bagdikian, "The Media Brokers: Concentration and Ownership of the Press," *Multinational Monitor*, September 1987, p. 10.

[28] Ben H. Bagdikian, *The Media Monopoly*, Third edition (Boston: Beacon Press, 1990), pp. 15-16.

[29] As quoted in Martin A. Lee and Norman Solomon, *Unreliable Sources: A Guide to Detecting Bias in News Media* (New York: Carol Publishing Group, 1990), p. 243.

[30] As quoted in Lee and Solomon, p. 243.

[31] Jonathan Tasini, *Lost in the Margins: Labor and the Media* (New York: Fairness and Accuracy in Reporting, 1990) cited in Holley Knaus, "Labor's Press," *Multinational Monitor*, Vol. 11, No. 11, November 1990, p. 7.

[32] Lee and Solomon, pp. 26-27.

[33] Susan J. Douglas, "The Representation of Women in the News Media," *Extra!* March/April 1991, p. 2.

[34] Lee and Solomon, p. 27.

[35] Lee and Solomon, p. 27.

[36] As quoted in Lee and Solomon, p. 29.

[37] Douglas, p. 2.

[38] Douglas, p. 2.

[39] Judy Southworth, "Women Media Workers: No Room at the Top," *Extra!* March/April 1991, p. 16.

[40] Lee and Solomon, p. 249.

[41] As quoted in Lee and Solomon, p. 248.

[42] James Donahue, *Audience Network Action Kit* (Washington, DC: Audience Network Action Project, 1991), p. 2.

[43] Bagdikian, *The Media Monopoly*, p. xix.

[44] Bagdikian, *The Media Monopoly*, p. 21.

[45] Bagdikian, "The Media Brokers," p. 7.

[46] Mintz and Cohen, p. 429; Bagdikian, *The Media Monopoly*, p. 201.

[47] Bagdikian, *The Media Monopoly*, p. xxi.

[48] Bagdikian, *The Media Monopoly*, pp. 199-200.

[49] Bagdikian, *The Media Monopoly*, p. 21.

[50] As quoted in Knaus, p. 7.

[51] Knaus, p. 7.

[52] Bagdikian, *The Media Monopoly*, p. 26.

[53] Bagdikian, *The Media Monopoly*, p. 26.

[54] Bagdikian, "The Media Brokers," p. 8.

[55] Bagdikian, *The Media Monopoly*, p. xix.

[56] Bagdikian, "The Media Brokers," p. 10.

[57] Bagdikian, "The Media Brokers," p. 10.

[58] Nader and Riley, p. 8.

[59] "Television," p. 5.

[60] Nader and Riley, pp. 67-86.

[61] Nader and Riley, pp. 67-86.

[62] Nader and Riley, pp. 67-86.

[63] Nader and Riley, pp. 67-86.

[64] Nader and Riley, pp. 60-64.

[65] "Television," p. 4.

[66] Action Kit (Washington, DC: Citizens for the Cable Consumer Participation Amendment, 1992).

[67] The broadcast of ABC World News Tonight, March 18, 1992, contained approximately 4,000 words. The front page of the *Washington Post*, March 18, 1992, contained approximately 1,800 words and several pictures.

[68] "America's Watching," The Roper Report (Television Information Office, 1991).

INDEX

376